standard catalog of®

Farm Toys

Identification and Price Guide

3rd Edition

Edited by
Karen O'Brien

Contributing Editor
Kate Bossen

©2007 Krause Publications

Published by

krause publications
An Imprint of F+W Publications

700 East State Street • Iola, WI 54990-0001
715-445-2214 • 888-457-2873
www.krausebooks.com

Library of Congress Control Number: 2007923819

ISBN-13: 978-0-89689-556-0
ISBN-10: 0-89689-556-4

Designed by Sandi Morrison
Edited by Karen O'Brien

Printed in the United States of America

On the Cover

Front: Farmall 806, 1:16-scale, Ertl, 1960s; John Deere 6410,
1:32-scale, Ertl, 2006; Matchbox Massey-Ferguson
Combine Harvester, Major Pack No. 5, 1950s

Spine: Arcade Oliver tractor, c.1940

Back: Upper Left: Hart-Parr 30-60, 1:16-scale, Scale Models, 1989
Upper Right: John Deere 4440, 1:16-scale, Ertl, 1979
Lower Left: Farmall B, 1:16-scale, Ertl, 2006
Lower Right: Case DC3, 1:16-scale, SpecCast, 2007

Dedication

This edition is dedicated to everyone who participates in toy shows. Attending shows provides the opportunity to renew acquaintances, network with like-minded collectors, and participate in this hobby on a personal level. Shows also remind us that it is the people we encounter along the collecting trail that make this hobby meaningful.

I'd also like to dedicate this edition to the wonderful dealers and exhibitors that reside in Hallway 2 of Beckman High School during the National Farm Toy Show in Dyersville, Iowa. Each year, these exceptional folks make the National a very educational and rewarding event for me, and I am deeply grateful for their generosity and kindness.

Acknowledgments

I must first acknowledge the achievements of the first edition. Editors Elizabeth Stephen and Dan Stearns assembled a remarkable first edition and this title would not be possible without their efforts. Farm toy collecting pioneers Bob Zarse and Eldon Trumm had the initial dedication to begin cataloging farm toys, and their books provide the solid foundation upon which this book is based. Jon Jacobson photographed most of the toys contained here. Ted Meyer, former director of the National Farm Toy Museum, allowed the photography of toys from the Museum's collection. And continued thanks to the first edition contributors: Tom Abarr, Chuck Burkholder, Ray Crilley, Tom Diers, Roy Ferguson, Doug Frey, Don Hoeck, and Keith Oltrogge, for their expertise.

This third edition is indebted to Contributing Editor Kate Bossen. Her genuine passion for farm toy collecting and encyclopedic knowledge of the hobby inspired many of the improvements you'll find in this edition. She provided new listings and pricing updates and her counsel throughout this project was much appreciated. She also let me borrow the beautiful Farmall 806 on the cover. If you're looking for farm toys, try her shop at:

Bossen Implement
Hwy. 187 South, 300 Washburn Ave.
Lamont, IA 50650
(563) 924-2880
www.bossenimp.com
email: sales@bossenimp.com

Thanks to the contributors to this edition. Chad Elmore wrote about the joys of real tractors and collecting their scale counterparts. Mark Rich updated the farm toy company listings and doubled the size of the farm animals section. I always enjoy my conversations with Cathy Scheibe—her insights on the hobby are invaluable. And I'd like to thank everyone who has generously taken the time to "talk toys" with me. Sharing your perspectives on the hobby makes this title stronger with each edition.

There are quite a few people at Krause Publications who deserve thanks as well. Sandi Morrison ran the database patterns and designed the book. Stacy Bloch assisted with design duties. Tom Nelson and Marilyn McGrane provided the book's cover. The scanning and production departments graciously handled the tight timeline. Tom Bartsch, editor of *Toy Shop* magazine, is a Milwaukee Brewers fan and will never sway my allegiance to the Chicago Cubs. Merry Dudley, editor of *Toy Cars & Models* magazine, volunteered the use of her family's Ford 8N for the photo in the Introduction that I called, "City Kid on Tractor." I had a lot of fun learning to drive the 8N!

And as always, special thanks to my family and friends for their love, encouragement, and inspiration.

Karen O'Brien
September 2007

Contents

Farm Toy Listings

Introduction

by Karen O'Brien

City Kid on Tractor

This edition is dedicated to everyone who attends and supports toy shows. I grew up attending toy shows with my dad, and those experiences forged me into the die-hard collector that I am today. In addition to establishing the love of the hobby, attending shows taught me life skills that I never would have learned in school.

For example, when planning a trip to a local show, dad always started with the show flyer and his road map. He figured out the directions and wrote down the route we would travel. I imagine you go through similar planning sessions when traveling, but when the show ended, did you ever toss the map to your nine-year-old daughter and tell her that it was up to her to find the way home?

At the time, I thought dad was just trying to teach me to read a map, but later I understood that it's the practical education we receive from participating in hobbies that helps to shape us as individuals. And that was the real lesson.

Practical education just might be the real theme of this edition. Check out the Toy Tractor Times Web site sometime (you'll find it at www.toytractortimes.com) and join in the farm toy discussions. I've learned a great deal from the online conversations of my fellow collectors and always enjoy the variety of topics that give the site a unique sense of community.

Speaking of practical education, while working on this edition I received a first-hand lesson on how to drive a Ford 8N—and I have the picture to prove it! Our offices are located in rural central Wisconsin, and Merry Dudley, editor of *Toy Cars & Models* magazine, said I could drive her family's Ford 8N. I had never driven a real tractor, so I jumped at the chance. Her dad was amused that the "city kid" wanted to drive a tractor. I was just hoping that I wouldn't grind the gears too much. After a short lesson on shifting, I was motoring around the fields. I included the picture on this page as photographic proof that city kids can drive tractors—and love every minute.

An Interesting Conversation

It's a real pleasure to "talk toys" with *Toy Farmer* publisher Cathy Scheibe. Her insights into farm toy collecting are always interesting and I thought I'd share some of those perspectives here. (For a more detailed look at the history of *Toy Farmer* and other perspectives, see "Toy Farmer: Perspectives from Cathy Scheibe" on page 8. Though produced for the 2nd edition of this book, the information is timeless and deserved an appearance here as well.)

Scheibe noted that the increasing popularity of 1:64-scale farm toys has a positive effect on the hobby—the affordability of the scale appeals to the younger collector, while the growing diorama-building segment appreciates the variety of offerings. The current appeal of these toys to young collectors bodes well for the future. "A lot of young people who have grown up with the hobby are staying with it," Scheibe said. "Some people that leave for various reasons always come back with a renewed interest. People remember the toys they had and come back, or the cycle repeats itself when they have kids of their own."

Collectors today are fortunate to enjoy a hobby climate that is open to all tastes and pocketbooks, making farm toy collecting more inclusive than ever. "We still see a great number of families participating in shows, especially at the Nationals," she said. "The beautiful farm displays entered for the competition get better every year, and many times whole families are pitching in to build them. I think it's great."

What's New?

Talking to other collectors is one of the great pleasures of this hobby, and I've received some terrific advice for additions, corrections, and improvements to this edition. Please keep those comments coming—this title gets better with each conversation, email, and letter I receive.

Continuing the efforts begun in the 2nd edition to make this book as user-friendly as possible, several enhancements were added to this edition. The most noticeable

"City kid" on tractor. I recently learned how to drive a Ford 8N!

Was the Fisher-Price Play Family Farm your first farm toy? The set was so popular that Fisher-Price produced it for twenty years. Fisher-Price offers Little People Farm sets today.

improvement is the addition of dark boxes in each chapter that contain the series of toy and scale. These boxes appear at the beginning of each series of listings. For example, in the John Deere chapter, the first box of the tractors series reads, "Tractors, 1:08-scale." The listings that follow are all of 1:08-scale John Deere tractors. When those listings conclude, another box announces the start of the next series. In this example, the next box reads, "Tractors, 1:128-scale."

A Farmall Note: The Farmall and McCormick listings have all been incorporated into the International Harvester chapter. I hope this change makes finding all of your "red" favorites a little easier.

A section on playsets debuts with this edition. One of my first toy farming adventures was with the Fisher-Price Play School Family Farm, and I'm sure many of you have fond memories of that toy. It was so popular, that the original version remained in production for more than twenty years. Conversations with other collectors revealed fond memories of their Marx farming playsets, and I thought this edition would be the ideal time to add a section just for those. I couldn't resist

including the Ertl Farm Country sets, and I know I wasn't able to find them all, so if you have information regarding sets not included, please let me know.

Become a Correspondent

Plans are already in action for the 4th edition and you can help by becoming a toy correspondent. Additional toy listings, more detailed information for the current listings, and photos are always needed, and you are invited to participate. If you know of toys not included here, please make a list and send it in.

Those of you attending shows as dealers or collectors are also welcome to submit show reports with your observations of the shows you attend. I'll include them on my new blog (see the address below). The blog is the most immediate way for me to communicate hobby news to collectors, so I update it frequently. We can't all attend every show, and this is an ideal way to share the hobby happenings in your area with your fellow collectors. Check back often and please send in those show reports!

We are always looking for color photos for our archives. Good quality color 35mm photos

or slides work best for reproduction in print. High-resolution digital images are welcome (at 300 ppi or higher at a 3" x 3" size), but low-resolution images, like the ones usually used for Web sites, are too small to use in print. If you have information for our listings, or photos of farm toys not pictured in this edition that you would like to donate to our archives, please contact me at the following address:

**Karen O'Brien
Krause Publications
700 E. State St.
IOLA, WI 54990
Phone: (715) 445-4612
Email: karen.obrien@fwpubs.com**

Be sure to visit my toy blog, "Babe in Toyland," at:
www.toyshopmag.com/toyland

Enjoy your collection, and make plans to attend a farm toy show in your area!

Karen O'Brien
September 2007

Toy Farmer

Perspectives from Cathy Scheibe

by Karen O'Brien

The farm toy hobby has grown up over the last 27 years, and *Toy Farmer* magazine has grown right along with it. Integral to the development of both, Cathy Scheibe has unique perspectives to share. She graciously discussed the magazine and the hobby, offered solid advice to collectors, and shared too many wonderful "toy stories" for me to include here.

As you'll discover, her passion for farm toy collecting is reflected not only in the pages of *Toy Farmer* but also through her love of communicating with hobbyists around the world.

The Beginning

Claire and Cathy Scheibe began their toy collection with the tractors Claire played with in childhood, and they soon accumulated enough toys that some had to go in order to make room for more. During the mid-1970s, there was no Internet, of course, so Claire assembled a list of tractors for sale and mailed it to other collectors. The favorable response led to more mailings, and in 1977, collectors urged the Scheibes to publish a farm toy newsletter.

"We started in January of 1978 with a four-page black-and-white newsletter," Cathy explained. "We had 17 subscribers who paid $7.50 for a year's subscription."

Printing the newsletter at their local newspaper, the Scheibes had no idea whether or not their *Toy Farmer* would succeed. Six months later, with more than 500 subscribers, the newsletter flourished.

"In January of 1986, we went from the newsletter to a color cover and the magazine format," Cathy continued. "At the time, we had about 8,000 subscribers. Within five years, we had 25,000 subscribers. In January of 2003,

we converted to full color, and this issue [October, 2004] has 104 pages. It only took us 27 years to get there!"

Trends in the Magazine

The magazine has adapted to the growing needs of its readers over the years.

"*Toy Farmer* has grown as the hobby has grown," Cathy explained. "But *Toy Farmer* brought the hobby together so that the communication [between collectors] could reach across the country.

"We've increased our international coverage. There was a time when we didn't cover any of that at all. We had an early impact, but there were publications before ours like Ray Crilley's *Miniature Tractors and Implements*. He did a black-and-white [newsletter] and had a lot of information because he collected the foreign tractors long before we were involved with writing about them. When he decided he didn't want to do the newsletter any longer, he sold it to us and then came back to writing for us. And that's when we started focusing more on the foreign tractors and when we started traveling to Europe to attend the toy shows."

Themed issues give the magazine a chance to offer a variety of perspectives on a single theme and have become increasingly popular with the readers.

"We have included two custom-built focus issues," Cathy remarked. We used to only have customs once a year. Now we have them twice a year because there are so many people out there customizing or scratch-building.

"One of the things that we feature now that we didn't do much with before is a special issue for layouts. And for the last four or five years, we have featured youth once a year. We get a good reaction from those layout and

youth issues, and that's just the online reaction. I go online sometimes to check and they'll say what the best issues are. It's the young people who are active online that are building, so they notice the layout issues and they notice the custom-built issues," Cathy said.

Hobby Trends

As the hobby developed, so did the number of toys available to collectors. The sheer volume requires most collectors to make tough decisions regarding the pieces they select for purchase and display.

"Through the years there has been much more specialization in collecting" Cathy explained. "When we first started, everybody that was collecting was collecting everything. And I'm talking every brand, John Deere, IH, Case, whatever. Gradually, more and more [toys were] being offered.

"Then came the specialization of collecting specific 'colors,' if you will, like International Harvester or John Deere. Then scale became a specialization. Originally most of the tractors were a 1:16 scale, and when they started making 1:64 scale, kids could collect because of the price point. Then came the toys created just for the collector market. Once so much was produced, most people started specializing because they didn't have the money or space to continue collecting absolutely everything."

It seems that a collection of farm toys can often spill over into a collection of real tractors "which they restore, display at shows, and store in great big buildings," Cathy commented.

Economic realities have produced changes in the manufacture of farm toys as well. "With the exception of Scale Models, all of the tractors are built in China now," Cathy said. "If toy quality goes up, then the price is higher. And competition among manufacturers has made the models better. When it was just Ertl, [the company] used to advertise that the toys were 'just like the real thing.' Now it's gotten to be more and more like the real thing. And with [Ertl's] Precision Classics, it's even better."

Significant growth of international interest in farm toys has led to an explosion of the hobby in Europe.

"It's like the beginning of the hobby over there," Cathy commented. "The International Farm Toy Show is on its 20th year in the Netherlands this year, but we see a real increase in customers from over there purchasing our tractors and also in visitors to our National Farm Toy Show. Every year there are more and more people, and I think it's partly because of [Toy Farmer] and it's partly because of the Internet. That's probably the biggest trend, the Internet—both from the standpoint of buying toys and selling toys. It can reach every corner of the world now."

Farm Toy Shows

The Scheibes founded the National Farm Toy Show in 1978. Held annually during the first weekend of November, the "Grandaddy of 'Em All" is one of the most highly-anticipated events of the year. Cathy's affection for attending shows hasn't diminished. "There's nothing like being able to go in and see

a toy and pick it up."

She shared some of the keys to being a successful dealer at shows.

"I think dealers still do pretty well at shows because over time they develop a loyal following of collectors who come to the show because a favorite dealer has items they like. I think if you're going to be in the toy-selling business; you have to find something that is somewhat a little bit different to sell from what everybody else has; you have to be willing to change what you're selling if its not working for you; you have to do toy shows, advertise in the magazines, sell on eBay—you should do all of those things if you want to be successful.

"There is a whole segment of the hobby that will not participate online, and if you ignore shows and magazines in favor of the Internet alone, you are missing out on some of the core audience. The more willing you are to think of your customer first, the better your business is going to be."

Collecting Advice

"I have advice for a grandfather who wants to introduce the grandkids to farm toys—take them to a farm toy show," declared Cathy. "We are seeing parents and grandparents bringing kids to the show. The advice I'd have for someone just starting out [in the hobby] is to buy your book [The Standard Catalog of Farm Toys]. I'm serious about that. They need to avail themselves of

your book, our magazine, the Internet, the whole thing."

Collecting advice isn't limited to the toys, either. Nostalgia develops one person at a time, one family at a time. Claire Scheibe's nostalgia for the toys of his youth led to the creation of the premiere magazine in the hobby. His passing in 2000 reminds us that we all have a role to play in handing down the love of this hobby to the next generation.

"It was his love of this hobby that really kept [Toy Farmer] going," recalled Cathy. "I encouraged him along the way to do the publication because I love journalism and I thought that way people would get to know about [the hobby]. But when it came to the hobby itself, he knew more about it than anybody I know. When people would interview him and ask, 'What's the most valuable tractor ever made?' or 'What's your favorite tractor?' he'd always reach behind his desk and pull out the one he played with as a kid. I think it's a John Deere A. It had one wheel broken off and the paint was almost all gone, but that was his most valuable and favorite tractor. That [tractor] was the answer to either question.

"Nostalgia was something that Claire always brought up. That's why I think it's important to make that relationship between parents and grandparents and children. It's a family hobby. It really is."

Red & Green

The Beginning...

by Chad Elmore

One of the toy farming hobby's most important partnerships began when a gold plastic tractor was exchanged between an Iowa man who collected only green equipment and a fellow in Indiana who gathered only red.

"I couldn't go to the auction, but I wanted a gold International Harvester tractor at the sale," recalls red collector Bob Zarse. "So I called a friend of mine, and asked him if he was going. He wasn't, but had a friend that was. That friend was Eldon Trumm. Eldon went to the auction and bought that gold IH tractor."

It was an event toy historians could take note of. Even today, Trumm's collection is focused on John Deere toys. No one at the auction could figure out why Trumm bought the International toy, a very rare dealer award issued in the 1950s.

"Well, Eldon didn't know who he bought it for. All he could say was 'some guy.' And we are talking about a $700 toy, way back then," says Zarse. "Trumm went home and told his wife what he had done, and that the guy was supposed to call tonight. She said, 'well, I hope he calls!' I called Eldon that night, and we've been good friends ever since. He's green and I'm red, but we've gotten along very well. We rib each other about the opposite color, and that's probably one of the reasons we get along."

Self-Publishing

By that time, Zarse had already written and self-published his first book. Published in 1982, the book was softbound and ran 117 pages. It covered the evolution of the International brand through toys,

Bob Zarse, one of the pioneers of farm toy collecting.

beginning with cast-iron horse-drawn implements. "A lot of people had questions about what tractors were available. I put the book together based on my collection and a couple others. The book was very amateurish, but it sold, and people still liked it."

After meeting Trumm and taking that gold International tractor off of his hands, Zarse suggested that Trumm write a similar book on John Deere, since he had one of the best collections of green tractors around. Trumm's subsequent book, on which he was the sole author, covered the evolution of Deere toys.

These early books were written at a time when farm toys were produced for—and worked hard in—1/16-scale sandbox fields maintained by children. That an adult would collect toys was practically unheard of, and

those who did talked about it only among themselves.

"We considered ourselves closet collectors," says Zarse. "Nobody talked about it. If someone visited an implement dealer, they said it was to buy a toy for their son."

Toys were in Zarse's genes, as a couple of relatives operated toy stores in the 1950s, and having been raised on a farm, farm toys were a natural. His collection probably began with toy International 560s that were given to his dad when he bought the real tractors in the 1950s, and occasionally an uncle would give him a toy of an Allis-Chalmers tractor. Once bitten by the collecting bug, there's no antidote. Zarse eventually began placing want ads seeking tractors for his collection. This collection led to a farm toy mail-order business that he operated on the farm, and eventually the books.

Trumm and Zarse teamed up as co-authors to tackle toy tractor subjects of different colors. "We've done a lot of hardbound and softcover books, one on White, one on pedal tractors, construction toys, and one on all types of Ertl farm toys. Eldon was one of the last people to go in and interview Fred Ertl, Sr. [who founded the Ertl toy company in 1945] before he passed away—that interview is in the book. We traveled all over the Midwest photographing the best toys we could. As we updated the books with new editions, we bought most of the toys or got them from the manufacturers." Eldon has estimated more than 50,000 copies of all titles are now on the shelves of collectors.

Full of photographs, the books written and published by Bob Zarse and Eldon Trumm provided a road map for collectors. For the first time, toy tractor fans knew what they needed to look for at shows and auctions in their quests for complete collections.

"Early on these books were more educational," says Zarse. "Back when we were doing these books, there were toys still being found that we didn't know were ever made."

It's appropriate that the work of Zarse and Trumm has become the foundation of a book in Krause Publication's Standard Catalog series. Covering a variety of subjects, the comprehensive Standard Catalogs have been an often-referenced guide in the libraries of collectors for decades. To Zarse and Trumm's original work, Krause Publications has added more information and updated the listings, ensuring that collectors will continue to approach the hobby well-informed. Dog-eared copies of the first *Standard Catalog of Farm Toys* can be found on the shelves and in the hands of collectors at shows around the world.

Sharing the Hobby

Most importantly, with this work Bob Zarse, Eldon Trumm, Krause Publications, and a number of contributors are helping to educate young collectors who are just beginning to see the number and variety of toy tractors available. For those beginning toy farmers, Zarse offers this advice:

"Never buy a toy because you think it will go up in value. Only buy a toy if you like it. I've never seen collectors who bought a toy they liked get disappointed if it goes down in value. They still like that toy. But if they buy a toy for $35 that they think will go to $65 but it drops to $25, they are upset. They never liked the toy. Buy what you like.

I have some pieces that I don't care whether they are worth $5 or $5,000. I have some other pieces that I bought that I would hope would appreciate, I won't deny that! And then I have a few pieces that are pretty sentimental. It's not got a

lot to do with the toys."

Bob's focus on a specific brand reflects one of the strongest drives behind any collector. "We farmed with International Harvesters; my dad started with a Farmall Regular after the horses. Specifically, I like anything that has to do with International 560s. My father had one. It's sentimental. I've moved more towards full-sized tractors, and I collect the ones from the late 1950s early, '60s. My toy collection is the same way. If I find something I really like from those years I buy it. However, my collecting bug hasn't stopped; it has gone from 1: 16-scale to full-scale. I've downsized a little bit, back to toys of the real tractors that we've owned. I try to keep a history from what dad started with up through what I farmed with."

While Zarse has pared down his toy collection to focus on the real thing, Trumm still collects John Deere toys, keeping his collection

current. Besides writing the books, Trumm has produced a line of toys himself over the years. He has made examples of the giant Big Bud tractors from Montana, and several licensed John Deere machines.

Although the tractors are the focus of the books, Zarse says they are not necessarily the most important part of the hobby.

"I have had this philosophy about collecting for a long time: The fun is in the hunt, and the hunt is all the people you meet during that hunt. It's all the other toy collectors," says Zarse.

"The toys were a medium to put people together. Do I like the toys? Yes. Do I like the toys more than the people? Absolutely not. I cherish the friends I've met through the toys. Without the toys I wouldn't have met Eldon. The whole thing has been quite an experience. We have a good time."

This Oliver 1655 from Ertl presents an opportunity to put Bob Zarse's advice to the test. If the tractor doesn't triple its value in 5 years, will you be disappointed with its original purchase, or glad to have such a finely-detailed 1:16-scale replica in your collection?

Collecting Diversity With Toys

by Chad Elmore

Nearly 10 years ago I gave my two-week's notice, hanging up my hat as an editor of an antique-car publication. The hat I put on was as editor for a magazine that deals with agricultural machinery. In making that switch some car guy friends suggested that I would soon be bored with the subject. They said there was so much variety in the automobile world that writing about farm tractors would quickly become monotonous. Although a lifelong car guy myself, I wasn't worried. Tractors weren't new to me. Plus, I knew they had the key components to ensure I would have fun with the subject: engines, wheels, a long and interesting history, and a little personal nostalgia.

New to the farm machinery hobby? One only has to flip quickly through the pages of this book to see that there is a lot of variety in the world of ag equipment. Collectors of full-sized equipment know that. Those who try to collect all of the examples produced by a certain make (such as Allis-Chalmers or International Harvester), a certain style (such as the streamlined orchard tractors or slow-moving crawlers), or simply farm tractors in general are soon talking about storage buildings that measure hundreds of feet in length.

Whether serious about filling a machine shed or a shelf, scale models give farm machinery collectors an opportunity to celebrate the nearly endless variety of agricultural equipment.

Like most collectors, I maintain a mental list of old tractors that I hope to own. Actually, I have two lists. The "Practical List" takes into account the available time, money, and storage space I have now and am likely to possess in the future. The other is the "Maybe List," the one I will use to cross off new acquisitions when I win the state lottery (although having never purchased a ticket, that's not too likely) or however else people suddenly find themselves with too much money.

For crossing off tractors on the Practical List, there are patience and being in the right place at the right time. For everything else there are scale tractor models. For me there's nothing like firing up my 1939 Sears Economy tractor (crossed off the Practical List years ago) and using it for light work around the yard. Later that day I might push my 1:16-scale UDLX (which is still on that other list, this one is courtesy of Scale Models rather than Minneapolis-Moline) across my desk while trying to work through a case of writer's block.

Beyond space and time, there's another positive to collecting scale farm tractors. Jim and Phyllis Hembrough have been selling farm toys at tractor shows throughout the Midwest for more than 25 years. For much of that time, Phyllis has written a column in *Belt Pulley* magazine—a publication that for 20 years has dealt primarily with antique full-sized farm machinery—called "These are easier to haul." For some of the machinery on that Maybe List—the early self-propelled Massey-Harris combines or the big four-wheel-drives of the 1970s—that helps make the high values for Ruehl's 1:20-scale harvesters or Ertl's dual-wheeled John Deere 8640s much more manageable.

Chad and his wife, Katie, publish Belt Pulley magazine (for more information on the see www.beltpulley. com). The all-brand, all antique farm machinery magazine is celebrating its 20th year of publication in 2007.

The National Farm Toy Museum

"If you build it, they will come."

As appropriate as that quote from the 1989 film, *Field of Dreams*, is to Kevin Costner's character, Ray Kinsella, it is even more poignant to Dyersville, Iowa. Not only is it home to the actual Field of Dreams, since 1986, Dyersville is the home of the National Farm Toy Museum.

Museum History

The idea to form the museum occurred in Dave Bell's living room in Iowa. One Sunday evening in the mid-1980s, following the National Farm Toy Show, Bell, the current owner and president of SpecCast, sat down with Claire Scheibe, owner of the show. The discussion turned to the growing show's need for more room, which in turn sparked the idea to found the museum.

They met with the Dyersville Industries Inc. Board of Directors and spoke with Fred Ertl at the Ertl Company, one of Dyersville's largest industries and a leading manufacturer of die-cast farm toys. The Board didn't immediately adopt the idea of building a museum because of the expense of constructing and maintaining the facility.

To solve the financial problem, a fund-raising campaign was designed around the creation of an exclusive series of collector tractors. The first series was a three-tractor set of Cockchutt tractors produced from 1986 through 1990. "We sold enough to pay for the museum," Bell said. Three sets of Cockshutt tractors were offered at $135 per set. According to Bell, it took $1 million to fund the museum, and the building was paid for in three years. Purchasers of those initial tractor sets are acknowledged on the Founding Collectors board located in the entrance to the museum.

The museum-edition tractor has become a tradition, and each year an exclusive collector's series tractor is released.

The Museum Today

The saying is true—they built it and the people really do come. The museum promotes the history of agriculture through toys, receives more than 30,000 guests each year, and is an integral part of the National Farm Toy Show.

The museum is host to more than 30,000 farm toys and one of the largest collections of cast-iron farm toys in the world. Tractors, implements, trucks, miniature farm dioramas, and pedal tractors are all on display between the museum's two floors.

Two remarkable Doug Schlesier sculptures and a plaque honoring the Ertl Company grace the entrance. Plaques honoring the National Farm Toy Hall of Fame inductees celebrate the achievements of dedicated individuals and remind us that this hobby is about people. Of course, when you see the wall devoted to explaining toy scale, you understand that the hobby is about the toys too—there is a life-sized John Deere depiction that houses scale replicas. Now that's putting things in perspective!

Other museum highlights include a forty-five-seat movie theater with multi-media show, a replicated farmhouse porch, and an actual die-cast and assembly machine used in the early years of the Ertl Company.

The museum's new Web site (www.nationalfarmtoymuseum.com) is full of interesting information and activities including a kid's corner, virtual tour of the museum, and message board. It's an excellent online avenue for collectors from around the world to stay in touch with the museum events and each other.

National Farm Toy Museum
1110 16th Ave. Ct. SE
Dyersville, Iowa 52040
USA
Phone: (563) 875-2727
Email: farmtoys@dyersville.com
Web site: www.nationalfarmtoymuseum.com

Hours of operation, admission charges, and driving directions are available online or by calling the phone number.

The National Farm Toy Museum
Hall of Fame

The National Farm Toy Museum Hall of Fame is dedicated to the pioneers in the farm toy world. It is located in what could be considered the center of the farm toy universe, in Dyersville, Iowa.

Fred and Gertrude Ertl
(inducted, 1992)

Fred and Gertrude Ertl, founders of the Ertl Company in early 1945, produced the first toy tractors in their Dubuque, Iowa basement. The company was later moved to Dyersville, Iowa and has since grown into the largest producer of farm toy replicas in the world by holding licenses to produce all major brands of farm toy tractors. The Ertl Company helped spur the growth of the farm toy hobby and has been most instrumental in the building of the National farm Toy Museum. The Ertls were a guiding force at the Ertl Company until they sold their business 1968.

Claire and Cathy Scheibe
(inducted, 1992)

It's unlikely that Claire and Cathy Scheibe realized the impact they would have on the farm toy hobby when they started a new magazine, *Toy Farmer* in January 1978. Toy Farmer has grown from a meager seventeen subscribers to 30,000 subscribers worldwide and has come to be regarded as the bible for farm toy collectors. Another project initiated by the Scheibes in 1978 was the first National farm Toy Show in Dyersville, Iowa, and annual event—like Toy Farmer—that has grown tremendously since its early years. In addition, the Scheibes lent their support and played a major role in establishment of the National Farm Toy Museum. Claire Scheibe passed away in 2000.

Ray Crilley
(inducted, 1993)

For many years, Ray Crilley was the editor and publisher of *Miniature Tractor and Implement*, a publication designed for farm toy collectors. In his unceasing efforts to gather information that could be used by collectors (including himself), Ray has co-authored several books on farm toys-most notable among those books was one entitled *Collecting Model Farm Toys of the World*. When it comes to top names in the farm toy hobby, Crilley ranks among the most knowledgeable.

Jim and Susan Higbee
(Inducted, 1994)

Jim and Susan Higbee took an early lead in farm toy display excellence by winning the "best of Show" award at the very first National Farm Toy Show, an honor they repeated in 1983. In the true and finest spirit of the farm toy hobby, Jim and Susan were always willing to help new or experienced collectors alike. In addition to their enthusiasm for farm toys, the Higbees demonstrated a devotion to American agriculture by helping with 4-H clubs.

Charles "Chuck" and Barb Burkholder
(inducted, 1994)

Burkholder Enterprises, established by Charles and Barb Burkholder, in the 1970s, has provided decals and parts available to farm toy collectors since the 1970s. Always in touch with the farm toy hobby, the Burkholders would attend numerous farm toy shows, big or small. Chuck also co-authored several books on farm toy collecting, including the highly regarded *Collecting Model Farm Toys of the World*.

Daryl A. Miller
(inducted, 1995)

Daryl Miller founded the first known publication entirely devoted to farm model collecting, *Toy Farm Equipment*, in late 1977. Miller, a fan of "real" farm machinery, started *Red Power Publication* in May of 1986.

Bob Heberer
(inducted, 1995)

Bob Heberer is one of the founders of the Gateway Mid-America Toy Show & Auction in St. Louis, Missouri and a charter member of the Gateway Toy Club also in the St. Louis area. Heberer has always been involved with agriculture, both through the agribusiness field and the support of various youth organizations.

Joseph Carter
(inducted, 1996)

Joseph Carter founded Carter Machine & Tool Company January 1, 1940. In 1956, Carter's company began manufacturing toys for original equipment manufacturers as well as being marketed them through Carter Tru-Scale, a name synonymous with quality scale farm models. The Carter Tru-Scale toys now stand as monuments to early die-cast and stamp-metal manufacturing of farm scale toys.

Roy Lee Baker
(inducted, 1996)

During the early years of his farm toy collecting, Roy Lee Baker was directly involved with manufacturing farm toy models, particularly 1:64-scale. Baker Manufacturing has provided scale model tractors for both the farm toy hobby and the Mid-America Toy Show held annually in St. Louis, Missouri.

Eldon Trumm
(inducted, 1997)

Eldon Trumm is known for his vast authoritative knowledge and collection of John Deere farm toys. He has authored and co-authored many informative books on the farm model hobby, including the *Trumm & Zarse* series of identification guides. Trumm is one of the original organizers of the Annual Plow City Farm Toy Show in Moline, Illinois.

Robert "Bob" Zarse
(inducted, 1997)

Bob Zarse has always been a person who has unselfishly shared his "International" knowledge with farm model collectors. Zarse was one of the original organizers of the Annual Lafayette Farm Toy Show in Lafayette, Indiana in 1979. He has authored and co-authored numerous books on the collecting farm toys, including the *Trumm & Zarse* series of identification guides. Zarse is one who labors endlessly in the pursuit for knowledge that can be shared throughout the farm toy collecting hobby.

Lyle Dingman
(inducted, 1998)

Considered a pioneer in farm model building business, Lyle Dingman, working hand in hand with Gilson Riecke, provided a steady stream of quality custom-made models that were not readily available from major farm toy manufacturers. Dingman was one who always had time to explain to collectors the How's, What's and Why's of farm toy collecting. Dingman passed away in 1992.

Gilson Riecke
(inducted, 1998)

Gilson Riecke's talent to build models "just like the real thing," has made him recognizable to farm toy collectors around the world. A dedicated artesian who never thought any detail was too small to display, Riecke was faced with many challenges during his early years. His work is now widely recognized as some of the finest in the farm toy collecting hobby today.

Wayne Samuelson
(inducted, 1999)

Wayne Samuelson has devoted many years of his collecting life both studying and identifying pedal tractors. Samuelson is now widely recognized as an expert in the pedal tractor area. Samuelson later established Samuelson's Pedal Tractor parts, a supplier of both parts and valuable information to the pedal tractor collector.

Joseph Ertl
(inducted, 1999)

Joseph Ertl founded Scale Models in 1978. Scale Models is devoted to smaller production runs of models, filling a niche for both the farm toy collector and original equipment manufacturers. Ertl has been an innovator of new models for the collecting hobby with Scale Model's large scale models (1:8-scale), the revision of pedal tractors and the reissue of past farm toys.

Graham and Michelle Miller
(inducted, 2000)

Graham and Michelle Miller have been a driving force in farm toy collecting both in Great Britain and Europe. Their desire to bring collectors together to share the hobby is quite well known. Their daily sharing of information about the farm toy hobby has generated thousands of new collectors. The Millers are also involved with the farm toy hobby in the United States as both importers and exporters. Each year they host an "open weekend" that brings collectors from near and far to share the farm toy experience.

Dave Bell
(inducted, 2001)

Having been involved with farming much of his life, Mr. Bell's knowledge and experience provides a sound basis for his later involvement with farm toy manufacturing. First with the Ertl Company and later and a CEO of his own company, SpecCast, his visions and dedication helped create the National Farm Toy Show and the National Farm Toy Museum. Farm toy collectors and Dyersville residents are thankful for Dave's untiring efforts.

Everett and Myra Weber
(inducted, 2001)

Ev and Myra Weber along with family members had created many award-winning exhibits depicting a wide variety of significant milestones in agricultural history. The Weber's use of hand crafted precisely detailed scale models having operating features makes exhibits almost come alive. Their dedication to accurate research and creativity is not only admired by farm toy collectors, but serves as a foundation for farm toy manufacturers' new products satisfying an ever more demanding market.

Dennis and Joan Parker
(inducted, 2002)

As early pioneers of building and customizing scale model farm toys, Dennis and Joan Parker paved the way in opening that facet of the hobby to all collectors. Realizing the need for custom and OEM parts, Dennis and Joan started Dakota Toys in 1981. The Parkers are recognized for simplifying the process of restoring and customizing farm toys by providing instructions and itemized parts lists in magazines and custom-building books. Dakota Toys' parts catalog has become the most recognized resource manual known to farm toy collectors. Since retiring in 2000, Dennis and Joan continue to share their knowledge of customized farm toys with collectors world wide.

Bob Condray
(inducted, 2003)

Bob Condray has had a lengthy and multi-faceted involvement in collecting and manufacturing farm toys. His interest in collecting was sparked in the early 1960s when he began repairing his children's toys. As Bob's knowledge of farm toys grew, he began to build custom scale-model toys. His toys are identified by their rich history and play value. Bob also contributed to the toy collecting hobby by organizing a popular toy show in Kansas City for 20 years. His support and passion for preserving a toy's story has been an inspiration to all enthusiasts of all ages.

The National Farm Toy Museum Hall of Fame

Doug Harke
(Inducted, 2003)

Doug Harke's enthusiasm for farm toys was sparked in his early childhood years. Growing up in Edmonton, Alberta Canada, the variety of model toys to collect was limited. He began attending toy shows in the eastern U.S. and eventually started to participate at shows as a dealer. His interest in collecting and restoring farm toys continued to grow and so did his interest in researching farm toys. Doug began writing for *Toy Tractor Times* in 1987 and *Toy Farmer* in 1992. As a teacher involved with academics, Doug enjoys research work necessary to write an informative article and finds it rewarding to educate new collectors.

Dick Sonnek
(Inducted 2004)

Dick Sonnek's interest in collecting toys began in 1968 when he attended his first auction. Though he was unsuccessful in his bid for the cast-iron Vindex toy, the experience opened his eyes to the value of collecting rare toys. In 1988, Dick compiled the first comprehensive price resource for Farm Toy Collectors, appropriately named, "Dick's Farm Toy Price Guide." The popularity of this guide was immediate. Now, over 4,500 copies are sold annually. Today, Dick continues to organize the long standing Mankato Toy Show and enjoys the quiet solitude of the family farm tending several acres of gardens and lawns near Mapelton, Minnesota.

Robert Earl Gray (Bob Gray)
1918-1983
(Inducted 2005)

Bob grew up on a farm near Eldora, IA and farmed there most of his life. He witnessed the early mechanization of farming and it left a distinct impression upon him. He carried those early memories with him all his life. His talents allowed him to make model toys from those memories. He began building those model toys in the early 50's and with encouragement from family and friends began to produce models for the public in 1968, under the name Pioneers of Power. Together with his wife Leona, they produced various "cast iron like" model toys until his death in 1983. His passion for Farm Toys lives on through his model toys today.

Fred Ertl Jr.
(Inducted 2005)

Fred was born in Dubuque, IA on 6-6-1930 to a German immigrant father and his mother, a Cascade IA farm girl. In September 1945, his father started the Ertl Co. in the basement of their Dubuque home. Since the beginning, Fred Jr. was continuously involved in the business until retirement 47 years later. Fred assumed the active management and Vice President position in September 1948 at the age of 18. He lead the continual growth, including the move to Dyersville, IA and sale of the company to Victor Comptometer in December 1967 when he became President. He continued in this position through the acquisition of Victor by Kiddie Corp. in December 1977 and Hanson PLC in September 1987. He became CEO in 1990 and retired on September 30, 1992. He was inducted into the Toy Manufacturers of America Hall of Fame in February 2000. He served on many Toy and Hobby industries Boards and was President of the Toy Manufacturers of America, 1970-71 and the Hobby Association in 1976. The Ertl Co. became and still is the heart of farm toy collecting worldwide.

Stan Krueger
(Inducted 2006)

Back in the '50s when Stan was about 10 growing up on the family farm, he began modifying toy trucks that he received as Christmas gifts at the Tonka Toys' Christmas Party. After working several jobs, a tour of Korea with the Army and college, his interest continued well into his adult years. By 1981 he along with his new wife, Sandi established Standi Toys, Inc., a husband and wife collaboration, which produces 1/64 scale toys & accessories, 1/16 replacement and custom parts. Stan, labeled "The Godfather of 1/64 Scale" in recognition of all the various parts Standi Toys has produced for that scale. Now, after more than 25 passionate years in the farm toy hobby, Stan is just as enthusiastic now as he was as a youngster. Stan is yet another example of turning his passion into a profession.

Farm Toys A to Z

An Introductory Guide to Farm Toy Manufacturers

by Mark Rich

Farm toys have appeared in great variety through the years, toy animals, implements, vehicles, farmer figures, and barns.

In dime stores, children and their parents could buy simple toy farm tractors without accessories, which were enough to conjure up an entire imaginary farm on the playroom floor…or pedal tractors that turned the backyard or sidewalk into imaginary cropland…or farm play sets, costing a few dimes or a dollar for a box or bag of farm figures and farm animals, in slush metal, cardboard, or plastic…or vehicle assortments, such as those sometimes produced by Hubley Mfg. Co., with tractors and machinery to be hitched behind…or truly complex play sets, such as the ones produced by Louis Marx & Co. in the 1950s through the '70s, with tin-litho farm buildings, various plastic vehicles and vehicle accessories, farm hands and farm families, farm animals, fences, feedsacks, and tiny pitchforks and shovels—and sometimes even miniature irrigation systems that would water seeds that would then, naturally, spring to life.

All reflected a fascination with the farm and rural life. If imaginary croplands and pastures counted in the tally, it would be a true statement to say that almost every child growing up in America worked on a farm—back in the good old days.

Advanced Products

Advanced made die-cast scale farm toys in the 1950s. Its line emphasized Massey-Ferguson model tractors.

Airfix

This British company, based in London, Airfix issued plastic kits from the early postwar years. It began producing plastic soldiers in the early 1960s. Its line included Western, World War II, Medieval, and space figures. While its specialty was in model kits of airplanes, boats, and military vehicles, its products would include items of farm-toy interest.

By mid-decade, Airfix Corp. of America was established at 421 E. Allegheny Ave., Philadelphia, Penn. It moved frequently, by 1966 becoming Airfix by Craft Master Corp., 126 Groesbeck Hwy., Mt. Clemens, Mich., then located in 1967 at 328 N. Westwood, Toledo, Ohio.

In the later 1970s it was distributed by USAirfix, a division of Ava International Inc., Waco, Texas.

Airfix bought the "Dinky" line in 1971, producing it through the end of the decade, when the factory making the line closed. Airfix also issued some large steel toys under the "Mogul" name.

Ajax Plastic Corp.

Founded in 1949, Ajax started its soft-plastic toy line with copies of "Beton" Western figures and Barclay soldiers. The company appears to have continued operations into the late '60s.

Alden Industries

A manufacturer of bagged and blister-packaged plastic toys, Alden Industries included farm toys in its line. The firm was located at 50 Beckwith Ave., Paterson, N.J., in the 1960s.

Amatoy Corp.

Located at 140 S. Dearborn St., Chicago, Ill., Amatoy made farm sets in the late 1940s.

American Precision Co.

American Precision issued toy tractors in the late 1940s and '50s, including the Allis-Chalmers C of 1949. The firm was located at 121 N. Broadway, Milwaukee, Wis., around 1947-49.

Amloid Co.

This manufacturer of plastic toy made farm toys, in addition to its many soldier, boat, vehicle and infant toys. It was making molded plastic toys at 81 Fifth St., Rochelle Park, N.J., from the late 1940s until the late '60s, when the address changed to Fifth St., Saddle Brook, N.J. Its early specialty of celluloid infant toys remained part of the Amloid line into the early '50s.

Animate Toy Co.

This New York City firm was established in the toy business as early as 1915, when it released its game, "Bugville Games." The company is best known as a manufacturer of tin wind-ups, with the most famous being its climbing tractors, starting with the "Baby Tractor" patented in 1916.

In the 1920s, the company was located at 31 E. 17th St., New York City. By the 1930s, when the firm had moved to 30 N. 15th St., East Orange, N.J., Animate was issuing both climbing tractors and tractor sets. The company also made toy road building and logging sets. In the later '30s, Animate Toy Co. closed its doors, and the "Animate" line of mechanical toys was issued by Woodhaven Metal Stamping Co., Inc.

Arcade Mfg. Co.

Arcade Manufacturing Co. of Freeport, Ill., made cast-iron toys from the late 1800s into the early 1940s. Its earliest toys included novelties, small stoves, banks, and floor trains. By the 1910s Arcade was producing horse-drawn vehicles, which were a major part of its toy line into the '30s. In 1922 the company made the move that would ensure the fame of its toy-making name. The toy proved popular and went through several versions. It introduced a Yellow Cab toy through an exclusive, mutually profitable arrangement with the Yellow Cab Company. Arcade also made Austins, Buicks, Chevrolets, and Fords, as well as Allis-Chalmers, Avery, Fordson, McCormick-Deering and Oliver farm equipment.

The slogan "They Look Real" was used on the "Arcade Cast Iron Toys"

line of the 1920s, when the Freeport, Ill., manufacturer was making doll house sets; McCormick Deering Threshers and International Harvester implements; Mack fire and dump trucks; Hotpoint stoves; the "Yellow Cab" and other "Yellow" truck and coach miniatures; and household hardware including coffee mills and mop sticks.

Among the best-selling items for the company in the years before the Great Depression were the McCormick-Deering Spreader, McCormick-Deering Wagon, Fordson Tractor and Plow, and Fordson Tractor and Trailer.

Arcade ranks among the most important manufacturers of cast-iron toys, having produced over 250 different models. It manufactured toys of miscellaneous materials during World War II, and closed in 1946.

Arco

See Auburn Rubber Co.

Armor Industries, Inc.

The "Slik-Toy" farm toys, cars and trucks of the late 1950s and '60s were made by this Lansing, Iowa, firm. It had its start around 1957. See also the original manufacturer, Lansing Co., Inc.

Auburn Rubber Co.

Considered the premiere manufacturer of rubber toys, Auburn Rubber Company of Auburn, Ind., began its toy-making days in 1935, although it had been in business since 1912. Both the Auburn Rubber and Double Fabric Tire Corp. names were used before 1935.

The company started with toy soldiers, and expanded its range the next year with the coffin-nosed Cord sedan, the first of many toy vehicles, all now highly prized by collectors. In addition to cars and toy soldiers, the company produced farm equipment, western figures, farm animals, pull-toys, toy tool kits, horseshoe games, emergency vehicles, trucks, airplanes, construction equipment, and motorcycles.

"Designed with plenty of juvenile Sales Appeal," Auburn Rubber boasted of its late '30s line of molded all-rubber toys. The line by 1939 included racers, automobiles, airplanes, trucks, tractors, farm implements, baseball players, soldiers, farm animals, brick

building blocks, sponge rubber blocks, available in both bulk and boxed sets. The former sold in the 5 to 50-cent range, while the later sold for prices from 50 cents to $1.00. Auburn ceased producing toys during wartime.

Most of the more distinctive figures Auburn released were the creative offspring of Roycroft-influenced illustrator Edward McCandlish, including farm animals and circus animals.

After using rubber for nearly two decades, in 1953 Auburn introduced vinyl, with the motorcycle of that year being possibly the first toy in that material. By 1955 the toy line was mostly vinyl, including the farm implements and animals.

Among the firm's most familiar toys are its toy tractors, featuring well-detailed farmer drivers at the wheel. In 1960, after moving to Deming, N.M., the firm's products were rubber and soft vinyl toys and novelties, sponge blocks, animals, building blocks, farm implements, and automobiles and other vehicles. It went out of business in 1969.

Bachmann Bros., Inc.

Bachmann manufactured a variety of plastic toys, and introduced its "Plasticville" miniature village around 1950. By the late '50s the company emphasized the usefulness of its Plasticville toys, including farm animals, for railroad layouts. It was located at 1400-38 E. Erle Ave., Philadelphia, Penn., from the late 1940s into the 1970s.

Banner Plastics Corp.

One of the most important manufacturers of smaller plastic toys from 1946 into the 1950s, Banner issued toy tractors, trucks, trains, boats, and a simple but popular circus train, also pulled by the farm tractor. The firm used trade names including "Bannertone" and "Bannerware." It was located at 80 Beckwith Ave., Paterson, N.J.

Banthrico

A company founded in 1931, and based on West Lake St., Chicago, Banthrico made die-cast savings banks and advertising novelties, with many John Deere items among them. It is best known for die-cast banks in vehicle designs, issued through the

Boomer years.

Bergen Toy & Novelty Co., Inc.

Established in Carlstadt, N.J., in the mid-1930s by Charles Marcak, Bergen's initial line consisted of lead soldiers. Beginning in 1938, in cooperation with the injection-molding firm Columbia Protektosite Co., Bergen issued the "Beton" acetate soldiers, cowboys and Indians, and railroad figures. The line, rather than being hampered by materials restrictions in wartime, enjoyed healthy growth as the metal toy soldier manufacturers ceased production.

Once Bergen moved to Hackettstown, N.J., after the war, it was producing all its own toys. "Beton Toys" sets included the "Dairy Farm and Cattle Range" and other farm sets of farm worker and animal toys. These retained their popularity through much of the 1950s. The toys were typically offered in polyethylene bags, as rack items, from the mid to late 50s.

During this time Louis Marx & Co. and other manufacturers had aggressively entered the world of plastic figure play sets. Bergen's assets were apparently acquired by Rel Manufacturing Corp., probably around 1958. The figures were also copied by other manufacturers.

Beton

See Bergen Toy & Novelty Co.

Bowman Bros.

In the late 1940s and early '50s, Bowman Bros. made toy tractors and farm implements, as well as water pistols, wheel goods, and roller skates. The firm was located at 1355 Market St., Merchandise Mart, San Francisco, Calif.

Milton Bradley Co.

Located at 74 Park St., Springfield, Mass., Milton Bradley was responsible for a number of farming-related toys and games, including the "Farm Friends" and "Farm Scenes" puzzles and "Farm Life" posters of the 1940s and early '50s, and the "Farm Toy Animals" of the early to mid-'50s.

William Britains Ltd.

A London, England, firm established around 1850 by William Britain, Sr., Britains manufactured small toys, including many mechanical items.

The founder's son, William Britain, Jr., developed the three-dimensional hollow-cast lead soldier in 1893. The firm produced faithful replicas of more than 100 British Army regiments in its first decade.

Britains grew to become the world's largest producer of lead toy soldiers, with many farm toys among them. Britains produced a variety of toy vehicles as well, including a series under the "Lilliput" name. Britains changed its production of toy soldiers from lead to plastic in 1966.

Bruder

This Fuerth, Germany, family firm was established in 1926 by Paul Bruder to make brass reeds for a toy trumpet manufacturer. After the interruption of WWII, Bruder resumed work, with son Heinz Bruder joining the business in 1954, eventually becoming sole owner in 1965. The firm, which had been making reeds, squeakers, and small toys by the early '50s, acquired an injection molding machine, and by the late '70s was issuing a full line of small toys, including vehicle toys. One of its important toys was the "Knallpistole," or "Pop Pistol," introduced in the mid-1960s.

By the end of the 20th century the firm's lines included infant toys, a "Profi" line of farm and construction vehicles, and "Roadmax," "Standard," and "Bruder Mini" lines of miscellaneous vehicles.

Built-Rite Toys

Located at 3200 South St., Lafayette, Ind., Built-Rite made "fibreboard model toys," including farm play sets, from 1941 through the war years. It became a division of Warren Paper Products Co. in the late 1940s, and continued making toys through the '50s and '60s.

During the years of World War II it was a major manufacturer of toy farm sets, including the "Ward's Modern Stock Farm" sets.

Burnett

A British manufacturer of lithographed tinplate toys, Burnett issued delivery vans and a series of simple "Ubilda" kits. The latter line was taken over by Chad Valley after WWII.

C.A.W. Novelty Co.

Active in the late 1930s, C.A.W. Novelty issued molded plastic and slush-metal toys, including automobiles, airplanes, and trucks. It was located at 614 Washington St., Clay Center, Kans., around 1937-39.

Carter Tru-Scale Machine Co.

This Rockford, Ill., firm specialized in miniature metal scale-model farm machinery, scale-model steel trucks, and die-cast trucks and farm toys in the postwar decades. It was especially known for 1:16-scale John Deere farm toys.

Carter Machine and Tool Co. was founded soon after the war by Joseph H. Carter, and first supplied stamped-steel toy implements to Eska Co. in 1946. Carter designed most pieces marketed by Eska, and acquired the company in 1950. The company was soon active in the toy industry under the Carter Tru-Scale Machine Co. name. Its farm implement toys were based on International-Harvester and John Deere models; its trucks were International Harvester. Carter patented a free-steering toy tractor.

The firm was located at 1916 Eleventh St., Rockford, in the 1950s and 60s. Ertl Co., q.v., bought Carter Tru-Scale in 1970.

Castoys

See Mettoy Co. Ltd.

Chad Valley

This venerable British firm was founded in 1849 by Joseph and Alfred Johnson as a printing business, which they named Chad Valley in 1897 when they built a new factory near Birmingham. They began making toys around this time, and started issuing dolls in 1917.

Chad Valley established a name for tin-plate and clockwork toys, and in the late '40s also introduced a line of die-cast vehicles with clockwork motors, mostly at 1:50-scale. Some were used as promotional models for automobile dealerships. The vehicle toys were produced into the '50s. In more recent decades the Chad Valley name has appeared on die-cast toys made in China.

Comet Metal Products Co.

Established in Queens, N.Y., in 1919 by Abraham Slonim as a die-casting firm, Comet Metal Products began issuing solid-cast toy figures around 1940, when its address was 521 W. 23rd St., New York City. The figures, apparently based on figures by William Britains, included farm animals.

Conrad

Vehicle models by Gescha appeared under the "Conrad" name after 1977. See Gescha.

Corgi Toys

See Mettoy.

Craftoys

Based in Omaha, Neb., from the late 1930s until the onset of WWII, Craftoys issued slush-metal toys vehicles, including a Fordson tractor, racers, and Freight Train. It acquired and began using some of Ralstoy's molds in 1940.

Cragstan

Issuing Japanese-made tinplate and plastic toys in the 1950s and '60s, Cragstan's most famous toys were battery-operated mechanical toys, such as "Mr. Robot," "Overland Stagecoach," and "Telly Bear." The company also issued the "Detroit Seniors," a die-cast vehicle toy line in 1:43 scale, manufactured by Habonim, q.v.

Crescent Toy Co., Ltd.

Established in 1922 in London, England, Crescent Toy Co. initially emphasized production of lead soldiers. After WWII, the firm acted as distributor of Die Casting Machine Tools, q.v. Crescent also established a new factory in Wales for making die-cast toy vehicles, and produced these toys through the 1950s. The line included an extensive series of farm vehicles.

Cursor

A German manufacturer, Cursor produced plastic vehicle toys in the 1960s, typically modeling them on German makes. The firm introduced die-cast to its production methods in 1969. Its models included Holder and Fendt farm tractors.

Walter Czuczka

Czuczka issued pre-school toys, including farm animal sets, in the early to mid-1950s. The firm was located at 328 Langdon Ave., Mount Vernon, N.Y.

D.C.M.T.

See Die Casting Machine Tools Ltd.

The Dent Hardware Co.

One of the major names in cast-iron toys, Dent, based in Fullerton, Penn., was founded in 1895 by Henry H. Dent. It made toys until 1937, and continued in the business of making cold-storage equipment into the 1970s.

Dent's toy line included vehicles with balloon type rubber wheels, including various kinds of trucks, steam shovels, roadsters, tractors, fire engines, hook and ladders. The "Pioneer" fire truck, Ford Tri-Motor, and large hook-and-ladder trucks were popular items. Dent also made aluminum toys, repeater pistols, penny-toy tools, jackstones, banks, and toy ranges, and assembled box assortments, including "Toyland Treasure Chests" in the 1930s.

Deoma Micromodels

An Italian firm, Deoma Micromodels issued small die-cast vehicle toys in the 1950s and early '60s. It used the "Microtoys" trade name.

Design Fabricators

A plastics manufacturer in the early 1950s, Design Fabricators issued plastic toys including 1:16 scale International Harvester Farmall Cub.

Diapet

See Yonezawa Toys.

Die Casting Machine Tools Ltd.

A firm based in North London, England, D.C.M.T. issued toys under the trade name "Lone Star" from the early 1950s through 1983, after which time the line was apparently sold to other toy concerns. Its toy vehicles included the "Road-masters" line, starting in 1956 (the name lost its hyphenation in 1962); and "Roadmaster Major," starting around 1969. The Farm King Tractor appeared in the latter line. The company's line of smaller, "Matchbox" style vehicles began with the "Impy" line, 1966-68, followed by the "Flyers," from '68 through the mid-'70s. It was again called the "Impy" line from 1976 into the '80s. The firm also made Western toys, including cap pistols.

The Dinky Collection

See Universal Toys.

Dinky Toys

See Meccano; also Solido; also Airfix.

Dowst Mfg. Co.

Brothers Charles and Samuel Dowst, trade-journal publishers, saw the Line-o-Type machine being demonstrated at the Chicago World's Columbian Exposition of 1893. Though the machine was designed to cast type for printing, the Dowsts saw its potential for other applications. Being publishers of the National Laundry Journal, the Dowst Bros. Co. first used the machine for making collar buttons and promotional trinkets, including miniature sadirons. By the turn of the century his company, based in Chicago, Ill., was focusing almost entirely on die-casting.

A major turning point came in the years 1910 and 1911, after years of making miniature objects used as premiums by various companies, including Rueckheim Bros. & Eckstein. In 1910, Dowst Bros. Co. made several size models of Louis Blériot's "aeroplane" which flew over the English Channel in 1909. It followed these toys with its 2-inch "Limousine," a fairly generic depiction of a contemporary luxury car. In 1914 the firm manufactured its first miniature car openly modeled on an existing car, its "Flivver," or 1914 Model T Ford convertible. This toy is considered the first die-cast model miniature of a real car made in America. It remained in production at Dowst until 1926. The names "Tootsie Toy" and "Tootsietoy" had started appearing on the firms toys by the early 1920s, the name itself reflecting the birth of a girl into the extended Dowst family, whose nickname was "Tootsie." The name was trademarked in 1924.

Two years later, Nathan Sure bought Dowst Bros. Co. and moved it adjacent to his Cosmo Toy & Novelty Co. He named the resulting firm Dowst Mfg. Co., a name it retained until the early 1960s.

By the early 1930s, the "Tootsietoy" line of metal automobiles, airplanes, doll house furniture, trains, and "5-cent and 10-cent goods" had high visibility in the toy world. The firm's line expanded to include toy "Buck Rogers" spaceships, toy dishes, "Basketball in Miniature," vending machine novelties, advertising novelties, and standard and special game markers, by the late 1930s.

In the Boomer years, Dowst's "Tootsietoy" line included die-cast metal automobiles, trucks, airplanes,

construction toys, farm toys, road-building toys, military toys, educational toys, party favors, doll accessories, bird feeder sets, and miniature novelties.

In 1961 the company bought the toy division of Strombeck-Becker Mfg. Co., and changed its name to Strombecker Corp., q.v. Farm toys continued to appear under the Tootsietoy name into the 2000s.

Dugu

Italian manufacturer Dugu, established in Varallo Sesia in the early 1960s, issued a variety of die-cast toy vehicle lines. The 1:43 "Miniautotoys" were introduced in 1963, and the "Museo" series, in 1964. Both lines continued to 1972. The "Sispla" line of 1:43-scale toys issued from 1974 were re-issues of the earlier Dugu toys. The same toys may have also appeared under the "Oldcars" name.

Eisele

A manufacturer of toy farm tractors in the 1950s, Eisele's models included Massey-Harris tractors.

Elastolin

The "Elastolin" line, produced by German firm O&M Hausser starting in 1901, enjoyed international popularity. Its wide range of composition toy figures included ones designed for barnyard scenes. The line was imported and distributed by Block House, Inc., of New York City in the 1920s and '30s. In 1947 the firm turned to plastic. It remained in operation until 1983.

Empire Plastic Corp.

Empire was located at 42-34 Bronx Blvd., Bronx, around 1948. At the top of its line were the "Havatoy" plastic toys, which included farm animals. Empire also made infant toys, banks, and balls. Around 1950-51, it moved to 375 E. 163rd St., Bronx, and at the same time appears to have dropped the Havatoy name.

Empire Plastic's toys included polyethylene riding toys for younger children, tractors among them. It also made dart games, water guns, and sports sets. The firm was based in Pelham Manor, N.Y.

The Ertl Co., Inc.

Founded in Dubuque, Iowa, by unemployed foundry worker Fred Ertl, Sr., the Ertl Co. began in 1945 as a family business. Ertl had learned sand-casting techniques in Germany. His son, Fred Ertl, Jr., began actively managing the company as early as 1948. The firm moved to Dyersville, Iowa, and grew to become the premiere 20th century manufacturer of toy farm equipment, which it based on the original blueprints for machinery and vehicles built by such companies as John Deere and International Harvester. In 1967, Victor Comptometer Corp. acquired Ertl. In the same year, Fred Ertl, Jr., became president of the company.

In the post-Boomer years, Ertl manufactured die-cast promotional toy banks based on vintage model vehicles, and promotional tractor-trailers. It also began issuing a variety of vehilces in 1:64-scale, some under the "Replicas" trade name.

Fred Ertl, Jr., was also instrumental in the effort to establish toy safety standards within the industry.

See also *Carter Tru-Scale Machine Co.*

Eska

Eska, based in Dubuque, Iowa, made chain-drive juvenile tractors and farm equipment in the 1950s and '60s. Its materials included cast aluminum. Beginning in 1946 it produced pressed-steel toy farm implements designed by Carter Machine and Tool Co. See also *Carter Tru-Scale Machine Co.*

Fisher-Price Toys, Inc.

Fisher-Price Toys was founded in 1931 in East Aurora, N.Y., near Buffalo. It produced miscellaneous farm-related numbers among its wood-and-litho pull toys, before and after World War II. In the 1960s F-P introduced the "Little People" toys, with the "Fisher-Price Play Family Farm" appearing in 1968.

Forma

An Italian manufacturer, Forma issued 1:43-scale toy vehicles in the 1970s, including numerous farm toys. See also *Yaxon.*

Friendly Acres

Barn sets; see *Kiddie Brush & Toy Co.*

Gama

A manufacturer of tinplate toys, Gama was named for Georg Adam Mangold, who established the firm in 1882 in Fürth, Germany. Die-cast vehicle toys became a part of its line

in 1959. In the 1990s, Gama issued "Schuco" toys.

Gamda

See Habonim.

Garton Toy Co.

A Sheboygan, Wis., manufacturer, Garton was one of the prominent names in juvenile toy vehicles. It established its name in the 1930s and '40s with pedal cars, coaster wagons, "Buddie Bikes," "Buddie Kars," wagons, velocipedes, Badger scooters, wheelbarrows, steering sleds, croquet sets, baby walkers, sidewalk cycles, and sand boxes, as well as outdoor furniture and lawn hose reels.

Through the Boomer years, Garton issued much the same line, adding outdoor and indoor golf sets and water skis.

Gescha

German manufacturer Gescha issued die-cast toy vehicles in the 1960s and '70s, issuing them under the "Conrad" name by 1978. Its toy cars were largely 1:43 scale, and its toy trucks, 1:50 scale.

Giordi

See Yaxon.

Graham & Matlack

This publisher issued Our Farmyard in 1915, a pop-up book. Also a manufacturer of pasteboard toy buildings, the firm may have made farms in its "Toytown" series.

Grey Iron Casting Co.

This toy-soldier firm, based in Mount Joy, Penn., produced farm sets around 1948.

Habonim

Located in Kibbutz Kfar Hanassi, Israel, Habonim manufactured die-cast toy vehicles in the 1950s, apparently using some molds from Die Casting Machine Tools Ltd. The toys were in 1:43 scale. In 1962 it issued new models under the "Gamda" name. It also combined with fellow Israeli company Koor to manufacture a series of 1:43 toy vehicles under the "Sabra" name, which were imported and sold as "Detroit Seniors" by Cragstan.

Hartland Plastics

Located in Hartland, Wis., this firm originally emphasized "Western Horses and Cowboys," as well as toy spurs, bridles, holsters, and guns in the mid-1950s. Around 1959 it became Hartland Plastics, Inc., and, possibly at the same time, became division of American Molded Plastics Co. When it was a division of Amerline Corp., which occurred by 1965, its focus had changed to emphasize model horse and cattle breeds. In 1970, the firm was located at 340 Maple Ave., and was employing 180 people making not only toys but also custom molding and industrial components.

Havatoy

Farm animals; see Empire Plastics Corp.

Hill-Standard Corp.

A manufacturer of juvenile vehicles since around 1900, Hill-Standard produced some farm-related toys, such as the "Junior Farm Wagon" of around 1934. Also a manufacturer of playground equipment, it was located in Anderson, Ind.

The Hubley Mfg. Co.

Founded in 1894 in Lancaster, Penn., by John E. Hubley, Hubley Mfg. Co. was one of the great names in cast-iron toys before World War II. In 1909 it purchased the Safety Buggy Co. factory. At the time it produced cast-iron toys, horse-drawn wagons and fire engines, circus trains, and cap guns. When the Great Depression hit, the firm survived by emphasizing the production of smaller, cheaper toys.

Hubley's 1930s output emphasized toy autos, buses, and trucks. The company also made banks, cap pistols, circus and fire toys, gas ranges, toy kitchen items, wheel toys, airplanes, motorcycles, and motorized toys.

Metal restrictions brought about by the advent of World War II brought Hubley's toy production to a halt in 1942. In the postwar years the firm's toys included die-cast and plastic toys, metal cap pistols and rifles, and leather holster sets.

Die-cast production had already begun to supplant cast-iron production as early as 1936, due to the increasing cost of shipping and increased competition from overseas manufacturers. Die-cast took a leading role after the war, and continued in importance after the company was purchased by Gabriel Industries in 1965. Both hard and soft plastic were also used for toy vehicles, including farm toys. "Hubley" die-cast toys were produced into the '70s, when Gabriel, a division of CBS, retired the name.

Husky

*See **Mettoy Co. Ltd.***

Husky Toy Co.

Based in Grand Rapids, Minn., Husky Toy Co. specialized in tractor construction toys, in the late 1950s and early '60s.

Ideal Novelty & Toy Co.

One of the most prominent toy manufacturers for much of the 20th century, Ideal was founded in 1903 in Brooklyn, N.Y., to manufacture dolls and stuffed toys. During the years around World War II, Ideal expanded its line to include plastic toy dishes and plastic toy boats, and was issuing plastic toy farm tractors and implements by the late 1940s.

Impy

Die-cast toy vehicles;
*see **Die Casting Machine Tools Ltd.***

Inter-Cars

*See **Nacoral.***

Intex Recreation Corp.

*See **Zee.***

Irwin Corp.

Based on West 20th St., New York City, Irwin made mechanical toys, celluloid infant's toys, moving picture projectors, cameras, and films in the late 1930s. In the Boomer years, it specialized in plastic toys, mechanical toys, dolls, pinwheels, tea sets, animals, roly-polys, floating toys, toy autos, whistles, and Easter novelties.

Irwin Toy Ltd.

*See **Joal.***

Jayline Mfg. Co., Inc.

A specialist in scale-model building construction sets, Jayline was founded around 1941, its first location being at the southeast corner of 55th and Wyalusing Ave., Philadelphia, Penn. It soon moved to 3915 Powelton Ave., Philadelphia, and then to Egg Harbor, N.J., in the later '40s. Best

known for its masonite doll houses, the company made farm sets until it closed its doors at the end of the 1940s.

Joal

Established in the late 1940s in Spain, Joal manufactured die-cast toy vehicles, mainly cars in 1:43 scale and trucks in 1:50 scale. By the 1990s, Irwin Toy Ltd. of Canada was issuing the "Joal" toys.

Jouef

A manufacturer based in Champagnole, France, Jouef issued plastic and die-cast model vehicles in 1:18 scale.

Jak-Pak-Inc.

This Milwaukee, Wis., firm had its start around 1950, based at 2631 S. 31 St., Milwaukee, Wis. While its initial rack-toy specialties included "Jak-Paks" jackstone sets, it made a variety of toys ranging from water pistols to police sets. It moved to 401 N. Water St. around 1953. The firm's line grew more varied during the mid-1960s, and in 1965-66 the firm changed its name to Jak-Pak, Inc., and its address to 120 E. Detroit St. The line included farm toys by at least 1967, by which time it was relocated at 236 N. Water St.

The Judy Co.

Located at 101 Third Ave. N., Minneapolis, Minn., Judy began issuing farm play sets in the early 1940s. After a move to 107 Third Ave. North, The company moved to 3120 N. Second St. in 1950.

"Judy's Farm" continued to be a part of the company's line into the early 1950s. The sets included people, farm animals, and vehicles made of thick rubber.

Kansas Toy & Novelty Co.

Based in Clifton, Kans., from its establishment in 1923, this specialist in slush-metal toys produced miniature airplanes, autos, racers, trucks, tractors, and steam rollers. Its eight-piece farm set was sold around 1935. The firm was founded by Arthur Haynes, an auto mechanic. In its heyday, the company ranked second to Barclay in the number and variety of its slush-metal toys, selling through stores including Woolworth's and Sears-Roebuck. Clayton Stevenson developed some molds for the firm.

Kellogg & Bulkeley

A publisher based in Hartford, Conn., in the 1850s, Kellogg & Bulkeley issued toys including "The Children's Farmyard," a farm play set of cut-outs.

The Kenton Hardware Co.

F.M. Perkins began manufacturing a patented line of refrigerator hardware in 1890, in Kenton, Ohio. The company began toy production in 1894 with a line of horse-drawn fire vehicles, toy stoves, and banks. The name became the Kenton Hardware Co. in 1900.

In the years 1903-1920 the Kenton name largely disappeared. In 1903, as part of the National Novelty Corp. merger, it produced toys under the name Wing Mfg. Co. After the break-up of National Novelty's trust, and several other takeover episodes, Kenton again emerged under its own name in 1920, and produced iron toys through the 1930s. Its line included banks, cap pistols, blank cartridge pistols, toy stoves and ranges, hook-and-ladder toys, automobiles, concrete mixers, airplanes, dirigibles, "Buckeye" ditchers, ladder toys, sand toys, and boxed assortments. A major manufacturer in the prewar years, Kenton maintained show offices in the Fifth Avenue Building.

Kenton continued in operation until 1952. A company called Littlestown Hardware & Foundry acquired the tooling for many Kenton toy designs and issued them under the brand name "Utexiqual" until that foundry closed in 1982.

Kiddie Brush & Toy Co.

This Jonesville, Mich., company made toy housecleaning sets in the 1930s. By the late prewar years its line included doll houses.

"Susy Goose," a trade name for the firm's toy sets, was introduced in the later '30s, and became the most prominent of the firm's trade names in the Boomer years. The name appeared on barn sets featuring tin buildings and plastic animals. The "Friendly Acres Dairy Farm" sets were also produced by the firm. The company used the slogan, "Toys That Mold Character."

Kiddie Toy

*See **Hubley Mfg. Co.***

Kilgore Mfg. Co., Inc.

A major toy manufacturer based in Westerville, Ohio, Kilgore began as a toy manufacturer in 1925 through the purchase of a kite-manufacturing business from the George D. Wanner Co.

Kilgore made its name in cast-iron toys, however, which it introduced in 1928. Its line included toy trucks, cars, fire engines, cap guns, and cannons. It produced toy paper caps after its merger with Andes Foundry and the Federal Toy Co. under the aegis of American Toy Co. The prestigious Butler Bros. Co. became its biggest distributor.

The 1930s Kilgore's line included single-shot and repeating cap pistols, using paper caps. It also made jackstones and toy vehicles with rubber tires. By the late '30s it was advertising play guns with "lustrous inlaid pearl grips," and "modern plastic toys." A major player in that decade, it maintained offices in the Fifth Avenue Building.

During wartime, the company was forced to cease manufacturing not only its cap pistols and paper caps, but also its plastic toys.

In the postwar years, Kilgore continued emphasizing toy cap pistols and paper caps, and added to its line mechanical and electronic toys and games.

The King Co.

Active in the late 1940s and '50s, the King Co. issued farm toys, including Massey-Harris tractor models.

LaKone

A small toy manufacturer of the 1950s, LaKone made farm toys including International Harvester Farmall models.

Lansing Co., Inc.

Established in Lansing, Iowa, in the prewar years, Lansing Co. initially specialized in button manufacture, using Mississippi River clam shells for material. Around 1940, Lansing introduced a line of farm toys. Although the well-known "Slik-Toy" line consisted of die-cast aluminum toy vehicles, the firm apparently also made steel toys. The aluminum toys were largely single-mold castings with black rubber tires.

The "Slik-Toy" line became a part of Armor Industries, q.v., in the 1950s, probably in 1956 when Lansing Co. ended toy production.

Lee Aluminum Foundry & Manufacturing

Located in New Albin, Iowa, Lee manufac990s.

Lesney Products

This London, England, die-casting firm was founded in 1947 by the unrelated friends Leslie Smith and Rodney Smith, joined later by John "Jack" Odell. The firm issued occasional die-cast toys, including an elaborate "Coronation Coach," until 1953, when the "Matchbox" line of miniature toy vehicles made its debut. Lesney established a 1 to 75 numbering system for the toys. Farm toys were an important part of the line, including both model tractors, combines, farm trailers, and farm trucks.

The 1-75 line was split into a United States numbering system and a rest-of-the-world system in 1981. In 1982, Universal Group bought the toy line. It changed hands again in 1992, after being bought by Tyco Toys, Inc.

Lido Toy Co.

Lido issued a diverse array of plastic toys through the 1950s and '60s, including bubble pipes, pick-up sticks, toy vehicles, tool sets, cowboy and Indian figures. Its hollow-plastic farm animals, sometimes in "Old MacDonald" packaging, were unmarked. In the 1950s it was located at 781 E. 135th St., New York City, relocating to 321 Rider Ave. by mid-decade. Becoming Lido Corp., it moved to 1340 Viele Ave., Bronx, N.Y., by the mid-1960s.

Lilliput

Die-cast toy vehicles; see **Britains.**

Lincoln Industries

Using molds that may have been acquired from Die Casting Machine Tools Ltd., Lincoln Industries issued die-cast toys in the 1950s. The firm was located in Auckland, New Zealand. In the later '50s it acquired molds for 1:43-scale vehicle toys. This tooling eventually became a part of Habonim's line, q.v.

Its 1:87-scale line included a Massey-Ferguson tractor.

Lincoln Specialties

A Canadian firm, Lincoln Specialties produced die-cast farm toys in the 1950s, including Massey-Harris tractors in 1:16 and 1:20 scales.

Lincoln Tool & Mfg. Co.

This Wisconsin firm made "Farmerette" miniature farm tools from around 1949 to around 1957-58. It was located at 1000 S. 5th St., Milwaukee.

Lincoln White Metal Works

Clayton and Ester Stevenson founded this Lincoln, Neb., firm in the early 1930s to manufacture slush-metal toy cars, buses, airplanes and trucks for sale through dime stores including Woolworth's and Kresges. The company continued through most or all of the decade.

Lines Bros.

Three brothers established Lines Bros. Ltd. in Britain in 1919, after separating from a family company involved in making toys and baby carriages. Its trademark depicted the three "lines" as sides of a triangle. In the 1920s the firm made wood pull toys, steel and wooden pedal cars, and other riding vehicles. By the later 1930s the firm had established a leading reputation in tinplate toys, under the "Tri-ang" trade name. Its "Tri-ang Minic Miniature Clockwork Vehicles" line consisted of pressed steel vehicles with spring motors, made especially notable in that all the line was made in the same scale. The initial line consisted of 14 models, from 3" to 7" in length. By wartime, the line had grown to some 70 models.

After the war, Lines Bros. issued toys essentially the same as its prewar line, adding new liveries to its trucks by 1947. These postwar models were exported to America in great numbers. Many of the toys became simpler in nature, with designs being altered, clockwork motors cut out, and plastic being employed. Lines Bros. remained the country's leading manufacturer of pedal cars.

In 1957, the firm introduced its "Scalextric" slot cars in 1:32 scale, featuring cars on an electrified track. In 1959 it launched the "Tri-ang Spot-On" line of 1:42-scale die-cast vehicle toys, manufacturing them in its Belfast, Northern Ireland, factory. The firm also introduced "Tommy Spot" play sets, including toy figures.

Lines Bros. bought Meccano in the early 1960s. By 1967 the firm phased out the "Spot-On" line in favor of the better established "Dinky Toys" line.

Lone Star

See Die Casting Machine Tools Ltd.

MPC

See **Multiple Products Corp.,** for plastic farm toys. The abbreviation was also used by Model Products Corp., a manufacturer of model kits, none being farm-related.

Majorette

This French manufacturer began issuing its die-cast toy vehicles in 1961 in Villeurbanne, suburb of Lyon. Its toys were based on European model cars and trucks, in scales ranging from about 1:50 to 1:90. They included farm tractors. Majorette purchased Solido in 1980.

Louis Marx & Co.

Louis Marx, born in 1896, entered the world of toy manufacturing within the organization of Ferdinand Strauss, who was "The Toy King" of the 1900s and 1910s. Parting ways in the 1910s, Marx established himself in the business in the late 1910s, finding in his brother a partner. In the 1920s and '30s Louis Marx & Co. emerged as a specialist in metal and mechanical toys.

Marx became a millionaire before age 30, due in great part to his practice of making less detailed, inexpensive versions of toys already popular, and issuing them in great quantity. Up through the Boomer years his company sold primarily through large department store chains and mail-order houses, making it unnecessary for him to advertise his wares.

Louis Marx & Co. issued a variety of farm-related toys, including both wind-up and battery-operated tractors, in both pressed steel and plastic. Its famous play sets of the 1950s and '60s included many with farm themes. Many were named simply called "Farm Set," while others appeared as the "Lazy Day" or "Happitime" farm sets. The "Happitime" series was sold through Sears, Roebuck and Co. Figures of the early '50s were made of a rubber-like

vinyl, soon replaced by a stiffer vinyl that lent itself to finer modeling details, and polyethylene.

Matai

See Micro Models.

Matchbox

See Lesney Products; also Universal Toys.

Maxwell Co.

The Maxwell Co. of Calcutta, India, manufactured die-cast toy cars and trucks beginning in the 1970s, apparently at first using the "Mini Auto Toys" trade name. Some of its toys were made from molds purchased from other manufacturers, including Lesney Products and Mettoy.

Mercury

Based in Turin, Italy, Mercury was founded in 1932 to manufacture die-cast toy vehicles. While primarily producing European models, Mercury did issue some U.S. models in its line. The models were issued in several scales, primarily 1:40 and 1:80. Some of the 1:40-scale models were issued with spring motors.

From 1954 to 1962 the company switched to 1:48 scale. Afterwards it produced models in the scale of 1:43, which had become standard. Later in the 1960s the firm attempted to compete with Lesney Products with its "Speedy" line in 1:66 scale, and in the late 1970s with the "Micro" line in a similar scale. The firm closed its doors around 1980.

See also *Scottoy.*

Meccano

Meccano of Liverpool, England, was founded in 1901 by Frank Hornby. Its specialty fell in the area of metal construction sets, of which the later "Erector" set of A.C. Gilbert was strongly reminiscent. In 1920, Hornby introduced "O" gauge toy trains to the line. In the 1930s the firm began producing metal miniature vehicles, in part as a way of providing accessories for the railway layouts and construction sets.

The first of the "Modelled Miniatures" were die-cast trains of the push-toy variety. By 1934 the company issued toy vehicles, and renamed the line "Dinky Toys." After WWII, Meccano added "Supertoys" to the Dinky line. These larger models of trucks were issued into the early 1950s.

In 1963 the company was bought by Lines Bros. The new owners introduced the "Mini Dinky" line in 1968, at a scale of about 1:65. The Dinky line ended in late 1979.

See also *Universal Toys*; also *Solido.*

Mettoy Playcraft Ltd.

Mettoy Playcraft Ltd. of Swansea, South Wales, was founded in 1943 and established its name in tinplate toys. In 1948, Mettoy introduced its "Castoys" line of die-cast toys with spring motors. In 1956, the firm inaugurated the "Corgi Toys" line, which featured miniature toy vehicles with die-cast bodies and clear plastic windows, which were a Mettoy innovation. The Corgi line included models from around the world. In the 1960s the line featured models based on television and movie vehicles, but also included many farm toys, including Massey Ferguson and Ford tractors, livestock transporters, and conveyors. Plastic animals were included with some of these toys. The "Husky" series of smaller die-cast toys made its debut in 1965. The name was changed to "Corgi Juniors" in 1970s. This line ended midway through the decade.

Micro Models

A Melbourne, Australia, manufacturer, Micro Models introduced its die-cast vehicle toy line in 1953, continuing it through the remainder the decade. In the mid-1970s the line was re-issued under the trade name of "Matai," and then again in New Zealand under the name "Torro." A third re-issue series appeared in the 1990s, under the name Micro Models Ltd. The line included a Ferguson tractor.

Micromodels

See Deoma Micromodels.
Micro Models of Australia may have also spelled its name this way on some toys.

Microtoys

See Deoma Micromodels.

Miner Industries

Miner became a manufacturer of farm toys with its acquisition of Multiple Toymakers in January 1968. See *Multiple Products Corp.*

Morgan Milton Pvt. Ltd.

Based in Calcutta, India, this

manufacturer of die-cast toy vehicles changed its name to Milton of Calcutta in the late 1970s or early '80s. It may have been associated with, or acquired by, Maxwell Co. Its toys, often in scales from 1:50 to 1:90, were issued in boxes under the "Mini Auto Cars" name.

Mini Auto Cars

See Morgan Milton Pvt. Ltd.

Mini Auto Toys

See Maxwell Co.

Miniautotoys

See Dugu.

Minic

See Lines Bros.

Minimac

These Brazilian-made toy military, construction, and farm vehicles were issued in 1:43 and 1:50 scales.

The Monarch Products Co.

Based in Tiffin, Ohio, Monarch made children's vehicles, scooters, "safety cycles," pedal cars, and baby walkers. Its lines included the mid-1930s "Monarch Master" velocipedes and "King Flyer" coaster wagons.

Morgan

See Morgan Milton Pvt. Ltd.

Mound Metalcraft Co.

See Tonka Toys, Inc.

Multiple Products Corp.

Located at 475 Fifth Ave., New York City, this company began around 1950 with such specialties as puzzles, "Magic Checkers," and Canasta card-shuffling trays. Its line began. It moved to 303 Fourth Ave. around 1953, expanding to include other toys in the mid-'50s, including toy pirate swords, bubble guns, and musical toys; then to 55 W. 13th St. around 1954.

Around 1956 Multiple started making the toys that became convenience-store staples across the country, from the later '50s into the '60s: "figures of pirates, animals, cowboys, Indians, farmers, soldiers, firemen," were listed in 1957. By that year both "farm animals" and "farm sets" were important items. Around 1964, the company became Multiple Products, Inc., and now based its operations at 1260 Zerega Ave., Bronx, N.Y.

It changed its name again in 1967 to Multiple Toymakers. In January 1968, it was acquired by Miner Industries, Inc.

The Murray-Ohio Mfg. Co.

The Murray Body Co. of Detroit, Mich., established this Cleveland, Ohio, subsidiary in 1919. Within four years the firm turned toward the making of juvenile autos, starting with vehicles based on White Truck Co. models. Through the 1920s it established its "Steelcraft" line, which enabled the firm to survive the Depression years. The "Steelcraft" pedal cars included Cadillacs, Huppmobiles, Lincolns, and Studebakers.

In the later 1930s and '40s it expanded its line, manufacturing toy automobiles, coaster wagons, scooters, steel toys, velocipedes, and sidewalk bicycles. It also established permanent display rooms in the Fifth Avenue Building.

After returning to the manufacture of wheel goods after WWII, Murray-Ohio moved to Nashville, Tenn., in 1957, and used the "Murray" trade name on its toys without eliminating the "Ohio" from its company name. It began manufacturing lightweight bicycles in 1965, and ceased producing pedal cars and other juvenile wheel goods in 1973.

Nacoral

A Spanish manufacturer of die-cast toy vehicles under the "Inter-Cars" trade name, Nacoral was established in the mide-1960s. Its line included both European and American makes of cars and trucks, with the cars produced in 1:43 scale, and the trucks in 1:50. Around 1970 the firm acquired the molds for the toy vehicles made by Belgian company Sablon.

National Playthings

A specialist in educational toys, novelty toys, and cap pistols, National Playthings also made farm sets in the late 1940s. It was located at 38 Prospect St., New Bedford, Mass.

National Sewing Machine Co.

In the 1930s and '40s, this Belvidere, Ill., manufacturer made iron toys under the "Vindex" name. Famous among collectors, these toys included buses, trucks, construction vehicles, racers, motorcycles, and

farm vehicles. The latter included a horse-drawn John Deere wagon.

Noma Electric Corp.

Located at 55 West 13th St., New York City, this specialist in Christmas lighting systems began making toys late during World War II. The line included a widely advertised 8-1/2" plastic "Farm Tractor." Animal toys included walking-action dog and duck. By 1947, the company was able to return to its original specialty.

Ny-Lint Tool & Mfg. Co.

Ny-Lint of Rockford, Ill., specialized in mechanical and scale-model toys. While its early toys in the late 1940s emphasized the mechanical end of the scale, including wind-ups, the company became best known for its heavy toy road-construction vehicles.

NZG

Established in 1968, German manufacturer Nurnberger Zinzdruckgussmodelle, or NZG, produced toy vehicles, including construction and farm equipment, in scales ranging from 1:24 to 1:87.

Ohio Art Co.

Ohio Art of Bryan, Ohio, is one of the best-known manufacturers of both prewar and postwar tin toys. In the 1930s its line included toy tea sets, trains, drums, laundry sets, washing machines, sand pails, sprinklers, and toy sweepers.

In the Boomer years the company's line continued expanding, with popular items including farm play sets with plastic toy tractors, plastic animals, and tin-litho barns. The toy animals were unmarked, and appeared in both hard-plastic and soft-plastic versions.

Old Cars

Established in 1975 in Turin, Italy, Old Cars issued die-cast and plastic vehicle toys in scales including 1:43 and 1:50. Its models were primarily truck and construction vehicles. The name was sometimes spelled as one word, "Oldcars."

Old Time Toys

Active in the late 1960s, Old Time Toys issued sand-cast copies of toys, including Arcade's Fordson F, in aluminum.

Penny

*Die-cast toy vehicles; see **Politoys**.*

Plasticville

*See **Bachmann Bros**.*

Plastine Mfg. Co.

Located at 207 E. 84th St., New York City, Plastine made molding activity sets with two-part molds, including the popular "Farm Animals" set of the early 1950s.

Playskool Institute, Inc.

A Milwaukee, Wis., firm, Playskool was producing high-quality pre-school playthings in the 1930s and '40s, when its line included home kindergarten equipment as well as educational toys and games. Its "Playskool Hammer-Nail" proved popular, with other toy titles including "Indian Beads," "Totem Pole," "Playskool Theatre," and "Playskool Pullman." Similar toys appeared with farm themes, through the years.

In the Boomer years, Playskool touted itself as the world's largest manufacturer of wood toys. It reached this point by acquiring other companies, which continued operating as divisions of this now Chicago, Ill., based company. These included Holgate Toys, Appleton Juvenile Furniture, Lincoln Logs, and Makit Toy. Its farm toys were numerous, such as the 1968 ride-on "Tot Tractor," made of wood and molded plastic for 2-5-year-olds.

Playskool Mfg. Co. was located at 3720 Kedzie Ave., Chicago, in the 1960s.

Polistil

*See **Politoys**.*

Politoys

A manufacturer of plastic toys established in 1960 in Italy, Politoys issued scale model vehicles in 1:41 scale. The firm introduced die-casting to its processes in the mid-1960s. Early models were in 1:43 scale, with a line in 1:66 scale issued by 1967 under the "Penny" name. The firm changed its name to Polistil in 1970. Tonka Toys acquired the line in the late 1980s.

Processed Plastic Co.

*See **Tim-Mee Toys**.*

Product Miniature Co., Inc.

Product Miniature, based at 2240 So. 54th St., Milwaukee, Wis., first made waves on the national toy scene with a plastic tractor and farm-trailer set, in the 1949-50 season. The item's name was anything but succinct: "Plastic Model of International Harvester Farmall Tractor and McCormick-Deering Tractor-Trailer." The tractor was 8" long, 3-1/2" high; the trailer, 6-1/2" long, not including the hitching pole, and 3-1/2" high.

Farm toys continued to be central to its success in the subsequent decade. It billed the toys as "Tru-Miniatures" by 1952, when its expanded line also featured an orange Allis-Chalmers "WD" Tractor (8" long) and wagon (6-7/8" long). These toys were made to scale, based on factory blueprints. By mid-decade, remote-control toy vehicles and plastic model kits, including farm-tractor kits, became important parts of the line.

In the later '50s, the firm moved to Pewaukee, Wis. The firm's "Action Toy" line included toy versions of the Wienermobile and Trailways bus, in addition to trucks and tractors.

In 1970, the company was located at 627 E. Capitol Drive, Pewaukee, and was employing 25 people in injection-molding, hot-stamping, and painting plastic parts, plastic panels, and plastic packaging.

Reich Bros., Ltd.

The Canadian toy firm Reich Brothers made farm sets in the 1970s, in addition to its toy trucks, dolls, holster sets, and games. It was located at 70 de Bresoles, Montreal, Quebec.

Rel Manufacturing Corp.

Located at 475 Boulevard, East Paterson, N.J., from around 1958 into the early '60s, Rel made play sets of plastic figures. See Bergen Toy & Novelty Co.

Reliable Toy Co., Ltd.

Reliable was a producer of plastic toys including trucks, flying saucers, beach toys, boats, rifles and housekeeping toys in the Boomer years. Its farm animals closely resembled Auburn farm animals. The undersides of the toys were sometimes marked. It was located at 258 Carlaw Ave., Toronto, Ontario, Canada.

Renwal Toy Corp.

Plastic toys of all kinds, including farm toys, comprised this Mineola, N.Y., firm's line from 1945 into the 1960s.

Replica

*Die-cast toy vehicles; see **The Ertl Co., Inc**.*

Rextoys

This German firm, founded under the name Rex, began issuing toy vehicles in the early 1960s. The company later moved to Lausanne, Switzerland. The firm's 1:43- and 1:87-scale models largely depicted American makes.

Reuhl Products, Inc.

Based in Madison, Wis., Reuhl Products manufactured scale-model construction and farm vehicle toys in the 1950s, which it sold as "put-together toy" kits requiring no glue or tools.

First located at 2609 Monroe St., Madison, Reuhl specialized from the beginning in modeling and "put-together" kits, as well as custom plastic molding. It moved to 4505 Belt Line Highway, Route 3, Madison, around 1951, where it continued into the mid-decade. The company had a particular specialty in Caterpillar tractors and scrapers.

Roadmasters

*Die-cast toy vehicles; see **Die Casting Machine Tools Ltd**.*

Scale Models, Inc.

Located in Dyersville, Iowa, Scale Models was established by the son of the Ertl Co. founder Fred Ertl, Joe Ertl. The firm makes farm tractors in 1:16 scale, of models including Allis-Chalmers, McCormick-Deering, International Harvester, John Deere, and Fordson. It also produces a wide variety of farm implements.

Scaledown Models

Located in East Susex, England, Scaledown is a contemporary manufacturer of die-cast kits for making farm tractors and machinery, in 1:32 scale.

Scottoy

An Italian firm founded in Genova, Italy, in 1993, Scottoy has reissued some of the toys first made by Mercury in the 1950s.

Selchow & Righter.

A famous manufacturer of games, Selchow & Righter's enormous list included such farm numbers as the "MacDonald's Farm" game of the mid-1950s.

Shinsei

A Japanese manufacturer established in the late 20th century, Shinsei issued construction and heavy equipment vehicle toys in scales including 1:43 and 1:64.

Siku

Established in 1921 in Germany by Richard Sieper, Siku manufactured plastic toys from 1949 to 1963, when the firm introduced die-casting to its manufacturing processes. Its toy vehicles were typically in 1:55 scale.

Sispla

See *Dugu.*

Slik-Toy

Metal farm toys; see *Lansing Co., Inc.;* also *Armor Industries.*

Smer

A Czechoslovakian firm active in the late 20th century, Smer issued die-cast models, in scales including 1:32.

Solido

Established in 1932 by Ferdinand de Vazeilles, Solido issued die-cast toys in three series: the "Major," "Junior," and "Baby." The firm abandoned the "Major" line after WWII. The "Junior" series was roughly 1:40 scale, and the "Baby," 1:50. The firm began issuing 1:66-scale models under the "Mosquito" series name. In 1957 the company began issuing "100" series 1:43-scale vehicle toys. The "200" series military models and "300" series commercial models were first issued in the early 1960s. Later it issued a low-cost, budget-minded "Cougar" series.

French company Majorette acquired Solido in 1980. Some of its models were marketed under the "Dinky" name in 1980 and '81. In 1993, along with Majorette, Solido became a part of the Ideal Loisirs Group. Among other lines, its later products included the "Nostalgia" and "Yesterday" models, featuring re-issues of earlier models.

Spec Cast

Founded in 1974 in Rockford, Ill., Spec Cast initially produced die-cast belt buckles, and gradually expanded its line to include desk items and still models. In 1986, after being purchased by David Bell, the firm moved to Dyersville, Iowa. The line expanded to include promotional models of cars, trucks, and tractor-trailers in addition to its expanding line of tractors.

"Spot-On"

See *Lines Bros.*

"Steelcraft"

Vehicle toys; see *Murray-Ohio Mfg. Co.*

Strombecker Corp.

In 1961, Dowst Mfg. Co. bought the toy division of Strombeck-Becker Mfg. Co. The resulting, enlarged company became Strombecker Corp. Although it did not abandon the manufacture of die-cast toy cars, a great deal of the company's energies went into the production of electrical car racing sets, which proved profitable until the later 1960s, when competition grew so severe that the company returned its primary focus to its original strength, manufacturing die-cast toy vehicles under the "Tootsietoy" trade name. Farm toys continued to appear from Strombecker, as they had from Dowst earlier. Among them were the Farm Tractor with Utility Wagon, in the "Collector Series" of around 1968.

Structo Mfg. Co.

Louis and Edward Strohacker and C.C. Thompson founded Structo Mfg. Co. in Freeport, Ill., in 1908. Structo started issuing the "Ready-Bilt" line of vehicle toys in 1920. Its early pressed-steel toy automobiles were based on the Stutz Bearcat. Perhaps most characteristic of the line, however, were the Belgian-style military tank and the farm tractor. Its extensive line of toy vehicles in the Boomer years featured a variety of farm-related toys, including farm play sets in the late 1950s that incorporated plastic animals used in Ohio Art barn sets.

In the 1960s, its Kompak series of 9" vehicles included farm sets, including the No. 163 Kompak Pony Van and No. 196 Animal Set, both of 1968.

The Superior Type Co.

The "Farm Life" printing toy was an important product of this printing-toy company through the 1930s and '40s. Another title was "Down on the Farm" game. It was located at 3940 Ravenswood Ave., Chicago, Ill., in the 1930s, moving to 1800 W. Larchmont Ave. in 1940. The firm became Superior Marking Equipment Co. in the late 1940s.

Susy Goose

Barn sets; see *Kiddie Brush & Toy Co.*

Tekno

Danish manufacturer Tekno was established in 1920 as a manufacturer of tinplate toys. The firm changed to Dutch ownership in the mid-1970s, and afterward introduced a line of 1:43-scale die-cast toy vehicles.

Tim-Mee Toys

Established as a part of Anchor Brush operations in Aurora, Ill., in 1948, Tim Mee specialized in plastic play set figures, including a farm set with tractor, farm workers, fencing, and animals. The farm figures were not marked with the company name.

Tim-Mee Toys, Inc., relocated to Montgomery, Ill., in the mid-1960s, after being bought by Processed Plastic Co., a specialist in plastic toy trucks and other vehicles, then located at 500 Rathbone Ave., Aurora, Ill. The new address of the Tim-Mee Toys division, 1001 Aucutt Road, Montgomery, also soon became the address of Processed Plastics.

Tomy

A Japanese manufacturer with a general toy line that became prominent in the 1960s, Tomy inaugurated a line of die-cast vehicles toys in 1971 reminiscent of the "Matchbox" 1-75 line, beginning with six cars in scales roughly 1:60 to 1:65, along with plastic accessories and buildings. Later vehicle scales ranged as small as 1:100. The line remained prominent through the '70s, with both domestic and foreign making appearances. The firm used the trade names "Tomica" and "Pocket Cars." The "Pocket Cars" were issued in packaging resembling a denim pocket. Tomy also issued the "Dandy" series of vehicle toys, in mixed scales from 1:40 to 1:50, in the 1970s.

Farm Toys A to Z

Tonka Toys, Inc.

Mound Metalcraft Co. was established in Mound, Minn., in 1946. Its steel vehicle toys, introduced in 1947, bore the "Tonka Toys" name. In 1955 the firm changed its name to Tonka Toys. Known for its larger truck toys, the company made many farm-related toys that were important to the firm's success, especially by around 1960. The firm introduced the smaller "Mini-Tonkas" in 1963. It became Tonka Corp. in 1965.

See also *Politoys*.

Tootsietoy

See Dowst Mfg. Co.; also Strombecker Corp.

Topping Models

A manufacturer of die-cast scale farm toys in the 1950s, Topping Models specialized in the Massey-Ferguson line.

Torro

See Micro Models.

Tri-ang

See Lines Bros.

Tru-Miniature

See Product Miniature Co.

Tru-Scale Toys

See Carter Tru-Scale Machine Co.

Tru-Toy

Die-cast farm toys and trucks; see Carter Tru-Scale Machine Co.

The Ullman Mfg. Co.

A major manufacturer of paint sets in the 1930s, Ullman produced farm-related items including the "Farm Life" coloring outfits. It was based in Brooklyn, N.Y.

Universal Toys

David Yeh's Hong Kong-based toy company, Universal Toys, or Universal Group, issued toys under the "Kidco" name beginning in 1977. It became majority owner of LJN Toys the next year. The firm bought Matchbox Toys Ltd., the company formed out of the bankruptcy of Lesney Products in 1982.

Besides farm toys in the Matchbox line, Universal made other die-cast toys of a farm-related nature.

In Europe, both Kidco and LJN lines were afterwards marketed under the "Matchbox" name. Universal expanded the company's toy line to include the "Voltron" line of changeable action figures, along the lines of "Transformers," the "Monster In My Pocket" line, and such licensed dolls as the "Pee Wee Herman" dolls of 1988 and "Freddy Krueger" of 1989. Universal also bought rights to the "Dinky" name in 1987, and issued the first toy cars in the "Dinky Collection," in 1:43 scale, in 1989.

In 1992, Tyco Toys bought the Universal Group.

Vindex

Iron toys; see National Sewing Machine Co.

Ward's Modern Stock Farm

Play sets, 1940s; see Built-Rite.

The A.C. Williams Co.

A major manufacturer of iron toys, the A.C. Williams Co. was founded in 1844 in Chagrin Falls, Ohio. The factory was twice destroyed by fire. After the 1889 fire the firm rebuilt its factory in Chagrin Falls, in 1890; after the 1892 fire, in Ravenna, Ohio, in 1893. It was incorporated in 1905.

From 1893 into the 1920s it produced numerous wheeled toys including horse-drawn rigs, automobiles, airplanes, and tractors.

In the 1930s, the simply named "Tractor" was issued in red, blue, green, and tan enamel, with rubber tires and cast-in driver. It was 5" long and 2-3/8" high. Williams also made Ford stake trucks.

Wolfe Products Co., Inc.

A company that made general toys including doll beds, plastic checkers, toy dog houses, and educational sand toys, Wolfe Products Co. began making farm sets around 1950-51. It specialized in "Massey-Harris model toys." It was located at 820 Penn Ave., Sheboygan, Wis. By 1952, Reuhl Products seems to have acquired rights for making the Massey-Harris toys, and Wolfe Products was concentrating on its toy dog houses and sand toys.

See also *Reuhl Products, Inc.*

Woodhaven Metal Stamping Co., Inc.

Located at 62 Schenectady Ave., Brooklyn, N.Y., Woodhaven Metal Stamping Co. took over the "Animate" line of mechanical toys around 1938. The firm moved to 234 Chestnut St., Brooklyn, around 1950. It ceased making climbing tractors around 1958, twenty years after taking on the line.

See also *Animate Toy Co.*

Yaxon

An Italian manufacturer, in 1978 Yaxon began issuing the line of vehicle toys originally manufactured by Forma. The toys were later issued under the "Giodi" name.

Yonezawa Toys

Japanese manufacturer Yonezawa Toys made some of the outstanding tinplate toys of the 1950s. In the mid-1960s, it introduced a series of plastic vehicle toys in scales under the "Diapet" trade name. In 1969 the firm introduced die-cast methods to the line. The line emphasized Japanese models, the cars in roughly 1:40 scale and trucks in 1:50 or 1:60 scale.

Zee Toys

A manufacturer of die-cast miniatures, Zee International, Inc., was located at 740 W. 190th St., Gardena, Calif., in the early 1970s. It became Zee Toys, Inc., around 1974, and around 1976 moved to 4130 Santa Fe Ave., Long Beach, Calif. The company seems to have become a subsidiary of Intex Recreation Corp. in the 1980s. Farm toys were included, as in the "Mini Macks" set of around 1981, with the "Farm Tractor."

Farm Toy Figures

by Mark Rich

Ajax

Ajax, horse, 4-1/2" long.
EX $.50 **NM $1** **NPF**

Auburn

Auburn, calf, vinyl, 2" long.
EX $.5 **NM $1** **MIP n/a**

Auburn, rooster, vinyl, 1-3/4" high;
hen, 1-1/4" high. Each:
EX $.25 **NM $.50** **MIP n/a**

Auburn, colt, vinyl, 2-5/16" long.
EX $.50 **NM $1** **MIP n/a**

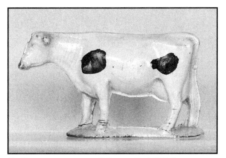

Auburn, cow, rubber, 3-1/2" long.
EX $10 **NM $15** **MIP n/a**

Auburn, cow, vinyl, open interior,
3-13/16" long.
EX $2 **NM $3** **MIP n/a**

Auburn, donkey, rubber, originally
with wheels, 3-3/4" long.
EX $10 **NM $15** **MIP n/a**

Auburn, donkey, vinyl, 2-3/8" long.
EX $2 **NM $3** **MIP n/a**

Auburn, duck, vinyl, 1-13/16" long.
EX $.25 **$.50** **n/a**

Farm Toy Figures

Auburn, farmer, vinyl, 3" high.
EX $2   **NM $4**   **MIP n/a**

Auburn, farmer carrying eggs, vinyl, 2-3/4" high.
EX $2   **NM $4**   **MIP n/a**

Auburn, boy carrying lunchbox, vinyl, 1-1/2" high.
EX $2   **NM $4**   **MIP n/a**

Auburn, goat, vinyl, 2-1/16" long.
EX $.50   **NM $1**   **MIP n/a**

Auburn, horse, rubber, originally with wheels, 3-3/4" long.
EX $10   **NM $15**   **MIP n/a**

Auburn, horse, vinyl, 3-3/4" long.
EX $1   **NM $3**   **MIP n/a**

Auburn, pig, rubber, 2-1/2" long.
EX $5   **NM $8**   **MIP n/a**

Auburn, pig, vinyl, 3-13/16" long.
EX $.5   **NM $1**   **MIP n/a**

Auburn, piglet, vinyl, 2-3/8" long.
EX $.25   **NM $.50**   **MIP n/a**

Auburn, pony, vinyl, 2-11/16" long.
EX $1   **NM $2**   **MIP n/a**

Auburn, sheep, vinyl, 1-15/16" long.
EX $.50   **NM $1**   **MIP n/a**

Auburn, turkey, vinyl, 1-3/4" high.
EX $.50   **NM $1**   **MIP n/a**

Bachmann

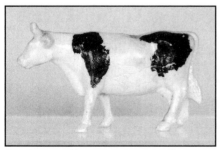

Bachmann Bros., cow, standing, hard plastic, 2-1/4" long.
EX $1   **NM $2**   **MIP n/a**

Bachmann Bros., cow, laying down, hard plastic, 2-1/4" long.
EX $1   **NM $2**   **MIP n/a**

Bachmann Bros., sheep, hard plastic, 1-3/8" long.
EX $1   **NM $2**   **MIP n/a**

Bergen

Bergen, billy goat, soft plastic, 2-1/8" long.
EX $2   **NM $3**   **MIP n/a**

Bergen, nanny goat, soft plastic, 2-1/8" long.
EX $2   **NM $3**   **MIP n/a**

Bergen, horse with saddle, hard plastic, 3-13/16" long.
EX $3   **NM $5**   **MIP n/a**

Bergen, ram, soft plastic, 2-1/4" long.
EX $2   **NM $3**   **MIP n/a**

Bergen, sheep, soft plastic, 2-1/4" long.
EX $2   **NM $3**   **MIP n/a**

Bergen, turkey, soft plastic, 1-1/4" long.
EX $1   **NM $3**   **MIP n/a**

Farm Toy Figures

Judy

Judy, goose, black rubber, 1-11/16" long.
EX $1   **NM $2**   **MIP n/a**

Judy, Pig, 1-11/16" long.
EX $2   **NM $4**   **MIP n/a**

Judy, sheep, black rubber, 1-15/16" long.
EX $2   **NM $4**   **MIP n/a**

Judy, farm truck, black rubber, 5-3/8" long.
EX $10   **NM $20**   **MIP n/a**

Kiddie

Kiddie Brush & Toy Co., dairy cow, "Friendly Acres Dairy Farm" or "Susie Goose," 2-1/4" long
EX $.50   **NM $1**   **MIP n/a**

Lido

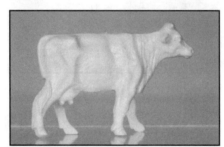

Lido, cow, hollow plastic, 2-5/8" long.
EX $.50   **NM $1**   **MIP n/a**

Marx

Marx, bale of hay, various colors, 1-15/16" long.
EX -   **NM $.50**   **MIP n/a**

Marx, calf, prancing, brown plastic, 2-5/16" long.
EX $1   **NM $2**   **MIP n/a**

Marx, collie, brown plastic, 2-5/16" long.
EX $1   **NM $2**   **MIP n/a**

Marx, colt, brown plastic, 2-11/16" long.
EX $1   **NM $2**   **MIP n/a**

Marx, "Prize Livestock" or "Blue Ribbon Livestock" Black Angus, 2-9/16" long.
EX $2   **NM $5**   **MIP n/a**

Marx, "Prize Livestock" or "Blue Ribbon Livestock" Brown Swiss, 3-1/4" long.
EX $2   **NM $5**   **MIP n/a**

Marx, "Prize Livestock" or "Blue Ribbon Livestock" American Guernsey, 3-1/8" long.
EX $2　　**NM $5**　　**MIP n/a**

Marx, hollow plastic, 3" long.
EX $1　　**NM $3**　　**MIP n/a**

Marx, hollow plastic, based on Prize Livestock Brown Swiss, 3" long.
EX $1　　**NM $3**　　**MIP n/a**

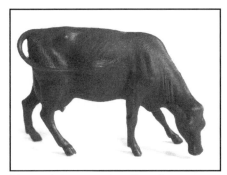

Marx, dairy cow, feeding, brown plastic, 3-3/16" long.
EX $1　　**NM $2**　　**MIP n/a**

Marx, dairy cow, lowing, brown plastic, 3-13/16" long.
EX $1　　**NM $2**　　**MIP n/a**

Marx, "Prize Livestock" or "Blue Ribbon Livestock" Hereford, 3" long.
EX $2　　**NM $5**　　**MIP n/a**

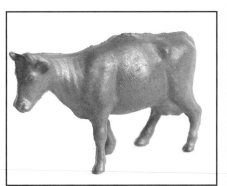

Marx, cow, "Chubby," 1950s, 3-1/8" long.
EX $2　　**NM $4**　　**MIP n/a**

Marx, longhorn steer, 3-3/4" long.
EX $2　　**NM $4**　　**MIP n/a**

Marx, farmer, pitchfork, 2-15/16" tall.
EX $1　　**NM $3**　　**MIP n/a**

Marx, farmer, hoe, 2-1/8" tall.
EX $1　　**NM $3**　　**MIP n/a**

Marx, farmer carrying chicken, 2-3/16" tall.
EX $1　　**NM $3**　　**MIP n/a**

Farm Toy Figures

Marx, farmer, feed sack, 2-1/8" tall.
EX $1   **NM $3**   **MIP n/a**

Marx, farmer boy, pail, 2" tall.
EX $1   **NM $3**   **MIP n/a**

Marx, farmer, wrench, 2-1/8" tall.
EX $1   **NM $3**   **MIP n/a**

Marx, farm woman, vinyl, early 1950s, 2-1/8" high.
EX $2   **NM $5**   **MIP n/a**

Marx, feed sack, 1-7/16" tall.
EX -   **NM $.50**   **MIP n/a**

Marx, goat, brown plastic, 1-7/16" long.
EX $1   **NM $2**   **MIP n/a**

Marx, horse, standing, "Chubby," 1950s, 2-13/16" long.
EX $2   **NM $4**   **MIP n/a**

Marx, horse, running, "Chubby," 1950s, 3-13/16" long.
EX $3   **NM $5**   **MIP n/a**

Marx, horse, 3-3/16" long.
EX $1   **NM $2**   **MIP n/a**

Marx, "Prize Livestock" or "Blue Ribbon Livestock" Clydesdale, 3-5/8" long.
EX $3   **NM $6**   **MIP n/a**

Marx, horse, brown plastic, 3-1/4" long.
EX $1 **NM $2** **MIP n/a**

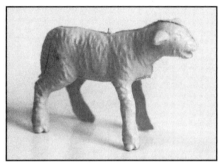

Marx, lamb, 1-3/16" long.
EX $.50 **NM $1** **MIP n/a**

Marx, pig, brown plastic, 1-11/16" long.
EX $1 **NM $2** **MIP n/a**

Marx, ranch hand with lasso, "chubby," 1950s, 2-1/2" tall.
EX $1 **NM $2** **MIP n/a**

Marx, rider with lasso, "chubby," 1950s, 2-5/16" tall.
EX $1 **NM $2** **MIP n/a**

Marx, rooster, 1-3/8" long.
EX $.50 **NM $1** **MIP n/a**

Marx, scarecrow, vinyl, early 1950s, 2-1/4" high, with Marx plastic bird on arm.
EX $2 **NM $5** **MIP n/a**

Marx, scarecrow, plastic, 2-1/4" high.
EX $1 **NM $2** **MIP n/a**

MPC

MPC, calf, 2-1/4" long.
EX $.25 **NM $.75** **MIP n/a**

MPC, cat, 2" long.
EX $.25 **NM $.75** **MIP n/a**

Farm Toy Figures

MPC, chickens: rooster, 1-5/8" high;
hen, 1-3/16" high; each:
EX $.10   **NM $.25**   **MIP n/a**

MPC, colt, 2-1/2" long.
EX $.25   **NM $.75**   **MIP n/a**

MPC, dog, 1-3/4" long.
EX $.25   **NM $.75**   **MIP n/a**

MPC, donkey, 2-1/2" long.
EX $.25   **NM $.75**   **MIP n/a**

MPC, goat, 1-3/4" long.
EX $.25   **NM $.75**   **MIP n/a**

MPC domestic fowl: goose, 1-3/4"
high; duck, 1-1/8" high; each:
EX $.10   **NM $.25**   **MIP n/a**

MPC, kitten, 1-3/16" long.
EX $.25   **NM $.50**   **MIP n/a**

MPC, pig, 1-15/16" long.
EX $.25   **NM $.50**   **MIP n/a**

MPC, piglet, 1-3/8" long.
EX $.25   **NM $.75**   **MIP n/a**

MPC, puppy, 1-1/2" long.
EX $.25   **NM $.50**   **MIP n/a**

MPC, rabbit, 1-1/4" long.
EX $.25   **NM $.50**   **MIP n/a**

MPC, sheep, 1-7/8" long.
EX $.25   **NM $.50**   **MIP n/a**

MPC, turkey, 1-1/2" high.
EX $.25   NM $.50   MIP n/a

Ohio Art

Ohio Art farm set, colt, 1-5/8" long.
EX $.25   NM $.50   MIP n/a

Ohio Art farm set, cow, 2-1/2" long.
EX $.25   NM $.50   MIP n/a

Ohio Art farm set, pig, 1-5/8" long.
EX $.25   NM $.50   NIP n/a

Ohio Art farm set, sheep, 1-5/8" long.
EX $.25   NM $.50   MIP n/a

Reliable

Reliable, chickens, soft plastic: rooster, 1-3/4" high; hen, 1-1/4" high; each:
EX $.25   NM $.50   MIP n/a

Reliable, duck, soft plastic, 1-3/8" high.
EX $.25   NM $.50   MIP n/a

Reliable, sheep, soft plastic, 2" long.
EX $.50   NM $1   MIP n/a

Tim-Mee

Tim-Mee, calf, 1-3/4" long.
EX $.25   NM $.50   MIP n/a

Tim-Mee, chickens, 2-3/16" long.
EX $.25   NM $.50   MIP n/a

Tim-Mee, dog, 1-3/4" long.
EX $.50   NM $.75   MIP n/a

Farm Toy Figures

Tim-Mee, farmer, shovel, 2-1/6" tall.
EX $.25   NM $.50   MIP n/a

Tim-Mee, goat, 1-3/4" long.
EX $.25   NM $.50   MIP n/a

Tim-Mee, pig, 1-1/2" long.
EX $.50   NM $.75   MIP n/a

Tim-Mee, farmer, hoe, 2-1/16" tall.
EX $.25   NM $.50   MIP n/a

Tim-Mee, horse, 2-11/16" long.
EX $.50   NM $1   MIP n/a

Tim-Mee, pig, 1-3/4" long.
EX $.25   NM $.50   MIP n/a

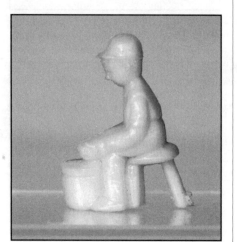

Tim-Mee, farmer milking, 1-1/2" high.
EX $.50   NM $1   MIP n/a

Tim-Mee, horse, feeding, 3" long.
EX $.50   NM $1   MIP n/a

Tim-Mee, sheep, 1-5/8" long.
EX $.50   NM $.75   MIP n/a

A Word About Scale

Toy Sizes for Miniature Farms

Scale is simply the size of a given toy stated in a ratio. For years, the most popular scale of farm toys has been 1:16-scale—1/16 the size of the real thing. Other toy tractors are either larger or smaller depending on the second number given. The higher the second number, the smaller the toy. This is the size most people think of when they consider "toy tractors." Why

1:16-scale? Probably because it's just a good-sized toy, especially for kids. Its scale allows for great detail, steerability, and tough construction. Naturally, there are some early farm toy exceptions.

Reuhl, for one, crafted much of their line in 1:20-scale. In construction toys, 1:50-scale is common—it allows enough room for plenty of detail and is still able to be stored on a shelf

easily. NZG Construction toys, for example, are most often produced in 1:50-scale. Moving into a yet smaller size, 1:87-scale—the size of HO model railroads—has also become popular. Mostly produced in plastic, these miniatures are made by many companies, Wiking of Germany being one of the most well-known.

1:64-scale   **1:43-scale**   **1:32-scale**   **1:16-scale**

1:64-scale

This small size has become a big-seller in the past twelve years or so. These "Matchbox-sized" toy tractors have nice detail, but don't dominate a den or basement quite like the 1:16-scale models do. Plus, they're an inexpensive collectible and easily modified. You see a lot of 1:64-scale layouts at the shows, featuring almost every variety of tractor imaginable. Some of the historical sets produced by Ertl in the early 1970s now command fairly high MIP prices.

1:43-scale

Another popular European scale, seen most often in Corgi, Dinky, and

some Matchbox farm equipment. Ertl also produced a nice line of tractors and automobiles in this scale beginning in 1988 and then returning with an expanded variety in the 1990s. Although not quite the 1:48-scale needed for O-scale model railroads, they add great detail to a layout.

1:32-scale

Popular in Europe, especially in the Britains line, 1:32-scale started making real inroads in the United States in the 1970s. Maybe with everyone scaling back because of the energy crisis, smaller-scale toys seemed to make sense. Ertl began mirroring its 1:16-scale

line in a downsized version, and in the 1980s released a series of 1:32-scale battery-operated tractors with working Power Take-Off.

1:16-scale

This scale is really the king of farm toy production. As far back as the 1920s, Vindex made cast-iron threshers and machinery in 1:16-scale, and it has remained a favorite ever since. The size is well suited for plenty of detail and play-use. After the Second World War, Eska, Ertl, and Carter Tru-Scale set the pattern for 1:16 to be the dominant farm toy scale in America.

How to Use this Book

Changes in the presentation of the listings in this book will make it easier to use, but will take a little getting used to.

The listing corresponding to a photo is located beneath that photo.

The header at the top of each page is organized like a dictionary; for a left page, the Make and Series listed are that of the listing in the top left corner of the page; for a right page, the Make and Series listed are that of the listing at the bottom right corner of the page.

The book is organized by:

Make: Beginning alphabetically with AGCO and ending with White, the listings are sorted first by manufacturer of the real tractor/implement. Identification of Make occurs in the header at the top of each page.

Series: Within in each make, listings are broken into sections including Banks, Construction Equipment, Implements, Lawn & Garden, Pedal Tractors, Tractors, and Trucks. Identification of Series occurs in the header at the top of each page.

Scale: Once you have the Make and Series you want, the toys are grouped by scale (1:08, 1:12, 1:16, 1:32, 1:43, 1:64, etc.). For example, once you arrive at the Ford Tractor pages, look for the scale you want next.

Model: When you arrive at the section containing the desired scale, listings are presented alphabetically by the Model name. For example, that Ford Tractor in 1:12 section begins with a Ford 2000. Number designations are presented before letter designations, so a 1:12-scale Ford NAA tractor is listed after the Ford 9700.

Company: For instances when multiple toys have the same model name, the listings are presented alphabetically by Company. There are two 1:12-scale Ford NAA tractors, the first listed was released by Franklin Mint and the second listed was released by Product Miniature.

Pedal Tractors

Pedal tractors are organized by make.

Collectors should also be aware that not all of the tractors were restored with the correct parts.

The grading used for Pedal tractors is slightly different than the rest of the book, although the values will still read as "EX," "NM," and "MIP."

The first value is for a good, unrestored example.

The second value is for a professionally restored value. Professional restoration is a wise investment for anyone with a vintage pedal tractor—poorly restored tractors just don't command the prices listed here.

The third value is for a Mint in Box example. When pedal tractor collecting became more popular, people did begin to save the original boxes, even though many were simply plain cardboard with black lettering.

Abbreviations

There are a few terms and abbreviations used in the descriptions that not everyone will know. The following is a short list:

n/a: not applicable. This is used when there isn't a value given for that toy in a certain condition grade.

npf: No Price Found. In some cases, a price cannot be found. Sometimes, there just aren't enough records on the sales of a particular model to make an honest evaluation of price. This doesn't always mean the toy is extremely valuable or not valuable at all, however.

w/ : with

w/o: without

ROPS: Rollover Protection System

PTO: Power Take Off

FWA: Front Wheel Assist

NF: Narrow Front

WF: Wide Front

MFD: Mechanical Front Drive

The three main pricing grades used are:

Excellent (EX): A toy that has seen some use and is starting to show its age. It will still be in perfect working order and have all its accessory parts when applicable. It will have some age soiling. Overall, it will have an appearance of freshness and be desirable to some collectors.

Near Mint (NM): A toy that practically looks like it just came from a toy store shelf, no matter what the age. Frequently, all that separates a near-mint piece and a mint in pack piece is simply the package itself. This value grade is one of the highest for older, cast-iron toys and for many custom-made toys. Many vintage toys either didn't come with a box or it is nearly impossible to find them in a box. Most custom-made toys did not come with a box.

❏ **John Deere 4430**, 1:16-scale, Ertl, green, small John Deere decal, International Harvester spindles, 1970s, No. 512

EX $28   **NM** $56   **MIP** $88

Mint in Pack (MIP): A Mint toy is in the condition in which it was originally issued regardless of age. It will also be complete with all accessory parts when applicable, and will look brand new. All toys in this category must be in perfect working condition. The original box in Mint condition will significantly enhance the value.

AGCO

BANKS 1:25-SCALE

❑ **AGCO Truck Bank**, 1:25-scale, Ertl, No. 2692 *(Photo by Ertl)*
EX $4   **NM** $12   **MIP** $18

IMPLEMENTS 1:24-SCALE

❑ **AGCO Combine, Gleaner R62**, 1:24-scale, Scale Models, included two heads, grain head shown, No. 2024 *(Photo by Scale Models)*
EX $36   **NM** $64   **MIP** $88

❑ **AGCO Combine, Gleaner R62**, 1:24-scale, Scale Models, corn and grain heads, 1994, No. FT-0444

(Photo by Bossen Implement)
EX $36   **NM** $64   **MIP** $88

❑ **AGCO Combine, Gleaner R65**, 1:24-scale, Scale Models, corn and grain heads, 2002, No. FT-0632
EX $37   **NM** $47   **MIP** $68

❑ **AGCO Combine, Gleaner R65**, 1:24-scale, Scale Models, corn and grain heads, chrome rims, 2002, No. FT-0641
EX $34   **NM** $57   **MIP** $72

❑ **AGCO Combine, Gleaner R72**, 1:24-scale, Scale Models, corn and grain heads, Collector Edition, 2001, No. FT-0603
EX $34   **NM** $43   **MIP** $62

IMPLEMENTS 1:64-SCALE

❑ **AGCO Combine, Gleaner R62**, 1:64-scale, Ertl, w/two heads, No. 1282 *(Photo by Kate Bossen)*
EX $12   **NM** $26   **MIP** $37

PEDAL TRACTORS

❑ **AGCO LT 85**, Scale Models, No. FT-0629
EX $102   **NM** $138   **MIP** $164

❑ **AGCO RT 150**, Scale Models, MFD, '04 AGCO Parts Expo, 2005, No. FT-0696
EX $99   **NM** $146   **MIP** $178

❑ **AGCO RT 150**, Scale Models, MFD, 2006, No. FT-0703
(Photo by Scale Models)
EX $96   **NM** $123   **MIP** $153

TRACTORS 1:16-SCALE

❑ **AGCO DT 225**, 1:16-scale, Scale Models, MFD, duals & ROPS, Collectors Edition, 2002, No. FT-0613
EX $32   **NM** $42   **MIP** $57

❑ **AGCO DT 225**, 1:16-scale, Scale Models, MFD, ROPS, 2002, No. FT-0614
EX $29   **NM** $38   **MIP** $52

❑ **AGCO DT 225**, 1:16-scale, Scale Models, MFD, duals & ROPS, '02, Louisville Edition, 2002, No. FB-2603
EX $32   **NM** $42   **MIP** $57

❑ **AGCO DT 240A**, 1:16-scale, Scale Models, MFD, duals front & rear, 2005, No. FT-0704
(Photo by Bossen Implement)
EX $29   **NM** $46   **MIP** $72

❑ **AGCO DT 240A**, 1:16-scale, Scale Models, MFD, "New Product Introduction," '05 Louisville, 2005, No. FB-2603
EX $27   **NM** $42   **MIP** $66

❑ **AGCO LT 70**, 1:16-scale, Scale Models, MFD, cab, '02, Louisville Edition, 2002, No. FB-2604
EX $23   **NM** $34   **MIP** $42

❑ **AGCO LT 70**, 1:16-scale, Scale Models, MFD, cab, 2002, No. FT-0630
EX $22   **NM** $33   **MIP** $42

❑ **AGCO LT 85**, 1:16-scale, Scale Models, MFD, w/ROPS, 2002, No. FT-0625
EX $23   **NM** $34   **MIP** $46

❑ **AGCO LT 90**, 1:16-scale, Scale Models, MFD, '04 AGCO Parts Expo, 2005, No. FT-0693 *(Photo by Bossen Implement)*
EX $22   **NM** $37   **MIP** $48

❑ **AGCO RT 120**, 1:16-scale, Scale Models, MFD, 2005, No. FT-0691
(Photo by Scale Models)
EX $26   **NM** $39   **MIP** $53

❑ **AGCO RT 145**, 1:16-scale, Scale Models, MFD, 2002, No. FT-0616
EX $28   **NM** $39   **MIP** $51

❑ **AGCO RT 145**, 1:16-scale, Scale Models, MFD, duals, ROPS, Collector Edition, 2002, No. FT-0615
EX $32   **NM** $42   **MIP** $57

❑ **AGCO RT 145**, 1:16-scale, Scale Models, MFD, duals, cab, '03, Louisville Edition, 2003, No. FB-2630
EX $32   **NM** $42   **MIP** $57

❑ **AGCO ST 45**, 1:16-scale, Scale Models, MFD, ROPS, Collector Edition, 2002, No. FT-0617
EX $23   **NM** $28   **MIP** $37

❑ **AGCO ST 45**, 1:16-scale, Scale Models, MFD, ROPS, 2002, No. FT-0602
EX $18   **NM** $23   **MIP** $32

❑ **AGCO Star 8425**, 1:16-scale, Scale Models, 4WD, duals, 1996, No. FT-0510 *(Photo by Scale Models)*
EX $102   **NM** $116   **MIP** $152

❑ **AGCO Star 8425**, 1:16-scale, Scale Models, 4WD, triples, '96 Louisville Edition, 1996, No. FB-2414
EX $108   **NM** $122   **MIP** $189

❑ **AGCO Star 8425**, 1:16-scale, Scale Models, 4WD, triples, 2000, No. FT-0590
EX $97   **NM** $113   **MIP** $144

TRACTORS 1:64-SCALE

❑ **AGCO Star 8425**, 1:64-scale, Scale Models, 4WD, duals, No. FT-0522 *(Photo by Scale Models)*
EX $8   **NM** $18   **MIP** $26

TRUCKS 1:64-SCALE

❑ **AGCO Dealer Dodge Pickup Dodge**, 1:64-scale, Ertl, 1997, No. 7067 *(Photo by Ertl)*
EX $1   **NM** $2   **MIP** $3

❑ **AGCO Dealer Pickup w/Minneapolis Moline G-55 on Trailer**, 1:64-scale, Ertl, No. 7054
(Photo by Ertl)
EX $4   **NM** $7   **MIP** $12

❑ **AGCO Hauling Set**, 1:64-scale, Ertl, No. 2306 *(Photo by Ertl)*
EX $8   **NM** $12   **MIP** $18

❑ **AGCO Semi w/AGCO Van Box**, 1:64-scale, Ertl, No. 2439 *(Photo by Ertl)*
EX $8   **NM** $12   **MIP** $18

AGCO-ALLIS

LAWN AND GARDEN 1:16-SCALE

❑ **AGCO-Allis 1616H**, 1:16-scale, Scale Models, No. FT-0460
EX $8   **NM** $16   **MIP** $24

❑ **AGCO-Allis 1920H**, 1:16-scale, Scale Models, 1994, No. FT-0458
EX $8   **NM** $16   **MIP** $24

❑ **AGCO-Allis 2025 GT**, 1:16-scale, Scale Models, w/mower deck, 1997, No. FT-0544 *(Photo by Scale Models)*
EX $8   **NM** $16   **MIP** $24

PEDAL TRACTORS

❑ **AGCO-Allis 8610**, Scale Models, 1994, No. FT-0436
EX $98   **NM** $132   **MIP** $169

❑ **AGCO-Allis 8765**, Scale Models, WF, 1998, No. FT-0559
EX $98   **NM** $122   **MIP** $159

❑ **AGCO-Allis 9815**, Scale Models, WF 2WD, 1996, No. FT-0513 *(Photo by Scale Models)*
EX $98   **NM** $148   **MIP** $188

TRACTORS 1:16-SCALE

❑ **AGCO-Allis 8630**, 1:16-scale, Scale Models, MFD, 3 point, windows, Collector Edition, 1992, No. FT-0447 *(Photo by Bossen Implement)*
EX $27   **NM** $36   **MIP** $47

❑ **AGCO-Allis 8630**, 1:16-scale, Scale Models, MFD, 1992, No. FT-0446 *(Photo by Scale Models)*
EX $22   **NM** $33   **MIP** $42

❑ **AGCO-Allis 8745**, 1:16-scale, Scale Models, MFD, 1999, No. FT-0575
EX $27   **NM** $36   **MIP** $47

❑ **AGCO-Allis 8765**, 1:16-scale, Scale Models, MFD, "New Product Intro Sept 1997", 1997, No. FT-0556
(Photo by Bossen Implement)
EX $28   **NM** $38   **MIP** $52

❑ **AGCO-Allis 8765**, 1:16-scale, Scale Models, MFD, 1998, No. FT-0557
EX $23   **NM** $33   **MIP** $47

❑ **AGCO-Allis 8785**, 1:16-scale, Scale Models, MFD, ROPS, 1999, No. FT-0558 *(Photo by Bossen Implement)*
EX $23   **NM** $32   **MIP** $43

❑ **AGCO-Allis 9650**, 1:16-scale, Scale Models, MFD, 1993, No. FT-0470 *(Photo by Scale Models)*
EX $22   **NM** $33   **MIP** $42

❑ **AGCO-Allis 9650**, 1:16-scale, Scale Models, MFD, Collectors Edition, 1994, No. FT-0480
EX $24   **NM** $36   **MIP** $48

❑ **AGCO-Allis 9650**, 1:16-scale, Scale Models, '95 Louisville Edition, 1995, No. FB-2363
EX $27   **NM** $38   **MIP** $55

❑ **AGCO-Allis 9655**, 1:16-scale, Scale Models, MFD, duals, Collector Edition, 1996, No. FT-0526
EX $26   **NM** $37   **MIP** $62

❑ **AGCO-Allis 9655**, 1:16-scale, Scale Models, MFD, 1997, No. FT-0532 *(Photo by Scale Models)*
EX $22   **NM** $31   **MIP** $46

❑ **AGCO-Allis 9735**, 1:16-scale, Scale Models, MFD, 1999, No. FT-0569
EX $23   **NM** $32   **MIP** $53

❑ **AGCO-Allis 9735**, 1:16-scale, Scale Models, MFD, '01 Farm Progress Show, 2001, No. FB-2571
EX $26   **NM** $37   **MIP** $62

❑ **AGCO-Allis 9775**, 1:16-scale, Scale Models, MFD, 1999, No. FT-0576
EX $23   **NM** $32   **MIP** $53

❑ **AGCO-Allis 9775**, 1:16-scale, Scale Models, MFD, duals, '00 Louisville Edition, 2000, No. FB-2551
EX $26   **NM** $37   **MIP** $62

❑ **AGCO-Allis 9815**, 1:16-scale, Scale Models, MFD, duals, Collector Edition, 1996, No. FT-0527
EX $26   **NM** $37   **MIP** $62

❑ **AGCO-Allis 9815**, 1:16-scale, Scale Models, MFD, 1997, No. FT-0508 *(Photo by Scale Models)*
EX $23   **NM** $32   **MIP** $53

TRACTORS 1:64-SCALE

❑ **AGCO-Allis 6670**, 1:64-scale, Ertl, 2WD, No. 1214
EX $2   **NM** $3   **MIP** $4

❑ **AGCO-Allis 6680**, 1:64-scale, Ertl, MFD, No. 1245
EX $2   **NM** $3   **MIP** $4

❑ **AGCO-Allis 6690**, 1:64-scale, Ertl, 2WD, duals, 4 post ROPS, No. 1215
EX $2   **NM** $3   **MIP** $4

❑ **AGCO-Allis 6690**, 1:64-scale, Ertl, 2WD, 4 post ROPS, No. 1239
EX $2   **NM** $3   **MIP** $4

❑ **AGCO-Allis 6690**, 1:64-scale, Ertl, MFD, 4 post ROPS, No. 1224
EX $2   **NM** $3   **MIP** $4

❑ **AGCO-Allis 6690**, 1:64-scale, Ertl, 2WD, duals, No. 1286
EX $2   **NM** $3   **MIP** $4

❑ **AGCO-Allis 6690**, 1:64-scale, Ertl, 2WD, duals, '94 Farm Show Edition, 1994, No. 1242FA
EX $2   **NM** $3   **MIP** $4

❑ **AGCO-Allis 8630**, 1:64-scale, Scale Models, 1992, No. FT-0452
(Photo by Scale Models)
EX $2   **NM** $4   **MIP** $6

❏ **AGCO-Allis 9455**, 1:64-scale, Scale Models, 2WD, duals, '96 Louisville Edition, 1996, No. FB-2413
EX $3   **NM** $6   **MIP** $8

❏ **AGCO-Allis 9650**, 1:64-scale, Scale Models, 2WD, duals, '95 Louisville Edition, 1995, No. FB-2359
EX $3   **NM** $6   **MIP** $8

❏ **AGCO-Allis 9650**, 1:64-scale, Scale Models, 2WD, duals, '95 Farm Progress Edition, 1995, No. FB-2400
EX $3   **NM** $6   **MIP** $8

❏ **AGCO-Allis 9650**, 1:64-scale, Scale Models, 1995, No. FT-0471
(Photo by Scale Models)
EX $2   **NM** $4   **MIP** $6

❏ **AGCO-Allis 9650**, 1:64-scale, Scale Models, MFD, '04 Farm Progress Edition, 2003, No. FT-0658
EX $3   **NM** $6   **MIP** $8

❏ **AGCO-Allis 9655**, 1:64-scale, Scale Models, 2WD, duals, '96 Farm Progress Edition, 1996, No. FT-0519
EX $3   **NM** $6   **MIP** $8

❏ **AGCO-Allis 9655**, 1:64-scale, Scale Models, 1996, No. FT-0533
(Photo by Scale Models)
EX $3   **NM** $6   **MIP** $8

❏ **AGCO-Allis 9675**, 1:64-scale, Ertl, MFD, w/duals, cab, 1997, No. 2685
EX $3   **NM** $4   **MIP** $6

❏ **AGCO-Allis 9675**, 1:64-scale, Ertl, 2WD, w/cab, 1998, No. 2693
EX $3   **NM** $4   **MIP** $6

❏ **AGCO-Allis 9695**, 1:64-scale, Ertl, MFD, cab, 1997, No. 7069
(Photo by Bossen Implement)
EX $3   **NM** $4   **MIP** $6

❏ **AGCO-Allis 9695**, 1:64-scale, Ertl, '98 Farm Show Edition, cab glass, 1998, No. 2848MA
EX $4   **NM** $8   **MIP** $11

❏ **AGCO-Allis 9815**, 1:64-scale, Scale Models, MFD, 1995, No. FT-0534 *(Photo by Scale Models)*
EX $3   **NM** $6   **MIP** $8

❏ **AGCO-Allis 9815**, 1:64-scale, Scale Models, MFD, '96 Louisville Edition, 1996, No. FB-2412
EX $3   **NM** $6   **MIP** $8

AGCO-WHITE

PEDAL TRACTORS

❏ **AGCO-White 145**, Scale Models, black, WF, 2WD, workhorse, 1993
EX $127   **NM** $183   **MIP** $297

❏ **AGCO-White 6215**, Scale Models, WF, No. 585
EX $116   **NM** $152   **MIP** $207

❏ **AGCO-White 6510**, Scale Models, WF, No. 604
EX $97   **NM** $113   **MIP** $155

❏ **White 6510**, Scale Models, silver, WF, 2WD, 1998
EX $108   **NM** $123   **MIP** $167

TRACTORS 1:16-SCALE

❏ **AGCO-White 170**, 1:16-scale, Scale Models, workhorse, black belly, 1992, No. FU-0552
(Photo by Bossen Implement)
EX $18   **NM** $27   **MIP** $43

❏ **AGCO-White 195**, 1:16-scale, Scale Models, workhorse, 2WD, duals, black belly, No. FU-0553
EX $18   **NM** $27   **MIP** $43

❏ **AGCO-White 6105**, 1:16-scale, Scale Models, MFD, Collector Edition, 1998, No. FU-0571
EX $26   **NM** $33   **MIP** $53

❏ **AGCO-White 6105**, 1:16-scale, Scale Models, MFD, 1998, No. FU-0572 *(Photo by Scale Models)*
EX $21   **NM** $29   **MIP** $47

❏ **AGCO-White 6195**, 1:16-scale, Scale Models, MFD, 1993, No. FU-0564 *(Photo by Scale Models)*
EX $22   **NM** $31   **MIP** $46

❏ **AGCO-White 6195**, 1:16-scale, Scale Models, MFD, '97 Farm Progress Edition, 1997, No. FB-2466
EX $26   **NM** $37   **MIP** $52

❏ **AGCO-White 6195**, 1:16-scale, Scale Models, MFD, duals, Collector Edition, 1998, No. FU-0586
EX $26   **NM** $37   **MIP** $52

❏ **AGCO-White 6215**, 1:16-scale, Scale Models, MFD, 1997, No. FU-0587 *(Photo by Scale Models)*
EX $22   **NM** $31   **MIP** $46

❏ **AGCO-White 6410**, 1:16-scale, Scale Models, MFD, 1999, No. FU-0609
EX $22   **NM** $31   **MIP** $46

❏ **AGCO-White 6510**, 1:16-scale, Scale Models, MFD, 1997, No. FU-0593
EX $22   **NM** $31   **MIP** $46

❏ **AGCO-White 6810**, 1:16-scale, Scale Models, MFD, ROPS, 1999, No. FU-0601
EX $22   **NM** $31   **MIP** $46

❏ **AGCO-White 8310**, 1:16-scale, Scale Models, MFD, 1999, No. FU-0602
EX $22   **NM** $31   **MIP** $46

❏ **AGCO-White 8710**, 1:16-scale, Scale Models, MFD, 1999, No. FU-0611
EX $22   **NM** $31   **MIP** $46

❏ **AGCO-White Silver Bullet**, 1:16-scale, SpecCast, silver, pulling tractor, 2003, No. SCT-214
EX $128   **NM** $178   **MIP** $262

TRACTORS 1:64-SCALE

❏ **AGCO-White 145**, 1:64-scale, Scale Models, No. FU-0561
(Photo by Scale Models)
EX $4   **NM** $6   **MIP** $8

❏ **AGCO-White 170**, 1:64-scale, Scale Models, No. FU-0559
(Photo by Scale Models)
EX $4   **NM** $6   **MIP** $8

❏ **AGCO-White 195**, 1:64-scale, Scale Models, No. FU-0560
(Photo by Scale Models)
EX $4   **NM** $6   **MIP** $8

❏ **AGCO-White 6105**, 1:64-scale, Scale Models, MFD, No. FU-0573
(Photo by Scale Models)
EX $3   **NM** $4   **MIP** $6

❏ **AGCO-White 6175**, 1:64-scale, Ertl, '99 Farm Show Edition, cab glass, 1999
EX $4   **NM** $8   **MIP** $11

❏ **AGCO-White 6175**, 1:64-scale, Scale Models, 2WD, 1997, No. FU-2847
EX $3   **NM** $4   **MIP** $6

❏ **AGCO-White 6195**, 1:64-scale, Scale Models, No. FU-0568
(Photo by Scale Models)
EX $3   **NM** $4   **MIP** $6

❏ **AGCO-White 6195**, 1:64-scale, Scale Models, '95 Farm Progress Edition, 1995, No. FB-2401
EX $3   **NM** $6   **MIP** $8

❏ **AGCO-White 6215**, 1:64-scale, Scale Models, '96 Louisville Edition, 1996, No. FB-2415
EX $3   **NM** $6   **MIP** $8

❏ **AGCO-White 6215**, 1:64-scale, Scale Models, MFD, 1996, No. FU-0588 *(Photo by Scale Models)*
EX $3   **NM** $6   **MIP** $8

ALLIS-CHALMERS

CONSTRUCTION EQUIPMENT 1:150-SCALE

❏ **Allis-Chalmers Crawler and Pan Scraper**, 1:150-scale, orange, "the ideal earthmoving package", 1950s
EX n/a   **NM** n/a   **MIP** npf

CONSTRUCTION EQUIPMENT 1:16-SCALE

❏ **Allis-Chalmers Crawler, 12G**, 1:16-scale, Ertl, yellow, 1960s, No. 198
EX $121   **NM** $263   **MIP** $477

❏ **Allis-Chalmers Crawler, H-3**, 1:16-scale, SpecCast, w/blade, metal track, 2005, No. SCT236
EX $28   **NM** $42   **MIP** $59

❏ **Allis-Chalmers Crawler, HD-3**, 1:16-scale, SpecCast, w/blade, metal track, 2006, No. SCT254
(Photo by SpecCast)
EX $28   **NM** $42   **MIP** $59

❏ **Allis-Chalmers Crawler, HD-3**, 1:16-scale, SpecCast, w/blade, metal track, back hoe, 2007, No. SCT277 *(Photo by SpecCast)*
EX $48   **NM** $63   **MIP** $98

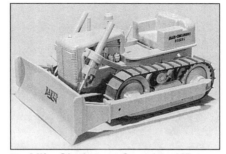

❏ **Allis-Chalmers Crawler, HD5**, 1:16-scale, Product Miniature, orange, 1950s
EX $126   **NM** $348   **MIP** $589

❏ **Allis-Chalmers Crawler, K**, 1:16-scale, SpecCast, metal track, side curtains, steering wheel, 2001, No. CUST703
EX $27   **NM** $39   **MIP** $52

❏ **Allis-Chalmers Crawler, K**, 1:16-scale, SpecCast, metal track, steering levers, 2002, No. SCT-199
EX $27   **NM** $39   **MIP** $52

❏ **Allis-Chalmers Crawler, K**, 1:16-scale, SpecCast, w/Bucyrus-Eric blade, metal tracks, 2002, No. SCT-211
EX $43   **NM** $58   **MIP** $72

❏ **Allis-Chalmers Crawler, K**, 1:16-scale, SpecCast, diesel, w/blade, 2005, No. SCT237
EX $34   **NM** $43   **MIP** $62

❏ **Monarch Crawler, 35**, 1:16-scale, SpecCast, metal track, steering wheel, gray, 2002, No. SCT-200
EX $28   **NM** $38   **MIP** $53

CONSTRUCTION EQUIPMENT 1:20-SCALE

❏ **Allis-Chalmers Crawler, HD-14**, 1:20-scale, Knecht, orange, paper weight, 1950s
EX $288   **NM** $593   **MIP** npf

❏ **Allis-Chalmers Crawler, HD-14**, 1:20-scale, Knecht, orange, paper weight, late 1940s to early 1950s
EX $296   **NM** $677   **MIP** npf

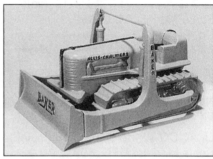

❏ **Allis-Chalmers Crawler, HD-14**, 1:20-scale, Knecht, orange, paper weight, late 1940s to early 1950s
EX $248   **NM** $596   **MIP** npf

❏ **Allis-Chalmers Crawler, HD-14**, 1:20-scale, Knecht, orange, paper weight, late 1940s to early 1950s
EX $288   **NM** $598   **MIP** npf

❏ **Allis-Chalmers Tractor, U**, 1:20-scale, Arcade, orange, red or green, w/bottom dump scraper, 1930s
EX $148   **NM** $279   **MIP** $748

CONSTRUCTION EQUIPMENT 1:25-SCALE

❑ **Allis-Chalmers Crawler, HD-21**, 1:25-scale, FG, w/blade, metal track, cable operated disc, 2006, No. 40-0126
EX $57   **NM** $86   **MIP** $143

CONSTRUCTION EQUIPMENT 1:30-SCALE

❑ **Allis-Chalmers Tractor, U**, 1:30-scale, Arcade, orange, w/bottom dump scraper, 1930s
EX $148   **NM** $279   **MIP** $748

CONSTRUCTION EQUIPMENT 1:43-SCALE

❑ **Allis-Chalmers Crawler, GU**, 1:43-scale, SpecCast, 1990s, No. DAC015
EX $6   **NM** $8   **MIP** $12

CONSTRUCTION EQUIPMENT 1:50-SCALE

❑ **Allis-Chalmers Crawler, HD-20**, 1:50-scale, Garrigan, orange, 1980s
EX n/a   **NM** n/a   **MIP** npf

CONSTRUCTION EQUIPMENT 1:60-SCALE

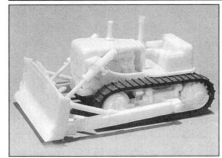

❑ **Allis-Chalmers Crawler**, 1:60-scale, Lionel, yellow, 1950s
EX $58   **NM** $127   **MIP** $228

❑ **Allis-Chalmers Crawler, HD-16**, 1:60-scale, Lionel, orange, 1950s
EX $58   **NM** $163   **MIP** $297

❑ **Allis-Chalmers Scraper**, 1:60-scale, Lionel, orange, pan scraper, 1950s
EX $63   **NM** $163   **MIP** $297

❑ **Allis-Chalmers Scraper**, 1:60-scale, Lionel, yellow, pan scraper, 1950s
EX $63   **NM** $138   **MIP** $253

❑ **Allis-Chalmers Scraper**, 1:60-scale, Lionel, orange, pan scraper, 1950s
EX $63   **NM** $163   **MIP** $297

CONSTRUCTION EQUIPMENT 1:80-SCALE

❑ **Allis-Chalmers Crawler**, 1:80-scale, Mercury (Italy), orange, 1950s
EX $200   **NM** $325   **MIP** $400

IMPLEMENTS 1:08-SCALE

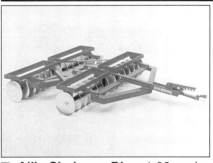

❑ **Allis-Chalmers Disc**, 1:08-scale, Scale Models, orange, No. FT-0528

(Photo by Scale Models)
EX $23   **NM** $48   **MIP** $77

❑ **Allis-Chalmers Wagon, Flare Box**, 1:08-scale, Scale Models, orange, 1990s, No. FT-0529

(Photo by Scale Models)
EX $23   **NM** $49   **MIP** $78

IMPLEMENTS 1:12-SCALE

❑ **Allis-Chalmers Combine, 60A**, 1:12-scale, Franklin Mint, all-crop harvester, 2002
EX $153 **NM** $176 **MIP** $248

❑ **Allis-Chalmers Disc**, 1:12-scale, orange, 1950s
EX $82 **NM** $227 **MIP** $342

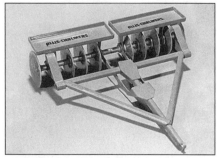

❑ **Allis-Chalmers Disc**, 1:12-scale, American Precision, orange, w/Allis, 1950s
EX $82 **NM** $227 **MIP** $342

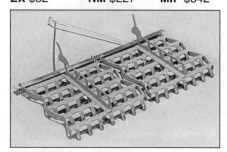

❑ **Allis-Chalmers Drag**, 1:12-scale, American Precision, orange, Drag Harrow, 1950s
EX $107 **NM** $257 **MIP** $414

❑ **Allis-Chalmers Plow**, 1:12-scale, American Precision, orange and silver, 1950s
EX $65 **NM** $163 **MIP** $274

❑ **Allis-Chalmers Plow**, 1:12-scale, American Precision, orange, 1950s
EX $65 **NM** $163 **MIP** $274

IMPLEMENTS 1:16-SCALE

❑ **Allis-Chalmers Baler, Roto**, 1:16-scale, Ertl, orange, red baler, 1989, No. 1244
EX $17 **NM** $36 **MIP** $63

❑ **Allis-Chalmers Baler, Roto**, 1:16-scale, Ertl, orange, special edition, red baler, 1989, No. 1244DA
EX $19 **NM** $37 **MIP** $63

❑ **Allis-Chalmers Baler, Roto**, 1:16-scale, Ertl, 50th Anniversary Edition, 1997, No. 2178DA
EX $18 **NM** $38 **MIP** $68

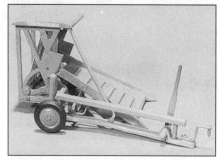

❑ **Allis-Chalmers Baler, Roto**, 1:16-scale, Jergensen (Custom), orange, did not come in box, 1980s
EX $27 **NM** $46 **MIP** n/a

❑ **Allis-Chalmers Chisel Plow**, 1:16-scale, Ertl, orange and cream rims, 1980s, No. 1222
EX $38 **NM** $46 **MIP** $73

❑ **Allis-Chalmers Combine**, 1:16-scale, Jergensen (Custom), orange, did not come in box, 1980s
EX $78 **NM** $114 **MIP** n/a

❑ **Allis-Chalmers Combine, 40**, 1:16-scale, SpecCast, '03 Orange Spectacular Edition, 2003, No. CUST769
EX $84 **NM** $102 **MIP** $198

❑ **Allis-Chalmers Combine, 60**, 1:16-scale, SpecCast, w/engine, 2005, No. SCT253 *(Photo by SpecCast)*
EX $52 **NM** $67 **MIP** $108

❑ **Allis-Chalmers Combine, 60**, 1:16-scale, SpecCast, w/PTO, 2007, No. SCT295 *(Photo by SpecCast)*
EX $52 **NM** $67 **MIP** $108

❏ **Allis-Chalmers Combine, 72**, 1:16-scale, Baird (Custom), orange, did not come in box, 1990
EX $153 **NM** $216 **MIP** n/a

❏ **Allis-Chalmers Corn Picker**, 1:16-scale, Ertl, D-17 #8 in Precision Series, 2001, No. 13191
EX $142 **NM** $182 **MIP** $268

❏ **Allis-Chalmers Disc**, 1:16-scale, Ertl, orange and cream rims, 1971
EX $14 **NM** $27 **MIP** $83

❏ **Allis-Chalmers Disc**, 1:16-scale, Ertl, orange w/folding wings, 1980s, No. 1217
EX $13 **NM** $26 **MIP** $76

❏ **Allis-Chalmers Loader**, 1:16-scale, Eisele, orange, 1940s
EX $78 **NM** $137 **MIP** $278

❏ **Allis-Chalmers Plow**, 1:16-scale, Ertl, orange, metal shares, die-cast rear rim, 4B, 1970s, No. 186
EX $21 **NM** $44 **MIP** $82

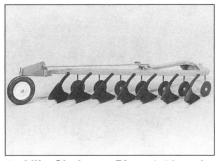

❏ **Allis-Chalmers Plow**, 1:16-scale, Ertl, orange, metal shares, 7B, 1970s, No. 186
EX $19 **NM** $43 **MIP** $113

❏ **Allis-Chalmers Plow**, 1:16-scale, Ertl, orange, metal shares, plastic rear rim, 4B, 1970s, No. 186
EX $17 **NM** $37 **MIP** $77

❏ **Allis-Chalmers Plow**, 1:16-scale, Ertl, orange, plastic shares, 4B, 1980s, No. 1216
EX $9 **NM** $22 **MIP** $46

❏ **Allis-Chalmers Spreader**, 1:16-scale, Ertl, orange, 1970s
EX $13 **NM** $27 **MIP** $43

❏ **Allis-Chalmers Wagon, Barge**, 1:16-scale, Ertl, orange, 1980s, No. 219
EX $7 **NM** $18 **MIP** $34

❏ **Allis-Chalmers Wagon, Barge**, 1:16-scale, Product Miniature, orange, barge, 1950
EX $43 **NM** $107 **MIP** $228

❏ **Allis-Chalmers Wagon, Flare Box**, 1:16-scale, Ertl, orange, 1970s
EX $8 **NM** $19 **MIP** $38

❑ **Allis-Chalmers Wagon, Flare Box**, 1:16-scale, Product Miniature, orange, flare box, 1948
EX $122   **NM** $326   **MIP** $894

❑ **Allis-Chalmers Wagon, Gravity**, 1:16-scale, Ertl, orange, 1980s, No. 1203
EX $14   **NM** $32   **MIP** $43

IMPLEMENTS 1:24-SCALE

❑ **Allis-Chalmers Combine, Gleaner**, 1:24-scale, Subbert (Custom), silver, did not come in box, 1980s
EX $7   **NM** $19   **MIP** n/a

❑ **Allis-Chalmers Combine, Gleaner N6**, 1:24-scale, Scale Models, silver and black, collector edition, 1980s, No. 6000
EX $73   **NM** $123   **MIP** $178

❑ **Allis-Chalmers Combine, Gleaner N6**, 1:24-scale, Scale Models, silver and black, large decal, 1980s, No. 6000
EX $38   **NM** $73   **MIP** $113

❑ **Allis-Chalmers Combine, Gleaner N6**, 1:24-scale, Scale Models, silver and black, small decal, 1980s, No. 6000
EX $38   **NM** $73   **MIP** $118

IMPLEMENTS 1:32-SCALE

❑ **Allis-Chalmers Chisel Plow**, 1:32-scale, Ertl, orange and cream rims, 1980s, No. 1956
EX $7   **NM** $14   **MIP** $28

❑ **Allis-Chalmers Combine, Gleaner F**, 1:32-scale, Ertl, silver, w/corn head & grain head, 4 windows, 1960s, No. 199
EX $68   **NM** $163   **MIP** $408

❑ **Allis-Chalmers Combine, Gleaner F**, 1:32-scale, Ertl, silver, closed reel, fixed head, 1960s, No. 195
EX $58   **NM** $114   **MIP** $328

❑ **Allis-Chalmers Combine, Gleaner F**, 1:32-scale, Ertl, silver, open reel, fixed head, 1960s, No. 195
EX $68   **NM** $172   **MIP** $374

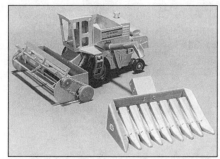

❑ **Allis-Chalmers Combine, Gleaner G**, 1:32-scale, Ertl, silver, w/corn head & grain head, 3 windows, 1970s
EX $58   **NM** $116   **MIP** $266

❑ **Allis-Chalmers Combine, Gleaner G**, 1:32-scale, Ertl, silver, 3 windows, grain head only, 1970s, No. 1202
EX $44   **NM** $88   **MIP** $178

❑ **Allis-Chalmers Combine, Gleaner L2**, 1:32-scale, Ertl, silver, 1980s, No. 1207
EX $22   **NM** $54   **MIP** $98

❑ **Allis-Chalmers Combine, Gleaner L3**, 1:32-scale, Ertl, silver, 1980s, No. 1207
EX $17   **NM** $48   **MIP** $77

❑ **Allis-Chalmers Disc**, 1:32-scale, Ertl, orange, 1980s
EX $3   **NM** $8   **MIP** $12

❑ **Allis-Chalmers Plow**, 1:32-scale, Ertl, orange, 1980s
EX $2   **NM** $6   **MIP** $9

❑ **Allis-Chalmers Wagon, Barge**, 1:32-scale, Ertl, orange, 1980s
EX $2   **NM** $6   **MIP** $8

IMPLEMENTS 1:64-SCALE

❑ **Allis-Chalmers Combine, Gleaner**, 1:64-scale, Subbert (Custom), silver, did not come in box
EX $27   **NM** $48   **MIP** n/a

LAWN AND GARDEN 1:16-SCALE

❑ **Allis-Chalmers 312-H**, 1:16-scale, Ertl, orange and white, 1970s, No. 151
EX $17   **NM** $42   **MIP** $76

❑ **Allis-Chalmers B-110**, 1:16-scale, Ertl, yellow, 1960s, No. 196
EX $88   **NM** $207   **MIP** $634

❑ **Allis-Chalmers B-112**, 1:16-scale, Ertl, yellow, came w/removable mower deck, 1960s, No. 197
EX $118   **NM** $297   **MIP** $834

PEDAL TRACTORS

❑ **Allis-Chalmers 190**, Ertl, orange, w/winged decal, tractor in original condition, 37", 1964
EX $357   **NM** $684   **MIP** $989

❑ **Allis-Chalmers 190 XT**, Ertl, orange, also available w/winged decal, tractor in original condition, 37", 1969, No. 190
EX $283   **NM** $427   **MIP** $582

❑ **Allis-Chalmers 200**, Ertl, orange, tractor in original condition, 37", 1960s, No. 190
EX $283   **NM** $427   **MIP** $582

❑ **Allis-Chalmers 7045**, Ertl, orange and black, 1978, No. 1210
EX $273   **NM** $318   **MIP** $437

❑ **Allis-Chalmers 7080**, Ertl, orange and maroon, tractor in original condition, 37", 1975, No. 1206
EX $281   **NM** $382   **MIP** $448

❑ **Allis-Chalmers 8070**, Ertl, orange and black, tractor in original condition, 37", 1982
EX $238   **NM** $282   **MIP** $363

❑ **Allis-Chalmers C**, Eska, orange, original tractor restored, 34", 1950s
EX $723   **NM** $923   **MIP** $1332

❑ **Allis-Chalmers CA**, Detail photo: Close-up of the square axle on the CA Pedal Tractor

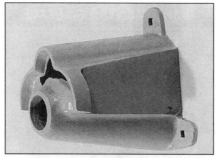

❑ **Allis-Chalmers CA**, Detail photo: Close-up of the round axle on the CA Pedal Tractor

❑ **Allis-Chalmers D-14**, Eska, orange, tractor in original condition, 38"
EX $712   **NM** $922   **MIP** $7787

❑ **Allis-Chalmers D-17**, Ertl, orange w/white wheels, tractor in original condition, 39", 1950s
EX $703   **NM** $932   **MIP** $1223

❑ **Allis-Chalmers Pedal Tractor Umbrella**, Heltrick, orange, in original condition, 1950s
EX $78   **NM** $169   **MIP** $283

❑ **Allis-Chalmers WD-45**, Scale Models, 50th Anniversary Edition, 2003, No. FT-0657
(Photo by Scale Models)
EX $98   **NM** $123   **MIP** $154

TRACTORS 1:08-SCALE

❑ **Allis-Chalmers WC**, 1:08-scale, Scale Models, diesel, Collector Edition, 2001, No. FT-0574
EX $86   **NM** $129   **MIP** $198

❑ **Allis-Chalmers WD-45**, 1:08-scale, Scale Models, No. FT-0511
(Photo by Scale Models)
EX $76   **NM** $122   **MIP** $198

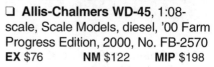

❑ **Allis-Chalmers WD-45**, 1:08-scale, Scale Models, diesel, '00 Farm Progress Edition, 2000, No. FB-2570
EX $76   **NM** $122   **MIP** $198

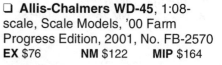

❑ **Allis-Chalmers WD-45**, 1:08-scale, Scale Models, '00 Farm Progress Edition, 2001, No. FB-2570
EX $76   **NM** $122   **MIP** $164

TRACTORS 1:12-SCALE

❑ **Allis-Chalmers C**, 1:12-scale, American Precision, orange, 1950s
EX $98   **NM** $183   **MIP** $367

❑ **Allis-Chalmers D-21**, 1:12-scale, Gubbels (Custom), orange, did not come in box, 1980s
EX $33   **NM** $47   **MIP** n/a

❑ **Allis-Chalmers WC**, 1:12-scale, Franklin Mint, on rubber, 2000
(Photo by Bossen Implement)
EX $53   **NM** $78   **MIP** $133

❑ **Allis-Chalmers WC**, 1:12-scale, Scale Models, orange, No. 1 of Collectors Series I, 3,000 made, 1980s
EX $29   **NM** $37   **MIP** $53

TRACTORS 1:16-SCALE

❑ **Allis-Chalmers 10-18**, 1:16-scale, Scale Models, green, 1990s
EX $46   **NM** $73   **MIP** $92

❑ **Allis-Chalmers 10-18**, 1:16-scale, Scale Models, '92 Farm Progress Edition, 1992, No. FB-1575
EX $46   **NM** $73   **MIP** $92

❑ **Allis-Chalmers 170**, 1:16-scale, SpecCast, WF, '91 Summer Toy Festival, 1991, No. DAC-407
(Photo by Bossen Implement)
EX $28   **NM** $32   **MIP** $52

❑ **Allis-Chalmers 170**, 1:16-scale, SpecCast, puller, 1998, No. SCT-163
EX $21   **NM** $33   **MIP** $52

❑ **Allis-Chalmers 175**, 1:16-scale, SpecCast, NF, Collector Edition, 1991, No. DAC-409
EX $21   **NM** $33   **MIP** $52

❑ **Allis-Chalmers 175**, 1:16-scale, SpecCast, WF, ROPS, '93 Crossroads USA Show, 1993, No. CUST263
EX $21   **NM** $33   **MIP** $52

❑ **Allis-Chalmers 175**, 1:16-scale, SpecCast, WF, ROPS, 1994, No. SCT-116
EX $21   **NM** $33   **MIP** $52

❑ **Allis-Chalmers 180**, 1:16-scale, SpecCast, 1990s
EX $23   **NM** $36   **MIP** $57

❑ **Allis-Chalmers 185**, 1:16-scale, Scale Models, WF, '03 Iowa FFA, 2003, No. FB-1683
EX $23   **NM** $36   **MIP** $57

❑ **Allis-Chalmers 185**, 1:16-scale, SpecCast, NF, ROPS, '94 Farm Progress Edition, 1994, No. SCT-311
EX $26   **NM** $33   **MIP** $49

❑ **Allis-Chalmers 190**, 1:16-scale, Ertl, orange, A-C diamond decal in grille, bar grille, 1960s, No. 192
EX $96   **NM** $221   **MIP** $743

❑ **Allis-Chalmers 190**, 1:16-scale, Ertl, orange, one-ninety winged decal, flat fenders, 1960s, No. 192
EX $63   **NM** $104   **MIP** $316

❑ **Allis-Chalmers 190**, 1:16-scale, Ertl, orange, black A over C decal in grille, bar grille, 1965, No. 192
EX $67   **NM** $143   **MIP** $402

❑ **Allis-Chalmers 190**, 1:16-scale, Scale Models, No. FF-0207
(Photo by Scale Models)
EX $22   **NM** $33   **MIP** $56

❏ **Allis-Chalmers 190**, 1:16-scale, Scale Models, '92 Farm Progress Edition, 1992, No. FB-1573
EX $20   **NM** $40   **MIP** $60

❏ **Allis-Chalmers 190**, 1:16-scale, Scale Models, WF, metal rims, 3 point, 1993, No. FT-0475
EX $22   **NM** $33   **MIP** $56

❏ **Allis-Chalmers 190**, 1:16-scale, Scale Models, '93 Farm Progress Edition, 1993, No. FT-0492
EX $20   **NM** $40   **MIP** $60

❏ **Allis-Chalmers 190**, 1:16-scale, Scale Models, Summer Open House, WF, cab, 1998, No. FB-2501
EX $20   **NM** $40   **MIP** $60

❏ **Allis-Chalmers 190XT**, 1:16-scale, Ertl, orange, 1960s, No. 192
EX $58   **NM** $98   **MIP** $257

❏ **Allis-Chalmers 190XT**, 1:16-scale, Ertl, orange, large wheels, Big Ace Puller, white outline around decal, 1970s, No. 2703
EX $58   **NM** $128   **MIP** $218

❏ **Allis-Chalmers 190XT**, 1:16-scale, Ertl, orange, small wheels, Big Ace Puller, 1970s, No. 2703
EX $76   **NM** $138   **MIP** $248

❏ **Allis-Chalmers 190XT**, 1:16-scale, Ertl, orange, Land Handler Series III, 1970s, No. 188
EX $146   **NM** $297   **MIP** $672

❏ **Allis-Chalmers 190XT**, 1:16-scale, Ertl, orange, large wheels, black decal, Big Ace Puller, 1970s, No. 2703
EX $76   **NM** $138   **MIP** $248

❏ **Allis-Chalmers 190XT**, 1:16-scale, Scale Models, orange, '05 Iowa FFA, 2005, No. FB-1708
EX $20   **NM** $38   **MIP** $55

❏ **Allis-Chalmers 200**, 1:16-scale, Ertl, orange, extra brace behind seat on right, 1970s, No. 152
EX $77   **NM** $146   **MIP** $254

❏ **Allis-Chalmers 200**, 1:16-scale, Ertl, orange, w/air cleaner, 1970s, No. 152
EX $73   **NM** $134   **MIP** $268

❏ **Allis-Chalmers 200**, 1:16-scale, Ertl, orange, 1970s, No. 152
EX $73   **NM** $134   **MIP** $248

❏ **Allis-Chalmers 200**, 1:16-scale, Scale Models, '00 Louisville Edition, w/cab, 2000, No. FB-2459
EX $15   **NM** $30   **MIP** $50

❏ **Allis-Chalmers 200**, 1:16-scale, Scale Models, WF, no cab, 2003, No. FT-0647
EX $15   **NM** $30   **MIP** $50

❏ **Allis-Chalmers 200**, 1:16-scale, Scale Models, cab, 2003, No. FT-0598
EX $21   **NM** $32   **MIP** $58

❏ **Allis-Chalmers 200**, 1:16-scale, Scale Models, no cab, 2003, No. FT-0647
EX $19   **NM** $31   **MIP** $52

❏ **Allis-Chalmers 210**, 1:16-scale, Ertl, '04 Summer Show Edition, metal rims, 2004, No. 16112A
EX $27   **NM** $36   **MIP** $57

❏ **Allis-Chalmers 210**, 1:16-scale, Ertl, 2WD, w/2 post ROPS, 2004, No. 13454
EX $21   **NM** $31   **MIP** $46

❏ **Allis-Chalmers 220**, 1:16-scale, Ertl, 2WD, '95 National Farm Toy Show, 1995, No. 2623PA
(Photo by Bossen Implement)
EX $37   **NM** $58   **MIP** $93

❑ **Allis-Chalmers 220**, 1:16-scale, Ertl, 2WD, 1996, No. 4755 *(Photo by Ertl)*
EX $14   **NM** $21   **MIP** $33

❑ **Allis-Chalmers 220**, 1:16-scale, Ertl, 2WD, Collector Edition, diesel, 1996, No. 2623DA
EX $32   **NM** $43   **MIP** $76

❑ **Allis-Chalmers 220**, 1:16-scale, Ertl, 2WD, '98 Farm Show Edition, w/duals, 1998, No. 2048TA
EX $27   **NM** $34   **MIP** $57

❑ **Allis-Chalmers 440**, 1:16-scale, Scale Models, 4WD, '04 AGCO Parts Expo, 2004, No. FT-0695
EX $93   **NM** $108   **MIP** $168

❑ **Allis-Chalmers 6060**, 1:16-scale, SpecCast, MFD, w/4-post ROPS, 2006, No. SCT266 *(Photo by SpecCast)*
EX $38   **NM** $52   **MIP** $78

❑ **Allis-Chalmers 6060**, 1:16-scale, SpecCast, 4WD, ROPS, canopy, loader, 2007, No. 266 *(Photo by SpecCast)*
EX $26   **NM** $38   **MIP** $52

❑ **Allis-Chalmers 6080**, 1:16-scale, SpecCast, MFD, cab, '06 Orange Spectacular, 2006, No. SCT265
(Photo by Bossen Implement)
EX $37   **NM** $43   **MIP** $66

❑ **Allis-Chalmers 7000**, 1:16-scale, Ertl, '01 CIFES 150th Anniversary, 2001, No. 29156P
EX $37   **NM** $51   **MIP** $73

❑ **Allis-Chalmers 7010**, 1:16-scale, Ertl, '99 Farm Progress Show, 1999, No. 13003A
EX $29   **NM** $37   **MIP** $58

❑ **Allis-Chalmers 7030**, 1:16-scale, Ertl, w/o cab, orange and maroon, 1974, No. 1201
EX $93   **NM** $177   **MIP** $262

❑ **Allis-Chalmers 7030**, 1:16-scale, Ertl, w/cab, orange and maroon, 1974, No. 1201
EX $97   **NM** $204   **MIP** $332

❑ **Allis-Chalmers 7030**, 1:16-scale, Ertl, black cab, wide duals, '03 Toy Tractor Times Anniversary, #18; 1,092 produced, 2003, No. 16111A
EX $28   **NM** $42   **MIP** $63

❑ **Allis-Chalmers 7040**, 1:16-scale, Ertl, orange and maroon, 1975, No. 1201
EX $79   **NM** $164   **MIP** $232

❑ **Allis-Chalmers 7045**, 1:16-scale, Ertl, orange and black, 1978, No. 1209
EX $42   **NM** $72   **MIP** $122

❑ **Allis-Chalmers 7045**, 1:16-scale, Ertl, w/cab and duals, '00 Toy Tractor Times Anniversary, #15; 2,000 produced, 2000, No. 29143A
EX $24   **NM** $48   **MIP** $64

❑ **Allis-Chalmers 7050**, 1:16-scale, Ertl, orange and maroon, 1970s, No. 1200
EX $89   **NM** $149   **MIP** $239

❏ **Allis-Chalmers 7060**, 1:16-scale, Ertl, orange and maroon, small front tires, w/air cleaner, 1970s, No. 1200
EX $89   **NM** $164   **MIP** $263

❏ **Allis-Chalmers 7060**, 1:16-scale, Ertl, orange and maroon, 1970s, No. 1200
EX $77   **NM** $152   **MIP** $238

❏ **Allis-Chalmers 7060**, 1:16-scale, Ertl, orange and black, 1970s, No. 1208
EX $42   **NM** $68   **MIP** $107

❏ **Allis-Chalmers 7060**, 1:16-scale, Ertl, orange and black, new style cab, 1970s
EX $42   **NM** $68   **MIP** $107

❏ **Allis-Chalmers 7060**, 1:16-scale, Ertl, orange and black, 1970s, No. 1208
EX $42   **NM** $68   **MIP** $107

❏ **Allis-Chalmers 7060**, 1:16-scale, Ertl, orange and maroon, no air cleaner, 1970s, No. 1200
EX $87   **NM** $156   **MIP** $243

❏ **Allis-Chalmers 7080**, 1:16-scale, Ertl, orange and black, 1970s, No. 1218
EX $47   **NM** $71   **MIP** $112

❏ **Allis-Chalmers 7080**, 1:16-scale, Ertl, orange and black, 1979 National Farm Toy Show, tractor dated 11-10-79, 1979, No. 1218
EX $274   **NM** $304   **MIP** $538

❏ **Allis-Chalmers 7080**, 1:16-scale, Ertl, '95 Summer Toy Show, triples, 1995, No. 2268BA
EX $32   **NM** $43   **MIP** $72

❏ **Allis-Chalmers 8010**, 1:16-scale, Ertl, orange and black, also available in a Collectors Series, 1983, No. 1221
EX $23   **NM** $38   **MIP** $63

❏ **Allis-Chalmers 8030**, 1:16-scale, Ertl, orange and black, also available in a Collectors Series, 1982, No. 1220
EX $23   **NM** $38   **MIP** $63

❏ **Allis-Chalmers 8070**, 1:16-scale, Ertl, MFD, duals, '92 National Farm Toy Museum, 1992, No. 2248PA
EX $42   **NM** $67   **MIP** $88

❏ **Allis-Chalmers A**, 1:16-scale, Gray (Custom), orange, did not come in box, 1970s
EX $27   **NM** $42   **MIP** n/a

❑ **Allis-Chalmers A**, 1:16-scale, Gray (Custom), orange, did come in box, 1970s
EX $27　　**NM** $42　　**MIP** n/a

❑ **Allis-Chalmers A**, 1:16-scale, SpecCast, w/accessories, 1995, No. SCT142 *(Photo by SpecCast)*
EX $22　　**NM** $32　　**MIP** $46

❑ **Allis-Chalmers A**, 1:16-scale, SpecCast, on steel, 1995, No. SCT-183
EX $16　　**NM** $28　　**MIP** $41

❑ **Allis-Chalmers A**, 1:16-scale, SpecCast, on rubber, 1995, No. SCT133 *(Photo by SpecCast)*
EX $16　　**NM** $28　　**MIP** $41

❑ **Allis-Chalmers B**, 1:16-scale, Pioneer Collectables, '87 Toy Tractor Times Anniversary Edition, #2; 1,820 produced, 1987, No. PC1987
EX $57　　**NM** $72　　**MIP** $94

❑ **Allis-Chalmers B**, 1:16-scale, Scale Models, 1991, No. FT-0431
EX $18　　**NM** $28　　**MIP** $44

❑ **Allis-Chalmers B**, 1:16-scale, Scale Models, orange, "Louisville Farm Machinery Show", 1991
EX $22　　**NM** $32　　**MIP** $47

❑ **Allis-Chalmers C**, 1:16-scale, Scale Models, NF, 1995, No. FT-0498 *(Photo by Scale Models)*
EX $14　　**NM** $19　　**MIP** $34

❑ **Allis-Chalmers C**, 1:16-scale, Scale Models, USA National Plowing Contest w/btm mounted plow, 2002, No. 2615
EX $28　　**NM** $47　　**MIP** $78

❑ **Allis-Chalmers CA**, 1:16-scale, Scale Models, 1996, No. FT-0530
EX $14　　**NM** $19　　**MIP** $34

❑ **Allis-Chalmers D-10**, 1:16-scale, SpecCast, orange, 1990, No. DAC405
EX $18　　**NM** $24　　**MIP** $38

❑ **Allis-Chalmers D-10**, 1:16-scale, SpecCast, high clearance, 1996, No. SCT-138
EX $18　　**NM** $24　　**MIP** $38

❑ **Allis-Chalmers D-10**, 1:16-scale, SpecCast, w/umbrella, 1997, No. SCT-146
EX $18　　**NM** $24　　**MIP** $38

❑ **Allis-Chalmers D-12**, 1:16-scale, SpecCast, orange, Series II, high clearance, 1990s, No. DAC406
EX $18　　**NM** $21　　**MIP** $38

❑ **Allis-Chalmers D-12**, 1:16-scale, SpecCast, orange, Paxton-Buckley-Loda FFA Chapter tractor, 1991
EX $18　　**NM** $28　　**MIP** $42

❑ **Allis-Chalmers D-12**, 1:16-scale, SpecCast, WF, 2002, No. SCT-208
EX $21　　**NM** $32　　**MIP** $44

❑ **Allis-Chalmers D-14**, 1:16-scale, SpecCast, NF, 1998, No. SCT-159
EX $18　　**NM** $21　　**MIP** $38

❑ **Allis-Chalmers D-14**, 1:16-scale, SpecCast, high crop, '05 National Farm Toy Museum, 2005, No. CUST851 *(Photo by SpecCast)*
EX $18　　**NM** $33　　**MIP** $43

❏ **Allis-Chalmers D-14 Series I**, 1:16-scale, SpecCast, orange, sold as set in walnut case, 1000 made, row crop, $153/set of four, 1990s
EX $17   **NM** $31   **MIP** n/a

❏ **Allis-Chalmers D-14 Series II**, 1:16-scale, SpecCast, orange, 1990s
EX $19   **NM** $21   **MIP** $38

❏ **Allis-Chalmers D-14 Series II**, 1:16-scale, SpecCast, orange, sold in walnut case, 1000 made, single fr. wheel, $153 for set of four, 1990s
EX $17   **NM** $31   **MIP** n/a

❏ **Allis-Chalmers D-15**, 1:16-scale, SpecCast, orange, Collector Edition, 1990s
EX $18   **NM** $21   **MIP** $38

❏ **Allis-Chalmers D-15**, 1:16-scale, SpecCast, WF, w/umbrella, 2000, No. SCT-190
EX $18   **NM** $21   **MIP** $38

❏ **Allis-Chalmers D-15 Series I**, 1:16-scale, SpecCast, orange, sold as set in walnut case, 1000 made, row crop, $153 for set of four, 1990s
EX $22   **NM** $34   **MIP** n/a

❏ **Allis-Chalmers D-15 Series II**, 1:16-scale, SpecCast, orange, "1989 Minnesota State Fair", 1989, No. DAC400
EX $22   **NM** $33   **MIP** $48

❏ **Allis-Chalmers D-15 Series II**, 1:16-scale, SpecCast, orange, sold in walnut case, 1000 made, single fr. wheel, $153/set of four, 1990s
EX $17   **NM** $31   **MIP** n/a

❏ **Allis-Chalmers D-15 Series II**, 1:16-scale, SpecCast, orange, 1992, No. DAC410
EX $18   **NM** $21   **MIP** $38

❏ **Allis-Chalmers D-17**, 1:16-scale, Ertl, #6 in Precision Series, 2000, No. 13008
EX $52   **NM** $74   **MIP** $128

❏ **Allis-Chalmers D-17**, 1:16-scale, Scale Models, regular rims, No. FF-0241 *(Photo by Scale Models)*
EX $22   **NM** $29   **MIP** $41

❏ **Allis-Chalmers D-17**, 1:16-scale, Scale Models, orange, "Louisville Farm Show February 14-17, 1990", 1990s
EX $23   **NM** $31   **MIP** $44

❑ **Allis-Chalmers D-17**, 1:16-scale, Scale Models, orange, 1990s
EX $21   **NM** $29   **MIP** $41

❑ **Allis-Chalmers D-17 Series I**, 1:16-scale, Ertl, orange, 1960s
EX $208   **NM** $421   **MIP** $1142

❑ **Allis-Chalmers D-17 Series II**, 1:16-scale, Ertl, orange, 1960s
EX $179   **NM** $358   **MIP** $982

❑ **Allis-Chalmers D-17 Series II**, 1:16-scale, Ertl, orange, 1960s
EX $172   **NM** $347   **MIP** $919

❑ **Allis-Chalmers D-17 Series III**, 1:16-scale, Ertl, orange, no headlights, 1960s
EX $176   **NM** $352   **MIP** $919

❑ **Allis-Chalmers D-17 Series III**, 1:16-scale, Ertl, orange, no headlights or breather, 1960s
EX $178   **NM** $339   **MIP** $926

❑ **Allis-Chalmers D-17 Series IV**, 1:16-scale, Scale Models, orange, No. FT-0536 *(Photo by Scale Models)*
EX $24   **NM** $38   **MIP** $48

❑ **Allis-Chalmers D-19**, 1:16-scale, Ertl, orange, special edition, singles, diesel, Collector's Edition, 1980s, No. 2220DA
EX $23   **NM** $33   **MIP** $48

❑ **Allis-Chalmers D-19**, 1:16-scale, Ertl, orange, 1989 National Show Tractor, 1980s, No. 2220PA
EX $22   **NM** $27   **MIP** $38

❑ **Allis-Chalmers D-19**, 1:16-scale, Ertl, orange, duals, diesel, '90 Minn. St. Fair edition, 1990, No. 2220Ya
EX $36   **NM** $47   **MIP** $73

❑ **Allis-Chalmers D-19**, 1:16-scale, Ertl, orange, 1990s, No. 2220DO
EX $18   **NM** $22   **MIP** $39

❑ **Allis-Chalmers D-19**, 1:16-scale, Ertl, w/loader, 1998, No. 2030
EX $19   **NM** $29   **MIP** $44

❑ **Allis-Chalmers D-19**, 1:16-scale, Ertl, high clearance '02 NFTM, 2002, No. 16098A
EX $26   **NM** $37   **MIP** $58

❑ **Allis-Chalmers D-19**, 1:16-scale, Ertl, high clearance, 2003, No. 13403
EX $18   **NM** $28   **MIP** $43

❑ **Allis-Chalmers D-19**, 1:16-scale, Ertl, w/loader, '05 World Pork Expo, 2005, No. 16140A
EX $27   **NM** $38   **MIP** $63

❑ **Allis-Chalmers D-21**, 1:16-scale, Ertl, orange, Collectors Edition, 1980s, No. 1283DA
EX $58   **NM** $63   **MIP** $78

❑ **Allis-Chalmers D-21**, 1:16-scale, Ertl, orange, 1980s, No. 1283
EX $27   **NM** $38   **MIP** $59

❑ **Allis-Chalmers D-21**, 1:16-scale, Ertl, orange, "Minnesota State Fair Tractor", 1980s, No. 1283TA
EX $57   **NM** $68   **MIP** $94

❑ **Allis-Chalmers D-21**, 1:16-scale, Ertl, w/duals, 2002, No. 13078
(Photo by Ertl)
EX $18   **NM** $28   **MIP** $46

❑ **Allis-Chalmers G**, 1:16-scale, Scale Models, bronze, 1980s, No. 402
EX $48   **NM** $63   **MIP** $102

❑ **Allis-Chalmers G**, 1:16-scale, Scale Models, orange, came w/plow, 1980s
EX $9   **NM** $16   **MIP** $21

❑ **Allis-Chalmers G**, 1:16-scale, Scale Models, orange, shelf, 1980s, No. 402
EX $12   **NM** $16   **MIP** $22

❑ **Allis-Chalmers G**, 1:16-scale, Scale Models, orange, no plow, Collector's Edition, 1980s, No. 404
EX $18   **NM** $27   **MIP** $38

❑ **Allis-Chalmers RC**, 1:16-scale, Scale Models, #12 in Collector Series I, 1984
EX $36   **NM** $47   **MIP** $78

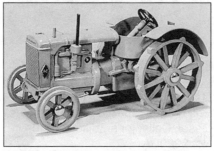

❑ **Allis-Chalmers U**, 1:16-scale, Marvil (Custom), orange, 1980s
EX $82   **NM** $122   **MIP** $178

❑ **Allis-Chalmers U**, 1:16-scale, Scale Models, on steel wheels, 1992, No. FT-0450
EX $19   **NM** $29   **MIP** $43

❑ **Allis-Chalmers U**, 1:16-scale, Scale Models, '00 Farm Progress Edition, 2000, No. FB-2572
EX $21   **NM** $32   **MIP** $44

❑ **Allis-Chalmers WC**, 1:16-scale, Arcade, orange, black rubber tires, 6-1/4" long, 1940s, No. 4060X
EX $119   **NM** $293   **MIP** $858

❑ **Allis-Chalmers WC**, 1:16-scale, Arcade, orange, also available w/front wheel centers painted orange, 7-3/4" long, 1941, No. 3740
EX $222   **NM** $468   **MIP** $1658

❑ **Allis-Chalmers WC**, 1:16-scale, Ertl, red, aluminum wheels, 1940s
EX $348   **NM** $798   **MIP** npf

❑ **Allis-Chalmers WC**, 1:16-scale, Ertl, on steel wheels, #1 in Precision Series, 1993, No. 2245
EX $98   **NM** $126   **MIP** $193

Photos by Jon Jacobson unless otherwise noted.

❏ **Allis-Chalmers WC**, 1:16-scale, Jergensen (Custom), orange, did not come in box, 1980s
EX $42   **NM** $63   **MIP** n/a

❏ **Allis-Chalmers WC**, 1:16-scale, Parker (Custom), orange, 1980s
EX $93   **NM** $132   **MIP** $168

❏ **Allis-Chalmers WC**, 1:16-scale, Scale Models, orange, Louisville Farm Show, 1980s
EX $24   **NM** $38   **MIP** $46

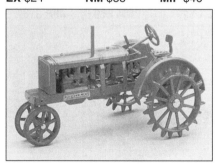

❏ **Allis-Chalmers WC**, 1:16-scale, Scale Models, orange, on steel wheels, 1993, No. FT-0477
(Photo by Scale Models)
EX $22   **NM** $32   **MIP** $47

❏ **Allis-Chalmers WC**, 1:16-scale, Scale Models, on rubber, 1996, No. FT-0531
EX $22   **NM** $32   **MIP** $47

❏ **Allis-Chalmers WD**, 1:16-scale, Ertl, #2 in Precision Series, 1994, No. 2252 *(Photo by Ertl)*
EX $98   **NM** $126   **MIP** $193

❏ **Allis-Chalmers WD**, 1:16-scale, Product Miniature, orange, 1950s
EX $87   **NM** $189   **MIP** $412

❏ **Allis-Chalmers WD**, 1:16-scale, Product Miniature, cream, 1950s
EX $87   **NM** $189   **MIP** $412

❏ **Allis-Chalmers WD**, 1:16-scale, Riecke (Custom), orange, row crop, did not come in box, 1980s
EX $226   **NM** $322   **MIP** n/a

❏ **Allis-Chalmers WD-45**, 1:16-scale, Ertl, w/wagon set, No. 1209
(Photo by Ertl)
EX $22   **NM** $38   **MIP** $48

❏ **Allis-Chalmers WD-45**, 1:16-scale, Ertl, orange, short and tall mufflers, 1980s, No. 1206
EX $18   **NM** $26   **MIP** $42

❏ **Allis-Chalmers WD-45**, 1:16-scale, Ertl, orange, Collectors edition, WF, 1980s, No. 1206DA
EX $46   **NM** $52   **MIP** $73

❏ **Allis-Chalmers WD-45**, 1:16-scale, Ertl, orange, "C.I.F.E.S. 1989 Special Edition", 1980s, No. 1206YA
EX $24   **NM** $37   **MIP** $54

❑ **Allis-Chalmers WD-45**, 1:16-scale, Ertl, Precision Series #3, WF, 1990s, No. 2253 *(Photo by Ertl)*
EX $138   **NM** $169   **MIP** $278

❑ **Allis-Chalmers WD-45**, 1:16-scale, Ertl, w/umbrella, '95 Iowa FFA Edition, 1995, No. 2670TA *(Photo by Ertl)*
EX $22   **NM** $36   **MIP** $46

❑ **Allis-Chalmers WD-45**, 1:16-scale, Ertl, w/umbrella '95 Farm Progress Edition, 1995, No. 1202DA

(Photo by Ertl)
EX $18   **NM** $26   **MIP** $36
❑ **Allis-Chalmers WD-45**, 1:16-scale, Ertl, Firestone Series 1 of 5000, 2000
EX $98   **NM** $126   **MIP** $192
❑ **Allis-Chalmers WD-45**, 1:16-scale, Ertl, diesel, NF, #7 in Precision Series, 2000, No. 13101
EX $53   **NM** $82   **MIP** $128
❑ **Allis-Chalmers WD-45**, 1:16-scale, Ertl, gas, NF, 50th Anniversary Precision Collector, 2003, No. 13384A
EX $53   **NM** $72   **MIP** $118
❑ **Allis-Chalmers WD-45**, 1:16-scale, Ertl, 2003, No. 13080
EX $9   **NM** $14   **MIP** $24

❑ **Allis-Chalmers WD-45**, 1:16-scale, Riecke (Custom), orange, w/wide front end, did not come in box, 1990s
EX $227   **NM** $327   **MIP** n/a

❑ **Allis-Chalmers WD-45**, 1:16-scale, SpecCast, "Best of Show" Series, 2000, No. SCT-174
EX $23   **NM** $38   **MIP** $66

❑ **Tractor Trailer**, 1:16-scale, Arcade, red tractor, green dump box trailer, rubber tires, 13" long, 1936, No. 2650
EX $63   **NM** $144   **MIP** $623

❑ **Tractor Trailer**, 1:16-scale, Arcade, similar to the 2650 but 12-3/4" long, same colors, 1937, No. 2657
EX $123   **NM** $264   **MIP** $738

TRACTORS 1:24-SCALE

❑ **Allis-Chalmers WC**, 1:24-scale, Arcade, red or orange, wood wheels, 1941 (war toy), No. 7341X
EX $96   **NM** $279   **MIP** npf

❑ **Allis-Chalmers WC**, 1:24-scale, Dent, orange, rubber wheels, painted driver casted separately, 1930s
EX $146   **NM** $373   **MIP** $1183

❑ **Allis-Chalmers WC**, 1:24-scale, Ertl, orange or red, rubber wheels, late 1940s
EX $388   **NM** $898   **MIP** npf

❑ **Allis-Chalmers WC**, 1:24-scale, Ertl, orange or red, mid to late 1940s
EX $388   **NM** $898   **MIP** npf

TRACTORS 1:25-SCALE

❑ **Allis-Chalmers D-14**, 1:25-scale, Strombecker, orange, 1960s
EX $27   **NM** $79   **MIP** $167

❑ **Allis-Chalmers D-14**, 1:25-scale, Strombecker, orange, 1960s
EX $27   **NM** $79   **MIP** $167

Photos by Jon Jacobson unless otherwise noted.

❑ **Allis-Chalmers D-14**, 1:25-scale, Yoder (Custom), orange, remake of Strombecker, 1980s
EX $24   **NM** $44   **MIP** $59

❑ **Allis-Chalmers D-15 Series II**, 1:25-scale, Yoder (Custom), orange, Beaver Falls Show Tractor, only 2000 made, 1980s
EX $27   **NM** $48   **MIP** $63

TRACTORS 1:32-SCALE

❑ **Allis-Chalmers 4W-305**, 1:32-scale, Ertl, orange and black, 1980s, No. 1225
EX $28   **NM** $42   **MIP** $58

❑ **Allis-Chalmers 4W-305**, 1:32-scale, Ertl, orange and black, Collector's Edition, 1980s, No. 1225DA
EX $32   **NM** $52   **MIP** $72

❑ **Allis-Chalmers 8550**, 1:32-scale, Ertl, orange and black, 1970s, No. 1213
EX $29   **NM** $54   **MIP** $77

❑ **Allis-Chalmers B**, 1:32-scale, Brown's Models, orange, model kit form, 1980s
EX $13   **NM** $27   **MIP** $44

TRACTORS 1:43-SCALE

❑ **Allis-Chalmers 190**, 1:43-scale, SpecCast, 1990s, No. DAC009
EX $6   **NM** $8   **MIP** $12

❑ **Allis-Chalmers 220**, 1:43-scale, Ertl, 1990s, No. 2336 *(Photo by Ertl)*
EX $4   **NM** $7   **MIP** $14

❑ **Allis-Chalmers 220**, 1:43-scale, Ertl, '95 LCN European Show Edition, 1995
EX $17   **NM** $27   **MIP** $44

❑ **Allis-Chalmers 220**, 1:43-scale, Ertl, 2WD, '95 National Farm Toy Show, 1995 *(Photo by Bossen Implement)*
EX $8   **NM** $18   **MIP** $24

❑ **Allis-Chalmers B**, 1:43-scale, SpecCast, orange, steel wheel, 1980s
EX $6   **NM** $8   **MIP** $12

❑ **Allis-Chalmers B**, 1:43-scale, SpecCast, rubber tires, 1990s, No. DAC002
EX $6   **NM** $8   **MIP** $12

❑ **Allis-Chalmers C**, 1:43-scale, Ertl, orange, narrow and wide front, 1980s, No. 2529
EX $4   **NM** $8   **MIP** $11

❑ **Allis-Chalmers D-12**, 1:43-scale, SpecCast, 1990s

EX $6   NM $8   MIP $12

❑ **Allis-Chalmers D-14**, 1:43-scale, SpecCast, 1990s, No. DAC008

EX $6   NM $8   MIP $12

❑ **Allis-Chalmers D-15**, 1:43-scale, SpecCast, 1990s, No. DAC016

EX $6   NM $8   MIP $12

❑ **Allis-Chalmers D-17**, 1:43-scale, SpecCast, 1990s

EX $6   NM $8   MIP $12

❑ **Allis-Chalmers D-19**, 1:43-scale, Ertl, orange, "1989 National Farm Tow Show", 1980s, No. 2566

EX $17   NM $23   MIP $38

❑ **Allis-Chalmers D-19**, 1:43-scale, Ertl, orange, 1980s, No. 2566

EX $6   NM $8   MIP $14

❑ **Allis-Chalmers D-21**, 1:43-scale, Ertl, orange, two different grille decals, 1980s, No. 2550

EX $4   NM $8   MIP $14

❑ **Allis-Chalmers U**, 1:43-scale, SpecCast, 1990s, No. DAC007

EX $6   NM $8   MIP $12

❑ **Allis-Chalmers WC**, 1:43-scale, SpecCast, 1990s, No. DAC006

EX $6   NM $8   MIP $12

❑ **Allis-Chalmers WD-45**, 1:43-scale, SpecCast, 1990s, No. DAC001

EX $6   NM $8   MIP $12

TRACTORS 1:64-SCALE

❑ **Allis-Chalmers 10-18**, 1:64-scale, Scale Models, Farm Progress Edition, 1990s, No. 1575

EX $4   NM $6   MIP $11

❑ **Allis-Chalmers 190**, 1:64-scale, Baker (Custom), orange and cream, 1980s

❑ **Allis-Chalmers 190**, 1:64-scale, Baker (Custom), orange and cream, did not come in box, 1980s

EX $3   NM $9   MIP n/a

Photos by Jon Jacobson unless otherwise noted.

❑ **Allis-Chalmers 190**, 1:64-scale, Baker (Custom), orange and cream, did not come in box, 1980s
EX $3   **NM** $9   **MIP** n/a

❑ **Allis-Chalmers 190**, 1:64-scale, Scale Models, No. FT-0476
EX $3   **NM** $6   **MIP** $9

❑ **Allis-Chalmers 190**, 1:64-scale, Scale Models, '92 Farm Progress Edition, 1992, No. FB-1576
EX $3   **NM** $6   **MIP** $9

❑ **Allis-Chalmers 190**, 1:64-scale, Scale Models, '93 Farm Progress Edition, 1993, No. FB-0493
EX $3   **NM** $6   **MIP** $9

❑ **Allis-Chalmers 190**, 1:64-scale, Scale Models, '93 Louisville Edition, 1993, No. FB-0449
EX $3   **NM** $6   **MIP** $9

❑ **Allis-Chalmers 190 XT**, 1:64-scale, Baker (Custom), orange and cream, did not come in box, 1980s
EX $3   **NM** $9   **MIP** n/a

❑ **Allis-Chalmers 190 XT**, 1:64-scale, Baker (Custom), orange and cream, did not come in box, 1980s
EX $3   **NM** $9   **MIP** n/a

❑ **Allis-Chalmers 190 XT**, 1:64-scale, Keith (Custom), orange and cream, did not come in box, 1980s
EX $3   **NM** $12   **MIP** n/a

❑ **Allis-Chalmers 190 XT**, 1:64-scale, Keith (Custom), orange and cream, did not come in box, 1980s
EX $3   **NM** $12   **MIP** n/a

❑ **Allis-Chalmers 190 XT**, 1:64-scale, Matsen (Custom), orange and cream, did not come in box, 1980s
EX $3   **NM** $12   **MIP** n/a

❑ **Allis-Chalmers 200**, 1:64-scale, Baker (Custom), orange, cream and black, did not come in box, 1980s
EX $3   **NM** $9   **MIP** n/a

❑ **Allis-Chalmers 200**, 1:64-scale, Baker (Custom), orange, cream and black, did not come in box, 1980s
EX $3   **NM** $9   **MIP** n/a

❑ **Allis-Chalmers 200**, 1:64-scale, Keith (Custom), orange, cream and black, did not come in box, 1980s
EX $3   **NM** $12   **MIP** n/a

❑ **Allis-Chalmers 200**, 1:64-scale, Matsen (Custom), orange, cream and black, did not come in box, 1980s
EX $3   **NM** $12   **MIP** n/a

❑ **Allis-Chalmers 200**, 1:64-scale, Matsen (Custom), orange, cream and black, did not come in box, 1980s
EX $3   **NM** $12   **MIP** n/a

Standard Catalog of Farm Toys 3rd Edition

❑ **Allis-Chalmers 200**, 1:64-scale, Scale Models, '00 Louisville Edition, 2000, No. FB-2550
EX $3   **NM** $6   **MIP** $9

❑ **Allis-Chalmers 220**, 1:64-scale, Gunning (Custom), orange and cream, did not come in box, 1980s
EX $3   **NM** $9   **MIP** n/a

❑ **Allis-Chalmers 7045**, 1:64-scale, Ertl, orange and black, rims are a bluish-white color, 1980s, No. 1623
EX $14   **NM** $24   **MIP** $57

❑ **Allis-Chalmers 7045**, 1:64-scale, Ertl, orange and black, front rims are spun-on, 1980s, No. 1623
EX $9   **NM** $19   **MIP** $24

❑ **Allis-Chalmers 7045**, 1:64-scale, Ertl, orange and black, rectangular decal, 1980s, No. 1623
EX $78   **NM** $123   **MIP** $184

❑ **Allis-Chalmers 7045**, 1:64-scale, Ertl, orange and black, front rims are pushed-on, 1980s, No. 1623
EX $9   **NM** $19   **MIP** $24

❑ **Allis-Chalmers 7045 variation photo**, 1:64-scale, The left rim is spun on, The right rim is pushed-on

❑ **Allis-Chalmers 7080**, 1:64-scale, Jarrett (Custom), orange and maroon, this is an Ertl unit repainted, did not come in box, 1980s
EX $12   **NM** $33   **MIP** n/a

❑ **Allis-Chalmers 7580**, 1:64-scale, Jarrett (Custom), orange and maroon, modifed Ertl unit, did not come in box, 1980
EX $13   **NM** $27   **MIP** n/a

❑ **Allis-Chalmers 8010**, 1:64-scale, Ertl, '91 Farm Progress Edition, 1991, No. 1819FA
EX $4   **NM** $9   **MIP** $14

❑ **Allis-Chalmers 8010**, 1:64-scale, Ertl, '92 NFTM, 1992, No. 1819MA
EX $8   **NM** $16   **MIP** $24

❑ **Allis-Chalmers 8070**, 1:64-scale, Ertl, orange and black, 1984 Kick-Off Meeting East Area, 1980s, No. 1819
EX $3   **NM** $4   **MIP** $9

❑ **Allis-Chalmers 8070**, 1:64-scale, Ertl, orange and black, 1980s, No. 1819
EX $3   **NM** $4   **MIP** $9

❑ **Allis-Chalmers 8070**, 1:64-scale, Ertl, orange and black, 1980s, No. 1819
EX $3   **NM** $4   **MIP** $9

❏ **Allis-Chalmers 8070**, 1:64-scale, Ertl, orange and black, 1980s, No. 1819
EX $3 **NM** $4 **MIP** $9

❏ **Allis-Chalmers 8550**, 1:64-scale, Jarrett (Custom), orange and maroon, modified Ertl unit, did not come in box, 1980s
EX $13 **NM** $27 **MIP** n/a

❏ **Allis-Chalmers B**, 1:64-scale, SpecCast, orange, 1980s
EX $4 **NM** $8 **MIP** $18

❏ **Allis-Chalmers C**, 1:64-scale, Scale Models, 1990s, No. FT-0499
(Photo by Scale Models)
EX $4 **NM** $6 **MIP** $9

❏ **Allis-Chalmers D-14**, 1:64-scale, SpecCast, WF, 1990s, No. 95001
EX $4 **NM** $6 **MIP** $11

❏ **Allis-Chalmers D-15**, 1:64-scale, SpecCast, NF, 1990s, No. 95000
EX $4 **NM** $6 **MIP** $11

❏ **Allis-Chalmers D-17**, 1:64-scale, Scale Models, 1990s, No. FT-0469
(Photo by Scale Models)
EX $4 **NM** $6 **MIP** $9

❏ **Allis-Chalmers D-19**, 1:64-scale, Ertl, 2001, No. 13077
EX $4 **NM** $6 **MIP** $9

❏ **Allis-Chalmers D-19**, 1:64-scale, Ertl, '02 NFTM, 2002, No. 16103A
EX $4 **NM** $6 **MIP** $9

❏ **Allis-Chalmers D-19**, 1:64-scale, Ertl, w/Hiniker cab, 2004, No. 13438
EX $4 **NM** $6 **MIP** $9

❏ **Allis-Chalmers D-21**, 1:64-scale, Gunning (Custom), orange and cream, did not come in box, 1980s
EX $4 **NM** $12 **MIP** n/a

❏ **Allis-Chalmers U**, 1:64-scale, Scale Models, on steel, No. FT-0451
(Photo by Scale Models)
EX $4 **NM** $6 **MIP** $9

❏ **Allis-Chalmers U**, 1:64-scale, Scale Models, '92 Louisville Edition, 1992, No. FB-0448
EX $4 **NM** $6 **MIP** $9

❏ **Allis-Chalmers WC**, 1:64-scale, Scale Models, orange, 1980, No. 478
EX $4 **NM** $6 **MIP** $9

❏ **Allis-Chalmers WC**, 1:64-scale, Scale Models, orange, 1980s, No. 478
EX $4 **NM** $6 **MIP** $9

❏ **Allis-Chalmers WC**, 1:64-scale, Scale Models, orange, 1980s, No. 478
EX $3 **NM** $4 **MIP** $6

❏ **Allis-Chalmers WC**, 1:64-scale, Scale Models, orange, 1980s, No. 478
EX $3 **NM** $4 **MIP** $6

❏ **Allis-Chalmers WC**, 1:64-scale, Scale Models, orange, on rubber, 1990, No. FT-0464 *(Photo by Scale Models)*
EX $4 **NM** $6 **MIP** $9

❏ **Allis-Chalmers WD-45**, 1:64-scale, Ertl, '95 Farm Show Edition, 1995, No. 1203FA
EX $3 **NM** $4 **MIP** $6

❏ **Allis-Chalmers WD-45**, 1:64-scale, Ertl, 2002, No. 13372
EX $3 **NM** $4 **MIP** $6

❏ **Allis-Chalmers WD-45**, 1:64-scale, Gunning (Custom), orange, did not come in box, 1980s
EX $4 **NM** $12 **MIP** n/a

❏ **Allis-Chalmers WD-45**, 1:64-scale, Gunning (Custom), orange, did not come in box, 1980s
EX $4 **NM** $12 **MIP** n/a

❏ **Allis-Chalmers WD-45**, 1:64-scale, Gunning (Custom), orange, first run, did not come in box, 1980s
EX $4 **NM** $12 **MIP** n/a

TRACTORS MICRO

❏ **Allis-Chalmers**, Micro, Micro Machines, orange, 1990s
EX $4 **NM** $6 **MIP** $9

TRUCKS 1:16-SCALE

❏ **Pickup, GMC**, 1:16-scale, Ertl, white, 1980s, No. 1202
EX $7 **NM** $16 **MIP** $26

TRUCKS 1:25-SCALE

❏ **Parts Express Semi**, 1:25-scale, Ertl, white, 1980s, No. 3118
EX $13 **NM** $47 **MIP** $72

ARTSWAY

IMPLEMENTS 1:64-SCALE

❏ **Artsway Mixer Mill**, 1:64-scale, Ertl, green and yellow, front decal has dark print, 1980s, No. 1051
EX $9 **NM** $17 **MIP** $22

❏ **Artsway Mixer Mill**, 1:64-scale, Ertl, green and yellow, front decal has light print, 1980s, No. 1051
EX $9 **NM** $17 **MIP** $22

❏ **Artsway Mixer Mill**, 1:64-scale, Ertl, 2004, No. 29298
EX $3 **NM** $6 **MIP** $8

❏ **Artsway Mixer Mill 475**, 1:64-scale, Ertl, green and yellow, 1980s, No. 9859
EX $4 **NM** $8 **MIP** $13

❏ **Artsway Mixer Mill 508A**, 1:64-scale, Ertl, 1980s, No. 9859
EX $3 **NM** $6 **MIP** $8

B.F. AVERY

TRACTORS 1:16-SCALE

❑ **B.F. Avery**, 1:16-scale, Scale Models, red, made for Tractor Supply Co., 1990s
EX $18   **NM** $33   **MIP** $53

TRACTORS

❑ **Avery Tractor**, Arcade, exposed engine, tall front stack, 3-1/8" tall, 1923
EX $78   **NM** $148   **MIP** $1

❑ **Avery Tractor**, Arcade, second version, hood over engine, short front stack, 3-1/8" tall, 1926
EX $93   **NM** $168   **MIP** $1

BADGER

IMPLEMENTS 1:64-SCALE

❑ **Badger Spreader, Liquid**, 1:64-scale, Mini Toys, green, 1980s, No. 811
EX $3   **NM** $4   **MIP** $8

❑ **Badger Spreader, Manure**, 1:64-scale, Mini Toys, green, 1980s, No. 812
EX $3   **NM** $4   **MIP** $8

BALZER

IMPLEMENTS 1:64-SCALE

❑ **Balzer Spreader, Liquid**, 1:64-scale, Mini Toys, green and orange, 1980s, No. 801
EX $3   **NM** $4   **MIP** $8

❑ **Balzer Spreader, Manure**, 1:64-scale, Mini Toys, green and orange
EX $3   **NM** $4   **MIP** $8

❑ **Spreader, Manure**, 1:64-scale, Ertl, various colors
EX $3   **NM** $4   **MIP** $8

BIG BUD

TRACTORS 1:16-SCALE

❑ **Big Bud**, 1:16-scale, Martin Fast, white, Montana 100th Anniversary Centennial Edition, limited to 200 units, 1990s
EX $933   **NM** $1072   **MIP** $1289

❑ **Big Bud 16V-747**, 1:16-scale, Diecast Promotions, original factory version, 700 HP engine, 2004, No. 40044
EX $276   **NM** $318   **MIP** $519

❑ **Big Bud 16V-900**, 1:16-scale, Diecast Promotions, restored version, 900 HP engine, 2004, No. 40045
EX $276   **NM** $318   **MIP** $569

❑ **Big Bud 600/50**, 1:16-scale, Martin Fast, w/duals, 1980s
EX $462   **NM** $533   **MIP** $828

❑ **Big Bud 650/84**, 1:16-scale, Martin Fast, orange, 1980s
EX $878   **NM** $933   **MIP** $1289

TRACTORS 1:32-SCALE

❑ **Big Bud 16V-747**, 1:32-scale, DieCast Promotions, original factory version, 700 HP engine, 2002, No. 40015
EX $78   **NM** $112   **MIP** $226

❑ **Big Bud 16V-900**, 1:32-scale, DieCast Promotions, restored version, 900 HP engine, 2002, No. 40017
EX $78   **NM** $112   **MIP** $256

❑ **Big Bud 370**, 1:32-scale, Ertl, w/duals, 1996, No. 4557
EX $33   **NM** $48   **MIP** $78

❑ **Big Bud 370**, 1:32-scale, Ertl, Bafus blue, w/duals, 1997, No. 2567
EX $33   **NM** $48   **MIP** $78

❑ **Big Bud 440**, 1:32-scale, Ertl, w/triples, 1998, No. 2569
EX $42   **NM** $54   **MIP** $89

❑ **Big Bud 500**, 1:32-scale, Ertl, w/duals, Komatsu engine, 1997, No. 2568
EX $33   **NM** $53   **MIP** $78

❑ **Big Bud 525/50**, 1:32-scale, Berg (Custom), black and white, 1980s
EX $523   **NM** $713   **MIP** $889

TRACTORS 1:64-SCALE

❑ **Big Bud 16-747**, 1:64-scale, Diecast Promotions, w;duals, original factory version, 2003, No. 40038

(Photo by Bossen Implement)

EX $17   **NM** $25   **MIP** $48

❑ **Big Bud 16-900**, 1:64-scale, Diecast Promotions, w/duals, restored version, 900 HP engine, 2003, No. 40039
EX $17   **NM** $28   **MIP** $58

❑ **Big Bud 370**, 1:64-scale, Ertl, w/duals, bafus blue, No. 4188
EX $16   **NM** $26   **MIP** $56

❑ **Big Bud 370**, 1:64-scale, Ertl, w/duals, No. 4187
EX $12   **NM** $17   **MIP** $46

❑ **Big Bud 400/20**, 1:64-scale, Ertl, black and white, 1987 Show Edition, 1987, No. 4197YA
EX $12   **NM** $17   **MIP** $27

❑ **Big Bud 400/30**, 1:64-scale, Ertl, gray, black and white, non-production run—did not come in box, 1980s
EX $1300   **NM** $2400   **MIP** n/a

❑ **Big Bud 400/30**, 1:64-scale, Ertl, black and white, 1980s, No. 4196
EX $12   **NM** $17   **MIP** $27

❑ **Big Bud 440**, 1:64-scale, Ertl, w/triples, No. 4186
EX $17   **NM** $22   **MIP** $57

❑ **Big Bud 500**, 1:64-scale, Ertl, w/duals, Komatsu engine, No. 4188
EX $16   **NM** $26   **MIP** $56

❑ **Big Bud 525/50**, 1:64-scale, Berg (Custom), white, did not come in box, 1980s
EX $22   **NM** $47   **MIP** n/a

❑ **Big Bud 525/50**, 1:64-scale, Ertl, gray, black and white, non-production run—did not come in box, 1980s
EX $1300   **NM** $2400   **MIP** n/a

❑ **Big Bud 525/50**, 1:64-scale, Ertl, black and gold, used by Toy Farmer in an awards program—did not come in box, 1980s
EX $527   **NM** $1289   **MIP** n/a

❑ **Big Bud 525/50**, 1:64-scale, Ertl, black and white, 1980s, No. 4197
EX $12   **NM** $17   **MIP** $27

❑ **Big Bud 525/50**, 1:64-scale, Ertl, black and white, 1987 Western Canada F.P.S., 1987, No. 4197YA
EX $12   **NM** $17   **MIP** $27

❑ **Big Bud 525/84**, 1:64-scale, Ertl, orange, 1980s, No. 4198
EX $12   **NM** $17   **MIP** $44

❑ **Big Bud 525/84**, 1:64-scale, Ertl, black and orange, 1980s, No. 4198
EX $12   **NM** $17   **MIP** $27

❑ **Big Bud 525/84**, 1:64-scale, Ertl, black and orange, w/loader, 1980s, No. 4199
EX $12   **NM** $17   **MIP** $27

❑ **Big Bud HN 250**, 1:64-scale, Mini Big Buds, 96 Great Falls, MT show
(Photo by Mini Big Buds)
EX $27   **NM** $43   **MIP** $74

❑ **Big Bud HN 250**, 1:64-scale, Mini Big Buds, 25th Anniversary Edition, 1980s
EX $27   **NM** $43   **MIP** $74

❑ **Big Bud HN 320**, 1:64-scale, Mini Big Buds
EX $27   **NM** $43   **MIP** $74

❑ **Big Bud HN 350**, 1:64-scale, Mini Big Buds, iranian yellow, 1990s
EX $122   **NM** $156   **MIP** $214

❑ **Big Bud HN 350**, 1:64-scale, Mini Big Buds, iranian bright yellow, 200 units wrong color, 1990s
EX $132   **NM** $162   **MIP** $298

❑ **Big Bud HN 360**, 1:64-scale, Mini Big Buds, bafus blue, 1990s
EX $132   **NM** $162   **MIP** $298

❑ **Big Bud KT 450**, 1:64-scale, Mini Big Buds, 1990s
EX $27   **NM** $43   **MIP** $74

❑ **Big Bud KT 525**, 1:64-scale, Mini Big Buds, Bicentennial
EX $27   **NM** $43   **MIP** $74

BLACK HAWK

TRACTORS 1:16-SCALE

❑ **Black Hawk 20**, 1:16-scale, Ertl, 1990 National Farm Toy Museum Set No. 5, wide front end, 1990
EX $33   **NM** $43   **MIP** $63

❑ **Black Hawk 40**, 1:16-scale, Ertl, 1986 National Farm Toy Museum Set No. 1, 1986, No. 4112PA
EX $33   **NM** $43   **MIP** $63

❑ **Black Hawk 50**, 1:16-scale, Ertl, 1990 National Farm Toy Museum Set No. 5, 1990
EX $33   **NM** $43   **MIP** $63

BOBCAT

CONSTRUCTION EQUIPMENT 1:50-SCALE

❑ **Bobcat Skid Steer Loader, 753**, 1:50-scale, Bobcat, No. 325
(Photo by Kate Bossen)
EX $4   **NM** $6   **MIP** $8

TRUCKS 1:25-SCALE

❑ **Bobcat Dealer Pickup**, 1:25-scale, Bobcat, No. 769 *(Photo by Kate Bossen)*
EX $8   **NM** $12   **MIP** $22

TRUCKS 1:50-SCALE

❑ **Bobcat Semi w/Four 753 Skid Steers**, 1:50-scale, Bobcat, No. 754
(Photo by Kate Bossen)
EX $19   **NM** $28   **MIP** $46

❑ **Bobcat Semi w/Four 753 Skid Steers**, 1:50-scale, Bobcat, No. 383
(Photo by Kate Bossen)
EX $18   **NM** $27   **MIP** $42

BRENT

IMPLEMENTS 1:16-SCALE

❑ **Brent Wagon, Gravity 450**, 1:16-scale, Ertl, red, No. 347
EX $26   **NM** $33   **MIP** $49

❑ **Brent Wagon, Gravity 450**, 1:16-scale, Ertl, green, No. 348
EX $26   **NM** $33   **MIP** $49

IMPLEMENTS 1:64-SCALE

❑ **Brent Gain Cart, 674**, 1:64-scale, SpecCast, red, 1995, No. CUST381
EX $16   **NM** $26   **MIP** $39

❑ **Brent Gain Cart, 674**, 1:64-scale, SpecCast, green, 1995, No. CUST366
EX $16   **NM** $26   **MIP** $39

❑ **Brent Grain Cart, Avalanche**, 1:64-scale, SpecCast, red, 2001, No. CUST666
EX $16   **NM** $22   **MIP** $34

❑ **Brent Grain Cart, Avalanche**, 1:64-scale, SpecCast, green, 2001, No. CUST665 *(Photo by Bossen Implement)*
EX $16   **NM** $22   **MIP** $34

❑ **Brent Wagon, Gravity 450**, 1:64-scale, Ertl, red and black, No. 9198
EX $12   **NM** $18   **MIP** $26

❑ **Brent Wagon, Gravity 450**, 1:64-scale, Ertl, green and black, No. 9197
EX $12   **NM** $18   **MIP** $26

❑ **Brent Wagon, Gravity 644**, 1:64-scale, SpecCast, red, dual wheels, 2000, No. CUST664

(Photo by Bossen Implement)
EX $16   **NM** $26   **MIP** $39

❑ **Brent Wagon, Gravity 644**, 1:64-scale, SpecCast, green, dual wheels, 2000, No. CUST663

(Photo by Bossen Implement)
EX $16   **NM** $26   **MIP** $39

BUSH HOG

IMPLEMENTS 1:16-SCALE

❑ **Bush Hog Mower**, 1:16-scale, SpecCast, rotary cutter, 1990s, No. SCT-290
EX $17   **NM** $22   **MIP** $32

❑ **Bush Hog Mower, #12**, 1:16-scale, Diecast Promotions, rotary cutter, 2000, No. 91586
EX $4   **NM** $7   **MIP** $13

❑ **Bush Hog Mower, 2615L Rotary**, 1:16-scale, Diecast Promotions, 2000, No. 91583 *(Photo by Diecast Promotions)*
EX $17   **NM** $22   **MIP** $32

IMPLEMENTS 1:64-SCALE

❑ **Bush Hog Mower, 2615**, 1:64-scale, SpecCast, rotary cutter, 1999, No. 91584
EX $3   **NM** $6   **MIP** $9

TRUCKS 1:64-SCALE

❑ **Semi, IH w/3 mowers**, 1:64-scale, SpecCast, 3 #2615 rotary cutter, 2000s, No. 30209
EX $37   **NM** $48   **MIP** $62

CALUMET

IMPLEMENTS 1:64-SCALE

❑ **Calumet 2250 Spreader, Liquid**, 1:64-scale, Ertl, red, 1980s, No. 9973
EX $4   **NM** $6   **MIP** $8

❑ **Calumet Liquid Spreader**, 1:64-scale, Mini Toys, red, 1980s, No. 821
EX $4   **NM** $6   **MIP** $8

CASE

BANKS 1:25-SCALE

❏ **Case Mack Truck Bank**, 1:25-scale, Ertl, black and white, 1980s, No. 216
EX $8　　**NM** $12　　**MIP** $18

BANKS

❏ **Case Bank**, only a few produced for the Case company, did not come in box, 1980s
EX $16　　**NM** $32　　**MIP** n/a

❏ **Mail Box Bank**, Ertl, white and orange, 1970s, No. 208
EX $9　　**NM** $14　　**MIP** $23

CONSTRUCTION EQUIPMENT 1:16-SCALE

❏ **Case Backhoe Loader**, 1:16-scale, Ertl, 40th Anniversary, Precision Series, 2006, No. 14511A
EX $75　　**NM** $100　　**MIP** $125

❏ **Case Backhoe, 580**, 1:16-scale, Tomy, yellow, 1960s
EX $262　　**NM** $388　　**MIP** $482

❏ **Case Backhoe, 580 B**, 1:16-scale, Gescha, yellow, 1970s
EX $229　　**NM** $311　　**MIP** $379

❏ **Case Backhoe, 580 B**, 1:16-scale, Gescha, yellow w/orange engine, 1970s
EX $258　　**NM** $447　　**MIP** $496

❏ **Case Backhoe, 580 E**, 1:16-scale, Ertl, tan and brown, 1980s, No. 287
EX $23　　**NM** $32　　**MIP** $39

❏ **Case Backhoe, 580 K**, 1:16-scale, Ertl, tan and brown, 1990s, No. 287
EX $23　　**NM** $32　　**MIP** $39

❏ **Case Backhoe, 580 Super M**, 1:16-scale, Ertl, #1 in Construction Precision Series, 2002, No. 14132
EX $78　　**NM** $102　　**MIP** $145

❏ **Case Crawler w/blade, 1450 B**, 1:16-scale, Ertl, tan and brown, 1980s, No. 608
EX $23　　**NM** $28　　**MIP** $39

❏ **Case Crawler w/blade, 1550**, 1:16-scale, Ertl, tan and brown, 1980s, No. 608
EX $23　　**NM** $28　　**MIP** $39

❏ **Case Crawler w/blade, 750**, 1:16-scale, Hong Kong, yellow and black. battery operated, 1960s
EX $293　　**NM** $722　　**MIP** $1026

❏ **Case Crawler, w/blade**, 1:16-scale, Ertl, No Model #, No. 608
(Photo by Bossen Implement)
EX $23　　**NM** $28　　**MIP** $39

❑ **Case Crawler, w/blade 850 G**,
1:16-scale, Ertl, tan and brown,
No. 608CP
EX $23   **NM** $28   **MIP** $39

❑ **Case Wheel Loader**, 1:16-scale,
Ertl, No Model #, tan and brown,
1990s, No. 625 *(Photo by Bossen Implement)*
EX $23   **NM** $34   **MIP** $39

❑ **Case Wheel Loader, W30**, 1:16-
scale, Ertl, tan and brown, 1980s,
No. 625
EX $23   **NM** $34   **MIP** $39

CONSTRUCTION EQUIPMENT 1:25-SCALE

❑ **Case Steam Roller**, 1:25-scale,
Irvin, black, 1970s
EX $28   **NM** $53   **MIP** $64

CONSTRUCTION EQUIPMENT 1:32-SCALE

❑ **Case Backhoe 580 K**, 1:32-scale,
Ertl, w/side shift backhoe, 1990s,
No. 4670
EX $8   **NM** $16   **MIP** $24

❑ **Case Backhoe, 580 K**, 1:32-scale,
Ertl, tan and brown, 1990s, No. 410
EX $7   **NM** $13   **MIP** $21

CONSTRUCTION EQUIPMENT 1:35-SCALE

❑ **Case Backhoe 580 K**, 1:35-scale,
Conrad, MFD, 1990s, No. 2934
EX $38   **NM** $52   **MIP** $78

❑ **Case Backhoe 580 Super K**,
1:35-scale, Conrad, gold colored case
150th Anniversary, 1990s, No. 2934
EX $38   **NM** $52   **MIP** $78

❑ **Case Backhoe, 580 C**, 1:35-
scale, Gescha, yellow and black, old
decals, 1970s
EX $27   **NM** $44   **MIP** $63

❑ **Case Backhoe, 580 C**, 1:35-scale,
Gescha, yellow and black, 1970s
EX $22   **NM** $33   **MIP** $48

❑ **Case Backhoe, 580 D**, 1:35-
scale, Conrad, silver and black, 25th
Anniversary Edition, 1980s,
No. 2931
EX $27   **NM** $44   **MIP** $53

❑ **Case Backhoe, 580 D**, 1:35-
scale, Conrad, yellow and black,
1980s, No. 2391
EX $22   **NM** $33   **MIP** $48

❑ **Case Backhoe, 580 E**, 1:35-
scale, Conrad, tan and brown, 1980s
EX $22   **NM** $33   **MIP** $48

❑ **Case Backhoe, 580 F**, 1:35-
scale, Gescha, yellow and black, old
decals, 1970s
EX $27   **NM** $44   **MIP** $63

❑ **Case Backhoe, 580 F**, 1:35-scale,
Gescha, yellow and black, 1970s
EX $23   **NM** $42   **MIP** $58

❏ **Case Backhoe, 580 G**, 1:35-scale, Conrad, silver and black, 25th Anniversary Edition, 1980s
EX $78   **NM** $189   **MIP** $247

❏ **Case Backhoe, 580 G**, 1:35-scale, Conrad, tan and brown, 1980s
EX $23   **NM** $42   **MIP** $58

❏ **Case Backhoe, 580 G**, 1:35-scale, Conrad, yellow and black, 1980s
EX $23   **NM** $42   **MIP** $58

❏ **Case Crawler w/blade, 850 B**, 1:35-scale, NZG, yellow and black, 1970s
EX $27   **NM** $44   **MIP** $53

❏ **Case Crawler w/blade, 850 B**, 1:35-scale, NZG, yellow and black, old decal, 1970s
EX $27   **NM** $44   **MIP** $53

❏ **Case Crawler w/blade, 850 B**, 1:35-scale, NZG, yellow and black, 1970s
EX $27   **NM** $44   **MIP** $53

❏ **Case Crawler w/blade, 850 B**, 1:35-scale, NZG, yellow and black, 1980s
EX $27   **NM** $44   **MIP** $53

❏ **Case Crawler w/blade, 850 C**, 1:35-scale, NZG, tan and brown, 1980s, No. 176
EX $27   **NM** $44   **MIP** $53

❏ **Case Crawler w/blade, 850 D**, 1:35-scale, NZG, tan and brown, 1980s
EX $23   **NM** $43   **MIP** $53

❏ **Case Crawler w/loader bucket, 850 B**, 1:35-scale, NZG, yellow and black, 1980s
EX $26   **NM** $42   **MIP** $53

❏ **Case Crawler w/loader bucket, 850 B**, 1:35-scale, NZG, yellow and black, 1980s
EX $26   **NM** $42   **MIP** $53

❏ **Case Crawler w/loader bucket, 850 C**, 1:35-scale, NZG, yellow and black, 1980s
EX $26   **NM** $42   **MIP** $53

❏ **Case Crawler w/loader bucket, 850 C**, 1:35-scale, NZG, yellow and black, 1980s
EX $26   **NM** $42   **MIP** $53

❏ **Case Crawler w/loader bucket, 855 C**, 1:35-scale, NZG, tan and brown, 1980s
EX $26   **NM** $42   **MIP** $53

❏ **Case Crawler w/loader bucket, 855 D**, 1:35-scale, NZG, tan and brown, 1980s
EX $24   **NM** $42   **MIP** $53

❏ **Case Excavator, 1085 B Cruz-Air**, 1:35-scale, Conrad, tan and brown, 1980s
EX $53   **NM** $89   **MIP** $117

❏ **Case Excavator, 125 B**, 1:35-scale, Conrad, tan and brown, 1980s
EX $53   **NM** $89   **MIP** $117

❏ **Case Excavator, 1280**, 1:35-scale, Conrad, tan and brown, 1980s, No. 2962
EX $63   **NM** $98   **MIP** $139

❏ **Case Excavator, 980 B**, 1:35-scale, Conrad, white and yellow, old decals, 1970s
EX $159   **NM** $273   **MIP** $334

❏ **Case Excavator, 980 B**, 1:35-scale, Conrad, yellow and black, 1970s
EX $157   **NM** $268   **MIP** $298

❏ **Case Excavator, Drott 50**, 1:35-scale, Conrad, white and yellow, muffler, 1970s
EX $159   **NM** $273   **MIP** $334

❏ **Case Excavator, Drott 50**, 1:35-scale, Conrad, white and yellow, 1970s
EX $157   **NM** $268   **MIP** $293

❏ **Case Roller, 1102**, 1:35-scale, Conrad, tan and brown, 1980s
EX $19   **NM** $29   **MIP** $36

❏ **Case Roller, 1601**, 1:35-scale, Conrad, yellow and black, 1980s, No. 2703
EX $26   **NM** $47   **MIP** $54

❑ **Case Skid Loader, 1845**, 1:35-scale, NZG, yellow and black, 1970s
EX $19   **NM** $41   **MIP** $52

❑ **Case Skid Loader, 1845 B**, 1:35-scale, NZG, tan and brown, 1980s, No. 196
EX $17   **NM** $28   **MIP** $39

❑ **Case Trencher, 760**, 1:35-scale, Conrad, tan and brown, 1980s
EX $18   **NM** $34   **MIP** $46

❑ **Case Trencher, DH4 B**, 1:35-scale, Conrad, tan and brown, 1980s
EX $19   **NM** $38   **MIP** $48

❑ **Case Wheel Loader, 740**, 1:35-scale, Zaragoza, yellow and black, 1970s
EX $289   **NM** $416   **MIP** $482

❑ **Case Wheel Loader, 740**, 1:35-scale, Zaragoza, yellow and black, 1970s
EX $289   **NM** $416   **MIP** $482

❑ **Case Wheel Loader, 740**, 1:35-scale, Zaragoza, yellow and black, 1970s
EX $289   **NM** $416   **MIP** $482

❑ **Case Wheel Loader, W20 B**, 1:35-scale, NZG, yellow and black, 1980s
EX $27   **NM** $44   **MIP** $57

❑ **Case Wheel Loader, W20 C**, 1:35-scale, NZG, yellow and black, 1980s, No. 214
EX $26   **NM** $42   **MIP** $54

❑ **Case Wheel Loader, W20 C**, 1:35-scale, NZG, tan and brown, 1980s
EX $24   **NM** $46   **MIP** $53

❑ **Vibromax Roller, 1601**, 1:35-scale, Conrad, yellow and black, 1970s
EX $24   **NM** $38   **MIP** $57

❑ **Vibromax Roller, 1601**, 1:35-scale, Conrad, tan and brown, 1980s
EX $24   **NM** $38   **MIP** $57

❏ **Vibromax Roller, 854**, 1:35-scale, Conrad, tan and brown, 1980s
EX $22　　**NM** $36　　**MIP** $46

CONSTRUCTION EQUIPMENT 1:40-SCALE

❏ **Case Wheel Loader, 621**, 1:40-scale, Ertl, tan and brown, 2001, No. 14233
EX $9　　**NM** $17　　**MIP** $28

CONSTRUCTION EQUIPMENT 1:43-SCALE

❏ **Case Backhoe/Loader, 580 K**, 1:43-scale, SpecCast, 1990s, No. ZJD18
EX $6　　**NM** $8　　**MIP** $12

❏ **Case Crawler w/blade**, 1:43-scale, SpecCast, gold-plated, 1980s, No. ZJD5
EX $6　　**NM** $8　　**MIP** $12

❏ **Case Crawler w/blade**, 1:43-scale, SpecCast, 1980s
EX $6　　**NM** $8　　**MIP** $12

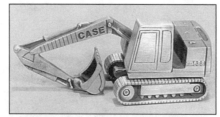

❏ **Case Excavator, 688**, 1:43-scale, SpecCast, 1990s, No. ZJD30
EX $6　　**NM** $8　　**MIP** $12

❏ **Case Wheel Loader, W30**, 1:43-scale, SpecCast, 1980s
EX $8　　**NM** $12　　**MIP** $18

CONSTRUCTION EQUIPMENT 1:50-SCALE

❏ **Case Backhoe 580 Super M**, 1:50-scale, Ertl, tan and brown, 2001, No. 14155
EX $8　　**NM** $12　　**MIP** $18

❏ **Case Backhoe and Excavator Set**, 1:50-scale, Ertl, No. 2360
(Photo by Ertl)
EX $8　　**NM** $12　　**MIP** $26

❏ **Case Backhoe, 580 E**, 1:50-scale, Artisans Guild, 1980s
EX $67　　**NM** $176　　**MIP** $214

❏ **Case Backhoe, 590**, 1:50-scale, Ertl, tan and brown, 1999, No. 14050
EX $8　　**NM** $12　　**MIP** $18

❏ **Case Crawler, w/blade 1850 K**, 1:50-scale, Ertl, tan and brown, 2003, No. 14306
EX $8　　**NM** $12　　**MIP** $18

❏ **Case Crawler, w/blade 650 H**, 1:50-scale, Ertl, tan and brown, 2001, No. 14104
EX $8　　**NM** $12　　**MIP** $18

❏ **Case Crawler, w/blade 750 H**, 1:50-scale, Ertl, tan and brown, 2002, No. 14125
EX $8　　**NM** $12　　**MIP** $18

❏ **Case Dump Truck, 330**, 1:50-scale, Ertl, orange, 2003, No. 14302
EX $8　　**NM** $12　　**MIP** $18

❏ **Case Excavator, 9030B**, 1:50-scale, Ertl, tan and brown, 2000, No. 4546
EX $8　　**NM** $12　　**MIP** $18

❏ **Case Excavator, CX-130**, 1:50-scale, Conrad, tan and brown, 2002, No. 2848
EX $28　　**NM** $42　　**MIP** $68

❏ **Case Excavator, CX-210**, 1:50-scale, Ertl, tan and brown, 2001, No. 14112
EX $8　　**NM** $12　　**MIP** $18

❏ **Case Skid Loader, 1845 C**, 1:50-scale, Ertl, tan and brown, No. 455
EX $4　　**NM** $6　　**MIP** $8

❑ **Case Skid Loader, 1845 C**, 1:50-scale, Ertl, tan and brown, 1980s
EX $4 **NM** $6 **MIP** $8

❑ **Case Wheel Loader, 621B**, 1:50-scale, Ertl, tan and brown, 1996, No. 4547
EX $8 **NM** $12 **MIP** $18

❑ **Case Wheel Loader, 621C**, 1:50-scale, Ertl, tan and brown, 1999, No. 14049
EX $8 **NM** $12 **MIP** $18

❑ **Case Wheel Loader, 621D**, 1:50-scale, Ertl, tan and brown, 2003, No. 14319
EX $8 **NM** $12 **MIP** $18

CONSTRUCTION EQUIPMENT 1:64-SCALE

❑ **Case Backhoe, 580 E**, 1:64-scale, Ertl, brown and tan, No. 202
EX $6 **NM** $12 **MIP** $16

CONSTRUCTION EQUIPMENT 1:82-SCALE

❑ **Case Crawler w/blade**, 1:82-scale, Matchbox, yellow and red, 1960s
EX $24 **NM** $38 **MIP** $48

❑ **Case Crawler w/blade**, 1:82-scale, Matchbox, red and yellow, 1960s
EX $19 **NM** $24 **MIP** $32

❑ **Case Crawler w/blade**, 1:82-scale, Matchbox, salmon and yellow, 1970s
EX $23 **NM** $37 **MIP** $46

CONSTRUCTION EQUIPMENT

❑ **Vibromax Rammer**, silver and black, 1960s
EX $29 **NM** $34 **MIP** $42

❑ **Vibromax Roller**, yellow and red, 1960s
EX $39 **NM** $47 **MIP** $53

❑ **Vibromax Walk Behind Roller**, yellow and red, 1960s
EX $39 **NM** $47 **MIP** $53

❑ **Vibromax Walk Behind Roller**, orange and black, 1970s
EX $29 **NM** $34 **MIP** $42

IMPLEMENTS 1:16-SCALE

❑ **Case Combine**, 1:16-scale, orange, did not come in box, 1980s
EX $79 **NM** $238 **MIP** n/a

❑ **Case Combine**, 1:16-scale, Vindex, silver w/red trim, early 1930s
EX $2238 **NM** $4859 **MIP** n/a

❏ **Case Disc**, 1:16-scale, Ertl,
orange, 1970s
EX $18   **NM** $42   **MIP** $79

❏ **Case Disc**, 1:16-scale, Ertl, red,
black discs, 1990s
EX $8   **NM** $16   **MIP** $24

❏ **Case Hammer Mill**, 1:16-scale,
Old Time Collectables (Custom),
orange, 1980s
EX $27   **NM** $59   **MIP** n/a

❏ **Case Hay Loader**, 1:16-scale,
Vindex, red w/pale green or yellow
wheels, early 1930s
EX $2296   **NM** $4633   **MIP** n/a

❏ **Case Minimum Tillage Plow**,
1:16-scale, Ertl, orange, 1980s,
No. 226
EX $32   **NM** $48   **MIP** $78

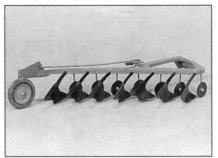

❏ **Case Plow**, 1:16-scale, Ertl,
orange, 7-bottom, 1970s
EX $12   **NM** $37   **MIP** $48

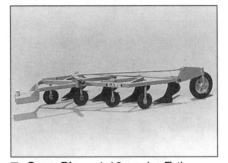

❏ **Case Plow**, 1:16-scale, Ertl,
orange, 4-bottom, 1970s
EX $9   **NM** $26   **MIP** $43

❏ **Case Plow**, 1:16-scale, Eska,
orange, 1950s
EX $79   **NM** $146   **MIP** $263

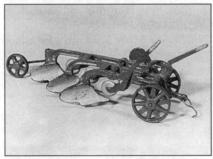

❏ **Case Plow**, 1:16-scale, Vindex,
red, 1930s
EX $612   **NM** $1193   **MIP** npf

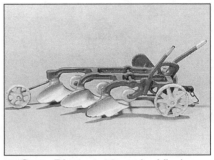

❏ **Case Plow**, 1:16-scale, Vindex,
red w/pale green or yellow wheels,
early 1930s
EX $612   **NM** $1193   **MIP** npf

❏ **Case Spreader**, 1:16-scale,
Monarch, orange, 1950s
EX $74   **NM** $182   **MIP** $362

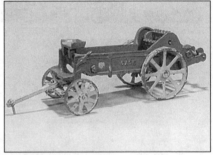

❏ **Case Spreader**, 1:16-scale,
Vindex, red, 1930s
EX $1398   **NM** $2318   **MIP** npf

❏ **Case Spreader**, 1:16-scale,
Vindex, red w/pale green or yellow
wheels, early 1930s
EX $1398   **NM** $2318   **MIP** npf

❑ **Case Wagon**, 1:16-scale, Eska, orange, tin rims, 1950s
EX $33   **NM** $77   **MIP** $192

❑ **Case Wagon, Barge**, 1:16-scale, Ertl, orange, die-cast rims, 1960s
EX $33   **NM** $74   **MIP** $148

❑ **Case Wagon, Barge**, 1:16-scale, Ertl, orange, plastic rims, 1970s
EX $23   **NM** $36   **MIP** $78

❑ **Case Wagon, Flare Box**, 1:16-scale, Ertl, orange, rubber wheels, 1970s
EX $31   **NM** $74   **MIP** $189

❑ **Case Wagon, Gravity**, 1:16-scale, Ertl, orange, 1980s, No. 350
EX $14   **NM** $22   **MIP** $36

IMPLEMENTS 1:25-SCALE

❑ **Case Thresher**, 1:25-scale, Irvin, silver, 1960s
EX $39   **NM** $57   **MIP** $73

❑ **Case Water Wagon**, 1:25-scale, Irvin, black, 1960s
EX $26   **NM** $49   **MIP** $59

IMPLEMENTS 1:32-SCALE

❑ **Case Disc**, 1:32-scale, Ertl, orange, 1980s
EX $4   **NM** $8   **MIP** $17

❑ **Case Minimum Till Plow**, 1:32-scale, Ertl, orange, 1980s
EX $13   **NM** $17   **MIP** $23

❑ **Case Plow**, 1:32-scale, Ertl, orange, 1980s
EX $4   **NM** $8   **MIP** $14

❑ **Case Wagon**, 1:32-scale, Ertl, orange, 1980s
EX $2   **NM** $4   **MIP** $9

IMPLEMENTS 1:43-SCALE

❑ **Case Combine**, 1:43-scale, Ertl, silver, 1990s, No. 2622
EX $7   **NM** $12   **MIP** $18

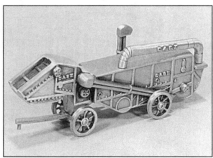

❏ **Case Threshing Machine**, 1:43-scale, SpecCast, 1990s, No. ZJD23
EX $8   **NM** $12   **MIP** $19

IMPLEMENTS 1:64-SCALE

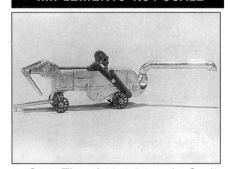

❏ **Case Thresher**, 1:64-scale, Scale Models, silver and red
EX $6   **NM** $8   **MIP** $12

MISCELLANEOUS

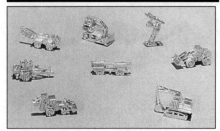

❏ **Case Charms for Charm Bracelet**, chrome plated, 1/2" long, 1980s
EX $14   **NM** $21   **MIP** $26

PEDAL TRACTORS

❏ **Case 30 Pleasure King**, Ertl, beige and orange, tractor in original condition
EX $489   **NM** $789   **MIP** n/a

❏ **Case 400**, Eska, beige and orange, tractor in original condition
EX $1289   **NM** $1979   **MIP** n/a

❏ **Case 580**, Scale Models, 2002, No. ZSM984
EX $93   **NM** $129   **MIP** $152

❏ **Case 580**, Scale Models, Collector Edition, 2002, No. ZSM972
EX $98   **NM** $132   **MIP** $159

❏ **Case 800 Case-O-Matic**, Eska, beige and orange, tractor in original condition
EX $789   **NM** $1292   **MIP** n/a

❏ **Case 90 Series**, Ertl, white and orange, tractor in original condition
EX $269   **NM** $352   **MIP** $469

❏ **Case 94 Series**, Ertl, white and black, tractor in original condition

EX $262   **NM** $349   **MIP** $459

❏ **Case Agri King 1070**, Ertl, desert tan and orange, tractor in original condition
EX $289   **NM** $517   **MIP** $778

❏ **Case Agri King 70 Series**, Ertl, white and orange, tractor in original condition
EX $269   **NM** $422   **MIP** $579

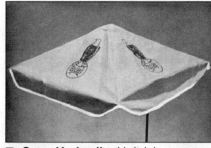

❏ **Case Umbrella**, Heltrick, orange, in original condition
EX $68   **NM** $159   **MIP** $273

❏ **Case VAC**, Eska, orange, tractor in original condition
EX $869   **NM** $1492   **MIP** n/a

TRACTORS 1:08-SCALE

❏ **Case 730**, 1:08-scale, Scale Models, beige and orange, NF, Comfort King, 2002, No. ZSM949
EX $82   **NM** $112   **MIP** $163

TRACTORS 1:12-SCALE

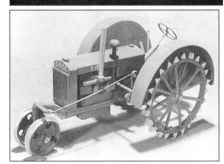

❏ **Case CC**, 1:12-scale, Kruse (Custom), gray, did not come in box, 1970s
EX $37   **NM** $56   **MIP** n/a

❏ **Case L**, 1:12-scale, Kruse (Custom), gray, did not come in box, 1970s
EX $37   **NM** $56   **MIP** n/a

❏ **Case SC**, 1:12-scale, Franklin Mint, 2001
EX $53   **NM** $78   **MIP** $133

TRACTORS 1:16-SCALE

❏ **Case 1030**, 1:16-scale, Ertl, #15 in Precision Series, wheatland, 2001, No. 14130
EX $56   **NM** $77   **MIP** $112

❏ **Case 1030**, 1:16-scale, Ertl, beige and orange, round fenders, late 1960s, No. 204
EX $132   **NM** $312   **MIP** $786

❏ **Case 1030**, 1:16-scale, Ertl, beige and orange, flat fenders, late 1960s, No. 204
EX $118   **NM** $186   **MIP** $472

❏ **Case 1070**, 1:16-scale, Ertl, 451 Cubes, beige and orange, no cab, small tires, early 1970s, No. 210
EX $123   **NM** $218   **MIP** $592

❏ **Case 1070**, 1:16-scale, Ertl, tan, no cab, early 1970s, No. 4556

(Photo by Ertl)
EX $18   **NM** $22   **MIP** $38

❏ **Case 1070**, 1:16-scale, Ertl, 451 Cubes, beige and orange, w/cab, singles, early 1970s
EX $122   **NM** $217   **MIP** $586

❏ **Case 1070**, 1:16-scale, Ertl, Agri King, beige and orange, w/cab, duals, small tires, early 1970s, No. 210
EX $138   **NM** $244   **MIP** $692

❏ **Case 1070**, 1:16-scale, Ertl, beige and orange, no cab, early 1970s
EX $123   **NM** $218   **MIP** $592

❏ **Case 1070**, 1:16-scale, Ertl, 451 Cubes, beige and orange, w/cab, duals, small tires, early 1970s, No. 210
EX $139   **NM** $246   **MIP** $693

❏ **Case 1070**, 1:16-scale, Ertl, 451 Cubes, beige and orange, no cab, small tires, early 1970s, No. 210
EX $123   **NM** $218   **MIP** $592

❑ **Case 1070 Demonstrator Black Knight**, 1:16-scale, Ertl, 451 Cubes, black and orange, 1970s, No. 210
EX $138   **NM** $389   **MIP** $868

❑ **Case 1070 Gold Demonstrator**, 1:16-scale, Ertl, black, beige, and orange, early 1970s, No. 210
EX $173   **NM** $698   **MIP** $1688

❑ **Case 1170**, 1:16-scale, Ertl, gold demostrator, '96 National Farm Toy Show, 1996, No. 475PA
EX $36   **NM** $42   **MIP** $68

❑ **Case 1170**, 1:16-scale, Ertl, Lowell Davis Series "Last Cowboy", 1997, No. 4301
EX $18   **NM** $27   **MIP** $48

❑ **Case 1170**, 1:16-scale, Ertl, Black Knight Collector Edition, 1997, No. 4255CA
EX $29   **NM** $42   **MIP** $68

❑ **Case 1170**, 1:16-scale, Ertl, w/cab, 2001, No. 14125
EX $17   **NM** $26   **MIP** $42

❑ **Case 1175**, 1:16-scale, Ertl, w/cab, '97 Toy Tractor Times Anniversary, #12; 2,500 produced, 1997, No. 3038TA
EX $36   **NM** $41   **MIP** $67

❑ **Case 1200**, 1:16-scale, Precision Engineering, on plaque, beige and orange, 1990s
EX $174   **NM** $212   **MIP** $267

❑ **Case 1200**, 1:16-scale, Precision Engineering, Black Knight, black and orange, 1990s
EX $174   **NM** $212   **MIP** $267

❑ **Case 1200**, 1:16-scale, Precision Engineering, beige and orange, 1990s
EX $173   **NM** $211   **MIP** $266

❑ **Case 12-20**, 1:16-scale, Conklin (Custom), gray, did not come in box, cross-mounted engine, 1980s
EX $177   **NM** $346   **MIP** n/a

❑ **Case 12-25**, 1:16-scale, Scale Models, green, 1980s, No. ZSM715
(Photo by Bossen Implement)
EX $43   **NM** $67   **MIP** $82

❑ **Case 1270**, 1:16-scale, Ertl, orange and yellow, w/cab, 1970s
EX $102   **NM** $227   **MIP** $579

❑ **Case 1270**, 1:16-scale, Ertl, 2006, No. 14460
EX $15   **NM** $24   **MIP** $35

❑ **Case 1270**, 1:16-scale, Ertl, 451 Turbo, beige and orange, large 1270 numbers, no cab, small tires, early 1970s
EX $104   **NM** $192   **MIP** $438

❑ **Case 1270**, 1:16-scale, Ertl, 451 Turbo, beige and orange, small 1270 numbers, no cab, small tires, early 1970s
EX $104   **NM** $192   **MIP** $438

❑ **Case 1370**, 1:16-scale, Ertl, Collector Edition, duals, 2007, No. 14458A
EX $18   **NM** $28   **MIP** $38

❑ **Case 1370**, 1:16-scale, Ertl, 504 Turbo, beige and orange, w/cab, large tires, early 1970s, No. 216
EX $108   **NM** $227   **MIP** $593

❑ **Case 1470**, 1:16-scale, Precision Engineering, beige and orange, with and without cab, 1998
(Photo by Bossen Implement)
EX $173   **NM** $212   **MIP** $267

❑ **Case 1470**, 1:16-scale, Precision Engineering, Black Knight, black and orange, 1998 *(Photo by Bossen Implement)*
EX $173 **NM** $212 **MIP** $267

❑ **Case 1470**, 1:16-scale, Precision Engineering, beige and orange on plaque, 1998 *(Photo by Bossen Implement)*
EX $173 **NM** $212 **MIP** $267

❑ **Case 15-27**, 1:16-scale, Pioneer Collectibles (Custom), gray, "1986 Waukee, IA Show," Cross-Mount, 1986
EX $69 **NM** $82 **MIP** $118

❑ **Case 15-27**, 1:16-scale, Scale Models, gray, cross mounted engine, 1980s, No. ZSM713
EX $69 **NM** $82 **MIP** $118

❑ **Case 1570**, 1:16-scale, Ertl, '05 Toy Tractor Times Annversary, #20; 5,500 produced, 2005, No. 16141A
EX $25 **NM** $55 **MIP** $85

❑ **Case 1570**, 1:16-scale, Ertl, Dealer Edition, 2007, No. 14461
EX $20 **NM** $40 **MIP** $60

❑ **Case 200**, 1:16-scale, SpecCast, beige and orange, w/eagle hitch, 2002, No. ZJD-146
EX $19 **NM** $28 **MIP** $42

❑ **Case 20-40**, 1:16-scale, Scale Models, green, 1980s, No. ZSM703
EX $53 **NM** $76 **MIP** $102

❑ **Case 2390**, 1:16-scale, Ertl, white and orange, black muffler, late 1970s, No. 268
EX $38 **NM** $67 **MIP** $86

❑ **Case 2390**, 1:16-scale, Ertl, white and orange, Collectors Edition, limited to 1,500 units, late 1970s, No. 268
EX $64 **NM** $104 **MIP** $142

❑ **Case 2390**, 1:16-scale, Ertl, white and orange, gray muffler, late 1970s, No. 268
EX $38 **NM** $67 **MIP** $86

❑ **Case 2390 variation photo**, 1:16-scale, Ertl, White and orange, notice difference in rear cab decal and frame, late 1970s

❑ **Case 2590**, 1:16-scale, Ertl, 1981 NFTS Tractor, 11-14-81, Toy Farmer Decal, engravings, 1,000 units, 1981, No. A104
EX $243 **NM** $369 **MIP** $547

❑ **Case 2590**, 1:16-scale, Ertl, new casting, 2002, No. 14237
EX $19 **NM** $28 **MIP** $42

❑ **Case 2590**, 1:16-scale, Ertl, gold plated, early 1980s, No. 269
EX $263 **NM** $423 **MIP** $982

❑ **Case 2590**, 1:16-scale, Ertl, white and orange, gray muffler, late 1970s, No. 269
EX $39 **NM** $68 **MIP** $86

❏ **Case 2590**, 1:16-scale, Ertl, white and orange, black muffler, late 1970s, No. 269
EX $39 **NM** $68 **MIP** $86

❏ **Case 2590**, 1:16-scale, Ertl, white and orange, Collectors Edition, limited to 1,500 units, late 1970s, No. 269
EX $66 **NM** $104 **MIP** $142

❏ **Case 2594**, 1:16-scale, Ertl, white and black, Collectors Edition, limited to forty-eight units per dealer, mid 1980s, No. 267TA
EX $28 **NM** $43 **MIP** $68

❏ **Case 2594**, 1:16-scale, Ertl, white and black, mid 1980s, No. 267
EX $23 **NM** $38 **MIP** $48

❏ **Case 300**, 1:16-scale, Siegel (Custom), orange and beige, narrow front, did not come in box, 1980s
EX $43 **NM** $98 **MIP** n/a

❏ **Case 300**, 1:16-scale, Siegel (Custom), orange and beige, wide front, 1980s
EX $43 **NM** $98 **MIP** n/a

❏ **Case 300**, 1:16-scale, Siegel (Custom), tan and orange, did not come in box, 1980s
EX $47 **NM** $98 **MIP** n/a

❏ **Case 300**, 1:16-scale, SpecCast, beige and orange, '98 Nashville Edition, 1998, No. ZJD-755

(Photo by SpecCast)
EX $26 **NM** $32 **MIP** $46

❏ **Case 300**, 1:16-scale, SpecCast, beige and orange, 1999, No. ZJD-782
EX $22 **NM** $28 **MIP** $42

❏ **Case 3294**, 1:16-scale, Ertl, white and black, mid 1980s, No. 266
EX $24 **NM** $38 **MIP** $48

❏ **Case 3294**, 1:16-scale, Ertl, white and black, Collectors Edition, limited to forty-eight units per dealer, mid 1980s, No. 266TA
EX $28 **NM** $43 **MIP** $68

❏ **Case 350**, 1:16-scale, Pioneer Implement, beige and orange, WMSTR, 150 yrs of Case, 1992
EX $22 **NM** $42 **MIP** $73

❏ **Case 400**, 1:16-scale, Parker (Custom), orange and beige, did not come in box, 1980s
EX $126 **NM** $173 **MIP** n/a

❑ **Case 400**, 1:16-scale, Yoder (Custom), Diesel, orange and beige, 1986 Lafayette Show Tractor, 1980s
EX $47   **NM** $64   **MIP** $88

❑ **Case 400**, 1:16-scale, Yoder (Custom), Super Diesel, orange and beige, 1980s
EX $46   **NM** $57   **MIP** $79

❑ **Case 400**, 1:16-scale, Yoder (Custom), black and orange, limited to 225 units, 1990s
EX $88   **NM** $112   **MIP** $148

❑ **Case 400**, 1:16-scale, Yoder (Custom), Diesel, orange, 1990s
EX $74   **NM** $106   **MIP** $138

❑ **Case 400 B**, 1:16-scale, SpecCast, beige and orange, NF, 1998, No. ZJD-764
EX $19   **NM** $28   **MIP** $52

❑ **Case 400 B**, 1:16-scale, SpecCast, beige and orange, WF, w/duals, 1999, No. ZJD-771
EX $23   **NM** $32   **MIP** $58

❑ **Case 500**, 1:16-scale, Ertl, orange, National Farm Toy Show Tractor 1985, 1985, No. 270PA
EX $33   **NM** $47   **MIP** $72

❑ **Case 530**, 1:16-scale, Siegel (Custom), tan and orange, did not come in box, 1980s
EX $62   **NM** $116   **MIP** n/a

❑ **Case 600**, 1:16-scale, Ertl, orange and beige, 1980s, No. 289
EX $21   **NM** $28   **MIP** $37

❑ **Case 600**, 1:16-scale, Ertl, orange and beige, Collectors Edition, 1980s, No. 289DA
EX $21   **NM** $32   **MIP** $38

❑ **Case 600**, 1:16-scale, Ertl, orange and tan, Tractors of the Past Set 1/16 & 1/43, 1980s, No. 213
EX $19   **NM** $24   **MIP** $43

❑ **Case 700**, 1:16-scale, Yoder (Custom), orange and beige, Beaver Falls Toys Show Tractor, 1980s
EX $46   **NM** $63   **MIP** $87

❑ **Case 700**, 1:16-scale, Yoder (Custom), Diesel, orange and tan, 1980s
EX $46   **NM** $57   **MIP** $79

❑ **Case 700**, 1:16-scale, Yoder (Custom), Diesel, black and orange, limited to 225 units, 1990s
EX $105   **NM** $144   **MIP** $178

❏ **Case 800**, 1:16-scale, Dingman (Custom), tan and orange, w/wide front end, did not come in box, 1990s
EX $279   **NM** $321   **MIP** n/a

❏ **Case 800**, 1:16-scale, Johan, orange and beige, w/model numbers, 1960s
EX $122   **NM** $289   **MIP** $547

❏ **Case 830**, 1:16-scale, Dingman (Custom), tan and orange, did not come in box, LP, 1990s
EX $283   **NM** $334   **MIP** n/a

❏ **Case 800**, 1:16-scale, Ertl, tan and orange, 1990s, No. 693
EX $18   **NM** $28   **MIP** $34

❏ **Case 800**, 1:16-scale, Warner (Custom), orange and beige, did not come in box, 1980s
EX $128   **NM** $238   **MIP** n/a

❏ **Case 9-18**, 1:16-scale, Scale Models, green, 1980s, No. ZSM710
(Photo by Bossen Implement)
EX $45   **NM** $63   **MIP** $82

❏ **Case 930**, 1:16-scale, Ertl, #12 in Precision Series, 1998, No. 4284
EX $67   **NM** $82   **MIP** $122

❏ **Case 800**, 1:16-scale, Ertl, tan and orange, "1990 National Farm Toy Show", 1990s, No. 693PA
EX $27   **NM** $38   **MIP** $47

❏ **Case 800**, 1:16-scale, Yoder (Custom), orange and tan, 1980s
EX $46   **NM** $62   **MIP** $86

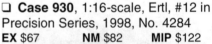
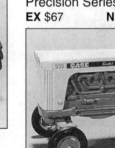

❏ **Case 930**, 1:16-scale, Ertl, beige and orange, all die-cast rims, mid 1960s, No. 204
EX $117   **NM** $234   **MIP** $796

❏ **Case 800**, 1:16-scale, Johan, orange and beige, w/o model numbers, 1960s
EX $117   **NM** $251   **MIP** $452

❏ **Case 800**, 1:16-scale, Yoder (Custom), orange and beige, 1980s
EX $46   **NM** $62   **MIP** $86

❏ **Case 930**, 1:16-scale, Ertl, beige and orange, plastic front rims w/die-cast rear rims, mid 1960s, No. 204
EX $102   **NM** $227   **MIP** $787

Photos by Jon Jacobson unless otherwise noted.

❏ **Case 970**, 1:16-scale, Ertl, beige and orange, 1998, No. 4279 *(Photo by Ertl)*
EX $17   **NM** $23   **MIP** $38

❏ **Case 970**, 1:16-scale, Ertl, gold demostrator, Collector Edition, 2002, No. 14193A
EX $29   **NM** $38   **MIP** $52

❏ **Case 970**, 1:16-scale, Ertl, beige w/one dual and w/4 bottom mounted plow, 2002, No. 14197
EX $27   **NM** $34   **MIP** $48

❏ **Case Agri King**, 1:16-scale, Ertl, Spirit of '76, white and orange w/red, white and dark blue decals, mid 1970s, No. 262
EX $103   **NM** $166   **MIP** $249

❏ **Case Agri King**, 1:16-scale, Ertl, white and orange, no cab, small tires, mid 1970s, No. 261
EX $57   **NM** $93   **MIP** $132

❏ **Case Agri King**, 1:16-scale, Ertl, white and orange, w/cab, decal variation, mid 1970s, No. 262
EX $59   **NM** $96   **MIP** $149

❏ **Case Agri King**, 1:16-scale, Ertl, white and orange, decal variation, mid 1970s, No. 261
EX $57   **NM** $93   **MIP** $132

❏ **Case Agri King**, 1:16-scale, Ertl, white and orange, w/cab, large tires, mid 1970s
EX $59   **NM** $96   **MIP** $149

❏ **Case Agri King**, 1:16-scale, Ertl, Spirit of '76, white and orange w/red, white and light blue decals, mid 1970s, No. 262
EX $103   **NM** $166   **MIP** $249

❏ **Case CC**, 1:16-scale, light gray, did not come in box, 1980s
EX $18   **NM** $32   **MIP** n/a

❏ **Case CC**, 1:16-scale, Jergensen (Custom), gray, did not come in box, 1980s
EX $48   **NM** $68   **MIP** n/a

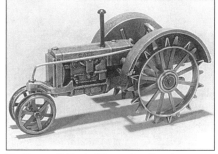

❏ **Case CC**, 1:16-scale, Scale Models, antique brass, 1980s
EX $53   **NM** $96   **MIP** $144

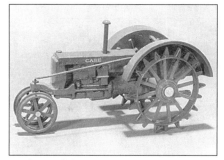

❏ **Case CC**, 1:16-scale, Scale Models, gray, No. 8 in Collector Series I, 1980s
EX $47   **NM** $59   **MIP** $78

❏ **Case CC**, 1:16-scale, Scale Models, gray, "1990 Beckman High School Fund", 1990s
EX $32   **NM** $48   **MIP** $63

❑ **Case D**, 1:16-scale, Dingman (Custom), orange, did not come in box, 1980s
EX $272   **NM** $409   **MIP** n/a

❑ **Case D**, 1:16-scale, Dingman (Custom), orange, did not come in box, 1980s
EX $276   **NM** $412   **MIP** n/a

❑ **Case D**, 1:16-scale, Dingman (Custom), orange, did not come in box, standard on steel, 1980s
EX $227   **NM** $398   **MIP** n/a

❑ **Case D**, 1:16-scale, SpecCast, gas, WF, 2007, No. 1546

(Photo by SpecCast)
EX $15   **NM** $30   **MIP** $45

❑ **Case DC**, 1:16-scale, Dingman (Custom), orange, did not come in box, LP, standard, 1980s
EX $286   **NM** $417   **MIP** n/a

❑ **Case DC**, 1:16-scale, Dingman (Custom), orange, did not come in box, NF, 1980s
EX $237   **NM** $384   **MIP** n/a

❑ **Case DC**, 1:16-scale, Dingman (Custom), orange, did not come in box, LP, row crop, 1980s
EX $242   **NM** $396   **MIP** n/a

❑ **Case DC**, 1:16-scale, Dingman (Custom), orange, did not come in box, standard on rubber, 1980s
EX $243   **NM** $411   **MIP** n/a

❑ **Case DC**, 1:16-scale, SpecCast, single front, Gateway Show Edition, 1990s, No. ZJD379
EX $22   **NM** $28   **MIP** $38

❑ **Case DC**, 1:16-scale, SpecCast, orange, WF on rubber, 1990s, No. ZJD736 *(Photo by Kate Bossen)*
EX $18   **NM** $26   **MIP** $38

❑ **Case DC**, 1:16-scale, SpecCast, orange, NF on rubber, 1990s, No. ZJD719 *(Photo by SpecCast)*
EX $16   **NM** $27   **MIP** $42

❑ **Case DC**, 1:16-scale, SpecCast, w/adjustable front axle, 1990s, No. ZJD150
EX $22   **NM** $28   **MIP** $38

❑ **Case DC**, 1:16-scale, SpecCast, puller, 1997, No. ZJD754

(Photo by Bossen Implement)
EX $23   **NM** $28   **MIP** $38

❑ **Case DC**, 1:16-scale, SpecCast, single front, on steel, case expo, 1997, No. ZJD746
EX $22   **NM** $28   **MIP** $38

❑ **Case DC**, 1:16-scale, SpecCast, w/eagle hitch, 2000, No. ZJD123
EX $22   **NM** $28   **MIP** $38

❏ **Case DC**, 1:16-scale, SpecCast, w/eagle hitch, 2001, No. ZJD144
EX $22   **NM** $28   **MIP** $38

❏ **Case DC-3**, 1:16-scale, SpecCast, WF, gas, eagle hitch, 2007, No. 1517 *(Photo by SpecCast)*
EX $15   **NM** $30   **MIP** $45

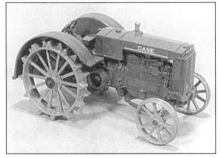

❏ **Case L**, 1:16-scale, Ertl, gray, "C.I.F.E.S. 1988 Special Edition" Canadian Show tractor, 3000 made, 1980s, No. 450TA
EX $16   **NM** $29   **MIP** $44

❏ **Case L**, 1:16-scale, Ertl, gray, Collectors Edition, 1980s, No. 450DA
EX $16   **NM** $27   **MIP** $43

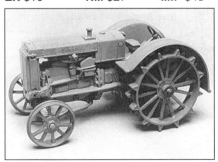

❏ **Case L**, 1:16-scale, Ertl, gray, 1980s, No. 450
EX $16   **NM** $26   **MIP** $36

❏ **Case L**, 1:16-scale, Ertl, 150th Anniversary of J.I. Case Corp., 1992, No. 252DA
EX $23   **NM** $33   **MIP** $43

❏ **Case L**, 1:16-scale, Old Time Collectables (Custom), gray, did not come in box, 1980s
EX $17   **NM** $34   **MIP** npf

❏ **Case L**, 1:16-scale, Vindex, gray w/red rims, nickel-plated driver, early 1930s
EX $346   **NM** $1047   **MIP** npf

❏ **Case LA**, 1:16-scale, orange, did not come in box, 1980s
EX $28   **NM** $57   **MIP** n/a

❏ **Case LA**, 1:16-scale, Dingman (Custom), orange, did not come in box, LP, 1980s
EX $236   **NM** $318   **MIP** n/a

❏ **Case LA**, 1:16-scale, Dingman (Custom), orange, did not come in box, 1980s
EX $227   **NM** $314   **MIP** n/a

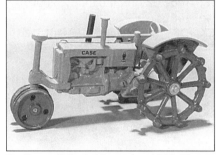

❏ **Case RC**, 1:16-scale, AT & T (custom), gray, did not come in box, 1980s
EX $19   **NM** $48   **MIP** n/a

❏ **Case SC**, 1:16-scale, Burkholder (Custom), orange, did not come in box, 1970s
EX $87   **NM** $153   **MIP** n/a

❏ **Case SC**, 1:16-scale, Monarch, orange, w/fenders, 1950s
EX $114   **NM** $263   **MIP** $388

❏ **Case SC**, 1:16-scale, Monarch, orange, w/o fenders, 1950s
EX $114   **NM** $273   **MIP** $388

❏ **Case Steam Engine**, 1:16-scale, Ertl, 6 HP, Millennium Edition, came with red, '02 green canopy, 2000, No. 14024
EX $70   **NM** $87   **MIP** $128

❏ **Case Steam Engine**, 1:16-scale, Scale Models, black, no canopy, No. ZSM701
EX $68   **NM** $94   **MIP** $128

❏ **Case Steam Engine**, 1:16-scale, Scale Models, #1, Case 150th Anniversary, 1990s, No. ZSM775
(Photo by Scale Models)
EX $32   **NM** $53   **MIP** $73

❏ **Case Steam Engine**, 1:16-scale, Scale Models, black, w/canopy, 1990s, No. ZSM712
EX $73   **NM** $116   **MIP** $168

❏ **Case VA**, 1:16-scale, Ertl, '92 Toy Tractor Times Anniversary, #7; 2,500 produced, 1992, No. 234TA
EX $25   **NM** $50   **MIP** $75

❏ **Case VAC**, 1:16-scale, Ertl, orange, 1980s, No. 632
EX $27   **NM** $46   **MIP** $64

❏ **Case VAC**, 1:16-scale, Ertl, orange, Collectors Edition, 1980s, No. 632DA
EX $28   **NM** $38   **MIP** $44

❏ **Case VAC**, 1:16-scale, Freiheit (Custom), orange, did not come in box, 1980s
EX $129   **NM** $183   **MIP** n/a

❏ **Case VAC**, 1:16-scale, Scale Models, orange, "JLE" stands for Joseph L. Ertl, 1986 Summer Show, 1986
EX $29   **NM** $37   **MIP** $59

❏ **Case 1412**, 1:25-scale, NZG, w/model numbers & ROPS, 1980s, No. 159
EX $16   **NM** $32   **MIP** $48

❏ **Case 1412**, 1:25-scale, NZG, white and orange, no model #'s, no ROPS, mid 1970s, No. 159
EX $16   **NM** $32   **MIP** $48

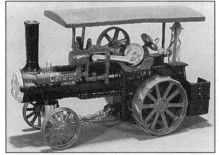

❏ **Case Steam Engine**, 1:25-scale, Irvin, black, 1970s
EX $29   **NM** $56   **MIP** $63

❏ **Case 1200**, 1:32-scale, Porasik (Custom), white and orange, duals, 1980s
EX $34   **NM** $63   **MIP** $88

❏ **Case 1200**, 1:32-scale, Porasik (Custom), white and orange, 1980s
EX $31   NM $59   MIP $82

❏ **Case 1690**, 1:32-scale, Ertl, white and orange, Collectors Edition, 1980s, No. 1787EA
EX $12   NM $22   MIP $37

❏ **Case 1690**, 1:32-scale, Ertl, white and orange, 1980s, No. 1787
EX $12   NM $19   MIP $33

❏ **Case 1690**, 1:32-scale, Ertl, white and orange, w/cab, 1980s, No. 1717
EX $12   NM $22   MIP $37

❏ **Case 1694**, 1:32-scale, Lone Star, white and black, 1980s
EX $8   NM $14   MIP $27

❏ **Case 1694**, 1:32-scale, Lone Star, white and black, 1980s
EX $8   NM $14   MIP $27

❏ **Case 2290**, 1:32-scale, Ertl, white and orange, 1980s, No. 1692
EX $12   NM $14   MIP $29

❏ **Case 2290**, 1:32-scale, Ertl, white and orange, Collectors Edition, 1980s, No. 1692EA
EX $12   NM $16   MIP $33

❏ **Case 2294**, 1:32-scale, Ertl, white and black, on plaque, Collectors Edition, 1980s, No. 261EA
EX $24   NM $48   MIP $64

❏ **Case 2294**, 1:32-scale, Ertl, white and black, Collectors Edition, 1980s, No. 1692TA
EX $16   NM $24   MIP $43

❏ **Case 2294**, 1:32-scale, Ertl, white and black, cab color reversed, 1980s, No. 261
EX $12   NM $14   MIP $34

❏ **Case 2294**, 1:32-scale, Ertl, beige and black, 1980s, No. 261
EX $1   NM $14   MIP $27

❏ **Case 4890**, 1:32-scale, Ertl, white and orange, Collectors Edition, 1980s, No. 1637EA
EX $38   **NM** $52   **MIP** $73

❏ **Case 4890**, 1:32-scale, Ertl, white and orange, 1980s, No. 1637
EX $32   **NM** $47   **MIP** $56

❏ **Case 4894**, 1:32-scale, Ertl, whtie and black, Collectors Edition, 1980s, No. 262EA
EX $24   **NM** $37   **MIP** $44

❏ **Case 4894**, 1:32-scale, Ertl, whtie and black, 1980s, No. 262
EX $21   **NM** $27   **MIP** $34

❏ **Case Pace Setter**, 1:32-scale, Pace Setter, orange and white, liquor bottle, 1980s
EX $23   **NM** $38   **MIP** $48

❏ **Cast Steam Engine**, 1:32-scale, Scale Models, No. ZSM724
EX $14   **NM** $23   **MIP** $37

TRACTORS 1:35-SCALE

❏ **Case 4890**, 1:35-scale, Conrad, white and orange, plastic cab lights, 1980s, No. 5010
EX $28   **NM** $52   **MIP** $77

❏ **Case 4890**, 1:35-scale, Conrad, white and orange, cast-in cab lights, 1980s, No. 5010
EX $27   **NM** $51   **MIP** $76

TRACTORS 1:40-SCALE

❏ **Case 2670**, 1:40-scale, NZG, white and orange, Traction King, 1970s, No. 154
EX $38   **NM** $62   **MIP** $88

TRACTORS 1:43-SCALE

❏ **Case 1170**, 1:43-scale, Ertl, gold demostrator, '96 National Farm Toy Show, 1996
EX $11   **NM** $16   **MIP** $23

❏ **Case 1170**, 1:43-scale, Ertl, Black Knight, '96 LCN European Edition, 1996
EX $18   **NM** $29   **MIP** $42

❏ **Case 1170**, 1:43-scale, Ertl, Black Knight Collector Edition, 1997, No. 4183EA
EX $18   **NM** $29   **MIP** $38

❏ **Case 500**, 1:43-scale, Ertl, orange, 1980s, No. 2510
EX $6   **NM** $8   **MIP** $13

❏ **Case 500**, 1:43-scale, Ertl, orange, National Farm Toy Show Tractor, part of three piece set, Collectors Edition, 1980s
EX $12   **NM** $16   **MIP** $43

❑ **Case 600**, 1:43-scale, Ertl, orange and tan, Tractors of the Past Set, 1980s
EX $4   **NM** $8   **MIP** n/a

❑ **Case 800**, 1:43-scale, Ertl, tan and orange, 1990 National Farm Toy Show, 1990, No. 2616MA
EX $8   **NM** $14   **MIP** $22

❑ **Case 800**, 1:43-scale, Ertl, tan and orange, 1990s, No. 2616
EX $4   **NM** $8   **MIP** $11

❑ **Case 830**, 1:43-scale, SpecCast, 1980s, No. ZJD2
EX $6   **NM** $8   **MIP** $12

❑ **Case 830**, 1:43-scale, SpecCast, 1980s, No. ZJD2
EX $6   **NM** $8   **MIP** $12

❑ **Case CC**, 1:43-scale, SpecCast, 1990s, No. ZJD35
EX $6   **NM** $8   **MIP** $12

❑ **Case Cross Mount**, 1:43-scale, SpecCast, 1980s, No. ZJD11
EX $6   **NM** $8   **MIP** $12

❑ **Case Cross Mount**, 1:43-scale, SpecCast, 1990s, No. ZJD11
EX $6   **NM** $8   **MIP** $12

❑ **Case DC**, 1:43-scale, SpecCast, 1980s, No. ZJD8
EX $6   **NM** $8   **MIP** $12

❑ **Case DC**, 1:43-scale, SpecCast, 1990s, No. ZJD8
EX $6   **NM** $8   **MIP** $12

❑ **Case L**, 1:43-scale, Ertl, gray, 1980s, No. 2554
EX $6   **NM** $8   **MIP** $13

❑ **Case L**, 1:43-scale, SpecCast, 1980s, No. ZJD4
EX $6   **NM** $8   **MIP** $12

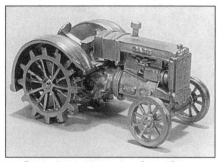

❏ **Case L**, 1:43-scale, SpecCast, 1990s, No. ZJD4
EX $6 **NM** $8 **MIP** $12

❏ **Case LA**, 1:43-scale, SpecCast, 1980s, No. ZJD26
EX $6 **NM** $8 **MIP** $12

❏ **Case RC**, 1:43-scale, SpecCast, 1990s, No. ZJD22
EX $6 **NM** $8 **MIP** $12

❏ **Case Steam Engine**, 1:43-scale, SpecCast, gold plated, 1980s
EX $18 **NM** $34 **MIP** $48

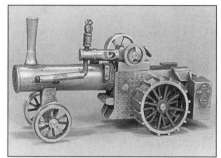

❏ **Case Steam Engine**, 1:43-scale, SpecCast, 1980s, No. ZJD6
EX $8 **NM** $11 **MIP** $13

❏ **Case Steam Engine**, 1:43-scale, SpecCast, 1990s, No. ZJ014
EX $8 **NM** $12 **MIP** $19

❏ **Case VAC**, 1:43-scale, SpecCast, 1990s, No. ZJD16
EX $6 **NM** $8 **MIP** $12

TRACTORS 1:64-SCALE

❏ **Case 1030**, 1:64-scale, Walters (Custom), orange and tan, 1980s
EX $6 **NM** $14 **MIP** $23

❏ **Case 1270 w/Disc Set**, 1:64-scale, Ertl, tractor and disc, 2007, No. 14480
EX $3 **NM** $6 **MIP** $9

❏ **Case 1470**, 1:64-scale, Ertl, Black Knight, 1997, No. 4368EA
EX $9 **NM** $18 **MIP** $27

❏ **Case 1470**, 1:64-scale, Ertl, later graphics, 2000, No. 4332 *(Photo by Ertl)*
EX $4 **NM** $6 **MIP** $8

❏ **Case 1470**, 1:64-scale, Ertl, early graphics, 2002, No. 14212
EX $4 **NM** $6 **MIP** $8

❏ **Case 2294**, 1:64-scale, Ertl, black and "pure" white, 1980s, No. 224
EX $11 **NM** $14 **MIP** $19

❏ **Case 2294**, 1:64-scale, Ertl, black and white, 1980s, No. 224
EX $6 **NM** $10 **MIP** $14

❏ **Case 2470**, 1:64-scale, Gunning (Custom), tan and orange, did not come in box, 1980s
EX $19 **NM** $24 **MIP** n/a

Photos by Jon Jacobson unless otherwise noted.

❑ **Case 2590**, 1:64-scale, Ertl, orange and white, rear axle is a rivet, 1970s, No. 1694
EX $9   **NM** $12   **MIP** $18

❑ **Case 2590**, 1:64-scale, Ertl, orange and white, rear axle is a steel-pin, 1970s, No. 1694
EX $9   **NM** $12   **MIP** $18

❑ **Case 2594**, 1:64-scale, Ertl, black and white, 1984s, No. 224
EX $4   **NM** $6   **MIP** $8

❑ **Case 2670**, 1:64-scale, Gunning (Custom), orange and white, did not come in box, 1980s
EX $19   **NM** $28   **MIP** n/a

❑ **Case 2870**, 1:64-scale, Gunning (Custom), orange and white, did not come in box, 1980s
EX $19   **NM** $28   **MIP** n/a

❑ **Case 4690**, 1:64-scale, Gunning (Custom), black and white, did not come in box, 1980s
EX $19   **NM** $28   **MIP** n/a

❑ **Case 4890**, 1:64-scale, Gunning (Custom), black and white, did not come in box, 1980s
EX $19   **NM** $28   **MIP** n/a

❑ **Case 500**, 1:64-scale, Ertl, 1999, No. 14096
EX $3   **NM** $4   **MIP** $6

❑ **Case 930**, 1:64-scale, Carlson (Custom), orange and tan, did not come in box
EX $6   **NM** $14   **MIP** n/a

❑ **Case 930**, 1:64-scale, Walters (Custom), orange and tan, 1980s
EX $6   **NM** $14   **MIP** $23

❑ **Case Agri King**, 1:64-scale, Ertl, orange and white, I-beam decal, 1970s, No. 1624
EX $26   **NM** $54   **MIP** $98

❑ **Case Agri King**, 1:64-scale, Ertl, orange and white, front rims are spun-on, 1970s, No. 1624
EX $11   **NM** $18   **MIP** $23

❑ **Case Agri King**, 1:64-scale, Ertl, orange and white, front rims are pushed-on, 1970s, No. 1624
EX $11   **NM** $18   **MIP** $23

❑ **Case CC**, 1:64-scale, Scale Models, gray, 1980s
EX $2   **NM** $3   **MIP** $4

❑ **Case CC**, 1:64-scale, Scale Models, gray, 1980s
EX $2   **NM** $3   **MIP** $4

❑ **Case CC**, 1:64-scale, Scale Models, orange, 1980s
EX $2   **NM** $3   **MIP** $6

❑ **Case CC**, 1:64-scale, Scale Models, five different chrome colors, 1980s
EX $2   **NM** $3   **MIP** $4

❑ **Case CC**, 1:64-scale, Scale Models, 1980s, No. ZSM846
(Photo by Scale Models)
EX $3   **NM** $4   **MIP** $6

❑ **Case DC-3**, 1:64-scale, SpecCast, NF, 2007, No. 1536 *(Photo by SpecCast)*
EX $7   **NM** $14   **MIP** $19

❑ **Case DC-3**, 1:64-scale, SpecCast, WF, high crop, 2007, No. 1537
(Photo by SpecCast)
EX $8   **NM** $14   **MIP** $19

❑ **Case L**, 1:64-scale, Ertl, 1999, No. 14095
EX $3   **NM** $4   **MIP** $6

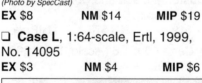

❑ **Case Steam Engine**, 1:64-scale, Scale Models, black and red, Trade Fair Houston 1987, w/Eagle on the front
EX $6   **NM** $11   **MIP** $17

❑ **Case Steam Engine**, 1:64-scale, Scale Models, black and red
EX $6   **NM** $11   **MIP** $17

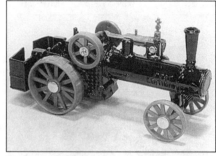

❑ **Case Steam Engine**, 1:64-scale, Scale Models, black and red, 1st Edition
EX $6   **NM** $11   **MIP** $17

❑ **Case Steam Engine**, 1:64-scale, Scale Models, black and red, 1st Edition/Eagle on the front
EX $6   **NM** $11   **MIP** $17

❑ **Case Steam Engine**, 1:64-scale, Scale Models, gold
EX $8   **NM** $22   **MIP** $33

❑ **Case Steam Engine**, 1:64-scale, Scale Models, black and red, Eagle on the front
EX $6   **NM** $11   **MIP** $17

❑ **Case Steam Engine**, 1:64-scale, Scale Models, black and red, 1st Edition, w/eagle on the front
EX $6   **NM** $11   **MIP** $17

❑ **Case Steam Engine**, 1:64-scale, Scale Models, black and red, 1986 St. Louis, Mo. Show Tractor, 1st. Edition, w/eagle on the front
EX $6   **NM** $11   **MIP** $17

❑ **Case Steam Engine**, 1:64-scale, Scale Models, black and red, 1st. Case Expo 1987, eagle on the front
EX $6   **NM** $11   **MIP** $17

TRACTORS 1:76-SCALE

❑ **Case Cross Mount**, 1:76-scale, VM Miniatures (Custom), gray, did not come in box, 1980s
EX $16   **NM** $32   **MIP** n/a

TRACTORS MICRO

❑ **Case 316**, Micro, Micro Machines, white, 1990s
EX $3   **NM** $6   **MIP** $8

TRUCKS 1:16-SCALE

❑ **Case Pickup**, 1:16-scale, Ertl, white, 1980s, No. 217
EX $9   **NM** $17   **MIP** $26

❑ **Case Semi**, 1:16-scale, Nylint, white, 1980s, No. 911
EX $27   **NM** $47   **MIP** $76

TRACTORS 1:16-SCALE

❑ **Case '57 Stake Truck**, 1:25-scale, Ertl, Prestige Series, No. 426
(Photo by Ertl)
EX $8   **NM** $16   **MIP** $32

❑ **Case Pickup**, 1:25-scale, Ertl, white, Hurricane, 1970s
EX $16   **NM** $28   **MIP** $74

❑ **Case Pickup**, 1:25-scale, Ertl, white, 1980s, No. 3830
EX $8   **NM** $16   **MIP** $23

❑ **Case Semi**, 1:25-scale, Ertl, white, Hurricane, 1970s
EX $49   **NM** $73   **MIP** $163

❏ **Case Semi**, 1:25-scale, Ertl, white, 1980s, No. 3117
EX $23   **NM** $42   **MIP** $63

TRUCKS 1:64-SCALE

❏ **Semi w/Case International Van Box**, 1:64-scale, Ertl, No. 425
(Photo by Ertl)
EX $6   **NM** $9   **MIP** $18

TRUCKS 1:87-SCALE

❏ **Semi w/Case Logo on Van Box '48 Peterbilt**, 1:87-scale, Ertl, 1990s, No. 4266 *(Photo by Kate Bossen)*
EX $3   **NM** $6   **MIP** $9

CASE-IH

BANKS

❏ **Case-IH Mailbox Bank**, Ertl, red, 1990s, No. 273
EX $9   **NM** $4   **MIP** $23

IMPLEMENTS 1:16-SCALE

❏ **Case-IH Baler**, 1:16-scale, Ertl, red and black, square, 1980s, No. 454
EX $13   **NM** $21   **MIP** $29

❏ **Case-IH Baler**, 1:16-scale, Ertl, w/4 plastic square bales, 1986, No. 454
EX $13   **NM** $21   **MIP** $28

❏ **Case-IH Baler, 8465 Round**, 1:16-scale, Ertl, w/plastic big round bale, 1995, No. 2811 *(Photo by Ertl)*
EX $14   **NM** $22   **MIP** $32

❏ **Case-IH Baler, 8575 Big Square**, 1:16-scale, Ertl, w/plastic big square bale, 1996, No. 4763 *(Photo by Ertl)*
EX $13   **NM** $26   **MIP** $34

❏ **Case-IH Combine, 2388**, 1:16-scale, Scale Models, Signature Series, 1998, No. ZSM910
EX $123   **NM** $162   **MIP** $228

❏ **Case-IH Combine, 2388**, 1:16-scale, Scale Models, corn head only, 1999, No. ZSM914
EX $123   **NM** $162   **MIP** $228

❏ **Case-IH Combine, 2388**, 1:16-scale, Scale Models, Silver Anniversary Edition, 2002, No. ZSM966
EX $138   **NM** $177   **MIP** $248

❏ **Case-IH Cotton Picker, 2555**, 1:16-scale, Scale Models, '97 Dealer Meeting, 1997, No. ZSM868
EX $123   **NM** $162   **MIP** $228

❏ **Case-IH Cotton Picker, 2555**, 1:16-scale, Scale Models, 1998, No. ZSM893
EX $123   **NM** $162   **MIP** $228

❏ **Case-IH Cotton Picker, 2555**, 1:16-scale, Scale Models, '98 Cotton Conference, 1998, No. ZSM892
EX $123   **NM** $162   **MIP** $228

❏ **Case-IH Cultivator, 1840**, 1:16-scale, Ertl, tool bar, 1998, No. 4292
EX $8   **NM** $13   **MIP** $23

❏ **Case-IH Disc**, 1:16-scale, Ertl, red, 2002, No. 14009
EX $8   **NM** $13   **MIP** $23

❏ **Case-IH Forage Harvestor**, 1:16-scale, Ertl, red, 1980s, No. 209
EX $13   **NM** $18   **MIP** $22

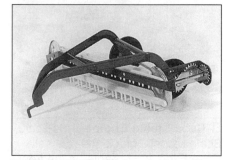

❏ **Case-IH Grain Drill, 5100**, 1:16-scale, Ertl, red, 1980s, No. 269
EX $11   **NM** $26   **MIP** $34

❏ **Case-IH Hay Rake**, 1:16-scale, Ertl, 1980s, No. 446 *(Photo by Ertl)*
EX $8   **NM** $12   **MIP** $21

❑ **Case-IH Hay Rake**, 1:16-scale, Ertl, 1994, No. 446 *(Photo by Bossen Implement)*
EX $8   **NM** $13   **MIP** $22

❑ **Case-IH Manure Spreader**, 1:16-scale, Ertl, No. 4207 *(Photo by Ertl)*
EX $8   **NM** $11   **MIP** $16

❑ **Case-IH Manure Spreader**, 1:16-scale, Ertl, dual axle, 1990s, No. 14305
EX $12   **NM** $16   **MIP** $22

❑ **Case-IH Mixer Mill**, 1:16-scale, Ertl, red and black, 1980s, No. 453
EX $12   **NM** $22   **MIP** $43

❑ **Case-IH Mixer Mill**, 1:16-scale, Ertl, no windows, 1999, No. 4356
EX $9   **NM** $18   **MIP** $27

❑ **Case-IH Mower, Rotary**, 1:16-scale, SpecCast, No. ZJD709

(Photo by SpecCast)
EX $9   **NM** $16   **MIP** $22

❑ **Case-IH Mower-Rotary**, 1:16-scale, Ertl, 2000, No. 14064
EX $8   **NM** $11   **MIP** $16

❑ **Case-IH Planter**, 1:16-scale, Ertl, no model #, likely a 900 or 955, 2006, No. 14490
EX $18   **NM** $27   **MIP** $34

❑ **Case-IH Planter, 900**, 1:16-scale, Ertl, 4-row, No. 609 *(Photo by Ertl)*
EX $18   **NM** $27   **MIP** $44

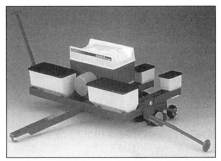

❑ **Case-IH Planter, 955**, 1:16-scale, Ertl, 4-row, 1997, No. 4416 *(Photo by Ertl)*
EX $18   **NM** $28   **MIP** $39

❑ **Case-IH Rotary Hoe**, 1:16-scale, Ertl, tool bar, 1998, No. 4434
EX $8   **NM** $13   **MIP** $23

❑ **Case-IH Tillage Tool, 5308**, 1:16-scale, Ertl, Ecolo-Tiger, 2002, No. 14118
EX $17   **NM** $28   **MIP** $43

❑ **Case-IH Wagon, Bale Throw**, 1:16-scale, Ertl, 1984, No. 439
EX $8   **NM** $16   **MIP** $22

❑ **Case-IH Wagon, Barge**, 1:12-scale, Ertl, No. 479 *(Photo by Ertl)*
EX $6   **NM** $9   **MIP** $14

❑ **Case-IH Wagon, Barge**, 1:12-scale, Ertl, red, large, 1980s, No. 636
EX $17   **NM** $29   **MIP** $42

❑ **Case-IH Wagon, Flare Box**, 1:16-scale, Ertl, red, 1980s, No. 635
EX $6   **NM** $9   **MIP** $14

❑ **Case-IH Wagon, Forage**, 1:16-scale, Ertl, 1984, No. 442

(Photo by Bossen Implement)
EX $8   **NM** $16   **MIP** $22

IMPLEMENTS 1:32-SCALE

❑ **Case-IH Big Baler**, 1:32-scale, Ertl, w/3 large bales, 2006, No. 14314
EX $8   **NM** $14   **MIP** $18

❑ **Case-IH Combine 8010AFX**, 1:32-scale, Ertl, European version w/grain tank covers, 2004, No. 40972
EX $22   **NM** $32   **MIP** $42

❑ **Case-IH Combine, 1680**, 1:32-scale, Ertl, red, two heads, 1980s, No. 443
EX $27   **NM** $68   **MIP** $93

❏ **Case-IH Combine, 2166**, 1:32-scale, Ertl, w/two heads, 1995, No. 291 *(Photo by Ertl)*
EX $22   **NM** $37   **MIP** $44

❏ **Case-IH Combine, 2188**, 1:32-scale, Ertl, St. Louis "1st Edition Introduction", 1995, No. 291PA

(Photo by Bossen Implement)
EX $73   **NM** $96   **MIP** $223

❏ **Case-IH Combine, 2188**, 1:32-scale, Ertl, Collectors Edition, 1995, No. 291DA *(Photo by Ertl)*
EX $22   **NM** $34   **MIP** $53

❏ **Case-IH Combine, 2188**, 1:32-scale, Ertl, AFS Edition, 1997, No. 4793DA
EX $24   **NM** $33   **MIP** $52

❏ **Case-IH Combine, 2366**, 1:32-scale, Ertl, red, 1998, No. 4613
EX $16   **NM** $28   **MIP** $42

❏ **Case-IH Combine, 2388**, 1:32-scale, Ertl, red, 1999, No. 14088
EX $14   **NM** $28   **MIP** $42

❏ **Case-IH Combine, 7010 Axial Flow**, 1:32-scale, Ertl, 2 heads, 2007, No. 14563A
EX $8   **NM** $16   **MIP** $24

❏ **Case-IH Combine, 8010**, 1:32-scale, Ertl, 2 heads, 2007, No. 14586
EX $8   **NM** $16   **MIP** $24

❏ **Case-IH Combine, AFX-8010**, 1:32-scale, Ertl, railings and window glass, Collector Edition, 2003, No. 14291A
EX $24   **NM** $33   **MIP** $52

❏ **Case-IH Combine, AFX-8010**, 1:32-scale, Ertl, red, 2003, No. 14290
EX $16   **NM** $28   **MIP** $42

IMPLEMENTS 1:64-SCALE

❏ **Case-IH Air Drill**, 1:64-scale, Ertl, revised graphics, 2002, No. 14210
EX $9   **NM** $16   **MIP** $28

❏ **Case-IH Air Drill, 8500**, 1:64-scale, Ertl, red and black, No. 444
EX $16   **NM** $33   **MIP** $63

❏ **Case-IH Baler**, 1:64-scale, Ertl, red, No. 482
EX $3   **NM** $4   **MIP** $6

❏ **Case-IH Baler**, 1:64-scale, Ertl, red, No. 482
EX $3   **NM** $4   **MIP** $6

❏ **Case-IH Baler**, 1:64-scale, Ertl, w/6 round bales, 2001, No. 14173
EX $3   **NM** $4   **MIP** $6

❏ **Case-IH Combine, 1660**, 1:64-scale, Ertl, red and black, No. 655
EX $8   **NM** $12   **MIP** $27

❏ **Case-IH Combine, 1660**, 1:64-scale, Ertl, red and black, 1988 Husker Harvest Days, 1988, No. 655EA
EX $12   **NM** $23   **MIP** $38

❏ **Case-IH Combine, 1666**, 1:64-scale, Ertl, No. 655EU
EX $12   **NM** $22   **MIP** $37

❏ **Case-IH Combine, 2166**, 1:64-scale, Ertl, red, 8 row corn head, Axial Flow, No. 4667 *(Photo by Ertl)*
EX $9   **NM** $12   **MIP** $22

❏ **Case-IH Combine, 2166**, 1:64-scale, Ertl, Ohio Science Review, No. 4262UA
EX $12   **NM** $22   **MIP** $37

❏ **Case-IH Combine, 2188**, 1:64-scale, Ertl, '95 Farm Show Edition, 1995, No. 4607MA
EX $16   **NM** $28   **MIP** $47

Photos by Jon Jacobson unless otherwise noted.

❑ **Case-IH Combine, 2366**, 1:64-scale, Ertl, 1998, No. 4614
EX $8   **NM** $12   **MIP** $19

❑ **Case-IH Combine, 2366**, 1:64-scale, Ertl, 100,000th Edition, 2000, No. 14089A
EX $8   **NM** $12   **MIP** $19

❑ **Case-IH Combine, 2388**, 1:64-scale, Ertl, 25th Anniversary of Axial Flow, chrome, No. 14190A
EX $8   **NM** $12   **MIP** $19

❑ **Case-IH Combine, 2388**, 1:64-scale, Ertl, w/12 row corn head and 30' grain platform, 2001, No. 14176
EX $8   **NM** $12   **MIP** $18

❑ **Case-IH Combine, 2388**, 1:64-scale, Ertl, model kit, 2001, No. 14164
EX $6   **NM** $9   **MIP** $12

❑ **Case-IH Combine, 7010**, 1:64-scale, Ertl, 2 heads, 2006, No. 14556
EX $8   **NM** $15   **MIP** $21

❑ **Case-IH Combine, AFX-8010**, 1:64-scale, Ertl, Collector Edition, 2003, No. 14289A
EX $9   **NM** $12   **MIP** $22

❑ **Case-IH Combine, AFX-8010**, 1:64-scale, Ertl, 2003, No. 14279
EX $8   **NM** $12   **MIP** $17

❑ **Case-IH Combine, AFX-8010**, 1:64-scale, Ertl, dealer ed, serial numbered 1300 units, 2003, No. 14266N
EX $112   **NM** $142   **MIP** $232

❑ **Case-IH Combine, AFX-8010**, 1:64-scale, Ertl, '03 Farm Show Edition, 2003, No. 14370X
EX $12   **NM** $17   **MIP** $27

❑ **Case-IH Cotton Picker, 1844**, 1:64-scale, Ertl, red and black, No. 211
EX $6   **NM** $8   **MIP** $16

❑ **Case-IH Cotton Picker, 2155**, 1:64-scale, Ertl, No. 4558 *(Photo by Ertl)*
EX $4   **NM** $8   **MIP** $12

❑ **Case-IH Cotton Picker, 2555**, 1:64-scale, Ertl, 1997, No. 4300
EX $4   **NM** $8   **MIP** $12

❑ **Case-IH Disc**, 1:64-scale, Ertl, 2007, No. 14587
EX $3   **NM** $4   **MIP** $6

❑ **Case-IH Forage Harvestor**, 1:64-scale, Ertl, red, No. 201
EX $3   **NM** $4   **MIP** $6

❑ **Case-IH Mixer Mill**, 1:64-scale, Ertl, red, No. 480
EX $3   **NM** $4   **MIP** $6

❑ **Case-IH Mower Conditioner**, 1:64-scale, Ertl, 1998, No. 4362
EX $3   **NM** $4   **MIP** $6

❑ **Case-IH Planter, 800**, 1:64-scale, Ertl, red and cream, No. 478
EX $3   **NM** $4   **MIP** $5

❑ **Case-IH Wagon, Bale Throw**, 1:64-scale, Ertl, No. 4427 *(Photo by Ertl)*
EX $3   **NM** $4   **MIP** $6

❑ **Case-IH Wagon, Flare Box**, 1:64-scale, Ertl, No. 465 *(Photo by Ertl)*
EX $3   **NM** $4   **MIP** $6

MISCELLANEOUS

❑ **Case-IH Farm Set**, Ertl, 1980s, No. 4410
EX $6   **NM** $8   **MIP** $19

❑ **Case-IH Service Center Set**, Ertl, 1980s, No. 4411
EX $6   **NM** $8   **MIP** $19

PEDAL TRACTORS

❑ **Case-IH**, Ertl, 2000, No. 14076
EX $78   **NM** $102   **MIP** $143

❑ **Case-IH 7130**, Ertl, 1991
EX $106   **NM** $156   **MIP** $211

❑ **Case-IH 7250**, Ertl, 1996, No. 671
(Photo by Ertl)
EX $98   **NM** $148   **MIP** $172

❑ **Case-IH 8950**, Ertl, red, 1997, No. 4560
EX $78   **NM** $102   **MIP** $157

❑ **Case-IH 94 Series**, Ertl, this Case tractor was painted red and black by the Ertl Company
EX $156   **NM** $189   **MIP** $298

❑ **Case-IH 94 Series**, Ertl, red and black, 1984, No. 612
EX $156   **NM** $189   **MIP** $298

❑ **Case-IH DX-33**, Scale Models, Collector Edition, 2001, No. ZSM941
EX $88   **NM** $112   **MIP** $163

❑ **Case-IH DX-33**, Scale Models, 2002, No. ZSM945
EX $78   **NM** $102   **MIP** $153

❑ **Case-IH MX-170**, Ertl, 2000, No. 14076
EX $76   **NM** $98   **MIP** $132

❑ **Case-IH MX-240**, Ertl, 2000, No. 14110
EX $78   **NM** $102   **MIP** $153

❑ **Case-IH MX-255**, Ertl, 100,000th Edition, 2003, No. 14287A
EX $124   **NM** $167   **MIP** $227

❑ **Case-IH MX-270**, Ertl, 1999, No. 4447
EX $78   **NM** $102   **MIP** $153

❑ **Case-IH MX-285**, Ertl, wide 2-3/4" tires, 2002, No. 14223
EX $78   **NM** $102   **MIP** $153

❑ **Case-IH MX-305**, Ertl, w/duals, Collector Edition, 2006, No. 14448
(Photo by Ertl)
EX $92   **NM** $126   **MIP** $198

❑ **Case-IH Puma 210**, Ertl, MFD, 2007, No. 14592
EX $100   **NM** $145   **MIP** $190

❑ **Case-IH STX-450**, Scale Models, w/duals, Collector Edition, 2002, No. ZSM965
EX $102   **NM** $138   **MIP** $248

❑ **Case-IH STX-450**, Scale Models, 2002, No. ZSM983
EX $78   **NM** $102   **MIP** $162

TRACTORS 1:128-SCALE

❑ **Case-IH Micro's**, 1:128-scale, Ertl, red and black, w/tractor, wagon and disk, 1990s, No. 461
EX $3   **NM** $6   **MIP** $9

TRACTORS 1:16-SCALE

❑ **Case-IH 2394**, 1:16-scale, Ertl, red and black, ground out, limited production, 1980s, No. 631
EX $19   **NM** $28   **MIP** $46

❑ **Case-IH 245**, 1:16-scale, Ertl, Dealer Edition, 2007, No. 14529
EX $20   **NM** $40   **MIP** $65

❑ **Case-IH 2594**, 1:16-scale, Ertl, red and black, 1980s, No. 600
EX $19   **NM** $26   **MIP** $36

❑ **Case-IH 2594**, 1:16-scale, Ertl, red and black, Collectors Edition, 1980s, No. 600TA
EX $19   **NM** $29   **MIP** $42

❑ **Case-IH 2594**, 1:16-scale, Ertl, red and black, Las Vegas February 22-28, Collectors Edition, 1980s
EX $42   **NM** $63   **MIP** $82

❑ **Case-IH 3294**, 1:16-scale, Ertl, red and black, Collectors Edition, 1980s, No. 601TA
EX $19   **NM** $29   **MIP** $42

❑ **Case-IH 3294**, 1:16-scale, Ertl, red and black, 1980s, No. 601
EX $19   **NM** $26   **MIP** $36

❑ **Case-IH 335 Magnum**, 1:16-scale, Ertl, Dealer Edition, 2007, No. 14576
EX $20   **NM** $40   **MIP** $60

❑ **Case-IH 4230**, 1:16-scale, Scale Models, w/ROPS MFD, No. ZSM828
(Photo by Kate Bossen)
EX $18   **NM** $22   **MIP** $36

❑ **Case-IH 4230**, 1:16-scale, Scale Models, gold plated, No. 1122

(Photo by Bossen Implement)

EX $82 **NM** $112 **MIP** $178

❑ **Case-IH 4230**, 1:16-scale, Scale Models, Same as FF-0221, w/ROPS 2WD, No. ZSM785 *(Photo by Scale Models)*

EX $14 **NM** $19 **MIP** $27

❑ **Case-IH 4230**, 1:16-scale, Scale Models, '95 Farm Progress Edition, 1995, No. FB-2360

EX $13 **NM** $18 **MIP** $27

❑ **Case-IH 480**, 1:16-scale, Ertl, Dealer Edition, front and rear duals, 2007, No. 14558

EX $20 **NM** $40 **MIP** $65

❑ **Case-IH 4994**, 1:16-scale, Ertl, red and black, Collectors Edition, 1980s, No. 206BA

EX $72 **NM** $93 **MIP** $127

❑ **Case-IH 4994**, 1:16-scale, Ertl, red and black, 1980s, No. 206

EX $46 **NM** $77 **MIP** $102

❑ **Case-IH 5120**, 1:16-scale, Ertl, red, 1990s, No. 634

EX $13 **NM** $21 **MIP** $28

❑ **Case-IH 5120**, 1:16-scale, Ertl, red and black, Collector Edition, 1990s, No. 634DA

EX $16 **NM** $23 **MIP** $34

❑ **Case-IH 5130**, 1:16-scale, Ertl, red and black, Kansas City edition, Collectors Edition, 1990s, No. 696NA

EX $22 **NM** $32 **MIP** $52

❑ **Case-IH 5130**, 1:16-scale, Ertl, red and black, 1990s, No. 696

EX $13 **NM** $21 **MIP** $28

❑ **Case-IH 5140**, 1:16-scale, Ertl, red and black, Collector Edition, 1990s, No. 696DA

EX $16 **NM** $23 **MIP** $32

❑ **Case-IH 5150**, 1:16-scale, Bruder, No. 8790

EX $8 **NM** $14 **MIP** $22

❑ **Case-IH 5150**, 1:16-scale, Bruder, black, 50,000th Edition, no box, new in plastic bag, 1998

(Photo by Bossen Implement)

EX $48 **NM** $72 **MIP** $92

❑ **Case-IH 5250**, 1:16-scale, Ertl, No. 676 *(Photo by Ertl)*

EX $16 **NM** $21 **MIP** $32

❑ **Case-IH 5250**, 1:16-scale, Ertl, Collector Edition, 1994, No. 676DA
EX $26 **NM** $37 **MIP** $57

❑ **Case-IH 5250**, 1:16-scale, Ertl, 50,000th Maxxum, 1996, No. 680TA
EX $24 **NM** $32 **MIP** $57

❑ **Case-IH 685**, 1:16-scale, Scale Models, '95 Ontario Show Edition, 1995, No. FB-2364
EX $48 **NM** $57 **MIP** $88

❑ **Case-IH 7120**, 1:16-scale, Ertl, red and black, 1980s, No. 620
EX $34 **NM** $53 **MIP** $54

❑ **Case-IH 7120**, 1:16-scale, Ertl, red and black, Collectors Edition, 1987, No. 620DA
EX $44 **NM** $53 **MIP** $72

❑ **Case-IH 7130**, 1:16-scale, Ertl, red and black, Denver Magnum, 1980s, No. 658TA
EX $68 **NM** $87 **MIP** $113

❑ **Case-IH 7130**, 1:16-scale, Ertl, red and black, "Strasbourg Magnum", 1980s, No. 619TA
EX $38 **NM** $48 **MIP** $72

❑ **Case-IH 7130**, 1:16-scale, Ertl, red and black, 1980s, No. 619
EX $34 **NM** $53 **MIP** $54

❑ **Case-IH 7140**, 1:16-scale, Ertl, red, Collectors Edition, 1980s, No. 619DA
EX $38 **NM** $58 **MIP** $74

❑ **Case-IH 7140**, 1:16-scale, Ertl, duals, 1992, No. 296
EX $32 **NM** $42 **MIP** $67

❑ **Case-IH 7150**, 1:16-scale, Ertl, 1992, No. 247
EX $24 **NM** $31 **MIP** $48

❑ **Case-IH 7150**, 1:16-scale, Ertl, Collector Edition, 1992, No. 247BA
EX $35 **NM** $46 **MIP** $73

❑ **Case-IH 7210**, 1:16-scale, Ertl, 1994, No. 4598 *(Photo by Ertl)*
EX $22 **NM** $34 **MIP** $46

❑ **Case-IH 7220**, 1:16-scale, Ertl, '96 Pennsylvania State Farm Show, 1 of 500, 1996, No. 4132TA
EX $92 **NM** $113 **MIP** $157

❑ **Case-IH 7240**, 1:16-scale, Ertl, Dealer Edition, w/duals, 1994, No. 4639TA
EX $56 **NM** $82 **MIP** $148

❑ **Case-IH 7240**, 1:16-scale, Ertl, '94 Farm Show Edition, 1994, No. 2258TA
EX $25 **NM** $37 **MIP** $53

❑ **Case-IH 7250**, 1:16-scale, Ertl, 50,000th Edition, Mark 50, 1994, No. 2258YA *(Photo by Ertl)*
EX $28 **NM** $53 **MIP** $78

❑ **Case-IH 7250**, 1:16-scale, Ertl, duals, 1994, No. 674 *(Photo by Ertl)*
EX $22 **NM** $38 **MIP** $53

❑ **Case-IH 8920**, 1:16-scale, Ertl, 1996, No. 4208
EX $23 **NM** $32 **MIP** $52

❑ **Case-IH 8940**, 1:16-scale, Ertl, red, 1997, No. 4374
EX $23 **NM** $32 **MIP** $52

❑ **Case-IH 8950**, 1:16-scale, Ertl, Collector Edition, 1997, No. 4792CA
EX $26 **NM** $42 **MIP** $67

❑ **Case-IH 9270**, 1:16-scale, Scale Models, duals, 1995, No. ZSM783

(Photo by Scale Models)

EX $64 **NM** $82 **MIP** $117

❑ **Case-IH 9280**, 1:16-scale, Scale Models, triples, Collector Edition, 1994, No. ZSM813

EX $138 **NM** $152 **MIP** $188

❑ **Case-IH 9370**, 1:16-scale, Scale Models, duals, '95 Farm Progress Show Edition, 1995, No. ZSM819

EX $83 **NM** $103 **MIP** $122

❑ **Case-IH 9370**, 1:16-scale, Scale Models, duals, 1996, No. ZSM816

(Photo by Scale Models)

EX $64 **NM** $82 **MIP** $117

❑ **Case-IH 9370**, 1:16-scale, Scale Models, duals, 40,000th Steiger, opening hood, 1998, No. ZSM890

EX $138 **NM** $152 **MIP** $188

❑ **Case-IH 9370**, 1:16-scale, Scale Models, Quad Track, Signature Series, 1998, No. ZSM905

EX $92 **NM** $113 **MIP** $162

❑ **Case-IH 9380**, 1:16-scale, Scale Models, triples, "A Powerfull Heritage, Fargo, ND 1995", 1995, No. ZSM817 *(Photo by Bossen Implement)*

EX $122 **NM** $142 **MIP** $173

❑ **Case-IH 9380**, 1:16-scale, Scale Models, quad track, 2000, No. ZSM931

EX $90 **NM** $102 **MIP** $143

❑ **Case-IH 9390**, 1:16-scale, Scale Models, wide duals, 1997, No. ZSM742

EX $90 **NM** $102 **MIP** $143

❑ **Case-IH 9390**, 1:16-scale, Scale Models, duals, 1998, No. ZSM885

(Photo by Kate Bossen)

EX $64 **NM** $82 **MIP** $127

❑ **Case-IH C-100**, 1:16-scale, Ertl, MFD, Collector Edition, 1998, No. 4906DA

EX $23 **NM** $38 **MIP** $58

❑ **Case-IH C-80**, 1:16-scale, Ertl, 2WD, w/ROPS, 1998, No. 4357

EX $18 **NM** $22 **MIP** $42

❑ **Case-IH C-90**, 1:16-scale, Ertl, MFD, ROPS, '98 Farm Show Edition, 1998, No. 4601TA

EX $38 **NM** $52 **MIP** $68

❑ **Case-IH C-90**, 1:16-scale, Ertl, w/loader, 1998, No. 4485

EX $22 **NM** $32 **MIP** $43

❑ **Case-IH C-90**, 1:16-scale, Ertl, w/loader, '00 California Show Edition, 2000, No. 4485

EX $77 **NM** $98 **MIP** $117

❑ **Case-IH CVT-170**, 1:16-scale, Bruder, MFD, removeable loader, 2001, No. 2092

EX $12 **NM** $18 **MIP** $28

❑ **Case-IH CVT-170**, 1:16-scale, Bruder, MFD, removeable duals and loader, 2001, No. 2093

EX $17 **NM** $22 **MIP** $34

❑ **Case-IH CVT-170**, 1:16-scale, Bruder, MFD, removeable duals, 2001, No. 2094

EX $12 **NM** $18 **MIP** $28

❑ **Case-IH CVT-170**, 1:16-scale, Bruder, MFD, 2001, No. 2090

EX $12 **NM** $16 **MIP** $24

❑ **Case-IH DX-33**, 1:16-scale, Scale Models, MFD, Collector Edition, 2001, No. ZSM938

EX $12 **NM** $22 **MIP** $29

❑ **Case-IH DX-33**, 1:16-scale, Scale Models, MFD, 2002, No. ZSM940

(Photo by Scale Models)

EX $11 **NM** $18 **MIP** $28

❑ **Case-IH DX-33**, 1:16-scale, Scale Models, "Farmall" on front of hood, 2004, No. ZSM1019

EX $12 **NM** $21 **MIP** $28

❑ **Case-IH Maxxum 140**, 1:16-scale, Ertl, Dealer Edition, 2007, No. 14585

EX $20 **NM** $40 **MIP** $60

❑ **Case-IH MX-110**, 1:16-scale, Ertl, 2WD, 1997, No. 4251 *(Photo by Ertl)*

EX $22 **NM** $33 **MIP** $46

❑ **Case-IH MX-110**, 1:16-scale, Ertl, 2WD, '98 "California Farm Equipment Show" 500 units made, 1998, No. 14023A

EX $38 **NM** $53 **MIP** $78

❑ **Case-IH MX-110**, 1:16-scale, Ertl, MFD, new graphics, 2000, No. 14107

EX $22 **NM** $33 **MIP** $46

❑ **Case-IH MX-120**, 1:16-scale, Ertl, '97 Farm Show Edition, 1997, No. 4487DA

EX $32 **NM** $42 **MIP** $67

❏ **Case-IH MX-125**, 1:16-scale, Ertl, '04 California Show Edition, 2004, No. 14268T
EX $62   **NM** $73   **MIP** $107

❏ **Case-IH MX-135**, 1:16-scale, Ertl, MFD, 1997, No. 4250
EX $19   **NM** $29   **MIP** $48

❏ **Case-IH MX-135**, 1:16-scale, Ertl, Phoenix Launch Dealer Edition, 1997, No. 4250PA
EX $48   **NM** $72   **MIP** $127

❏ **Case-IH MX-210**, 1:16-scale, Ertl, MFD, duals, '05 Farm Progress Edition, 2005, No. 14485A
EX $26   **NM** $37   **MIP** $68

❏ **Case-IH MX-220**, 1:16-scale, Ertl, MFD, duals, 1999, No. 4195
EX $23   **NM** $34   **MIP** $47

❏ **Case-IH MX-220**, 1:16-scale, Ertl, MFD, '99 Farm Show Edition, 1999, No. 4195CA
EX $47   **NM** $67   **MIP** $88

❏ **Case-IH MX-220**, 1:16-scale, Ertl, MFD, duals, '99 California Show Edition, 1999, No. 4195
EX $93   **NM** $102   **MIP** $138

❏ **Case-IH MX230**, 1:16-scale, Ertl, 2005, No. 14343
EX $15   **NM** $22   **MIP** $30

❏ **Case-IH MX-235**, 1:16-scale, Ertl, MFD, flotation tires, 2005, No. 14343
EX $26   **NM** $32   **MIP** $48

❏ **Case-IH MX-240**, 1:16-scale, Ertl, MFD, and rear duals, '99 California Show Edition, 1999, No. 4160
EX $62   **NM** $83   **MIP** $117

❏ **Case-IH MX-240**, 1:16-scale, Ertl, MFD, radio control, 1999, No. 14048
EX $18   **NM** $33   **MIP** $48

❏ **Case-IH MX-240**, 1:16-scale, Ertl, MFD, and rear duals, Collector Edition, 1999, No. 4160CA
EX $33   **NM** $46   **MIP** $98

❏ **Case-IH MX-240**, 1:16-scale, Ertl, front and rear duals, 2001, No. 14120
EX $28   **NM** $42   **MIP** $78

❏ **Case-IH MX-255**, 1:16-scale, Ertl, MFD, 2004, No. 14347
EX $18   **NM** $28   **MIP** $43

❏ **Case-IH MX-270**, 1:16-scale, Dicki, MFD, duals, radio control, 2000, No. 19716
EX $53   **NM** $88   **MIP** $223

❏ **Case-IH MX-270**, 1:16-scale, Dicki, MFD, singles, w/wagon, radio control, 2000, No. 19717
EX $53   **NM** $88   **MIP** $158

❏ **Case-IH MX-270**, 1:16-scale, Ertl, MFD, radio control, 1999, No. 14047
EX $18   **NM** $33   **MIP** $48

❏ **Case-IH MX-270**, 1:16-scale, Ertl, MFD, Dealer Edition, 1999, No. 14030A
EX $198   **NM** $257   **MIP** $333

❏ **Case-IH MX-270**, 1:16-scale, Ertl, MFD, front and rear duals, Collector's Edition, 2002, No. 14101A *(Photo by Bossen Implement)*
EX $53   **NM** $62   **MIP** $88

❏ **Case-IH MX-275**, 1:16-scale, Ertl, 2006, No. 14444
EX $27   **NM** $38   **MIP** $59

❏ **Case-IH MX-285**, 1:16-scale, Ertl, MFD, front and rear duals, 2002, No. 14262
EX $26   **NM** $37   **MIP** $58

❏ **Case-IH MX-285**, 1:16-scale, Ertl, MFD, duals, 2003 California Show Edition, 2003, No. 14262A
EX $73   **NM** $97   **MIP** $128

❏ **Case-IH MX-285**, 1:16-scale, Ertl, MFD, front and rear duals, 100,000th Magnum, 2003, No. 14267A
EX $42   **NM** $56   **MIP** $69

❏ **Case-IH MX-305**, 1:16-scale, Ertl, MFD, duals, Collector Edition, 2006, No. 14424A
EX $33   **NM** $57   **MIP** $83

❏ **Case-IH MXU-125**, 1:16-scale, Ertl, w/loader, MFD, 2003, No. 14259
EX $24   **NM** $32   **MIP** $44

❏ **Case-IH MXU-125**, 1:16-scale, Ertl, MFD, singles, Collector Edition, 2003, No. 14268A
EX $27   **NM** $38   **MIP** $53

❏ **Case-IH MXU-125**, 1:16-scale, Ertl, MFD, European wide tires, 2004, No. 14260
EX $23   **NM** $31   **MIP** $42

❏ **Case-IH MXU-125**, 1:16-scale, Ertl, w/loader, MFD, '04 World Park Expo Edition, 2004, No. 16125A
EX $28   **NM** $38   **MIP** $58

❏ **Case-IH Quadtrac**, 1:16-scale, Scale Models, Collector Edition, 1996, No. ZSM841
EX $88   **NM** $113   **MIP** $158

❏ **Case-IH Quadtrac**, 1:16-scale, Scale Models, '96 Farm Progress Edition, 1996, No. ZSM844
EX $88   **NM** $113   **MIP** $158

❏ **Case-IH Quadtrac**, 1:16-scale, Scale Models, 1997, No. ZSM861
(Photo by Scale Models)
EX $72   **NM** $93   **MIP** $148

❏ **Case-IH STX-375**, 1:16-scale, Ertl, w/duals, 2000, No. 14003 *(Photo by Ertl)*
EX $41   **NM** $53   **MIP** $78

❏ **Case-IH STX-375**, 1:16-scale, Ertl, Quad Trac, 2001, No. 14153
EX $38   **NM** $57   **MIP** $78

❏ **Case-IH STX-375**, 1:16-scale, Ertl, w/duals, '01 California Show Edition, 2001, No. 14003A
EX $67   **NM** $98   **MIP** $126

❏ **Case-IH STX-440**, 1:16-scale, Ertl, Quad Trac, Collector Edition, 2000, No. 14038A
EX $43   **NM** $57   **MIP** $88

❏ **Case-IH STX-440**, 1:16-scale, Ertl, w/triples, Collector Edition, 2001, No. 14002A
EX $52   **NM** $64   **MIP** $92

❏ **Case-IH STX-450**, 1:16-scale, Ertl, red, 2002, No. 14226
EX $41   **NM** $53   **MIP** $84

❏ **Case-IH STX-450**, 1:16-scale, Ertl, Quad Trac, "'02 World Ag Expo", 2002, No. 14225A
EX $83   **NM** $108   **MIP** $137

❏ **Case-IH STX-450**, 1:16-scale, Ertl, Quad Trac, 2002, No. 14225
EX $41   **NM** $53   **MIP** $78

❑ **Case-IH STX-480**, 1:16-scale, Ertl, 4WD, duals, 2006, No. 14422

(Photo by Bossen Implement)

EX $34   **NM** $58   **MIP** $93

❑ **Case-IH STX-480**, 1:16-scale, Ertl, Quad Trac, 2006, No. 14423

EX $33   **NM** $56   **MIP** $88

❑ **Case-IH STX-500**, 1:16-scale, Ertl, 4WD, duals, 2002, No. 14348

EX $33   **NM** $56   **MIP** $88

❑ **Case-IH STX-500**, 1:16-scale, Ertl, Quad Trac, 2004, No. 14288

EX $28   **NM** $48   **MIP** $78

❑ **Case-IH STX-500**, 1:16-scale, Ertl, w/1/64 chrome STX-500, Collector Edition, 2004, No. 14286A

EX $48   **NM** $64   **MIP** $93

❑ **Case-IH STX-500**, 1:16-scale, Ertl, Quad Trac, 50,000th Edition, Ertl 60th Anniversary, 2005, No. 14455

EX $33   **NM** $56   **MIP** $88

❑ **Case-IH STX-500**, 1:16-scale, Ertl, Quad Trac, World Ag Expo, 2005, No. 14288

EX $43   **NM** $66   **MIP** $116

❑ **Case-IH STX-530**, 1:16-scale, Ertl, 4WD, duals, Collector Edition, 2006, No. 14421A

EX $43   **NM** $66   **MIP** $98

❑ **Case-IH STX-530**, 1:16-scale, Ertl, Quad Trac, Farm Progress Edition, 2006, No. 14432A

(Photo by Bossen Implement)

EX $43   **NM** $66   **MIP** $98

TRACTORS 1:32-SCALE

❑ **Case-IH**, 1:32-scale, Lone Star, red, 1980s

EX $8   **NM** $14   **MIP** $22

❑ **Case-IH**, 1:32-scale, Lone Star, red, 1980s

EX $8   **NM** $14   **MIP** $22

❑ **Case-IH 2294**, 1:32-scale, Ertl, w/loader, No. 4608

EX $8   **NM** $14   **MIP** $22

❑ **Case-IH 2294**, 1:32-scale, Ertl, red and black, 1980s, No. 265

EX $6   **NM** $9   **MIP** $16

❑ **Case-IH 2294**, 1:32-scale, Ertl, red and black, w/lift hitch, 1980s, No. 257

EX $6   **NM** $9   **MIP** $16

❑ **Case-IH 2294**, 1:32-scale, Ertl, w/loader and loader attachments, 1991, No. 663

EX $9   **NM** $16   **MIP** $26

❑ **Case-IH 245**, 1:32-scale, Ertl, 2007, No. 14532

EX $7   **NM** $14   **MIP** $20

❑ **Case-IH 2594**, 1:32-scale, Ertl, red and black, motorized, 1980s, No. 4096

EX $6   **NM** $9   **MIP** $16

❑ **Case-IH 305**, 1:32-scale, Ertl, Dealer Edition, duals, 2007, No. 14571

EX $8   **NM** $16   **MIP** $25

❑ **Case-IH 4894**, 1:32-scale, Ertl, red and black, special collectors edition "1985", 1980s, No. 222EA

EX $13   **NM** $27   **MIP** $33

❑ **Case-IH 4894**, 1:32-scale, Ertl, red and black, 1980s, No. 222

EX $9   **NM** $17   **MIP** $27

❏ **Case-IH 4994**, 1:32-scale, Ertl, red and black, battery operated, 1980s, No. 610
EX $13   **NM** $27   **MIP** $33

❏ **Case-IH 5120**, 1:32-scale, Ertl, MFD, w/loader and attachments, No. 675
EX $9   **NM** $16   **MIP** $26

❏ **Case-IH 5120**, 1:32-scale, Ertl, red and black, 1990s, No. 427
EX $6   **NM** $9   **MIP** $16

❏ **Case-IH 5130**, 1:32-scale, Ertl, red, battery operated, 1990s, No. 698
EX $8   **NM** $12   **MIP** $16

❏ **Case-IH 5140**, 1:32-scale, Ertl, red and black, Collector Edition, 1990s, No. 427EA
EX $12   **NM** $22   **MIP** $28

❏ **Case-IH 5230**, 1:32-scale, Ertl, w/loader, No. 456 *(Photo by Ertl)*
EX $4   **NM** $9   **MIP** $17

❏ **Case-IH 5230**, 1:32-scale, Ertl, MFD, w/loader, 1994, No. 733
EX $8   **NM** $14   **MIP** $22

❏ **Case-IH 5230**, 1:32-scale, Ertl, MFD, w/loader, 1996, No. 456
EX $8   **NM** $14   **MIP** $22

❏ **Case-IH 5240**, 1:32-scale, Ertl, 1994, No. 734
EX $6   **NM** $8   **MIP** $14

❏ **Case-IH 5240**, 1:32-scale, Ertl, 1996, No. 452 *(Photo by Ertl)*
EX $6   **NM** $8   **MIP** $14

❏ **Case-IH 9150**, 1:32-scale, Ertl, w/duals, Collector Edition, No. 641DA
EX $19   **NM** $26   **MIP** $38

❏ **Case-IH 9150**, 1:32-scale, Ertl, red and black, w/PTO and hitch, 1980s, No. 641
EX $17   **NM** $24   **MIP** $36

❏ **Case-IH 9270**, 1:32-scale, Scale Models, w/duals, 1996, No. ZSM829
(Photo by Bossen Implement)
EX $18   **NM** $24   **MIP** $36

❏ **Case-IH 9370**, 1:32-scale, Scale Models, duals, No. ZSM825
(Photo by Scale Models)
EX $18   **NM** $24   **MIP** $36

❏ **Case-IH 9370**, 1:32-scale, Scale Models, '95 Farm Progress Show Edition, 1995, No. ZSM820
EX $18   **NM** $24   **MIP** $36

❏ **Case-IH 9380**, 1:32-scale, Scale Models, w/duals, "A Powerful Heritage, Fargo, ND", 1995, No. ZSM823
EX $18   **NM** $24   **MIP** $36

❏ **Case-IH 9380**, 1:32-scale, Scale Models, Quad Track, 2000, No. ZSM932
EX $18   **NM** $24   **MIP** $36

❏ **Case-IH 9390**, 1:32-scale, Scale Models, triples, No. ZSM886
(Photo by Kate Bossen)
EX $18   **NM** $24   **MIP** $36

❏ **Case-IH 9390**, 1:32-scale, Scale Models, w/duals, 1996, No. ZSM829
EX $18   **NM** $24   **MIP** $36

❑ **Case-IH 9390**, 1:32-scale, Scale Models, w/triples, 1998, No. ZSM886
EX $18   **NM** $24   **MIP** $36

❑ **Case-IH 956 XL**, 1:32-scale, Ertl, red and black, 1990s, No. 661
EX $4   **NM** $9   **MIP** $17

❑ **Case-IH 956XL**, 1:32-scale, Ertl, w/loader and attachments, No. 664
EX $9   **NM** $16   **MIP** $26

❑ **Case-IH Maxxum 140**, 1:32-scale, Ertl, 2007, No. 14596
EX $7   **NM** $13   **MIP** $16

❑ **Case-IH MX275 w/Disc Harrow**, 1:32-scale, Ertl, set, 2006, No. 14513
EX $8   **NM** $14   **MIP** $18

❑ **Case-IH MX305**, 1:32-scale, Ertl, 2006, No. 14447
EX $8   **NM** $14   **MIP** $18

❑ **Case-IH MXU135**, 1:32-scale, Ertl, 2006, No. 14475
EX $8   **NM** $14   **MIP** $18

❑ **Case-IH Puma 180**, 1:32-scale, Ertl, '07 Farm Progress edition, 2007, No. 14610A
EX $8   **NM** $16   **MIP** $24

❑ **Case-IH Puma 195**, 1:32-scale, Ertl, 2007, No. 14531
EX $7   **NM** $14   **MIP** $20

❑ **Case-IH Quadtrac**, 1:32-scale, Scale Models, Denver Summit, August 1996, 1996, No. ZSM855

(Photo by Scale Models)
EX $38   **NM** $67   **MIP** $98

❑ **Case-IH Quadtrac**, 1:32-scale, Scale Models, 1997, No. 859
EX $18   **NM** $24   **MIP** $36

TRACTORS 1:35-SCALE

❑ **Case-IH 4994**, 1:35-scale, Conrad, red and black, 1980s
EX $21   **NM** $32   **MIP** $42

TRACTORS 1:43-SCALE

❑ **Case-IH Magnum**, 1:43-scale, SpecCast, 1990s, No. ZJD33
EX $7   **NM** $9   **MIP** $13

TRACTORS 1:64-SCALE

❑ **Case-IH 2394**, 1:64-scale, Ertl, '87 Plowing Match, 1987, No. 473FP
EX $6   **NM** $9   **MIP** $14

❑ **Case-IH 2594**, 1:64-scale, Ertl, red and black, 1985 Farm Show Edition, 1985, No. 227FA
EX $3   **NM** $8   **MIP** $14

❑ **Case-IH 2594**, 1:64-scale, Ertl, red and black, w/Loader, 1986, No. 212
EX $4   **NM** $6   **MIP** $7

❑ **Case-IH 2594**, 1:64-scale, Ertl, red and black, 1986, No. 227
EX $3   **NM** $4   **MIP** $6

❑ **Case-IH 2594**, 1:64-scale, Ertl, red and black, duals, 2WD, 1986, No. 204
EX $3   **NM** $4   **MIP** $6

❑ **Case-IH 2594**, 1:64-scale, Ertl, red and black, 1986, No. 227
EX $3   **NM** $4   **MIP** $6

❑ **Case-IH 2594**, 1:64-scale, Ertl, w/loader, 1986, No. 212
EX $4   **NM** $6   **MIP** $7

❑ **Case-IH 2594**, 1:64-scale, Ertl, red and black, 1987 Western Canada F.P.S., 1987, No. 204FA
EX $3   **NM** $4   **MIP** $8

❑ **Case-IH 2594**, 1:64-scale, Ertl, w/loader, '87 Corn Husker Harvest Edition, 1987, No. 212FP
EX $4   **NM** $6   **MIP** $8

❑ **Case-IH 3294**, 1:64-scale, Ertl, red and black, 1980s, No. 205
EX $3   **NM** $4   **MIP** $6

❑ **Case-IH 3394**, 1:64-scale, Ertl, red and black, No. 288
EX $3   **NM** $4   **MIP** $6

❑ **Case-IH 3394**, 1:64-scale, Ertl, red and black, 1986 Farm Show Edition, 1986, No. 288YA
EX $3   **NM** $6   **MIP** $9

❑ **Case-IH 3394**, 1:64-scale, Ertl, red and black, plowing match, 1986, No. 288FA
EX $3   **NM** $4   **MIP** $9

❑ **Case-IH 4230**, 1:64-scale, Scale Models, 1995, No. ZSM784

(Photo by Scale Models)
EX $3   **NM** $4   **MIP** $6

❑ **Case-IH 4694**, 1:64-scale, Gunning (Custom), red and black, did not come in box
EX $19   **NM** $28   **MIP** n/a

❑ **Case-IH 480 Quad Trac**, 1:64-scale, Ertl, 2007, No. 14584
EX $3   **NM** $6   **MIP** $9

❑ **Case-IH 4894**, 1:64-scale, Gunning (Custom), red and black, did not come in box
EX $19   **NM** $28   **MIP** n/a

❑ **Case-IH 5120**, 1:64-scale, Ertl, w/duals, 1991, No. 241
EX $3   **NM** $4   **MIP** $6

❑ **Case-IH 5130**, 1:64-scale, Ertl, 2WD, 1991, No. 229
EX $3   **NM** $4   **MIP** $6

❑ **Case-IH 5130**, 1:64-scale, Ertl, w/loader, '91 Farm Show Edition, 1991, No. 222FP
EX $4   **NM** $5   **MIP** $6

❑ **Case-IH 5130**, 1:64-scale, Ertl, w/loader, 1992, No. 242
EX $4   **NM** $6   **MIP** $7

❑ **Case-IH 5130**, 1:64-scale, Ertl, w/loader, '93 CI Trade Fair Edition, 1993, No. 229YA
EX $4   **NM** $6   **MIP** $9

❑ **Case-IH 5140**, 1:64-scale, Ertl, MFD, 1991, No. 240
EX $3   **NM** $4   **MIP** $6

❑ **Case-IH 7120**, 1:64-scale, Ertl, red and black, MFD
EX $3   **NM** $4   **MIP** $6

❑ **Case-IH 7120**, 1:64-scale, Ertl, red and black
EX $3   **NM** $4   **MIP** $6

❑ **Case-IH 7120**, 1:64-scale, Ertl, red and black, 1987 Farm Show Edition, 1987, No. 495FP
EX $3   **NM** $4   **MIP** $8

❑ **Case-IH 7120**, 1:64-scale, Ertl, red and black, duals, 1988, No. 626
EX $3   **NM** $4   **MIP** $6

❑ **Case-IH 7120**, 1:64-scale, Ertl, w/loader, 1993, No. 460
EX $4   NM $6   MIP $8

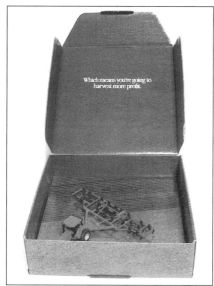

❑ **Case-IH 7130**, 1:64-scale, Ertl, w/field cultivator *(Photo by Bossen Implement)*
EX $22   NM $48   MIP $78

❑ **Case-IH 7130**, 1:64-scale, Ertl, red and black, 1987, No. 458
EX $3   NM $4   MIP $6

❑ **Case-IH 7130**, 1:64-scale, Ertl, red and black, w/Loader, 1987, No. 460
EX $4   NM $6   MIP $8

❑ **Case-IH 7130**, 1:64-scale, Ertl, red and black, 1988 Farm Show Edition, 1988, No. 616FR
EX $3   NM $4   MIP $8

❑ **Case-IH 7130**, 1:64-scale, Ertl, red and black, 1988 Farm Show Edition, note size of model numbers, 1988, No. 616FR
EX $3   NM $4   MIP $8

❑ **Case-IH 7130**, 1:64-scale, Ertl, on stocking stuffer card, 1989, No. 458
(Photo by Bossen Implement)
EX $3   NM $4   MIP $6

❑ **Case-IH 7140**, 1:64-scale, Ertl, red and black
EX $3   NM $4   MIP $6

❑ **Case-IH 7140**, 1:64-scale, Ertl, red and black, 1989, No. 616
EX $3   NM $4   MIP $6

❑ **Case-IH 7150**, 1:64-scale, Ertl, '92 Farm Show Edition, 1992, No. 285FA
EX $3   NM $6   MIP $8

❑ **Case-IH 7210**, 1:64-scale, Ertl, 2WD, 1994, No. 458FU
EX $3   NM $4   MIP $6

❑ **Case-IH 7220**, 1:64-scale, Ertl, w/loader, 1994, No. 460FU
EX $4   NM $6   MIP $8

❑ **Case-IH 7240**, 1:64-scale, Ertl, '94 CI Trade Fair Edition, 1994, No. 458MA
EX $3   NM $9   MIP $17

❑ **Case-IH 7240**, 1:64-scale, Ertl, MFD, 1994, No. 616FU
EX $3   NM $4   MIP $6

❑ **Case-IH 7240**, 1:64-scale, Ertl, friction drive, 1994, No. 4617
EX $3   NM $4   MIP $6

❑ **Case-IH 7250**, 1:64-scale, Ertl, MFD, '94 Farm Show Edition, 1994, No. 4757MA
EX $3   NM $4   MIP $8

❑ **Case-IH 7250**, 1:64-scale, Ertl, w/duals, 1994, No. 626FU
EX $3   NM $4   MIP $6

❑ **Case-IH 7250**, 1:64-scale, Ertl, w/sound chip, 1994, No. 4407
EX $3   NM $4   MIP $6

❑ **Case-IH 7250 and MX-285**, 1:64-scale, Ertl, Mark 50 and 100,000th, sold as a set, 2003, No. 14030
EX $4   NM $8   MIP $22

❑ **Case-IH 8920**, 1:64-scale, Ertl, 2WD, w/loader, 1996, No. 4289A
EX $4   NM $6   MIP $8

❑ **Case-IH 8920**, 1:64-scale, Ertl, 2WD, 1999, No. 4616
EX $4   NM $6   MIP $8

❑ **Case-IH 8940**, 1:64-scale, Ertl, MFD, 1996, No. 4209
EX $4   NM $6   MIP $8

❑ **Case-IH 8950**, 1:64-scale, Ertl, MFD and duals, 1997, No. 4612
EX $6   NM $9   MIP $18

❑ **Case-IH 8950**, 1:64-scale, Ertl, triples, '98 Farm Show Edition, 1998, No. 4602FA
EX $9   NM $22   MIP $38

❑ **Case-IH 9250**, 1:64-scale, Ertl, rigid frame, 1994, No. 231EP
EX $4   NM $9   MIP $14

❑ **Case-IH 9250 w/Planter Set**, 1:64-scale, Ertl, 1990s, No. 4446

(Photo by Ertl)

EX n/a   **NM** n/a   **MIP** $17

❑ **Case-IH 9260**, 1:64-scale, Ertl, rigid frame, '93 Farm Show Edition, 1993, No. 231FP

EX $4   **NM** $9   **MIP** $14

❑ **Case-IH 9260**, 1:64-scale, Ertl, rigid frame, 1993, No. 231FP

EX $4   **NM** $9   **MIP** $14

❑ **Case-IH 9370**, 1:64-scale, Scale Models, duals, 1995, No. ZSM824

(Photo by Scale Models)

EX $6   **NM** $8   **MIP** $14

❑ **Case-IH 9380**, 1:64-scale, Scale Models, Quad Trac, 1999, No. ZSM933

EX $4   **NM** $9   **MIP** $14

❑ **Case-IH 9390**, 1:64-scale, Scale Models, w/duals, No. ZSM857

EX $4   **NM** $9   **MIP** $14

❑ **Case-IH 9390**, 1:64-scale, Scale Models, w/duals, 1997, No. ZSM744

EX $4   **NM** $9   **MIP** $14

❑ **Case-IH 9390**, 1:64-scale, Scale Models, w/wide duals, 1998, No. ZSM887

EX $4   **NM** $9   **MIP** $14

❑ **Case-IH 9390**, 1:64-scale, Scale Models, triples, '99 Farm Show Edition, 1999, No. ZSM930

EX $4   **NM** $9   **MIP** $14

❑ **Case-IH Historical Toy Set**, 1:64-scale, Ertl, Case L, Case 600, Farmall H, McC WD-9 4-piece set, 1989, No. 4400 *(Photo by Ertl)*

EX n/a   **NM** n/a   **MIP** $13

❑ **Case-IH Magnum, 305**, 1:64-scale, Ertl, 2006, No. 14553

EX $4   **NM** $6   **MIP** $8

❑ **Case-IH Maxxum 140**, 1:64-scale, Ertl, 2007, No. 14554

EX $2   **NM** $4   **MIP** $6

❑ **Case-IH Puma 180**, 1:64-scale, Ertl, '07 Farm Progress edition, 2007, No. 14614A

EX $3   **NM** $6   **MIP** $9

❑ **Case-IH Puma 210**, 1:64-scale, Ertl, 2007, No. 14533

EX $3   **NM** $6   **MIP** $9

❑ **Case-IH Quadtrac**, 1:64-scale, Scale Models, No. ZSM860

(Photo by Scale Models)

EX $6   **NM** $8   **MIP** $14

❑ **Case-IH Quadtrac**, 1:64-scale, Scale Models, Collector Edition, 1996, No. ZSM858

EX $4   **NM** $9   **MIP** $14

❑ **Case-IH Quadtrac**, 1:64-scale, Scale Models, 1997, No. ZSM860

EX $4   **NM** $9   **MIP** $14

❑ **Case-IH Quadtrac**, 1:64-scale, Scale Models, '98 Farm Show Edition, 1998, No. ZSM909

EX $4   **NM** $9   **MIP** $14

❑ **Case-IH Steiger 530**, 1:64-scale, Ertl, front and rear duals, 2006, No. 14555

EX $4   **NM** $7   **MIP** $10

❑ **Case-IH STX375 w/Grain Cart**, 1:64-scale, Ertl, 2005, No. 14397

EX $4   **NM** $8   **MIP** $12

❑ **Case-IH STX500**, 1:64-scale, Ertl, front and rear duals, 2005, No. 14360

EX $4   **NM** $7   **MIP** $12

❑ **Case-IH VAC and Farmall F-20 Set**, 1:64-scale, Ertl, gray, 1990s, No. 238 *(Photo by Ertl)*

EX $3   **NM** $6   **MIP** $9

TRACTORS MICRO

❑ **Case-IH 2594**, Micro, Micro Machines, red and black, part of set— did not come in individual box, 1990s

EX $1   **NM** $2   **MIP** n/a

TRUCKS 1:16-SCALE

❑ **Case-IH Ford F-150 Pickup**, 1:16-scale, Ertl, 1990s, No. 4650

(Photo by Ertl)

EX $6   **NM** $12   **MIP** $19

TRUCKS 1:25-SCALE

❑ **Case-IH Semi**, 1:25-scale, Ertl, white, 1980s, No. 484

EX $9   **NM** $18   **MIP** $29

Photos by Jon Jacobson unless otherwise noted.

TRUCKS 1:43-SCALE

❑ **Case-IH Van Model T**, 1:43-scale, SpecCast, 1990s, No. ZJD24
EX $6   **NM** $8   **MIP** $12

TRUCKS 1:64-SCALE

❑ **Case-IH Hauling Set**, 1:64-scale, Ertl, 1990s, No. 2642
EX $9   **NM** $13   **MIP** $24

❑ **Case-IH Hauling Set**, 1:64-scale, Ertl, 1995, No. 4562
EX $8   **NM** $14   **MIP** $24

CATERPILLAR

BANKS 1:25-SCALE

❑ **Caterpillar '57 Stake Truck**, 1:25-scale, Ertl, Prestige Series, No. 2013 *(Photo by Ertl)*
EX $4   **NM** $12   **MIP** $18

❑ **Caterpillar Truck Bank**, 1:25-scale, Ertl, No. 2440 *(Photo by Ertl)*
EX $4   **NM** $12   **MIP** $18

❑ **Caterpillar Truck Bank**, 1:25-scale, Ertl, No. 2353 *(Photo by Ertl)*
EX $4   **NM** $12   **MIP** $18

CONSTRUCTION EQUIPMENT 1:16-SCALE

❑ **Caterpillar Challenger 35**, 1:16-scale, NZG, 1996, No. 118
EX $106   **NM** $147   **MIP** $196

❑ **Caterpillar Challenger 45**, 1:16-scale, NZG, 1996, No. 119
EX $106   **NM** $147   **MIP** $196

❑ **Caterpillar Challenger 55**, 1:16-scale, NZG, 1996, No. 120
EX $106   **NM** $147   **MIP** $196

❑ **Caterpillar Crawler, 2-Ton**, 1:16-scale, Ertl, 1993, No. 2438 *(Photo by Ertl)*
EX $12   **NM** $17   **MIP** $27

❑ **Caterpillar Roller**, 1:16-scale, Brudor, asphalt drum compactor, 2004, No. 2434
EX $4   **NM** $9   **MIP** $14

CONSTRUCTION EQUIPMENT 1:50-SCALE

❑ **Caterpillar Front Shovel, 5090**, 1:50-scale, Ertl, 1997, No. 2676
(Photo by Ertl)
EX $14   **NM** $18   **MIP** $26

CONSTRUCTION EQUIPMENT 1:64-SCALE

❑ **Caterpillar Challenger, 35**, 1:64-scale, Ertl, '96 Farm Progress Show Edition, 1996, No. 2345MA
EX $6   **NM** $14   **MIP** $22

❑ **Caterpillar Challenger, 45**, 1:64-scale, Ertl, 1994, No. 2441 *(Photo by Ertl)*
EX $4   **NM** $6   **MIP** $9

❑ **Caterpillar Challenger, 45**, 1:64-scale, Ertl, '94 Farm Progress Show Edition, 1994, No. 2441MA
EX $6   **NM** $13   **MIP** $22

❑ **Caterpillar Challenger, 45**, 1:64-scale, Ertl, w/implements set, 1997, No. 2834 *(Photo by Ertl)*
EX n/a   **NM** n/a   **MIP** $18

❑ **Caterpillar Challenger, 55**, 1:64-scale, Ertl, No. 2441
EX $4   **NM** $6   **MIP** $9

❑ **Caterpillar Challenger, 55**, 1:64-scale, Ertl, '95 Farm Progress Show Edition, 1995, No. 2441PA
EX $6   **NM** $13   **MIP** $22

❑ **Caterpillar Challenger, 65**, 1:64-scale, Ertl, Caterpillar Yellow and black, regular edition, 1989, No. 2415
EX $6   **NM** $9   **MIP** $16

❑ **Caterpillar Challenger, 65**, 1:64-scale, Ertl, Caterpillar yellow and black, 1st edition, 1 of 5000, 1989, No. 2415EA
EX $6   **NM** $9   **MIP** $22

❑ **Caterpillar Challenger, 65D**, 1:64-scale, Ertl, '97 Farm Progress Show Edition, 1997, No. 2830MA
EX $6   **NM** $9   **MIP** $22

❑ **Caterpillar Challenger, 65D**, 1:64-scale, Ertl, w/wing disc set, 1997, No. 2835 *(Photo by Ertl)*
EX $6   **NM** $9   **MIP** $12

❑ **Caterpillar Challenger, 75**, 1:64-scale, Ertl, '90 Farm Progress Show Edition, 1990, No. 2415ER
EX $8   **NM** $13   **MIP** $26

❑ **Caterpillar Challenger, 75**, 1:64-scale, Ertl, '92 Farm Progress Show Edition, 1992, No. 2413EA
EX $8   **NM** $13   **MIP** $26

❑ **Caterpillar Challenger, 85C**, 1:64-scale, Ertl, 1994, No. 2404
(Photo by Ertl)
EX $4   **NM** $8   **MIP** $16

❑ **Caterpillar Challenger, 85C**, 1:64-scale, Ertl, 1994, No. 2404
(Photo by Kate Bossen)
EX $6   **NM** $8   **MIP** $16

❑ **Caterpillar Challenger, 85D**, 1:64-scale, Ertl, 1996, No. 2404
(Photo by Kate Bossen)
EX $6   **NM** $8   **MIP** $11

❑ **Caterpillar Challenger, 85D**, 1:64-scale, Norscott, 1999, No. 55959 *(Photo by Kate Bossen)*
EX $4   **NM** $6   **MIP** $11

❑ **Caterpillar Combine, 485**, 1:64-scale, Norscott, Lexion, w/corn and grain platform, 1999, No. 55028
(Photo by Bossen Implement)
EX $11   **NM** $22   **MIP** $38

❑ **Caterpillar Crawler, w/blade, D6H**, 1:64-scale, Ertl, No. 1846
EX $6   **NM** $8   **MIP** $11

❑ **Caterpillar Dump Truck, D25D**, 1:64-scale, Ertl, No. 2417
EX $6   **NM** $8   **MIP** $11

❑ **Caterpillar Excavator**, 1:64-scale, Brudor, 2004, No. 2439
EX $17   **NM** $28   **MIP** $46

❑ **Caterpillar Grader**, 1:64-scale, Brudor, 2003, No. 2437
EX $14   **NM** $24   **MIP** $42

❑ **Caterpillar Grader, 12G**, 1:64-scale, Ertl, camouflage, No. 1034
EX $9   **NM** $16   **MIP** $26

❑ **Caterpillar Grader, 12G**, 1:64-scale, Ertl, industrial yellow, No. 1848
EX $6   **NM** $8   **MIP** $11

❑ **Caterpillar Scraper, 613C**, 1:64-scale, Ertl, No. 2419
EX $6   **NM** $8   **MIP** $11

❑ **Caterpillar Skid Loader**, 1:64-scale, Brudor, 2003, No. 2435
EX $4   **NM** $9   **MIP** $16

❑ **Caterpillar Wheel Loader, 950 E**, 1:64-scale, Ertl, No. 2418
EX $6   **NM** $8   **MIP** $11

IMPLEMENTS 1:64-SCALE

❑ **Caterpillar Auger Cart**, 1:64-scale, Ertl, on Cat track system, 1995, No. 2323 *(Photo by Ertl)*
EX $3   **NM** $4   **MIP** $6

❑ **Caterpillar Dry Fertilizer Spreader**, 1:64-scale, Ertl, on Cat track system, 1996, No. 2328

(Photo by Ertl)

EX $3   **NM** $4   **MIP** $6

❑ **Caterpillar Liquid Fertilizer Sprayer**, 1:64-scale, Ertl, on Cat track system, 1996, No. 2327 *(Photo by Ertl)*

EX $3   **NM** $4   **MIP** $6

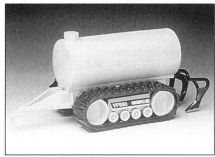

❑ **Caterpillar Liquid Manure Spreader**, 1:64-scale, Ertl, on Cat track system, 1995, No. 2324

(Photo by Ertl)

EX $3   **NM** $4   **MIP** $6

❑ **Caterpillar Wagon, Gravity**, 1:64-scale, Ertl, on Cat track system, 1996, No. 2326 *(Photo by Ertl)*

EX $3   **NM** $4   **MIP** $6

❑ **Caterpillar Wing Disc**, 1:64-scale, Ertl, 1996, No. 2333 *(Photo by Ertl)*

EX $3   **NM** $4   **MIP** $6

PEDAL TRACTORS

❑ **Caterpillar D4 w/ and w/o blade**, New London Metal Processing Corp, yellow, can be found powered by pedal, gas engine, or electric, in original condition

EX $1960   **NM** $3289   **MIP** n/a

TRACTORS 1:16-SCALE

❑ **Caterpillar Tractor**, 1:16-scale, Arcade, green w/gold trim and red spoke wheels, nickel-plated driver, 7-1/2" long, 1930, No. 271X

EX $2233   **NM** $3772   **MIP** n/a

❑ **Caterpillar Tractor**, 1:16-scale, Arcade, red, blue or green w/gold trim; chain-link tracks, 6-7/8" long, 1931, No. 269X

EX $198   **NM** $442   **MIP** n/a

❑ **Caterpillar Tractor**, 1:16-scale, Arcade, green w/gold trim and red spoke wheels, nickel piece added to radiator, driver, 7-1/2" long, 1931, No. 272X

EX $515   **NM** $1078   **MIP** $3105

❑ **Caterpillar Tractor Diesel**, 1:16-scale, Arcade, yellow w/black trim, black rubber tread, nickel-plated engine and driver, 7-3/4" long; 1937 version identical but numbered 2700Y, 1936, No. 270Y

EX $515   **NM** $1058   **MIP** $3095

TRACTORS

❑ **Caterpillar Tractor**, Arcade, red, blue, or green; chain-link tracks, 5-5/8" long, 1931, No. 268X

EX n/a   **NM** n/a   **MIP** n/a

❑ **Caterpillar Tractor**, Arcade, red, blue, or green; no trim color, chain-link tracks, 3-7/8" long, 1931, No. 267X

EX n/a   **NM** n/a   **MIP** n/a

❑ **Caterpillar Tractor**, Arcade, chain-link tracks, pull toy, 3" long, 1931, No. 266X

EX n/a   **NM** n/a   **MIP** n/a

TRUCKS 1:25-SCALE

❑ **Caterpillar Straight Truck w/Van Box**, 1:25-scale, Ertl, No. 2420

(Photo by Ertl)

EX $6   **NM** $11   **MIP** $18

TRUCKS 1:64-SCALE

❑ **Caterpillar Hauling Set w/45s**, 1:64-scale, Ertl, No. 2412 *(Photo by Ertl)*

EX $11   **NM** $16   **MIP** $27

❑ **Caterpillar Semi w/CAT Van Box**, 1:64-scale, Ertl, No. 7705 *(Photo by Ertl)*

EX $8   **NM** $13   **MIP** $18

CENTURY

IMPLEMENTS 1:64-SCALE

❑ **Century Sprayer**, 1:64-scale, Ertl, yellow and red, 1980s, No. 1003
EX $3   **NM** $4   **MIP** $7

❑ **Century Sprayer**, 1:64-scale, Ertl, yellow and red, first 5,000, 1980s, No. 1003
EX $3   **NM** $4   **MIP** $8

CEREAL

IMPLEMENTS 1:64-SCALE

❑ **Cereal Swather, 722**, 1:64-scale, Scale Models, green, did not come in box, 1980s
EX $17   **NM** $38   **MIP** n/a

CHALLENGER

PEDAL TRACTORS

❑ **Challenger**, Scale Models, '02 Farm Progress Show Edition, 2002, No. FT-0636
EX $98   **NM** $126   **MIP** $168

❑ **Challenger**, Scale Models, 2003, No. FT-0642
EX $89   **NM** $102   **MIP** $152

TRACTORS 1:16-SCALE

❑ **Challenger MT-255**, 1:16-scale, Scale Models, '03 Louisville Show Edition, 2003, No. FB-2625
(Photo by Scale Models)
EX $18   **NM** $29   **MIP** $47

❑ **Challenger MT-265**, 1:16-scale, Scale Models, '02 Farm Progress Show Edition, 2002, No. FT-0635
(Photo by Bossen Implement)
EX $16   **NM** $24   **MIP** $42

❑ **Challenger MT-295**, 1:16-scale, Scale Models, 2003, No. FT-0649
EX $16   **NM** $24   **MIP** $42

❑ **Challenger MT-455**, 1:16-scale, Scale Models, '03 Louisville Show Edition, 2003, No. FB-2624
(Photo by Bossen Implement)
EX $18   **NM** $33   **MIP** $48

❑ **Challenger MT-455B**, 1:16-scale, Scale Models, MFD, ROPS, 2006, No. FT-0690
EX $16   **NM** $24   **MIP** $43

❑ **Challenger MT-465**, 1:16-scale, Scale Models, '02 Farm Progress Show Edition, 2002, No. FT-0634
EX $18   **NM** $29   **MIP** $47

❑ **Challenger MT-465B**, 1:16-scale, Scale Models, MFD, 3-point hitch, 2006, No. FT-0707
EX $16   **NM** $24   **MIP** $44

❑ **Challenger MT-4665B**, 1:16-scale, Scale Models, MFD, duals, 3-point hitch, 2006, No. FT-0708
(Photo by Bossen Implement)
EX $11   **NM** $24   **MIP** $44

❑ **Challenger MT-655**, 1:16-scale, Scale Models, '03 Louisville Show Edition, 2003, No. FB-2623
(Photo by Bossen Implement)
EX $19   **NM** $28   **MIP** $52

❑ **Challenger MT-665**, 1:16-scale, Scale Models, '02 Farm Progress Show Edition, 2002, No. FT-0633
EX $18   **NM** $27   **MIP** $51

❑ **Challenger MT-765**, 1:16-scale, Scale Models, Collector Edition, 2003, No. FT-656 *(Photo by Scale Models)*
EX $89   **NM** $102   **MIP** $173

❑ **Challenger MT-765**, 1:16-scale, Scale Models, '03 Farm Progress Show Edition, 2003, No. FT-0659
EX $89   **NM** $102   **MIP** $166

❏ **Challenger MT-975B**, 1:16-scale, Scale Models, 4WD, triples, 2006, No. FT-0721 *(Photo by Bossen Implement)*
EX $83   **NM** $102   **MIP** $168

TRACTORS 1:64-SCALE

❏ **Challenger**, 1:64-scale, Scale Models, MFD, w/duals, 2003, No. 13388
EX $6   **NM** $8   **MIP** $12

❏ **Challenger, MT-765**, 1:64-scale, Scale Models, Collector Edition, 2003, No. FT-0655
EX $6   **NM** $8   **MIP** $12

❏ **Challenger, MT-765**, 1:64-scale, Scale Models, '03 Farm Progress Show Edition, 2003, No. FT-0660
EX $6   **NM** $8   **MIP** $12

CLAY

IMPLEMENTS 1:64-SCALE

❏ **Clay Liquid Spreader**, 1:64-scale, Ertl, cream and black
EX $4   **NM** $6   **MIP** $8

❏ **Clay Liquid Spreader**, 1:64-scale, Mini Toys, orange and black
EX $4   **NM** $6   **MIP** $8

COCKSHUTT

IMPLEMENTS 1:16-SCALE

❏ **Cockshutt Wagon**, 1:16-scale, Advance Products, red, 1950s
EX $93   **NM** $178   **MIP** $319

❏ **Cockshutt Wagon**, 1:16-scale, Advance Products, red, 1950s
EX $93   **NM** $178   **MIP** $319

❏ **Cockshutt Wagon**, 1:16-scale, Kemp, red, 1950s
EX $122   **NM** $277   **MIP** $548

MISCELLANEOUS

❏ **Cockshutt Puzzle**, 1950s
EX $48   **NM** $56   **MIP** $78

TRACTORS 1:16-SCALE

❏ **Cockshutt 1555**, 1:16-scale, Ertl, C.I.F.E.S., '94 Candian Show Edition, 1994, No. 4124TA
EX $16   **NM** $24   **MIP** $47

❏ **Cockshutt 1555**, 1:16-scale, Ertl, ROPS, International Cockshutt Club 1 of 500, 1994, No. 4105TA
EX $32   **NM** $42   **MIP** $63

❏ **Cockshutt 1555**, 1:16-scale, Ertl, NF w/ROPS Collector Edition, 1994, No. 4124DA *(Photo by Ertl)*
EX $26   **NM** $38   **MIP** $52

❏ **Cockshutt 1655**, 1:16-scale, Ertl, ROPS and duals, '94 Sugar Valley Toy Show, 1994, No. 4527TA

(Photo by Ertl)
EX $26   **NM** $38   **MIP** $52

❏ **Cockshutt 1655**, 1:16-scale, Ertl, 1994, No. 4179 *(Photo by Ertl)*
EX $26   **NM** $38   **MIP** $52

❏ **Cockshutt 1755**, 1:16-scale, Scale Models, red, 1980s
EX $18   **NM** $28   **MIP** $37

❏ **Cockshutt 1850**, 1:16-scale, Ertl, red, plastic rims, 1960s
EX $98   **NM** $188   **MIP** $492

❏ **Cockshutt 1850**, 1:16-scale, Ertl, red, die-cast rear rims, plastic fronts, 1960s
EX $98   **NM** $188   **MIP** $492

❏ **Cockshutt 1850**, 1:16-scale, Ertl, tan over red, fenders, die-cast rear rims, plastic fronts, 1960s
EX $148   **NM** $289   **MIP** $834

❏ **Cockshutt 1850**, 1:16-scale, Ertl, tan over red, no fenders, die-cast rear rims, plastic fronts, 1960s
EX $148   **NM** $289   **MIP** $834

❏ **Cockshutt 1855**, 1:16-scale, Scale Models, Heritage
EX $22   **NM** $32   **MIP** $42

❏ **Cockshutt 1855**, 1:16-scale, Scale Models, red, Ontario Farm Toy Show 8-12-88 Woodstock, 1980s
EX $178   **NM** $223   **MIP** $288

❏ **Cockshutt 1855 Heritage**, 1:16-scale, Scale Models, red, 1980s
EX $18   **NM** $28   **MIP** $37

❏ **Cockshutt 1950T**, 1:16-scale, Ertl, 2003, No. 13383
EX $22   **NM** $32   **MIP** $48

❏ **Cockshutt 20**, 1:16-scale, Ertl, 1989 National Farm Toy Museum Set No. 4, narrow front end, 1989, No. 4126PA
EX $23   **NM** $37   **MIP** $67

❏ **Cockshutt 20 Deluxe**, 1:16-scale, Ertl, tan and red, 1989 National Farm Toy Museum Set No. 4, 1989, No. 4127PA
EX $23   **NM** $37   **MIP** $57

❏ **Cockshutt 30**, 1:16-scale, Advance Products, red, steerable, 1950s
EX $138   **NM** $263   **MIP** $606

❏ **Cockshutt 30**, 1:16-scale, Advance Products, red, non-steerable, 1950s
EX $138   **NM** $263   **MIP** $606

❏ **Cockshutt 30**, 1:16-scale, Kemp, red, 1950s
EX $248   **NM** $1082   **MIP** $2332

❏ **Cockshutt 30**, 1:16-scale, Lincoln, red, decals and tires possible restored, 1950s
EX $163   **NM** $252   **MIP** $588

❏ **Cockshutt 30**, 1:16-scale, Scale Models, red, Gambles Farmcrest, 1980s
EX $23   **NM** $32   **MIP** $39

❏ **Cockshutt 40**, 1:16-scale, Ertl, 1986 National Farm Toy Museum Set No. 1, 1986, No. 4110PA
EX $23   **NM** $47   **MIP** $67

❏ **Cockshutt 40**, 1:16-scale, Scale Models, 1987 Summer Toy Festival Show Tractor, 1987
EX $23   **NM** $32   **MIP** $39

❏ **Cockshutt 50**, 1:16-scale, Ertl, 1986 National Farm Toy Museum Set No. 1, 1986, No. 4111PA
EX $23   **NM** $47   **MIP** $67

❏ **Cockshutt 540**, 1:16-scale, Advance Products, tan, 1950s
EX $163   **NM** $252   **MIP** $542

❏ **Cockshutt 550**, 1:16-scale, C & M Farm Toys, red and tan, did not come in box, 1980s
EX $88   **NM** $133   **MIP** n/a

❏ **Cockshutt 550**, 1:16-scale, SpecCast, 1999, No. SCT-172
EX $18   **NM** $28   **MIP** $38

❏ **Cockshutt 550**, 1:16-scale, Yoder (Custom), red, 1990s
EX $48   **NM** $98   **MIP** $123

❏ **Cockshutt 560**, 1:16-scale, Ertl, tan and red, 1987 National Farm Toy Museum Set No. 2, 1987, No. 4114PA
EX $23   **NM** $37   **MIP** $57

❏ **Cockshutt 560**, 1:16-scale, Ertl, tan, Diesel, 1990 National Farm Toy Museum Set No. 5, 1990, No. 4137PA
EX $23   **NM** $37   **MIP** $57

❏ **Cockshutt 560**, 1:16-scale, Ertl, 1998, No. 2034DA
EX $23   **NM** $37   **MIP** $57

❏ **Cockshutt 570**, 1:16-scale, Ertl, tan and red, 1987 National Farm Toy Museum Set No. 2, 1987, No. 4115PA
EX $23   **NM** $37   **MIP** $57

❏ **Cockshutt 570 Super**, 1:16-scale, Ertl, tan and red, 1987 National Farm Toy Museum Set No. 2, 1987, No. 4116PA
EX $23   **NM** $37   **MIP** $57

❑ **Cockshutt 580 Super**, 1:16-scale, Ertl, tan and red, 12th Anniversary Marion County Show, 1980s, No. 4131QA
EX $33   **NM** $47   **MIP** $57

❑ **Cockshutt 60**, 1:16-scale, SpecCast, 2002, No. SCT-207
EX $22   **NM** $32   **MIP** $42

❑ **Cockshutt 70**, 1:16-scale, Scale Models, steerable, w/rubber tires, 1980s
EX $13   **NM** $26   **MIP** $33

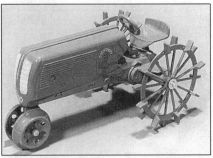

❑ **Cockshutt 70**, 1:16-scale, Scale Models, red, 1980s
EX $18   **NM** $28   **MIP** $38

❑ **Cockshutt Golden Arrow**, 1:16-scale, Scale Models, 1987 Ontario Farm Toy Show, 1987
EX $178   **NM** $212   **MIP** $243

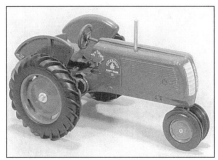

❑ **Cockshutt Hart-Parr 70**, 1:16-scale, Scale Models, 1990 Ontario Toy Show, 1990s
EX $178   **NM** $212   **MIP** $263

❑ **Spirit of Cockshutt**, 1:16-scale, Scale Models, red, new cab and top, 1990s
EX $18   **NM** $32   **MIP** $48

TRACTORS 1:32-SCALE

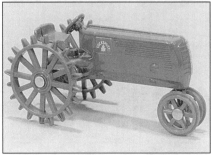

❑ **Cockshutt 70**, 1:32-scale, Scale Models, red, steel wheels, 1980s
EX $4   **NM** $6   **MIP** $8

❑ **Cockshutt 70**, 1:32-scale, Scale Models, red, rubber tires, 1980s
EX $4   **NM** $6   **MIP** $8

TRACTORS 1:64-SCALE

❑ **Cockshutt 1650**, 1:64-scale, Walters (Custom), red and white
EX $9   **NM** $12   **MIP** $16

❑ **Cockshutt 1650**, 1:64-scale, Walters (Custom), red and white
EX $9   **NM** $12   **MIP** $16

❑ **Cockshutt 1755**, 1:64-scale, Scale Models, red and cream
EX $3   **NM** $6   **MIP** $9

❑ **Cockshutt 1850**, 1:64-scale, Walters (Custom), red and white
EX $9   **NM** $12   **MIP** $16

❑ **Cockshutt 1850**, 1:64-scale, Walters (Custom), red and white
EX $9   **NM** $12   **MIP** $16

❑ **Cockshutt 1855**, 1:64-scale, Scale Models, red and white
EX $3   **NM** $6   **MIP** $9

❑ **Cockshutt 70**, 1:64-scale, Scale Models, red
EX $4   **NM** $6   **MIP** $9

❑ **Cockshutt 1850**, 1:64-scale, Walters (Custom), red and white
EX $9   **NM** $12   **MIP** $16

❑ **Cockshutt 1855**, 1:64-scale, Scale Models, red and white, 1988 World Ag-Expo
EX $3   **NM** $6   **MIP** $9

❑ **Cockshutt 1950T**, 1:64-scale, Ertl, 2003, No. 13387
EX $4   **NM** $6   **MIP** $8

❑ **Cockshutt 70**, 1:64-scale, Scale Models, red
EX $3   **NM** $6   **MIP** $8

❑ **Cockshutt 1855**, 1:64-scale, Scale Models, red and cream
EX $3   **NM** $6   **MIP** $9

❑ **Cockshutt 70**, 1:64-scale, Scale Models, red
EX $3   **NM** $6   **MIP** $8

❑ **Cockshutt 70**, 1:64-scale, Scale Models, red
EX $4   **NM** $6   **MIP** $9

❑ **Cockshutt 1855**, 1:64-scale, Scale Models, red and cream
EX $3   **NM** $6   **MIP** $9

❑ **Cockshutt 70**, 1:64-scale, Scale Models, red, C.L.A.T.S. "1988"
EX $4   **NM** $6   **MIP** $9

CO-OP

IMPLEMENTS 1:16-SCALE

❑ **Co-Op Wagon**, 1:16-scale, Advance Products, orange, 1950s
EX $63   **NM** $138   **MIP** $266

TRACTORS 1:16-SCALE

❑ **Co-Op E-2**, 1:16-scale, Ertl, orange, 1989 National Farm Toy Museum Set No. 4, narrow front end, No. 4128PA
EX $23   **NM** $37   **MIP** $57

❑ **Co-Op E-3**, 1:16-scale, Advance Products, orange, 1950s
EX $98   **NM** $222   **MIP** $462

❑ **Co-Op E-3**, 1:16-scale, Advance Products, orange, original tractor, decals missing, 1950s
EX $98   **NM** $222   **MIP** $462

❑ **Co-Op E-4**, 1:16-scale, Scale Models, red, 1980s, No. 1307
EX $16   **NM** $33   **MIP** $48

❑ **Co-Op No. 1**, 1:16-scale, SpecCast, 1999, No. CUST618
EX $13   **NM** $27   **MIP** $47

❑ **Co-Op No. 3**, 1:16-scale, Scale Models, red, Tractor Supply Co., 1980s
EX $23   **NM** $33   **MIP** $42

❑ **Co-Op No. 3**, 1:16-scale, SpecCast, No. CUST002

(Photo by Bossen Implement)

EX $18   **NM** $29   **MIP** $42

❑ **Co-Op No. 3 LP**, 1:16-scale, SpecCast, red, 1980s, No. Cust005
EX $18   **NM** $29   **MIP** $42

TRACTORS 1:43-SCALE

❑ **Co-Op No. 3**, 1:43-scale, SpecCast, red, 1980s
EX $6   **NM** $8   **MIP** $12

❑ **Co-Op No. 3**, 1:43-scale, SpecCast, 1980s
EX $6   **NM** $8   **MIP** $12

❑ **Co-Op No. 3 LP**, 1:43-scale, SpecCast, red, 1980s
EX $6   **NM** $8   **MIP** $12

❑ **Co-Op No. 3 LP**, 1:43-scale, SpecCast, 1980s
EX $6   **NM** $8   **MIP** $12

TRACTORS 1:64-SCALE

❑ **Co-Op**, 1:64-scale, SpecCast, red
EX $6   **NM** $9   **MIP** $18

❑ **Co-Op**, 1:64-scale, SpecCast, red, 1988 KFYR Ag-Expo
EX $6   **NM** $16   **MIP** $24

❑ **Co-Op**, 1:64-scale, SpecCast, red
EX $6   **NM** $9   **MIP** $18

DAVID BRADLEY

IMPLEMENTS 1:32-SCALE

❑ **Cultipacker**, 1:32-scale, Auburn Rubber, red w/white discs, 4" long
EX n/a   **NM** n/a   **MIP** n/a

❑ **Disc Harrow**, 1:32-scale, Auburn Rubber, red w/white discs, 2-1/2" long
EX n/a   **NM** n/a   **MIP** n/a

❑ **Hay Wagon**, 1:32-scale, Auburn Rubber, red w/black wheels,
EX n/a   **NM** n/a   **MIP** n/a

❑ **Mower**, 1:32-scale, Auburn Rubber, cuts to side, red w/black wheels, 3" long
EX n/a   **NM** n/a   **MIP** n/a

❑ **Plow**, 1:32-scale, Auburn Rubber, red w/2 blades, 4-3/4" long
EX n/a   **NM** n/a   **MIP** n/a

❑ **Spreader**, 1:32-scale, Auburn Rubber, red, 4-3/4" long
EX n/a   **NM** n/a   **MIP** n/a

DAVID BROWN

CONSTRUCTION EQUIPMENT 1:16-SCALE

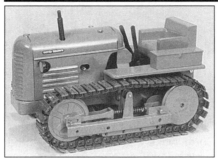

❑ **David Brown Crawler**, 1:16-scale, Chad Valley, red, wind-up, mid 1950s
EX $327   **NM** $1024   **MIP** $1342

TRACTORS 1:16-SCALE

❑ **David Brown 25D**, 1:16-scale, Denzil Skinner, red, mid 1950s
EX $288   **NM** $924   **MIP** $1134

❑ **David Brown Cropmaster**, 1:16-scale, red, mid 1950s
EX $298   **NM** $827   **MIP** $988

TRACTORS 1:25-SCALE

❑ **David Brown 1412**, 1:25-scale, NZG, white and orange, front wheel variation, mid 1970s
EX $18   **NM** $32   **MIP** $57

❑ **David Brown 1412**, 1:25-scale, NZG, white and orange, front wheel variation, mid 1970s, No. 156
EX $18   **NM** $32   **MIP** $57

TRACTORS 1:32-SCALE

❑ **David Brown 1690**, 1:32-scale, Ertl, white and orange, 1980s, No. 1716
EX $18   **NM** $24   **MIP** $37

❑ **David Brown 1690**, 1:32-scale, Ertl, white and orange, Collectors Edition, 1980s, No. 1716EA
EX $19   **NM** $26   **MIP** $39

❑ **David Brown 1694**, 1:32-scale, Lone Star, white and black, 1980s
EX $11　　**NM** $16　　**MIP** $27

❑ **David Brown 1694**, 1:32-scale, Lone Star, white and red, 1980s
EX $8　　**NM** $14　　**MIP** $24

❑ **David Brown 1694**, 1:32-scale, Lone Star, white and red, 1980s
EX $8　　**NM** $14　　**MIP** $24

❑ **David Brown 990**, 1:32-scale, Ertl, red and yellow, 1990s, No. 4180
EX $8　　**NM** $12　　**MIP** $23

TRACTORS 1:40-SCALE

❑ **David Brown 1412**, 1:40-scale, Corgi, white and orange, w/mounted combine, mid 1970s
EX $46　　**NM** $68　　**MIP** $118

❑ **David Brown 1412**, 1:40-scale, Corgi, white and orange, mid 1970s
EX $16　　**NM** $34　　**MIP** $46

TRACTORS 1:43-SCALE

❑ **David Brown 990**, 1:43-scale, Dinky, white and red, mid 1960s
EX $33　　**NM** $63　　**MIP** $89

❑ **David Brown 990**, 1:43-scale, Dinky, white and red, mid 1960s
EX $33　　**NM** $63　　**MIP** $89

❑ **David Brown 990**, 1:43-scale, Dinky, red and yellow, mid 1960s
EX $126　　**NM** $174　　**MIP** $228

❑ **David Brown 995**, 1:43-scale, Dinky, white and red, mid 1970s
EX $33　　**NM** $63　　**MIP** $89

❑ **David Brown 995**, 1:43-scale, Dinky, white and red, mid 1970s
EX $33　　**NM** $63　　**MIP** $89

TRACTORS 1:72-SCALE

❑ **David Brown Taskmaster**, 1:72-scale, Air Fix, gray, model kit, mid 1970s
EX $19　　**NM** $53　　**MIP** $98

DEUTZ

PEDAL TRACTORS

❏ **Deutz 5006**, Rolly Toys of Germany, dark green, tractor in original condition
EX $188 **NM** $233 **MIP** n/a

❏ **Deutz 5006**, Rolly Toys of Germany, light green, tractor in original condition
EX $188 **NM** $233 **MIP** n/a

❏ **Deutz DX 110**, Rolly Toys of Germany, dark green, tractor in original condition
EX $48 **NM** $77 **MIP** n/a

❏ **Deutz DX 110**, Rolly Toys of Germany, dark green, tractor in original condition
EX $48 **NM** $77 **MIP** n/a

TRACTORS 1:16-SCALE

❏ **Bauernschlepper**, 1:16-scale, Scale Models, 1936, Bauernschlepper, 1986, No. 410
(Photo by Bossen Implement)
EX $16 **NM** $22 **MIP** $37

❏ **Deutz 200**, 1:16-scale, Bruder, agrotron, w/duals and loader, 2002, No. 02073
EX $14 **NM** $22 **MIP** $32

❏ **Deutz 200**, 1:16-scale, Bruder, agrotron, w/loaders, 2002, No. 02072
EX $12 **NM** $17 **MIP** $27

❏ **Deutz 200**, 1:16-scale, Bruder, agrotron, w/duals, removeable, 2002, No. 02074 *(Photo by Bruder)*
EX $12 **NM** $17 **MIP** $27

❏ **Deutz 200**, 1:16-scale, Bruder, agrotron, 2002, No. 02070
(Photo by Bossen Implement)
EX $9 **NM** $13 **MIP** $22

TRACTORS 1:32-SCALE

❏ **Deutz 210**, 1:32-scale, Siku, agrotron, No. 3253 *(Photo by Bossen Implement)*
EX $9 **NM** $16 **MIP** $24

❏ **Deutz 6.95**, 1:32-scale, Siku, agrotron, No. 2958 *(Photo by Bossen Implement)*
EX $8 **NM** $14 **MIP** $22

❏ **Deutz D9005**, 1:32-scale, Siku, 2003, No. 3462
EX $8 **NM** $14 **MIP** $22

DEUTZ-ALLIS

BANKS 1:16-SCALE

❏ **Deutz-Allis Truck Bank**, 1:16-scale, Ertl, orange, 1990s, No. 2209
EX $6 **NM** $8 **MIP** $13

IMPLEMENTS 1:16-SCALE

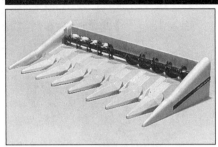

❑ **Deutz-Allis Corn Head**, 1:16-scale, Scale Models, green decals, only came w/Gleaner Combine, 1980s
EX npf   **NM** npf   **MIP** npf

❑ **Deutz-Allis Disc**, 1:16-scale, Ertl, green, folding wings, 1980s
EX $12   **NM** $22   **MIP** $32

❑ **Deutz-Allis Manure Spreader**, 1:16-scale, Ertl, green, 1980s, No. 2242
EX $12   **NM** $23   **MIP** $32

❑ **Deutz-Allis Minimum Tillage Plow**, 1:16-scale, Ertl, green, 1980s
EX $26   **NM** $53   **MIP** $82

❑ **Deutz-Allis Mixer Mill**, 1:16-scale, Ertl, green, 1980s
EX $16   **NM** $28   **MIP** $42

❑ **Deutz-Allis Wagon, Gravity**, 1:16-scale, Ertl, green, 1980s, No. 1270
EX $18   **NM** $26   **MIP** $37

IMPLEMENTS 1:24-SCALE

❑ **Deutz-Allis Gleaner, Combine**, 1:24-scale, Scale Models, w/Hawk decals, silver plated for Deutz-Allis T.A.P.S. Program, 1990s
EX $221   **NM** $265   **MIP** $319

❑ **Deutz-Allis Gleaner, Combine R6**, 1:24-scale, Scale Models, green decals, 1980s, No. 406
EX $32   **NM** $53   **MIP** $84

❑ **Deutz-Allis Gleaner, Combine R6**, 1:24-scale, Scale Models, green decals, 1980s, No. 406
EX $34   **NM** $56   **MIP** $89

IMPLEMENTS 1:32-SCALE

❑ **Deutz-Allis Combine, L3**, 1:32-scale, Ertl, green decals, 1980s, No. 1275
EX $23   **NM** $47   **MIP** $58

IMPLEMENTS 1:64-SCALE

❑ **Deutz-Allis Gleaner Combine, R50**, 1:64-scale, Ertl, green, No. 1284
EX $9   **NM** $16   **MIP** $24

❑ **Deutz-Allis Mixmill**, 1:64-scale, Ertl, green, No. 2208
EX $4   **NM** $6   **MIP** $12

❑ **Deutz-Allis Planter**, 1:64-scale, Ertl, Deutz-Allis Green, No. 2240
EX $4   **NM** $8   **MIP** $14

LAWN AND GARDEN 1:16-SCALE

❑ **Deutz-Allis**, 1:16-scale, Scale Models, No. 412
EX $9   **NM** $16   **MIP** $22

❑ **Deutz-Allis 1920 LGT**, 1:16-scale, Scale Models, green, 1980s, No. 412
EX $9   **NM** $16   **MIP** $22

PEDAL TRACTORS

❑ **Deutz-Allis 7085**, Ertl, 1990
EX $172   **NM** $233   **MIP** $362

❑ **Deutz-Allis 8070**, Ertl, orange, tractor in original condition
EX $198   **NM** $289   **MIP** $333

TRACTORS 1:128-SCALE

❑ **Deutz-Allis Micro's**, 1:128-scale, Ertl, green, w/tractor, wagon and disk, 1990s, No. 2221
EX $3   **NM** $6   **MIP** $8

TRACTORS 1:16-SCALE

❑ **Deutz-Allis 6240**, 1:16-scale, Ertl, green, w/ROPS, 1980s, No. 1269
EX $9   **NM** $17   **MIP** $27

❑ **Deutz-Allis 6240**, 1:16-scale, Ertl, Collector Edition, 1986, No. 1269DA
(Photo by Bossen Implement)
EX $11   **NM** $22   **MIP** $32

❑ **Deutz-Allis 6260**, 1:16-scale, Ertl, green, 1980s, No. 1261
EX $9   **NM** $17   **MIP** $27

❑ **Deutz-Allis 6260**, 1:16-scale, Ertl, Collector Edition, 1986, No. 1261DA
(Photo by Bossen Implement)
EX $11   **NM** $22   **MIP** $32

❑ **Deutz-Allis 8010**, 1:16-scale, Ertl, orange, FWA, 1980s, No. 1251
EX $22   **NM** $33   **MIP** $46

❑ **Deutz-Allis 8010**, 1:16-scale, Ertl, Collector Edition, 1985, No. 1251DA
EX $28   **NM** $38   **MIP** $56

❑ **Deutz-Allis 8030**, 1:16-scale, Ertl, orange, w/duals, 1980s, No. 1250
EX $22   **NM** $33   **MIP** $46

❑ **Deutz-Allis 8030**, 1:16-scale, Ertl, Collector Edition, 1985, No. 1250DA
EX $28   **NM** $38   **MIP** $56

❑ **Deutz-Allis 9150**, 1:16-scale, Ertl, green, FWA, 1980s, No. 1281
EX $16   **NM** $28   **MIP** $36

❑ **Deutz-Allis 9150**, 1:16-scale, Ertl, green, FWA, Collectors Edition, 1980s, No. 1281DA
EX $18   **NM** $29   **MIP** $42

❑ **Deutz-Allis 9150**, 1:16-scale, Ertl, green, Collectors Edition, 1980s, No. 1280DA
EX $18   **NM** $29   **MIP** $42

❑ **Deutz-Allis 9150**, 1:16-scale, Ertl, green, 1980s, No. 1281
EX $16   **NM** $28   **MIP** $36

❑ **Deutz-Allis 9150**, 1:16-scale, Ertl, orange, FWA, Collectors Edition, 1990s, No. 2227DA
EX $28   **NM** $34   **MIP** $49

❑ **Deutz-Allis 9150**, 1:16-scale, Ertl, orange and blue, Collectors Edition, 1990s, No. 2228DA
EX $28   **NM** $34   **MIP** $49

TRACTORS 1:32-SCALE

❑ **Deutz-Allis 4WD-305**, 1:32-scale, Ertl, orange, 1980s, No. 1276
EX $33   **NM** $48   **MIP** $77

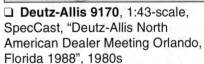
TRACTORS 1:43-SCALE

❑ **Deutz-Allis 9170**, 1:43-scale, SpecCast, "Deutz-Allis North American Dealer Meeting Orlando, Florida 1988", 1980s
EX $6   **NM** $9   **MIP** $14

❑ **Deutz-Allis 9170**, 1:43-scale, SpecCast, 1990s, No. DAC004
EX $5   **NM** $9   **MIP** $12

TRACTORS 1:64-SCALE

❑ **Deutz-Allis 6260**, 1:64-scale, Ertl, green, FWA, 1980s, No. 1241
EX $3   **NM** $4   **MIP** $6

❑ **Deutz-Allis 6260**, 1:64-scale, Ertl, green, FWA, 1980s, No. 2232
EX $3   **NM** $4   **MIP** $5

❑ **Deutz-Allis 6260**, 1:64-scale, Ertl, green, 1987 Farm Show Edition, 1987, No. 2232FA
EX $3   **NM** $4   **MIP** $6

❑ **Deutz-Allis 6265**, 1:64-scale, Scale Models, green, 1987 Louisvlle, 1980s
EX $3   **NM** $4   **MIP** $6

❑ **Deutz-Allis 6265**, 1:64-scale, Scale Models, green, 1980s
EX $3   **NM** $4   **MIP** $6

❑ **Deutz-Allis 6265**, 1:64-scale, Scale Models, green, 1980s
EX $3   **NM** $4   **MIP** $6

❑ **Deutz-Allis 6265**, 1:64-scale, Scale Models, green, 1980s
EX $3   **NM** $4   **MIP** $6

❑ **Deutz-Allis 6265**, 1:64-scale, Scale Models, chrome, Christmas 1986, 1986
EX $3 **NM** $4 **MIP** $6

❑ **Deutz-Allis 6275**, 1:64-scale, Scale Models, green, 1987 Louisville, 1987
EX $3 **NM** $4 **MIP** $6

❑ **Deutz-Allis 6275**, 1:64-scale, Scale Models, green, 1988 Minnesota State Fair, 1988
EX $3 **NM** $4 **MIP** $6

❑ **Deutz-Allis 6265**, 1:64-scale, Scale Models, green, 1987 Minnesota State Fair, 1987
EX $3 **NM** $4 **MIP** $6

❑ **Deutz-Allis 6275**, 1:64-scale, Scale Models, chrome, Christmas 1987, 1987
EX $3 **NM** $4 **MIP** $6

❑ **Deutz-Allis 6275**, 1:64-scale, Scale Models, chrome, Orlando 1988, 1988
EX $3 **NM** $16 **MIP** $22

❑ **Deutz-Allis 6265**, 1:64-scale, Scale Models, green, 1988 Minnesota State Fair, 1988
EX $3 **NM** $4 **MIP** $6

❑ **Deutz-Allis 6275**, 1:64-scale, Scale Models, green, 1987 Minnesota State Fair, 1987
EX $3 **NM** $4 **MIP** $6

❑ **Deutz-Allis 7085**, 1:64-scale, Ertl, green, 1980s, No. 1260
EX $3 **NM** $4 **MIP** $6

❑ **Deutz-Allis 6275**, 1:64-scale, Scale Models, green
EX $3 **NM** $4 **MIP** $6

❑ **Deutz-Allis 6275**, 1:64-scale, Scale Models, chrome, Christmas 1988, 1988
EX $3 **NM** $4 **MIP** $6

❑ **Deutz-Allis 7085**, 1:64-scale, Ertl, green, 1980s, No. 2234
EX $3 **NM** $4 **MIP** $6

❑ **Deutz-Allis 7085**, 1:64-scale, Ertl, green w/Loader, 1980s, No. 2233
EX $4   NM $6   MIP $6

❑ **Deutz-Allis 7085**, 1:64-scale, Ertl, green, 1988 Farm Show Edition, 1988, No. 2234FA
EX $3   NM $4   MIP $6

❑ **Deutz-Allis 8030**, 1:64-scale, Ertl, orange, 1980s, No. 1259
EX $3   NM $6   MIP $14

❑ **Deutz-Allis 8030**, 1:64-scale, Ertl, orange, duals, 1980s, No. 1259
EX $3   NM $6   MIP $14

❑ **Deutz-Allis 8070**, 1:64-scale, Ertl, orange, no model numbers, 1980s, No. 1277
EX $3   NM $6   MIP $9

❑ **Deutz-Allis 8070**, 1:64-scale, Ertl, orange w/Loader, 1980s, No. 1226
EX $4   NM $6   MIP $9

❑ **Deutz-Allis 8070**, 1:64-scale, Ertl, orange, w/model numbers, 1980s, No. 1277
EX $3   NM $6   MIP $9

TRUCKS 1:43-SCALE

❑ **Deutz-Allis Ford Van**, 1:43-scale, SpecCast, 1990s
EX $4   NM $9   MIP $12

DRESSER

CONSTRUCTION EQUIPMENT 1:50-SCALE

❑ **Dresser Pay Loader**, 1:50-scale, Conrad, brown and white, 1980s
EX $78   NM $106   MIP $133

CONSTRUCTION EQUIPMENT 1:64-SCALE

❑ **Dresser Crawler w/blade, TD-20E**, 1:64-scale, Ertl, dark yellow, 1980s, No. 1851
EX $9   NM $16   MIP $26

❑ **Dresser Pay Loader, 560B**, 1:64-scale, Ertl, dark yellow, 1980s, No. 1852
EX $9   NM $16   MIP $26

❑ **Dresser Pay Loader, 560B**, 1:64-scale, Ertl, brown, 1980s, No. 1852
EX $9   NM $16   MIP $26

❏ **Dresser Scraper, 412B**, 1:64-scale, Ertl, dark yellow, 1980s, No. 1855
EX $9   **NM** $16   **MIP** $26

FARM SERVICE (FS)

IMPLEMENTS 1:64-SCALE

❏ **FS Anhydrous Tank**, 1:64-scale, Ertl, white and gray, 1980s, No. 9241
EX $4   **NM** $6   **MIP** $8

❏ **FS Fertilizer Spreader**, 1:64-scale, Ertl, gray and white, 1980s
EX $4   **NM** $6   **MIP** $9

❏ **FS Grain Auger**, 1:64-scale, Ertl, white and gray, plastic tires, 1980s, No. 9182
EX $4   **NM** $6   **MIP** $8

❏ **FS Mixmill**, 1:64-scale, Ertl, white, 1980s, No. 9242
EX $4   **NM** $6   **MIP** $12

❏ **FS Sprayer**, 1:64-scale, Ertl, white and gray, 1980s, No. 9243
EX $4   **NM** $6   **MIP** $9

❏ **FS Wagon, Gravity**, 1:64-scale, Ertl, white, 1980s
EX $6   **NM** $12   **MIP** $18

FARMTOY

TRACTORS 1:16-SCALE

❏ **Farmall 806**, 1:16-scale, Scale Models, red, Lafayette Farm Toy Show, Farm Toy decals, 1980s
EX $18   **NM** $33   **MIP** $58

❏ **Farmall 806**, 1:16-scale, Scale Models, red, Gateway Mid-America Toy Show, Farm Toy decals, 1980s
EX $18   **NM** $33   **MIP** $58

FERGUSON

IMPLEMENTS 1:12-SCALE

❏ **Ferguson Plow**, 1:12-scale, Topping, gray, plow fits Ferguson 30 tractor by Topping, 1950s
EX $147   **NM** $263   **MIP** $521

TRACTORS 1:12-SCALE

❏ **Ferguson**, 1:12-scale, Advanced, gray, 1950s
EX $122   **NM** $271   **MIP** $493

❏ **Ferguson TO-30**, 1:12-scale, Topping, gray, 1950s
EX $225   **NM** $526   **MIP** $988

TRACTORS 1:16-SCALE

❑ **Ferguson 30**, 1:16-scale, SpecCast, green, 1990s, No. SCT-2708 *(Photo by Bossen Implement)*
EX $22   **NM** $32   **MIP** $48

❑ **Ferguson 30**, 1:16-scale, SpecCast, gray, 1993, No. SCT-137
(Photo by Bossen Implement)
EX $21   **NM** $28   **MIP** $42

❑ **Ferguson TO-20**, 1:16-scale, NBTK, 1000 units producted, 1988
(Photo by Bossen Implement)
EX $58   **NM** $73   **MIP** $108

❑ **Ferguson TO-20**, 1:16-scale, Scale Models, '93 Farm Progress Show Edition, 1993, No. FB-1616
EX $22   **NM** $37   **MIP** $58

❑ **Ferguson TO-20**, 1:16-scale, Scale Models, no 3 point, no exhaust, also stock #230, 1994, No. 806 *(Photo by Bossen Implement)*
EX $9   **NM** $17   **MIP** $27

❑ **Ferguson TO-30**, 1:16-scale, Chad Valley, gray, 1950s
EX $258   **NM** $542   **MIP** $1092

TRACTORS 1:20-SCALE

❑ **Ferguson**, 1:20-scale, Triton, gray, 1960s
EX npf   **NM** npf   **MIP** npf

TRACTORS 1:32-SCALE

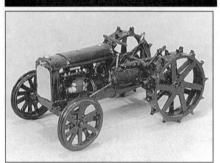

❑ **Ferguson Black**, 1:32-scale, Browns Models, model kit, 1980s
EX $56   **NM** $198   **MIP** $253

❑ **Ferguson Brown**, 1:32-scale, Browns Models, model kit, 1980s
EX $22   **NM** $37   **MIP** $68

❑ **Ferguson Brown**, 1:32-scale, Browns Models, model kit, 1980s
EX $22   **NM** $37   **MIP** $68

TRACTORS 1:35-SCALE

❑ **Ferguson**, 1:35-scale, Conrad, gray, 1980s
EX $63   **NM** $94   **MIP** $148

TRACTORS 1:43-SCALE

❑ **Ferguson**, 1:43-scale, Replica, gray, 1980s
EX npf   **NM** npf   **MIP** npf

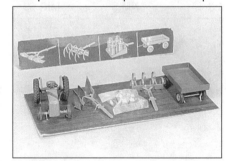

❑ **Ferguson**, 1:43-scale, Tekno, gray, 1950s
EX $188   **NM** $269   **MIP** $437

Photos by Jon Jacobson unless otherwise noted.

TRACTORS 1:64-SCALE

❑ **Ferguson TO-20**, 1:64-scale, Scale Models, 1995, No. FT-0809

(Photo by Scale Models)
EX $4   **NM** $6   **MIP** $9

FIAT

TRACTORS 1:16-SCALE

❑ **Fiat 44-23**, 1:16-scale, Scale Models, orange, black and cream, 1980s
EX $148   **NM** $238   **MIP** $323

❑ **Fiat F-110**, 1:16-scale, Scale Models, '94 Farm Progress Show Edition, 1993, No. FB-2382
EX $22   **NM** $32   **MIP** $48

❑ **Fiat F-110**, 1:16-scale, Scale Models, brown, 1994, No. FD-1635

(Photo by Bossen Implement)
EX $22   **NM** $32   **MIP** $48

❑ **Fiat F-130**, 1:16-scale, Scale Models, brown, 1994, No. FD-1637

(Photo by Bossen Implement)
EX $22   **NM** $32   **MIP** $48

❑ **Fiat G-240**, 1:16-scale, SpecCast, MFD, 1994, No. 9624711
EX $22   **NM** $32   **MIP** $53

TRACTORS 1:32-SCALE

❑ **Fiat G-240**, 1:32-scale, Ertl, MFD, w/loader, No. 327
EX $11   **NM** $18   **MIP** $27

❑ **Fiat G-240**, 1:32-scale, Ertl, MFD, No. 324
EX $9   **NM** $17   **MIP** $22

❑ **Fiat L-85**, 1:32-scale, Ertl, MFD, 1999, No. 9489
EX $4   **NM** $8   **MIP** $12

❑ **Fiat M-160**, 1:32-scale, Ertl, MFD, 1999, No. 9490
EX $4   **NM** $8   **MIP** $12

TRACTORS 1:43-SCALE

❑ **Fiat M-115**, 1:43-scale, Ertl, 1997 LCN Show Edition, 1997, No. 3050YR *(Photo by Kate Bossen)*
EX $8   **NM** $19   **MIP** $28

FIAT-ALLIS

CONSTRUCTION EQUIPMENT 1:16-SCALE

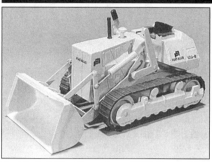

❑ **Fiat-Allis Crawler, 12G-B**, 1:16-scale, Ertl, yellow, 1970s
EX $104   **NM** $219   **MIP** $387

CONSTRUCTION EQUIPMENT 1:24-SCALE

❑ **Fiat-Allis Crawler, FL 10B**, 1:24-scale, Mini Auto, yellow, also one w/just Fiat grille decal and FL 10, 1970s
EX $30   **NM** $50   **MIP** $65

CONSTRUCTION EQUIPMENT 1:50-SCALE

❑ **Fiat-Allis Crawler, 41-B**, 1:50-scale, Conrad, first orange then brown, 1980s
EX $150   **NM** $195   **MIP** $250

❑ **Fiat-Allis Crawler, F 20**, 1:50-scale, Old Car, military color, plastic individual link track, 1980s
EX $30   **NM** $50   **MIP** $65

❑ **Fiat-Allis Crawler, FL 20**, 1:50-scale, Old Car, fire brigade red, plastic individual link track, 1980s
EX $30   **NM** $50   **MIP** $65

❑ **Fiat-Allis Crawler, FL 20**, 1:50-scale, Old Car, yellow, also ROPS instead of cab, plastic individual link track, 1980s
EX $30   **NM** $50   **MIP** $65

❑ **Fiat-Allis Crawler, FL20**, 1:50-scale, Old Car, yellow, steel, plastic or rubber tracks, 1980s
EX $30   **NM** $50   **MIP** $65

❑ **Fiat-Allis Loader, FR 20**, 1:50-scale, Old Car, military color, 1980s
EX $30   **NM** $50   **MIP** $65

❑ **Fiat-Allis Loader, FR 20**, 1:50-scale, Old Car, red or yellow, 1980s
EX $30   **NM** $50   **MIP** $65

❑ **Fiat-Allis Log Loader, FR 20**, 1:50-scale, Old Car, yellow, 1980s
EX $30   **NM** $50   **MIP** $65

CONSTRUCTION EQUIPMENT

❑ **Fiat-Allis Excavator, FE 40**, Old Car, yellow, rubber tracks or individual plastic link track, 1980s
EX $30   **NM** $50   **MIP** $65

TRUCKS 1:16-SCALE

❑ **Pickup**, 1:16-scale, Nylint, white, 1980s
EX $8   **NM** $16   **MIP** $23

TRUCKS 1:43-SCALE

❑ **Fiat-Allis Van**, 1:43-scale, Old Car, white w/brown strip, 1980s
EX $9   **NM** $19   **MIP** $29

❑ **Fiat-Allis Van**, 1:43-scale, Old Car, orange, 1980s
EX $9   **NM** $19   **MIP** $29

TRUCKS 1:50-SCALE

❑ **Iveco Semi w/FL 20 Crawler**, 1:50-scale, Old Car, all red, blue or military color, 1980s
EX $60   **NM** $90   **MIP** $120

❑ **Iveco Semi w/FL 20 Crawler**, 1:50-scale, Old Car, all white or white semi w/brown FL 20 loader, 1980s
EX $60   **NM** $90   **MIP** $120

❑ **Iveco Semi w/FR 20 Loader**, 1:50-scale, Old Car, white cab w/brown trailer, FR 20 Loader. Also white, red, blue or military color, 1980s
EX $60   **NM** $90   **MIP** $120

❑ **Iveco-Fiat-Allis Semi**, 1:50-scale, Old Car, white, 1980s
EX $29   **NM** $49   **MIP** $64

FORD

BANKS 1:25-SCALE

❑ **Ford Runabout Bank**, 1:25-scale, Ertl, white and blue, 1980s, No. 870
EX $4   **NM** $12   **MIP** $18

❑ **Ford Truck Bank**, 1:25-scale, Ertl, No. 813 *(Photo by Ertl)*
EX $4   **NM** $12   **MIP** $18

❑ **Ford Truck Bank**, 1:25-scale, Ertl, white and blue, 1980s, No. 865
EX $4   **NM** $12   **MIP** $18

CONSTRUCTION EQUIPMENT 1:12-SCALE

❑ **Ford Backhoe, 750**, 1:12-scale, Ertl, yellow, 1970s, No. 820
EX $38   **NM** $79   **MIP** $119

❑ **Ford Backhoe, 755 A**, 1:12-scale, Ertl, yellow, 1980s, No. 820
EX $36   **NM** $77   **MIP** $117

CONSTRUCTION EQUIPMENT 1:16-SCALE

❑ **Ford Fork Lift, 4000**, 1:16-scale, Cragstan, yellow, 1970s
EX $78   **NM** $163   **MIP** $337

❑ **Ford Loader and Backhoe**, 1:16-scale, Cragstan, red, remote control, 1970s
EX $177   **NM** $223   **MIP** $389

❑ **Ford Skid Loader, CL-25**, 1:16-scale, Ertl, yellow, 1980s, No. 840
EX $16   **NM** $29   **MIP** $48

CONSTRUCTION EQUIPMENT 1:32-SCALE

❑ **Ford Backhoe, 555**, 1:32-scale, Ertl, yellow, 1980s, No. 1456
EX $8   **NM** $13   **MIP** $18

❑ **Ford Backhoe, 555 A**, 1:32-scale, Ertl, yellow, 1980s, No. 1456
EX $7   **NM** $12   **MIP** $16

❑ **Ford Tractors 5000**, 1:32-scale, Corgi, yellow, 1970s
EX $17   **NM** $27   **MIP** $37

CONSTRUCTION EQUIPMENT 1:35-SCALE

❑ **Ford Backhoe**, 1:35-scale, NZG, yellow, w/Loader, 1970s, No. 130
EX $76   **NM** $128   **MIP** $177

❑ **Ford Backhoe**, 1:35-scale, NZG, yellow, w/Loader, 1980s, No. 161
EX $76   **NM** $128   **MIP** $177

CONSTRUCTION EQUIPMENT 1:64-SCALE

❑ **Ford Backhoe**, 1:64-scale, Ertl, industrial yellow, No. 885
EX $6   **NM** $8   **MIP** $12

❑ **Ford Backhoe, 555 B**, 1:64-scale, Ertl, yellow body & cab, 1989, No. 885
EX $4   **NM** $6   **MIP** $8

❑ **Ford Tractor, 4000**, 1:64-scale, Ertl, yellow, 1999, No. 13506
EX $3   **NM** $4   **MIP** $6

IMPLEMENTS 1:08-SCALE

❑ **Ford Dearborn Flare Box Wagon**, 1:08-scale, Scale Models, 1997, No. 404 *(Photo by Scale Models)*
EX $23   **NM** $47   **MIP** $77

IMPLEMENTS 1:12-SCALE

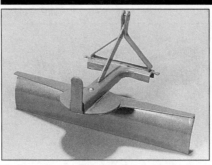

❑ **Dearborn Blade, Rear Mount**, 1:12-scale, Hubley, red, attachment for 507, 1960-61, No. 758
EX $122   **NM** $211   **MIP** $396

❑ **Dearborn Plow**, 1:12-scale, Hubley, red, 1950s
EX $86   **NM** $128   **MIP** $254

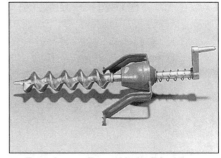

❑ **Dearborn Post Hole Digger**, 1:12-scale, Hubley, red, attachment for 507, 1960-61, No. 757
EX $96   **NM** $188   **MIP** $343

❑ **Ford Wagon, Barge**, 1:12-scale, Ertl, blue, 1980s, No. 806
EX $14   **NM** $42   **MIP** $73

IMPLEMENTS 1:16-SCALE

❑ **Ford Chisel Plow**, 1:16-scale, Ertl, blue, 1980s, No. 838
EX $36   **NM** $62   **MIP** $73

❏ **Ford Disc**, 1:16-scale, Ertl, blue, 1980s, No. 824
EX $8   **NM** $17   **MIP** $38

❏ **Ford Spreader**, 1:16-scale, Ertl, blue, 1980s, No. 822
EX $7   **NM** $22   **MIP** $39

❏ **Ford Wagon, Gravity**, 1:16-scale, Ertl, blue, 1980s, No. 827
EX $12   **NM** $34   **MIP** $58

IMPLEMENTS 1:32-SCALE

❏ **Ford Implement Set**, 1:16-scale, Scale Models, three-piece, No. 327

(Photo by Scale Models)

EX n/a   **NM** n/a   **MIP** $17

❏ **Ford Wagon, Bale**, 1:16-scale, Ertl, blue, 1980s, No. 809
EX $8   **NM** $22   **MIP** $28

❏ **Ford Chisel Plow**, 1:32-scale, Ertl, blue, 1980s
EX $8   **NM** $16   **MIP** $26

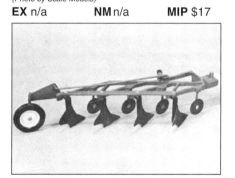

❏ **Ford Plow**, 1:16-scale, Ertl, blue, 1970s
EX $12   **NM** $27   **MIP** $46

❏ **Ford Wagon, Flare Box**, 1:16-scale, Ertl, blue, 1970s
EX $12   **NM** $18   **MIP** $49

❏ **Ford Disc**, 1:32-scale, Ertl, blue, 1980s
EX $4   **NM** $12   **MIP** $18

❏ **Ford Plow**, 1:16-scale, Ertl, blue, 1980s
EX $8   **NM** $22   **MIP** $36

❏ **Ford Wagon, Flare Box**, 1:16-scale, Ertl, blue, 1980s
EX $6   **NM** $12   **MIP** $24

❏ **Ford Plow**, 1:32-scale, Ertl, blue, 1980s
EX $3   **NM** $7   **MIP** $14

❑ **Ford Wagon, Barge**, 1:32-scale, Ertl, blue, 1980s
EX $4   **NM** $8   **MIP** $12

LAWN AND GARDEN 1:12-SCALE

❑ **Ford LGT 12**, 1:12-scale, Ertl, blue and white, also available in a collectors series, 1980s, No. 808
EX $13   **NM** $27   **MIP** $42

❑ **Ford LGT 145**, 1:12-scale, Ertl, blue, w/or w/o hydrostat decal, 1970s, No. 814
EX $14   **NM** $48   **MIP** $67

LAWN AND GARDEN 1:16-SCALE

❑ **Ford 18H**, 1:16-scale, Scale Models, 1992, No. JLE323
EX $9   **NM** $14   **MIP** $22

❑ **Ford GT 95**, 1:16-scale, Scale Models, w/mower deck, No. 370
(Photo by Scale Models)
EX $9   **NM** $14   **MIP** $22

PEDAL TRACTORS

❑ **Ford 6000**, Ertl, blue and gray, early-style grille and decal, tractor in original condition, 1964, No. Commander
EX $1952   **NM** $2492   **MIP** n/a

❑ **Ford 6000**, Ertl, blue and gray, later-style grille and decal, tractor in original condition, 1966, No. Commander
EX $952   **NM** $1492   **MIP** n/a

❑ **Ford 7740**, Ertl, 1990s, No. 344
EX $78   **NM** $132   **MIP** $243

❑ **Ford 8000**, Ertl, blue, tractor in original condition, 1969, No. 810
EX $269   **NM** $389   **MIP** $498

❑ **Ford 8630**, Scale Models, 1990
EX $78   **NM** $132   **MIP** $193

❑ **Ford 8730**, Scale Models, 1990s, No. JLE235
EX $78   **NM** $122   **MIP** $193

❑ **Ford 8N**, Scale Models, red and gray fenders, 2001, No. JLE461
EX $78   **NM** $112   **MIP** $168

❑ **Ford 900**, Graphic Reproductions, red and gray, stamped steel fenders, available w/two or three bolt axle mounting bracket, original tractor restored, 1954
EX $2247   **NM** $3429   **MIP** n/a

❑ **Ford 901**, Graphic Reproductions, red and gray, die-cast fenders, bar grille, original tractor restored, 1958
EX $333   **NM** $4178   **MIP** n/a

❑ **Ford Trailer**, Graphic Reproductions, red w/white Ford covered wagon canopy, made for use w/the 900 Ford pedal tractors, trailer and canopy in original condition
EX $448   **NM** $868   **MIP** $1389

❑ **Ford TW-20**, Ertl, blue, tractor in original condition, 1980, No. 810
EX $98   **NM** $289   **MIP** $343

❏ **Ford TW-35**, Scale Models, blue, tractor in original condition, 2003, No. 487
EX $98 **NM** $152 **MIP** $189

❏ **Ford TW-5**, Ertl, blue, w/dark TW-5 decal and red trim, tractor in original condition
EX $112 **NM** $189 **MIP** $343

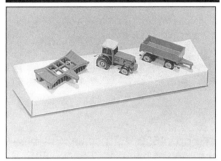

❏ **Ford TW-5**, Ertl, blue, w/light blue TW-5 decal, tractor in original condition
EX $112 **NM** $189 **MIP** $343

TRACTORS 1:08-SCALE

❏ **Ford 4000**, 1:08-scale, Scale Models, 2000, No. JLE433
EX $78 **NM** $102 **MIP** $153

❏ **Ford 8N**, 1:08-scale, Scale Models, 1997, No. JLE407
EX $78 **NM** $102 **MIP** $153

TRACTORS 1:128-SCALE

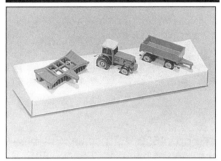

❏ **Ford Micros**, 1:128-scale, Ertl, blue, w/tractor, wagon and disk, 1990s, No. 874
EX $3 **NM** $6 **MIP** $12

TRACTORS 1:12-SCALE

❏ **Ford 2000**, 1:12-scale, Scale Models, blue, Show Tractor 1986
EX $18 **NM** $27 **MIP** $33

❏ **Ford 4000**, 1:12-scale, Ertl, blue,split grille, 1960s, No. 805
EX $74 **NM** $144 **MIP** $259

❏ **Ford 4000**, 1:12-scale, Ertl, blue, 1970s, No. 805
EX $24 **NM** $54 **MIP** $94

❏ **Ford 4000**, 1:12-scale, Hubley, gray and red, 1960s, No. 1506
EX $63 **NM** $134 **MIP** $248

❏ **Ford 4000**, 1:12-scale, Hubley, gray and red, 1960s, No. 1506
EX $68 **NM** $134 **MIP** $248

❏ **Ford 4000**, 1:12-scale, Hubley, gray and blue, NF, 1963, No. 1507
EX $87 **NM** $166 **MIP** $339

❏ **Ford 4000**, 1:12-scale, Hubley, gray and blue, WF, 1964, No. 1508
EX $89 **NM** $168 **MIP** $349

❏ **Ford 4000**, 1:12-scale, Scale Models, NF, No. FH-411

(Photo by Scale Models)

EX $18   **NM** $21   **MIP** $29

❏ **Ford 4000**, 1:12-scale, Scale Models, same as 389, No. FF-0249

(Photo by Scale Models)

EX $18   **NM** $21   **MIP** $29

❏ **Ford 4400**, 1:12-scale, Ertl, yellow and blue, 1970s, No. 812

EX $59   **NM** $129   **MIP** $264

❏ **Ford 4600**, 1:12-scale, Ertl, blue, 1970s, No. 805

EX $16   **NM** $37   **MIP** $63

❏ **Ford 4600**, 1:12-scale, Ertl, blue, three-point hitch, 1970s, No. 805

EX $18   **NM** $39   **MIP** $68

❏ **Ford 600**, 1:12-scale, Product Miniature, gray and red, 1950s

EX $148   **NM** $333   **MIP** $659

❏ **Ford 6000**, 1:12-scale, Hubley, gray and blue, Commander, w/stacks, 1960s, No. 1509

EX $69   **NM** $117   **MIP** $237

❏ **Ford 6000**, 1:12-scale, Hubley, gray and blue, metal exhaust, Diesel, 1960s, No. 509

EX $129   **NM** $242   **MIP** $494

❏ **Ford 6000**, 1:12-scale, Hubley, gray and red, metal exhaust, Diesel, functional steering, 12" long, 1962-65, No. 509

EX $149   **NM** $276   **MIP** $519

❏ **Ford 6000**, 1:12-scale, Hubley, gray and blue, Commander, w/o stacks, 1970s

EX $49   **NM** $86   **MIP** $143

❏ **Ford 7700**, 1:12-scale, Ertl, blue, 1970s, No. 819

EX $46   **NM** $89   **MIP** $156

❏ **Ford 8000**, 1:12-scale, Ertl, blue, w/small Ford 8000 decal, 1970s

EX $42   **NM** $147   **MIP** $289

❑ **Ford 8000**, 1:12-scale, Ertl, blue, 1970s
EX $38   **NM** $76   **MIP** $143

❑ **Ford 8000**, 1:12-scale, Ertl, blue, 1970s
EX $38   **NM** $76   **MIP** $143

❑ **Ford 8600**, 1:12-scale, Ertl, blue, 1970s, No. 800
EX $37   **NM** $59   **MIP** $113

❑ **Ford 8600**, 1:12-scale, Ertl, blue, all white rear rim, 1970s, No. 800
EX $36   **NM** $57   **MIP** $133

❑ **Ford 8N**, 1:12-scale, AMT/MPC, gray and red, also w/windup clock work, 1950s
EX $116   **NM** $218   **MIP** $388

❑ **Ford 8N**, 1:12-scale, Product Miniature, gray and red, 1950s
EX $98   **NM** $122   **MIP** $289

❑ **Ford 900**, 1:12-scale, Hubley, gray and red, 1950s
EX $48   **NM** $123   **MIP** $268

❑ **Ford 900**, 1:12-scale, Product Miniature, gray and red, 1950s
EX $244   **NM** $543   **MIP** $1159

❑ **Ford 901**, 1:12-scale, Scale Models, Powermaster, red and gray, 9th Annual Show Tractor, w/wide front end, 1980s
EX $18   **NM** $27   **MIP** $33

❑ **Ford 9600**, 1:12-scale, Ertl, blue, 1970s
EX $69   **NM** $126   **MIP** $233

❑ **Ford 961**, 1:12-scale, Hubley, gray and red, Powermaster, functional steering, 10-1/2" long, 1958-61, No. 507
EX $116   **NM** $203   **MIP** $436

❑ **Ford 961**, 1:12-scale, Hubley, gray and red, Select-O-Speed, 1960s, No. 508
EX $112   **NM** $198   **MIP** $372

❏ **Ford 961**, 1:12-scale, Hubley, gray and red, Select-O-Speed, 1960s, No. 508
EX $112   **NM** $198   **MIP** $372

❏ **Ford 9700**, 1:12-scale, Ertl, blue, 1970s, No. 818
EX $46   **NM** $84   **MIP** $146

❏ **Ford NAA**, 1:12-scale, Franklin Mint, Gold Jubliee, 2000
EX $53   **NM** $78   **MIP** $133

❏ **Ford NAA**, 1:12-scale, Product Miniature, gray and red, 1950s
EX $123   **NM** $258   **MIP** $524

❏ **Ford TW-10**, 1:12-scale, Ertl, blue, 1980s, No. 819
EX $34   **NM** $58   **MIP** $97

❏ **Ford TW-15**, 1:12-scale, Ertl, blue, red decals, 1980s
EX $33   **NM** $57   **MIP** $73

❏ **Ford TW-15**, 1:12-scale, Ertl, blue, white decals, 1980s, No. 818
EX $33   **NM** $57   **MIP** $93

❏ **Ford TW-20**, 1:12-scale, Ertl, blue, 1980s, No. 818
EX $34   **NM** $58   **MIP** $86

❏ **Ford TW-25**, 1:12-scale, Ertl, blue, 1980s, No. 819
EX $29   **NM** $52   **MIP** $83

❏ **Ford TW-35**, 1:12-scale, Ertl, blue, 1980s, No. 818
EX $33   **NM** $57   **MIP** $84

❏ **Ford TW-5**, 1:12-scale, Ertl, blue, 1980s, No. 848
EX $29   **NM** $52   **MIP** $83

❏ **Ford TW-5**, 1:12-scale, Ertl, blue, 1980s, No. 819
EX $29   **NM** $52   **MIP** $83

❏ **Ford TW-5**, 1:12-scale, Ertl, blue, 1980s, No. 847
EX $29   **NM** $52   **MIP** $83

TRACTORS 1:16-SCALE

❏ **Ford**, 1:16-scale, Chrome loader, plastic wheels and tires, toy mfr. not known, 1980s
EX npf   **NM** npf   **MIP** npf

❏ **Ford**, 1:16-scale, Strike, blue, stripe, made in Republic of South Africa, 1980s
EX $17   **NM** $36   **MIP** $48

❏ **Ford 1156**, 1:16-scale, Scale Models, blue and white, 1991, No. FH-302
EX $76   **NM** $98   **MIP** $159

❏ **Ford 1710**, 1:16-scale, Ertl, blue, Collectors Edition, 1980s, No. 831TA
EX $9   **NM** $23   **MIP** $44

❏ **Ford 1710**, 1:16-scale, Ertl, blue, 1980s, No. 831
EX $8   **NM** $16   **MIP** $37

❏ **Ford 1920**, 1:16-scale, Scale Models, blue and gray, w/plow, 1980s, No. 307
EX $12   **NM** $17   **MIP** $26

❏ **Ford 1920**, 1:16-scale, Scale Models, MFD w/ROPS, 1980s, No. FF-0118 *(Photo by Scale Models)*
EX $14   **NM** $19   **MIP** $26

❏ **Ford 1920**, 1:16-scale, Scale Models, blue and gray, 1980s, No. FH-118
EX $13   **NM** $18   **MIP** $26

❏ **Ford 2N**, 1:16-scale, Ertl, Precision Series, gray, 1995, No. 354 *(Photo by Ertl)*
EX $62   **NM** $109   **MIP** $157

❏ **Ford 4630**, 1:16-scale, Scale Models, same as 225, 1990s, No. FF-0220 *(Photo by Scale Models)*
EX $8   **NM** $11   **MIP** $19

❏ **Ford 4630**, 1:16-scale, Scale Models, 1994, No. 371 *(Photo by Scale Models)*
EX $8   **NM** $13   **MIP** $23

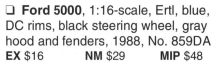

❏ **Ford 5000**, 1:16-scale, Ertl, blue, DC rims, black steering wheel, gray hood and fenders, 1988, No. 859DA
EX $16   **NM** $29   **MIP** $48

❏ **Ford 5000**, 1:16-scale, Ertl, gray and blue, Collectors Edition, Super Major, 1990s, No. 307DA
EX $23   **NM** $36   **MIP** $46

❏ **Ford 5000**, 1:16-scale, Ertl, #7 Precision Series, 2000, No. 13503
EX $76   **NM** $118   **MIP** $223

❏ **Ford 5640**, 1:16-scale, Ertl, Collector Edition, 1994, No. 329TA
EX $16   **NM** $28   **MIP** $43

❏ **Ford 621**, 1:16-scale, Ertl, workmaster, red, 1999, No. 13529
EX $14   **NM** $22   **MIP** $33

❏ **Ford 640**, 1:16-scale, Ertl, 1999, No. 3054
EX $14   **NM** $22   **MIP** $33

❏ **Ford 640**, 1:16-scale, Ertl, #8 Precision Series, 2002, No. 13574
EX $67   **NM** $82   **MIP** $118

❏ **Ford 641**, 1:16-scale, Ertl, '98 Toy Tractor Times Anniversary, #13; 1,300 produced, 1998, No. 16036

(Photo by Bossen Implement)

EX $16   **NM** $28   **MIP** $48

❏ **Ford 641**, 1:16-scale, Ertl, w/725 loader, #6 Precision Series, 1999, No. 383
EX $82   **NM** $102   **MIP** $147

❏ **Ford 6640**, 1:16-scale, Ertl, MFD, 1992, No. 873 *(Photo by Ertl)*
EX $23   **NM** $32   **MIP** $41

❏ **Ford 7710**, 1:16-scale, Ertl, blue, red decal, 1980s, No. 849
EX $18   **NM** $28   **MIP** $44

❏ **Ford 7710**, 1:16-scale, Ertl, blue, also available in a collectors series, white decal, 1980s, No. 836
EX $19   **NM** $29   **MIP** $44

❏ **Ford 7710**, 1:16-scale, Ertl, blue, 1983 National Farm Toy Show Tractor, 1983, No. 1522
EX $197   **NM** $237   **MIP** $358

❏ **Ford 7740**, 1:16-scale, Ertl, Collector Edition, 1992, No. 873DA
EX $22   **NM** $33   **MIP** $47

❏ **Ford 7740**, 1:16-scale, Ertl, 1994, No. 329
EX $17   **NM** $28   **MIP** $43

❏ **Ford 7740**, 1:16-scale, Ertl, w/hay wagon, 1995, No. 3027 *(Photo by Ertl)*
EX $21   **NM** $32   **MIP** $46

❏ **Ford 7840**, 1:16-scale, Ertl, Collector Edition, 1994, No. 338TA
EX $22   **NM** $33   **MIP** $47

❏ **Ford 8240**, 1:16-scale, Ertl, 1993, No. 877 *(Photo by Ertl)*
EX $23   **NM** $32   **MIP** $41

❏ **Ford 8340**, 1:16-scale, Ertl, Collector Edition, 1993, No. 877DA
EX $21   **NM** $33   **MIP** $47

❏ **Ford 8340**, 1:16-scale, Ertl, ROPS, 1994, No. 338
EX $23   **NM** $32   **MIP** $41

❏ **Ford 846**, 1:16-scale, Scale Models, duals, 4WD w/duals, 1992, No. 356 *(Photo by Scale Models)*
EX $48   **NM** $67   **MIP** $117

❏ **Ford 8670**, 1:16-scale, SpecCast, 1990s, No. 9624883
EX $24   **NM** $33   **MIP** $58

❏ **Ford 8730**, 1:16-scale, Scale Models, same as FH-315, 1990s, No. JLE315 *(Photo by Scale Models)*
EX $18   **NM** $24   **MIP** $36

❑ **Ford 8730**, 1:16-scale, Scale Models, blue and white, w/duals, 1990s, No. FH-315
EX $22   **NM** $31   **MIP** $38

❑ **Ford 8730**, 1:16-scale, Scale Models, blue and white, 1990s, No. FH-214
EX $21   **NM** $29   **MIP** $36

❑ **Ford 8770**, 1:16-scale, SpecCast, singles, 1996, No. 962483
EX $24   **NM** $33   **MIP** $52

❑ **Ford 8770**, 1:16-scale, SpecCast, duals, 1996, No. 962484
EX $24   **NM** $33   **MIP** $52

❑ **Ford 8830**, 1:16-scale, Scale Models, MFD, 1991, No. FH-343
EX $17   **NM** $28   **MIP** $43

❑ **Ford 8830**, 1:16-scale, Scale Models, w/cab, 1992, No. FH-314
EX $17   **NM** $28   **MIP** $43

❑ **Ford 8830**, 1:16-scale, Scale Models, w/cab with windows, 1994, No. FH-353
EX $22   **NM** $34   **MIP** $46

❑ **Ford 8830**, 1:16-scale, Scale Models, MFD, 1996, No. 353
(Photo by Scale Models)
EX $22   **NM** $34   **MIP** $46

❑ **Ford 8870**, 1:16-scale, SpecCast, MFD, "End of an Era", 1996, No. 9673563
EX $24   **NM** $33   **MIP** $63

❑ **Ford 8970**, 1:16-scale, SpecCast, MFD, duals, Collector Edition, 1994, No. 9624710
EX $24   **NM** $33   **MIP** $52

❑ **Ford 8N**, 1:16-scale, Ertl, gray and red, w/plow, 1980s, No. 841
EX $18   **NM** $33   **MIP** $43

❑ **Ford 8N**, 1:16-scale, Ertl, gray and red, Collectors Edition, 1980s, No. 841DA
EX $30   **NM** $52   **MIP** $68

❑ **Ford 8N**, 1:16-scale, Ertl, 1984, No. 843 *(Photo by Ertl)*
EX $8   **NM** $14   **MIP** $22

❑ **Ford 8N**, 1:16-scale, Ertl, w/wagon set, 1990s, No. 309 *(Photo by Kate Bossen)*
EX $14   **NM** $22   **MIP** $28

❑ **Ford 8N**, 1:16-scale, Ertl, Precision Series #3, 1996, No. 362
(Photo by Ertl)
EX $126   **NM** $177   **MIP** $243

❑ **Ford 8N**, 1:16-scale, Ertl, w/canopy and plow, 1998, No. 3346DA
EX $16   **NM** $28   **MIP** $47

❑ **Ford 8N**, 1:16-scale, SpecCast, on plaque "Best of Show", 2001, No. 1001
EX $18   **NM** $26   **MIP** $43

❑ **Ford 901**, 1:16-scale, Ertl, Powermaster, gold plated, National Toy Show Tractor "1986", No. 424PA
EX $126   **NM** $178   **MIP** $378

❑ **Ford 901**, 1:16-scale, Ertl, gray and red, Select-O-Speed, 1980s, No. 868
EX $17   **NM** $26   **MIP** $37

❑ **Ford 901**, 1:16-scale, Ertl, red and gray, Select-O-Speed, Collectors Edition, 1980s, No. 868TA
EX $18   **NM** $27   **MIP** $39

❑ **Ford 901**, 1:16-scale, Ertl, Powermaster, gray and red, 1986 National Farm Toy Show Tractor, 1986, No. 424PA
EX $19   **NM** $33   **MIP** $43

❑ **Ford 901**, 1:16-scale, Ertl, Gold Colored Collectors Edition, 1995, No. 363TA *(Photo by Ertl)*
EX $22   **NM** $43   **MIP** $63

❑ **Ford 901**, 1:16-scale, Ertl, Foxfire Farm w/Jim Babcock, 1996, No. 3092
EX $14   **NM** $22   **MIP** $33

❑ **Ford 961**, 1:16-scale, Ertl, red and gray, 2002, No. 13569
EX $12   **NM** $19   **MIP** $28

❑ **Ford 9880**, 1:16-scale, Scale Models, w/duals, Collector Edition, 1994, No. JLE383
EX $72   **NM** $93   **MIP** $129

❑ **Ford 9880**, 1:16-scale, Scale Models, duals, 4WD w/duals, 1995, No. 384 *(Photo by Scale Models)*
EX $62   **NM** $88   **MIP** $127

❑ **Ford 9N**, 1:16-scale, Arcade, blue, 1940s
EX $193   **NM** $464   **MIP** $1493

❑ **Ford 9N**, 1:16-scale, Arcade, gray, w/plow attached, (w/out plow is #7200), 6-1/2" long, 1941, No. 7220
EX $238   **NM** $464   **MIP** $1287

❑ **Ford 9N**, 1:16-scale, Ertl, gray, Collectors Edition, 1980s, No. 842TA
EX $24   **NM** $34   **MIP** $48

❑ **Ford 9N**, 1:16-scale, Ertl, w/nickel hood, '93 Toy Tractor Times Anniversary, #8; 1,548 produced, 1993, No. 4924TA
EX $22   **NM** $37   **MIP** $58

❑ **Ford 9N**, 1:16-scale, Ertl, Precision Series #1, 1995, No. 352
(Photo by Ertl)
EX $73   **NM** $117   **MIP** $217

❑ **Ford 9N**, 1:16-scale, Ertl, '95 National Farm Toy Museum, 1995, No. 3010PA
EX $17   **NM** $27   **MIP** $43

❑ **Ford 9N**, 1:16-scale, Pioneer of Power, gray, did not come in box, 1970s
EX $18   **NM** $36   **MIP** n/a

❑ **Ford 9N/Plow**, 1:16-scale, Ertl, gray, 50th Anniversary Ford 9N 1939-1989, 1980s, No. 833DA
EX $24   **NM** $36   **MIP** $48

❑ **Ford NAA**, 1:16-scale, Ertl, red and gray, Collectors Edition, Golden Jubilee, 1980s, No. 803TA
EX $16   **NM** $32   **MIP** $44

❑ **Ford NAA**, 1:16-scale, Ertl, gray and red, Jubilee, 1980s, No. 803
EX $16   **NM** $28   **MIP** $36

❏ **Ford NAA**, 1:16-scale, Ertl, w/canopy, 2001, No. 13561
EX $9 **NM** $17 **MIP** $28

❏ **Ford NAA**, 1:16-scale, Ertl, Gold Jubilee 50th Anniversary, Percision Series, 2003, No. 13630A
EX $68 **NM** $89 **MIP** $122

❏ **Ford TW-25**, 1:16-scale, Scale Models, 1989, No. FF-0194

(Photo by Scale Models)
EX $18 **NM** $23 **MIP** $38

❏ **Ford TW-25**, 1:16-scale, Scale Models, blue and white, 1990s
EX $21 **NM** $29 **MIP** $39

❏ **Ford TW-25**, 1:16-scale, Scale Models, blue and white, w/duals, 1990s, No. 117
EX $21 **NM** $29 **MIP** $39

❏ **Ford 3600**, 1:20-scale, Maxwell, blue, 1970s
EX $16 **NM** $32 **MIP** $54

❏ **Ford 3600**, 1:20-scale, Milton, blue, 1980s
EX $13 **NM** $28 **MIP** $54

❏ **Ford**, 1:32-scale, blue and white, 1980s
EX $4 **NM** $17 **MIP** $38

❏ **Ford 1156**, 1:32-scale, Scale Models, 1991, No. 340
EX $16 **NM** $27 **MIP** $33

❏ **Ford 256**, 1:32-scale, Scale Models, blue and white, 1989 Nashville Dealer Meeting, 1990s, No. FH-334
EX $3 **NM** $9 **MIP** $16

❏ **Ford 276**, 1:32-scale, Scale Models, blue and white, Bi-Directional, 1990s, No. FH-334
EX $2 **NM** $8 **MIP** $14

❏ **Ford 5000**, 1:32-scale, Britains, blue, 1970s
EX $18 **NM** $37 **MIP** $47

❏ **Ford 5000**, 1:32-scale, Ertl, Super Major, 1991, No. 802

(Photo by Bossen Implement)
EX $6 **NM** $12 **MIP** $16

❏ **Ford 5000**, 1:32-scale, Ertl, 2007, No. 13700
EX $8 **NM** $16 **MIP** $22

❏ **Ford 6600**, 1:32-scale, Britains, blue, 1980s
EX $13 **NM** $19 **MIP** $27

❑ **Ford 6600**, 1:32-scale, Britains, blue, 1980s
EX $12   NM $18   MIP $26

❑ **Ford 7610**, 1:32-scale, Lone Star, blue, 1980s, No. 1750
EX $6   NM $12   MIP $16

❑ **Ford 7710**, 1:32-scale, Britains, yellow, 1980s
EX $8   NM $13   MIP $16

❑ **Ford 7710**, 1:32-scale, Ertl, blue, friction tractor, 1980s, No. 4097
EX $4   NM $11   MIP $18

❑ **Ford 846**, 1:32-scale, Scale Models, 1989 Nashville Dealer Meeting, 1980s, No. FH-333
EX $9   NM $18   MIP $33

❑ **Ford 8630**, 1:32-scale, Ertl, 1990s, No. 1830
EX $4   NM $8   MIP $14

❑ **Ford 8630**, 1:32-scale, Ertl, w/loader and attachments, 1991, No. 304
EX $9   NM $16   MIP $27

❑ **Ford 8670**, 1:32-scale, Ertl, 1994, No. 313
EX $4   NM $8   MIP $12

❑ **Ford 8870**, 1:32-scale, Ertl, w/loader, 1994, No. 317 *(Photo by Ertl)*
EX $4   NM $9   MIP $17

❑ **Ford 9030**, 1:32-scale, Scale Models, Bi-directional, w/attachments set, No. 338 *(Photo by Scale Models)*
EX n/a   NM n/a   MIP $28

❑ **Ford FW-60**, 1:32-scale, Ertl, blue, out by Toy Farmer, 1980s, No. 3092
EX $17   NM $38   MIP $72

❑ **Ford FW-60**, 1:32-scale, Ertl, blue, available in collectors and non-collectors series, 1980s, No. 1926
EX $26   NM $54   MIP $67

❑ **Ford NAA**, 1:32-scale, Nostalig, gray and red, 1980s
EX $43   NM $78   MIP $122

❑ **Ford NAA**, 1:32-scale, Tootsietoy, red, 1960s
EX $6   NM $29   MIP $74

❑ **Ford TW-15**, 1:32-scale, Ertl, blue, white decal, 1980s, No. 1643
EX $6 **NM** $17 **MIP** $26

❑ **Ford TW-15**, 1:32-scale, Ertl, blue, red decal, 1980s, No. 881
EX $4 **NM** $9 **MIP** $14

❑ **Ford TW-15**, 1:32-scale, Ertl, radio control, 1980s, No. 4789
EX $7 **NM** $18 **MIP** $29

❑ **Ford TW-15**, 1:32-scale, Ertl, blue, radio control, 1980s, No. 4789
EX $7 **NM** $18 **MIP** $29

❑ **Ford TW-20**, 1:32-scale, Britains, blue, 1980s
EX $6 **NM** $11 **MIP** $16

❑ **Ford TW-20**, 1:32-scale, Ertl, blue, 1980s, No. 1643
EX $6 **NM** $17 **MIP** $27

❑ **Ford TW-35**, 1:32-scale, Siku, blue, 1980s
EX $9 **NM** $14 **MIP** $22

❑ **Ford TW-5**, 1:32-scale, Ertl, blue, 1980s, No. 881
EX $6 **NM** $9 **MIP** $14

TRACTORS 1:32-SCALE

❑ **Ford 8N**, 1:32-scale, Scale Models, gray, give-away at Scale Model open house, did not come in box, 1980s
EX $1 **NM** $2 **MIP** n/a

TRACTORS 1:41-SCALE

❑ **Ford 8700**, 1:41-scale, Polistil, blue, 1980s
EX $4 **NM** $7 **MIP** $16

❑ **Ford 8700**, 1:41-scale, Polistil, blue, 1980s
EX $6 **NM** $9 **MIP** $17

TRACTORS 1:43-SCALE

❑ **Ford 5000**, 1:43-scale, Corgi, yellow, 1970s
EX $38 **NM** $57 **MIP** $78

❑ **Ford 5000**, 1:43-scale, Corgi, yellow, 1970s
EX $38 **NM** $57 **MIP** $78

❑ **Ford 5000**, 1:43-scale, Maxwell, yellow, made in India, 1980s
EX $19   **NM** $37   **MIP** $54

❑ **Ford 5000**, 1:43-scale, Maxwell, blue, made in India, 1980s
EX $18   **NM** $34   **MIP** $54

❑ **Ford 8N**, 1:43-scale, Ertl, gray and red, only available in a set w/1:16-scale 8N Ford (gray loader), 1980s, No. 867
EX $12   **NM** $24   **MIP** $42

❑ **Ford 8N**, 1:43-scale, Ertl, gray and red, red loader, 1980s, No. 2512
EX $4   **NM** $8   **MIP** $14

❑ **Ford 8N**, 1:43-scale, Ertl, gray and red, 1980s, No. 2520
EX $9   **NM** $16   **MIP** $24

❑ **Ford 901**, 1:43-scale, Ertl, Powermaster, gray and red, 1986 National Farm Toy Show Tractor, part of set, 1980s
EX $8   **NM** $17   **MIP** $27

❑ **Ford 901**, 1:43-scale, Ertl, Powermaster, gray and red, 1980s, No. 2508
EX $4   **NM** $8   **MIP** $13

❑ **Ford 901 Select-O-Speed**, 1:43-scale, Ertl, gray and red, 1980s, No. 2564
EX $4   **NM** $8   **MIP** $13

TRACTORS 1:56-SCALE

❑ **Ford 5000**, 1:56-scale, Matchbox, yellow and blue, also available in all blue, 1960s
EX $17   **NM** $27   **MIP** $37

TRACTORS 1:64-SCALE

❑ **Ford 2000**, 1:64-scale, Ertl, 2000, No. 13552
EX $4   **NM** $6   **MIP** $8

❑ **Ford 4000**, 1:64-scale, Ertl, 1996, No. 3024 *(Photo by Ertl)*
EX $4   **NM** $6   **MIP** $8

❑ **Ford 5000**, 1:64-scale, Ertl, chrome, did not come in box, 1990s, No. 3048MA
EX $4   **NM** $9   **MIP** n/a

❑ **Ford 5000**, 1:64-scale, Ertl, Super Major, 1995, No. 928 *(Photo by Ertl)*
EX $4   **NM** $6   **MIP** $8

❑ **Ford 5000**, 1:64-scale, Ertl, 1998, No. 3293
EX $4   **NM** $6   **MIP** $8

❑ **Ford 5000**, 1:64-scale, Ertl, '99 National Farm Toy Museum, 1999, No. 16017HA
EX $4   **NM** $6   **MIP** $8

Photos by Jon Jacobson unless otherwise noted.

❑ **Ford 5640**, 1:64-scale, Ertl, ROPS, w/loader, 1992, No. 334
EX $4   **NM** $6   **MIP** $8

❑ **Ford 6640**, 1:64-scale, Ertl, ROPS, 1992, No. 332
EX $4   **NM** $5   **MIP** $7

❑ **Ford 681**, 1:64-scale, Ertl, workmaster, 2000, No. 13509
EX $4   **NM** $6   **MIP** $8

❑ **Ford 7740**, 1:64-scale, Ertl, cab w/loader, 1992, No. 387
EX $4   **NM** $6   **MIP** $8

❑ **Ford 7740**, 1:64-scale, Ertl, ROPS, 1992, No. 333
EX $4   **NM** $6   **MIP** $7

❑ **Ford 7840**, 1:64-scale, Ertl, cab, 1992, No. 336
EX $4   **NM** $6   **MIP** $7

❑ **Ford 7840**, 1:64-scale, Ertl, ROPS, w/duals, 1992, No. 335
EX $4   **NM** $6   **MIP** $7

❑ **Ford 8240**, 1:64-scale, Ertl, MFD, cab, 1993, No. 389
EX $4   **NM** $6   **MIP** $7

❑ **Ford 8340**, 1:64-scale, Ertl, duals, cab, 1992, No. 388
EX $4   **NM** $6   **MIP** $7

❑ **Ford 8730**, 1:64-scale, Ertl, w/loader, 1991, No. 303
EX $4   **NM** $6   **MIP** $8

❑ **Ford 8770**, 1:64-scale, Ertl, 2WD, 1995, No. 391
EX $4   **NM** $6   **MIP** $7

❑ **Ford 8830**, 1:64-scale, Ertl, MFD, 1991, No. 854
EX $4   **NM** $6   **MIP** $7

❑ **Ford 8830**, 1:64-scale, Ertl, duals, 1991, No. 879
EX $4   **NM** $6   **MIP** $7

❑ **Ford 8870**, 1:64-scale, Ertl, MFD, 1995, No. 392
EX $4   **NM** $6   **MIP** $7

❑ **Ford 8870**, 1:64-scale, Ertl, MFD, duals, Collector Edition, 1995, No. 394FA
EX $4   **NM** $6   **MIP** $7

❑ **Ford 8870**, 1:64-scale, Ertl, 2WD, 1995, No. 391
EX $4   **NM** $6   **MIP** $7

❑ **Ford 8970**, 1:64-scale, Ertl, MFD w/duals, 1995, No. 394 *(Photo by Kate Bossen)*
EX $4   **NM** $6   **MIP** $7

❑ **Ford 8N**, 1:64-scale, Ertl, also as stock #13620, 2000, No. 13551
EX $3   **NM** $4   **MIP** $6

❑ **Ford 8N**, 1:64-scale, Ertl, '02 Holiday Ornament, 2001, No. 135848
EX $4   **NM** $8   **MIP** $12

❑ **Ford 8N**, 1:64-scale, Gunning (Custom), red and gray, did not come in box, 1980s
EX $3   **NM** $12   **MIP** n/a

❑ **Ford 901**, 1:64-scale, Ertl, 1995, No. 927 *(Photo by Ertl)*
EX $3   **NM** $4   **MIP** $6

❑ **Ford 901**, 1:64-scale, Ertl, power master, gold, 1997, No. 3018EA
EX $3   **NM** $4   **MIP** $6

❑ **Ford 9700**, 1:64-scale, Tractor on left has dome wheels, tractor on right has regular wheels

❑ **Ford 9700**, 1:64-scale, Tractor on left has a PTO, tractor on right does not

❑ **Ford 9700**, 1:64-scale, Ertl, blue and white, silver grille/PTO, dome-wheels, 1970s, No. 1621
EX $58   **NM** $83   **MIP** $98

❑ **Ford 9700**, 1:64-scale, Ertl, blue and white, silver grille/PTO, 1970s, No. 1621
EX $16   **NM** $27   **MIP** $38

❑ **Ford 9700**, 1:64-scale, Ertl, blue and white, dark grille, can be found w/ or w/o PTO, 1970s, No. 1621
EX $16   **NM** $27   **MIP** $38

❑ **Ford 9880**, 1:64-scale, Scale Models, '96 Farm Progress Show Edition, 1996, No. FG-2432
EX $8   **NM** $13   **MIP** $18

❑ **Ford 9N**, 1:64-scale, Ertl, '95 National Farm Toy Museum, 1995, No. 3006MA
EX $3   **NM** $4   **MIP** $6

❑ **Ford 9N**, 1:64-scale, Ertl, 1995, No. 926 *(Photo by Ertl)*
EX $3   **NM** $4   **MIP** $6

❑ **Ford 9N**, 1:64-scale, Gunning (Custom), gray, did not come in box, 1980s
EX $3   **NM** $12   **MIP** n/a

❑ **Ford 9N**, 1:64-scale, Scale Models, '96 Farm Progress Show Edition, 1996, No. FB-2431
EX $3   **NM** $4   **MIP** $6

❑ **Ford FW-60**, 1:64-scale, Ertl, blue and white, white spun-on wheels, clear windows, 1980s, No. 1528
EX $17   **NM** $27   **MIP** $37

❑ **Ford FW-60**, 1:64-scale, Ertl, blue and white, gray riveted wheels, 1980s, No. 1528
EX $17   **NM** $27   **MIP** $37

❑ **Ford FW-60**, 1:64-scale, Ertl, blue and white, gray spun-on wheels, 1980s, No. 1528
EX $17   **NM** $27   **MIP** $37

❑ **Ford FW-60**, 1:64-scale, Ertl, blue and white, white spun-on wheels, dark windows, 1980s, No. 1528
EX $17   **NM** $27   **MIP** $37

❑ **Ford NAA**, 1:64-scale, Ertl, 2000, No. 13524
EX $4   **NM** $6   **MIP** $7

❑ **Ford NAA**, 1:64-scale, Ertl, Gold Jubilee, also stock #13634, 2000, No. 13555
EX $4   **NM** $6   **MIP** $7

❑ **Ford Set**, 1:64-scale, Ertl, Fordson F, 8N, Super Major, 981, 1990s, No. 862
EX n/a   **NM** n/a   **MIP** $18

❑ **Ford Set**, 1:64-scale, Ertl, 860 w/wagon, 2002, No. 13582
EX n/a   **NM** n/a   **MIP** $9

❑ **Ford Set**, 1:64-scale, Ertl, Ford NAA, 8N, 7840, 901, 2002, No. 13590
EX n/a   **NM** n/a   **MIP** $18

❑ **Ford TW-20**, 1:64-scale, Ertl, blue and white, 1980s, No. 1621
EX $4   **NM** $6   **MIP** $9

❑ **Ford TW-25**, 1:64-scale, Ertl, blue and white, 1980s, No. 896
EX $4   **NM** $6   **MIP** $8

❑ **Ford TW-35**, 1:64-scale, Ertl, blue and white, 1980s, No. 832
EX $4   **NM** $6   **MIP** $8

❑ **Ford TW-35**, 1:64-scale, Ertl, blue and white, w/Loader, 1980s, No. 897
EX $4 **NM** $6 **MIP** $9

❑ **Ford TW-35**, 1:64-scale, Ertl, blue and white, dark grille, Pow-R-Pull, 1980s, No. 4094
EX $4 **NM** $6 **MIP** $8

❑ **Ford TW-35**, 1:64-scale, Ertl, blue and white, light grille, Pow-R-Pull, different tires, 1980s, No. 4094
EX $4 **NM** $6 **MIP** $9

❑ **Ford TW-35**, 1:64-scale, Ertl, blue and white, 1980s, No. 832
EX $3 **NM** $4 **MIP** $6

❑ **Ford TW-35**, 1:64-scale, Ertl, blue and white, 1980s, No. 896
EX $4 **NM** $6 **MIP** $9

❑ **Ford TW-35**, 1:64-scale, Ertl, blue and white, w/Loader, 1980s, No. 897
EX $4 **NM** $6 **MIP** $9

❑ **Ford TW-35**, 1:64-scale, Ertl, blue, red decal, 1986, No. 899
EX $3 **NM** $4 **MIP** $8

❑ **Ford TW-35**, 1:64-scale, Ertl, blue, w/duals, 1986, No. 895
EX $4 **NM** $6 **MIP** $9

TRACTORS

❑ **Tractor 960**, Hubley, red/gray, functional steering, spring seat, 12" long, 1957-61, No. 525
EX $124 **NM** $224 **MIP** n/a

❑ **Tractor 960**, Hubley, red/gray, functional steering, 11" long, 1965, No. 1506
EX $124 **NM** $224 **MIP** n/a

TRUCKS 1:64-SCALE

❑ **Ford CL-9000 w/Flatbed and 9700s**, 1:64-scale, Ertl, white cab w/red trailer, no PTOs on tractors, No. 1405
EX $18 **NM** $42 **MIP** $50

❑ **Ford CL-9000 w/Flatbed and 9700s**, 1:64-scale, Ertl, white cab w/red trailer, tractors have PTOs, No. 1405
EX $20 **NM** $46 **MIP** $52

❑ **Ford CL-9000 w/Flatbed and I-Beam**, 1:64-scale, Ertl, silver cab w/orange trailer, No. 1455
EX $16 **NM** $29 **MIP** $32

❑ **Ford CL-9000 w/Flatbed and I-Beam**, 1:64-scale, Ertl, brown cab w/red trailer, No. 1450
EX $12 **NM** $28 **MIP** $30

❑ **Ford CL-9000 w/Flatbed and TW-20s**, 1:64-scale, Ertl, white cab w/red trailer, No. 1405
EX $21 **NM** $27 **MIP** $44

❏ **Ford CL-9000 w/Grain Trailer,**
1:64-scale, Ertl, brown cab w/silver
trailer, No. 1451
EX $15   **NM** $23   **MIP** $26

❏ **Ford CL-9000 w/Van Trailer,**
1:64-scale, Ertl, Yellow cab w/yellow
(painted) trailer, No. 1312
EX $12   **NM** $18   **MIP** $22

❏ **Ford CL-9000 w/Van Trailer,**
1:64-scale, Ertl, all white w/light blue
decals, No. 1452
EX $10   **NM** $18   **MIP** $20

❏ **Ford CL-9000 w/Grain Trailer,**
1:64-scale, Ertl, brown cab, silver
trailer, brown tractor frame, No. 1454
EX $14   **NM** $24   **MIP** $25

❏ **Ford CL-9000 w/Van Trailer,**
1:64-scale, Ertl, yellow cab w/yellow
(molded) trailer, No. 1312
EX $12   **NM** $17   **MIP** $21

❏ **Ford CL-9000 w/Van Trailer,**
1:64-scale, Ertl, white cab w/white
(smooth) trailer, dark blue decals,
No. 1453
EX $10   **NM** $20   **MIP** $22

❏ **Ford CL-9000 w/Grain Trailer,**
1:64-scale, Ertl, brown cab w/silver
trailer, silver tractor frame, No. 1454
EX $12   **NM** $22   **MIP** $24

❏ **Ford CL-9000 w/Van Trailer,**
1:64-scale, Ertl, all yellow, No. 1370
EX $12   **NM** $27   **MIP** $30

❏ **Ford CL-9000 w/Van Trailer,**
1:64-scale, Ertl, all red, No. 1360
EX $50   **NM** $200   **MIP** $250

❏ **Ford CL-9000 w/Van Trailer,**
1:64-scale, Ertl, all white, No. 1335
EX $8   **NM** $14   **MIP** $15

❏ **Ford CL-9000 w/Van Trailer,**
1:64-scale, Ertl, white cab w/white
(ribbed) trailer, dark blue decals,
No. 1453
EX $10   **NM** $22   **MIP** $25

❏ **Ford CL-9000 w/Van Trailer,**
1:64-scale, Ertl, all white, No. 1652
EX $10   **NM** $28   **MIP** $30

❑ **Ford CL-9000 w/Van Trailer**, 1:64-scale, Ertl, all white, No. 1338
EX $10   **NM** $81   **MIP** $85

❑ **Ford CL-9000 w/Van Trailer**, 1:64-scale, Ertl, gray cab w/white trailer, No. 1343
EX $12   **NM** $70   **MIP** $74

❑ **Ford CL-9000 w/Van Trailer**, 1:64-scale, Ertl, all white, No. 1313
EX $12   **NM** $47   **MIP** $50

❑ **Ford CL-9000 w/Van Trailer**, 1:64-scale, Ertl, all white, No. 1313
EX $10   **NM** $49   **MIP** $55

❑ **Ford LTL-9000 w/Drop Center Trailer and TW-35s**, 1:64-scale, Ertl, white cab w/gray trailer, No. 858
EX $14   **NM** $21   **MIP** $24

❑ **Ford LTL-9000 w/Drop Center Trailer and TW-35s**, 1:64-scale, Ertl, white cab w/gray trailer, No. 858
EX $15   **NM** $22   **MIP** $25

❑ **Ford LTL-9000 w/Drop Center Trailer**, 1:64-scale, Ertl, white cab w/gray trailer, two 8730 Tractors, small nos. on tractors, No. 858
EX $12   **NM** $25   **MIP** $28

❑ **Ford LTL-9000 w/Drop Center Trailer, Ford**, 1:64-scale, Ertl, white cab w/gray trailer, w/two 8730 Tractors, No. 858
EX $10   **NM** $23   **MIP** $26

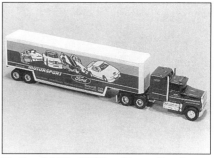

❑ **Ford LTL-9000 w/Drop Deck Van Trailer, Ford Motor Sport**, 1:64-scale, Ertl, all blue, No. 1315
EX $12   **NM** $37   **MIP** $41

❑ **Ford LTL-9000 w/Tanker Trailer**, 1:64-scale, Ertl, red cab w/gray tank, No. 9733
EX $10   **NM** $25   **MIP** $28

❑ **Ford LTL-9000 w/Tanker Trailer**, 1:64-scale, Ertl, blue cab w/gray tank, No. 1184
EX $10   **NM** $15   **MIP** $18

❑ **Ford LTL-9000 w/Van Trailer**, 1:64-scale, Ertl, all white, No. 9872
EX $12   **NM** $41   **MIP** $45

❏ **Ford LTL-9000 w/Van Trailer**, 1:64-scale, Ertl, all white, No. 9874
EX $35   **NM** $140   **MIP** $155

❏ **Ford LTL-9000 w/Van Trailer**, 1:64-scale, Ertl, blue cab w/white trailer, No. 9867
EX n/a   **NM** $15   **MIP** $10

❏ **Ford LTL-9000 w/Van Trailer**, 1:64-scale, Ertl, all white, No. 9884
EX $10   **NM** $17   **MIP** $20

❏ **Ford LTL-9000 w/Van Trailer**, 1:64-scale, Ertl, all white, No. 9812
EX $10   **NM** $15   **MIP** $18

❏ **Ford LTL-9000 w/Van Trailer**, 1:64-scale, Ertl, all black, No. 31500
EX $12   **NM** $17   **MIP** $20

❏ **Ford LTL-9000 w/Van Trailer**, 1:64-scale, Ertl, all white, No. 9453
EX $10   **NM** $45   **MIP** $50

❏ **Ford LTL-9000 w/Van Trailer**, 1:64-scale, Ertl, all white, No. 9866
EX $8   **NM** $12   **MIP** $15

❏ **Ford LTL-9000 w/Van Trailer**, 1:64-scale, Ertl, all white, No. 9487
EX $12   **NM** $18   **MIP** $22

❏ **Ford LTL-9000 w/Van Trailer**, 1:64-scale, Ertl, all white, No. 371
EX $10   **NM** $12   **MIP** $15

❏ **Ford LTL-9000 w/Van Trailer**, 1:64-scale, Ertl, red cab w/white trailer, No. 9868
EX $10   **NM** $15   **MIP** $18

❏ **Ford LTL-9000 w/Van Trailer**, 1:64-scale, Ertl, all white, No. 9811
EX $11   **NM** $16   **MIP** $18

❏ **Ford LTL-9000 w/Van Trailer**, 1:64-scale, Ertl, all white, No. 9177
EX $10   **NM** $12   **MIP** $15

❏ **Ford LTL-9000 w/Van Trailer**, 1:64-scale, Ertl, all white, No. 9705
EX $10 **NM** $17 **MIP** $21

❏ **Ford LTL-9000 w/Van Trailer, Big Foot**, 1:64-scale, Ertl, all white, No. 2613
EX $10 **NM** $27 **MIP** $32

❏ **Ford LTL-9000 w/Van Trailer, Ford Heavy Duty Truck Parts**, 1:64-scale, Ertl, all white, No. 9646
EX $10 **NM** $31 **MIP** $35

❏ **Ford LTL-9000 w/Van Trailer, ABC Groff**, 1:64-scale, Ertl, all white
EX $10 **NM** $18 **MIP** $22

❏ **Ford LTL-9000 w/Van Trailer, Citgo**, 1:64-scale, Ertl, all white, No. 2463
EX $10 **NM** $31 **MIP** $35

❏ **Ford LTL-9000 w/Van Trailer, Ford New Holland Parts**, 1:64-scale, Ertl, all black, No. 31500
EX $11 **NM** $15 **MIP** $21

❏ **Ford LTL-9000 w/Van Trailer, ABC Groff**, 1:64-scale, Ertl, all white, anniversary date on trailer, No. 9409
EX $11 **NM** $17 **MIP** $21

❏ **Ford LTL-9000 w/Van Trailer, Cummins**, 1:64-scale, Ertl, all white, No. 2149UP
EX $12 **NM** $37 **MIP** $40

❏ **Ford LTL-9000 w/Van Trailer, Garst Seeds**, 1:64-scale, Ertl, all white, No. 7643
EX $21 **NM** $37 **MIP** $40

❏ **Ford LTL-9000 w/Van Trailer, Agri Pro Seeds**, 1:64-scale, Ertl, all white, No. 9003
EX $18 **NM** $32 **MIP** $35

❏ **Ford LTL-9000 w/Van Trailer, Farris Truck Stop**, 1:64-scale, Ertl, red cab w/white trailer, No. 9382
EX $10 **NM** $21 **MIP** $25

❏ **Ford LTL-9000 w/Van Trailer, Heritage Seed Inc.**, 1:64-scale, Ertl, blue cab w/white trailer, No. 1331
EX $16 **NM** $34 **MIP** $39

❏ **Ford LTL-9000 w/Van Trailer, Illinois FFA**, 1:64-scale, Ertl, all white, No. 95329

EX $12   **NM** $38   **MIP** $43

❏ **Ford LTL-9000 w/Van Trailer, J.F. Good Co.**, 1:64-scale, Ertl, blue cab w/white trailer, No. 9867

EX $12   **NM** $25   **MIP** $29

❏ **Ford LTL-9000 w/Van Trailer, Noble Bear Seeds**, 1:64-scale, Ertl, all white, No. 9337

EX $10   **NM** $23   **MIP** $25

❏ **Ford LTL-9000 w/Van Trailer, Indiana FFA**, 1:64-scale, Ertl, all white, No. 9010

EX $12   **NM** $37   **MIP** $42

❏ **Ford LTL-9000 w/Van Trailer, Kory Farm Equipment**, 1:64-scale, Ertl, all white

EX $40   **NM** $120   **MIP** $150

❏ **Ford LTL-9000 w/Van Trailer, Publix**, 1:64-scale, Ertl, green cab w/white trailer, No. 7692

EX $9   **NM** $12   **MIP** $15

❏ **Ford LTL-9000 w/Van Trailer, Iowa FFA**, 1:64-scale, Ertl, all white, No. 9527

EX $12   **NM** $70   **MIP** $78

❏ **Ford LTL-9000 w/Van Trailer, M.M. Weaver and Sons**, 1:64-scale, Ertl, all white, No. 9079

EX $10   **NM** $20   **MIP** $24

❏ **Ford LTL-9000 w/Van Trailer, Rainbow Machine Shop**, 1:64-scale, Ertl, all white

EX $10   **NM** $22   **MIP** $27

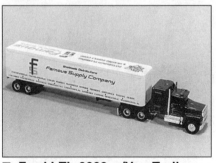

❏ **Ford LTL-9000 w/Van Trailer, J.F. Good Co.**, 1:64-scale, Ertl, blue cab w/white trailer, No. 9867

EX $12   **NM** $25   **MIP** $29

❏ **Ford LTL-9000 w/Van Trailer, McCubbin Seed Farm**, 1:64-scale, Ertl, all white, No. 9214

EX $12   **NM** $33   **MIP** $38

❏ **Ford LTL-9000 w/Van Trailer, Ralphs**, 1:64-scale, Ertl, red cab w/white trailer, No. 7563

EX $11   **NM** $24   **MIP** $28

❑ **Ford LTL-9000 w/Van Trailer, Sidney Truck**, 1:64-scale, Ertl, red cab w/white trailer, No. 9076
EX $12   **NM** $27   **MIP** $31

❑ **Ford LTL-9000 w/Van Trailer, Sieben Seeds**, 1:64-scale, Ertl, all white, No. 9239
EX $20   **NM** $37   **MIP** $41

❑ **Ford LTL-9000 w/Van Trailer, Steelcase**, 1:64-scale, Ertl, blue and silver, No. 9602
EX $12   **NM** $25   **MIP** $30

❑ **Ford LTL-9000 w/Van Trailer, Stow and Davis**, 1:64-scale, Ertl, blue and silver, No. 9132
EX $10   **NM** $22   **MIP** $27

❑ **Ford LTL-9000 w/Van Trailer, Stow and Davis**, 1:64-scale, Ertl, blue and silver, first run, decals on truck and trailer, No. 9132
EX $10   **NM** $21   **MIP** $25

❑ **Ford LTL-9000 w/Van Trailer, Thackery Custom Baling**, 1:64-scale, Ertl, red cab w/white trailer, No. 2974
EX $10   **NM** $15   **MIP** $20

❑ **Ford LTL-9000 w/Van Trailer, U.S. Mail**, 1:64-scale, Ertl, all white, No. 7650
EX $21   **NM** $37   **MIP** $41

❑ **Ford LTL-9000 w/Van Trailer, Van's Cabinet Inc.**, 1:64-scale, Ertl, all white, No. 9580
EX $9   **NM** $15   **MIP** $18

❑ **Ford LTL-9000 w/Van Trailer, Walcott Trucker's Jamboree 1990**, 1:64-scale, Ertl, blue cab w/white trailer
EX $10   **NM** $21   **MIP** $25

FORD NEW HOLLAND

BANKS 1:25-SCALE

❑ **Ford New Holland Ford Model T Bank**, 1:25-scale, Ertl, blue and white, 1990s
EX $6   **NM** $11   **MIP** $18

BANKS

❑ **Ford New Holland Mailbox Bank**, Ertl, blue, 1990s
EX $9   **NM** $14   **MIP** $23

TRUCKS 1:64-SCALE

❑ **Semi w/Ford/New Holland Van Box**, 1:64-scale, Ertl, 1980s, No. JLE315 *(Photo by Kate Bossen)*
EX $4   **NM** $8   **MIP** $14

FORD VERSATILE

IMPLEMENTS 1:64-SCALE

❑ **Ford Versatile 4700 Swather**, 1:64-scale, Scale Models, red, black, and lemon yellow, 1980s
EX $6   **NM** $13   **MIP** $17

TRACTORS 1:64-SCALE

❑ **Ford Versatile 936**, 1:64-scale, Scale Models, red, black, and lemon yellow, 1980s
EX npf   **NM** npf   **MIP** npf

❑ **Ford/Versatile 836**, 1:64-scale, Scale Models, red, black and lemon yellow, 1980
EX $22   **NM** $29   **MIP** $37

❑ **Ford/Versatile 836**, 1:64-scale, Scale Models, red, black and lemon yellow, 1980s
EX $22   **NM** $29   **MIP** $37

❑ **Ford/Versatile 836**, 1:64-scale, Scale Models, red, black and lemon yellow, 1980s
EX $22   **NM** $29   **MIP** $37

❑ **Ford/Versatile 836**, 1:64-scale, Scale Models, red, black and lemon yellow, 1988 Reno, 1988
EX $22   **NM** $29   **MIP** $37

❑ **Ford/Versatile 846**, 1:64-scale, Scale Models, red, black and lemon yellow, 1980s
EX $22   **NM** $29   **MIP** $37

❑ **Ford/Versatile 846**, 1:64-scale, Scale Models, red, black and lemon yellow, 1988 W. Brooklyn F.P.S., 1988
EX $22   **NM** $29   **MIP** $37

❑ **Ford/Versatile 876**, 1:64-scale, Scale Models, red, black and lemon yellow, 1980s
EX $22   **NM** $29   **MIP** $37

❑ **Ford/Versatile 876**, 1:64-scale, Scale Models, red, black and lemon yellow, 1980s
EX $22   **NM** $29   **MIP** $37

❑ **Ford/Versatile 876**, 1:64-scale, Scale Models, red, black and lemon yellow, 1980s
EX $22   **NM** $29   **MIP** $37

❑ **Ford/Versatile 936**, 1:64-scale, Scale Models, red, black and lemon yellow, 1980
EX $22   **NM** $29   **MIP** $37

❑ **Ford/Versatile 936**, 1:64-scale, Scale Models, red, black and lemon yellow, 1980s
EX $22   **NM** $29   **MIP** $37

❑ **Ford/Versatile 936**, 1:64-scale, Scale Models, red, black and lemon yellow, 1980s
EX $22   **NM** $29   **MIP** $37

FORD/VERSATILE

TRACTORS 1:16-SCALE

❑ **Ford/Versatile 935**, 1:16-scale, Scale Models, red and yellow, Coming on Strong Boston, 1990s
EX $98   **NM** $133   **MIP** $162

FORDSON

TRACTORS 1:16-SCALE

❑ **Fordson**, 1:16-scale, Ertl, gray, open engine casting, 1960s, No. 804
EX $12   **NM** $18   **MIP** $34

❑ **Fordson**, 1:16-scale, Ertl, gray, closed engine casting, 1970s, No. 804
EX $12   **NM** $16   **MIP** $26

❑ **Fordson**, 1:16-scale, Kenton, gray, 1930s
EX $48   **NM** $112   **MIP** $318

❑ **Fordson All Around**, 1:16-scale, Scale Models, gray, 1890-1990 Idaho Centennial Celebrate Idaho, 1990s
EX $21   **NM** $38   **MIP** $46

❑ **Fordson E27-N**, 1:16-scale, Chad Valley, blue gray, 1950s
EX $198   **NM** $422   **MIP** $722

❑ **Fordson F**, 1:16-scale, Ertl, gray, w/fenders, 1990s, No. 872
EX $14   **NM** $19   **MIP** $26

❑ **Fordson F**, 1:16-scale, Ertl, gray, Collectors Edition, 1990s, No. 872TA
EX $19   **NM** $36   **MIP** $42

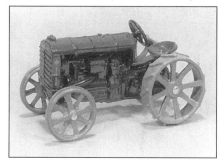

❑ **Fordson F**, 1:16-scale, Ertl, blue and orange, C.I.F.E.S. 1990 Special Edition, 1990s, No. 853YA
EX $24   **NM** $32   **MIP** $48

❑ **Fordson Major**, 1:16-scale, Chad Valley, blue, wind-up, hood opens, 1950s
EX $178   **NM** $324   **MIP** $671

❏ **Fordson Major**, 1:16-scale, Ertl, blue, Super Major, Collectors Edition, 1990s, No. 307DA
EX $18 **NM** $29 **MIP** $47

❏ **Fordson Major**, 1:16-scale, Ertl, blue, Super Major, 1990s, No. 859
EX $22 **NM** $37 **MIP** $42

❏ **Fordson N**, 1:16-scale, Scale Models, blue, No. 14 in Collectors Series No. 1, limited to 3500 units made, 1990s
EX $21 **NM** $38 **MIP** $46

❏ **Fordson N**, 1:16-scale, Scale Models, blue, orange wheels, '96 Farm Progress Show, 1996, No. FB-2429
EX $23 **NM** $37 **MIP** $48

❏ **Fordson N**, 1:16-scale, Scale Models, blue, orange wheels, 1997, No. 408
EX $23 **NM** $37 **MIP** $48

❏ **Fordson/Whitehead & Kales**, 1:16-scale, Arcade, gray, disk wheels w/raised "W&K", 1923-30s
EX $66 **NM** $156 **MIP** $422

TRACTORS 1:20-SCALE

❏ **Fordson Major**, 1:20-scale, M W, blue gray, 1960s
EX $43 **NM** $78 **MIP** $122

TRACTORS 1:25-SCALE

❏ **Fordson Major**, 1:25-scale, Cresent, gray, 1960s
EX $43 **NM** $78 **MIP** $122

TRACTORS 1:32-SCALE

❏ **Fordson**, 1:32-scale, Arcade, gray, 1930s
EX $23 **NM** $56 **MIP** $244

❏ **Fordson**, 1:32-scale, Hubley, gray, 1930s
EX $23 **NM** $56 **MIP** $253

❏ **Fordson E27-N**, 1:32-scale, Britains, blue gray, 1950s
EX $26 **NM** $52 **MIP** $78

❏ **Fordson E27-N**, 1:32-scale, Britains, blue gray, 1950s
EX $26 **NM** $52 **MIP** $78

❏ **Fordson E27-N**, 1:32-scale, Brown's Models, blue gray, model kit form, 1980s
EX $24 **NM** $36 **MIP** $42

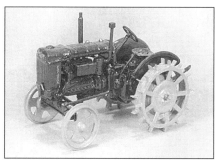

❏ **Fordson E27-N**, 1:32-scale, Brown's Models, blue gray, model kit form, 1980s
EX $24   **NM** $36   **MIP** $42

❏ **Fordson Major**, 1:32-scale, Brown's Models, blue gray, model kit form, 1980s
EX $24   **NM** $36   **MIP** $42

❏ **Fordson Major**, 1:32-scale, Scaledown, blue gray, 1980s
EX $26   **NM** $36   **MIP** $42

❏ **Fordson Major**, 1:32-scale, Scaledown, blue gray, 1980s
EX $26   **NM** $36   **MIP** $42

❏ **Fordson Major**, 1:32-scale, Scaledown, blue gray, 1980s
EX $26   **NM** $42   **MIP** $54

❏ **Fordson Major**, 1:32-scale, Scaledown, blue gray, 1980s
EX $26   **NM** $36   **MIP** $42

❏ **Fordson Major**, 1:32-scale, Scaledown, blue gray, 1980s
EX $26   **NM** $36   **MIP** $42

❏ **Fordson Major**, 1:32-scale, Scaledown, blue gray, 1980s
EX $26   **NM** $36   **MIP** $42

❏ **Fordson Super Major**, 1:32-scale, Ertl, blue and gray, steerable front wheels, 1990, No. 802
EX $5   **NM** $9   **MIP** $17

TRACTORS 1:43-SCALE

❏ **Fordson**, 1:43-scale, Corgi, gray, 1960s
EX $38   **NM** $57   **MIP** $78

❏ **Fordson**, 1:43-scale, Ertl, blue, English Fordson, 1990s, No. 2526
EX $4   **NM** $8   **MIP** $13

❏ **Fordson F**, 1:43-scale, Ertl, gray, 1980s
EX $4   **NM** $8   **MIP** $13

❑ **Fordson Major**, 1:43-scale, Corgi, gray, 1960s
EX $38   **NM** $57   **MIP** $78

❑ **Fordson Major**, 1:43-scale, Matchbox, blue with red or orange wheels, shown with trailer, gray and blue, Super Major, 1960s
EX $16   **NM** $29   **MIP** $44

❑ **Fordson Major**, 1:43-scale, Matchbox, blue with red or orange wheels, Super Major, 1960s
EX $16   **NM** $29   **MIP** $44

TRACTORS 1:64-SCALE

❑ **Fordson**, 1:64-scale, Baker (Custom), red and gray, did not come in box, 1960s
EX $6   **NM** $12   **MIP** n/a

❑ **Fordson**, 1:64-scale, Baker (Custom), silver, did not come in box, 1960s
EX $6   **NM** $12   **MIP** n/a

❑ **Fordson**, 1:64-scale, Scale Models, red and gray, 1960s
EX $4   **NM** $5   **MIP** $7

❑ **Fordson**, 1:64-scale, Scale Models, red and gray, plastic, 1960s
EX $3   **NM** $4   **MIP** $6

❑ **Fordson**, 1:64-scale, Scale Models, red and gray, plastic, 1960s
EX $3   **NM** $4   **MIP** $6

❑ **Fordson**, 1:64-scale, Scale Models, red and gray, die-cast, 1980s
EX $3   **NM** $4   **MIP** $6

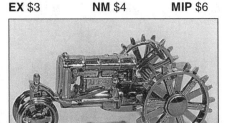

❑ **Fordson**, 1:64-scale, Scale Models, five different chrome colors, sold as a Christmas ornament, 1980s
EX $3   **NM** $4   **MIP** $5

TRACTORS

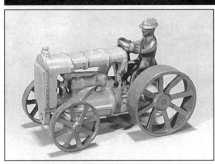

❑ **Fordson**, Arcade, gray, w/out lugs on wheels, cast in driver, 6" long, 1923-30s, No. 275
EX $24   **NM** $46   **MIP** $243

❑ **Fordson**, Arcade, gray, w/lugs on wheels, cast in driver, 6" long, 1923-30s, No. 275
EX $24   **NM** $46   **MIP** $243

Photos by Jon Jacobson unless otherwise noted.

❑ **Fordson**, Arcade, gray w/red wheels, lug wheels, driver, 3-7/8" long; Model 273X available in red or green body color, 1928, No. 273
EX $48   **NM** $89   **MIP** $326

❑ **Fordson**, Arcade, gray w/red wheels, lug wheels, driver, 4-3/4" long; Model 274X available in red or green body color, 1928, No. 274
EX $56   **NM** $116   **MIP** $338

❑ **Fordson**, Arcade, gray w/red wheels, rubber tires, driver, 6" long, 1928, No. 275
EX $56   **NM** $116   **MIP** $338

❑ **Fordson**, Kenton, red, available in four sizes, nickel-plated driver, nickel-plated spoke wheels, 1928, No. 2806
EX $39   **NM** $98   **MIP** n/a

GRAHAM-BRADLEY

IMPLEMENTS 1:32-SCALE

❑ **Trailer**, 1:32-scale, Auburn Rubber, 4 wheels, 4-3/4" long
EX $4   **NM** $16   **MIP** $27

❑ **Trailer**, 1:32-scale, Auburn Rubber, 2 wheels, 5-3/4" long
EX $4   **NM** $16   **MIP** $27

TRACTORS 1:16-SCALE

❑ **Graham-Bradley**, 1:16-scale, Die-Cast Promotions, NF, opening hood panels, 2002, No. 40028
EX $26   **NM** $32   **MIP** $54

❑ **Graham-Bradley**, 1:16-scale, Die-Cast Promotions, WF, opening hood panels, 2004, No. 40029
EX $26   **NM** $32   **MIP** $54

TRACTORS 1:32-SCALE

❑ **Tractor**, 1:32-scale, Auburn Rubber, red w/black wheels, 4-1/4" long
EX $6   **NM** $18   **MIP** $33

HART-PARR

TRACTORS 1:16-SCALE

❑ **Hart-Parr #3**, 1:16-scale, SpecCast, 1000 units made, 2003, No. CUST778
EX $97   **NM** $123   **MIP** $189

❑ **Hart-Parr 18-27**, 1:16-scale, Scale Models, '90 Farm Progress Show Edition, 1990
EX $38   **NM** $53   **MIP** $82

❑ **Hart-Parr 18-36**, 1:16-scale, Teeswater Custom Toys, 2002
EX $76   **NM** $113   **MIP** $158

❑ **Hart-Parr 28-40**, 1:16-scale, Bob Gray (Custom), 1978
EX $23   **NM** $48   **MIP** n/a

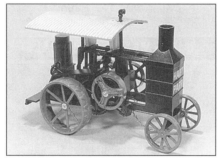

❑ **Hart-Parr 28-44**, 1:16-scale, Scale Models, 1991 *(Photo by Bossen Implement)*
EX $27   **NM** $42   **MIP** $74

❑ **Hart-Parr 30-60**, 1:16-scale, Scale Models, black, 1990s
EX $89   **NM** $117   **MIP** $168

❑ **Hart-Parr 70**, 1:16-scale, Scale Models, '90 Ontario Show Edition, 1990
EX $162   **NM** $198   **MIP** $247

❑ **Hart-Parr 90**, 1:16-scale, Scale Models, #19 in Collector Series I, 1992 *(Photo by Bossen Implement)*
EX $62   **NM** $72   **MIP** $98

TRACTORS 1:64-SCALE

❑ **Hart-Parr 30-60**, 1:64-scale, Walters (Custom), black and red, 1980s
EX $6   **NM** $12   **MIP** $24

HEIDER

TRACTORS 1:16-SCALE

❑ **Heider C**, 1:16-scale, SpecCast, Rock Island Plow Company, w/belt buckle, 1986 *(Photo by Bossen Implement)*
EX $72   **NM** $106   **MIP** $134

❑ **Heider D**, 1:16-scale, SpecCast, Rock Island Plow Company, w/belt buckle, 1987 *(Photo by Bossen Implement)*
EX $72   **NM** $106   **MIP** $135

TRACTORS 1:64-SCALE

❑ **Heider C**, 1:64-scale, SpecCast, green, silver, and red, 1988 Quad-City Show Tractor, 1980s
EX $6   **NM** $12   **MIP** $23

❏ **Heider D**, 1:64-scale, SpecCast, green, silver, and red, 1980s
EX $6   **NM** $12   **MIP** $23

HESSTON

CONSTRUCTION EQUIPMENT 1:50-SCALE

❏ **Hesston, Skid Loader**, 1:50-scale, Ertl, 1990s, No. 2267
EX $4   **NM** $6   **MIP** $9

IMPLEMENTS 1:16-SCALE

❏ **Hesston Baler, 4755**, 1:16-scale, Ertl, Big Square, 1997, No. 7061
(Photo by Ertl)
EX $12   **NM** $22   **MIP** $32

❏ **Hesston Baler, 560**, 1:16-scale, Ertl, Round, 1995, No. 207 *(Photo by Ertl)*
EX $9   **NM** $18   **MIP** $28

❏ **Hesston Baler, 565 A**, 1:16-scale, Ertl, Round, 1997, No. 207DP
(Photo by Bossen Implement)
EX $9   **NM** $18   **MIP** $28

❏ **Hesston Forage Harvester**, 1:16-scale, Ertl, pull type, 1990s, No. 2293
EX $9   **NM** $16   **MIP** $28

❏ **Hesston Wagon, Forage**, 1:16-scale, Ertl, 1990s, No. 2294
EX $9   **NM** $16   **MIP** $28

IMPLEMENTS 1:64-SCALE

❏ **Hesston Bale-Grinder, BP20**, 1:64-scale, Ertl, Autumn-red and white, 1986, No. 7335
EX $3   **NM** $4   **MIP** $12

❏ **Hesston Baler, 4600**, 1:64-scale, Mini Toys, Autumn-red and white/Plastic, Big Square Bales, 1980s, No. 340
EX $9   **NM** $19   **MIP** $28

❏ **Hesston Baler, 565**, 1:64-scale, Ertl, round, 1994, No. 2263
EX $4   **NM** $6   **MIP** $8

❏ **Hesston Baler, 565 A**, 1:64-scale, Ertl, round, 1998, No. 2263
EX $4   **NM** $6   **MIP** $8

❏ **Hesston Fertilizer Spreader**, 1:64-scale, Ertl, autumn red and white, 1986, No. 7395
EX $4   **NM** $6   **MIP** $9

❏ **Hesston Fertilizer Spreader IMC**, 1:64-scale, Ertl, green and white, 1986
EX $4   **NM** $6   **MIP** $9

❏ **Hesston Liquid Spreader**, 1:64-scale, Ertl, white and Autumn-red, 1986, No. 7394
EX $4   **NM** $6   **MIP** $11

❏ **Hesston Liquid Spreader**, 1:64-scale, Mini Toys, autumn red, 1986, No. 7394
EX $4   **NM** $6   **MIP** $11

❏ **Hesston Manure Spreader**, 1:64-scale, Ertl, autumn red and white, 1986, No. 7396
EX $4   **NM** $6   **MIP** $11

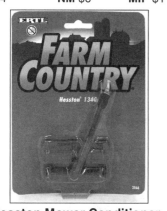

❏ **Hesston Mower Conditioner, 1340**, 1:64-scale, Ertl, 1998, No. 2068 *(Photo by Bossen Implement)*
EX $4   **NM** $6   **MIP** $7

❏ **Hesston Swatler, 8400**, 1:64-scale, Ertl, windrower, self-propelled, 1993, No. 2261 *(Photo by Bossen Implement)*
EX $12   **NM** $26   **MIP** $34

❏ **Hesston Wagon, Forage**, 1:64-scale, Ertl, autumn red and white, 1986, No. 7389
EX $4   **NM** $6   **MIP** $8

❏ **Hesston, Baling Set**, 1:64-scale, Ertl, 2002, No. 13085
EX $3   **NM** $4   **MIP** $11

❏ **Hesston, Disc**, 1:64-scale, Ertl, wing disc without wheels, 1986, No. 7397 *(Photo by Bossen Implement)*
EX $4   **NM** $6   **MIP** $8

❏ **Hesston, Forage Harvester**, 1:64-scale, Ertl, pull type, 1993, No. 2262
EX $4   **NM** $6   **MIP** $8

❏ **Hesston, Mininum Tillage Plow**, 1:64-scale, Ertl, 1986, No. 7398
EX $14   **NM** $22   **MIP** $33

❏ **Hesston, Sprayer**, 1:64-scale, Ertl, pull type, 1986, No. 7399
EX $4   **NM** $6   **MIP** $8

❏ **Hesston, Wagon, Anhydrous Ammonia**, 1:64-scale, Ertl, 1986, No. 7392
EX $4   **NM** $6   **MIP** $8

❏ **Hesston, Wagon, Hay**, 1:64-scale, Ertl, 1986, No. 7391
EX $4   **NM** $6   **MIP** $8

TRACTORS 1:16-SCALE

❏ **Hesston 100-90**, 1:16-scale, Scale Models, autumn red, 1980s
EX $18   **NM** $23   **MIP** $36

❏ **Hesston 1380**, 1:16-scale, Scale Models, on plaque, Dealer Edition, 1980s
EX $27   **NM** $36   **MIP** $53

❏ **Hesston 1380**, 1:16-scale, Scale Models, autumn red, cab decal, 1980s
EX $18   **NM** $23   **MIP** $36

❏ **Hesston 1380**, 1:16-scale, Scale Models, autumn red, 1980s
EX $18   **NM** $23   **MIP** $36

❏ **Hesston 140-90**, 1:16-scale, Scale Models, autumn red, 1980s
EX $18   **NM** $23   **MIP** $36

❏ **Hesston 980**, 1:16-scale, Scale Models, autumn red, 1980s
EX $18   **NM** $23   **MIP** $36

❏ **Hesston 980 DT**, 1:16-scale, Scale Models, on plaque, Dealer Edition, 1980s
EX $27   **NM** $36   **MIP** $53

❑ **Hesston 980 DT**, 1:16-scale, Scale Models, autumn red, cab decal, 1980s
EX $18   **NM** $23   **MIP** $36

❑ **Hesston 980 DT**, 1:16-scale, Scale Models, autumn red, DT is Hesston's designation for front wheel assist, 1980s
EX $18   **NM** $23   **MIP** $36

TRACTORS 1:32-SCALE

❑ **Hesston 800 DT 5**, 1:32-scale, Yaxon, autumn red, 1980s
EX $4   **NM** $8   **MIP** $12

TRACTORS 1:64-SCALE

❑ **Hesston 100-90**, 1:64-scale, Ertl, autumn red and black, w/Loader, 1980s, No. 7213
EX $4   **NM** $6   **MIP** $9

❑ **Hesston 100-90**, 1:64-scale, Ertl, autumn red, 1985, No. 7207
EX $3   **NM** $4   **MIP** $9

❑ **Hesston 100-90**, 1:64-scale, Ertl, autumn red and black, plastic tires, w/Loader, 1985, No. 7213
EX $4   **NM** $6   **MIP** $9

❑ **Hesston 100-90**, 1:64-scale, Ertl, autumn red and black, Farm Show Edition "1986" w/ Loader, 1986, No. 7213
EX $4   **NM** $6   **MIP** $9

❑ **Hesston 100-90**, 1:64-scale, Mini Toys, autumn red, 1984, No. 308
EX $3   **NM** $4   **MIP** $9

❑ **Hesston 100-90 DT**, 1:64-scale, Ertl, autumn red, 1980s, No. 7206
EX $3   **NM** $4   **MIP** $9

❑ **Hesston 100-90 DT**, 1:64-scale, Mini Toys, autumn red, 1980s, No. 307
EX $3   **NM** $4   **MIP** $9

❑ **Hesston 1180**, 1:64-scale, Mini Toys, autumn red, 1980s, No. 304
EX $4   **NM** $6   **MIP** $14

❑ **Hesston 1180**, 1:64-scale, Mini Toys, autumn red, 1980s, No. 306
EX $4   **NM** $6   **MIP** $14

❑ **Hesston 1180**, 1:64-scale, Mini Toys, autumn red, special edition 1 of 5,000, 1980s, No. 313
EX $12   **NM** $17   **MIP** $27

❑ **Hesston 1180 DT**, 1:64-scale, Mini Toys, autumn red, 1980s, No. 303
EX $4   **NM** $6   **MIP** $14

❑ **Hesston 1180 DT**, 1:64-scale, Mini Toys, autumn red, 1980s, No. 305
EX $4   **NM** $6   **MIP** $14

❑ **Hesston 130-90**, 1:64-scale, Ertl, autumn red, 1980s, No. 7209
EX $4   **NM** $6   **MIP** $9

❑ **Hesston 130-90**, 1:64-scale, Ertl, autumn red, 1980s, No. 7211
EX $4   **NM** $6   **MIP** $9

❑ **Hesston 130-90**, 1:64-scale, Mini Toys, autumn red, 1980s, No. 312
EX $4   **NM** $6   **MIP** $9

❑ **Hesston 130-90**, 1:64-scale, Mini Toys, autumn red, 1980s, No. 310
EX $4   **NM** $6   **MIP** $9

❑ **Hesston 130-90 DT**, 1:64-scale, Ertl, autumn red, 1980s, No. 7208
EX $4   **NM** $6   **MIP** $9

❑ **Hesston 130-90 DT**, 1:64-scale, Ertl, autumn red, 1980s, No. 7210
EX $4   **NM** $6   **MIP** $9

❑ **Hesston 130-90 DT**, 1:64-scale, Mini Toys, autumn red, 1980s, No. 309
EX $4   **NM** $6   **MIP** $9

❑ **Hesston 130-90 DT**, 1:64-scale, Mini Toys, autumn red, 1980s, No. 311
EX $4   **NM** $6   **MIP** $9

❑ **Hesston 180-90**, 1:64-scale, Ertl, autumn red, 1987 Farm Show Edition, 1980s, No. 7214
EX $4   **NM** $6   **MIP** $9

❏ **Hesston 180-90**, 1:64-scale, Ertl, autumn red, 1980s, No. 7216
EX $4 **NM** $6 **MIP** $9

❏ **Hesston 180-90**, 1:64-scale, Ertl, autumn red, 1980s, No. 7215
EX $4 **NM** $6 **MIP** $9

❏ **Hesston 80-90**, 1:64-scale, Ertl, autumn red, 1980s
EX $4 **NM** $6 **MIP** $9

❏ **Hesston 980**, 1:64-scale, Mini Toys, autumn red, 1980s, No. 302
EX $4 **NM** $6 **MIP** $14

❏ **Hesston 980 DT**, 1:64-scale, Mini Toys, autumn red, 1980s, No. 301
EX $4 **NM** $6 **MIP** $14

HOLT

CONSTRUCTION EQUIPMENT 1:16-SCALE

❏ **Holt 2-Ton**, 1:16-scale, Ertl, white, 1993, No. 2438
EX $9 **NM** $18 **MIP** $32

TRACTORS 1:32-SCALE

❏ **Holt 77**, 1:32-scale, SpecCast, 100th Anniversary of Caterpillar, 2005
EX $83 **NM** $112 **MIP** $163

HOUGH

CONSTRUCTION EQUIPMENT 1:130-SCALE

❏ **Hough Pay Loader**, 1:130-scale, Mercury, yellow, 1960s
EX $22 **NM** $53 **MIP** $78

CONSTRUCTION EQUIPMENT 1:64-SCALE

❏ **Hough Crawler w/blade, TD-20E**, 1:64-scale, Ertl, light yellow, 1980s, No. 1851
EX $9 **NM** $16 **MIP** $26

❏ **Hough Crawler w/blade, TD-20E**, 1:64-scale, Ertl, dark yellow, 1980s, No. 1851
EX $9 **NM** $16 **MIP** $26

❏ **Hough Scraper, 412B**, 1:64-scale, Ertl, light yellow, 1980s, No. 1855
EX $9 **NM** $16 **MIP** $26

❏ **Hough Scraper, 412B**, 1:64-scale, Ertl, dark yellow, 1980s, No. 1855
EX $9 **NM** $16 **MIP** $26

HUBER

TRACTORS 1:16-SCALE

❏ **Huber L**, 1:16-scale, Scale Models, #16 in Collector Series I, 1987 *(Photo by Bossen Implement)*
EX $28 **NM** $47 **MIP** $77

TRACTORS 1:64-SCALE

❏ **Huber HK**, 1:64-scale, Rock Ridge Casting, green and red, M.O.T. 1988
EX $16   **NM** $28   **MIP** $48

TRACTORS

❏ **Huber Steam Roller**, Hubley, olive or green, 1920s
EX $142   **NM** $222   **MIP** $682

HUSKEY

IMPLEMENTS 1:64-SCALE

❏ **Husky Liquid Spreader**, 1:64-scale, Ertl, various colors w/o tube on top of the tank, 1980s
EX $4   **NM** $6   **MIP** $11

❏ **Husky Liquid Spreader**, 1:64-scale, Ertl, various colors, w/tube on top of the tank, 1980s
EX $4   **NM** $6   **MIP** $11

❏ **Husky Liquid Spreader**, 1:64-scale, Mini Toys, green, 1980s
EX $4   **NM** $6   **MIP** $11

❏ **Husky Liquid Spreader Alma Ontario**, 1:64-scale, Ertl, green, 1980s
EX $4   **NM** $6   **MIP** $11

IMC

IMPLEMENTS 1:64-SCALE

❏ **IMC Anhydrous Tank**, 1:64-scale, Ertl, white and green, 1980s
EX $4   **NM** $6   **MIP** $12

❏ **IMC Grain Cart**, 1:64-scale, Ertl, white and green, 1980s
EX $4   **NM** $6   **MIP** $12

INTERNATIONAL HARVESTER

BANKS 1:25-SCALE

❏ **Farmall Truck Bank**, 1:25-scale, Ertl, No. 968 *(Photo by Ertl)*
EX $4   **NM** $12   **MIP** $18

❏ **Farmall Truck Bank**, 1:25-scale, Ertl, No. 440 *(Photo by Ertl)*
EX $4   **NM** $12   **MIP** $18

❏ **Farmall Truck Bank M**, 1:25-scale, Ertl, No. 474 *(Photo by Ertl)*
EX $4   **NM** $12   **MIP** $18

BANKS

❏ **Mailbox Bank**, Ertl, red, 1970s
EX $8   **NM** $14   **MIP** $22

❏ **Mailbox Bank**, Ertl, red, 1970s, No. 420
EX $22   **NM** $38   **MIP** $57

CONSTRUCTION EQUIPMENT 1:16-SCALE

❏ **International Backhoe**, 1:16-scale, Ertl, yellow, red or black decals, two front wheel variations, 1970s, No. 472
EX $33   **NM** $62   **MIP** $98

❏ **International Backhoe**, 1:16-scale, Ertl, yellow, 1970s, No. 472
EX $33   **NM** $63   **MIP** $98

❏ **International Backhoe**, 1:16-scale, Ertl, plastic, brown, 1980s
EX $24   **NM** $73   **MIP** $96

❏ **International Backhoe**, 1:16-scale, Ertl, yellow, 1980s
EX $24   **NM** $73   **MIP** $96

❏ **International Backhoe, 3414**, 1:16-scale, Ertl, yellow, 1960s, No. 428
EX $88   **NM** $206   **MIP** $463

❏ **International Backhoe, 3444**, 1:16-scale, Ertl, yellow, 1970s, No. 428
EX $68   **NM** $138   **MIP** $282

❏ **International Crawler Diesel**, 1:16-scale, Arcade, red, 1940s
EX $419   **NM** $1089   **MIP** $2983

❏ **International Crawler Diesel**, 1:16-scale, Arcade, orange, 1940s
EX $419   **NM** $1089   **MIP** $2983

❏ **International Crawler T-340**, 1:16-scale, Deyen (Custom), red and white, did not come in box, 1980s
EX $93   **NM** $164   **MIP** n/a

❏ **International Crawler TD 18 Diesel**, 1:16-scale, Arcade, red, 1940s, No. 7120
EX $437   **NM** $1057   **MIP** $3114

❏ **International Crawler TD 18 Diesel**, 1:16-scale, Arcade, orange, 1940s, No. 7120
EX $437   **NM** $1057   **MIP** $3114

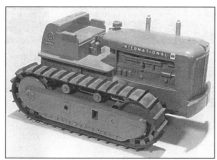

❏ **International Crawler TD 24 Diesel**, 1:16-scale, Product Miniature, red, 1950s
EX $98   **NM** $236   **MIP** $442

❏ **International Crawler TD 24 Diesel**, 1:16-scale, Product Miniature, red, 1950s
EX $98   **NM** $236   **MIP** $442

❏ **International Crawler TD 24 Diesel**, 1:16-scale, Product Miniature, red, wire control, 1950s
EX $133   **NM** $328   **MIP** $582

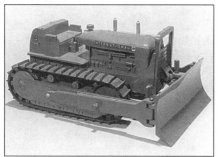

❏ **International Crawler w/Blade TD 24 Diesel**, 1:16-scale, Product Miniature, red, 1950s
EX $173   **NM** $386   **MIP** $842

❏ **International Crawler w/Blade TD 24 Diesel**, 1:16-scale, Product Miniature, red, 1950s
EX $173   **NM** $386   **MIP** $842

❏ **International Crawler, T-340**, 1:16-scale, Ertl, metal tracks, Collectors Edition, 1996, No. 4592DA
(Photo by Ertl)
EX $28   **NM** $38   **MIP** $47

❏ **International Crawler, T-340**, 1:16-scale, Ertl, red rubber track, 1996, No. 4734 *(Photo by Ertl)*
EX $12   **NM** $18   **MIP** $27

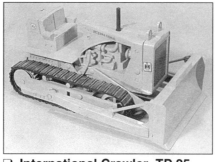

❏ **International Crawler, TD 25**, 1:16-scale, Ertl, yellow, lights on top, two decal variations, 1960s, No. 427
EX $168   **NM** $293   **MIP** $646

❏ **International Crawler, TD 25**, 1:16-scale, Ertl, yellow, lights on side, 1970s, No. 452
EX $53   **NM** $113   **MIP** $172

❏ **International Engine UD 24 Diesel**, 1:16-scale, Product Miniature, red, cigarette dispenser, 1950s
EX $118   **NM** $238   **MIP** $372

❏ **International Hough Pay Loader**, 1:16-scale, Ertl, yellow, 1970s
EX $263   **NM** $482   **MIP** $627

❏ **International Hough Pay Loader**, 1:16-scale, Ertl, yellow or brown, 1970s
EX $263   **NM** $482   **MIP** $627

❏ **International Loader, 2644**, 1:16-scale, Ertl, yellow, non-removable loader, 1970s, No. 421
EX $93 **NM** $268 **MIP** $892

❏ **International Loader, 544**, 1:16-scale, Ertl, white, non-removable loader, 1970s, No. 418
EX $53 **NM** $92 **MIP** $189

❏ **International Pay Hauler**, 1:16-scale, Ertl, yellow, also came w/exhaust coming out of right side of hood, 1960s, No. 419
EX $323 **NM** $689 **MIP** $1543

❏ **International Tractor, 2504**, 1:16-scale, Ertl, yellow, 1960s, No. 434
EX $117 **NM** $342 **MIP** $1388

❏ **International Tractor, 2504**, 1:16-scale, Ertl, yellow, decaled white side panels, 1960s, No. 434
EX $117 **NM** $342 **MIP** $1388

❏ **International Tractor, 2644**, 1:16-scale, Ertl, yellow, 1970s, No. 416
EX $98 **NM** $257 **MIP** $793

❏ **International Tractor, 340**, 1:16-scale, Ertl, yellow, 1950s
EX $223 **NM** $493 **MIP** $1899

❏ **International Tractor, 660**, 1:16-scale, Ertl, yellow, 2002, No. 14217
EX $11 **NM** $22 **MIP** $33

❏ **McCormick Trac-Tractor**, 1:16-scale, Arcade, red, nickeled driver, 7-1/2" long, 1941, No. 7120
EX $428 **NM** $913 **MIP** $3092

❏ **International Crawler TD-24 w/Cable Blade**, 1:25-scale, SpecCast, umbrella, 2007, No. 1533
EX $38 **NM** $54 **MIP** $84

❏ **International Hough Pay Loader**, 1:25-scale, Prieser, yellow or army green, 1980s, No. 426
EX $22 **NM** $73 **MIP** $122

❏ **International Pay Hauler**, 1:25-scale, Ertl, yellow, 1970s
EX $96 **NM** $132 **MIP** $189

❏ **International Pay Hauler**, 1:25-scale, Ertl, yellow, 1960s, No. 425
EX $23 **NM** $72 **MIP** $122

❑ **International Pay Hauler**, 1:25-scale, Ertl, yellow w/white cab, 1970s, No. 425
EX $23　　**NM** $72　　**MIP** $122

CONSTRUCTION EQUIPMENT 1:50-SCALE

❑ **International Crawler TD-24 w/Hydraulic Blade**, 1:50-scale, SpecCast, 2007, No. 1553
EX $15　　**NM** $25　　**MIP** $35

❑ **International Excavator**, 1:50-scale, Solido, yellow, "Yumbo" metal tracks, 1970s
EX $53　　**NM** $100　　**MIP** $162

❑ **International Excavator, 3984**, 1:50-scale, Solido, yellow, "Yumbo" w/metal tracks, 1970s
EX $53　　**NM** $106　　**MIP** $162

❑ **International Hough Pay Loader, 560**, 1:50-scale, West Germany, yellow, 1970s
EX $178　　**NM** $382　　**MIP** $462

❑ **International Pay Loader 510**, 1:50-scale, Diapet, brown and white, 1980s
EX $53　　**NM** $106　　**MIP** $162

❑ **International Pay Loader, 510**, 1:50-scale, Diapet, brown and white, 1980s
EX $53　　**NM** $106　　**MIP** $162

❑ **International Pay Loader, 560**, 1:50-scale, Diapet, orange, 1980s
EX $53　　**NM** $106　　**MIP** $162

CONSTRUCTION EQUIPMENT 1:64-SCALE

❑ **International Backhoe**, 1:64-scale, Ertl, dark yellow w/dark yellow rims, No. 1853
EX $9　　**NM** $16　　**MIP** $26

❑ **International Backhoe**, 1:64-scale, Ertl, dark yellow w/white rims, No. 1853
EX $9　　**NM** $16　　**MIP** $26

❑ **International Backhoe**, 1:64-scale, Ertl, light yellow w/white rims, No. 1853
EX $9　　**NM** $16　　**MIP** $26

❑ **International Backhoe**, 1:64-scale, Ertl, light yellow w/yellow rims, No. 1853
EX $9　　**NM** $16　　**MIP** $26

❑ **International Crawler**, 1:64-scale, Keith (Custom), red and white, did not come in box
EX $9　　**NM** $22　　**MIP** n/a

❏ **International Crawler w/Blade,**
1:64-scale, Ertl, camouflage,
No. 1031
EX $9   **NM** $16   **MIP** $26

❏ **International Crawler w/blade,**
TD-20, 1:64-scale, Ertl, dark yellow,
No. 1851
EX $9   **NM** $16   **MIP** $26

❏ **International Crawler w/blade,**
TD-20, 1:64-scale, Ertl, light yellow,
No. 1851
EX $9   **NM** $16   **MIP** $26

❏ **International Excavator, 640,**
1:64-scale, Ertl, light yellow, No. 1854
EX $9   **NM** $16   **MIP** $26

❏ **International Excavator, 640,**
1:64-scale, Ertl, dark yellow, No. 1854
EX $9   **NM** $16   **MIP** $26

❏ **International Scraper, 412**, 1:64-
scale, Ertl, light yellow, No. 1855
EX $9   **NM** $16   **MIP** $26

❏ **International Scraper, 412**, 1:64-
scale, Ertl, dark yellow, No. 1855
EX $9   **NM** $16   **MIP** $26

❏ **International Scraper, 412**, 1:64-
scale, Ertl, industrial yellow, black
belt, No. 1855
EX $9   **NM** $16   **MIP** $26

❏ **International Tractor, 4100**,
1:64-scale, Keith (Custom), industrial
yellow, did not come in box, 1980s
EX $16   **NM** $27   **MIP** n/a

❏ **International Tractor, 4156**,
1:64-scale, Keith (Custom), industrial
yellow and white, did not come in
box, 1980s
EX $16   **NM** $27   **MIP** n/a
❏ **International Tractor, 660**, 1:64-
scale, Ertl, yellow, 2002, No. 14216
EX $4   **NM** $6   **MIP** $8

CONSTRUCTION EQUIPMENT 1:80-SCALE

❏ **International Crawler**, 1:80-
scale, Matchbox, red w/green tracks,
1970s
EX $42   **NM** $58   **MIP** $73

❏ **International Pay Hauler**, 1:80-
scale, Ertl, olive drab, 1980s, No. 1033
EX $9   **NM** $16   **MIP** $26

❑ **International Pay Hauler, 350**, 1:80-scale, Ertl, light yellow, no decals, No. 1852
EX $9   **NM** $16   **MIP** $26

❑ **International Pay Hauler, 350**, 1:80-scale, Ertl, light yellow, No. 1852
EX $9   **NM** $16   **MIP** $26

❑ **International Pay Hauler, 350**, 1:80-scale, Ertl, dark yellow, No. 1852
EX $9   **NM** $16   **MIP** $26

❑ **International Pay Hauler, 350**, 1:80-scale, Ertl, yellow, 1980s
EX $9   **NM** $16   **MIP** $26

❑ **International Pay Hauler, 350**, 1:80-scale, Ertl, brown, 1980s
EX $9   **NM** $16   **MIP** $26

❑ **International Pay Hauler, 350**, 1:80-scale, Ertl, yellow, no IH decal, 1980s
EX $9   **NM** $16   **MIP** $26

❑ **International Pay Hauler, 350**, 1:80-scale, Ertl, brown, 1980s
EX $9   **NM** $16   **MIP** $26

❑ **International Pay Hauler, 350**, 1:80-scale, Ertl, brown, no IH decal, 1980s
EX $9   **NM** $16   **MIP** $26

❑ **International Pay Loader**, 1:80-scale, Ertl, olive drab, 1980s, No. 1032
EX $9   **NM** $16   **MIP** $26

❑ **International Pay Loader, 560**, 1:80-scale, Ertl, dark yellow, No. 1850
EX $9   **NM** $16   **MIP** $26

❑ **International Pay Loader, 560**, 1:80-scale, Ertl, dark yellow, No. 1850
EX $9   **NM** $16   **MIP** $26

❑ **International Pay Loader, 560**, 1:80-scale, Ertl, light yellow, No. 1850
EX $9   **NM** $16   **MIP** $26

❑ **International Pay Loader, 560**, 1:80-scale, Ertl, light yellow, No. 1850
EX $9   **NM** $16   **MIP** $26

❑ **International Pay Loader, 560**, 1:80-scale, Ertl, brown, 1980s
EX $9   **NM** $16   **MIP** $26

❑ **International Payloader**, 1:80-scale, Ertl, camouflage, No. 1032
EX $9   **NM** $16   **MIP** $26

❑ **International Pay Loader, 560**, 1:80-scale, Ertl, yellow, 1980s
EX $9   **NM** $16   **MIP** $26

❑ **International Payhauler**, 1:80-scale, Ertl, camouflage, No. 1033
EX $9   **NM** $16   **MIP** $26

❑ **International w/Drott 4 in 1**, 1:80-scale, Mercury, yellow, 1970s
EX $22   **NM** $53   **MIP** $78

❑ **International Pay Loader, 560**, 1:80-scale, Ertl, brown, 1980s
EX $9   **NM** $16   **MIP** $26

❑ **International Payhauler**, 1:80-scale, Ertl, dark yellow, No. 1852
EX $9   **NM** $16   **MIP** $26

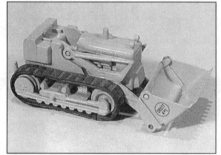

❑ **International w/Drott 4 in 1**, 1:80-scale, Mercury, orange, 1970s
EX $22   **NM** $53   **MIP** $78

❑ **International Pay Loader, 560**, 1:80-scale, Ertl, yellow, 1980s
EX $9   **NM** $16   **MIP** $26

❑ **International Payhauler 350**, 1:80-scale, Ertl, dark yellow, No. 1852
EX $9   **NM** $16   **MIP** $26

CONSTRUCTION EQUIPMENT 1:87-SCALE

❑ **International Crawler**, 1:87-scale, Mercury, yellow, 1970s
EX $22   **NM** $53   **MIP** $78

CONSTRUCTION EQUIPMENT

❑ **International Crawler**, Hong Kong, 3" long, yellow, 1970s
EX $4   **NM** $18   **MIP** $27

❑ **International Crawler**, Hong Kong, 3" long, yellow, 1970s
EX $4   **NM** $18   **MIP** $27

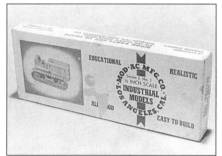

❑ **McCormick Crawler**, Mod-ac, 4' long wood kit, 1950s
EX $53   **NM** $68   **MIP** $109

IMPLEMENTS 1:06-SCALE

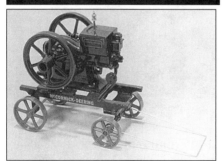

❑ **McCormick Engine**, 1:06-scale, Ertl, green w/red trim, collector's edition, 1990s, No. 4651DA
EX $8   **NM** $16   **MIP** $22

❑ **McCormick Engine, Model M**, 1:06-scale, Ertl, green, No. 4651
EX $8   **NM** $16   **MIP** $22

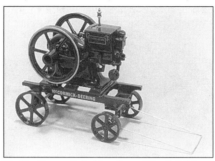

❑ **McCormick Engine, Model M**, 1:06-scale, Ertl, green w/gold trim, 1990s, No. 4651
EX $8   **NM** $16   **MIP** $22

IMPLEMENTS 1:16-SCALE

❑ **International Corn Picker, PR-1**, 1:16-scale, Ertl, red and white, 1-row, 1990s, No. 666
EX $16   **NM** $31   **MIP** $48

❑ **International Corn Picker, PR-1**, 1:16-scale, Ertl, red and white, 1-row, Collector Edition, 1990s, No. 666DA
EX $16   **NM** $32   **MIP** $58

❑ **International Disc**, 1:16-scale, Ertl, red, C hitch, 1960s
EX $22   **NM** $57   **MIP** $88

❑ **International Disc**, 1:16-scale, Ertl, red, w/wings, 1960s, No. 449
EX $22   **NM** $57   **MIP** $92

❑ **International Disc**, 1:16-scale, Ertl, red, plastic hitch, 1970s
EX $11   **NM** $26   **MIP** $48

❑ **International Disc**, 1:16-scale, Ertl, red, w/wings, 1980s, No. 493
EX $11   **NM** $26   **MIP** $48

❑ **International Gas Engine**, 1:16-scale, Riecke (Custom), red, 1990s
EX $34   **NM** $58   **MIP** n/a

❑ **International Grain Drill**, 1:16-scale, Ertl, white and red, die-cast lid, crank hitch, 1960s, No. 448
EX $37   **NM** $73   **MIP** $162

❑ **International Grain Drill**, 1:16-scale, Ertl, white and red, plastic lid, C hitch, 1970s-80s, No. 448
EX $22   **NM** $46   **MIP** $78

❑ **International Grinder Mixer**, 1:16-scale, Ertl, 2007, No. 14551
EX $15   **NM** $20   **MIP** $25

❑ **International Harvester Combine, 82**, 1:16-scale, SpecCast, 2007, No. 1519
EX $50   **NM** $85   **MIP** $110

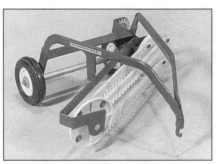

❑ **International Hay Rake**, 1:16-scale, Ertl, red w/white teeth, 1960s, No. 446
EX $26   **NM** $52   **MIP** $136

❑ **International Hay Rake**, 1:16-scale, Ertl, red w/blue teeth, 1970s, No. 446
EX $22   **NM** $52   **MIP** $78

❑ **International Hay Rake**, 1:16-scale, Ertl, red w/blue teeth, 1980s-90s, No. 446
EX $8   **NM** $27   **MIP** $32

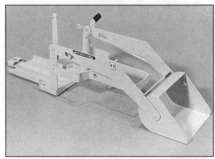

❑ **International Loader**, 1:16-scale, Ertl, white, fits 806, 1960s, No. 444
EX $48   **NM** $82   **MIP** $238

❑ **International Manure Spreader, 200**, 1:16-scale, Ertl, Precision Series #9, No. 4201 *(Photo by Ertl)*
EX $62   **NM** $83   **MIP** $132

❑ **International Minimum-Till Plow**, 1:16-scale, Ertl, red, 1980s, No. 498
EX $38   **NM** $67   **MIP** $88

❑ **International Mixer Mill**, 1:16-scale, Ertl, red, 1980s, No. 325
EX $22   **NM** $42   **MIP** $57

❑ **International Mower**, 1:16-scale, Ertl, red, C hitch, 1960s, No. 445
EX $37   **NM** $73   **MIP** $128

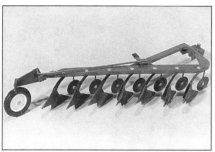

❏ **International Plow**, 1:16-scale, Ertl, red, 7 bottom, metal, 1960s, No. 441
EX $22   **NM** $57   **MIP** $113

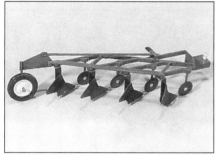

❏ **International Plow**, 1:16-scale, Ertl, red, 4 bottom, decal variations, wheel, die-cast white, plastic red or white, 1960s, No. 442
EX $17   **NM** $57   **MIP** $118

❏ **International Plow**, 1:16-scale, Ertl, red, 3 bottom, 1960s
EX $17   **NM** $48   **MIP** npf

❏ **International Plow**, 1:16-scale, Ertl, red, 4 bottom, reset, 1970s, No. 476
EX $16   **NM** $27   **MIP** $48

❏ **International Plow**, 1:16-scale, Ertl, 6 bottom, 2007, No. 14535
EX $15   **NM** $20   **MIP** $25

❏ **International Spreader**, 1:16-scale, Ertl, red w/white rims, spring driver, 1960s, No. 443
EX $22   **NM** $54   **MIP** $146

❏ **International Spreader**, 1:16-scale, Ertl, red and white, crank hitch, belt drive, 1960s, No. 443
EX $22   **NM** $54   **MIP** $146

❏ **International Spreader**, 1:16-scale, Ertl, red and white, chain drive, C hitch, 1960s, No. 443
EX $16   **NM** $48   **MIP** $96

❏ **International Spreader**, 1:16-scale, Ertl, red w/red rims, spring driver, 1960s, No. 443
EX $22   **NM** $54   **MIP** $146

❏ **International Spreader**, 1:16-scale, Ertl, red and white, 1980s, No. 492
EX $9   **NM** $22   **MIP** $42

❏ **International Wagon**, 1:16-scale, Ertl, red and white, w/Hoist, 1970s, No. 478
EX $18   **NM** $53   **MIP** $118

❏ **International Wagon**, 1:16-scale, Ertl, red and white, removable bed and sides, 1970s, No. 438
EX $18   **NM** $27   **MIP** $88

❏ **International Wagon**, 1:16-scale, Ertl, red and white, plastic rims, 1970s, No. 438
EX $18   **NM** $27   **MIP** $88

❑ **International Wagon**, 1:16-scale, Ertl, red and white, 1970s, No. 478
EX $18   **NM** $27   **MIP** $53

❑ **International Wagon**, 1:16-scale, Ertl, red and white, 1970s, No. 478
EX $18   **NM** $27   **MIP** $53

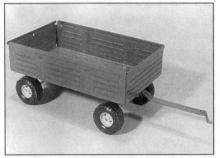

❑ **International Wagon**, 1:16-scale, Ertl, red and white, 1980s, No. 479
EX $6   **NM** $9   **MIP** $14

❑ **International Wagon, Bale**, 1:16-scale, Ertl, red and white, 1980s, No. 439
EX $8   **NM** $12   **MIP** $21

❑ **International Wagon, Forage**, 1:16-scale, Ertl, red and white, 1980s, No. 442
EX $8   **NM** $12   **MIP** $21

❑ **International Wagon, Gravity**, 1:16-scale, Ertl, red and white, w/crank, 1970s, No. 350
EX $22   **NM** $48   **MIP** $89

❑ **McCormick Combine, 76**, 1:16-scale, Baird (Custom), red, did not come in box, 1980s
EX $198   **NM** $273   **MIP** n/a

❑ **McCormick Combine, 76**, 1:16-scale, Baird (Custom), white, demonstrator, did not come in dox, 1990s
EX $198   **NM** $273   **MIP** n/a

❑ **McCormick Combine, 76**, 1:16-scale, Baird (Custom), red, pull type, did not come in box, 1990s
EX $198   **NM** $273   **MIP** n/a

❑ **McCormick Deering Box Wagon**, 1:16-scale, Arcade, green box, red running gear, 1930s
EX $148   **NM** $303   **MIP** $1127

❑ **McCormick Deering Box Wagon**, 1:16-scale, Arcade, green box/red running gear, 1930s
EX $148   **NM** $303   **MIP** $1127

❑ **McCormick Deering Combine, 20**, 1:16-scale, Montana Harvest (Custom), silver, 1990s
EX $389   **NM** $492   **MIP** $562

❑ **McCormick Deering Combine, 22**, 1:16-scale, Montana Harvest, silver, 1990s
EX $389   **NM** $492   **MIP** $562

❑ **McCormick Deering Cream Separator**, 1:16-scale, Arcade, black, 1930s
EX $143   **NM** $323   **MIP** $947

❑ **McCormick Deering Plow**, 1:16-scale, Arcade, red frame, yellow wheels, 7-3/4" long, 1926, No. 283R
EX $93   **NM** $246   **MIP** $822

❑ **McCormick Deering Plow**, 1:16-scale, Arcade, red, 1930s
EX $93   **NM** $246   **MIP** $822

❑ **McCormick Deering Plow**, 1:16-scale, Riecke (Custom), red, blue, black, did not come in box, 1990s
EX $148   **NM** $192   **MIP** n/a

❑ **McCormick Deering Plow**, 1:16-scale, Riecke (Custom), red, blue, black, did not come in box, 1990s
EX $148   **NM** $192   **MIP** n/a

❑ **McCormick Deering Plow**, 1:16-scale, Riecke (Custom), red, blue, black, did not come in box, 1990s
EX $148   **NM** $192   **MIP** n/a

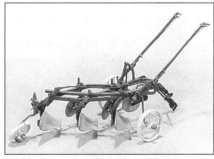

❑ **McCormick Deering Plow**, 1:16-scale, Riecke (Custom), red, blue, black, did not use box, 1990s
EX $148   **NM** $192   **MIP** n/a

❑ **McCormick Deering Spreader**, 1:16-scale, Arcade, red box, blue shields, yellow tongue, 2 black horses, 15" long, 1929, No. 402
EX $215   **NM** $443   **MIP** $982

❑ **McCormick Deering Spreader**, 1:16-scale, Arcade, red box, blue shields, yellow tongue, 1930s
EX $182   **NM** $389   **MIP** $859

❑ **McCormick Deering Thresher Large**, 1:16-scale, Arcade, gray, red trim, yellow wheels, 12" long, 1927, No. 451
EX $193   **NM** $392   **MIP** $932

❑ **McCormick Deering Thresher Small**, 1:16-scale, Arcade, red, green, blue, yellow, 1930s, No. 450
EX $172   **NM** $422   **MIP** $979

❏ **McCormick Deering Wagon**, 1:16-scale, Product Miniature, red, 1950s
EX $28 **NM** $76 **MIP** $158

❏ **McCormick Deering Weber Wagon**, 1:16-scale, Arcade, green wagon w/red wheels, 2 black horses, no driver, buck seat, 12-1/8" long, 1927
EX $193 **NM** $373 **MIP** n/a

❏ **McCormick Disc**, 1:16-scale, Carter, red w/blue or black plastic blades, 1950s
EX $48 **NM** $103 **MIP** $207

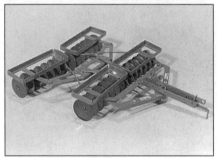

❏ **McCormick Disc**, 1:16-scale, Carter, red w/blue metal blades, 1950s
EX $48 **NM** $103 **MIP** $227

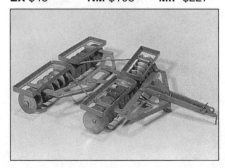

❏ **McCormick Disc**, 1:16-scale, Carter, red w/blue metal blades, 1950s
EX $48 **NM** $103 **MIP** $227

❏ **McCormick Disc**, 1:16-scale, Carter, red w/black plastic blades, fast hitch, 1960s
EX $92 **NM** $178 **MIP** $227

❏ **McCormick Disc**, 1:16-scale, Carter, red w/blue metal blades, fast hitch, 1960s
EX $106 **NM** $182 **MIP** $322

❏ **McCormick Disc**, 1:16-scale, Carter, red w/blue plastic blades, fast hitch, 1960s
EX $92 **NM** $178 **MIP** $227

❏ **McCormick Elevator, 456**, 1:16-scale, Carter, red, 1950s
EX $22 **NM** $77 **MIP** $262

❏ **McCormick International Baler**, 1:16-scale, Ertl, red, 1960s, No. 447
EX $22 **NM** $47 **MIP** $78

❏ **McCormick International Disc**, 1:16-scale, Ertl, red, C hitch, 1960s, No. 439
EX $22 **NM** $73 **MIP** $152

❏ **McCormick International Disc**, 1:16-scale, Ertl, red, crank hitch, 1960s, No. 439
EX $22 **NM** $73 **MIP** $152

❏ **McCormick International Mower**, 1:16-scale, Ertl, red, crank hitch, 1960s
EX $37 **NM** $73 **MIP** $146

❑ **McCormick Loader**, 1:16-scale, Product Miniature, red, 1950s
EX $118   **NM** $148   **MIP** $223

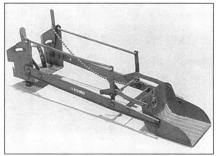

❑ **McCormick Loader Long**, 1:16-scale, Ertl, red, fits Farmall 560, IH decal in bucket, 1950s
EX $48   **NM** $118   **MIP** $233

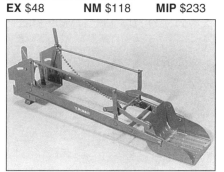

❑ **McCormick Loader Long**, 1:16-scale, Ertl, red, fits Farmall 560, 1950s
EX $48   **NM** $98   **MIP** $212

❑ **McCormick Loader Short**, 1:16-scale, Ertl, red, fits Farmall 400 or 450, 1950s
EX $56   **NM** $102   **MIP** $212

❑ **McCormick Mower, 27**, 1:16-scale, Nygren (Custom), red, 1980s
EX $48   **NM** $82   **MIP** npf

❑ **McCormick Plow**, 1:16-scale, Carter, red, 2 bottom, solid rubber tail wheel, 1950s
EX $53   **NM** $118   **MIP** $289

❑ **McCormick Plow**, 1:16-scale, Carter, red, 3 bottom, fast hitch, metal tail wheel, 1950s
EX $108   **NM** $189   **MIP** $342

❑ **McCormick Plow**, 1:16-scale, Carter, red, 3 bottom, fast hitch, plastic tail wheel, 1950s
EX $108   **NM** $217   **MIP** $467

❑ **McCormick Plow**, 1:16-scale, Carter, red, 2 bottom, white tail wheel, 1950s
EX $53   **NM** $142   **MIP** $342

❑ **McCormick Plow**, 1:16-scale, Carter, red, 2 bottom, red tail wheel, 1950s
EX $53   **NM** $118   **MIP** $289

❑ **McCormick Plow**, 1:16-scale, Carter, red, 2 bottom, red tail wheel, 1950s
EX $53   **NM** $118   **MIP** $289

❑ **McCormick Plow, Little Genius**, 1:16-scale, Riecke (Custom), red, did not come w/box, 1980s
EX $148   **NM** $192   **MIP** n/a

❑ **McCormick Plow, Little Genius**, 1:16-scale, Riecke (Custom), red, did not come w/box, 1980s

EX $148   **NM** $192   **MIP** n/a

❑ **McCormick Plow, Little Genius 3-bottom**, 1:16-scale, Ertl, Precision Classic, No. 233 *(Photo by Ertl)*

EX $77   **NM** $148   **MIP** $248

❑ **McCormick Reaper**, 1:16-scale, McCormick Works, natural wood, 1931

EX $1382   **NM** $1926   **MIP** npf

❑ **McCormick Spreader**, 1:16-scale, Carter, red and white, 1950s

EX $48   **NM** $93   **MIP** $218

❑ **McCormick Spreader**, 1:16-scale, Carter, red and white, 1950s

EX $48   **NM** $93   **MIP** $218

❑ **McCormick Spreader**, 1:16-scale, Carter, red, white wheels, 1950s

EX $48   **NM** $93   **MIP** $218

❑ **McCormick Spreader**, 1:16-scale, Carter, red, red wheels, 1950s

EX $48   **NM** $93   **MIP** $218

❑ **McCormick Spreader**, 1:16-scale, Carter, red, solid rubber tires, 1950s

EX $48   **NM** $93   **MIP** $218

❑ **McCormick Wagon**, 1:16-scale, red, 1950s

EX $119   **NM** $172   **MIP** n/a

❑ **McCormick Wagon**, 1:16-scale, Ertl, red and white, removable bed and sides, tin wheels, decals vary, 1950s, No. 438

EX $22   **NM** $35   **MIP** $132

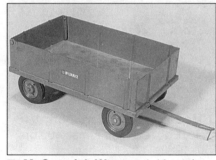

❑ **McCormick Wagon**, 1:16-scale, Ertl, red and white, removable bed and sides, tin wheels, decals vary, 1950s, No. 438

EX $22   **NM** $53   **MIP** $132

❑ **McCormick Wagon**, 1:16-scale, Ertl, red, removable bed and sides, tin wheels, decals vary, 1950s, No. 438

EX $28   **NM** $87   **MIP** $182

❑ **McCormick Wagon**, 1:16-scale, Ertl, red and white, removable bed and sides, tin wheels, decals vary, 1960s, No. 438
EX $22   **NM** $53   **MIP** $132

❑ **McCormick Wagon**, 1:16-scale, Product Miniature, red, 1950s
EX $28   **NM** $76   **MIP** $158

❑ **Trac-Trailer**, 1:16-scale, Arcade, red, 1930s
EX $428   **NM** $913   **MIP** $3092

IMPLEMENTS 1:24-SCALE

❑ **International Combine, 915**, 1:24-scale, Ertl, red and white, smooth or knobby rear tires, plastic reel, silver steering column, 1960s, No. 400
EX $98   **NM** $248   **MIP** $432

❑ **International Combine, 915**, 1:24-scale, Ertl, red and white, silver column for steering wheel, 1960s, No. 400
EX $98   **NM** $248   **MIP** $432

❑ **International Combine, 915**, 1:24-scale, Ertl, red and white, no dual exhaust stacks, plastic reel, 1970s, No. 400
EX $98   **NM** $248   **MIP** $432

❑ **International Combine, 915**, 1:24-scale, Ertl, white and red, red steering column, 1970s, No. 400
EX $98   **NM** $248   **MIP** $432

IMPLEMENTS 1:25-SCALE

❑ **International Plow, 710**, 1:25-scale, Ertl, red, 6 bottom, 1970s, No. 8011
EX $8   **NM** $22   **MIP** $37

❑ **International Wagon**, 1:25-scale, Ertl, red, w/hoist, 1970s, No. 8004
EX $4   **NM** $11   **MIP** $24

IMPLEMENTS 1:28-SCALE

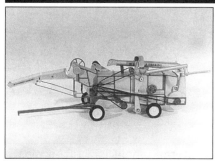

❑ **McCormick Thresher**, 1:28-scale, SpecCast, No. ZJD731 *(Photo by Kate Bossen)*
EX $33   **NM** $54   **MIP** $66

IMPLEMENTS 1:32-SCALE

❑ **International Baler, 2400**, 1:32-scale, Ertl, red w/white or red rims (correct rims), 1980s, No. 1642
EX $4   **NM** $14   **MIP** $22

❑ **International Baler, 2400**, 1:32-scale, Ertl, red w/orange rims (incorrect rims), 1980s, No. 1642
EX $4   **NM** $14   **MIP** $22

❏ **International Combine**, 1:32-scale, Ertl, red, red or black ladder, Axial Flow, 1970s, No. 413
EX $22   **NM** $47   **MIP** $62

❏ **International Disc**, 1:32-scale, Ertl, red, 1970s, No. 1553
EX $4   **NM** $8   **MIP** $14

❏ **International Disc**, 1:32-scale, Ertl, red, w/wings, 1980s, No. 1553
EX $1   **NM** $2   **MIP** $6

❏ **International Minimum-Till Plow**, 1:32-scale, Ertl, red, 1980s, No. 1552
EX $14   **NM** $27   **MIP** $38

❏ **International Plow**, 1:32-scale, Ertl, red, 6 bottom, 1970s, No. 1641
EX $4   **NM** $8   **MIP** $14

❏ **International Plow**, 1:32-scale, Ertl, red, 4 bottom, 1980s, No. 43
EX $4   **NM** $8   **MIP** $14

❏ **International Spreader**, 1:32-scale, Ertl, red and white, 1970s, No. 44
EX $4   **NM** $8   **MIP** $14

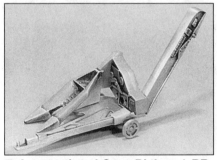

❏ **International Wagon**, 1:32-scale, Ertl, red, 1970s, No. 41
EX $4   **NM** $8   **MIP** $14

❏ **International Wagon**, 1:32-scale, Ertl, red, 1980s, No. 1639
EX $2   **NM** $3   **MIP** $6

❏ **McCormick Deering Thresher Small**, 1:32-scale, Arcade, red, green, blue, yellow; 9-1/2" long, 1930, No. 450
EX $172   **NM** $422   **MIP** $979

IMPLEMENTS 1:43-SCALE

❏ **International Corn Picker, 1-PR**, 1:43-scale, Ertl, red/white, No. 2621
EX $6   **NM** $12   **MIP** $18

❏ **International Corn Picker, 1-PR**, 1:43-scale, SpecCast, 1990s
EX $6   **NM** $8   **MIP** $12

Photos by Jon Jacobson unless otherwise noted.

IMPLEMENTS 1:64-SCALE

❏ **International 2400 Baler**, 1:64-scale, Variation photo: Baler on the left has hydraulic hoses, baler on the right does not

❏ **International Baler, 2400**, 1:64-scale, Ertl, red, w/o Right side hydraulic hoses, No. 1758
EX $3   **NM** $4   **MIP** $9

❏ **International Baler, 2400**, 1:64-scale, Ertl, red w/gray rims, No. 1758
EX $3   **NM** $4   **MIP** $9

❏ **International Baler, 2400**, 1:64-scale, Ertl, red w/red rims, No. 1758
EX $3   **NM** $4   **MIP** $9

❏ **International Combine**, 1:64-scale, Gunning (Custom), red and white, did not come in box
EX $27   **NM** $48   **MIP** n/a

❏ **International Combine 815**, 1:64-scale, Ertl, 1998, No. 4354
EX $4   **NM** $6   **MIP** $9

❏ **International Corn Picker**, 1:64-scale, Nygren (Custom), red and white, did not come in box
EX $11   **NM** $33   **MIP** n/a

❏ **International Corn Picker**, 1:64-scale, Nygren (Custom), red, did not come in box
EX $11   **NM** $33   **MIP** n/a

❏ **International Corn Picker**, 1:64-scale, Nygren (Custom), red, did not come in box
EX $11   **NM** $33   **MIP** n/a

❏ **International Flare Wagon**, 1:64-scale, Nygren (Custom), red, did not come in box
EX $6   **NM** $12   **MIP** n/a

❏ **International Harvestor Disc**, 1:64-scale, Matsen (Custom), red and black, did not come in box
EX $12   **NM** $27   **MIP** n/a

❏ **International Mixmill**, 1:64-scale, Ertl, red, may have white or cream-rims, No. 1551
EX $4   **NM** $5   **MIP** $13

❏ **International Picker**, 1:64-scale, Walters (Custom), red and white
EX $11   **NM** $33   **MIP** n/a

❏ **International Picker-Sheller**, 1:64-scale, Nygren (Custom), red and white, did not come in box
EX $11   **NM** $33   **MIP** n/a

❏ **International Planter, 800**, 1:64-scale, Ertl, red and white, hinges on the seed-hopper may be to the front or rear, No. 1579
EX $3   **NM** $4   **MIP** $12

❏ **International Planter, 800**, 1:64-scale, Ertl, red and cream, hinges on the seed-hopper may be to the front or rear, No. 1579
EX $3   **NM** $4   **MIP** $6

❏ **International Sickle Mower**, 1:64-scale, Nygren (Custom), red and silver, did not come in box
EX $4   **NM** $9   **MIP** n/a

❏ **International Sickle Mower**, 1:64-scale, Van Hove (Custom), red and black, did not come in box
EX $4   **NM** $9   **MIP** n/a

❏ **McCormick Baler**, 1:64-scale, Nygren (Custom), red, did not come in box
EX $6   **NM** $9   **MIP** n/a

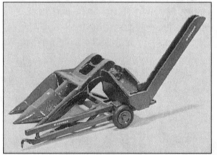

❏ **McCormick Picker**, 1:64-scale, Nygren (Custom), red, did not come in box
EX $6   **NM** $9   **MIP** n/a

❏ **McCormick Wagon, Flare Box**, 1:64-scale, Nygren (Custom), red, did not come in box
EX $2   **NM** $12   **MIP** n/a

IMPLEMENTS 1:80-SCALE

❏ **International Combine**, 1:80-scale, Ertl, red and white, No. 408
EX $12   **NM** $19   **MIP** $29

❏ **International Combine**, 1:80-scale, Ertl, red and white, No. 1520
EX $12   **NM** $19   **MIP** $29

❏ **International Combine**, 1:80-scale, Ertl, red and white, large International Harvester decal, No. 1520
EX $12   **NM** $19   **MIP** $29

❏ **International Combine**, 1:80-scale, Ertl, red and white, small International Harvester decal, No. 1520
EX $12   **NM** $19   **MIP** $29

❑ **International Combine**, 1:80-scale, Ertl, red and white, black auger, non-production run, did not come in box
EX $19   **NM** $48   **MIP** n/a

LAWN AND GARDEN 1:16-SCALE

❑ **Cub Cadet 122**, 1:16-scale, Ertl, white hood w/yellow body, w/blade and cart, 1960s, No. 432
EX $92   **NM** $242   **MIP** $783

❑ **Cub Cadet 122**, 1:16-scale, Ertl, white hood w/yellow body, 1960s, No. 432
EX $73   **NM** $176   **MIP** $682

❑ **Cub Cadet 125**, 1:16-scale, Ertl, white hood w/yellow body, 1960s
EX $88   **NM** $192   **MIP** $682

❑ **Cub Cadet 125**, 1:16-scale, Ertl, white hood w/yellow body, w/blade and cart, 1960s
EX $92   **NM** $226   **MIP** $853

❑ **Cub Cadet 126**, 1:16-scale, Ertl, white hood w/yellow body, 1970s
EX $53   **NM** $126   **MIP** $333

❑ **Cub Cadet 126**, 1:16-scale, Ertl, white hood w/yellow body, w/blade and cart, 1970s
EX $58   **NM** $128   **MIP** $433

❑ **Cub Cadet 129**, 1:16-scale, Ertl, white hood w/yellow body, w/blade and cart, 1970s, No. 433
EX $38   **NM** $63   **MIP** $162

❑ **Cub Cadet 129**, 1:16-scale, Ertl, white hood w/yellow body, 1970s, No. 432
EX $33   **NM** $58   **MIP** $133

❑ **Cub Cadet 1650**, 1:16-scale, Ertl, white hood w/yellow body, 1970s, No. 435
EX $22   **NM** $43   **MIP** $73

❑ **Cub Cadet 1650**, 1:16-scale, Ertl, white hood w/yellow body, w/blade and cart, 1970s, No. 436
EX $27   **NM** $58   **MIP** $88

❑ **Cub Cadet 1650**, 1:16-scale, Ertl, 1650 Cub Cadet w/129 Cub Cadet decals, white hood w/yellow body, w/blade and cart, 1970s, No. 436
EX $27   **NM** $59   **MIP** $88

❑ **Cub Cadet 682**, 1:16-scale, Ertl, red, Collectors Edition, also available in non-collectors, 1980s, No. 459DA
EX $16   **NM** $37   **MIP** $58

❑ **Cub Cadet LGT**, 1:16-scale, Scale Models, white and yellow, 1990s, No. FR-1904
EX $6   **NM** $14   **MIP** $23

❑ **Louisville Cubs**, gold, price is for each, holding toy, January 1949
EX $47   **NM** $98   **MIP** $238

PEDAL TRACTORS

❑ **Cub Cadet**, Ertl, WF, 2000, No. 13115
EX $92   **NM** $187   **MIP** $233

❑ **Cub Cadet**, Scale Models, NF, 1997, No. 1907
EX $122   **NM** $174   **MIP** $262

❑ **Cub Cadet 682**, 1:16-scale, Ertl, red, w/blade cart, 1980s, No. 465
EX $18   **NM** $47   **MIP** $58

❑ **Cub Cadet Spirit of '76**, 1:16-scale, Ertl, white hood w/red body, 1976, No. 432
EX $67   **NM** $154   **MIP** $264

MISCELLANEOUS

❑ **Farmall 1206**, Scale Models, 2006, No. 1068 *(Photo by Scale Models)*
EX $86   **NM** $112   **MIP** $156

❑ **Cub Cadet 682**, 1:16-scale, Ertl, white hood w/yellow body, Collectors Edition, also available in non-collectors, 1980s, No. 466DA
EX $16   **NM** $37   **MIP** $58

❑ **Farmall Farm Management Game**, Big Top Games, 1970s
EX $8   **NM** $22   **MIP** $133

❑ **Cub Cadet GT**, 1:16-scale, Scale Models, wo/mower deck, 1990s, No. FR-1903 *(Photo by Scale Models)*
EX $6   **NM** $9   **MIP** $18

❑ **Louisville Cadet**, gold/one was chrome plated, September 14, 1974
EX $189   **NM** $322   **MIP** $678

❑ **Farmall 400**, Eska, red, original tractor restored, 1950s
EX $448   **NM** $769   **MIP** $2388

❑ **Farmall 450**, Eska, red w/decal grille, original tractor restored, 1957
EX $478   **NM** $769   **MIP** $2388

❑ **Farmall 460**, Scale Models, 2006, No. 1061
EX $86   **NM** $112   **MIP** $156

❑ **Farmall 560**, Eska, red w/white decal, original tractor restored, 1958
EX $377   **NM** $792   **MIP** $1622

❑ **Farmall 560**, Scale Models, NF, 2000, No. ZSM939
EX $92   **NM** $118   **MIP** $153

❑ **Farmall 706**, Scale Models, WF, '03 Farm Progress Show Edition, 2003, No. ZSM1014
EX $98   **NM** $123   **MIP** $168

❑ **Farmall 806**, Ertl, red w/white decal, original tractor restored, 1964
EX $383   **NM** $592   **MIP** $1469

❑ **Farmall 806**, Scale Models, NF, w/muffler, Collector Edition, 2003, No. ZSM994
EX $98   **NM** $123   **MIP** $168

❑ **Farmall 826**, Scale Models, Hydro, Gold Demonstrator, 2004, No. 1026
EX $86   **NM** $112   **MIP** $156

❑ **Farmall F-20**, Ertl, NF, red, 2001, No. 14147
EX $102   **NM** $156   **MIP** $207

❑ **Farmall F-20**, Ertl, NF, gray, Collector Edition, 2001, No. 14224A
EX $123   **NM** $182   **MIP** $289

❑ **Farmall H**, Scale Models, muffler, fenders, Farm Progress Show Edition, 2005, No. 1042
EX $86   **NM** $112   **MIP** $166

❑ **Farmall H Mid Size**, Eska, red, closed grille, low steering post, original tractor restored, IH decal placed away from tractor name, 1951
EX $622   **NM** $789   **MIP** $2489

❑ **Farmall H Mid Size**, Eska, red, high steering post, closed grille, tractor in original condition, 1952
EX $622   **NM** $789   **MIP** $2489

❑ **Farmall H Mid Size**, Eska, red, w/open grille, original tractor restored, 1952
EX $769   **NM** $789   **MIP** $2489

❑ **Farmall H Small Version**, Eska, red, open grille, tractor in original condition, 1949
EX $769   **NM** $789   **MIP** $2692

❑ **Farmall H Small Version**, Eska, red, w/radiator cap, decal placed wrong, original tractor restored, 1949
EX $769   **NM** $789   **MIP** $2692

❑ **Farmall M**, Scale Models, NF, red, '03 Farm Progress Show Edition, 1998, No. FB-2503
EX $96   **NM** $162   **MIP** $222

❑ **Farmall M**, Scale Models, NF, white, "Demonstrator," Collector Edition, 20001, No. ZSM944
EX $85   **NM** $122   **MIP** $176

❑ **Farmall M Large Version**, Eska, red, original condition; different engine casting, rear axle housings cast in one piece w/body casting, 1953
EX $1892   **NM** $3972   **MIP** $4492

Photos by Jon Jacobson unless otherwise noted.

❏ **Farmall M Large Version**, Eska, red, closed grille, rear axle housings are bolted to the body casting, original tractor restored, 1954
EX $669   **NM** $1163   **MIP** $2683

❏ **Farmall Super H**, Scale Models, 2006, No. 1062
EX $86   **NM** $112   **MIP** $156

❏ **Farmall Super M**, Scale Models, NF, w/muffler, Collector Edition, 1999, No. ZSM912
EX $98   **NM** $123   **MIP** $168

❏ **Farmall Super M**, Scale Models, NF, no muffler, 1999, No. ZSM919
EX $92   **NM** $118   **MIP** $153

❏ **Farmall Super M**, Scale Models, NF, '01 Farm Progress Show Edition, 2001, No. ZSM964
EX $98   **NM** $123   **MIP** $168

❏ **Farmall Super MTA**, Scale Models, Red Power Round-Up, 2004, No. 1040
EX $86   **NM** $112   **MIP** $156

❏ **International 1026**, Ertl, red w/white decal, original tractor restored, 1970, No. 450
EX $236   **NM** $389   **MIP** $732

❏ **International 1255**, Rolly Toys, red, not marketed in the USA, tractor in original condition
EX $338   **NM** $462   **MIP** n/a

❏ **International 2+2 Ride On**, Ertl, red, tractor in original condition
EX $14   **NM** $47   **MIP** $113

❏ **International 50 Series**, Ertl, red and black, tractor in original condition, 1986
EX $48   **NM** $162   **MIP** $198

❏ **International 66 Series**, Ertl, red w/white decal, tractor in original condition, 1971
EX $143   **NM** $289   **MIP** $529

❏ **International 856**, Ertl, red w/white decal, original tractor restored, 1967, No. 450
EX $229   **NM** $339   **MIP** $734

❏ **International 86 Series**, Ertl, red w/black stripe decal, tractor in original condition, 1978, No. 612
EX $142   **NM** $283   **MIP** $442

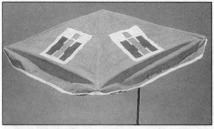

❏ **International Umbrella**, Heltrick, red, umbrella in original condition
EX $138   **NM** $327   **MIP** $398

❏ **McCormick MTX-140**, Scale Models, red, '02 Farm Progress Show Edition, 2002, No. FB-1300
EX $118   **NM** $132   **MIP** $168

TRACTORS 1:08-SCALE

❏ **Farmall 1206**, 1:08-scale, Scale Models, 1999, No. ZSM913
EX $67   **NM** $92   **MIP** $153

❏ **Farmall 400**, 1:08-scale, Scale Models, NF, gas, 1998, No. ZSM904
EX $67   **NM** $92   **MIP** $153

❏ **Farmall 450**, 1:08-scale, Scale Models, NF, gas, 2002, No. ZSM982
EX $67   **NM** $92   **MIP** $153

❏ **Farmall 560**, 1:08-scale, Scale Models, No. ZSM848 *(Photo by Scale Models)*
EX $67   **NM** $92   **MIP** $143

❏ **Farmall 560**, 1:08-scale, Scale Models, NF, gas, 1997, No. ZSM848
EX $67   **NM** $92   **MIP** $143

❑ **Farmall 806**, 1:08-scale, Scale Models, gold demonstrator, 2001, No. ZSM948
EX $67   **NM** $92   **MIP** $153

❑ **Farmall 856**, 1:08-scale, Scale Models, '99 Farm Progress Show Edition, 1999, No. ZSM921
EX $67   **NM** $92   **MIP** $153

❑ **Farmall M**, 1:08-scale, Scale Models, No. ZSM836 *(Photo by Scale Models)*
EX $67   **NM** $92   **MIP** $143

TRACTORS 1:12-SCALE

❑ **International Cub Mower**, 1:12-scale, Riecke (Custom), red, fits IH Cub, 1980s
EX $88   **NM** $126   **MIP** npf

❑ **International Cub Plow**, 1:12-scale, Riecke (Custom), red, fits IH Cub, did not come in box, 1980s
EX $98   **NM** $137   **MIP** n/a

❑ **McCormick 624**, 1:12-scale, Mont Blanc, red, 1960s
EX $188   **NM** $269   **MIP** $346

TRACTORS 1:16-SCALE

❑ **Farmall 100**, 1:16-scale, Dingman (Custom), red, did not come in box, 1990s
EX $167   **NM** $262   **MIP** n/a

❑ **Farmall 100**, 1:16-scale, Ertl, high clear, '93 Summer Show Edition, 1993, No. 4614RA
EX $26   **NM** $37   **MIP** $53

❑ **Farmall 100**, 1:16-scale, Ertl, high clear, Collector Edition, 2002, No. 4614RC
EX $18   **NM** $29   **MIP** $43

❑ **Farmall 100**, 1:16-scale, Florida Classics, red, 1980s
EX $16   **NM** $24   **MIP** $32

❑ **Farmall 1206**, 1:16-scale, Burnett/Snyder, red, 10th Annual Michigan Farm Toy Show, 1990s
EX $53   **NM** $72   **MIP** $122

❑ **Farmall 1206**, 1:16-scale, Dressler (Custom), red, did not come in box, 1990s
EX $82   **NM** $178   **MIP** n/a

❑ **Farmall 1206**, 1:16-scale, Ertl, red, 1960s, No. 436
EX $122   **NM** $289   **MIP** $959

❑ **Farmall 1206**, 1:16-scale, Ertl, '95 LaFayette Show Edition, 1995, No. 491PA
EX $48   **NM** $73   **MIP** $117

❑ **Farmall 1206**, 1:16-scale, Ertl, Foxfire Farm, w/Warren, 1998, No. 4440
EX $18   **NM** $28   **MIP** $42

❑ **Farmall 1206**, 1:16-scale, Ertl, '98 IA FFA, 1998, No. 16003A
EX $23   **NM** $32   **MIP** $58

❑ **Farmall 1206**, 1:16-scale, Ertl, 100th Anniversary Edition, 2002, No. 14196A
EX $48   **NM** $73   **MIP** $102

❑ **Farmall 1206**, 1:16-scale, Ertl, duals, 40th Anniversary, 2005, No. 14487A
EX $19   **NM** $27   **MIP** $43

❑ **Farmall 1206**, 1:16-scale, Ertl, #1 in Key Precision Series, 2005, No. 14408 *(Photo by Bossen Implement)*
EX $68   **NM** $82   **MIP** $128

❑ **Farmall 1206**, 1:16-scale, Scale Models, '93 Ontario Show Edition, 1993, No. FB-1612
EX $67   **NM** $82   **MIP** $123

❑ **Farmall 1206**, 1:16-scale, Scale Models, MFD, '04 Ontario Show Edition, 2004
EX $53   **NM** $72   **MIP** $118

❑ **Farmall 130**, 1:16-scale, Dingman (Custom), red, did not come in box, 1990s
EX $167   **NM** $222   **MIP** n/a

❑ **Farmall 130**, 1:16-scale, Ertl, '93 LaFayette Show Edition, 1993, No. 254TA
EX $23   **NM** $33   **MIP** $53

❑ **Farmall 130**, 1:16-scale, Ertl, high clear, '01 National Farm Toy Museum, 2001, No. 16085A
EX $16   **NM** $27   **MIP** $42

❑ **Farmall 130**, 1:16-scale, Florida Classics, red and white, Penn's Cave Show Tractor, 1980s
EX $22   **NM** $36   **MIP** $52

❑ **Farmall 140**, 1:16-scale, Ertl, '94 LaFayette Show Edition, 1994, No. 4742TA *(Photo by Ertl)*
EX $18   **NM** $28   **MIP** $38

❑ **Farmall 140**, 1:16-scale, Ertl, late version, 1995, No. 4754 *(Photo by Ertl)*
EX $14   **NM** $21   **MIP** $32

❑ **Farmall 140**, 1:16-scale, Ertl, '95 Farm Show Edition, 1995, No. 4741TA
EX $14   **NM** $21   **MIP** $33

❑ **Farmall 140**, 1:16-scale, Ertl, Replica Magazine Edition, 1 of 5000, 1996, No. 2321TA
EX $16   **NM** $23   **MIP** $38

❑ **Farmall 140**, 1:16-scale, Florida Classics, red, 3rd Grand National Toy Show, 1980s
EX $22   **NM** $27   **MIP** $42

❑ **Farmall 140**, 1:16-scale, Florida Classics, yellow, 16th Annual 1990 Penn's Cave Pennsylvania Show and Sale, 1990s
EX $22   **NM** $27   **MIP** $42

❑ **Farmall 140**, 1:16-scale, Florida Classics, yellow, 16th Annual 1990 Penn's Cave Pennsylvania Show and Sale, 1990s
EX $22   **NM** $27   **MIP** $42

❑ **Farmall 140**, 1:16-scale, Freiheit (Custom), red, did not come in box, rubber rear tires, 1980s
EX $167   **NM** $242   **MIP** n/a

❑ **Farmall 140**, 1:16-scale, Freiheit (Custom), red, did not come in box, plastic rear tires, 1980s

❏ **Farmall 1456**, 1:16-scale, Ertl, 1997, No. 2311 *(Photo by Ertl)*
EX $18   **NM** $27   **MIP** $42

❏ **Farmall 200**, 1:16-scale, Classic Farm Toys, red, 1980s
EX $22   **NM** $33   **MIP** $46

❏ **Farmall 200**, 1:16-scale, Ertl, '00 LaFayette Show Edition, 2000, No. 16030A
EX $16   **NM** $27   **MIP** $43

❏ **Farmall 200**, 1:16-scale, Florida Classics, red, did not come in box, 1980s
EX $23   **NM** $42   **MIP** n/a

❏ **Farmall 200**, 1:16-scale, Lakone, red, 1950s
EX $148   **NM** $382   **MIP** $986

❏ **Farmall 230**, 1:16-scale, Classic Farm Toys, red, 1980s
EX $22   **NM** $33   **MIP** $46

❏ **Farmall 230**, 1:16-scale, Ertl, NF, '99 Toy Tractor Times Anniversary, #14; 2,500 produced, 1999, No. 16019A
EX $22   **NM** $33   **MIP** $58

❏ **Farmall 230**, 1:16-scale, Ertl, WF, 2000, No. 14040
EX $11   **NM** $17   **MIP** $32

❏ **Farmall 230**, 1:16-scale, Florida Classics, red, 1980s
EX $22   **NM** $29   **MIP** $42

❏ **Farmall 230**, 1:16-scale, Freiheit (Custom), red, did not come in box, 1980s
EX $142   **NM** $189   **MIP** n/a

❏ **Farmall 230**, 1:16-scale, Lakone, red, 1950s
EX $148   **NM** $382   **MIP** $986

❏ **Farmall 300**, 1:16-scale, Ertl, red, 1984 National Farm Toy Show Tractor, 1984, No. 417PA
EX $33   **NM** $52   **MIP** $98

❏ **Farmall 300**, 1:16-scale, Ertl, NF, 1998, No. 14000
EX $11   **NM** $17   **MIP** $32

❏ **Farmall 300**, 1:16-scale, Freiheit (Custom), red, did not come in box, 1980s
EX $142   **NM** $189   **MIP** n/a

❏ **Farmall 300**, 1:16-scale, SpecCast, NF, gas, 2003, No. ZJD159
EX $19   **NM** $28   **MIP** $43

❏ **Farmall 340**, 1:16-scale, SpecCast, NF, gas, 2006, No. 1507
EX $18   **NM** $26   **MIP** $44

❏ **Farmall 340**, 1:16-scale, SpecCast, NF, diesel, LaFayette, Indiana show, 2006, No. 1502
EX $22   **NM** $33   **MIP** $53

❏ **Farmall 350**, 1:16-scale, Ertl, red, WF, 1980s, No. 418
EX $14   **NM** $19   **MIP** $28

❏ **Farmall 350**, 1:16-scale, Ertl, red, Collectors Edition, 1980s, No. 418DA
EX $18   **NM** $26   **MIP** $42

❏ **Farmall 350**, 1:16-scale, Ertl, red, '86 Canadian Farm Show Edition, 1986, No. 422UA
EX $22   **NM** $33   **MIP** $42

❏ **Farmall 350**, 1:16-scale, Ertl, WF, '91 Iowa FFA Edition, 1991, No. 4979TA
EX $19   **NM** $28   **MIP** $43

❏ **Farmall 350**, 1:16-scale, Freiheit (Custom), red, did not come in box, 1980s
EX $147   **NM** $202   **MIP** n/a

❏ **Farmall 350**, 1:16-scale, SpecCast, WF, LP, high clear, '04 LaFayette Show Edition, 2004, No. ZJD160
EX $19   **NM** $38   **MIP** $53

❏ **Farmall 350**, 1:16-scale, SpecCast, NF, LP, 2004, No. ZJD165
EX $19   **NM** $28   **MIP** $43

❏ **Farmall 400**, 1:16-scale, Ertl, red, 1950s
EX $198   **NM** $432   **MIP** $1432

❏ **Farmall 400**, 1:16-scale, Ertl, red, split rims on rear, 1950s
EX $222   **NM** $472   **MIP** $1973

❏ **Farmall 400**, 1:16-scale, Ertl, NF, gas, #13 Precision Series, 2000, No. 14007
EX $62   **NM** $77   **MIP** $117

❏ **Farmall 400**, 1:16-scale, Ertl, w/cultivator, 50th Anniversary, Precision Series, 2004, No. 14333A
EX $82   **NM** $156   **MIP** $328

❏ **Farmall 400**, 1:16-scale, SpecCast, WF, gas, Claire Scheibe Memorial Edition, 2002, No. CUST729
EX $32   **NM** $48   **MIP** $68

❏ **Farmall 400**, 1:16-scale, SpecCast, NF, diesel, '02 Toy Tractor Times Anniversary, #17; 564 produced, 2002, No. CUST745
EX $23   **NM** $35   **MIP** $52

❏ **Farmall 400**, 1:16-scale, SpecCast, NF, diesel, 2002, No. ZJD155
EX $19   **NM** $28   **MIP** $43

❏ **Farmall 400**, 1:16-scale, SpecCast, gas, high crop, '03 LaFayette Show Edition, 2003, No. ZJD157
EX $23   **NM** $32   **MIP** $48

❏ **Farmall 400**, 1:16-scale, SpecCast, NF, '04 Mason City, IA Show Edition, 2004, No. CUST805
EX $23   **NM** $32   **MIP** $48

❏ **Farmall 400**, 1:16-scale, SpecCast, gas, NF, 2004, No. ZJD166
EX $19   **NM** $28   **MIP** $43

❏ **Farmall 400**, 1:16-scale, SpecCast, gas, w/loader, 2006, No. 1526 *(Photo by SpecCast)*
EX $27   **NM** $34   **MIP** $53

❏ **Farmall 400**, 1:16-scale, SpecCast, gas, w/"Electrall" side-mount generator, 2006, No. 1525

(Photo by SpecCast)
EX $26   **NM** $33   **MIP** $44

❏ **Farmall 404**, 1:16-scale, Ertl, red, NF, white rims, 1960s
EX $48   **NM** $157   **MIP** $588

❏ **Farmall 404**, 1:16-scale, Ertl, red, w/Ertl Toy decals, 1960s
EX $273   **NM** $392   **MIP** $1589

Photos by Jon Jacobson unless otherwise noted.

❏ **Farmall 404**, 1:16-scale, Ertl, red, NF, die-cast rims, red rims, 1960s, No. 437
EX $83   **NM** $257   **MIP** $872

❏ **Farmall 404**, 1:16-scale, Ertl, red, plastic front rims, die-cast rear rims, 1960s
EX $83   **NM** $257   **MIP** $772

❏ **Farmall 404**, 1:16-scale, Ertl, red, NF, plastic front rims, die-cast rear rims, International decal, 1960s
EX $98   **NM** $257   **MIP** $772

❏ **Farmall 404**, 1:16-scale, Ertl, red, NF, all plastic rims, 1960s, No. 437
EX $83   **NM** $257   **MIP** $872

❏ **Farmall 404**, 1:16-scale, Ertl, red, does not have lights in the grille, utility, 1960s
EX $167   **NM** $387   **MIP** $1359

❏ **Farmall 404**, 1:16-scale, Ertl, red, w/ and w/o three-point hitch, utility, 1960s
EX $98   **NM** $257   **MIP** $772

❏ **Farmall 450**, 1:16-scale, Ertl, red, 1950s
EX $227   **NM** $672   **MIP** $1923

❏ **Farmall 450**, 1:16-scale, Ertl, NF, Precision Series, 50th Anniversary, 2005, No. 14426A
EX $62   **NM** $89   **MIP** $142

❏ **Farmall 450**, 1:16-scale, SpecCast, NF, gas, '02 LaFayette Show Edition, brass tacks demonstrator, 2002, No. CUST724
EX $23   **NM** $32   **MIP** $48

❏ **Farmall 450**, 1:16-scale, SpecCast, NF, 2002, No. ZJD153
EX $19   **NM** $28   **MIP** $43

❏ **Farmall 450**, 1:16-scale, SpecCast, WF, LP, '03 Mason City Show Edition, 2003, No. CUST761
EX $23   **NM** $32   **MIP** $48

❏ **Farmall 450**, 1:16-scale, SpecCast, WF, LP, 2003, No. ZJD161
EX $19   **NM** $28   **MIP** $43

❏ **Farmall 460**, 1:16-scale, Ertl, red, w/ and w/o two-point hitch, also w/plastic front rims, 1960s
EX $98   **NM** $277   **MIP** $869

❏ **Farmall 460**, 1:16-scale, Ertl, NF, gas, #11 Precision Series, 1998, No. 4355
EX $62   **NM** $77   **MIP** $117

❏ **Farmall 504**, 1:16-scale, SpecCast, gas, NF, round fenders, 2005, No. 186
EX $22   **NM** $33   **MIP** $46

❏ **Farmall 504**, 1:16-scale, SpecCast, gas, NF, flat fenders, LaFayette, Indiana show, 2005, No. 184
EX $22   **NM** $33   **MIP** $48

❏ **Farmall 504**, 1:16-scale, SpecCast, gas, WF, flat fenders, 2005, No. 190
EX $22   **NM** $33   **MIP** $46

❏ **Farmall 504**, 1:16-scale, SpecCast, diesel, WF, round fenders, 2007, No. 1547
EX $22   **NM** $33   **MIP** $46

❏ **Farmall 560**, 1:16-scale, Ertl, red, NF, two-point hitch, belt pulley, 400-style front rims, 1950s
EX $137   **NM** $377   **MIP** $1273

❏ **Farmall 560**, 1:16-scale, Ertl, red, NF, two-point hitch, w/and w/o belt pulley, 1960s, No. 408
EX $98   **NM** $277   **MIP** $989

❏ **Farmall 560**, 1:16-scale, Ertl, red, red plastic rims, plastic grille, 1970s, No. 408
EX $67   **NM** $198   **MIP** $784

❏ **Farmall 560**, 1:16-scale, Ertl, red, puller, small front wheels, 1970s, No. 2701
EX $83   **NM** $187   **MIP** $354

❏ **Farmall 560**, 1:16-scale, Ertl, red, no two-point or belt pulley, plastic red front rims, 1960s, No. 408
EX $67   **NM** $198   **MIP** $782

❏ **Farmall 560**, 1:16-scale, Ertl, red, white plastic rims, no 560 decal, 1970s, No. 408
EX $67   **NM** $198   **MIP** $736

❏ **Farmall 560**, 1:16-scale, Ertl, red, puller, large front wheels, 1970s, No. 2701
EX $83   **NM** $187   **MIP** $374

❏ **Farmall 560**, 1:16-scale, Ertl, red, white plastic rims, 1970s, No. 408
EX $67   **NM** $198   **MIP** $636

❏ **Farmall 560**, 1:16-scale, Ertl, red, 1970s, No. 409
EX $102   **NM** $298   **MIP** $1363

❏ **Farmall 560**, 1:16-scale, Ertl, red, white plastic rims, cab, 1970s, No. 409
EX $98   **NM** $298   **MIP** $989

❏ **Farmall 560**, 1:16-scale, Ertl, red, white plastic rims, duals, 1970s, No. 460
EX $98   **NM** $257   **MIP** $787

❏ **Farmall 560**, 1:16-scale, Ertl, maroon, puller, small front wheels, 1970s, No. 2701
EX $83   **NM** $187   **MIP** $278

❏ **Farmall 560**, 1:16-scale, Ertl, red, 1978 National Farm Toy Show Tractor, limited to 500 units, 1978, No. 1978
EX $493   **NM** $682   **MIP** $1144

❑ **Farmall 560**, 1:16-scale, Ertl, red, produced for Toy Farmer, duals, limited to 500 units, 1979, No. 1979
EX $493   **NM** $682   **MIP** $1144

❑ **Farmall 560**, 1:16-scale, Ertl, w/2MH corn picker, #14 Precision Series, 2000, No. 14060
EX $126   **NM** $152   **MIP** $248

❑ **Farmall 560**, 1:16-scale, Ertl, Demonstrator, '01 LaFayette Show Edition, 2001, No. 16029A
EX $18   **NM** $28   **MIP** $48

❑ **Farmall 560**, 1:16-scale, Ertl, NF, diesel, #19 Precision Series, 2001, No. 14276
EX $62   **NM** $77   **MIP** $117

❑ **Farmall 560**, 1:16-scale, SpecCast, on base, "Best of Show", 2001, No. ZJD119
EX $16   **NM** $28   **MIP** $43

❑ **Farmall 560 2-Point Hitch**, 1:16-scale, Ertl, red, solid drawbar cut off, 1960s

❑ **Farmall 560 2-Point Hitch**, 1:16-scale, Ertl, red, smooth rear end housing, 1960s

❑ **Farmall 560 Solid Drawbar**, 1:16-scale, Ertl, red, no two-point hitch, 1960s

❑ **Farmall 656**, 1:16-scale, Scale Models, '96 Ontario Show Edition, 1996, No. FB-2424
EX $63   **NM** $82   **MIP** $118

❑ **Farmall 656**, 1:16-scale, Scale Models, '98 Ontario Show Edition, 1998, No. FB-2499
EX $56   **NM** $72   **MIP** $118

❑ **Farmall 656**, 1:16-scale, Scale Models, '01 Ontario Show Edition, Demonstrator, 2001, No. FB-2595
EX $52   **NM** $67   **MIP** $103

❑ **Farmall 706**, 1:16-scale, Ertl, 1995, No. 2307 *(Photo by Ertl)*
EX $16   **NM** $27   **MIP** $37

❑ **Farmall 706**, 1:16-scale, Ertl, '95 Toy Tractor Times Edition, #10; 3,500 produced, 1995, No. 421TA
EX $27   **NM** $38   **MIP** $43

❑ **Farmall 706**, 1:16-scale, Ertl, '96 IA FFA, 1996, No. 482TA
EX $23   **NM** $32   **MIP** $48

❑ **Farmall 706**, 1:16-scale, Ertl, '98 LaFayette Show Edition, 1998, No. 4769TA
EX $27   **NM** $36   **MIP** $58

❑ **Farmall 706**, 1:16-scale, Ertl, WF, #16 Precision Series, 2002, No. 14129
EX $62   **NM** $77   **MIP** $117

❑ **Farmall 706**, 1:16-scale, Scale Models, '92 Ontario Show Edition, 1992, No. FB-1592
EX $92   **NM** $107   **MIP** $163

❑ **Farmall 806**, 1:16-scale, Burnett/Snyder, red, 1990s
EX $78   **NM** $112   **MIP** $152

❑ **Farmall 806**, 1:16-scale, Dressler (Custom), red, did not come in box, 1990s
EX $89   **NM** $212   **MIP** n/a

❑ **Farmall 806**, 1:16-scale, Ertl, red, w/die-cast or plastic rims, NF, flat fenders, 1960s, No. 435
EX $78   **NM** $257   **MIP** $772

❑ **Farmall 806**, 1:16-scale, Ertl, red, die-cast rear rims, round fenders, 1960s, No. 435
EX $78   **NM** $257   **MIP** $822

❑ **Farmall 806**, 1:16-scale, Ertl, '97 LaFayette Show Edition, 1997, No. 4779TA
EX $34   **NM** $48   **MIP** $68

❑ **Farmall 806**, 1:16-scale, Ertl, WF, 1997, No. 4406 *(Photo by Ertl)*
EX $22   **NM** $32   **MIP** $48

❑ **Farmall 806**, 1:16-scale, Ertl, '00 IA FFA, 2000, No. 16044
EX $72   **NM** $96   **MIP** $153

❑ **Farmall 806**, 1:16-scale, Ertl, NF, duals, 2005, No. 14501
EX $17   **NM** $27   **MIP** $38

❑ **Farmall 806**, 1:16-scale, Ertl, #4 in Key Precision Series, WF, diesel, 3-point hitch, 2007, No. 14530
EX $85   **NM** $110   **MIP** $130

❑ **Farmall 806**, 1:16-scale, Scale Models, '91 Ontario Show Edition, 1991 *(Photo by Bossen Implement)*
EX $122   **NM** $162   **MIP** $248

❑ **Farmall 806**, 1:16-scale, Scale Models, Collector Edition, 1997, No. ZSM869
EX $72   **NM** $96   **MIP** $153

❑ **Farmall 806**, 1:16-scale, Scale Models, '03 Ontario Show Edition, 2003
EX $56   **NM** $72   **MIP** $98

❑ **Farmall 806**, 1:16-scale, Scale Models, National Assoc. of Farm Broadcasters, w/fender mount radio, 2004, No. 1045
EX $23   **NM** $33   **MIP** $48

❑ **Farmall 806**, 1:16-scale, Scale Models, MFD, ROPS, canopy, Red Power Round-Up, 2006, No. 1066
EX $22   **NM** $33   **MIP** $63

❑ **Farmall 826**, 1:16-scale, Dressler (Custom), red, did not come in box, 1990s
EX $87   **NM** $212   **MIP** n/a

❑ **Farmall 826**, 1:16-scale, Ertl, gold demonstrator, 1995, No. 4652DA
EX $23   **NM** $32   **MIP** $48

❑ **Farmall 826**, 1:16-scale, Ertl, Foxfire Farm, w/Miss Charlotte, 1996, No. 4273
EX $23   **NM** $32   **MIP** $43

❑ **Farmall 826**, 1:16-scale, Ertl, w/ROPS, 1996, No. 2312 *(Photo by Ertl)*
EX $16   **NM** $27   **MIP** $38

❑ **Farmall 856**, 1:16-scale, Ertl, '95 Summer Show Edition, 1995, No. 409TA
EX $31   **NM** $48   **MIP** $63

❑ **Farmall 856**, 1:16-scale, Ertl, w/cab, '97 IH Winter Convention, 1997, No. 4934TA
EX $22   **NM** $33   **MIP** $48

❑ **Farmall 856**, 1:16-scale, Ertl, w/Hiniker cab, Collector Edition, 2000, No. 14090A
EX $27   **NM** $38   **MIP** $48

❑ **Farmall 856**, 1:16-scale, Scale Models, '00 Ontario Show Edition, 2000, No. FB-2563
EX $63   **NM** $87   **MIP** $119

❑ **Farmall 856**, 1:16-scale, Scale Models, WF, duals, Iowa FFA, 2006, No. 1717
EX $26   **NM** $38   **MIP** $59

❑ **Farmall A**, 1:16-scale, Dingman (Custom), red, did not come in box, 1980s
EX $162   **NM** $248   **MIP** n/a

❑ **Farmall A**, 1:16-scale, Ertl, red, '91 Toy Tractor Times Anniversary, #6; 5,000 produced, 1991, No. 250PA
EX $25   **NM** $50   **MIP** $75

❑ **Farmall A**, 1:16-scale, Florida Classics, red, Official 1988 Lebanon Show Tractor, 1980s
EX $22   **NM** $36   **MIP** $42

❑ **Farmall A**, 1:16-scale, Florida Classics, white, 1980s
EX $22   **NM** $36   **MIP** $42

❑ **Farmall AV**, 1:16-scale, Florida Classics, red, 3rd Anniversary Western Show, 1990s
EX $22   **NM** $36   **MIP** $42

❑ **Farmall B**, 1:16-scale, Dingman (Custom), red, did not come in box, 1980s
EX $162   **NM** $248   **MIP** n/a

❑ **Farmall B**, 1:16-scale, Dingman (Custom), red, did not come in box, 1980s
EX $162   **NM** $248   **MIP** n/a

❑ **Farmall B**, 1:16-scale, Florida Classics, red, 1st Grand National Farm Toy Show Tractor, 1980s
EX $22   **NM** $36   **MIP** $42

❑ **Farmall B**, 1:16-scale, Florida Classics, Demonstrator, white, only 600 made, 1980s
EX $22   **NM** $36   **MIP** $42

❑ **Farmall C**, 1:16-scale, Florida Classics, white, 1980s
EX $22   **NM** $36   **MIP** $42

❑ **Farmall C**, 1:16-scale, Florida Classics, white, demonstrator, 1980s
EX $22   **NM** $36   **MIP** $42

❑ **Farmall C**, 1:16-scale, Jouef, red, 1970s
EX $97   **NM** $268   **MIP** $652

❑ **Farmall C**, 1:16-scale, Jouef, red, 1970s
EX $97   **NM** $268   **MIP** $652

❑ **Farmall Cub**, 1:16-scale, red, 1950s
EX $238   **NM** $732   **MIP** npf

❑ **Farmall Cub**, 1:16-scale, Design Fabricators, red, Farmall was decalled, 1950s
EX $89   **NM** $221   **MIP** $478

❑ **Farmall Cub**, 1:16-scale, Design Fabricators, red, 1950s
EX $89   **NM** $221   **MIP** $478

❑ **Farmall Cub**, 1:16-scale, Design Fabricators, red, 1950s
EX $89   **NM** $221   **MIP** $478

❑ **Farmall Cub**, 1:16-scale, Ertl, gold plated, Collectors Series, 1980s
EX $189   **NM** $283   **MIP** $329

❑ **Farmall Cub**, 1:16-scale, Ertl, red, first in a series, Collectors Series, upright exhaust, 1990s, No. 689DA
EX $38   **NM** $56   **MIP** $88

❑ **Farmall Cub**, 1:16-scale, Ertl, Bar Grill, red w/white, white side decals, red in grill, forth in a series, 1990s, No. 652
EX $16   **NM** $26   **MIP** $48

❑ **Farmall Cub**, 1:16-scale, Ertl, red, second in a series, indented for side decal, 1990s, No. 689
EX $16   **NM** $26   **MIP** $43

❑ **Farmall Cub**, 1:16-scale, Ertl, silver plated, 1990s
EX $169   **NM** $263   **MIP** $312

❑ **Farmall Cub**, 1:16-scale, Ertl, red and white, third in a series, white grill, 1990s, No. 235
EX $16   **NM** $26   **MIP** $43

❑ **Farmall Cub**, 1:16-scale, Ertl, red, second in a series, hood from third in a series Cub, 1990s, No. 689
EX $16   **NM** $26   **MIP** $48

❑ **Farmall Cub**, 1:16-scale, Riecke (Custom), red, 1980s
EX $182   **NM** $267   **MIP** n/a

❑ **Farmall Cub**, 1:16-scale, Riecke (Custom), white, did not come in box, 1980s
EX $182   **NM** $267   **MIP** n/a

❑ **Farmall Cub**, 1:16-scale, Riecke (Custom), white/yellow, 1980s
EX $182   **NM** $267   **MIP** n/a

❑ **Farmall Cub**, 1:16-scale, Riecke (Custom), red, did not come in box, 1980s
EX $182   **NM** $267   **MIP** n/a

❑ **Farmall Cultivision A**, 1:16-scale, Arcade, red, black rubber wheels, 7-1/2" long, 1941, No. 7050
EX $293   **NM** $778   **MIP** $3223

Photos by Jon Jacobson unless otherwise noted.

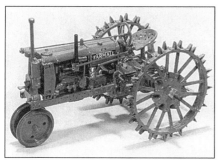

❏ **Farmall F-12**, 1:16-scale, Riecke (Custom), red, did not come in box, 1990s
EX $182   **NM** $323   **MIP** n/a

❏ **Farmall F-12**, 1:16-scale, Riecke (Custom), gray, on rubber, did not come in box, 1990s
EX $182   **NM** $323   **MIP** n/a

❏ **Farmall F-12**, 1:16-scale, Riecke (Custom), gray, on rubber, did not come in box, 1990s
EX $182   **NM** $323   **MIP** n/a

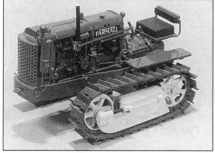

❏ **Farmall F-12 Crawler**, 1:16-scale, Riecke (Custom), red, did not come in box, 1990s
EX $182   **NM** $323   **MIP** n/a

❏ **Farmall F-14**, 1:16-scale, Riecke (Custom), red, did not come in box, 1990s
EX $182   **NM** $323   **MIP** n/a

❏ **Farmall F-20**, 1:16-scale, Ertl, Precision Series, WF, red, No. 299
(Photo by Ertl)
EX $62   **NM** $89   **MIP** $168

❏ **Farmall F-20**, 1:16-scale, Ertl, Precision Series, NF, red, No. 294
EX $68   **NM** $89   **MIP** $168

❏ **Farmall F-20**, 1:16-scale, Ertl, red, 1980s, No. 437
EX $16   **NM** $24   **MIP** $42

❏ **Farmall F-20**, 1:16-scale, Ertl, red, Collectors Edition, metal rims, 1980s, No. 437DA
EX $16   **NM** $27   **MIP** $42

❏ **Farmall F-20**, 1:16-scale, Riecke (Custom), gray, did not come in box, 1980s
EX $214   **NM** $298   **MIP** n/a

❏ **Farmall F-20**, 1:16-scale, Riecke (Custom), red, did not come in box, 1980s
EX $214   **NM** $298   **MIP** n/a

❏ **Farmall F-20**, 1:16-scale, Riecke (Custom), gray, did not come in box, 1980s
EX $214   **NM** $298   **MIP** n/a

❏ **Farmall F-20**, 1:16-scale, Riecke (Custom), red, did not come in box, 1980s
EX $214   **NM** $298   **MIP** n/a

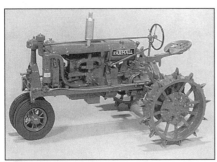

❏ **Farmall F-20**, 1:16-scale, Riecke (Custom), red, did not come in box, 1980s
EX $214   **NM** $298   **MIP** n/a

❏ **Farmall F-30**, 1:16-scale, Gray (Custom), gray, did not come in a box, 1970s
EX $23   **NM** $44   **MIP** n/a

❏ **Farmall H**, 1:16-scale, Ertl, red, Collectors Edition, 1985, No. 414DA
EX $22   **NM** $38   **MIP** $58

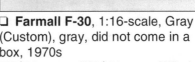

❏ **Farmall F-20**, 1:16-scale, Riecke (Custom), red, did not come in box, 1980s
EX $214   **NM** $298   **MIP** n/a

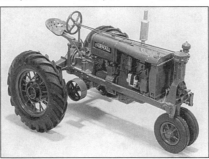

❏ **Farmall F-30**, 1:16-scale, Riecke (Custom), red, did not come in box, 1990s
EX $289   **NM** $402   **MIP** n/a

❏ **Farmall H**, 1:16-scale, Ertl, red, 1986, 1988, No. 414
EX $18   **NM** $29   **MIP** $38

❏ **Farmall F-20**, 1:16-scale, Riecke (Custom), red, did not come in box, 1980s
EX $214   **NM** $298   **MIP** n/a

❏ **Farmall H**, 1:16-scale, Dressler (Custom), red, did not come in box, 1990s
EX $98   **NM** $187   **MIP** n/a

❏ **Farmall H**, 1:16-scale, Ertl, Ertl 50th Anniversary Edition, w/man, 1995, No. 4453DA *(Photo by Ertl)*
EX $16   **NM** $26   **MIP** $39

❏ **Farmall F-20 Set**, 1:16-scale, Ertl, w/wagon set, No. 4227 *(Photo by Ertl)*
EX $12   **NM** $22   **MIP** $38

❏ **Farmall H**, 1:16-scale, Ertl, red, 1950s
EX $289   **NM** $593   **MIP** npf

❏ **Farmall H**, 1:16-scale, Ertl, w/man, gold-plated, Employee Edition, 1995, No. 4555MA *(Photo by Ertl)*
EX $82   **NM** $143   **MIP** $189

❑ **Farmall H**, 1:16-scale, Freiheit (Custom), red, did not come in box, 1982
EX $167   **NM** $242   **MIP** n/a

❑ **Farmall H**, 1:16-scale, Scale Models, various colors, 1980s
EX $17   **NM** $27   **MIP** $43

❑ **Farmall H**, 1:16-scale, Scale Models, red, serial numbered, 1980s
EX $17   **NM** $27   **MIP** $43

❑ **Farmall International 340**, 1:16-scale, Ertl, red, smooth or ribbed front tires, one has word McCormick above International, one doesn't, 1960s
EX $189   **NM** $483   **MIP** $1188

❑ **Farmall M**, 1:16-scale, Arcade, red, cast-in driver, 1940s
EX $97   **NM** $227   **MIP** $727

❑ **Farmall M**, 1:16-scale, Arcade, red, 1940s
EX $97   **NM** $227   **MIP** $727

❑ **Farmall M**, 1:16-scale, Arcade, red, separate driver, 1941, No. 7070
EX $238   **NM** $656   **MIP** $2602

❑ **Farmall M**, 1:16-scale, Arcade, red, 1941, No. 7070
EX $238   **NM** $656   **MIP** $2602

❑ **Farmall M**, 1:16-scale, Baker (Custom), red, did not come in box, 1980s
EX $98   **NM** $133   **MIP** n/a

❑ **Farmall M**, 1:16-scale, Dressler (Custom), red, did not come in box, 1990s
EX $133   **NM** $212   **MIP** n/a

❑ **Farmall M**, 1:16-scale, Ertl, Precision Series, No. 4610 *(Photo by Ertl)*
EX $117   **NM** $164   **MIP** $223

❑ **Farmall M**, 1:16-scale, Ertl, red/yellow rims, 1950s
EX $438   **NM** $842   **MIP** $1969

❑ **Farmall M**, 1:16-scale, Ertl, IH 100th Anniversary, #4 of 4, NF, 2002, No. 14239A

❑ **Farmall M**, 1:16-scale, Ertl, NF, 2007, No. 14524
EX $15   **NM** $20   **MIP** $25

❑ **Farmall M**, 1:16-scale, Product Miniature, white, 1950s
EX $146   **NM** $392   **MIP** $987

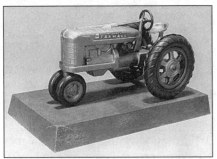

❑ **Farmall M**, 1:16-scale, Product Miniature, gold, can also be found in silver, 1950s
EX $983   **NM** $1216   **MIP** $1532

❑ **Farmall M**, 1:16-scale, Product Miniature, red, 1950s
EX $48   **NM** $118   **MIP** $267

❑ **Farmall M**, 1:16-scale, Product Miniature, red, 1950s
EX $48   **NM** $118   **MIP** $267

❑ **Farmall M**, 1:16-scale, Product Miniature, red, 1950s
EX $48   **NM** $118   **MIP** $267

❑ **Farmall M**, 1:16-scale, Product Miniature, red, 1950s
EX $48   **NM** $118   **MIP** $267

❑ **Farmall M**, 1:16-scale, Riecke (Custom), red, did not come in box, 1990s
EX $233   **NM** $322   **MIP** n/a

❑ **Farmall M**, 1:16-scale, Scale Models, red, 1980s
EX $22   **NM** $37   **MIP** $42

❑ **Farmall M**, 1:16-scale, Scale Models, red, 1980s
EX $22   **NM** $37   **MIP** $42

❑ **Farmall M**, 1:16-scale, Scale Models, red, 1980s
EX $8   **NM** $14   **MIP** $22

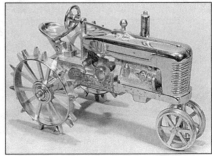

❑ **Farmall M**, 1:16-scale, Scale Models, gold, employee edition, 1980s
EX $98   **NM** $162   **MIP** $233

❑ **Farmall M**, 1:16-scale, Scale Models, red, 50th Anniversary Farmall M, 1980s
EX $22   **NM** $33   **MIP** $44

❑ **Farmall M**, 1:16-scale, Tru-Scale, red, 1950s
EX $67   **NM** $178   **MIP** $634

❑ **Farmall M Restoration**, 1:16-scale, Ertl, tractor plus tool box, air compressor, jacks, tools, 2007, No. 14593
EX $15   **NM** $20   **MIP** $26

❑ **Farmall MTA**, 1:16-scale, Ertl, No. 445 *(Photo by Ertl)*
EX $22   **NM** $34   **MIP** $42

❑ **Farmall MTA**, 1:16-scale, Riecke (Custom), red, did not come in box, 1990s
EX $167   **NM** $272   **MIP** n/a

❑ **Farmall Regular**, 1:16-scale, Arcade, green w/red lug wheels, nickel-plated driver, 6" long, 1929, No. 279
EX $388   **NM** $792   **MIP** $2989

❑ **Farmall Regular**, 1:16-scale, Arcade, red, white rubber tires, red wheels, 6-1/4" long, 1937, No. 2790
EX $388   **NM** $792   **MIP** $2989

❑ **Farmall Regular**, 1:16-scale, Old Time Collectables (Custom), red, did not come in box, 1970s
EX $18   **NM** $38   **MIP** n/a

❑ **Farmall Regular**, 1:16-scale, Scale Models, gray, No. 10 in Collectors Series, 1980s
EX $18   **NM** $32   **MIP** $47

❑ **Farmall Super A**, 1:16-scale, Florida Classics, red, w/sickle mower, 1980s
EX $22   **NM** $36   **MIP** $52

❑ **Farmall Super C**, 1:16-scale, Classic Farm Toys, red, 1980s
EX $22   **NM** $36   **MIP** $42

❑ **Farmall Super C**, 1:16-scale, Florida Classics, red, did not come in box, 1980s
EX $22   **NM** $36   **MIP** n/a

❑ **Farmall Super C**, 1:16-scale, Freiheit (Custom), white, 1980s
EX $167   **NM** $242   **MIP** n/a

❑ **Farmall Super C**, 1:16-scale, Lakone, red, 1950s
EX $116   **NM** $278   **MIP** $683

❏ **Farmall Super H**, 1:16-scale, Freiheit (Custom), red, did not come in box, 1980s
EX $167   **NM** $242   **MIP** n/a

❏ **Farmall Super M**, 1:16-scale, Ertl, Precision Series, No. 4615 *(Photo by Ertl)*
EX $98   **NM** $157   **MIP** $228

❏ **Farmall Super M**, 1:16-scale, Riecke (Custom), red, did not come in box, LP, 1990s
EX $187   **NM** $267   **MIP** n/a

❏ **Farmall Super M**, 1:16-scale, Riecke (Custom), red, did not come in box, High Crop, 1990s
EX $187   **NM** $267   **MIP** n/a

❏ **Farmall Super M**, 1:16-scale, Riecke (Custom), red, did not come in box, 1990s
EX $187   **NM** $267   **MIP** n/a

❏ **Farmall Super M**, 1:16-scale, Riecke (Custom), red, did not come in box, 1990s
EX $187   **NM** $267   **MIP** n/a

❏ **Farmall Super MTA**, 1:16-scale, Ertl, WF, No. 4528 *(Photo by Ertl)*
EX $18   **NM** $27   **MIP** $36

❏ **Farmall Super MTA**, 1:16-scale, Ertl, IH 100th Anniversary, #2 of 4, 2002, No. 14243A
EX n/a   **NM** n/a   **MIP** $135

❏ **Farmall Super MTA**, 1:16-scale, Ertl, WF, 2007, No. 14562
EX $10   **NM** $16   **MIP** $22

❏ **Farmall Super MTA**, 1:16-scale, Freiheit (Custom), red, did not come in box, 1980s
EX $167   **NM** $242   **MIP** n/a

❏ **Farmall Super MTA**, 1:16-scale, Parker (Custom), red, did not come in box, 1980s
EX $98   **NM** $167   **MIP** n/a

❏ **Farmall Super MTA**, 1:16-scale, Riecke (Custom), red, did not come in box, 1990s
EX $187   **NM** $267   **MIP** n/a

❏ **Farmall Super MTA**, 1:16-scale, Yoder (Custom), white, 1980s
EX $67   **NM** $96   **MIP** $142

❏ **Farmall Super MTA**, 1:16-scale, Yoder (Custom), red, gas tractor, 1980s
EX $32   **NM** $47   **MIP** $66

Photos by Jon Jacobson unless otherwise noted.

❏ **Farmall Super MTA**, 1:16-scale, Yoder (Custom), white, 1980s
EX $67   **NM** $96   **MIP** $142

❏ **Farmall Super MTA**, 1:16-scale, Yoder (Custom), red, gas tractor, 1990s
EX $32   **NM** $47   **MIP** $66

❏ **International**, 1:16-scale, Berg (Custom), yellow, did not come in box, 1980s
EX $244   **NM** $489   **MIP** n/a

❏ **International**, 1:16-scale, Ertl, red, 1980s
EX $26   **NM** $52   **MIP** $62

❏ **International 1026**, 1:16-scale, Ertl, red, Hydro, 1960s, No. 419
EX $98   **NM** $417   **MIP** $673

❏ **International 1026**, 1:16-scale, Ertl, Hydro 100, under slung fuel tank, 1991, No. 4623DA
EX $18   **NM** $32   **MIP** $43

❏ **International 1026**, 1:16-scale, Ertl, gold demonstrator, 1996, No. 4653DA
EX $26   **NM** $37   **MIP** $48

❏ **International 1026**, 1:16-scale, Ertl, w/one dual, '97 Summer Show Edition, 1997, No. 417TA
EX $27   **NM** $38   **MIP** $57

❏ **International 1066**, 1:16-scale, Ertl, red, two front wheel variations, w/cab, 1970s, No. 411
EX $73   **NM** $137   **MIP** $262

❏ **International 1066**, 1:16-scale, Ertl, red, w/ROPS, 1970s, No. 402
EX $73   **NM** $167   **MIP** $326

❏ **International 1066**, 1:16-scale, Ertl, red and white, 1 of 5,000,000, 1990s, No. 4620DA
EX $66   **NM** $106   **MIP** $138

❏ **International 1066**, 1:16-scale, Ertl, red, black stripe decal, w/ROPS, 1990s, No. 4621DA
EX $22   **NM** $37   **MIP** $48

❏ **International 1066**, 1:16-scale, Ertl, cab, '06 Toy Tractor Times Anniversary, #21; 5,900 produced, 2006, No. 16156A
EX $25   **NM** $55   **MIP** $85

❏ **International 1066**, 1:16-scale, Ertl/Toy Farmer, red, built for Toy Farmer, 1970s
EX $73   **NM** $253   **MIP** $457

❏ **International 1086**, 1:16-scale, Ertl, '04 Toy Tractor Times Anniversary, #19; 4,000 produced, No. 16130A
EX $25   **NM** $55   **MIP** $85

❏ **International 1086**, 1:16-scale, Ertl, red, two front wheel variations, 1970s, No. 462
EX $27   **NM** $57   **MIP** $88

❏ **International 1086**, 1:16-scale, Ertl, red, radio controlled, 1980s, No. 29
EX $22   **NM** $57   **MIP** $97

❏ **International 1086**, 1:16-scale, Ertl, WF, cab, removable front wieghts, Red Power, 2006, No. 14497A
EX $24   **NM** $33   **MIP** $48

❏ **International 1206**, 1:16-scale, Ertl, IH 100th Anniversary, #3 of 4, ROPS, 2002, No. 14196A
EX n/a   **NM** n/a   **MIP** $175

❏ **International 1256**, 1:16-scale, Ertl, red, 1960s, No. 420
EX $98   **NM** $258   **MIP** $877

❏ **International 1256**, 1:16-scale, Ertl, '98 Summer Show Edition, 1998, No. 419TA
EX $26   **NM** $38   **MIP** $53

❏ **International 1256**, 1:16-scale, Ertl, slant cab, 2002, No. 14198
EX $24   **NM** $33   **MIP** $43

❏ **International 1256**, 1:16-scale, Ertl, w/slant cab, 2002, No. 14198
EX $21   **NM** $32   **MIP** $43

❏ **International 1256**, 1:16-scale, Scale Models, '02 Ontario Show Edition, 2002
EX $63   **NM** $72   **MIP** $98

❏ **International 1456**, 1:16-scale, Ertl, red, 1960s, No. 420
EX $98   **NM** $257   **MIP** $772

❏ **International 1456**, 1:16-scale, Ertl, gold demonstrator, 1995, No. 4651DA
EX $34   **NM** $52   **MIP** $77

❏ **International 1456**, 1:16-scale, Ertl, '96 Toy Tractor Times Anniversary, #11, 1996, No. 2310TA
EX $26   **NM** $43   **MIP** $54

❏ **International 1466**, 1:16-scale, Ertl, red, made for Toy Farmer, limited to 500 units, 1970s
EX $223   **NM** $289   **MIP** $433

❏ **International 1466**, 1:16-scale, Ertl, red, two front wheel variations, 1970s, No. 403
EX $53   **NM** $97   **MIP** $186

❏ **International 1466**, 1:16-scale, Ertl, Turbo, red, w/cab, collector insert, revised casting, 1990s, No. 4622DA
EX $34   **NM** $52   **MIP** $68

❏ **International 1466**, 1:16-scale, Ertl, #18 in Precision Sereis, 2002, No. 14204
EX $82   **NM** $97   **MIP** $138

❏ **International 1468**, 1:16-scale, Ertl, red cab, no windows, 1993, No. 4601DA
EX $38   **NM** $56   **MIP** $77

❏ **International 1468**, 1:16-scale, Ertl, white cab, w/windows, 1993, No. 4600DA
EX $44   **NM** $62   **MIP** $88

❏ **International 1468**, 1:16-scale, Ertl, ROPS, '94 LaFayette, 1994, No. 4613TA
EX $42   **NM** $54   **MIP** $73

❏ **International 1468**, 1:16-scale, Ertl, no cab, duals, '95 Blue River, 1995, No. 4697RA
EX $37   **NM** $48   **MIP** $77

❏ **International 1468**, 1:16-scale, Ertl, #3 in Key Precision Series, 2006, No. 14481
EX $62   **NM** $87   **MIP** $133

❏ **International 1486**, 1:16-scale, Ertl, w/dark, red power decal, 2003, No. 14340
EX $21   **NM** $31   **MIP** $42

❏ **International 1566**, 1:16-scale, Ertl, w/under slung fuel tank, 1990, No. 4625DA
EX $28   **NM** $38   **MIP** $48

❏ **International 1568**, 1:16-scale, Ertl, 1994, No. 4603DA
EX $26   **NM** $37   **MIP** $48

❏ **International 1568**, 1:16-scale, Ertl, '94 WI Farm Progress Days, 1994, No. 622TA
EX $67   **NM** $83   **MIP** $128

❏ **International 1568**, 1:16-scale, Ertl, red cab, 1994, No. 4602DA
EX $26   **NM** $37   **MIP** $48

❏ **International 1586**, 1:16-scale, Ertl, red, two front wheel variations, duals, 1970s, No. 463
EX $22   **NM** $37   **MIP** $52

❏ **International 1586**, 1:16-scale, Ertl, red, 1980s, No. 463
EX $18   **NM** $28   **MIP** $33

❏ **International 1586**, 1:16-scale, Ertl, red and white, w/engine block casting change, 1990s, No. 463
EX $12   **NM** $21   **MIP** $27

❏ **International 1586**, 1:16-scale, Ertl, red and white, w/Loader, 1990s, No. 416
EX $12   **NM** $27   **MIP** $38

❏ **International 186 Hydro**, 1:16-scale, Ertl, 2007, No. 14538
EX $15   **NM** $20   **MIP** $25

❏ **International 240**, 1:16-scale, Ertl, red, 404-style rear rims, 1950s
EX $189   **NM** $483   **MIP** $1492

❏ **International 240**, 1:16-scale, Ertl, red, smooth or ribbed front tires, one with McCormick above International, one without, 1960s
EX $189   **NM** $483   **MIP** $1492

❏ **International 300**, 1:16-scale, Deyen (Custom), red, 1980s
EX $143   **NM** $186   **MIP** n/a

❏ **International 300**, 1:16-scale, Ertl, utility, underslung exhaust, diecut rims, 50th Anniversary, 2005, No. 14426A
EX $19   **NM** $22   **MIP** $43

❏ **International 3088**, 1:16-scale, Ertl, red, one engraved and given to Ertl employees for a safety award, one w/o engraving, 1980s, No. 415
EX $22   **NM** $38   **MIP** $56

❏ **International 3088**, 1:16-scale, Ertl, red, Central Tractor Parts, 1980s, No. 415
EX $4   **NM** $9   **MIP** $16

❏ **International 3088**, 1:16-scale, Ertl, red, 1980s, No. 415
EX $4   **NM** $9   **MIP** $16

❏ **International 3088**, 1:16-scale, Ertl, red, 1980s, No. 415
EX $6   **NM** $8   **MIP** $16

❑ **International 3088 Set**, 1:16-scale, Ertl, red, Campbell's Soup w/wagon, 1980s, No. 415
EX $28   **NM** $34   **MIP** $48

❑ **International 340**, 1:16-scale, Ertl, red, 404-style rear rims, 1960s
EX $212   **NM** $483   **MIP** $1188

❑ **International 340**, 1:16-scale, SpecCast, diesel, utility, LaFayette, Indiana show, 2007, No. 1528
EX $26   **NM** $33   **MIP** $53

❑ **International 340**, 1:16-scale, SpecCast, gas, WF, utility, 2007, No. 1529
EX $24   **NM** $31   **MIP** $47

❑ **International 350**, 1:16-scale, Deyen (Custom), red, did not come in box, 1980s
EX $172   **NM** $232   **MIP** n/a

❑ **International 3588**, 1:16-scale, Ertl, red, First Edition, a variation exists that has the words "1st Edition" ground out, 1970s, No. 464DA
EX $164   **NM** $203   **MIP** $378

❑ **International 3588**, 1:16-scale, Ertl, red, 1970s, No. 464
EX $67   **NM** $102   **MIP** $168

❑ **International 3588**, 1:16-scale, Ertl, #2 in Key Precision Series, 2005, No. 14350
EX $62   **NM** $87   **MIP** $138

❑ **International 4166**, 1:16-scale, Berg (Custom), red, did not come in box, 1980s
EX $244   **NM** $489   **MIP** n/a

❑ **International 4366**, 1:16-scale, Scale Models, 1999, No. ZSM920
EX $123   **NM** $162   **MIP** $248

❑ **International 460**, 1:16-scale, Deyen (Custom), red, did not come in box, 1980s
EX $174   **NM** $223   **MIP** n/a

❑ **International 5088**, 1:16-scale, Ertl, red, also available special edition 12-81, 1980s, No. 468
EX $27   **NM** $42   **MIP** $58

❑ **International 5288**, 1:16-scale, Ertl, red, Collectors Edition, 1980s, No. 409TW
EX $37   **NM** $53   **MIP** $82

❑ **International 5288**, 1:16-scale, Ertl, red, also available Kansas City 9-81, 1980s, No. 487
EX $28   **NM** $44   **MIP** $62

❑ **International 5288**, 1:16-scale, Ertl, 2004, No. 14346
EX $23   **NM** $32   **MIP** $47

❏ **International 544**, 1:16-scale, Ertl, red, WF, red rims, 1960s, No. 414
EX $72   **NM** $159   **MIP** $284

❏ **International 544**, 1:16-scale, Ertl, red, 1970s, No. 415
EX $9   **NM** $24   **MIP** $68

❏ **International 544**, 1:16-scale, Ertl, red, NF, w/duals, white rims, 1970s, No. 417
EX $57   **NM** $176   **MIP** $486

❏ **International 544**, 1:16-scale, Ertl, red, NF, wide plastic tires, white rims, 1970s, No. 415
EX $8   **NM** $12   **MIP** $17

❏ **International 5488**, 1:16-scale, Ertl, red, 1980s, No. 409
EX $37   **NM** $48   **MIP** $77

❏ **International 5488**, 1:16-scale, Ertl, red, Collectors Edition, 1980s, No. 409PA
EX $64   **NM** $124   **MIP** $172

❏ **International 5488**, 1:16-scale, Ertl, IH 100th Anniversary, #1 of 4, 2002, No. 14240A
EX n/a   **NM** n/a   **MIP** $150

❏ **International 5488**, 1:16-scale, Ertl, 100th Anniversary Edition, 2002, No. 14240A
EX $46   **NM** $72   **MIP** $102

❏ **International 560**, 1:16-scale, Ertl, gas, Wheatland, 2000, No. 14035
EX $17   **NM** $22   **MIP** $34

❏ **International 560**, 1:16-scale, Snyder (Custom), red, South Indiana Show Edition 10F 500, 1980s
EX $36   **NM** $63   **MIP** $87

❏ **International 600**, 1:16-scale, Ertl, 1994, No. 282 *(Photo by Ertl)*
EX $17   **NM** $23   **MIP** $38

❏ **International 600**, 1:16-scale, Ertl, w/wheel inserts, 1995, No. 248
(Photo by Bossen Implement)
EX $16   **NM** $23   **MIP** $38

❏ **International 606**, 1:16-scale, Deyen (Custom), red, did not come in box, 1980s
EX $73   **NM** $128   **MIP** n/a

❏ **International 606**, 1:16-scale, Scale Models, gold plated, 1990s
EX $82   **NM** $117   **MIP** $188

❏ **International 606**, 1:16-scale, Scale Models, w/3 point, '91 Farm Progress Show Edition, 1991, No. FB-1535
EX $18   **NM** $26   **MIP** $42

❏ **International 606**, 1:16-scale, Scale Models, same as FF-0226, 1994, No. ZSM805 *(Photo by Scale Models)*
EX $14   **NM** $19   **MIP** $27

❏ **International 606**, 1:16-scale, Scale Models, under slung exhaust, '03 Open House Edition, 2003, No. ZSM1017
EX $18   **NM** $26   **MIP** $42

❏ **International 6388**, 1:16-scale, Ertl, red, 1980s, No. 464
EX $53   **NM** $83   **MIP** $142

❏ **International 650**, 1:16-scale, Ertl, Standard, 1995, No. 246

(Photo by Kate Bossen)

EX $18   **NM** $22   **MIP** $38

❏ **International 660**, 1:16-scale, Ertl, '99 National Farm Toy Show Edition, 1999, No. 16020A
EX $27   **NM** $42   **MIP** $68

❏ **International 660 Wheatland**, 1:16-scale, Snyder (Custom), red, 9th Annual Michigan Farm Toy Show Tractor, 1989
EX $78   **NM** $112   **MIP** $133

❏ **International 666**, 1:16-scale, Wolfe (Custom), red, did not come in box, 1980s
EX $57   **NM** $186   **MIP** n/a

❏ **International 684**, 1:16-scale, Scale Models, '97 Ontario Show Edition, 1997, No. FB-2474
EX $53   **NM** $92   **MIP** $128

❏ **International 7488**, 1:16-scale, Ertl, red, 1980s, No. 467
EX $57   **NM** $88   **MIP** $153

❏ **International 7488**, 1:16-scale, Ertl, red, Collectors Edition, 1980s, No. 467PA
EX $118   **NM** $238   **MIP** $373

❏ **International 756**, 1:16-scale, Ertl, WF, 1996, No. 2308
EX $16   **NM** $22   **MIP** $38

❏ **International 756**, 1:16-scale, Ertl, '96 Farm Show Edition, 1996, No. 4719TA
EX $22   **NM** $32   **MIP** $48

❏ **International 756**, 1:16-scale, Ertl, '97 IA FAA, 1997, No. 4303TA
EX $22   **NM** $32   **MIP** $48

❏ **International 756**, 1:16-scale, Ertl, w/Hiniker cab, 2001, No. 14124
EX $16   **NM** $22   **MIP** $42

❏ **International 756**, 1:16-scale, Scale Models, '94 Ontario Show Edition, 1994, No. FB-1642
EX $32   **NM** $48   **MIP** $93

❏ **International 784**, 1:16-scale, Scale Models, '99 Ontario Show Edition, 1999, No. FB-2543
EX $62   **NM** $78   **MIP** $128

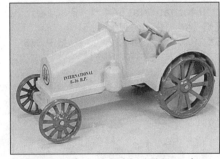

❏ **International 8-16**, 1:16-scale, Ebersol (Custom), gray, did not come in box, 1980s
EX $27   **NM** $48   **MIP** n/a

❏ **International 8-16**, 1:16-scale, Scale Models, gray, Kerosene, 1992, No. ZSM895
EX $9   **NM** $18   **MIP** $27

❏ **International 8-16**, 1:16-scale, Scale Models, green, Kerosene, 1994, No. ZSM733
EX $9   **NM** $18   **MIP** $27

❏ **International 856**, 1:16-scale, Ertl, red, 1960s, No. 419
EX $98   **NM** $257   **MIP** $772

❑ **International 856**, 1:16-scale, Ertl, Dealer Edition, duals, 2007, No. 14567

EX $25   **NM** $45   **MIP** $60

❑ **International 88 Series**, 1:16-scale, Pace Setter, red, liquor decanter, 1980s

EX $16   **NM** $32   **MIP** $48

❑ **International 886**, 1:16-scale, Ertl, red, two front wheel variations, 1970s, No. 461

EX $29   **NM** $53   **MIP** $82

❑ **International 966**, 1:16-scale, Ertl, red, two front wheel variations, Hydro, 1970s, No. 401

EX $42   **NM** $98   **MIP** $162

❑ **International 966**, 1:16-scale, Ertl, red, white front rims, Hydro, 1970s, No. 401

EX $63   **NM** $157   **MIP** $273

❑ **International 966**, 1:16-scale, Ertl, red, black stripe decals, 1990s, No. 4624

EX $22   **NM** $37   **MIP** $53

❑ **International 966**, 1:16-scale, Scale Models, NF, '05 Ontario Show Edition, 2005, No. 1059

EX $27   **NM** $38   **MIP** $88

❑ **International 966**, 1:16-scale, Scale Models, NF, sandbox toy, 2006, No. 1063

EX $8   **NM** $12   **MIP** $19

❑ **International 986**, 1:16-scale, Ertl, w/loader, 2002, No. 14238

EX $13   **NM** $22   **MIP** $37

❑ **International Pedal Tractor**, 1:16-scale, Riecke (Custom), red, did not come in box, 1990s

EX $18   **NM** $28   **MIP** n/a

❑ **International Titan 10-20**, 1:16-scale, Scale Models, green, 1990s, No. ZSM706

EX $33   **NM** $52   **MIP** $73

❑ **McCormick 10-20**, 1:16-scale, Gray (Custom), gray, did not come in box, 1970s

EX $26   **NM** $44   **MIP** n/a

❑ **McCormick 10-20**, 1:16-scale, Kilgore, gray, 1930s

EX $489   **NM** $1189   **MIP** npf

❑ **McCormick 10-20**, 1:16-scale, Kilgore, gray, 1930s

EX $489   **NM** $1189   **MIP** npf

❑ **McCormick 10-20**, 1:16-scale, Scale Models, No. ZSM707

(Photo by Scale Models)

EX $28   **NM** $42   **MIP** $67

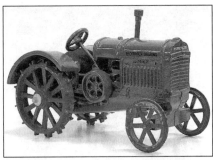

❏ **McCormick 10-20**, 1:16-scale, Scale Models, #13 in Collector Series I, 1980s *(Photo by Bossen Implement)*
EX $32   **NM** $46   **MIP** $73

❏ **McCormick 15-30**, 1:16-scale, Scale Models, 1980s, No. ZSM722

(Photo by Scale Models)
EX $19   **NM** $28   **MIP** $48

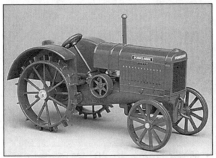

❏ **McCormick 22-36**, 1:16-scale, Scale Models, 1990s, No. ZSM735

(Photo by Scale Models)
EX $26   **NM** $43   **MIP** $73

❏ **McCormick C-100**, 1:16-scale, Scale Models, red, '02 Farm Progress Show Edition, 2002, No. FB-1301 *(Photo by Bossen Implement)*
EX $28   **NM** $62   **MIP** $88

❏ **McCormick C-70**, 1:16-scale, Scale Models, red, '02 Louisville Show Edition, 2002, No. FB-2609
EX $28   **NM** $62   **MIP** $88

❏ **McCormick Deering 10-20**, 1:16-scale, Arcade, gray, w/ or w/out lug wheels, 1925
EX $168   **NM** $389   **MIP** $1624

❏ **McCormick MTX-140**, 1:16-scale, Scale Models, red, '02 Farm Progress Show Edition, 2002, No. FB-1303
EX $32   **NM** $66   **MIP** $113

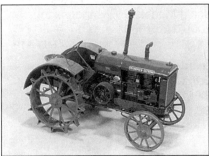

❏ **McCormick W-30**, 1:16-scale, Missouri Basin, gray or red, 1990s
EX $342   **NM** $492   **MIP** $689

❏ **McCormick W-30**, 1:16-scale, SpecCast, No. SCT734

(Photo by SpecCast)
EX $18   **NM** $27   **MIP** $42

❏ **McCormick W-30**, 1:16-scale, SpecCast, No. ZJD735 *(Photo by Kate Bossen)*
EX $18   **NM** $24   **MIP** $42

❏ **McCormick W-4**, 1:16-scale, C & M Farm Toys, red, 12th Annual Lafayette Farm Toy Show, 1990s
EX $67   **NM** $102   **MIP** $162

❏ **McCormick W-6**, 1:16-scale, Hasty (Custom), red, did not come in box, 1980s
EX $26   **NM** $48   **MIP** n/a

❏ **McCormick W-6, Super**, 1:16-scale, Graves (Custom), red, did not come in box, 1980s
EX $26   **NM** $48   **MIP** n/a

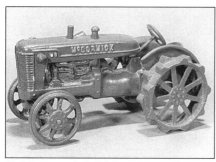

❑ **McCormick W-9**, 1:16-scale, Gray (Custom), red, did not come in box, 1970s
EX $26   **NM** $48   **MIP** n/a

❑ **McCormick WD-9**, 1:16-scale, Ertl, red, Collectors Edition, 1980s, No. 633DA
EX $22   **NM** $38   **MIP** $48

❑ **McCormick WD-9**, 1:16-scale, Ertl, red, 1980s, No. 633
EX $22   **NM** $36   **MIP** $43

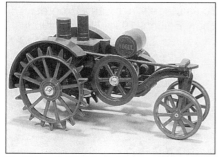

❑ **Mogul 10-20**, 1:16-scale, Scale Models, green, red wheels, 1990s, No. ZSM705
EX $33   **NM** $48   **MIP** $78

❑ **Mogul 12-25**, 1:16-scale, Scale Models, green, 1990s, No. ZSM709
EX $33   **NM** $48   **MIP** $78

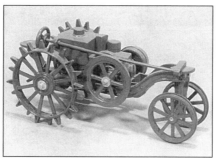

❑ **Mogul 8-16**, 1:16-scale, Scale Models, green, red wheels, 1980s, No. ZSM704
EX $33   **NM** $52   **MIP** $73

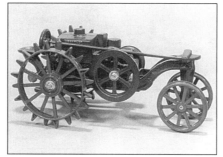

❑ **Mogul 8-16**, 1:16-scale, Scale Models, green, red wheels, 1980s, No. ZSM704
EX $33   **NM** $52   **MIP** $73

❑ **Titan**, 1:16-scale, Scale Models, green, 1980s, No. ZSM702
EX $37   **NM** $63   **MIP** $87

❑ **Titan**, 1:16-scale, Scale Models, black and silver, 1990s, No. ZSM702
EX $42   **NM** $73   **MIP** $97

❑ **Farmall M**, 1:25-scale, Slik, red, 1940s
EX $4   **NM** $22   **MIP** $43

❑ **Farmall M**, 1:25-scale, Slik, red, 1960s
EX $4   **NM** $22   **MIP** $43

❑ **International 1466**, 1:25-scale, Ertl, red, plastic model kit, 1970s, No. 8003
EX $22   **NM** $46   **MIP** $82

❑ **International 275**, 1:25-scale, Makindra, red, 1980s
EX $48   **NM** $63   **MIP** $97

TRACTORS 1:30-SCALE

❏ **International 844 S**, 1:30-scale, Bruder, red, 1980s

EX $4   **NM** $16   **MIP** $27

❏ **International B-434**, 1:30-scale, Leckno, red, the brush is removable and can be replaced w/a blade, 1970s

EX $187   **NM** $222   **MIP** $274

❏ **McCormick B-434**, 1:30-scale, Leckno, red, 1960s

EX $147   **NM** $173   **MIP** $218

❏ **McCormick B-434**, 1:30-scale, Leckno, red, the brush is removable and can be replaced w/a blade, 1970s

EX $187   **NM** $222   **MIP** $274

TRACTORS 1:32-SCALE

❏ **Farmall**, 1:32-scale, red, 1950s

EX $4   **NM** $22   **MIP** $46

❏ **Farmall 300**, 1:32-scale, Ertl, red, Ertl Replica magazine edition, 1980s, No. 4646FA

EX $8   **NM** $18   **MIP** $27

❏ **Farmall 350**, 1:32-scale, Ertl, 1992, No. 4616

EX $9   **NM** $16   **MIP** $22

❏ **Farmall 656**, 1:32-scale, Ertl, red, 1970s, No. 40

EX $4   **NM** $22   **MIP** $48

❏ **Farmall 656**, 1:32-scale, Ertl, red, 1970s, No. 40

EX $4   **NM** $22   **MIP** $48

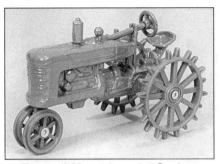

❏ **Farmall M**, 1:32-scale, Scale Models, red, 1980s

EX $3   **NM** $8   **MIP** $12

❏ **Farmall M**, 1:32-scale, Scale Models, red, 1980s

EX $3   **NM** $8   **MIP** $12

❏ **Farmall M**, 1:32-scale, Scale Models, white demonstrator, 2002, No. ZSM997

EX $6   **NM** $9   **MIP** $13

❏ **Farmall Super H**, 1:32-scale, Scale Models, '01 Farm Progress Show Edition, 1991, No. ZSM962

EX $6   **NM** $9   **MIP** $13

❏ **International**, 1:32-scale, Pace Setter, red, liquor decanter, 1980s

EX $16   **NM** $22   **MIP** $36

❑ **International**, 1:32-scale, Polistil, red, 1980s
EX $4   **NM** $14   **MIP** $22

❑ **International 240**, 1:32-scale, Universal, red, 1970s
EX $38   **NM** $52   **MIP** $87

❑ **International 423**, 1:32-scale, Elastolin, red, 1980s
EX $57   **NM** $74   **MIP** $98

❑ **International 4366**, 1:32-scale, Ertl, front and rear duals, 2007, No. 14570
EX $8   **NM** $15   **MIP** $20

❑ **International 656**, 1:32-scale, Ertl, implement set, No. 683 *(Photo by Ertl)*
EX n/a   **NM** n/a   **MIP** $22

❑ **International 656**, 1:32-scale, Ertl, red, 1970s, No. 405
EX $4   **NM** $12   **MIP** $22

❑ **International 656**, 1:32-scale, Ertl, red, 1970s, No. 40
EX $4   **NM** $12   **MIP** $28

❑ **International 656 Set**, 1:32-scale, Ertl, w/wagon set, No. 52 *(Photo by Ertl)*
EX $3   **NM** $6   **MIP** $12

❑ **International 784**, 1:32-scale, Ertl, red, 1970s, No. 1638
EX $6   **NM** $17   **MIP** $33

❑ **International 946**, 1:32-scale, Lone Star, red and white, 1980s
EX $6   **NM** $16   **MIP** $27

❑ **International 946**, 1:32-scale, Lone Star, red, 1980s
EX $6   **NM** $16   **MIP** $27

❑ **McCormick**, 1:32-scale, red, 1960s
EX $6   **NM** $18   **MIP** $43

❑ **McCormick CX-100**, 1:32-scale, Cerberus, red, 2002

(Photo by Bossen Implement)
EX $13   **NM** $22   **MIP** $37

❑ **McCormick Farmall M**, 1:32-scale, Auburn Rubber, red w/black wheels, 4" long
EX n/a   **NM** n/a   **MIP** n/a

❏ **McCormick MTX-175**, 1:32-scale, Universal Hobbies, red, 2003, No. 02395
EX $9   **NM** $18   **MIP** $33

TRACTORS 1:37-SCALE

❏ **McCormick B-250**, 1:37-scale, Matchbox, red, several wheel rim colors, 1960s
EX $12   **NM** $21   **MIP** $29

TRACTORS 1:40-SCALE

❏ **International 6388**, 1:40-scale, Ertl, red, radio controlled, 1980s, No. 4791
EX $8   **NM** $18   **MIP** $36

TRACTORS 1:43-SCALE

❏ **Farmall 1206**, 1:43-scale, SpecCast, 1980s
EX $6   **NM** $8   **MIP** $12

❏ **Farmall 1206**, 1:43-scale, SpecCast, gold plated, 1980s
EX $6   **NM** $8   **MIP** $12

❏ **Farmall 300**, 1:43-scale, Ertl, red, National Farm Toy Show Tractor. Also came in set of three, MIB value for set, 1980s, No. 2524VA
EX $22   **NM** $34   **MIP** $57

❏ **Farmall 300**, 1:43-scale, Ertl, NF, 1985, No. 2513
EX $6   **NM** $8   **MIP** $13

❏ **Farmall 350**, 1:43-scale, Ertl, WF, also sold under part #33534, 1980s, No. 2244
EX $6   **NM** $8   **MIP** $13

❏ **Farmall 350 Set**, 1:43-scale, Ertl, red, came only as a boxed set w/Farmall 350, Tractors of the Past set, 1980s, No. 630
EX $22   **NM** $32   **MIP** $47

❏ **Farmall 560**, 1:43-scale, SpecCast, 1990s
EX $6   **NM** $8   **MIP** $12

❏ **Farmall 806**, 1:43-scale, SpecCast, 1990s
EX $6   **NM** $8   **MIP** $12

❏ **Farmall A**, 1:43-scale, SpecCast, only 7500 made, 1990s
EX $6   **NM** $8   **MIP** $12

❏ **Farmall B**, 1:43-scale, SpecCast, 1990s
EX $6   **NM** $8   **MIP** $12

❑ **Farmall C**, 1:43-scale, SpecCast, 1990s
EX $6   **NM** $8   **MIP** $12

❑ **Farmall H**, 1:43-scale, SpecCast, only 7500 made, 1990s
EX $6   **NM** $8   **MIP** $12

❑ **International 3180**, 1:43-scale, NPS, red and white, 1980s
EX $2   **NM** $3   **MIP** $6

❑ **Farmall Cub**, 1:43-scale, SpecCast, 1990s
EX $6   **NM** $8   **MIP** $12

❑ **Farmall M**, 1:43-scale, SpecCast, 1980s
EX $6   **NM** $8   **MIP** $12

❑ **International 3180**, 1:43-scale, NPS, blue and white, 1980s
EX $2   **NM** $3   **MIP** $6

❑ **Farmall F-12**, 1:43-scale, SpecCast, 1990s
EX $6   **NM** $8   **MIP** $12

❑ **Farmall M**, 1:43-scale, SpecCast, 1990s
EX $6   **NM** $8   **MIP** $12

❑ **International 400**, 1:43-scale, SpecCast, 1990s
EX $6   **NM** $8   **MIP** $12

❑ **Farmall F-30**, 1:43-scale, SpecCast, 1980s
EX $6   **NM** $8   **MIP** $12

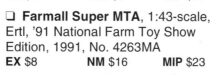

❑ **Farmall Regular**, 1:43-scale, Ertl, gray, 1980s, No. 2527
EX $4   **NM** $8   **MIP** $11

❑ **Farmall Super MTA**, 1:43-scale, Ertl, '91 National Farm Toy Show Edition, 1991, No. 4263MA
EX $8   **NM** $16   **MIP** $23

❑ **Farmall Super MTA**, 1:43-scale, Ertl, 1999, No. 33535
EX $6   **NM** $8   **MIP** $13

❑ **International 460**, 1:43-scale, SpecCast, Utility, 1990s
EX $6   **NM** $8   **MIP** $12

❏ **International 844**, 1:43-scale, Diano, red, 1970s
EX $22   **NM** $37   **MIP** $42

❏ **International 955**, 1:43-scale, Yaxon, red, 1980s
EX $6   **NM** $17   **MIP** $28

❏ **McCormick 10-20**, 1:43-scale, SpecCast, 1990s
EX $6   **NM** $8   **MIP** $12

❏ **McCormick F-20**, 1:43-scale, SpecCast, 1980s
EX $6   **NM** $8   **MIP** $28

❏ **McCormick WD-9**, 1:43-scale, SpecCast, 1990s
EX $6   **NM** $8   **MIP** $12

TRACTORS 1:64-SCALE

❏ **Farmall 1206**, 1:64-scale, Keith (Custom), red and white, did not come in box, 1980s
EX $6   **NM** $22   **MIP** n/a

❏ **Farmall 1206**, 1:64-scale, Keith (Custom), red and white, did not come in box, 1980s
EX $6   **NM** $22   **MIP** n/a

❏ **Farmall 1206**, 1:64-scale, Keith (Custom), red and white, did not come in box, 1980s
EX $6   **NM** $22   **MIP** n/a

❏ **Farmall 1206**, 1:64-scale, Matsen (Custom), red and white, did not come in box, 1980s
EX $6   **NM** $22   **MIP** n/a

❏ **Farmall 1206**, 1:64-scale, Matsen (Custom), red and white, did not come in box, 1980s
EX $6   **NM** $22   **MIP** n/a

❏ **Farmall 1206**, 1:64-scale, Matsen (Custom), red and white, did not come in box, 1980s
EX $6   **NM** $22   **MIP** n/a

❏ **Farmall 300**, 1:64-scale, Baker (Custom), red, did not come in box, 1980s
EX $3   **NM** $12   **MIP** n/a

❑ **Farmall 300**, 1:64-scale, Baker (Custom), red, did not come in box, 1980s

EX $3   **NM** $9   **MIP** n/a

❑ **Farmall 460**, 1:64-scale, Ertl, 1999, No. 4577

EX $4   **NM** $5   **MIP** $6

❑ **Farmall 560**, 1:64-scale, Ertl, WF, 1999, No. 4973

EX $4   **NM** $5   **MIP** $6

❑ **Farmall 560**, 1:64-scale, Ertl, w/corn picker and flare box wagon, 2000, No. 14073

EX $4   **NM** $6   **MIP** $9

❑ **Farmall 560**, 1:64-scale, Keith (Custom), red and white, did not come in box, 1980s

EX $6   **NM** $22   **MIP** n/a

❑ **Farmall 560**, 1:64-scale, Keith (Custom), red and white, did not come in box, 1980s

EX $6   **NM** $22   **MIP** n/a

❑ **Farmall 560**, 1:64-scale, Keith (Custom), red and white, did not come in box, 1980s

EX $6   **NM** $22   **MIP** n/a

❑ **Farmall 560**, 1:64-scale, Keith (Custom), red and white, did not come in box, 1980s

EX $6   **NM** $22   **MIP** n/a

❑ **Farmall 560**, 1:64-scale, Matsen (Custom), red and white, did not come in box, 1980s

EX $6   **NM** $22   **MIP** n/a

❑ **Farmall 560**, 1:64-scale, Matsen (Custom), red and white, did not come in box, 1980s

EX $6   **NM** $22   **MIP** n/a

❑ **Farmall 706**, 1:64-scale, Keith (Custom), red and white, did not come in box, 1980s

EX $6   **NM** $22   **MIP** n/a

❑ **Farmall 806**, 1:64-scale, Ertl, NF, 2002, No. 14211

EX $4   **NM** $5   **MIP** $6

❑ **Farmall 806**, 1:64-scale, Keith (Custom), red and white, did not come in box, 1980s

EX $6   **NM** $22   **MIP** n/a

❑ **Farmall 806**, 1:64-scale, Keith (Custom), red and white, did not come in box, 1980s

EX $6   **NM** $22   **MIP** n/a

❑ **Farmall 806**, 1:64-scale, Matsen (Custom), red and white, did not come in box, 1980s

EX $6   **NM** $22   **MIP** n/a

❏ **Farmall 806**, 1:64-scale, Matsen (Custom), red and white, did not come in box, 1980s

EX $6   **NM** $22   **MIP** n/a

❏ **Farmall 806**, 1:64-scale, Scale Models, green, 1980s

EX $4   **NM** $6   **MIP** $8

❏ **Farmall 806**, 1:64-scale, Scale Models, red, 1980s

EX $4   **NM** $6   **MIP** $8

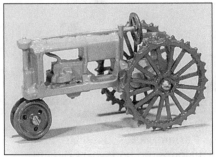

❏ **Farmall F-12**, 1:64-scale, Baker (Custom), gray and red, did not come in box, 1980s

EX $6   **NM** $12   **MIP** n/a

❏ **Farmall F-12**, 1:64-scale, Scale Models, '91 Farm Progress Show Edition, 1991, No. FB-1537

EX $4   **NM** $5   **MIP** $8

❏ **Farmall F-12**, 1:64-scale, Scale Models, 1996, No. ZSM850

(Photo by Scale Models)

EX $4   **NM** $6   **MIP** $8

❏ **Farmall F-20**, 1:64-scale, Ertl, 1998, No. 14094

EX $4   **NM** $5   **MIP** $6

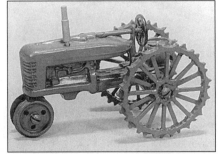

❏ **Farmall H**, 1:64-scale, Baker (Custom), red, did not come in box, 1980s

EX $6   **NM** $12   **MIP** n/a

❏ **Farmall H**, 1:64-scale, Ertl, red, "Farmall" is a decal, 1980s, No. 1747

EX $4   **NM** $6   **MIP** $27

❏ **Farmall H**, 1:64-scale, Ertl, red, "Farmall" is painted on, 1980s, No. 1747

EX $4   **NM** $6   **MIP** $27

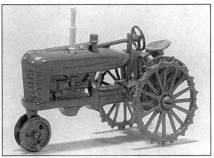

❏ **Farmall M**, 1:64-scale, Baker (Custom), red, did not come in box, 1980s

EX $6   **NM** $12   **MIP** n/a

❏ **Farmall M**, 1:64-scale, Baker (Custom), red, did not come in box, 1980s

EX $6   **NM** $12   **MIP** n/a

❏ **Farmall M**, 1:64-scale, Baker (Custom), red, did not come in box, 1980s

EX $6   **NM** $12   **MIP** n/a

❏ **Farmall M**, 1:64-scale, Ertl, single front wheel, 1995, No. 4684 *(Photo by Ertl)*

EX $4   **NM** $6   **MIP** $7

❏ **Farmall M**, 1:64-scale, Ertl, 1998, No. 4404

EX $4   **NM** $5   **MIP** $6

❏ **Farmall M**, 1:64-scale, Ertl, '98 National Farm Toy Museum, 1998, No. 16001HA
EX $4   **NM** $5   **MIP** $6

❏ **Farmall M**, 1:64-scale, Ertl, '01 National Farm Toy Museum, 2001, No. 16086A
EX $4   **NM** $5   **MIP** $7

❏ **Farmall M**, 1:64-scale, Ertl, 2001 Holiday Ornament, 2001, No. 14234P
EX $4   **NM** $6   **MIP** $11

❏ **Farmall M**, 1:64-scale, Ertl, white demonstrator, 2002, No. ZSM998
EX $4   **NM** $5   **MIP** $6

❏ **Farmall M**, 1:64-scale, Scale Models, red, 1980s
EX $3   **NM** $4   **MIP** $6

❏ **Farmall M**, 1:64-scale, Scale Models, five different chrome colors, sold as a Christmas ornament, 1980s
EX $3   **NM** $4   **MIP** $6

❏ **Farmall M**, 1:64-scale, Scale Models, red, 1980s
EX $3   **NM** $4   **MIP** $6

❏ **Farmall M**, 1:64-scale, Walters (Custom), red, did not come in box, 1980s
EX $6   **NM** $12   **MIP** n/a

❏ **Farmall M Set**, 1:64-scale, Ertl, M, Set #2, 1995, No. 4567
EX n/a   **NM** n/a   **MIP** $23

❏ **Farmall M Set**, 1:64-scale, Ertl, M, Set #1, 1995, No. 4559
EX n/a   **NM** n/a   **MIP** $23

❏ **Farmall M Set**, 1:64-scale, Ertl, M, Set #4, 1996, No. 4542EA *(Photo by Ertl)*
EX n/a   **NM** n/a   **MIP** $23

❏ **Farmall M Set**, 1:64-scale, Ertl, M, Set #3, 1996, No. 4559EA *(Photo by Ertl)*
EX n/a   **NM** n/a   **MIP** $23

❏ **Farmall M w/'50 Chevy Truck Set**, 1:64-scale, Ertl, tractor sits in pickup bed, 2007, No. 14543
EX $3   **NM** $6   **MIP** $9

❏ **Farmall MD**, 1:64-scale, Ertl, diesel, 1999, No. 4404
EX $3   **NM** $4   **MIP** $6

❏ **Farmall Set**, 1:64-scale, Ertl, 100, 200, 300, 400, 2004, No. 14332A
EX n/a   **NM** n/a   **MIP** $22

❏ **Farmall Super H**, 1:64-scale, Scale Models, '01 Farm Progress Show Edition, 2001, No. ZSM963
EX $4   **NM** $5   **MIP** $6

❏ **Farmall Super M**, 1:64-scale, Ertl, 2001, No. 14171
EX $4   **NM** $5   **MIP** $6

❏ **International 1026**, 1:64-scale, Keith (Custom), red and white, did not come in box, 1980s
EX $6   **NM** $22   **MIP** n/a

❏ **International 1066**, 1:64-scale, Gunning (Custom), red and white, 1989 Hannibal, Missouri Show Tractor, no box included, 1980s
EX $6   **NM** $22   **MIP** n/a

❏ **International 1066**, 1:64-scale, Gunning (Custom), red and white, did not come in box, 1980s
EX $6   **NM** $22   **MIP** n/a

❑ **International 1066**, 1:64-scale, Gunning (Custom), red and white, 1980s

EX $6   **NM** $22   **MIP** n/a

❑ **International 1456**, 1:64-scale, Keith (Custom), red and white, did not come in box, 1980s

EX $6   **NM** $22   **MIP** n/a

❑ **International 1466**, 1:64-scale, Ertl, red w/cream cab, white decals, 1970s, No. 1355

EX $23   **NM** $48   **MIP** $72

❑ **International 1086**, 1:64-scale, Ertl, red and cream, IH Historical card, 1970s, No. 1620

EX $17   **NM** $24   **MIP** $28

❑ **International 1456**, 1:64-scale, Keith (Custom), gold and red, gold demonstrator, did not come in box, 1980s

EX $6   **NM** $22   **MIP** n/a

❑ **International 1466**, 1:64-scale, Ertl, red w/white cab, may have white or cream decals, 1970s, No. 1355

EX $23   **NM** $48   **MIP** $72

❑ **International 1086**, 1:64-scale, Ertl, red and white, die-cast card, 1980s, No. 1620

EX $17   **NM** $24   **MIP** $28

❑ **International 1456**, 1:64-scale, Keith (Custom), red and white, did not come in box, 1980s

EX $6   **NM** $22   **MIP** n/a

❑ **International 1468**, 1:64-scale, Gunning (Custom), red and white, 1980s

EX $6   **NM** $22   **MIP** n/a

❑ **International 350 w/Picker & Wagon Set**, 1:64-scale, Ertl, mounted corn picker, wagon, 2007, No. 14544

EX $3   **NM** $6   **MIP** $9

❑ **International 1086**, 1:64-scale, Ertl, red and white, Farm Machines of the World card, 1980s, No. 1620

EX $17   **NM** $24   **MIP** $32

❑ **International 1206**, 1:64-scale, Ertl, ROPS, No. 14281

EX $4   **NM** $5   **MIP** $6

❑ **International 1466**, 1:64-scale, Ertl, red w/cream cab, white or cream decals, spun on or riveted rear axle, 1970s, No. 1355

EX $23   **NM** $48   **MIP** $72

❑ **International 3588**, 1:64-scale, Ertl, red, black, and white, steel pin used for rear axle, 1980s, No. 1526
EX $48　　**NM** $77　　**MIP** $92

❑ **International 3588**, 1:64-scale, Ertl, red, black, and white, rivet used for rear axle, 1980s, No. 1526
EX $48　　**NM** $77　　**MIP** $92

❑ **International 4166**, 1:64-scale, Keith (Custom), red and white, cab is cast to the tractor, did not come in box, 1980s
EX $16　　**NM** $27　　**MIP** n/a

❑ **International 4166**, 1:64-scale, Keith (Custom), red and white, cab is separate from the tractor, did not come in box, 1980s
EX $16　　**NM** $27　　**MIP** n/a

❑ **International 4186**, 1:64-scale, Matsen (Custom), red and white, did not come in box, 1980s
EX $16　　**NM** $27　　**MIP** n/a

❑ **International 4366**, 1:64-scale, Ertl, front and rear duals, 2007, No. 14573
EX $3　　**NM** $6　　**MIP** $9

❑ **International 4786**, 1:64-scale, Gunning (Custom), red and black, did not come in box, 1980s
EX $16　　**NM** $27　　**MIP** n/a

❑ **International 4786**, 1:64-scale, Gunning (Custom), red, black, and white, did not come in box, 1980s
EX $16　　**NM** $27　　**MIP** n/a

❑ **International 5088**, 1:64-scale, Ertl, red and black, gray rims and black cab posts, 1980s, No. 1797
EX $4　　**NM** $6　　**MIP** $9

❑ **International 5088**, 1:64-scale, Ertl, red and black, red rims and red cab posts, 1980s, No. 1797
EX $6　　**NM** $9　　**MIP** $16

❑ **International 5088**, 1:64-scale, Ertl, red and black, gray rear rims and white front rims, 1980s
EX $4　　**NM** $6　　**MIP** $9

❑ **International 5088**, 1:64-scale, Ertl, red and black, red rims and black cab posts, 1980s, No. 1797
EX $6　　**NM** $9　　**MIP** $14

❑ **International 5088**, 1:64-scale, Ertl, red and black w/John Deere front-end, 1980s
EX $4　　**NM** $4　　**MIP** $9

❏ **International 5088**, 1:64-scale, Ertl, red & black, Pow-R-Pull, International Harvester grill decal, right or left, 1980s, No. 4091
EX $4   **NM** $4   **MIP** $9

❏ **International 5088**, 1:64-scale, Ertl, red and black, gray rims and red cab posts, 1980s, No. 1797
EX $6   **NM** $9   **MIP** $12

❏ **International 5488**, 1:64-scale, Ertl, red and black, Pow-R-Pull, 1980s, No. 4091
EX $4   **NM** $4   **MIP** $9

❏ **International 5488**, 1:64-scale, Ertl, red and black, Pow-R-Pull, red cab posts and different tires, 1980s, No. 4091
EX $4   **NM** $6   **MIP** $9

❏ **International 560**, 1:64-scale, Ertl, gas, 1998, No. 4830
EX $4   **NM** $5   **MIP** $6

❏ **International 6388**, 1:64-scale, Variation photo: Tractor on left has large IH on grille, tractor on right has small IH on grille

❏ **International 6388**, 1:64-scale, Ertl, red and black, long rear axle, may or may not have spacers, 1980s, No. 1526
EX $26   **NM** $32   **MIP** $42

❏ **International 6388**, 1:64-scale, Ertl, red and black, clear rear lights, round rivet in front of cab, 1980s, No. 1526
EX $26   **NM** $32   **MIP** $42

❏ **International 6388**, 1:64-scale, Ertl, red and black, clear rear lights, flat rivet in front of cab, 1980s, No. 1526
EX $26   **NM** $32   **MIP** $42

❏ **International 6388**, 1:64-scale, Ertl, Variation—red and black, white rear lights and small IH on grille, 1980s, No. 1526
EX $26   **NM** $32   **MIP** $42

❏ **International 6388**, 1:64-scale, Ertl, red and black, white rear lights and large IH on grille, 1980s, No. 1526
EX $26   **NM** $32   **MIP** $42

❏ **International 660**, 1:64-scale, Ertl, '99 National Farm Toy Show, 1999, No. 16022A
EX $8   **NM** $16   **MIP** $27

❏ **International 660**, 1:64-scale, Ertl, 2000, No. 14042
EX $4   **NM** $5   **MIP** $6

❏ **International 856**, 1:64-scale, Ertl, w/Hiniker cab, 2001, No. 14170
EX $4   **NM** $5   **MIP** $6

❏ **International 856**, 1:64-scale, Keith (Custom), red and white, did not come in box, 1980s
EX $6   **NM** $22   **MIP** n/a

Photos by Jon Jacobson unless otherwise noted.

❏ **International 856**, 1:64-scale, Keith (Custom), red and white, did not come in box, 1980s
EX $6   **NM** $22   **MIP** n/a

❏ **International 966**, 1:64-scale, Gunning (Custom), red and black, did not come in box, 1970s
EX $6   **NM** $22   **MIP** $88

❏ **International 966**, 1:64-scale, Gunning (Custom), red, black and white, did not come in box, 1980s
EX $6   **NM** $22   **MIP** n/a

❏ **International Mogul**, 1:64-scale, Scale Models, green w/red wheels, 1980s
EX $4   **NM** $8   **MIP** $11

❏ **International Set**, 1:64-scale, Ertl, 66 Series Set #1, 966, 966, 1066, 1466, 1992, No. 4630
EX n/a   **NM** n/a   **MIP** $27

❏ **International Set**, 1:64-scale, Ertl, 66 Series Set #2, 966, 1066, 1066, 1466, 1992, No. 4637
EX n/a   **NM** n/a   **MIP** $27

❏ **International Set**, 1:64-scale, Ertl, 66 Series Set #3, 966, 966, 1066, 1466, 1992, No. 4636
EX n/a   **NM** n/a   **MIP** $27

❏ **International Set**, 1:64-scale, Ertl, 66 Series Set #5, 966, 1066, 1066, 1466, 1993, No. 4643
EX n/a   **NM** n/a   **MIP** $27

❏ **International Set**, 1:64-scale, Ertl, 66 Series Set #6, 966, 1066, 1066, 1466, 1993, No. 4672
EX n/a   **NM** n/a   **MIP** $27

❏ **International Set**, 1:64-scale, Ertl, 66 Series Set #7, 966, 1066, 1466, 1566, 1993, No. 4677
EX n/a   **NM** n/a   **MIP** $27

❏ **International Set**, 1:64-scale, Ertl, 66 Series Set #4, 966, 966, 1066, 1466, 1993, No. 4642
EX n/a   **NM** n/a   **MIP** $27

❏ **International Set**, 1:64-scale, Ertl, 66 Series Set #8, 966, 1066, 1466, 1566, 1994, No. 4683
EX n/a   **NM** n/a   **MIP** $27

❏ **International Set**, 1:64-scale, Ertl, 66 Series Set #9, 966, 1066, 1466, 1566, 1994, No. 4693
EX n/a   **NM** n/a   **MIP** $27

❏ **International Set**, 1:64-scale, Ertl, 66 Series Set #10, 1066, 5 Millionth, 1994, No. 4590
EX n/a   **NM** n/a   **MIP** $23

❏ **International Set**, 1:64-scale, Ertl, 460 NF, 460 standard, 560 NF, 560 standard, 1997, No. 441
EX n/a   **NM** n/a   **MIP** $23

❏ **International Set**, 1:64-scale, Ertl, 708, 806, 1206, 2001, No. 14133
EX n/a   **NM** n/a   **MIP** $22

❏ **International Set**, 1:64-scale, Ertl, 460, 560, 660, 2003, No. 14366
EX n/a   **NM** n/a   **MIP** $22

❏ **International Titan**, 1:64-scale, Scale Models, No. ZSM766

(Photo by Scale Models)

EX $4   **NM** $8   **MIP** $11

❏ **International Titan 10-20**, 1:64-scale, Ertl, gray and red, "Titan 10-20" is a decal, 1980s, No. 1748
EX $4   **NM** $6   **MIP** $27

❏ **International Titan 10-20**, 1:64-scale, Ertl, gray and red, "Titan 10-20" is painted on, 1980s, No. 1748
EX $4   **NM** $6   **MIP** $27

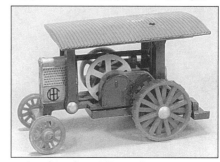

❏ **International Type A**, 1:64-scale, Ertl, green w/red top and wheels, flywheel is gray, 1980s, No. 1750
EX $4   **NM** $8   **MIP** $24

❏ **International Type A**, 1:64-scale, Ertl, green w/red top and wheels, green flywheel, 1980s, No. 1750
EX $4   **NM** $8   **MIP** $27

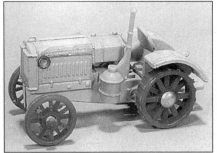

❏ **McCormick Deering**, 1:64-scale, Ertl, gray and red, name is a decal, 1980s, No. 1749
EX $4   **NM** $6   **MIP** $27

❏ **McCormick Deering**, 1:64-scale, Ertl, gray and red, name is painted on, 1980s, No. 1749
EX $4   **NM** $6   **MIP** $27

❏ **McCormick Farmall Regular**, 1:64-scale, Ertl, gray and red, 1980s, No. 1751
EX $4   **NM** $6   **MIP** $27

TRACTORS 1:87-SCALE

❏ **International 844**, 1:87-scale, Preiser, red, model kit, 1980s
EX $4   **NM** $14   **MIP** $23

TRACTORS

❏ **International 1256—Variations 56 Series**, Large front spindle

❏ **International 1256—Variations 56 Series**, Small front spindle

❏ **International 1466 —Front Wheel Variations 66 Series**, Inside center of rim is red, seen on 1466 model

❏ **International 1466—Front Wheel Variations 66 Series**, Inside center of rim is black, seen on 966

❏ **International 6388**, Variation photo: Tractor on left does not have spacers. Tractor on right has spacers

❏ **International 6388**, Variation photo: Tractor on left has clear rear lights. Tractor on right has white rear lights

TRUCKS 1:16-SCALE

❏ **International Low Bed 95 Trailer**, 1:16-scale, Ertl, red and white, crank hitch, 1960s, No. 24
EX $32   **NM** $72   **MIP** $162

❑ **International Low Bed Trailer**, 1:16-scale, Ertl, red and white, C-hitch, 1970s, No. 454
EX $32   **NM** $72   **MIP** $162

TRUCKS 1:25-SCALE

❑ **International '40 Ford Pickup**, 1:25-scale, Ertl, Prestige Series, No. 4367 *(Photo by Ertl)*
EX $12   **NM** $18   **MIP** $28

TRUCKS 1:64-SCALE

❑ **International—Early 1970s Semi-Truck Wheel**, 1:64-scale, Ertl, only found on early Transtars

❑ **International—Late 1970s and 1980s Semi-Truck Wheel**, 1:64-scale, Ertl, speed wheel

❑ **International—Late 1980s Semi-Truck Wheel**, 1:64-scale, Ertl, bud-style rim, rubber tire

❑ **International 4300 Eagle w/Flatbed and I-Beam**, 1:64-scale, Ertl, all red, No. 1412
EX $11   **NM** $26   **MIP** $29

❑ **International 4300 Eagle w/Grain Trailer**, 1:64-scale, Ertl, orange cab w/silver trailer w/o flaps on trailer, No. 1413
EX $15   **NM** $20   **MIP** $23

❑ **International 4300 Eagle w/Grain Trailer**, 1:64-scale, Ertl, orange cab w/silver trailer w/mud flaps, No. 1413
EX $16   **NM** $21   **MIP** $24

❑ **International 4300 Eagle w/Tanker Trailer**, 1:64-scale, Ertl, red cab w/white trailer, writing on cab doors
EX $10   **NM** $21   **MIP** $25

❑ **International 4300 Eagle w/Tanker Trailer**, 1:64-scale, Ertl, red cab w/white tank, No. 1427
EX $11   **NM** $16   **MIP** $20

❑ **International 4300 Eagle w/Tanker Trailer**, 1:64-scale, Ertl, red cab w/white tank, No. 1414
EX $10   **NM** $14   **MIP** $18

❑ **International 4300 Eagle w/Tanker Trailer**, 1:64-scale, Ertl, red cab w/white tank, No. 1414
EX $12   **NM** $15   **MIP** $21

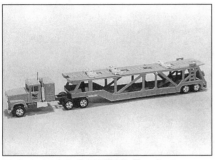

❑ **International 4300 Eagle
w/Transport Trailer**, 1:64-scale,
Ertl, all orange, No. 1426
EX $20   **NM** $38   **MIP** $45

❑ **International 4300 Eagle w/Van
Trailer**, 1:64-scale, Ertl, all black,
No. 1313EH
EX $15   **NM** $120   **MIP** $125

❑ **International 4300 Eagle w/Van
Trailer**, 1:64-scale, Ertl, white cab
w/white (ribbed) trailer, No. 1428
EX $10   **NM** $28   **MIP** $31

❑ **International 4300 Eagle w/Van
Trailer**, 1:64-scale, Ertl, white cab
w/white (smooth) trailer, No. 1428
EX $10   **NM** $27   **MIP** $30

❑ **International 4300 Eagle w/Van
Trailer**, 1:64-scale, Ertl, blue cab
w/white trailer, No. 1411
EX $10   **NM** $22   **MIP** $24

❑ **International 4300 Eagle w/Van
Trailer**, 1:64-scale, Ertl, blue cab
w/white trailer, No. 1411
EX $10   **NM** $18   **MIP** $20

❑ **International Conventional
w/Drop Center Trailer and 130-90s**,
1:64-scale, Ertl, white cab w/gray
trailer, No. 7315
EX $15   **NM** $30   **MIP** $35

❑ **International Conventional
w/Drop Center Trailer and 2294s
cream**, 1:64-scale, Ertl, white cab
w/gray trailer, No. 1412
EX $14   **NM** $35   **MIP** $42

❑ **International Conventional
w/Drop Center Trailer and 2594s**,
1:64-scale, Ertl, white cab w/gray
trailer, No. 1236
EX $14   **NM** $33   **MIP** $38

❑ **International Conventional
w/Drop Center Trailer and 2594s**,
1:64-scale, Ertl, white cab w/gray
trailer, No. 1412
EX $14   **NM** $36   **MIP** $43

❑ **International Conventional
w/Drop Center Trailer and 4450s**,
1:64-scale, Ertl, white cab w/gray
trailer, No. 5530
EX $15   **NM** $31   **MIP** $35

❑ **International Conventional
w/Drop Center Trailer and 4450s**,
1:64-scale, Ertl, white cab w/gray
trailer, No. 5530
EX $15   **NM** $31   **MIP** $35

❏ **International Conventional w/Drop Center Trailer and 4450s**, 1:64-scale, Ertl, white cab w/gray trailer, No. 5502

EX $15   **NM** $25   **MIP** $30

❏ **International Conventional w/Drop Center Trailer and 4450s**, 1:64-scale, Ertl, white cab w/gray trailer, No. 5530

EX $15   **NM** $29   **MIP** $33

❏ **International Conventional w/Drop Center Trailer and 4450s**, 1:64-scale, Ertl, white cab w/gray trailer, No. 5530

EX $15   **NM** $39   **MIP** $33

❏ **International Conventional w/Drop Center Trailer and 5088/2594**, 1:64-scale, Ertl, white cab w/gray trailer, No. 474

EX $15   **NM** $34   **MIP** $40

❏ **International Conventional w/Drop Center Trailer and 5088/2594**, 1:64-scale, Ertl, white cab w/gray trailer, No. 474

EX $16   **NM** $35   **MIP** $41

❏ **International Conventional w/Drop Center Trailer and 5088/2594**, 1:64-scale, Ertl, white cab w/gray trailer, No. 1236

EX $15   **NM** $35   **MIP** $40

❏ **International Conventional w/Drop Center Trailer and 699s**, 1:64-scale, Ertl, white cab w/gray trailer, No. 1411

EX $15   **NM** $28   **MIP** $32

❏ **International Conventional w/Drop Center Trailer and 8070s**, 1:64-scale, Ertl, white cab w/gray trailer, No. 1288

EX $16   **NM** $41   **MIP** $49

❏ **International Conventional w/Drop Center Trailer and 8070s**, 1:64-scale, Ertl, white cab w/gray trailer, No. 1288

EX $14   **NM** $38   **MIP** $45

❏ **International Conventional w/Drop Center Trailer and 8070s**, 1:64-scale, Ertl, white cab w/gray trailer, No. 1288

EX $15   **NM** $42   **MIP** $50

❏ **International Conventional w/Drop Center Trailer, Case-International Harvester**, 1:64-scale, Ertl, white cab w/gray trailer

EX $10   **NM** $18   **MIP** $22

❏ **International Conventional w/Drop Center Trailer, John Deere**, 1:64-scale, Ertl, white cab w/gray trailer, w/two 4450 tractors

EX $10   **NM** $21   **MIP** $25

❑ **International Conventional w/Trailer, Case-International**, 1:64-scale, Ertl, white cab w/gray trailer, w/Case 2594 and IH 5088

EX $12   **NM** $20   **MIP** $25

❑ **International Conventional w/Van Trailer**, 1:64-scale, Ertl, all white, can have either black or silver trailer frame, No. 9200

EX $8   **NM** $10   **MIP** $12

❑ **International Conventional w/Van Trailer**, 1:64-scale, Ertl, all tan, No. 1400

EX $5   **NM** $10   **MIP** $15

❑ **International Conventional w/Van Trailer**, 1:64-scale, Ertl, all tan, No. 1400

EX $5   **NM** $11   **MIP** $16

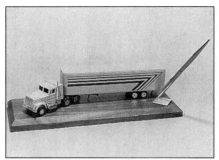

❑ **International Conventional w/Van Trailer**, 1:64-scale, Ertl, all tan, No. 86

EX $10   **NM** $18   **MIP** $20

❑ **International Conventional w/Van Trailer**, 1:64-scale, Ertl, all tan, No. 9484

EX $10   **NM** $38   **MIP** $45

❑ **International Conventional w/Van Trailer**, 1:64-scale, Ertl, all tan, No. 9807

EX $10   **NM** $35   **MIP** $42

❑ **International Conventional w/Van Trailer**, 1:64-scale, Ertl, all white, No. 9453

EX $9   **NM** $30   **MIP** $35

❑ **International Conventional w/Van Trailer**, 1:64-scale, Ertl, all white, No. 9388

EX $15   **NM** $100   **MIP** $150

❑ **International Conventional w/Van Trailer**, 1:64-scale, Ertl, all white, No. 483

EX $5   **NM** $9   **MIP** $10

❑ **International Conventional w/Van Trailer**, 1:64-scale, Ertl, all white, No. 483

EX $6   **NM** $10   **MIP** $12

❑ **International Conventional w/Van Trailer**, 1:64-scale, Ertl, all white, No. 5535

EX $4   **NM** $9   **MIP** $10

❑ **International Conventional w/Van Trailer**, 1:64-scale, Ertl, all white, No. 5535
EX $4 **NM** $10 **MIP** $12

❑ **International Conventional, Allis-Chalmers**, 1:64-scale, Ertl, white, cab only, boxed w/o trailer
EX $5 **NM** $8 **MIP** $10

❑ **International Navistar S-Series Cement Mixer, Flynn Ready Mix**, 1:64-scale, Ertl, green and white, No. 4296
EX $9 **NM** $16 **MIP** $20

❑ **International Navistar S-Series Straight Truck, Publix**, 1:64-scale, Ertl, green cab w/white box, No. 7691
EX $5 **NM** $7 **MIP** $8

❑ **International Navistar S-Series Straight Truck, Shop Rite**, 1:64-scale, Ertl, red cab w/white box, No. 7634
EX $5 **NM** $6 **MIP** $8

❑ **International Navistar S-Series Straight Truck, Tegeler's Dairy Products**, 1:64-scale, Ertl, blue and white, No. 4295
EX $10 **NM** $23 **MIP** $25

❑ **International Navistar S-Series Straight Truck, U.S. Mail**, 1:64-scale, Ertl, all white, No. 2134
EX $9 **NM** $18 **MIP** $21

❑ **International Navistar S-Series Van**, 1:64-scale, Ertl, all white, No. 7618
EX $5 **NM** $12 **MIP** $17

❑ **International Navistar S-Series Wrecker, Deutmeyer Bros.**, 1:64-scale, Ertl, red and white, No. 4297
EX $10 **NM** $17 **MIP** $23

❑ **International Navistar w/Drop Center Trailer and 7130s**, 1:64-scale, Ertl, white cab w/gray trailer, No. 607
EX $15 **NM** $23 **MIP** $25

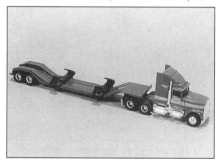

❑ **International Navistar w/Drop Center Trailer, C.B. Hoober**, 1:64-scale, Ertl, red cab w/gray trailer, No. 9592
EX $11 **NM** $15 **MIP** $21

❑ **International Navistar w/Drop Center Trailer, Messick Farm Equipment**, 1:64-scale, Ertl, red cab w/gray trailer, No. 2960
EX $10 **NM** $15 **MIP** $20

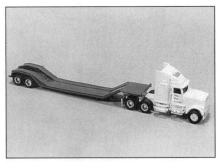

❑ **International Navistar w/Drop Center Trailer, Yuba**, 1:64-scale, Ertl, white cab w/gray trailer
EX $12   **NM** $15   **MIP** $20

❑ **International Navistar w/Grain Trailer**, 1:64-scale, Ertl, red cab w/gray trailer, No. 1187
EX $15   **NM** $22   **MIP** $25

❑ **International Navistar w/Refrigerated Van Trailer, McCollisters Moving and Storage, Atlanta, GA**, 1:64-scale, Ertl, all white
EX $15   **NM** $41   **MIP** $45

❑ **International Navistar w/Drop Deck Van Trailer**, 1:64-scale, Ertl, all white, No. 9885
EX $12   **NM** $18   **MIP** $21

❑ **International Navistar w/Refrigerated Trailer, Minn Tex**, 1:64-scale, Ertl, red cab w/white trailer, No. 9936
EX $12   **NM** $27   **MIP** $30

❑ **International Navistar w/Refrigerated Van Trailer, McCollisters Moving and Storage, Boston, MA**, 1:64-scale, Ertl, all white
EX $15   **NM** $41   **MIP** $45

❑ **International Navistar w/Drop Deck Van Trailer, Iowa FFA**, 1:64-scale, Ertl, all white, No. 9222
EX $13   **NM** $24   **MIP** $30

❑ **International Navistar w/Refrigerated Van Trailer, Ardmore Farms**, 1:64-scale, Ertl, all white, No. 9593
EX $14   **NM** $32   **MIP** $37

❑ **International Navistar w/Refrigerated Van Trailer, McCollisters Moving and Storage, Burlington, NJ**, 1:64-scale, Ertl, all white
EX $15   **NM** $41   **MIP** $45

❑ **International Navistar w/Drop Deck Van Trailer, FedEx/Frito Lay**, 1:64-scale, Ertl, all white, FedEx tractor w/Frito Lay trailer, No. 9324
EX $15   **NM** $18   **MIP** $20

❑ **International Navistar w/Refrigerated Van Trailer, Flav-O-Rich Dairy**, 1:64-scale, Ertl, all white, No. 9098
EX $12   **NM** $21   **MIP** $26

❑ **International Navistar w/Refrigerated Van Trailer, McCollisters Moving and Storage, Chicago, IL**, 1:64-scale, Ertl, all white
EX $15   **NM** $41   **MIP** $45

AGCO produced its RT150 from 2004-05, and Scale Models released this pedal tractor in 2006.

EX $96   **NM $123**   **MIP $153**

This AGCO-Allis 9655 was released by Scale Models in 1:64-scale.

EX $3   **NM $6**   **MIP $8**

The AGCO LT90 debuted in 2004, the same year that Scale Models released this 1:16-scale replica.

EX $22   **NM $37**   **MIP $48**

The AGCO-White 170 was produced from 1990-92 and carried an original sticker price of $66,000. More easily obtainable is the 1:16-scale replica from Scale Models.

EX $18   **NM $27**   **MIP $43**

Scale Models released this AGCO-Allis 9650 in 1:16-scale. The full sized 156-hp AGCO-Allis 9650 was produced from 1994-95.

EX $22   **NM $33**   **MIP $42**

The AGCO-White 6105 was produced from 1992-97 and this 1:16-scale tractor was released by Scale Models in 1998.

EX $21   **NM $29**   **MIP $47**

A total of 10,126 Allis-Chalmers 200s were produced from 1972-75. Ertl released this 1:16-scale tractor w/air cleaner in 1972.

EX $73　　　　**NM $134**　　　　**MIP $268**

Ertl released this 1:16-scale Allis-Chalmers 7050 in 1974, the only year the real tractor was made.

EX $89　　　　**NM $149**　　　　**MIP $239**

Ertl released this Collector's Edition Allis-Chalmers 8030 in 1:16-scale in 1982, the same year the real tractor debuted.

EX $23　　　　**NM $38**　　　　**MIP $63**

Located in West Allis, Wis., the Allis-Chalmers Co. produced 23,050 D-14 tractors between 1957-60. This high crop model in 1:16-scale was the official 2005 National Farm Toy Museum tractor.

EX $18　　　　**NM $33**　　　　**MIP $43**

Allis-Chalmers produced 84,914 of its popular D-17 from 1958-67. Ertl released this 1:16-scale version w/ headlights and large "Allis-Chalmers" decal in 1960.

EX $172　　　　**NM $347**　　　　**MIP $919**

With an original sticker price of $2,400, the Allis-Chalmers WD-45 was a brisk seller from 1953-57. The Ertl Co. released this 1:16-scale WD-45 as #3 in its Precision Series in 1995.

EX $138　　　　**NM $169**　　　　**MIP $238**

Powered by a Komatsu engine, the Big Bud 370 was available from 1986-89 and really made 370 hp. Ertl released this 1:64-scale Bafus Blue replica in 1993.

EX $33   **NM $48**   **MIP $78**

The Havre, Mont., factory produced only one of the Big Bud 16-747 tractors in 1978. Die-Cast Promotions released this 1:64-scale model in 2003.

EX $17   **NM $22**   **MIP $38**

The three-wheeled Case 10-20 was issued as a four-cylinder light tractor during the World War I period. Scale Models released this 1:16-scale Case 10-20 in 1993.

EX $32   **NM $63**   **MIP $90**

Case produced its popular VA line of tractors from 1942-55, of which the VAC is a variant designed for row crop use. This 1:16-scale model from Ertl was released in 1988.

EX $28   **NM $38**   **MIP $44**

The Case 400 was available from 1955-58. SpecCast released this 1:16-scale tractor with a narrow front in 1998.

EX $19   **NM $28**   **MIP $52**

J.I. Case manufactured its 102 hp 1030 model from 1966-69. Ertl released this 1:16-scale square fendered 1030 in 1967.

EX $118   **NM $186**   **MIP $472**

Scale Models released this 1:16-scale Case 12-25 in 1990.

EX $53   **NM $67**   **MIP $82**

This 1:16-scale Case-IH Big Square Baler was released by Ertl in 1996.

EX $13   **NM $26**   **MIP $34**

The red, white, and blue color scheme of the Case Agri-King Spirit of '76 edition make this 1:16-scale replica from Ertl a favorite among collectors.

EX $103   **NM $166**   **MIP $249**

In 1997, Ertl added the Case-IH Cotton Picker to its growing line of 1:64-scale implements.

EX $4   **NM $8**   **MIP $12**

Case produced the 2294 from 1983-87. Ertl released this 1:64-scale 2294 in black and cream.

EX $11   **NM $14**   **MIP $19**

The Case-IH 3294 was available from 1983-86 at a list price of $67,600. Ertl released its 3294 in 1:16-scale in 1986.

EX $19   **NM $26**   **MIP $36**

The Case-IH 4994 was produced from 1984-87. Ertl released its Collector's Edition 1:16-scale version in 1986.

EX $72   **NM $93**   **MIP $127**

The enormous Case-IH 9380 made 400 hp and was produced from 1996-2000. Scale Models released this special edition 1:16-scale 9380 with triples in 1995, "A Powerful Heritage, Fargo, ND 1995."

EX $122   **NM $142**   **MIP $173**

The Case-IH MX-200 was first released in 1999. Ertl released this MX-200 in 1:64-scale.

EX $1   **NM $2**   **MIP $4**

This 1:16-scale Challenger MT-465B was produced by Scale Models in 2006.

EX $16   **NM $24**   **MIP $44**

Less than 140 Cockshutt Golden Arrow tractors were ever manufactured, making them a rare addition to any collection. Scale Models released this Cockshutt Golden Arrow in 1:16-scale as the 1987 Ontario Show edition.

EX $178   **NM $212**   **MIP $243**

The style of the Cockshutt 70 is unmistakable from its cousin, the Oliver 70. Scale Models released this 1:16-scale Cockshutt 70 on steel wheels in 1983.

EX $18   **NM $28**   **MIP $38**

Made for the needs of small farms, the Deutz Model FIM 414 debuted in 1936 and contributed to the mechanization of rural Germany. Also known as the Deutz Bauernschlepper, the tractor was offered in 1:16-scale by Scale Models in 1986.

EX $10   **NM $22**   **MIP $37**

This 1:16-scale Deutz 200 was produced by Bruder in 2002.

EX $9   **NM $13**   **MIP $22**

The Deutz-Allis 6260 was produced from 1986-90. Ertl released this 1:16-scale Collector's Edition tractor in 1986.

EX $18   **NM $28**   **MIP $42**

Tractor salesman Harry Ferguson was the inventor of the "Ferguson System" for attaching implements to tractors. Today, we know his invention as the 3-point hitch. Ferguson also released a limited number of tractors before his company was purchased by Massey-Harris in 1953. Here is SpecCast's 1:16-scale Ferguson 30.

EX $22   **NM $32**   **MIP $48**

The Fordson F was produced in factories in Detroit, Mich., and Cork, Ireland from 1917-28. Ertl released this no fenders version of the 1:16-scale Forsson F in 1969.

EX $62   **NM $80**   **MIP $100**

The Fordson Super Major was manufactured in the Dagenham, England plant from 1961-64. Ertl released this 1:16-scale Super Major in the 1990s.

EX $22   **NM $37**   **MIP $42**

The charming Ford 8N was manufactured from 1947-52, replacing the Ford 2N. Ertl's 1:16-scale Ford 8N was released in 1984.

EX $18   **NM $33**   **MIP $43**

The Ford/New Holland 4630 was produced from 1990-99. Scale Models released this Ford 4630 in 1:16-scale.

EX $8   **NM $11**   **MIP $19**

Produced as part of the Workmaster series, the Ford 641 was manufactured from 1957-61. This 1:16-scale Ford 641 was released as the 1998 Toy Tractor Times edition.

EX $16   **NM $28**   **MIP $48**

Ford produced its 106 hp 8340 tractor from 1992-97. Ertl released this Collector Edition 8340 in 1:16-scale.

EX $21   **NM $33**   **MIP $47**

The diesel-engined Ford TW-25 was produced from 1983-89. Scale Models released this 1:16-scale Ford TW-25 in 1989.

EX $18   **NM $23**   **MIP $38**

The Ford 8770 was in production from 1993-2000. This 1:16-scale 8770 with duals was released by SpecCast in 1996.

EX $24   **NM $33**   **MIP $52**

Manufactured in International Harvester's Chicago, Ill., plant, the Farmall B was available for just $770 from 1939-47. I couldn't resist adding this 1:16-scale Farmall B from Ertl to my collection in 2006.

EX $12   **NM $18**   **MIP $24**

Though the vast majority of Farmall F-12 tractors were manufactured at the Chicago plant, International Harvester produced F-12 tractors for the European market at its plant in Neuss, Germany. Scale Models released this 1:16-scale Farmall F-12 in 1996.

EX $21   **NM $32**   **MIP $43**

From 1939-52, the Farmall M was the bedrock of the International Harvester line. It is one of the most oft-produced "red" toy tractors and received a special edition from Ertl in 1:16-scale to commemorate International Harvester's one-millionth tractor.

EX $65   **NM $90**   **MIP $125**

A total of 9,197 Farmall 130 tractors were built from 1956-58. This is the 1:16-scale highcrop Farmall 130 National Farm Toy Museum edition that Ertl released in 2001.

EX $16   **NM $27**   **MIP $42**

The Farmall 350 tractor was available from 1956-58. SpecCast released this 1:16-scale Farmall 350 with wide front in 2004 as the LaFayette Show edition.

EX $19   **NM $38**   **MIP $53**

International Harvester sold 65,982 Farmll 560 tractors from 1958-63. This rare 1:16-scale Farmall 560 with duals is the 1979 Toy Farmer edition from Ertl.

EX $493   **NM $682**   **MIP $1,144**

This is the International Harvester 915 Combine that was released in 1:24-scale in the 1970s.

EX $98   **NM $248**   **MIP $432**

The IH Mogul 8-16 was a kerosene-powered tractor offered from 1917-22. Scale Models released this 1:16-scale Mogul 8-16 in 1981.

EX $33   **NM $52**   **MIP $73**

Ertl released this 1:16-scale Gravity Wagon in the 1970s.

EX $22   **NM $48**   **MIP $89**

The gasoline-powered International Harvester 600 was manufactured from 1956-57. Ertl released this 1:16-scale IH 600 in 1994.

EX $17   **NM $23**   **MIP $38**

Despite the merging of the McCormick and Deering companies under the International Harvester name, both divisions kept unique tractor models well in to the 1920s. "Titan" models were Deering offerings, while "Mogul" models were found at McCormick locations. This is the 1:16-scale IH Titan produced by Scale Models in 1982.

EX $33   **NM $67**   **MIP $87**

The International Harvester 1026 was offered for only two years, 1970-71. This 1:16-scale IH 1026 with "Hydro" on hood was released by Ertl in 1970.

EX $98   **NM $417**   **MIP $673**

The International Harvester 1456 was manufactured from 1969-71. Ertl released this 1:16-scale IH 1456 with duals in 1970.

EX $98 **NM $257** **MIP $772**

Available from 1971-76, the International Harvester 1466 was capable of 133 horsepower. Ertl released this 1:16-scale IH 1466, No. 4622, in 1990 with a collector's insert.

EX $34 **NM $52** **MIP $68**

The International Harvester 5488 was manufactured from 1981-85. Another 2002 release commemorating the IH's 100th anniversary was this 1:16-scale IH 5488 from Ertl.

EX $46 **NM $72** **MIP $102**

The International Harvester 4366 was built at the Fargo, ND, Steiger plant from 1973-76. This is the 1:64-scale IH 4366 2006 National Farm Toy Show edition from Ertl.

EX $7 **NM $11** **MIP $15**

International Harvester released the 30 hp McCormick-Deering 15-30 from 1923-29. In 1992, Scale Models produced this McCormick 15-30 in 1:16-scale.

EX $19 **NM $28** **MIP $48**

During its production run from 1931-39, International Harvester sold 32,541 of its McCormick-Deering W-30 tractors. SpecCast released this 1:16-scale McCormick W-30 in 1997.

EX $18 **NM $24** **MIP $42**

Part of the New Generation series, the John Deere 4020 was released in a variety of styles. Ertl produced this John Deere 4020 pedal tractor in 1991.

EX $173   **NM $322**   **MIP $396**

Ertl released the 1:32-scale John Deere Forage Harvestor 6650 with corn head in 1999.

EX $8   **NM $14**   **MIP $28**

This is the 1:16-scale John Deere Combine 12-A that Ertl released in 1991.

EX $18   **NM $34**   **MIP $48**

Waterloo Boy tractors were manufactured from 1913 until 1924 when John Deere introduced the Model D. This is Ertl's 1:16-scale Waterloo Boy R from 1988.

EX $22   **NM $31**   **MIP $39**

Ertl produced this 1:08-scale John Deere Stationary Gas Engine Waterloo Boy in 1992.

EX $6   **NM $11**   **MIP $22**

The John Deere A was one of John Deere Co.'s longest-running production tractors. It remained in production from 1934 to 1952. This early 1:16-scale Ertl John Deere A has a closed flywheel and was made in the 1940s.

EX $82   **NM $198**   **MIP $677**

Ertl released this high post 1:16-scale John Deere A in the 1950s.

EX $114   **NM $268**   **MIP $689**

The two-cylinder gas-powered John Deere L was produced from 1937-46. SpecCast offered this 1:16-scale John Deere L as the first of a series of six tractors in 2001.

EX $16   **NM $22**   **MIP $33**

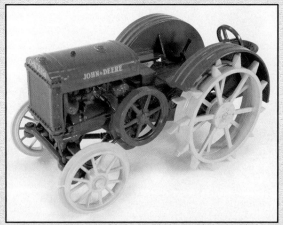

John Deere built more than 160,000 model D tractors during its long production run from 1923-1953. This 1:16-scale John Deere D from Ertl is the 1998 Two Cylinder Club edition.

EX $42   **NM $67**   **MIP $98**

More than 45,000 John Deere M tractors were manufactured between 1947-52. SpecCast released this wide front 1:16-scale John Deere M with a 2-bottom mounted plow in 2007.

EX $16   **NM $28**   **MIP $37**

Deere & Co. began development of its own tractors in 1912, and the only one to go into production was the Dain in 1918. Named for its engineer, Joseph Dain, very few were released because Deere acquired the Waterloo Engine Co. that year and its Waterloo Boy tractors became the staple in the John Deere line. This 1:16-scale John Deere Dain was produced by Scale Models in 2000.

EX $32   **NM $56**   **MIP $78**

The John Deere 620 was produced from 1956-58. Ertl released this wide front 1:16-scale John Deere 620 in 2002.

EX $8   **NM $13**   **MIP $26**

The John Deere 2755 was manufactured at plants in Germany and Mexico from 1984-92. Ertl released this 1:16-scale John Deere 2755 in 1989.

EX $12   **NM $26**   **MIP $34**

The 225 hp John Deere 8400 was available between 1994-98. This is Ertl's 1:16-scale John Deere 8400T Collector's Edition trac tractor from 1998.

EX $33   **NM $58**   **MIP $87**

The six-cylinder John Deere 4250 made 121 hp and was manufactured from 1983-88. Ertl produced this 1:16-scale John Deere 4250 as the 1982 National Farm Toy Show edition.

EX $238   **NM $422**   **MIP $563**

The John Deere 7800 was manufactured from 1992-96. Ertl released this 1:64-scale John Deere 7800 in 1992.

EX $4   **NM $5**   **MIP $6**

John Deere's Waterloo, Iowa plant produced more than 13,000 John Deere 5020 tractors between 1965-72. Ertl released this John Deere 5020 without air cleaner in the 1960s.

EX $33   **NM $57**   **MIP $87**

The 205 hp John Deere 8310 was produced from 1999-2002. Ertl's 1:64-scale John Deere 8310 is a favorite of diorama builders.

EX $4   **NM $5**   **MIP $6**

Ertl released this 1:16-scale Massey-Ferguson 595 in 1977.

EX $36　　　　**NM $82**　　　　**MIP $116**

The Massey-Harris 55 was produced from 1946-52 and carried a hefty original sticker price at $3,848. Ertl released this 1:16-scale Massey-Harris 55 in 1994.

EX $12　　　　**NM $18**　　　　**MIP $27**

The Massey-Ferguson 1100 was manufactured from 1964-72. Scale Models produced this 1:16-scale Massey-Ferguson 1100 in 1995.

EX $18　　　　**NM $23**　　　　**MIP $42**

SpecCast released this 1:16-scale Massey-Harris 101 on steel wheels in 2003.

EX $18　　　　**NM $26**　　　　**MIP $37**

The Massey-Ferguson 2805 was manufactured from 1976-83. Ertl released this 1:20-scale Massey-Ferguson 2805 with duals in 1979.

EX $18　　　　**NM $36**　　　　**MIP $47**

The Massey-Harris Colt was produced from 1952-54. SpecCast issued this charming 1:16-scale Massey-Harris Colt in 2002.

EX $18　　　　**NM $32**　　　　**MIP $43**

Minneapolis-Moline was formed in 1929 with the merger of three companies. Scale Models released this 1:16-scale Minneapolis-Moline J in 1981 as the fifth model in its Collector Series.

EX $23　　　　**NM $56**　　　　**MIP $72**

The Minneapolis-Moline 4 Star replaced the 445 and was manufactured from 1959-63. SpecCast released this 1:16-scale Minneapolis-Moline 4 Star as the 2005 Iowa FFA edition.

EX $21　　　　**NM $32**　　　　**MIP $44**

The New Holland TV-140 was manufactured from 2001-02. Scale Models released this 1:16-scale New Holland TV-140 Bi-Directional in 1998.

EX $19　　　　**NM $28**　　　　**MIP $53**

Ertl released this enormous 1:16-scale New Holland TJ-480 with triples as the 2006 Farm Progress Show edition tractor.

EX $48　　　　**NM $72**　　　　**MIP $97**

The Oliver 1655 was produced from 1969-75. Ertl released this 1:16-scale Oliver 1655 in 1995 as a Collector Edition.

EX $22　　　　**NM $34**　　　　**MIP $58**

The Oliver 2255 was available from 1972-76. Ertl released this 1:16-scale Oliver 2255 in 1998.

EX $19　　　　**NM $32**　　　　**MIP $48**

Famous for its cast-iron toys, Arcade produced a variety of farm tractors and implements. Arcade first released its Oliver 70 tractors in 1937 with white tires. This later model is c.1940 and has black tires. Though it's not the oldest Arcade in my collection, this charming Oliver is certainly among my favorites.

EX $48   NM $113   MIP $424

Steiger debuted its Panther 1000 tractors in 1986. Scale Models released this 1:16-scale Steiger Panther 1000 with triples as the 1995 Heritage Fargo, ND edition.

EX $78   NM $118   MIP $153

Epitomizing the art-deco inspired designs of the World War II era, the Oliver 70 was manufactured from 1937-48. SpecCast issued this patriotic 1:16-scale Oliver 70 with single front wheel in 2006.

EX $32   NM $53   MIP $98

The 330 hp Versatile 935 was manufactured from 1978-82. Scale Models released this 1:16-scale Versatile 935 in 1991.

EX $98   NM $133   MIP $153

Steiger manufactured its Cougar tractors in its Fargo, North Dakota plant. Ertl released this Steiger Cougar 1000 in 1:32-scale.

EX $28   NM $46   MIP $93

The White 2-135 was manufactured from 1976-87. Scale Models issued this 1:16-scale White 2-135 in 1995 to commemorate the 25th anniversary of JLE, Inc.

EX $18   NM $28   MIP $43

❑ **International Navistar w/Refrigerated Van Trailer, McCollisters Moving and Storage, Dallas, TX**, 1:64-scale, Ertl, all white
EX $15 **NM** $41 **MIP** $45

❑ **International Navistar w/Refrigerated Van Trailer, McCollisters Moving and Storage, Poughkeepsie, NY**, 1:64-scale, Ertl, white
EX $15 **NM** $41 **MIP** $45

❑ **International Navistar w/Refrigerated Van Trailer, Monfort**, 1:64-scale, Ertl, all white, No. 2128
EX $15 **NM** $40 **MIP** $47

❑ **International Navistar w/Refrigerated Van Trailer, Spanglers Markets**, 1:64-scale, Ertl, red cab w/white trailer, No. 7528
EX $18 **NM** $19 **MIP** $27

❑ **International Navistar w/Trailer, Case International w/two 7130 tractors**, 1:64-scale, Ertl, white cab w/gray trailer, No. 607
EX $12 **NM** $20 **MIP** $25

❑ **International Navistar w/Trailer, Caterpillar**, 1:64-scale, Ertl, white cab w/gray trailer, w/Caterpillar 65 Challenger, No. 7711
EX $12 **NM** $16 **MIP** $21

❑ **International Navistar w/Van Trailer**, 1:64-scale, Ertl, black cab w/white trailer, No. 9025
EX $10 **NM** $71 **MIP** $75

❑ **International Navistar w/Van Trailer**, 1:64-scale, Ertl, all white, No. 9021
EX $5 **NM** $8 **MIP** $10

❑ **International Navistar w/Van Trailer**, 1:64-scale, Ertl, all white, No. 9615
EX $10 **NM** $18 **MIP** $22

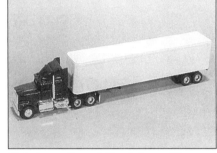

❑ **International Navistar w/Van Trailer**, 1:64-scale, Ertl, blue cab w/white trailer, No. 9886
EX $11 **NM** $16 **MIP** $18

❑ **International Navistar w/Van Trailer**, 1:64-scale, Ertl, all white, No. 9488
EX $10 **NM** $18 **MIP** $25

❑ **International Navistar w/Van Trailer**, 1:64-scale, Ertl, all white, No. 9833
EX $11 **NM** $17 **MIP** $24

❑ **International Navistar w/Van Trailer**, 1:64-scale, Ertl, all white, No. 9788
EX $10   **NM** $18   **MIP** $20

❑ **International Navistar w/Van Trailer**, 1:64-scale, Ertl, all white, No. 9875
EX $9   **NM** $18   **MIP** $20

❑ **International Navistar w/Van Trailer**, 1:64-scale, Ertl, all yellow, No. 9790
EX $11   **NM** $15   **MIP** $18

❑ **International Navistar w/Van Trailer**, 1:64-scale, Ertl, red cab w/white trailer, No. 9864
EX $12   **NM** $17   **MIP** $19

❑ **International Navistar w/Van Trailer**, 1:64-scale, Ertl, all white, No. 9887
EX $8   **NM** $17   **MIP** $21

❑ **International Navistar w/Van Trailer**, 1:64-scale, Ertl, all white, No. 9607
EX $12   **NM** $50   **MIP** $52

❑ **International Navistar w/Van Trailer**, 1:64-scale, Ertl, all white, No. 9798
EX $8   **NM** $16   **MIP** $18

❑ **International Navistar w/Van Trailer**, 1:64-scale, Ertl, all white, No. 9892
EX $11   **NM** $38   **MIP** $40

❑ **International Navistar w/Van Trailer**, 1:64-scale, Ertl, all white, No. 9865
EX $12   **NM** $16   **MIP** $18

❑ **International Navistar w/Van Trailer**, 1:64-scale, Ertl, all white, No. 9809
EX $10   **NM** $20   **MIP** $22

❑ **International Navistar w/Van Trailer**, 1:64-scale, Ertl, all beige, No. 9769
EX $10   **NM** $100   **MIP** $145

❑ **International Navistar w/Van Trailer, A.L. Herr**, 1:64-scale, Ertl, all white, No. 7568
EX $12   **NM** $22   **MIP** $25

❑ **International Navistar w/Van Trailer, Agri Gold 1991**, 1:64-scale, Ertl, all white, No. 9351
EX $12   **NM** $35   **MIP** $38

❑ **International Navistar w/Van Trailer, American Home Foods**, 1:64-scale, Ertl, all white, No. 1325
EX $10   **NM** $27   **MIP** $31

❑ **International Navistar w/Van Trailer, Clark Transfer**, 1:64-scale, Ertl, red cab w/white trailer, No. 7648
EX $12   **NM** $27   **MIP** $31

❑ **International Navistar w/Van Trailer, Agri Pro Seeds**, 1:64-scale, Ertl, all white, No. 9242
EX $18   **NM** $41   **MIP** $48

❑ **International Navistar w/Van Trailer, Binkley and Hurst Equipment**, 1:64-scale, Ertl, all white, No. 9075
EX $12   **NM** $21   **MIP** $24

❑ **International Navistar w/Van Trailer, Cummins**, 1:64-scale, Ertl, all white, No. 2149US
EX $13   **NM** $47   **MIP** $52

❑ **International Navistar w/Van Trailer, ALTA**, 1:64-scale, Ertl, all white, No. 9942
EX $10   **NM** $27   **MIP** $31

❑ **International Navistar w/Van Trailer, Buckeye Pet Foods**, 1:64-scale, Ertl, all white, No. 9515
EX $12   **NM** $24   **MIP** $28

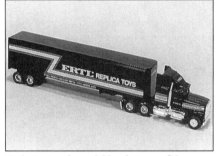

❑ **International Navistar w/Van Trailer, Ertl Replica Toys**, 1:64-scale, Ertl, all black, No. 7538
EX $10   **NM** $30   **MIP** $35

❑ **International Navistar w/Van Trailer, AM Best Truck Stops**, 1:64-scale, Ertl, all white, No. 7552
EX $11   **NM** $20   **MIP** $24

❑ **International Navistar w/Van Trailer, CAT**, 1:64-scale, Ertl, all white, No. 7709
EX $10   **NM** $20   **MIP** $22

❑ **International Navistar w/Van Trailer, Express Mail**, 1:64-scale, Ertl, blue cab w/white trailer, No. 7651
EX $15   **NM** $40   **MIP** $46

❑ **International Navistar w/Van Trailer, F.W. Newcomb**, 1:64-scale, Ertl, red cab w/white trailer, No. 1367
EX $10   **NM** $30   **MIP** $36

❑ **International Navistar w/Van Trailer, Gully Transport**, 1:64-scale, Ertl, all white, No. 9223
EX $13   **NM** $28   **MIP** $31

❑ **International Navistar w/Van Trailer, Hiner Transportation**, 1:64-scale, Ertl, all white, No. 9312
EX $12   **NM** $31   **MIP** $35

❑ **International Navistar w/Van Trailer, Fore Way**, 1:64-scale, Ertl, red cab w/white trailer, No. 2967
EX $14   **NM** $61   **MIP** $65

❑ **International Navistar w/Van Trailer, Gutwein Seeds**, 1:64-scale, Ertl, all white, No. 7547
EX $12   **NM** $34   **MIP** $38

❑ **International Navistar w/Van Trailer, Holiday Inn, Hannibal, Missouri**, 1:64-scale, Ertl, red cab w/white trailer, No. 9131
EX $10   **NM** $20   **MIP** $25

❑ **International Navistar w/Van Trailer, Golden Harvest Seeds**, 1:64-scale, Ertl, all white, No. 9758
EX $15   **NM** $38   **MIP** $42

❑ **International Navistar w/Van Trailer, Hayworth Inc.**, 1:64-scale, Ertl, all burgundy, No. 2970
EX $12   **NM** $29   **MIP** $34

❑ **International Navistar w/Van Trailer, Holiday Inn, Hannibal, Missouri**, 1:64-scale, Ertl, all white, No. 9131
EX $10   **NM** $20   **MIP** $25

❑ **International Navistar w/Van Trailer, Griffith Seed**, 1:64-scale, Ertl, red cab w/white trailer, No. 2138
EX $18   **NM** $31   **MIP** $36

❑ **International Navistar w/Van Trailer, Heineken Beer**, 1:64-scale, Ertl, all white, No. 9355
EX $14   **NM** $32   **MIP** $38

❑ **International Navistar w/Van Trailer, Hoober Parts Express**, 1:64-scale, Ertl, red cab w/white trailer, No. 9756
EX $10   **NM** $21   **MIP** $23

❑ **International Navistar w/Van Trailer, HWI Hardware**, 1:64-scale, Ertl, orange, white, silver and black, No. 9664
EX $10   **NM** $25   **MIP** $30

❑ **International Navistar w/Van Trailer, Hyman Freight**, 1:64-scale, Ertl, all white, No. 2980
EX $12   **NM** $30   **MIP** $35

❑ **International Navistar w/Van Trailer, J.H. Ware**, 1:64-scale, Ertl, red cab w/white trailer, No. 7642
EX $14   **NM** $37   **MIP** $41

❑ **International Navistar w/Van Trailer, J.M. Schultz Seed**, 1:64-scale, Ertl, all white, No. 9508
EX $20   **NM** $30   **MIP** $34

❑ **International Navistar w/Van Trailer, K-May Construction**, 1:64-scale, Ertl, red cab w/white trailer, No. 7630
EX $10   **NM** $20   **MIP** $23

❑ **International Navistar w/Van Trailer, Marlboro**, 1:64-scale, Ertl, all white, No. 7500
EX $20   **NM** $57   **MIP** $61

❑ **International Navistar w/Van Trailer, Mason Dixon**, 1:64-scale, Ertl, red cab w/white trailer, No. 7674
EX $24   **NM** $58   **MIP** $62

❑ **International Navistar w/Van Trailer, Mike Brooks Transportation**, 1:64-scale, Ertl, red cab w/white trailer, No. 9220
EX $15   **NM** $29   **MIP** $33

❑ **International Navistar w/Van Trailer, Moormans Mfg.**, 1:64-scale, Ertl, red cab w/white trailer, No. 7544
EX $12   **NM** $31   **MIP** $35

❑ **International Navistar w/Van Trailer, Motorola**, 1:64-scale, Ertl, all white, No. 9449
EX $12   **NM** $38   **MIP** $41

❑ **International Navistar w/Van Trailer, National Tractor Pulling Championships**, 1:64-scale, Ertl, blue cab w/white trailer, No. 1363
EX $10   **NM** $23   **MIP** $27

❑ **International Navistar w/Van Trailer, National Tractor Pulling Championships**, 1:64-scale, Ertl, red cab w/white trailer, No. 1364
EX $10   **NM** $22   **MIP** $26

❑ **International Navistar w/Van Trailer, National Tractor Pulling Championships**, 1:64-scale, Ertl, all white, No. 1362

EX $10   **NM** $21   **MIP** $25

❑ **International Navistar w/Van Trailer, ORTX**, 1:64-scale, Ertl, blue cab w/white trailer, No. 9564

EX $12   **NM** $34   **MIP** $37

❑ **International Navistar w/Van Trailer, PPG**, 1:64-scale, Ertl, all white, No. 9225

EX $12   **NM** $38   **MIP** $44

❑ **International Navistar w/Van Trailer, Priority Mail**, 1:64-scale, Ertl, red cab w/white trailer, No. 7649

EX $15   **NM** $45   **MIP** $50

❑ **International Navistar w/Van Trailer, Rural King Supply**, 1:64-scale, Ertl, all white, No. 9087

EX $10   **NM** $22   **MIP** $25

❑ **International Navistar w/Van Trailer, Sheffer Beer**, 1:64-scale, Ertl, all white, No. 7526

EX $12   **NM** $26   **MIP** $31

❑ **International Navistar w/Van Trailer, Sigco Research**, 1:64-scale, Ertl, all white, No. 9219

EX $10   **NM** $25   **MIP** $31

❑ **International Navistar w/Van Trailer, Stoller**, 1:64-scale, Ertl, all white, No. 9218

EX $12   **NM** $27   **MIP** $32

❑ **International Navistar w/Van Trailer, Stroh's Beer**, 1:64-scale, Ertl, blue cab w/white trailer, No. 7677

EX $10   **NM** $28   **MIP** $32

❑ **International Navistar w/Van Trailer, Sun Prairie Seed**, 1:64-scale, Ertl, all white, No. 1368

EX $12   **NM** $38   **MIP** $41

❑ **International Navistar w/Van Trailer, Turkey Hill**, 1:64-scale, Ertl, red cab w/white trailer, No. 7520

EX $11   **NM** $21   **MIP** $25

❑ **International Navistar w/Van Trailer, Walnut Grove**, 1:64-scale, Ertl, blue cab w/white trailer, No. 9569

EX $12   **NM** $28   **MIP** $33

❑ **International Paystar 5000 Cement Mixer**, 1:64-scale, Ertl, orange and white, No. 1422
EX $55   **NM** $68   **MIP** $75

❑ **International Paystar 5000 Cement Mixer**, 1:64-scale, Ertl, orange and white, No. 1422
EX $55   **NM** $68   **MIP** $75

❑ **International Paystar 5000 w/Flatbed and I-Beam**, 1:64-scale, Ertl, all red, No. 1429
EX $12   **NM** $27   **MIP** $30

❑ **International Paystar 5000 Cement Mixer**, 1:64-scale, Ertl, orange and white, No. 1401
EX $50   **NM** $65   **MIP** $72

❑ **International Paystar 5000 Dump**, 1:64-scale, Ertl, orange cab and yellow box w/black top board, No. 1410
EX $76   **NM** $91   **MIP** $101

❑ **International Paystar 5000 w/Gravel Trailer**, 1:64-scale, Ertl, green and white cab/silver trailer, No. 1403
EX $50   **NM** $74   **MIP** $84

❑ **International Paystar 5000 Cement Mixer**, 1:64-scale, Ertl, orange and white, No. 1422
EX $55   **NM** $69   **MIP** $76

❑ **International Paystar 5000 Dump**, 1:64-scale, Ertl, orange cab w/white box, No. 1410
EX $80   **NM** $95   **MIP** $110

❑ **International Paystar 5000 w/Gravel Trailer**, 1:64-scale, Ertl, green cab w/silver trailer, No. 1419
EX $50   **NM** $81   **MIP** $90

❑ **International Paystar 5000 Cement Mixer**, 1:64-scale, Ertl, orange and white, No. 1422
EX $55   **NM** $69   **MIP** $79

❑ **International Paystar 5000 Dump**, 1:64-scale, Ertl, orange cab and yellow box w/reddish top board, No. 1410
EX $81   **NM** $98   **MIP** $112

❑ **International Paystar 5000 w/Gravel Trailer**, 1:64-scale, Ertl, green cab w/silver trailer, No. 1419
EX $50   **NM** $78   **MIP** $89

❑ **International Paystar 5000 w/Log Trailer**, 1:64-scale, Ertl, blue cab w/white trailer, No. 1420
EX $40   **NM** $62   **MIP** $70

❑ **International Paystar 5000 Wrecker**, 1:64-scale, Ertl, red and white, No. 1402
EX npf   **NM** npf   **MIP** npf

❑ **International S-series Flatbed**, 1:64-scale, Ertl, white and black, No. 5542
EX $3   **NM** $6   **MIP** $10

❑ **International Paystar 5000 w/Log Trailer**, 1:64-scale, Ertl, blue and white cab w/white trailer, No. 1404
EX $42   **NM** $70   **MIP** $75

❑ **International Paystar 5000 Wrecker**, 1:64-scale, Ertl, red and white, No. 1421
EX $45   **NM** $60   **MIP** $65

❑ **International S-series Flatbed**, 1:64-scale, Ertl, white and black, No. 645
EX $3   **NM** $5   **MIP** $8

❑ **International Paystar 5000 w/Van Trailer**, 1:64-scale, Ertl, all orange w/red hood, No. 1658
EX $15   **NM** $85   **MIP** $92

❑ **International S-series Flatbed**, 1:64-scale, Ertl, white and black, No. 2204
EX $3   **NM** $5   **MIP** $8

❑ **International S-series Flatbed**, 1:64-scale, Ertl, white and brown, No. 7316
EX $3   **NM** $6   **MIP** $9

❑ **International Paystar 5000 Wrecker**, 1:64-scale, Ertl, red and white, No. 1421
EX $39   **NM** $56   **MIP** $60

❑ **International S-series Flatbed**, 1:64-scale, Ertl, white and black, No. 1098
EX $3   **NM** $5   **MIP** $8

❑ **International S-series Grain Hauler**, 1:64-scale, Ertl, black and white, No. 5543
EX $5   **NM** $11   **MIP** $13

❏ **International S-series Grain Hauler**, 1:64-scale, Ertl, red and white, No. 646
EX $6   **NM** $12   **MIP** $14

❏ **International S-series Milk Truck**, 1:64-scale, Ertl, Deutz-Allis blue and gray, No. 2207
EX $3   **NM** $4   **MIP** $7

❏ **International S-series Spray Truck**, 1:64-scale, Ertl, white and gray, No. 5544
EX $3   **NM** $5   **MIP** $9

❏ **International S-series Grain Hauler**, 1:64-scale, Ertl, Deutz-Allis blue and white, No. 2205
EX $5   **NM** $10   **MIP** $12

❏ **International S-series Milk Truck**, 1:64-scale, Ertl, red and gray, No. 648
EX $3   **NM** $5   **MIP** $9

❏ **International S-series Spray Truck**, 1:64-scale, Ertl, white and gray, No. 9764
EX $4   **NM** $8   **MIP** $12

❏ **International S-series Grain Hauler**, 1:64-scale, Ertl, red and white, has a red tarp, No. 4253
EX $4   **NM** $12   **MIP** $15

❏ **International S-series Milk Truck, Tegeler's Dairy**, 1:64-scale, Ertl, blue w/chrome tank, No. 4255
EX $6   **NM** $20   **MIP** $25

❏ **International S-series Spray Truck**, 1:64-scale, Ertl, red and gray, No. 647
EX $4   **NM** $7   **MIP** $10

❏ **International S-series Milk Truck**, 1:64-scale, Ertl, white and gray, No. 5545
EX $3   **NM** $5   **MIP** $8

❏ **International S-series Spray Truck**, 1:64-scale, Ertl, white and gray, No. 2206
EX $3   **NM** $6   **MIP** $10

❏ **International S-series Spray Truck, Alpine Fertilizers**, 1:64-scale, Ertl, white and gray, No. 4254
EX $5   **NM** $12   **MIP** $15

❏ **International Transtar II Van Trailer**, 1:64-scale, Ertl, blue cab w/white trailer, Autolite decal on left, Fram decal on right, No. 1331
EX $10   **NM** $70   **MIP** $85

❏ **International Transtar II Van Trailer**, 1:64-scale, Ertl, blue cab w/white trailer, No. 1415
EX $11   **NM** $21   **MIP** $25

❏ **International Transtar II Van Trailer**, 1:64-scale, Ertl, blue cab w/white trailer, Autolite decal on left, Fram decal on right, No. 1331
EX $10   **NM** $70   **MIP** $85

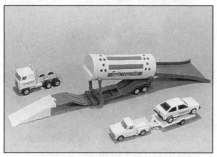

❏ **International Transtar II w/Drop Center Trailer**, 1:64-scale, Ertl, white cab w/blue and white trailer, Joie Chitwood playset, No. 9415
EX $50   **NM** $175   **MIP** $200

❏ **International Transtar II w/Drop Center Trailer and 1086s**, 1:64-scale, Ertl, blue cab w/gray trailer, IH dealership playset, No. 1904
EX $30   **NM** $95   **MIP** $112

❏ **International Transtar II w/Drop Center Trailer and 5088s**, 1:64-scale, Ertl, blue cab w/gray trailer, red rims on tractor, No. 1409
EX $15   **NM** $25   **MIP** $30

❏ **International Transtar II w/Drop Center Trailer and 5088s**, 1:64-scale, Ertl, blue cab w/gray trailer, tractors have gray rims, No. 1409
EX $12   **NM** $21   **MIP** $27

❏ **International Transtar II w/Drop Center Trailer and 5088s**, 1:64-scale, Ertl, blue cab, gray trailer; tractors, red rims and gray rims, No. 1409
EX $15   **NM** $22   **MIP** $28

❏ **International Transtar II w/Flatbed**, 1:64-scale, Ertl, blue cab w/red trailer, No. 1358
EX $10   **NM** $32   **MIP** $35

❏ **International Transtar II w/Flatbed and I-Beam**, 1:64-scale, Ertl, blue cab w/red trailer, No. 1416
EX $10   **NM** $21   **MIP** $25

❏ **International Transtar II w/Flatbed and I-Beam**, 1:64-scale, Ertl, blue cab w/red trailer, No. 1416
EX $10   **NM** $25   **MIP** $27

❏ **International Transtar II w/Flatbed and Shuttle**, 1:64-scale, Ertl, white cab w/red trailer, No. 9523
EX $27   **NM** $126   **MIP** $130

❏ **International Transtar II w/Flatbed and Shuttle**, 1:64-scale, Ertl, blue cab w/red trailer, No. 9523
EX $25 **NM** $120 **MIP** $125

❏ **International Transtar II w/Grain Trailer**, 1:64-scale, Ertl, blue cab w/silver trailer, No. 1423
EX $15 **NM** $24 **MIP** $27

❏ **International Transtar II w/Livestock Trailer**, 1:64-scale, Ertl, green cab w/gray trailer, No. 1424
EX $10 **NM** $16 **MIP** $21

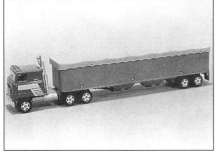

❏ **International Transtar II w/Grain Trailer**, 1:64-scale, Ertl, blue cab w/silver trailer w/trailer w/mud flaps, No. 1417
EX $25 **NM** $42 **MIP** $50

❏ **International Transtar II w/Grain Trailer**, 1:64-scale, Ertl, blue cab w/silver trailer, No. 1417
EX $15 **NM** $22 **MIP** $25

❏ **International Transtar II w/Tanker Trailer**, 1:64-scale, Ertl, blue cab w/white tank, No. 1418
EX $10 **NM** $25 **MIP** $30

❏ **International Transtar II w/Grain Trailer**, 1:64-scale, Ertl, red cab w/silver trailer, No. 1238
EX $15 **NM** $24 **MIP** $27

❏ **International Transtar II w/Grain Trailer**, 1:64-scale, Ertl, blue cab w/silver trailer w/o flaps on trailer, No. 1417
EX $15 **NM** $22 **MIP** $25

❏ **International Transtar II w/Tanker Trailer**, 1:64-scale, Ertl, blue cab w/white tank, No. 1418
EX $10 **NM** $14 **MIP** $20

❏ **International Transtar II w/Grain Trailer**, 1:64-scale, Ertl, blue cab w/silver trailer, No. 1238
EX $15 **NM** $25 **MIP** $28

❏ **International Transtar II w/Livestock Trailer**, 1:64-scale, Ertl, blue cab w/gray trailer, painted on stripes, No. 1424
EX $10 **NM** $15 **MIP** $20

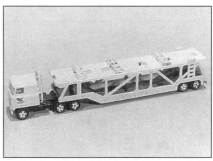

❏ **International Transtar II w/Transport Trailer**, 1:64-scale, Ertl, all yellow w/black frame, No. 9398
EX $12 **NM** $26 **MIP** $30

❑ **International Transtar II w/Transport Trailer**, 1:64-scale, Ertl, all yellow, Speedway playset, No. 9398
EX $20   **NM** $130   **MIP** $140

❑ **International Transtar II w/Van Trailer**, 1:64-scale, Ertl, all yellow w/black cab frame, No. 1654
EX $11   **NM** $38   **MIP** $42

❑ **International Transtar II w/Van Trailer**, 1:64-scale, Ertl, all black, No. 9213
EX $10   **NM** $22   **MIP** $24

❑ **International Transtar II w/Van Trailer**, 1:64-scale, Ertl, all black, No. 9213
EX $10   **NM** $20   **MIP** $22

❑ **International Transtar II w/Van Trailer**, 1:64-scale, Ertl, blue cab w/white trailer, No. 9450
EX $10   **NM** $18   **MIP** $21

❑ **International Transtar II w/Van Trailer**, 1:64-scale, Ertl, blue cab w/white trailer, No. 1415
EX $10   **NM** $18   **MIP** $20

❑ **International Transtar II w/Van Trailer**, 1:64-scale, Ertl, all white, No. 1605
EX $13   **NM** $90   **MIP** $95

❑ **International Transtar II w/Van Trailer**, 1:64-scale, Ertl, metallic blue cab w/white trailer, No. 1357
EX $5   **NM** $10   **MIP** $25

❑ **International Transtar II w/Van Trailer**, 1:64-scale, Ertl, all white, black grille and stacks, No. 1330
EX $10   **NM** $101   **MIP** $125

❑ **International Transtar II w/Van Trailer**, 1:64-scale, Ertl, all white, No. 1651
EX $10   **NM** $92   **MIP** $112

❑ **International Transtar II w/Van Trailer**, 1:64-scale, Ertl, blue cab w/white trailer, No. 1653
EX $10   **NM** $90   **MIP** $98

❑ **International Transtar II w/Van Trailer**, 1:64-scale, Ertl, blue cab w/white trailer, No. 1653
EX $11   **NM** $84   **MIP** $95

❏ **International Transtar II w/Van Trailer**, 1:64-scale, Ertl, all white, can also be found on a desk set
EX $5   **NM** $20   **MIP** $25

❏ **International Transtar II w/Van Trailer**, 1:64-scale, Ertl, all yellow w/silver cab frame, No. 8-1654
EX $10   **NM** $36   **MIP** $40

❏ **International Transtar II w/Van Trailer**, 1:64-scale, Ertl, white cab w/white (smooth) trailer, No. 1425
EX $10   **NM** $38   **MIP** $45

❏ **International Transtar II w/Van Trailer**, 1:64-scale, Ertl, all white, No. 1347
EX $5   **NM** $10   **MIP** $15

❏ **International Transtar II w/Van Trailer**, 1:64-scale, Ertl, white cab w/white (smooth) trailer, No. 86
EX $12   **NM** $80   **MIP** $85

❏ **International Transtar II w/Van Trailer**, 1:64-scale, Ertl, white cab w/white (ribbed) trailer, No. 1425
EX $11   **NM** $39   **MIP** $47

❏ **International Transtar II w/Van Trailer**, 1:64-scale, Ertl, all yellow w/silver cab frame and ribbed trailer, No. 8-1654
EX $10   **NM** $35   **MIP** $39

❏ **International Transtar II w/Van Trailer**, 1:64-scale, Ertl, white cab w/white (ribbed) trailer, No. 86
EX $13   **NM** $81   **MIP** $86

❏ **International Transtar II w/Van Trailer**, 1:64-scale, Ertl, red cab w/white trailer, No. 1325
EX $10   **NM** $28   **MIP** $30

❏ **International Transtar II w/Van Trailer**, 1:64-scale, Ertl, all white, No. 1311
EX $12   **NM** $76   **MIP** $81

❏ **International Transtar II w/Van Trailer**, 1:64-scale, Ertl, all white, No. 1338
EX $12   **NM** $90   **MIP** $95

❏ **International Transtar II w/Van Trailer**, 1:64-scale, Ertl, yellow cab w/white trailer, No. 1660
EX $12   **NM** $36   **MIP** $40

❏ **International Transtar II w/Van Trailer**, 1:64-scale, Ertl, blue cab w/white trailer, No. 1357
EX $4   NM $9   MIP $24

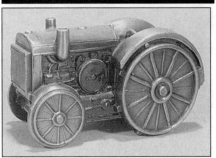

❏ **International Transtar II w/Van Trailer**, 1:64-scale, Ertl, all white, No. 1668
EX $15   NM $101   MIP $110

JOHN DEERE

BANKS 1:16-SCALE

❏ **John Deere D Bank**, 1:16-scale, Banithrico, 1980s
EX $6   NM $9   MIP $13

BANKS 1:25-SCALE

❏ **John Deere Chevy Bank**, 1:25-scale, Ertl, green and yellow, 1980s, No. 5621
EX $4   NM $12   MIP $18

❏ **John Deere Lubicants Truck Bank**, 1:25-scale, Ertl, No. 5957
(Photo by Ertl)
EX $8   NM $12   MIP $27

❏ **John Deere Mack Bank**, 1:25-scale, Ertl, green and yellow, No. 103, 1980s, No. 5564
EX $8   NM $26   MIP $33

❏ **John Deere Mack Bank**, 1:25-scale, Ertl, dark green and light green, No. 101, 1980s, No. 531
EX $23   NM $57   MIP $86

❏ **John Deere Mack Truck Bank**, 1:25-scale, Ertl, green and yellow, No. 102, 1980s, No. 5534
EX $32   NM $48   MIP $72

❏ **John Deere Truck Prestige Series**, 1:25-scale, Ertl, No. 5944
(Photo by Ertl)
EX $8   NM $12   MIP $22

BANKS 10" TALL, APPROX.

❏ **John Deere Mechanical Bank**, 10" tall, approx., Taiwan, green w/blue and tan man, reproduction of original, 1980s
EX $8   NM $17   MIP $23

BANKS 3" TALL

❏ **John Deere Drum Bank**, 3" tall, John Deere, green, for John Deere Centennial, 1937
EX npf   NM npf   MIP npf

BANKS 5-1/2" LONG

❏ **John Deere Mail Box Bank**, 5-1/2" long, Ertl, green, 1970s
EX $87   NM $176   MIP $296

❑ **John Deere Mail Box Bank**, 5-1/2" long, Ertl, green, plastic flag, decal on door, 1980s, No. 5505
EX $8   **NM** $13   **MIP** $26

❑ **John Deere Mail Box Bank**, 5-1/2" long, Ertl, green, 1980s, No. 5505
EX $46   **NM** $98   **MIP** $176

BANKS

❑ **John Deere Mailbox Bank**, Ertl, green and yellow, 1990s, No. 5589
EX $9   **NM** $14   **MIP** $23

CONSTRUCTION 1:16-SCALE

❑ **John Deere 440**, 1:16-scale, Ertl, yellow, w/o three-point hitch, 1950s
EX $267   **NM** $473   **MIP** $1059

❑ **John Deere 4430**, 1:16-scale, Argentina, yellow, no three-point hitch, 1970s
EX $54   **NM** $76   **MIP** $88

CONSTRUCTION EQUIPMENT 1:08-SCALE

❑ **John Deere Tractor, D**, 1:08-scale, Scale Models, yelllow, 2002, No. FY-1024
EX $78   **NM** $102   **MIP** $153

CONSTRUCTION EQUIPMENT 1:16-SCALE

❑ **John Deere Backhoe**, 1:16-scale, Ertl, yellow, new style front rims, 1970s, No. 589
EX $23   **NM** $68   **MIP** $98

❑ **John Deere Backhoe**, 1:16-scale, Ertl, yellow, 1970s, No. 589
EX $23   **NM** $68   **MIP** $98

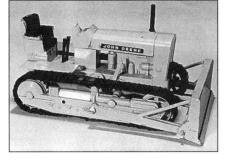

❑ **John Deere Crawler, 1010**, 1:16-scale, Ertl, yellow, 1960s, No. 526
EX $218   **NM** $372   **MIP** $967

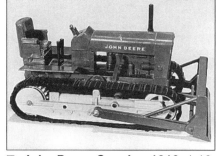

❑ **John Deere Crawler, 1010**, 1:16-scale, Ertl, green, 1960s
EX $316   **NM** $986   **MIP** $1987

❑ **John Deere Crawler, 1010**, 1:16-scale, Ertl, green, no blade, rubber tracks, 2001, No. 15191
EX $9   **NM** $17   **MIP** $26

❑ **John Deere Crawler, 1010**, 1:16-scale, Ertl, yellow, w/blade, metal tracks, Collector Edition, 2001, No. 15190A
EX $12   **NM** $28   **MIP** $43

❑ **John Deere Crawler, 1010**, 1:16-scale, Ertl, green, no blade, metal tracks, ripper, '02 Plow City Show Edition, 2002, No. 16093A
EX $33   **NM** $52   **MIP** $68

❑ **John Deere Crawler, 1010**, 1:16-scale, Ertl, yellow, no blade, rubber tracks, 2002, No. 15384
EX $9   **NM** $16   **MIP** $23

❑ **John Deere Crawler, 2010**, 1:16-scale, Ertl, green, w/blade, metal tracks, '03 Plow City Show Edition, 2003, No. 16074A *(Photo by Bossen Implement)*
EX $29   **NM** $47   **MIP** $58

❑ **John Deere Crawler, 2010**, 1:16-scale, Ertl, green, no blade, rubber tracks, 2003, No. 15482
EX $9   **NM** $16   **MIP** $23

❑ **John Deere Crawler, 2010**, 1:16-scale, Ertl, yellow, w/blade, metal tracks, ripper, Collector Edition, 2003, No. 15472A
EX $13   **NM** $32   **MIP** $47

❑ **John Deere Crawler, 2010**, 1:16-scale, Ertl, yellow, 2005, No. 15634
EX $15   **NM** $24   **MIP** $32

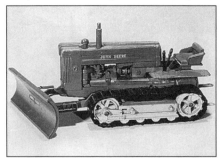

❑ **John Deere Crawler, 40**, 1:16-scale, Ertl, green, with blade, rubber track, 1950s
EX $156   **NM** $276   **MIP** $678

❑ **John Deere Crawler, 40**, 1:16-scale, Ertl, yellow, with blade, rubber track, 1950s
EX $178   **NM** $321   **MIP** $889

❑ **John Deere Crawler, 40**, 1:16-scale, Ertl, green, no blade, rubber track, 1999, No. 5072
EX $9   **NM** $16   **MIP** $23

❑ **John Deere Crawler, 40**, 1:16-scale, Ertl, green, blade, metal tracks, '99 Plow City Show Edition, 1999, No. 16010A
EX $28   **NM** $42   **MIP** $63

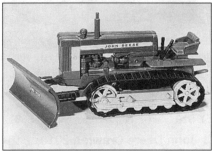

❑ **John Deere Crawler, 420**, 1:16-scale, Ertl, green, 1950s
EX $148   **NM** $268   **MIP** $563

❑ **John Deere Crawler, 420**, 1:16-scale, Ertl, green, no blade, 2 point hitch, metal track, '98 Plow City Show Edition, 1998, No. 5996TA
EX $28   **NM** $42   **MIP** $62

❑ **John Deere Crawler, 420**, 1:16-scale, Ertl, green, #62 blade, metal track, #22A ripper, Collector Edition, 1998, No. 15441A
EX $13   **NM** $32   **MIP** $47

❑ **John Deere Crawler, 420**, 1:16-scale, Ertl, yellow, #62 blade, metal tracks, Collector Edition, 1998, No. 5067DA *(Photo by Bossen Implement)*
EX $26   **NM** $38   **MIP** $48

❑ **John Deere Crawler, 430**, 1:16-scale, Ertl, yellow, no blade, metal tracks, grille guard, '97 Toy Truck and Construction Show, 1997, No. 481TA *(Photo by Bossen Implement)*
EX $26   **NM** $38   **MIP** $52

❑ **John Deere Crawler, 430**, 1:16-scale, Ertl, green, no blade, metal tracks, Collector Edition, 1997, No. 5941DA
EX $28   **NM** $42   **MIP** $62

❑ **John Deere Crawler, 430**, 1:16-scale, Ertl, yellow, no blade, rubber tracks, 1997, No. 5771
EX $9   **NM** $16   **MIP** $28

❑ **John Deere Crawler, 430**, 1:16-scale, Ertl, green, w/blade, metal tracks, '00 Plow City Show Edition, 2000, No. 16042A *(Photo by Bossen Implement)*
EX $26   **NM** $38   **MIP** $57

❑ **John Deere Crawler, 430**, 1:16-scale, Ertl, yellow, w/blade, rubber tracks, 2001, No. 15234
EX $9   **NM** $16   **MIP** $28

❑ **John Deere Crawler, 430**, 1:16-scale, E-Tee's, green, 1980s
EX $22   **NM** $32   **MIP** $42

❑ **John Deere Crawler, 430**, 1:16-scale, E-Tee's, yellow, 1980s
EX $22   **NM** $32   **MIP** $42

❑ **John Deere Crawler, 430**, 1:16-scale, Nygren (Custom), green, did not come in box, 1980s
EX $276   **NM** $456   **MIP** n/a

❑ **John Deere Crawler, 430**, 1:16-scale, Nygren (Custom), green, did not come in box, 1980s
EX $276   **NM** $456   **MIP** n/a

Photos by Jon Jacobson unless otherwise noted.

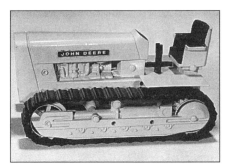

❏ **John Deere Crawler, 440**, 1:16-scale, Ertl, yellow, 1950s
EX $178 **NM** $292 **MIP** $664

❏ **John Deere Crawler, 450**, 1:16-scale, Ertl, yellow, two levers on right side, black grille decal, 1960s, No. 546
EX $78 **NM** $147 **MIP** $382

❏ **John Deere Crawler, 450**, 1:16-scale, Ertl, yellow, no levers, silver grille decal, 1960s, No. 546
EX $78 **NM** $147 **MIP** $342

❏ **John Deere Crawler, 450**, 1:16-scale, Ertl, yellow, winch, black seat, 1970s, No. 554
EX $68 **NM** $126 **MIP** $446

❏ **John Deere Crawler, 450**, 1:16-scale, Ertl, yellow, 1970s, No. 521
EX $57 **NM** $98 **MIP** $127

❏ **John Deere Crawler, 650 H**, 1:16-scale, Ertl, yellow, w/blade, metal tracks, #1 on Construction Precision Series, 2002, No. 15410
EX $77 **NM** $98 **MIP** $133

❏ **John Deere Crawler, Lindeman**, 1:16-scale, Riecke (Custom), green, did not come in box, 1980s
EX $326 **NM** $392 **MIP** n/a

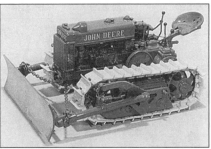

❏ **John Deere Crawler, Lindeman**, 1:16-scale, Riecke (Custom), green, did not come in box, 1990s
EX $326 **NM** $392 **MIP** n/a

❏ **John Deere Crawler, Lindeman**, 1:16-scale, SpecCast, green, no blade, metal tracks, 1998, No. JDM116 *(Photo by Bossen Implement)*
EX $13 **NM** $32 **MIP** $46

❏ **John Deere Crawler, Lindeman**, 1:16-scale, SpecCast, green, w/blade, metal tracks, 2000, No. JDM135
EX $24 **NM** $36 **MIP** $48

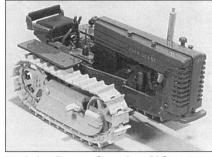

❏ **John Deere Crawler, MC**, 1:16-scale, Riecke (Custom), green, did not come in box, 1990s
EX $323 **NM** $388 **MIP** n/a

❏ **John Deere Crawler, MC**, 1:16-scale, SpecCast, green, w/blade, metal tracks, '95 Plow City Show edition, 1995, No. CUST365
EX $22 **NM** $32 **MIP** $47

❏ **John Deere Crawler, MC**, 1:16-scale, SpecCast, on rubber track, 1996, No. JDM076 *(Photo by SpecCast)*
EX $13 **NM** $23 **MIP** $32

❏ **John Deere Crawler, MC**, 1:16-scale, SpecCast, green, w/blade, rubber tracks, 1996, No. JDM096
EX $13 **NM** $32 **MIP** $42

❏ **John Deere Crawler, MC**, 1:16-scale, SpecCast, green, metal tracks, 2001, No. JDM164
EX $13 **NM** $32 **MIP** $42

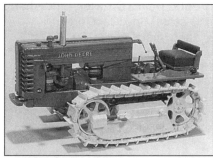

❏ **John Deere Crawler, MI**, 1:16-scale, Riecke (Custom), green, did not come in box, 1980s
EX $323   **NM** $388   **MIP** n/a

❏ **John Deere Crawler, MI**, 1:16-scale, Riecke (Custom), yellow, did not come in box, 1990s
EX $323   **NM** $388   **MIP** n/a

❏ **John Deere Grader, 772 B**, 1:16-scale, Ertl, yellow, 1980s, No. 511
EX $34   **NM** $59   **MIP** $102

❏ **John Deere Grader, 772 BH**, 1:16-scale, Ertl, yellow, 1995, No. 511
EX $34   **NM** $59   **MIP** $82

❏ **John Deere Grader, 772 BH**, 1:16-scale, Ertl, yellow, plastic blade, updated graphics, 2003, No. 15233
EX $21   **NM** $32   **MIP** $62

❏ **John Deere Log Skidder, 740**, 1:16-scale, Ertl, yellow, 1970s, No. 590
EX $64   **NM** $213   **MIP** $233

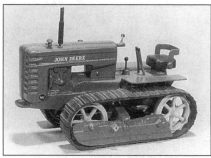

❏ **John Deere MC Crawler**, 1:16-scale, S & K Sandcasting, green, did not come in box, 1980s
EX $23   **NM** $46   **MIP** n/a

❏ **John Deere Skid Loader**, 1:16-scale, Ertl, green w/yellow wheels, short decal, large lettering, 1970s, No. 571
EX $9   **NM** $19   **MIP** $24

❏ **John Deere Skid Loader**, 1:16-scale, Ertl, green w/white rims, 1970s, No. 569
EX $14   **NM** $26   **MIP** $36

❏ **John Deere Skid Loader**, 1:16-scale, Ertl, green w/yellow rims, 1970s, No. 569
EX $9   **NM** $19   **MIP** $24

❏ **John Deere Skid Loader**, 1:16-scale, Ertl, yellow, 1980s, No. 571
EX $9   **NM** $19   **MIP** $26

❏ **John Deere Skid Loader**, 1:16-scale, Ertl, green, pre-production run, did not come in box, 1980s
EX $9   **NM** $22   **MIP** n/a

❏ **John Deere Skid Loader**, 1:16-scale, Ertl, green and black, 1980s, No. 569
EX $9   **NM** $19   **MIP** $24

❏ **John Deere Skid Loader**, 1:16-scale, Ertl, yellow, 1980s, No. 554
EX $9   **NM** $19   **MIP** $24

❏ **John Deere Skid Loader, 250**, 1:16-scale, Ertl, yellow, 2000, No. 15011
EX $9   **NM** $16   **MIP** $24

❏ **John Deere Tractor, 2755**, 1:16-scale, Ertl, yellow, w/loader, 1991, No. 5677
EX $17   **NM** $32   **MIP** $48

❏ **John Deere Tractor, 440**, 1:16-scale, Ertl, yellow, w/three-point hitch, 1950s
EX $267   **NM** $452   **MIP** $983

❏ **John Deere Tractor, 5010**, 1:16-scale, Ertl, yellow, Industrial, 1980s, No. 5629
EX $26   **NM** $38   **MIP** $58

❏ **John Deere Tractor, 6410 Set**, 1:16-scale, Ertl, yellow, w/yellow MX7 rotary mower, 2003, No. 15504
EX n/a   **NM** n/a   **MIP** $38

❏ **John Deere Tractor, 720**, 1:16-scale, Yoder (Custom), yellow, w/electric start, 1995
EX $26   **NM** $48   **MIP** $62

❏ **John Deere Tractor, 720**, 1:16-scale, Yoder (Custom), yellow, w/pony start, 1995
EX $26   **NM** $48   **MIP** $62

❏ **John Deere Tractor, 730**, 1:16-scale, Yoder (Custom), yellow, 1980s
EX $26   **NM** $48   **MIP** $62

❏ **John Deere Tractor, 80**, 1:16-scale, Trumm (Custom), yellow, did not come in box, 1980s
EX $34   **NM** $74   **MIP** n/a

❏ **John Deere Tractor, 80**, 1:16-scale, Trumm (Custom), yellow, did not come in box, 1980s
EX $34   **NM** $74   **MIP** n/a

❏ **John Deere Tractor, 820**, 1:16-scale, Trumm (Custom), yellow, did not come in box, 1980s
EX $34   **NM** $74   **MIP** n/a

❏ **John Deere Tractor, 820**, 1:16-scale, Trumm (Custom), yellow, did not come in box, 1980s
EX $34   **NM** $74   **MIP** n/a

❏ **John Deere Tractor, 830**, 1:16-scale, Stephan Manufacturing, yellow, limited to 500 units, 1990s
EX $198   **NM** $351   **MIP** $563

❏ **John Deere Tractor, 830**, 1:16-scale, Trumm (Custom), yellow, did not come in box, 1980s
EX $73   **NM** $94   **MIP** n/a

❏ **John Deere Tractor, BI**, 1:16-scale, Ertl, yellow, 1997, No. 5730
EX $9   **NM** $16   **MIP** $27

❏ **John Deere Tractor, LA**, 1:16-scale, Riecke (Custom), orange, did not come in box, 1980s
EX $198   **NM** $289   **MIP** n/a

❏ **John Deere Tractor, LI**, 1:16-scale, SpecCast, yellow, 1995, No. JDM069
EX $16   **NM** $22   **MIP** $28

❏ **John Deere Tractor, LI**, 1:16-scale, SpecCast, yellow, 2003, No. JDM175
EX $16   **NM** $22   **MIP** $33

❏ **John Deere Tractor, MI**, 1:16-scale, Ertl, orange, 1990, No. 5628
EX $11   **NM** $22   **MIP** $33

❑ **John Deere Tractor, MI**, 1:16-scale, Riecke (Custom), yellow, did not come in box, 1980s
EX $186   **NM** $227   **MIP** n/a

❑ **John Deere Tractor, MI**, 1:16-scale, Riecke (Custom), orange, did not come in box, 1980s
EX $186   **NM** $237   **MIP** n/a

❑ **John Deere Tractor, MI**, 1:16-scale, SpecCast, yellow, Collector Edition, 1997, No. JDM113
EX n/a   **NM** n/a   **MIP** n/a

❑ **John Deere Wheel Loader, 544J**, 1:16-scale, Ertl, Precision Series, 2006, No. 15774
EX $55   **NM** $85   **MIP** $110

CONSTRUCTION EQUIPMENT 1:20-SCALE

❑ **John Deere Skid Loader**, 1:20-scale, Ertl, yellow, 2003, No. 15423
EX $4   **NM** $6   **MIP** $11

CONSTRUCTION EQUIPMENT 1:25-SCALE

❑ **John Deere Backhoe, 310**, 1:25-scale, Ertl, yellow, model kit, 1970s, No. 8015
EX $12   **NM** $22   **MIP** $43

❑ **John Deere Backhoe, 310**, 1:25-scale, Ertl, yellow, model kit, reissue, new box, 1999, No. 15043
EX $12   **NM** $22   **MIP** $33

❑ **John Deere Excavator, 690**, 1:25-scale, Ertl, yellow, 1970s, No. 505
EX $27   **NM** $83   **MIP** $118

❑ **John Deere Grader, 590**, 1:25-scale, Ertl, yellow, cross bar in cab door has been reinforced, 1980s, No. 504
EX $28   **NM** $68   **MIP** $92

❑ **John Deere Grader, 590**, 1:25-scale, Ertl, yellow, 1980s, No. 502
EX $28   **NM** $68   **MIP** $122

❑ **John Deere Scraper**, 1:25-scale, Ertl, Elevating, yellow, windshield, no muffler, 1970s, No. 506
EX $93   **NM** $196   **MIP** $347

❑ **John Deere Scraper**, 1:25-scale, Ertl, Elevating, yellow, ROPS, 1970s, No. 508
EX $64   **NM** $138   **MIP** $228

❑ **John Deere Scraper**, 1:25-scale, Ertl, Elevating, yellow, windshield, 1970s, No. 506
EX $93   **NM** $196   **MIP** $347

❑ **John Deere Wheel Loader, 644**, 1:25-scale, Ertl, yellow, w/ROPS, 1970s, No. 507
EX $16   **NM** $29   **MIP** $46

❑ **John Deere Wheel Loader, 644**, 1:25-scale, Ertl, yellow, 1970s, No. 503
EX $48   **NM** $62   **MIP** $86

❑ **John Deere Wheel Loader, 644 G**, 1:25-scale, Ertl, yellow, w/ROPS, 1990, No. 507
EX $9   **NM** $16   **MIP** $27

❑ **John Deere Wheel Loader, 644 G**, 1:25-scale, Ertl, yellow, w/ROPS, no model #'s, revised graphics, 2003, No. 37011
EX $4   **NM** $8   **MIP** $13

CONSTRUCTION EQUIPMENT 1:32-SCALE

❑ **John Deere Backhoe, 310**, 1:32-scale, Ertl, yellow, 1980s, No. 5520
EX $8   **NM** $16   **MIP** $22

❑ **John Deere Backhoe, 310 D**, 1:32-scale, Ertl, yellow, 1980s, No. 5520 *(Photo by Ertl)*
EX $7   **NM** $13   **MIP** $18

❑ **John Deere Backhoe, 310 SE**, 1:32-scale, Ertl, yellow, 1994, No. 5220
EX $7   **NM** $13   **MIP** $18

❑ **John Deere Backhoe, 3185**, 1:32-scale, Hong Kong, green, w/blade, 1980s
EX $3   **NM** $7   **MIP** $11

❑ **John Deere Crawler, 550G**, 1:32-scale, Ertl, yellow, 1990s, No. 5573
EX $6   **NM** $11   **MIP** $18

❑ **John Deere Log Skidder, 648 E**, 1:32-scale, Ertl, yellow, 1991, No. 5644 *(Photo by Ertl)*
EX $8   **NM** $12   **MIP** $21

❑ **John Deere Log Skidder, 648 G**, 1:32-scale, Ertl, yellow, 1997, No. 5644
EX $6   **NM** $8   **MIP** $14

❑ **John Deere Log Skidder, 648 G**, 1:32-scale, Ertl, yellow, no model #'s, revised graphics, 2003, No. 37011
EX $4   **NM** $8   **MIP** $13

❑ **John Deere Log Skidder, 648G III**, 1:32-scale, Ertl, 2007, No. 15776
EX $10   **NM** $20   **MIP** $30

❑ **John Deere Material Handler, 3200**, 1:32-scale, Ertl, green, Telehandler, 2002, No. 40062
EX $4   **NM** $8   **MIP** $13

❑ **John Deere Skid Loader, 6675**, 1:32-scale, Ertl, yellow, 2000, No. 5790
EX $4   **NM** $7   **MIP** $11

❑ **John Deere Tractor, 3185**, 1:32-scale, Hong Kong, yellow, w/power tiller, 1980s
EX $3   **NM** $7   **MIP** $11

CONSTRUCTION EQUIPMENT 1:50-SCALE

❑ **John Deere Backhoe Loader, 310SJ**, 1:50-scale, Ertl, singles, 2007, No. 15889
EX $5   **NM** $10   **MIP** $16

❑ **John Deere Backhoe, 310 SE**, 1:50-scale, Ertl, yellow, 1997, No. 5769
EX $4   **NM** $9   **MIP** $16

❑ **John Deere Backhoe, 310 SG**, 1:50-scale, Ertl, yellow, 2002, No. 15231
EX $4   **NM** $9   **MIP** $16

❑ **John Deere Bulldozer, 650J**, 1:50-scale, Ertl, Dealer Edition, 2007, No. 15887
EX $10   **NM** $20   **MIP** $30

❑ **John Deere Crawler, 550 G**, 1:50-scale, Ertl, yellow, w/blade, rubber tracks, 1990, No. 5573
EX $4   **NM** $9   **MIP** $16

❑ **John Deere Crawler, 650 H**, 1:50-scale, Ertl, yellow, w/blade, rubber tracks, 2004, No. 15631
EX $4   **NM** $9   **MIP** $16

❑ **John Deere Crawler, 2850 C**, 1:50-scale, Ertl, yellow, w/blade, rubber tracks, 1996, No. 5261
EX $4   **NM** $9   **MIP** $16

❑ **John Deere Crawler, 850 C**, 1:50-scale, Ertl, yellow, Series II, 2001, No. 15232
EX $4   **NM** $9   **MIP** $16

❑ **John Deere Dump Truck, 400 D**, 1:50-scale, Ertl, yellow, articulated, 2002, No. 15386
EX $4   **NM** $9   **MIP** $16

❑ **John Deere Excavator, 200 LC**, 1:50-scale, Ertl, yellow, 1997, No. 5260
EX $4   **NM** $9   **MIP** $16

❑ **John Deere Feller Bucher, 843L**, 1:50-scale, Ertl, 2007, No. 15911
EX $12   **NM** $18   **MIP** $24

❑ **John Deere Grader, 772 CH**, 1:50-scale, Ertl, yellow, 1999, No. 15039
EX $4   **NM** $9   **MIP** $16

❑ **John Deere Grader, 772 CH**, 1:50-scale, Ertl, yellow, updated graphics, 2003, No. 15527
EX $4   NM $9   MIP $16

❑ **John Deere Log Skidder, 648 G**, 1:50-scale, Ertl, yellow, Series III, 2004, No. 15662
EX $4   NM $9   MIP $16

❑ **John Deere Log Skidder, 848H**, 1:50-scale, Ertl, duals, 2007, No. 15888
EX $6   NM $9   MIP $14

❑ **John Deere Skid Loader, 675**, 1:50-scale, Ertl, yellow and black, 1986, No. 5536
EX $4   NM $6   MIP $9

❑ **John Deere Wheel Loader, 744 H**, 1:50-scale, Ertl, yellow, 1998, No. 5085
EX $4   NM $9   MIP $16

❑ **John Deere Wheel Loader, 744 H**, 1:50-scale, Ertl, yellow, updated graphics, 2003, No. 15528
EX $4   NM $9   MIP $16

❑ **John Deere Wheel Loader, 824J**, 1:50-scale, Ertl, yellow, 2004, No. 15633
EX $4   NM $9   MIP $16

❑ **John Deere Wheel Loader, 824J w/Log Forks**, 1:50-scale, Ertl, 2007, No. 15912
EX $9   NM $14   MIP $23

CONSTRUCTION EQUIPMENT 1:64-SCALE

❑ **John Deere Backhoe**, 1:64-scale, Ertl, industrial yellow, 1983, No. 5521
EX $4   NM $6   MIP $9

❑ **John Deere Backhoe, 310 D**, 1:64-scale, Ertl, yellow, 1997, No. 5521
EX $4   NM $6   MIP $8

❑ **John Deere Crawler**, 1:64-scale, Ertl, industrial yellow, No. 568
EX $4   NM $6   MIP $8

❑ **John Deere Crawler**, 1:64-scale, Ertl, yellow, w/blade, 1985, No. 568
EX $4   NM $6   MIP $8

❑ **John Deere Crawler**, 1:64-scale, Ertl, yellow, w/blade, revised graphics, 1995, No. 568
EX $4   NM $6   MIP $8

❑ **John Deere Crawler, 430**, 1:64-scale, Ertl, green, no blade, rubber tracks, 1997, No. 5616
EX $3   NM $4   MIP $6

❑ **John Deere Crawler, 430**, 1:64-scale, Ertl, yellow, on furrow magazine card, 2000, No. 15156
EX $3   NM $4   MIP $6

❑ **John Deere Crawler, 430**, 1:64-scale, Keith/Trumm (Custom), yellow, did not come in box, 1980s
EX $3   NM $4   MIP $6

❑ **John Deere Crawler, 430**, 1:64-scale, Keith/Trumm (Custom), green and yellow, 1988 Moline, Illinois Show Tractor, no box, 1988
EX $3   NM $4   MIP $6

❑ **John Deere Excavator, 690 C**, 1:64-scale, Ertl, yellow, 1986, No. 579
EX $3   NM $4   MIP $6

❑ **John Deere Excavator, 690 C**, 1:64-scale, Ertl, yelllow, 1995, No. 579
EX $3   NM $4   MIP $6

❑ **John Deere Grader, 772 B**, 1:64-scale, Ertl, yellow, 1988, No. 5540
EX $3   NM $4   MIP $6

❑ **John Deere Grader, 772 BH**, 1:64-scale, Ertl, yelllow, 1995, No. 5540
EX $3   NM $4   MIP $6

❑ **John Deere Log Skidder, 648 E**, 1:64-scale, Ertl, yelllow, 1991, No. 5605
EX $3   NM $4   MIP $6

❑ **John Deere Log Skidder, 648 G**, 1:64-scale, Ertl, yelllow, 1997, No. 5605
EX $3   NM $4   MIP $6

❑ **John Deere Semi w/Log Skidder, 648G III Set**, 1:64-scale, Ertl, white loboy semi hauls log skidder, 2007, No. 15933
EX n/a   NM n/a   MIP n/a

❑ **John Deere Skid Loader, 6675**, 1:64-scale, Ertl, yelllow, 2000, No. 5925
EX $3   NM $4   MIP $6

❏ **John Deere Tractor, 5010**, 1:64-scale, Ertl, yelllow, w/wing disc, w/wheels, 1998, No. 5198
EX $3　　**NM** $4　　**MIP** $6

❏ **John Deere Wheel Loader, 544 E**, 1:64-scale, Ertl, yellow, 1980s, No. 5539
EX $3　　**NM** $6　　**MIP** $11

❏ **John Deere Wheel Loader, 544 G**, 1:64-scale, Ertl, yelllow, 1995, No. 5539
EX $3　　**NM** $4　　**MIP** $6

CONSTRUCTION EQUIPMENT 4-1/2" LONG

❏ **John Deere Crawler, 850**, 4-1/2" long, Precision Engineering, 1980s
EX $28　　**NM** $68　　**MIP** $127

❏ **John Deere Wheel Loader 544B**, 4-1/2" long, Precision Engineering, 1980s
EX $28　　**NM** $68　　**MIP** $127

IMPLEMENTS 1:08-SCALE

❏ **John Deere Disc, KBA**, 1:08-scale, Ertl, green, 1999, No. FY-1007
EX $33　　**NM** $46　　**MIP** $77

❏ **John Deere Manure Spreader**, 1:08-scale, Scale Models, green, 1998, No. FY-1006
EX $42　　**NM** $67　　**MIP** $98

❏ **John Deere Plow**, 1:08-scale, Ertl, green, 4 bottom, 1999, No. FY-1012
EX $53　　**NM** $72　　**MIP** $123

❏ **John Deere Stationary Gas Engine**, 1:08-scale, Ertl, green, battery operated, No. 4969 *(Photo by Ertl)*
EX $12　　**NM** $18　　**MIP** $26

❏ **John Deere Stationary Gas Engine**, 1:08-scale, Ertl, red, Waterloo Boy, '92 JD Nashville Parts Expo, 1992, No. 5645DA
EX $13　　**NM** $18　　**MIP** $33

❏ **John Deere Stationary Gas Engine**, 1:08-scale, Ertl, red, Waterloo Boy, 1992, No. 5645
(Photo by Bossen Implement)
EX $6　　**NM** $11　　**MIP** $22

❏ **John Deere Wagon, Flare Box**, 1:08-scale, Scale Models, green, 1996, No. FY-1001 *(Photo by Kate Bossen)*
EX $33　　**NM** $46　　**MIP** $77

IMPLEMENTS 1:128-SCALE

❏ **John Deere Combine**, 1:128-scale, Micro Machines, green, from set, 1980s
EX $2　　**NM** $6　　**MIP** npf

IMPLEMENTS 1:12-SCALE

❏ **John Deere Stationary Engine Waterloo Boy Engine**, 1:12-scale, SpecCast, No. JDM071
(Photo by Kate Bossen)
EX $6　　**NM** $8　　**MIP** $16

❏ **John Deere Stationary Gas Engine**, 1:12-scale, Old Time Collectables (Custom), green, 1970s
EX $22　　**NM** $47　　**MIP** npf

❏ **John Deere Stationary Gas Engine**, 1:12-scale, SpecCast, No. JDM064 *(Photo by SpecCast)*
EX $6　　**NM** $11　　**MIP** $18

❑ **John Deere Stationary Gas Engine**, 1:12-scale, Vindex, green w/silver trim on pulley and flywheel, 1930s
EX $321 **NM** $727 **MIP** npf

❑ **John Deere Waterloo Boy Stationary Engine**, 1:12-scale, SpecCast, No. JDM042 *(Photo by SpecCast)*
EX $6 **NM** $11 **MIP** $18

IMPLEMENTS 1:12-SCALE

❑ **John Deere Stationary Gas Engine**, 1:12-scale, Gray (Custom), green, did not come in box, 1970s
EX $22 **NM** $47 **MIP** n/a

❑ **John Deere Stationary Gas Engine**, 1:12-scale, Vindex, green w/silver trim on pulley and flywheel, 1930s
EX $321 **NM** $727 **MIP** npf

IMPLEMENTS 1:16-SCALE

❑ **John Deere Ammonia Tank**, 1:16-scale, Ertl, white and green, reissued in 1999 as stock 15010, 1980s, No. 5636
EX $12 **NM** $17 **MIP** $23

❑ **John Deere Auger**, 1:16-scale, Ertl, 2004, No. 15551
EX $8 **NM** $16 **MIP** $25

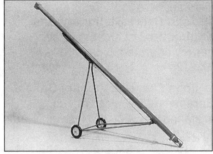

❑ **John Deere Auger**, 1:16-scale, Nygren (Custom), green, did not come in box, 1980s
EX $36 **NM** $82 **MIP** n/a

❑ **John Deere Backhoe**, 1:16-scale, Ertl, green, slides on draw bar, 2002, No. 12196G
EX $4 **NM** $9 **MIP** $16

❑ **John Deere Bale Mover**, 1:16-scale, Ertl, green, slides on draw bar, 2002, No. 15041
EX $4 **NM** $8 **MIP** $13

❑ **John Deere Baler, 14T**, 1:16-scale, Eska, green, metal teeth in pickup, 1950s
EX $83 **NM** $172 **MIP** $368

❑ **John Deere Baler, 14T**, 1:16-scale, Eska, green, plastic teeth in pickup, available w/or w/o hitch on the side of the bale chamber, 1950s
EX $78 **NM** $223 **MIP** $467

❑ **John Deere Baler, 214-T**, 1:16-scale, Ertl, green, #11 in Precision Classic Series, 1997, No. 5770
EX $72 **NM** $98 **MIP** $123

❑ **John Deere Baler, 24T**, 1:16-scale, Ertl, green, 1960s, No. 545
EX $36 **NM** $78 **MIP** $163

❑ **John Deere Baler, 336**, 1:16-scale, Ertl, green and yellow, green hitch, 1970s, No. 585
EX $12 **NM** $27 **MIP** $36

❑ **John Deere Baler, 336**, 1:16-scale, Ertl, green and yellow, black hitch, 1970s, No. 585
EX $12 **NM** $27 **MIP** $58

❑ **John Deere Baler, 348**, 1:16-scale, Ertl, green, small square bales, 1995, No. 5911 *(Photo by Ertl)*
EX $11　　**NM** $17　　**MIP** $27

❑ **John Deere Baler, 348**, 1:16-scale, Ertl, green, w/small square bales, revised graphics, 2002, No. 15518
EX $8　　**NM** $14　　**MIP** $26

❑ **John Deere Baler, 566**, 1:16-scale, Ertl, green, w/large plastic bale, 1980s, No. 592
EX $13　　**NM** $27　　**MIP** $38

❑ **John Deere Baler, 566**, 1:16-scale, Ertl, green, revised graphics, w/round bale, 1999, No. 5919
EX $9　　**NM** $16　　**MIP** $29

❑ **John Deere Baler, 567**, 1:16-scale, Ertl, green, w/round plastic bale, 2000, No. 15176
EX $8　　**NM** $14　　**MIP** $23

❑ **John Deere Carry Scraper, K9**, 1:16-scale, Ertl, green, C-type hitch, two-piece lift lever, two legged deer, 1960s, No. 549
EX $96　　**NM** $197　　**MIP** $356

❑ **John Deere Carry Scraper, K9**, 1:16-scale, Ertl, green, C-type hitch, one-piece lift lever, four legged deer, 1960s, No. 549
EX $96　　**NM** $197　　**MIP** $356

❑ **John Deere Carry Scraper, K9**, 1:16-scale, Ertl, green, crank-type hitch, one-piece lift lever, four legged deer, 1960s, No. 549
EX $103　　**NM** $202　　**MIP** $387

❑ **John Deere Combine**, 1:16-scale, Vindex, silver w/green trim and yellow wheels, blue driver, 1930s
EX $2856　　**NM** $6836　　**MIP** npf

❑ **John Deere Combine**, 1:16-scale, Vindex, silver, 1930s
EX $2856　　**NM** $6836　　**MIP** npf

❑ **John Deere Combine, 12-A**, 1:16-scale, Ertl, green, 50th Anniversary Collector Edition, brown reel, 1990s, No. 5601DA
EX $23　　**NM** $37　　**MIP** $53

❑ **John Deere Combine, 12-A**, 1:16-scale, Ertl, green, 1991, No. 5601 *(Photo by Bossen Implement)*
EX $18　　**NM** $34　　**MIP** $48

❑ **John Deere Combine, 12-A**, 1:16-scale, Eska, green, lift lever made like the ones on the grain drills, 1950s
EX $96　　**NM** $183　　**MIP** $383

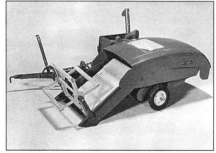

❑ **John Deere Combine, 12-A**, 1:16-scale, Eska, green, lift lever made like the ones on the two bottom plows, 1950s
EX $96　　**NM** $183　　**MIP** $383

❑ **John Deere Combine, 30**, 1:16-scale, Eska, green, auger feed, 1950s
EX $173   **NM** $548   **MIP** $1262

❑ **John Deere Combine, 42**, 1:16-scale, Baird (Custom), green, did not come in box, 1980s
EX $213   **NM** $263   **MIP** n/a

❑ **John Deere Combine, 45**, 1:16-scale, Ertl, green, Prestige Series, 2001, No. 15195
EX $48   **NM** $72   **MIP** $97

❑ **John Deere Combine, 55**, 1:16-scale, Cleek (Custom), green, did not come in box, 1980s
EX $197   **NM** $259   **MIP** n/a

❑ **John Deere Combine, 55**, 1:16-scale, Cottonwood Acres, green, 1980s
EX $386   **NM** $489   **MIP** $593

❑ **John Deere Combine, 55**, 1:16-scale, Kaufman (Custom), green, did not come in box, 1970s
EX $223   **NM** $283   **MIP** n/a

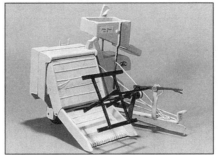

❑ **John Deere Combine, 6**, 1:16-scale, Jergensen (Custom), gray, 1980s
EX $36   **NM** $87   **MIP** npf

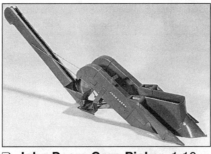

❑ **John Deere Corn Picker**, 1:16-scale, Eska, green, square letter decal, fits 60-, 620- and 730-style tractors, 1950s
EX $157   **NM** $238   **MIP** $438

❑ **John Deere Corn Picker**, 1:16-scale, Eska, green, early decal, fits 60- and 620-style tractors, 1950s
EX $157   **NM** $238   **MIP** $438

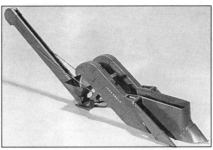

❑ **John Deere Corn Picker**, 1:16-scale, Eska, green, long-nosed picker that fits the 3010-style tractor, 1960s
EX $218   **NM** $347   **MIP** $767

❑ **John Deere Cotton Picker, 9920**, 1:16-scale, Lemmond, green, 1980s
EX $387   **NM** $482   **MIP** $892

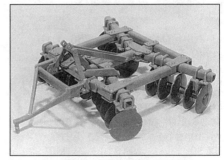

❑ **John Deere Disc**, 1:16-scale, Argentina, green, w/hitch, 1970s
EX $33   **NM** $49   **MIP** $74

❑ **John Deere Disc**, 1:16-scale, Ertl, green, "C"-type hitch riveted in place, w/wings riveted plastic wheels, wings, 1960s, No. 556
EX $54   **NM** $123   **MIP** $205

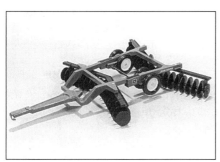

❑ **John Deere Disc**, 1:16-scale, Ertl, green and black, 1990s, No. 5602
EX $8   **NM** $13   **MIP** $24

❑ **John Deere Disc**, 1:16-scale, Ertl, green, 1999, No. 15054
EX $6   **NM** $11   **MIP** $24

❑ **John Deere Disc, 220**, 1:16-scale, Ertl, green and yellow, 1970s, No. 583
EX $43   **NM** $86   **MIP** $133

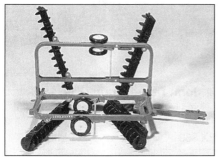

❑ **John Deere Disc, 220**, 1:16-scale, Ertl, green and black, 1970s, No. 583
EX $22   **NM** $48   **MIP** $86

❑ **John Deere Disc, 220**, 1:16-scale, Ertl, green, w/chrome gangs, Dealer Award, 1970s, No. 583
EX $233   **NM** $437   **MIP** $682

❑ **John Deere Disc, E**, 1:16-scale, Argentina, green, 3 point mounted, 1970s, No. 2530
EX $34   **NM** $52   **MIP** $76

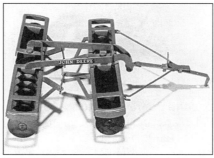

❑ **John Deere Disc, KBA**, 1:16-scale, Eska, green, old-style decal, 1950s
EX $78   **NM** $133   **MIP** $243

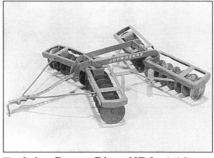

❑ **John Deere Disc, KBA**, 1:16-scale, Eska, green, new-style decal, 1950s
EX $78   **NM** $133   **MIP** $243

❑ **John Deere Disc, RWA**, 1:16-scale, Argentina, green, crank-type hitch, cast in place, 1970s, No. 2700
EX $34   **NM** $73   **MIP** $129

❑ **John Deere Disc, RWA**, 1:16-scale, Ertl, green, crank-type hitch, die-cast wheels, 1950s
EX $77   **NM** $146   **MIP** $344

❑ **John Deere Disc, RWA**, 1:16-scale, Ertl, green, crank-type hitch, cast in place, 1950s
EX $34   **NM** $73   **MIP** $166

❑ **John Deere Disc, RWA**, 1:16-scale, Ertl, green, "C"-type hitch, plastic wheels, no cylinder brackets, 1960s
EX $33   **NM** $66   **MIP** $109

❑ **John Deere Disc, RWA**, 1:16-scale, Ertl, green, "C"-type hitch, plastic wheels, 1960s, No. 528
EX $33   **NM** $66   **MIP** $139

❑ **John Deere Disc, RWA**, 1:16-scale, Ertl, green, "C"-type hitch, push nuts on axle, 1960s
EX $33   **NM** $66   **MIP** $139

❏ **John Deere Disc, RWA**, 1:16-scale, Eska, green, tin wheel rims, w/strap, 1950s
EX $86   **NM** $182   **MIP** $364

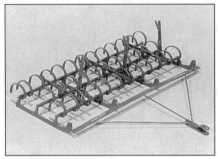

❏ **John Deere Drag**, 1:16-scale, Nygren (Custom), green, did not come in box, 1980s
EX $23   **NM** $78   **MIP** n/a

❏ **John Deere Drag**, 1:16-scale, Nygren (Custom), green, did not come in box, 1980s
EX $23   **NM** $78   **MIP** n/a

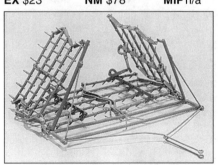

❏ **John Deere Drag**, 1:16-scale, Nygren (Custom), green, did not come in box, 1980s
EX $27   **NM** $79   **MIP** n/a

❏ **John Deere Elevator**, 1:16-scale, Ertl, black and gray, w/square hay bales, 1990s, No. 5069
EX $14   **NM** $22   **MIP** $28

❏ **John Deere Elevator**, 1:16-scale, Eska, green, 1950s
EX $77   **NM** $203   **MIP** $432

❏ **John Deere Flail Chopper**, 1:16-scale, Nygren (Custom), green, did not come in box, 1980s
EX $18   **NM** $36   **MIP** n/a

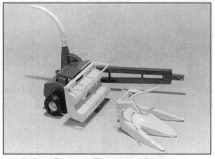

❏ **John Deere Forage Harvestor**, 1:16-scale, Ertl, green, interchangeable heads, yellow hands, 1980s, No. 509
EX $16   **NM** $22   **MIP** $36

❏ **John Deere Forage Harvestor**, 1:16-scale, Ertl, green, w/green interchangeable heads, 1996, No. 509DP
EX $13   **NM** $19   **MIP** $26

❏ **John Deere Forage Harvestor**, 1:16-scale, Ertl, green, revised graphics, green heads, 2003, No. 15523
EX $13   **NM** $19   **MIP** $26

❏ **John Deere Forage Wagon**, 1:16-scale, Ertl, green, 2004, No. 15524
EX $8   **NM** $16   **MIP** $24

❏ **John Deere Frontier Blade**, 1:16-scale, Ertl, green, 2004, No. 15680
EX $8   **NM** $16   **MIP** $24

❏ **John Deere Grain Binder**, 1:16-scale, Lowry (Custom), green, did not come in box, 1980s
EX $48   **NM** $86   **MIP** n/a

❏ **John Deere Grain Drill**, 1:16-scale, Eska, green, new-style decal, 1950s
EX $86   **NM** $193   **MIP** $346

❏ **John Deere Grain Drill**, 1:16-scale, Eska, green, old-style decal, 1950s
EX $86   **NM** $193   **MIP** $346

❑ **John Deere Grain Drill**, 1:16-scale, Eska, green w/yellow lids, silver disc, 1950s
EX $96   **NM** $246   **MIP** $493

❑ **John Deere Grain Drill**, 1:16-scale, Eska, green w/yellow lids, green disc, 1950s
EX $96   **NM** $223   **MIP** $442

❑ **John Deere Grain Drill**, 1:16-scale, Vindex, red w/yellow wheels, nickel-plated disc, Van Brunt, 1930s
EX $958   **NM** $2667   **MIP** npf

❑ **John Deere Grain Drill, 1590**, 1:16-scale, Ertl, green, 2002, No. 15350
EX $14   **NM** $21   **MIP** $32

❑ **John Deere Grain Drill, 452**, 1:16-scale, Ertl, green and yellow, 1990s, No. 580
EX $8   **NM** $21   **MIP** $32

❑ **John Deere Gravity Wagon, Frontier**, 1:16-scale, Ertl, green "Frontier" logos, 2004, No. 15681
EX $8   **NM** $16   **MIP** $24

❑ **John Deere Grinder Mixer**, 1:16-scale, Ertl, green, 1999, No. 5002
EX $9   **NM** $18   **MIP** $27

❑ **John Deere Grinder Mixer**, 1:16-scale, Kruger (Custom), green, 1980s
EX $23   **NM** $49   **MIP** n/a

❑ **John Deere Hammer Mill**, 1:16-scale, Old Time Collectables (Custom), green, did not come in box, 1970s
EX $63   **NM** $92   **MIP** n/a

❑ **John Deere Hay Elevator**, 1:16-scale, Ertl, w/plastic hay bales, 2004, No. 15552
EX $7   **NM** $14   **MIP** $21

❑ **John Deere Hay Loader**, 1:16-scale, Rouch (Custom), green and yellow, did not come in box, 1990s
EX $236   **NM** $467   **MIP** n/a

❑ **John Deere Hay Loader**, 1:16-scale, Vindex, red w/yellow wheels, 1930s
EX $1632   **NM** $4489   **MIP** npf

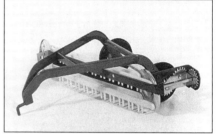

❑ **John Deere Hay Rake**, 1:16-scale, Ertl, No. 5686 *(Photo by Ertl)*
EX $8   **NM** $14   **MIP** $27

❑ **John Deere Hay Rake**, 1:16-scale, Ertl, 2004, No. 15484
EX $7   **NM** $14   **MIP** $21

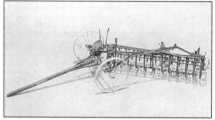

❑ **John Deere Hay Rake**, 1:16-scale, Rouch (Custom), green and yellow, did not come in box, 1990s
EX $233   **NM** $427   **MIP** n/a

❑ **John Deere Hay Wagon**, 1:16-scale, Ertl, Precision Classics #19, 2004, No. 15134
EX $20   **NM** $40   **MIP** $60

❑ **John Deere Hayrack and Team**, 1:16-scale, Vindex, green rack w/red running gear, running gear has long tongue, 1930s
EX $1062   **NM** $1889   **MIP** npf

❏ **John Deere Hydra Spreader**, 1:16-scale, Ertl, green, 4 wheels, 2004, No. 549
EX $8   **NM** $16   **MIP** $24

❏ **John Deere Implement Trailer**, 1:16-scale, Ertl, green, flatbed w/ramp, 2004, No. 15204
EX $8   **NM** $16   **MIP** $24

❏ **John Deere Loader**, 1:16-scale, Argentina (Sigomac), green, 1970s
EX $78   **NM** $94   **MIP** $131

❏ **John Deere Loader**, 1:16-scale, Eisele, green, 1950s
EX $156   **NM** $283   **MIP** $356

❏ **John Deere Loader**, 1:16-scale, Eisele, green, fits on A-style tractor, 1950s
EX $156   **NM** $283   **MIP** $356

❏ **John Deere Loader**, 1:16-scale, Eisele, green, fits on A-style tractor, 1950s
EX $156   **NM** $283   **MIP** $356

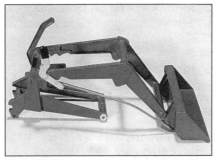

❏ **John Deere Loader**, 1:16-scale, Ertl, green, fits 3010 - 3020 tractors, 1960s
EX $72   **NM** $103   **MIP** $154

❏ **John Deere Loader**, 1:16-scale, Eska, green, fits 620-style tractor, 1950s
EX $68   **NM** $138   **MIP** $243

❏ **John Deere Loader**, 1:16-scale, Eska, green, sits 60-style tractor, has clips that swing down behind axle to hold loader, 1950s
EX $76   **NM** $167   **MIP** $283

❏ **John Deere Machinery Trailer**, 1:16-scale, Ertl, yellow, 1980s, No. 594
EX $13   **NM** $18   **MIP** $26

❏ **John Deere Manure Spreader**, 1:16-scale, Ertl, green, hydra push, 1980s, No. 549
EX $9   **NM** $16   **MIP** $27

❏ **John Deere Manure Spreader**, 1:16-scale, Vindex, red box, yellow wheels, green seat and beaters, 1930s
EX $942   **NM** $2236   **MIP** npf

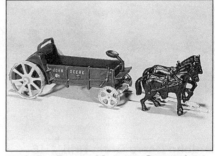

❏ **John Deere Manure Spreader**, 1:16-scale, Vindex, red box, yellow wheels, green seat and beaters, 1930s
EX $942   **NM** $2236   **MIP** npf

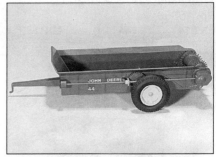

❏ **John Deere Manure Spreader**, 44, 1:16-scale, Ertl, green, die-cast rims, crank type hitch, gear drive, 1960s, No. 534
EX $56   **NM** $127   **MIP** $298

❏ **John Deere Manure Spreader, 44**, 1:16-scale, Ertl, green, C-type hitch, wider support on tongue, die-cast rims, 1960s, No. 534
EX $36   **NM** $58   **MIP** $106

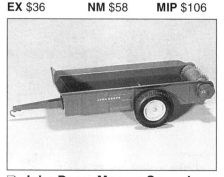

❏ **John Deere Manure Spreader, 44**, 1:16-scale, Ertl, green, C-type hitch, 1960s, No. 534
EX $36   **NM** $58   **MIP** $106

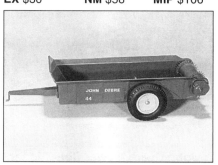

❏ **John Deere Manure Spreader, 44**, 1:16-scale, Ertl, green, crank-type hitch, 1960s, No. 534
EX $36   **NM** $48   **MIP** $106

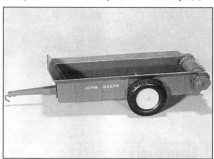

❏ **John Deere Manure Spreader, 44**, 1:16-scale, Ertl, green, C-type hitch, plastic wheels rims, 1970s, No. 534
EX $19   **NM** $38   **MIP** $67

❏ **John Deere Manure Spreader, E**, 1:16-scale, Rouch (Custom), red, did not come in box, 1990s
EX $239   **NM** $489   **MIP** n/a

❏ **John Deere Manure Spreader, E**, 1:16-scale, Rouch (Custom), red, did not come in box, 1990s
EX $239   **NM** $489   **MIP** n/a

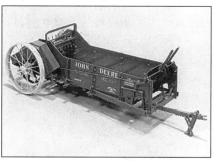

❏ **John Deere Manure Spreader, E**, 1:16-scale, Rouch (Custom), green and yellow, did not come in box, 1990s
EX $239   **NM** $489   **MIP** n/a

❏ **John Deere Manure Spreader, E**, 1:16-scale, Rouch (Custom), green, did not come in box, 1990s
EX $239   **NM** $489   **MIP** n/a

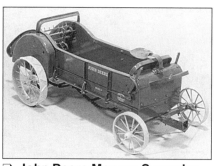

❏ **John Deere Manure Spreader, H**, 1:16-scale, Rouch (Custom), green, did not come in box, 1990s
EX $239   **NM** $489   **MIP** n/a

❏ **John Deere Manure Spreader, H**, 1:16-scale, Rouch (Custom), green, did not come in box, 1990s
EX $239   **NM** $489   **MIP** n/a

❏ **John Deere Manure Spreader, H**, 1:16-scale, Rouch (Custom), green, did not come in box, 1990s
EX $239   **NM** $489   **MIP** n/a

❏ **John Deere Manure Spreader, H**, 1:16-scale, Rouch (Custom), green, did not come in box, 1990s
EX $239   **NM** $489   **MIP** n/a

❏ **John Deere Manure Spreader, K**, 1:16-scale, Eska, green, short levers, all rubber tires, 1950s
EX $61 NM $109 MIP $248

❏ **John Deere Manure Spreader, K**, 1:16-scale, Eska, green, short levers, 1950s
EX $61 NM $109 MIP $248

❏ **John Deere Manure Spreader, L**, 1:16-scale, Eska, green, long levers, square letter decal, 1950s
EX $61 NM $109 MIP $268

❏ **John Deere Manure Spreader, L**, 1:16-scale, Eska, green, long levers, 1950s
EX $61 NM $109 MIP $268

❏ **John Deere Mower**, 1:16-scale, Ertl, green, crank-type hitch, cast in place, metal wheel sickle drive, 1960s, No. 546
EX $34 NM $88 MIP $176

❏ **John Deere Mower**, 1:16-scale, Ertl, green, "C"-type riveted hitch, plastic wheel drive, black divider board, 1960s, No. 546
EX $34 NM $82 MIP $146

❏ **John Deere Mower**, 1:16-scale, Ertl, green, "C"-type pinion hitch, plastic wheel drive, green divider board, 1960s, No. 546
EX $34 NM $82 MIP $146

❏ **John Deere Mower**, 1:16-scale, Nygren (Custom), green, did not come in box, 1980s
EX $48 NM $86 MIP n/a

❏ **John Deere Mower**, 1:16-scale, Nygren (Custom), green, did not come in box, 1980s
EX $48 NM $82 MIP n/a

❏ **John Deere Mower**, 1:16-scale, SpecCast, rotary, 1992, No. JDM046
(Photo by SpecCast)
EX $9 NM $16 MIP $22

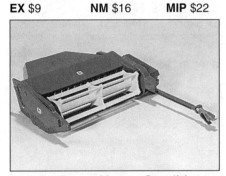

❏ **John Deere Mower Conditioner**, 1:16-scale, Ertl, green, 1970s, No. 596
EX $13 NM $19 MIP $34

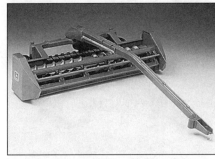

❏ **John Deere Mower Conditioner, 1600**, 1:16-scale, Ertl, green, 1991, No. 5630 *(Photo by Ertl)*
EX $8 NM $14 MIP $23

Photos by Jon Jacobson unless otherwise noted.

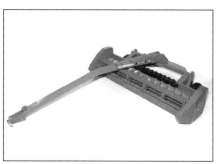

❏ **John Deere Mower Conditioner, 1600**, 1:16-scale, Ertl, green, revised graphics, 1996, No. 5630

(Photo by Bossen Implement)

EX $8   **NM** $14   **MIP** $23

❏ **John Deere Mower, 5**, 1:16-scale, Nygren (Custom), green, did not come in box, 1980s

EX $48   **NM** $82   **MIP** n/a

❏ **John Deere Mower, 7**, 1:16-scale, Nygren (Custom), green, did not come in box, 1980s

EX $48   **NM** $82   **MIP** n/a

❏ **John Deere Mower, MX7**, 1:16-scale, Ertl, green, slides on draw bar, 2000, No. 15074

EX $4   **NM** $11   **MIP** $17

❏ **John Deere Mulch Master**, 1:16-scale, Ertl, 1999, No. 5711 *(Photo by Ertl)*

EX $12   **NM** $16   **MIP** $27

❏ **John Deere Mulch Master**, 1:16-scale, Ertl, Dealer Edition, 2007, No. 15866

EX $12   **NM** $24   **MIP** $38

❏ **John Deere Mulch Ripper, 2700**, 1:16-scale, Ertl, green, 2002, No. 15356

EX $12   **NM** $21   **MIP** $42

❏ **John Deere Planter, 1700**, 1:16-scale, Ertl, green, tool bar grow, 1998, No. 5177

EX $9   **NM** $17   **MIP** $34

❏ **John Deere Planter, 1700**, 1:16-scale, Ertl, 2006, No. 15825

EX $8   **NM** $14   **MIP** $19

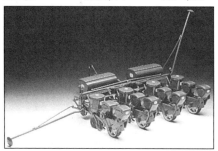

❏ **John Deere Planter, 494A**, 1:16-scale, Ertl, Precision Classic #9, No. 5838 *(Photo by Ertl)*

EX $63   **NM** $89   **MIP** $133

❏ **John Deere Planter, 495**, 1:16-scale, Ertl, green, two-legged decal, plastic wheels, clank hitch, static marker disc, 1960s, No. 539

EX $56   **NM** $93   **MIP** $228

❏ **John Deere Planter, 495**, 1:16-scale, Ertl, 4-leg decal, crank-type cast hitch, tongue cross-brace, marker disc turns, 1970s, No. 539

EX $56   **NM** $93   **MIP** $228

❏ **John Deere Planter, 495**, 1:16-scale, Ertl, green, two legged decal, plastic wheels, C-type hitch, static marker disc, 1970s, No. 539

EX $56   **NM** $83   **MIP** $189

❏ **John Deere Planter, 495**, 1:16-scale, Ertl, 4-leg decal, cast crank-type hitch, 2 tongue braces, marker disc turns, 1970s, No. 539

EX $56   **NM** $93   **MIP** $228

❏ **John Deere Planter, 7000**, 1:16-scale, Ertl, green, 1970s, No. 595

EX $28   **NM** $54   **MIP** $72

❏ **John Deere Plow**, 1:16-scale, Argentina, green, 5 bottom, mounted, no tail wheel, 1960s, No. 2800

EX $33   **NM** $48   **MIP** $73

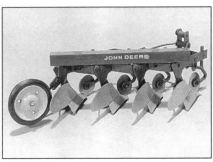

❑ **John Deere Plow**, 1:16-scale, Argentina, green, 4 bottom, mounted, 1970s
EX $43   **NM** $56   **MIP** $73

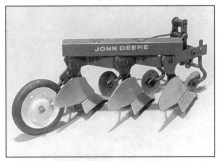

❑ **John Deere Plow**, 1:16-scale, Argentina, green, 3 bottom, mounted, w/tail wheel, 1970s, No. 2803
EX $43   **NM** $56   **MIP** $73

❑ **John Deere Plow**, 1:16-scale, Argentina, green, 3 bottom, mounted, 1970s
EX $43   **NM** $56   **MIP** $73

❑ **John Deere Plow**, 1:16-scale, Ertl, 4 bottom, wrap-around coulter supports like two bottom plow, mounted, 1950s
EX $97   **NM** $156   **MIP** $213

❑ **John Deere Plow**, 1:16-scale, Ertl, green, 4 bottom, single coulter support, mounted, 1950s
EX $97   **NM** $156   **MIP** $213

❑ **John Deere Plow**, 1:16-scale, Ertl, green, 4 bottom, plastic rims, no angle brace, 1950s, No. 527
EX $68   **NM** $98   **MIP** $203

❑ **John Deere Plow**, 1:16-scale, Ertl, green, 4 bottom, die-cast wheel rims, 1950s, No. 527
EX $98   **NM** $173   **MIP** $348

❑ **John Deere Plow**, 1:16-scale, Ertl, green, 4 bottom, narrow plastic wheels w/angle braces in frame, 1960s, No. 527
EX $68   **NM** $93   **MIP** $156

❑ **John Deere Plow**, 1:16-scale, Ertl, green, 4 bottom, wide rubber tires on plastic rims, angle brace in frame, 1960s, No. 527
EX $67   **NM** $98   **MIP** $177

❑ **John Deere Plow**, 1:16-scale, Ertl, green, 4 bottom, wide plastic rims, w/angle braces in frame, 1970s, No. 527
EX $67   **NM** $89   **MIP** $134

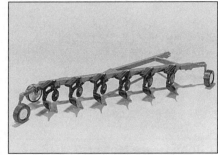

❑ **John Deere Plow**, 1:16-scale, Ertl, green, 6 bottom, front & rear wheels could lock in transport position, rear wheel free to swivel, 1970s, No. 525
EX $26   **NM** $33   **MIP** $89

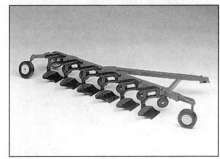

❑ **John Deere Plow**, 1:16-scale, Ertl, 6 bottom, 1980s, No. 525 *(Photo by Ertl)*
EX $8   **NM** $23   **MIP** $34

❏ **John Deere Plow**, 1:16-scale, Eska, green, 2 bottom, lever & cylinder, 1950s
EX $93　　**NM** $219　　**MIP** $388

❏ **John Deere Plow**, 1:16-scale, Eska, green, 2 bottom, metal rim tail wheel, crank & cylinder, 1950s
EX $66　　**NM** $159　　**MIP** $293

❏ **John Deere Plow**, 1:16-scale, Eska, green, 2 bottom, smooth tires, rubber tail wheel, crank & cylinder, 1950s
EX $66　　**NM** $159　　**MIP** $298

❏ **John Deere Plow**, 1:16-scale, Eska, green, 2 bottom, ribbed tires, lever & cylinder, 1950s
EX $93　　**NM** $219　　**MIP** $388

❏ **John Deere Plow**, 1:16-scale, Eska, green, 2 bottom, wooden tail wheel, smooth tires, crank & cylinder, 1950s
EX $67　　**NM** $162　　**MIP** $311

❏ **John Deere Plow**, 1:16-scale, Riecke (Custom), green, did not come in box, 1990s
EX $127　　**NM** $164　　**MIP** n/a

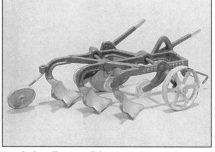

❏ **John Deere Plow**, 1:16-scale, Vindex, green w/yellow wheels, 1930s
EX $737　　**NM** $1772　　**MIP** npf

❏ **John Deere Plow**, 1:16-scale, Vindex, green, 1930s
EX $737　　**NM** $1772　　**MIP** npf

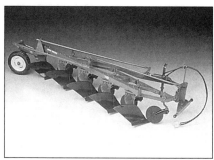

❏ **John Deere Plow, F-145**, 1:16-scale, Ertl, 5 Bottom, Precision Classics, #6, 1994, No. 5763 *(Photo by Ertl)*
EX $68　　**NM** $93　　**MIP** $164

❏ **John Deere Round Baler, 567**, 1:16-scale, Ertl, green, new graphics, 2004, No. 15689
EX $8　　**NM** $16　　**MIP** $24

❏ **John Deere Round Baler, 567**, 1:16-scale, Ertl, 2005, No. 15681
EX $12　　**NM** $15　　**MIP** $19

❏ **John Deere Stationary Gas Engine**, 1:16-scale, Riecke (Custom), green, 1980s
EX $38　　**NM** $66　　**MIP** n/a

❏ **John Deere Stationary Gas Engine**, 1:16-scale, Riecke (Custom), green, push button, minor turns, did not come in box, 1980s
EX $48　　**NM** $86　　**MIP** n/a

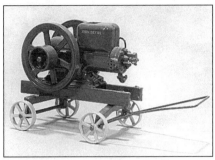

❑ **John Deere Stationary Gas Engine**, 1:16-scale, Riecke (Custom), green, did not come in box, 1980s

EX $38   **NM** $52   **MIP** n/a

❑ **John Deere Thresher**, 1:16-scale, Vindex, silver w/green trim and yellow wheels, 1930s

EX $1416   **NM** $2844   **MIP** npf

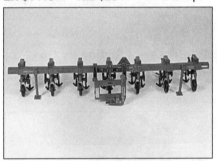

❑ **John Deere Tool Bar Cultivator**, 1:16-scale, Ertl, No. 5920

(Photo by Kate Bossen)

EX $8   **NM** $13   **MIP** $26

❑ **John Deere Tool Bar Rotary Hoe**, 1:16-scale, Ertl, No. 5918 *(Photo by Ertl)*

EX $12   **NM** $18   **MIP** $27

❑ **John Deere Wagon Buckboard**, 1:16-scale, Scale Models, green, 1990s

EX $12   **NM** $18   **MIP** $28

❑ **John Deere Wagon Running Gear**, 1:16-scale, Arcade, green, one-piece steel tongue, 1940s

EX $221   **NM** $387   **MIP** $859

❑ **John Deere Wagon, Bale**, 1:16-scale, Ertl, green, 1980s, No. 522

EX $6   **NM** $11   **MIP** $22

❑ **John Deere Wagon, Barge**, 1:16-scale, Ertl, green, sand cast, removable box, spring mounted bolsters, 1950s

EX $82   **NM** $148   **MIP** $323

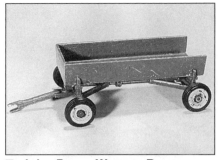

❑ **John Deere Wagon, Barge**, 1:16-scale, Ertl, green, sand cast, removable box, spring mounted bolsters, 1950s

EX $82   **NM** $148   **MIP** $323

❑ **John Deere Wagon, Barge**, 1:16-scale, Ertl, green, slotted wheel rims, diecast box, 1970s

EX $8   **NM** $13   **MIP** $26

❑ **John Deere Wagon, Barge**, 1:16-scale, Ertl, green, green hitch, diecast box, 1970s

EX $8   **NM** $13   **MIP** $26

❑ **John Deere Wagon, Barge**, 1:16-scale, Ertl, green, black hitch, flotation tires, diecast box, 1970s

EX $8   **NM** $13   **MIP** $22

❑ **John Deere Wagon, Barge,**
1:16-scale, Ertl, green, 1980s
EX $6 **NM** $11 **MIP** $18

❑ **John Deere Wagon, Barge,**
1:16-scale, Ertl, green, #16 Precision
Series, 2000, No. 15133
EX $18 **NM** $26 **MIP** $68

❑ **John Deere Wagon, Barge,**
1:16-scale, Ertl, green, 2001,
No. 15203
EX $4 **NM** $8 **MIP** $16

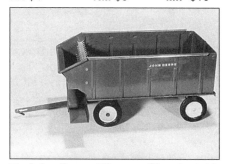

❑ **John Deere Wagon, Chuck,** 1:16-
scale, Ertl, green, 1960s, No. 533
EX $23 **NM** $37 **MIP** $88

❑ **John Deere Wagon, Chuck,**
1:16-scale, Ertl, green, stamped
steel floor, 1970s, No. 533
EX $23 **NM** $37 **MIP** $88

❑ **John Deere Wagon, Chuck,**
1:16-scale, Ertl, green, channel iron-
type tongue, 1970s, No. 533
EX $23 **NM** $37 **MIP** $88

❑ **John Deere Wagon, Chuck,**
1:16-scale, Ertl, green, stamped
steel front wheel assembly, 1970s,
No. 533
EX $23 **NM** $37 **MIP** $88

❑ **John Deere Wagon, Chuck 112,**
1:16-scale, Ertl, green, plastic rims
w/die-cast front spindles, 1950s,
No. 533
EX $33 **NM** $67 **MIP** $158

❑ **John Deere Wagon, Chuck 112,**
1:16-scale, Ertl, green, die-cast rims
like 430 w/die-cast front spindles,
1950s, No. 533
EX $67 **NM** $168 **MIP** $383

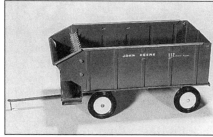

❑ **John Deere Wagon, Chuck 112,**
1:16-scale, Ertl, green, flat spot
where John Deere decal goes,
1950s, No. 533
EX $33 **NM** $67 **MIP** $158

❑ **John Deere Wagon, Flare Box,**
1:16-scale, Arcade/Strombecker,
green, cast-iron running gear, wood
box, 1940s
EX $192 **NM** $294 **MIP** $769

❑ **John Deere Wagon, Flare Box,**
1:16-scale, Argentina, yellow, 1980s
EX $12 **NM** $32 **MIP** $46

❑ **John Deere Wagon, Flare Box,**
1:16-scale, Argentina, green, 1980s
EX $12 **NM** $32 **MIP** $46

❑ **John Deere Wagon, Flare Box,**
1:16-scale, Ertl, green, die-cast rims
like 430 tractor box, not removable,
edges not rolled, 1950s, No. 529
EX $54 **NM** $98 **MIP** $247

❏ **John Deere Wagon, Flare Box**, 1:16-scale, Ertl, green, plastic wheel rims, die-cast front spindles, 1960s, No. 529
EX $12   **NM** $21   **MIP** $32

❏ **John Deere Wagon, Flare Box**, 1:16-scale, Ertl, green, stamped steel front end assembly, 1970s, No. 529
EX $8   **NM** $16   **MIP** $27

❏ **John Deere Wagon, Flare Box**, 1:16-scale, Ertl, green, w/o Ertl name in front and rear, 1980s, No. 529
EX $8   **NM** $16   **MIP** $27

❏ **John Deere Wagon, Flare Box**, 1:16-scale, Ertl, green, stake appearance sides and Ertl stamped in front and rear of wagon, 1980s, No. 529
EX $8   **NM** $16   **MIP** $27

❏ **John Deere Wagon, Flare Box**, 1:16-scale, Eska, green, smooth tires, 1950s
EX $44   **NM** $98   **MIP** $167

❏ **John Deere Wagon, Flare Box**, 1:16-scale, Eska, green, ribbed tires, 1950s, No. 529
EX $44   **NM** $83   **MIP** $167

❏ **John Deere Wagon, Flare Box**, 1:16-scale, Eska, green, die-cast wheel rims like 730 tractor, 1950s, No. 529
EX $44   **NM** $98   **MIP** $167

❏ **John Deere Wagon, Flare Box**, 1:16-scale, Eska, green, solid rubber tires, one-piece tongue w/tin or aluminum box, 1950s
EX $46   **NM** $96   **MIP** $166

❏ **John Deere Wagon, Flare Box**, 1:16-scale, Eska, green, solid rubber tires, one piece tongue, 1950s
EX $46   **NM** $96   **MIP** $166

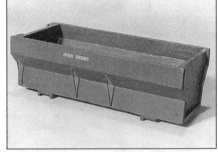

❏ **John Deere Wagon, Flare Box**, 1:16-scale, Strombecker, wood, fits Arcade running gear, came in a kit w/decals, 1940s
EX $42   **NM** $94   **MIP** $269

❏ **John Deere Wagon, Forage**, 1:16-scale, Ertl, green, 1980s, No. 510
EX $6   **NM** $12   **MIP** $18

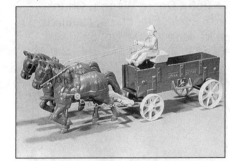

❏ **John Deere Wagon, Grain**, 1:16-scale, Gray (Custom), green and yellow, brown horses, did not come in box, licensed by John Deere, 1970s
EX $68   **NM** $118   **MIP** n/a

Photos by Jon Jacobson unless otherwise noted.

❏ **John Deere Wagon, Grain**, 1:16-scale, Vindex, green box w/red running gear, short tongue, cast iron, 1930s
EX $627   **NM** $1232   **MIP** npf

❏ **John Deere Wagon, Grain**, 1:16-scale, Vindex, green box w/red running gear, running gear has short tongue, 1930s
EX $627   **NM** $1232   **MIP** npf

❏ **John Deere Wagon, Gravity**, 1:16-scale, Ertl, green, small wheels, 1980s, No. 5061 (Photo by Ertl)
EX $6   **NM** $8   **MIP** $16

❏ **John Deere Wagon, Gravity**, 1:16-scale, Ertl, green, big floatation tires, 2000, No. 15125
EX $8   **NM** $14   **MIP** $22

❏ **John Deere Wagon, Hay**, 1:16-scale, Ertl, No. 5674 (Photo by Kate Bossen)
EX $6   **NM** $13   **MIP** $22

❏ **John Deere Wagon, Hay**, 1:16-scale, Ertl, green, #19 Precision Series, 2001, No. 15134
EX $18   **NM** $26   **MIP** $48

❏ **John Deere Wagon, Hay**, 1:16-scale, Ertl, green, running gear, 2003, No. 15485
EX $6   **NM** $12   **MIP** $18

❏ **John Deere Wagon, Hay**, 1:16-scale, Vindex, green rack, red running gear, long tongue, cast iron, 1930s
EX $1062   **NM** $1889   **MIP** npf

IMPLEMENTS 1:24-SCALE

❏ **John Deere Combine, 6600**, 1:24-scale, Ertl, green, plastic gear driven auger & plastic reel, four-wheel drive style rear wheels, 1970s, No. 558
EX $76   **NM** $169   **MIP** $324

❏ **John Deere Combine, 6600**, 1:24-scale, Ertl, green, plastic gear driven auger and reel, plastic reel, 1970s, No. 558
EX $72   **NM** $124   **MIP** $223

❏ **John Deere Combine, 6600**, 1:24-scale, Ertl, green, chain driven auger, metal gear drive to metal reel, 1970s, No. 558
EX $93   **NM** $182   **MIP** $357

❏ **John Deere Combine, 6600**, 1:24-scale, Ertl, green, chain drive auger & reel, no silver bar through center of metal reel, 1970s, No. 558
EX $113   **NM** $246   **MIP** $412

❏ **John Deere Combine, 6600**, 1:24-scale, Ertl, green, chain drive auger & reel, silver bar through center of metal reel, 1970s, No. 558
EX $113   **NM** $246   **MIP** $412

❏ **John Deere Combine, Titan**, 1:24-scale, Ertl, green, supports in feeder house hold head when you pick up combine, 1970s, No. 524
EX $32   **NM** $68   **MIP** $112

❏ **John Deere Combine, Titan**, 1:24-scale, Ertl, green, no feeder house supports, header drops when you pick up toy, 1970s, No. 524
EX $32   **NM** $68   **MIP** $112

❏ **John Deere Combine, Titan**, 1:24-scale, Ertl, green, quick change, corn or grain head, 1980s, No. 536
EX $28   **NM** $62   **MIP** $92

❏ **John Deere Combine, Titan II**, 1:24-scale, Ertl, green, w/green cab top, 1980s, No. 582
EX $23   **NM** $58   **MIP** $82

IMPLEMENTS 1:25-SCALE

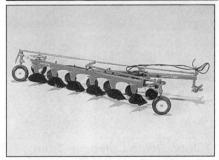

❏ **John Deere Plow**, 1:25-scale, Ertl, green, model kit, 1970s, No. 8012
EX $6   **NM** $21   **MIP** $56

❏ **John Deere Wagon**, 1:25-scale, Ertl, green, model kit, 1970s, No. 8006
EX $4   **NM** $11   **MIP** $19

IMPLEMENTS 1:28-SCALE

❏ **John Deere Combine**, 1:28-scale, Ertl, green, top brace on feeder house, right feeder house has more head movement, 1990s
EX npf   **NM** npf   **MIP** npf

❏ **John Deere Combine, 9500**, 1:28-scale, Ertl, green, 1980s, No. 546
EX $22   **NM** $34   **MIP** $47

❏ **John Deere Combine, 9510**, 1:28-scale, Ertl, green, 1998, No. 5171
(Photo by Ertl)
EX $22   **NM** $34   **MIP** $47

❏ **John Deere Combine, 9600**, 1:28-scale, Ertl, green, Collectors Edition, 1980s, No. 546DA
EX $23   **NM** $47   **MIP** $61

❏ **John Deere Stationary Gas Engine**, 1:28-scale, Turtle Creek, green, Model "E", 2003
EX $9   **NM** $18   **MIP** $32

❏ **John Deere Thresher**, 1:28-scale, SpecCast, silver, on steel wheels, 1992, No. JDM039 *(Photo by SpecCast)*
EX $27   **NM** $42   **MIP** $67

❏ **John Deere Threshers**, 1:28-scale, SpecCast, silver, on rubber tires, 1996, No. JDM079
EX $27   **NM** $42   **MIP** $67

IMPLEMENTS 1:32-SCALE

❏ **John Deere Combine, 2266**, 1:32-scale, Ertl, green, European w/grain head only, 2000, No. 12017
(Photo by Ertl)
EX $9   **NM** $18   **MIP** $28

❏ **John Deere Combine, 530**, 1:32-scale, Smer of West Germany, green, not 1/32 scale 8-1/2" long, 1970s
EX $392   **NM** $596   **MIP** $942

❏ **John Deere Combine, 9750**, 1:32-scale, Ertl, green, #1 in Precision Series II, 2000, No. 15036
EX $64   **NM** $73   **MIP** $137

❏ **John Deere Combine, 9760**, 1:32-scale, Ertl, green, 2004, No. 15358
EX $16   **NM** $23   **MIP** $42

❏ **John Deere Combine, 9760STS**, 1:32-scale, Ertl, 2005, No. 15358
EX $15   **NM** $20   **MIP** $25

❏ **John Deere Combine, 9760STS**, 1:32-scale, Ertl, Collector Edition, 2006, No. 15127A
EX $15   **NM** $25   **MIP** $35

❑ **John Deere Combine, 9860**, 1:32-scale, Ertl, green, Collector Edition, 2003, No. 15520A
EX $18 **NM** $26 **MIP** $48

❑ **John Deere Combine, 9860STS**, 1:32-scale, Ertl, 2 heads, 2006, No. 15798
EX $15 **NM** $20 **MIP** $25

❑ **John Deere Forage Harvestor, 6650**, 1:32-scale, Ertl, green, w/corn head, European version, 1999, No. 15129 *(Photo by Bossen Implement)*
EX $8 **NM** $14 **MIP** $28

❑ **John Deere Forage Harvestor, 7500**, 1:32-scale, Siku, green, w/yellow corn head, 2002, No. 4056

(Photo by Bossen Implement)
EX $24 **NM** $32 **MIP** $53

❑ **John Deere Forage Harvestor, 7500**, 1:32-scale, Siku, green, w/yellow hay head, 2004, No. 4057

(Photo by Siku)
EX $24 **NM** $32 **MIP** $53

❑ **John Deere Forage Havester, 6850**, 1:32-scale, Ertl, self-propelled, reissued under part #15644, 1998, No. 5129 *(Photo by Ertl)*
EX $8 **NM** $14 **MIP** $28

❑ **John Deere Lanz Combine**, 1:32-scale, Rex of West Germany, green, not 1/32 scale 7" long, 1960s
EX $388 **NM** $593 **MIP** $938

❑ **John Deere Manure Spreader**, 1:32-scale, Ertl, green, hydro push, PTO for 8960 4x4 tractor, 1980s, No. 5577
EX $3 **NM** $6 **MIP** $8

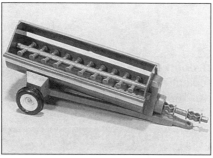

❑ **John Deere Manure Spreader**, 1:32-scale, Ertl, green and yellow, European-style, PTO, side discharge, 1990, No. 5625
EX $3 **NM** $6 **MIP** $8

❑ **John Deere Marston Trailer**, 1:32-scale, Ertl, green, 2004, No. 40609
EX $7 **NM** $14 **MIP** $21

❑ **John Deere Mower**, 1:32-scale, Lanz, green, plastic tractor, wood mower, 1960s
EX $392 **NM** $597 **MIP** npf

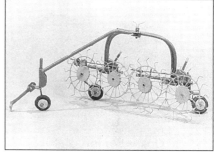

❑ **John Deere Rake**, 1:32-scale, Lanz, green and yellow, 1960s
EX $98 **NM** $148 **MIP** $247

❑ **John Deere Shredder**, 1:32-scale, Lanz, green, 1960s
EX $292 **NM** $387 **MIP** $594

❑ **John Deere Wagon, Barge**, 1:32-scale, Argentina, green, 1980s
EX $3 **NM** $6 **MIP** $12

❏ **John Deere Wagon, Barge**, 1:32-scale, Argentina, yellow, 1980s
EX $3   NM $6   MIP $12

❏ **John Deere Wagon, Barge**, 1:32-scale, Ertl, green, PTO fits 8960 tractor, 1980s, No. 5623
EX $3   NM $6   MIP $8

❏ **John Deere Wagon, Hay**, 1:32-scale, Ertl, green, 1994, No. 5694
EX $3   NM $6   MIP $8

IMPLEMENTS 1:43-SCALE

❏ **John Deere Manure Spreader**, 1:43-scale, Ertl, green, 1992, No. 5654
EX $2   NM $3   MIP $6

❏ **John Deere Wagon, Flare Box**, 1:43-scale, Ertl, green, reissued under stock #33530, 1992, No. 5637
EX $2   NM $3   MIP $6

IMPLEMENTS 1:50-SCALE

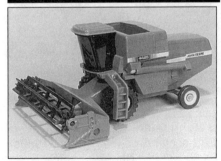

❏ **John Deere Combine, 4425**, 1:50-scale, Ertl, green, 1980, No. 506
EX $8   NM $13   MIP $22

❏ **John Deere Combine, 965**, 1:50-scale, Ertl, green, reversed decal, Hydro/4, 1980s, No. 1994
EX $8   NM $13   MIP $22

❏ **John Deere Combine, 965**, 1:50-scale, Ertl, green, Hydro/4, 1980s, No. 1994
EX $8   NM $13   MIP $22

❏ **John Deere Combine, 985**, 1:50-scale, Ertl, green, Hydro/4, 1980s, No. 1634
EX $8   NM $13   MIP $22

IMPLEMENTS 1:64-SCALE

❏ **John Deere 637 Disc w/200 Seed Bed Finisher**, 1:64-scale, Ertl, 2007, No. 15922
EX $4   NM $8   MIP $12

❏ **John Deere Bale-Grinder**, 1:64-scale, Ertl, green and yellow, 1987, No. 5568
EX $4   NM $5   MIP $6

❏ **John Deere Baler**, 1:64-scale, Ertl, can be either light or dark green, no model #15, 1983, No. 577
EX $4   NM $5   MIP $9

❏ **John Deere Baler**, 1:64-scale, Nygren (Custom), green, did not come in box
EX $3   NM $9   MIP n/a

❏ **John Deere Baler, 338**, 1:64-scale, Ertl, green with green pickup, 1996, No. 5646
EX $4   NM $5   MIP $6

❏ **John Deere Baler, 348**, 1:64-scale, Ertl, green, square, yellow pickup, 1993, No. 5646 *(Photo by Ertl)*
EX $4   NM $5   MIP $6

❏ **John Deere Baler, 535**, 1:64-scale, Ertl, green with yellow pickup, 1985, No. 577
EX $4   NM $5   MIP $6

❏ **John Deere Baler, 535**, 1:64-scale, Ertl, green with green pickup, 1996, No. 577
EX $4   NM $5   MIP $6

❏ **John Deere Baler, 566**, 1:64-scale, Ertl, green with green pickup, 1997, No. 577
EX $4 **NM** $5 **MIP** $6

❏ **John Deere Combine**, 1:64-scale, Gunning (Custom), green and yellow, did not come in box
EX $27 **NM** $48 **MIP** n/a

❏ **John Deere Combine**, 1:64-scale, Gunning (Custom), green and yellow, did not come in box
EX $27 **NM** $48 **MIP** n/a

❏ **John Deere Combine**, 1:64-scale, Gunning (Custom), green, did not come in box
EX $27 **NM** $48 **MIP** n/a

❏ **John Deere Combine**, 1:64-scale, Gunning (Custom), green and yellow, did not come in box
EX $9 **NM** $27 **MIP** n/a

❏ **John Deere Combine, 95**, 1:64-scale, Ertl, w/corn head only, 1996, No. 5819 *(Photo by Ertl)*
EX $4 **NM** $6 **MIP** $12

❏ **John Deere Combine, 9500**, 1:64-scale, Ertl, w/corn head and grain platform, 1989, No. 5604

(Photo by Kate Bossen)
EX $6 **NM** $8 **MIP** $16

❏ **John Deere Combine, 9610**, 1:64-scale, Ertl, w/corn head and grain platform, 1998, No. 5809 *(Photo by Ertl)*
EX $6 **NM** $8 **MIP** $12

❏ **John Deere Combine, 9860STS**, 1:64-scale, Ertl, 2 heads, 2006, No. 15800
EX $8 **NM** $16 **MIP** $22

❏ **John Deere Combine, CTS**, 1:64-scale, Ertl, rice, grain platform only, 1996, No. 5029 *(Photo by Ertl)*
EX $6 **NM** $9 **MIP** $12

❏ **John Deere Combine, CTS II**, 1:64-scale, Ertl, green, rice, grain platform only, 1998, No. 5172
EX $6 **NM** $9 **MIP** $12

❏ **John Deere Commodity Cart, 1900**, 1:64-scale, Ertl, green with yellow tanks, 2000, No. 15082
EX $4 **NM** $5 **MIP** $6

❏ **John Deere Corn Picker**, 1:64-scale, Nygren (Custom), green, did not come in box
EX $4 **NM** $9 **MIP** n/a

❏ **John Deere Corn Picker**, 1:64-scale, Nygren (Custom), green, did not come in box, picker/sheller
EX $11 **NM** $33 **MIP** n/a

❏ **John Deere Corn Picker**, 1:64-scale, Nygren (Custom), green, did not come in box
EX $11 **NM** $33 **MIP** n/a

Photos by Jon Jacobson unless otherwise noted.

❏ **John Deere Corn-Sheller**, 1:64-scale, Nygren (Custom), green, did not come in box
EX $9   **NM** $22   **MIP** n/a

❏ **John Deere Cotton Picker, 9976**, 1:64-scale, Ertl, green, 1997, No. 5765
EX $4   **NM** $8   **MIP** $16

❏ **John Deere Cotton Picker, 9986**, 1:64-scale, Ertl, green, 2002, No. 15440
EX $4   **NM** $7   **MIP** $14

❏ **John Deere Disc**, 1:64-scale, Matsen (Custom), green and black, did not come in box
EX $9   **NM** $12   **MIP** n/a

❏ **John Deere Disc**, 1:64-scale, Matsen (Custom), green, yellow, and black, did not come in box
EX $9   **NM** $18   **MIP** n/a

❏ **John Deere Forage Blower**, 1:64-scale, Ertl, green, No. 5728 *(Photo by Ertl)*
EX $3   **NM** $4   **MIP** $6

❏ **John Deere Forage Harvester**, 1:64-scale, Nygren (Custom), green, did not come in box
EX $4   **NM** $9   **MIP** n/a

❏ **John Deere Forage Harvester, 6910**, 1:64-scale, Ertl, self propelled, 1990s, No. 5658 *(Photo by Kate Bossen)*
EX $6   **NM** $12   **MIP** $23

❏ **John Deere Forage Harvestor**, 1:64-scale, Ertl, green and yellow, silver border around the decal, 1980, No. 566
EX $4   **NM** $5   **MIP** $6

❏ **John Deere Forage Harvestor**, 1:64-scale, Ertl, green and yellow, w/o silver border around the decal, 1980, No. 566
EX $4   **NM** $5   **MIP** $7

❏ **John Deere Forage Harvestor**, 1:64-scale, Ertl, green, green heads, 1996, No. 566
EX $4   **NM** $5   **MIP** $6

❏ **John Deere Forage Harvestor, 7500**, 1:64-scale, Ertl, green, came w/two forage wagons, 2003, No. 15494
EX n/a   **NM** n/a   **MIP** $16

❏ **John Deere Grain Cart, 500**, 1:64-scale, Ertl, 1989, No. 5565 *(Photo by Ertl)*
EX $4   **NM** $5   **MIP** $6

❏ **John Deere Grain Drill**, 1:64-scale, Ertl, 1980s, No. 5528 *(Photo by Ertl)*
EX $4   **NM** $5   **MIP** $6

❏ **John Deere Grain Drill, 1590**, 1:64-scale, Ertl, green, 1999, No. 15016
EX $4   **NM** $5   **MIP** $6

❏ **John Deere Hay Rake**, 1:64-scale, Ertl, 1990s, No. 5751 *(Photo by Ertl)*
EX $3   **NM** $4   **MIP** $5

❏ **John Deere Manure Spreader**, 1:64-scale, Ertl, green, plastic tires, 1980s, No. 7300
EX $4   **NM** $5   **MIP** $6

❑ **John Deere Manure Spreader**, 1:64-scale, Ertl, hydra push, 1985, No. 574 *(Photo by Ertl)*
EX $3   **NM** $4   **MIP** $5

❑ **John Deere Manure Spreader**, 1:64-scale, Ertl, V-tank, 1996, No. 5928 *(Photo by Ertl)*
EX $3   **NM** $4   **MIP** $5

❑ **John Deere Mix Mill**, 1:64-scale, Ertl, green and yellow, 1980s, No. 5554
EX $4   **NM** $5   **MIP** $6

❑ **John Deere Mower**, 1:64-scale, Ertl, Bat Wing, Rotary mower, No. 5600 *(Photo by Ertl)*
EX $3   **NM** $4   **MIP** $5

❑ **John Deere Mower**, 1:64-scale, Ertl, green, flex wing rotary cutter, 1993, No. 5600
EX $3   **NM** $4   **MIP** $5

❑ **John Deere Mower**, 1:64-scale, Nygren (Custom), green and yellow, did not come in box
EX $3   **NM** $9   **MIP** n/a

❑ **John Deere Mower**, 1:64-scale, Nygren (Custom), green and yellow, did not come in box
EX $3   **NM** $9   **MIP** n/a

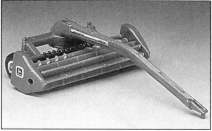

❑ **John Deere Mower Conditioner**, 1:64-scale, Ertl, 1992, No. 5657

(Photo by Ertl)
EX $4   **NM** $5   **MIP** $6

❑ **John Deere Mulch Master**, 1:64-scale, Ertl, 1994, No. 5727 *(Photo by Ertl)*
EX $3   **NM** $4   **MIP** $6

❑ **John Deere Mulch Ripper, 2700**, 1:64-scale, Ertl, green, 2003, No. 15491
EX $4   **NM** $5   **MIP** $8

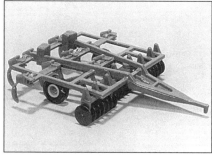

❑ **John Deere Mulch-Tiller**, 1:64-scale, Ertl, green, reissued as stock #15337, 1986, No. 578
EX $2   **NM** $3   **MIP** $4

❑ **John Deere Planter**, 1:64-scale, Matsen (Custom), green and yellow, various sizes, did not come in box
EX $9   **NM** $24   **MIP** n/a

❑ **John Deere Planter, 1790**, 1:64-scale, Ertl, green, 16 row, 2002, No. 15380
EX $4   **NM** $6   **MIP** $9

❑ **John Deere Planter, 7200**, 1:64-scale, Ertl, green and yellow, No. 576
EX $6   **NM** $11   **MIP** $16

❑ **John Deere Shredder**, 1:64-scale, Matsen (Custom), green, did not come in box
EX $3   **NM** $6   **MIP** n/a

❏ **John Deere Shredder**, 1:64-scale, Matsen (Custom), green and yellow, did not come in box
EX $3   **NM** $12   **MIP** n/a

❏ **John Deere Shredder**, 1:64-scale, Nygren (Custom), green, did not come in box
EX $3   **NM** $9   **MIP** n/a

❏ **John Deere Shredder**, 1:64-scale, Nygren (Custom), green, did not come in box
EX $3   **NM** $6   **MIP** n/a

❏ **John Deere Sprayer, 4700**, 1:64-scale, Ertl, green, self propelled, No. 5752 *(Photo by Ertl)*
EX $4   **NM** $6   **MIP** $9

❏ **John Deere Sprayer, 4710**, 1:64-scale, Ertl, green, 2000, No. 15180
EX $4   **NM** $6   **MIP** $9

❏ **John Deere Wagon, Bale Throw**, 1:64-scale, Ertl, No. 5755
(Photo by Ertl)
EX $4   **NM** $5   **MIP** $6

❏ **John Deere Wagon, Barge**, 1:64-scale, Argentina, green
EX $18   **NM** $26   **MIP** $37

❏ **John Deere Wagon, Barge**, 1:64-scale, Argentina, yellow
EX $18   **NM** $26   **MIP** $37

❏ **John Deere Wagon, Barge**, 1:64-scale, Ertl, green, 1980s, No. 5529
EX $3   **NM** $4   **MIP** $6

❏ **John Deere Wagon, Flare Box**, 1:64-scale, Nygren (Custom), green, did not come in box
EX $6   **NM** $12   **MIP** n/a

❏ **John Deere Wagon, Flare Box**, 1:64-scale, Standi (Custom), various colors, various tire sizes
EX $3   **NM** $4   **MIP** $5

❏ **John Deere Wagon, Forage**, 1:64-scale, Ertl, green and yellow, w/o silver border around the decal, 1980s, No. 1519
EX $4   **NM** $6   **MIP** $8

❏ **John Deere Wagon, Forage**, 1:64-scale, Ertl, green and yellow, silver border around the decal, 1980s, No. 567
EX $4   **NM** $6   **MIP** $8

Photos by Jon Jacobson unless otherwise noted.

❏ **John Deere Wagon, Forage**, 1:64-scale, Standi (Custom), green, 1980s
EX $3   **NM** $6   **MIP** $9

❏ **John Deere Wagon, Gravity**, 1:64-scale, Ertl, green, 1980s, No. 5552
EX $4   **NM** $6   **MIP** $8

❏ **John Deere/Bauer Built Planter, 36 Row**, 1:64-scale, SpecCast, folds out to 36 rows, 2007, No. 206

(Photo by SpecCast)
EX $35   **NM** $50   **MIP** $65

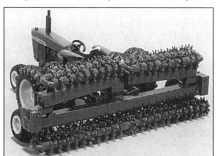

❏ **Rotary-Hoe John Deere**, 1:64-scale, Matsen (Custom), green, did not come in box
EX $13   **NM** $26   **MIP** n/a

IMPLEMENTS 1:80-SCALE

❏ **John Deere Combine, Titan**, 1:80-scale, Ertl, green and yellow, grain head only, 1982, No. 1519
EX $12   **NM** $22   **MIP** $33

❏ **John Deere Combine, Titan**, 1:80-scale, Ertl, green and yellow, yellow reel and black auger, 1982, No. 1519
EX $37   **NM** $58   **MIP** $74

❏ **John Deere Combine, Titan**, 1:80-scale, Ertl, green and yellow, 2 heads, 1983, No. 537
EX $12   **NM** $22   **MIP** $33

❏ **John Deere Combine, Titan II**, 1:80-scale, Ertl, green, 2 heads, 1986, No. 550
EX $12   **NM** $22   **MIP** $27

❏ **John Deere Cotton Picker**, 1:80-scale, Ertl, green, yellow and black, front tires may be either hard or soft rubber, 1980s, No. 1000
EX $6   **NM** $8   **MIP** $16

IMPLEMENTS 1:87-SCALE

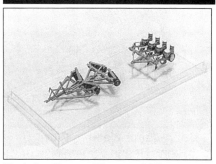

❏ **John Deere Disc and Planter**, 1:87-scale, Woodland Scenes, green, kit, 1970s
EX $6   **NM** $12   **MIP** $27

IMPLEMENTS 10" LONG

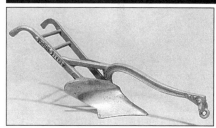

❏ **John Deere Walking Plow**, 10" long, John Deere, nickel plated, 1940s
EX $182   **NM** $236   **MIP** npf

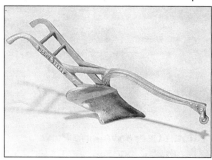

❏ **John Deere Walking Plow**, 10" long, John Deere, nickel plated, also available in brass, 1940s
EX $182   **NM** $236   **MIP** npf

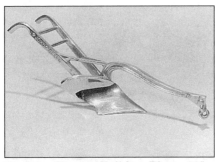

❑ **John Deere Walking Plow**, 10" long, John Deere, marked "The local chapter of FFA" on the landslide, 1970s
EX $182   **NM** $236   **MIP** npf

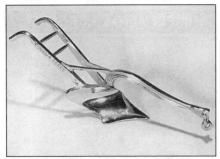

❑ **John Deere Walking Plow**, 10" long, John Deere, chrome plated, "The local Chapter of FFA" on the landslide, 1970s
EX $182   **NM** $236   **MIP** npf

❑ **John Deere Walking Plow**, 10" long, McCenning, 1980s
EX $18   **NM** $37   **MIP** npf

❑ **John Deere Walking Plow w/Team**, 10" long, Lalonda, made for John Deere's 150th Anniversary, 1980s
EX npf   **NM** npf   **MIP** npf

IMPLEMENTS 7" LONG

❑ **John Deere Walking Plow**, 7" long, Argentina, chrome plated on wood plaque, 1980s
EX npf   **NM** npf   **MIP** npf

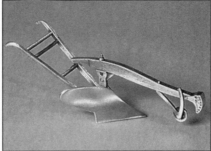

❑ **John Deere Walking Plow**, 7" long, SpecCast, No. JDM065
(Photo by SpecCast)
EX $8   **NM** $12   **MIP** $19

LAWN AND GARDEN 1:08-SCALE

❑ **John Deere Gator**, 1:08-scale, Scale Models, yellow, work site version, 2001, No. FY-1023
EX $32   **NM** $46   **MIP** $73

❑ **John Deere Gator**, 1:08-scale, Scale Models, dark green, trail version, 2001, No. FY-1022
EX $32   **NM** $46   **MIP** $73

❑ **John Deere Gator**, 1:08-scale, Scale Models, green, 2001, No. FY-1020
EX $32   **NM** $46   **MIP** $73

LAWN AND GARDEN 1:16-SCALE

❑ **John Deere 110 L & G**, 1:16-scale, Ertl, green, half of seat painted yellow, 1960s, No. 538
EX $54   **NM** $126   **MIP** $238

❑ **John Deere 110 L & G**, 1:16-scale, Ertl, green, model no. 5, 1960s, No. 538
EX $54   **NM** $126   **MIP** $238

❑ **John Deere 110 L & G**, 1:16-scale, Ertl, green, one lever, 1960s, No. 538
EX $54   **NM** $126   **MIP** $238

❑ **John Deere 110 L & G**, 1:16-scale, Ertl, green, whole seat painted yellow, 1960s, No. 538
EX $54   **NM** $126   **MIP** $238

❑ **John Deere 110 L & G**, 1:16-scale, Ertl, green, w/cart #1 in Precision Series, 2001, No. 15213
EX $26   **NM** $33   **MIP** $52

❑ **John Deere 140 L & G**, 1:16-scale, Ertl, green, die-cast trailer, w/lever dump latch, 1960s
EX $56 **NM** $88 **MIP** $288

❑ **John Deere 140 L & G**, 1:16-scale, Ertl, orange and white w/black grille, 1960s, No. 571
EX $103 **NM** $214 **MIP** $384

❑ **John Deere 140 L & G**, 1:16-scale, Ertl, red and white w/black grille, 1960s, No. 574
EX $103 **NM** $214 **MIP** $384

❑ **John Deere 140 L & G**, 1:16-scale, Ertl, blue and white w/black grille, 1960s, No. 572
EX $103 **NM** $214 **MIP** $384

❑ **John Deere 140 L & G**, 1:16-scale, Ertl, green, metal steering wheel, 1960s, No. 550
EX $43 **NM** $97 **MIP** $189

❑ **John Deere 140 L & G**, 1:16-scale, Ertl, yellow and white w/black grille, 1960s, No. 573
EX $103 **NM** $214 **MIP** $384

❑ **John Deere 140 L & G**, 1:16-scale, Ertl, green, lever on left side only, plastic trailer, 1970s
EX $53 **NM** $122 **MIP** $268

❑ **John Deere 140 L & G**, 1:16-scale, Ertl, green and white trailer, blade riveted to the front of tractor, 1970s, No. 515
EX $93 **NM** $162 **MIP** $276

❑ **John Deere 140 Maintenance Set**, 1:16-scale, Ertl, green tractor, white loader, scraper, yellow blade, broom, black grille, 1960s, No. 580
EX $246 **NM** $457 **MIP** $843

❑ **John Deere 200**, 1:16-scale, Ertl, green, 1980s, No. 5594
EX $17 **NM** $24 **MIP** $36

❑ **John Deere 200**, 1:16-scale, Ertl, green, plastic yellow mower, 1980s, No. 5591
EX $16 **NM** $22 **MIP** $32

❑ **John Deere 200**, 1:16-scale, Ertl, green, w/mower, 1990s, No. 5591
EX $9 **NM** $23 **MIP** $37

❑ **John Deere 200**, 1:16-scale, Ertl, green, w/trailer and yellow mower, 1990s, No. 5594
EX $7   **NM** $13   **MIP** $21

❑ **John Deere 300**, 1:16-scale, Ertl, green, die-cast trailer w/friction dump latch, 1970s, No. 598
EX $52   **NM** $86   **MIP** $238

❑ **John Deere 320**, 1:16-scale, Ertl, green, Foxfire Friends, "Pumpkin Patch", 1988, No. 5164
EX $12   **NM** $16   **MIP** $24

❑ **John Deere 325**, 1:16-scale, Ertl, green, w/mower deck, tiller and dump cart, 2001, No. 15199
EX $7   **NM** $11   **MIP** $16

❑ **John Deere 345**, 1:16-scale, Ertl, green, w/mower deck, snow blower and blade, 1997, No. 5079
(Photo by Bossen Implement)
EX $8   **NM** $12   **MIP** $18

❑ **John Deere 400**, 1:16-scale, Ertl, green, light bar decal, w/cart, 1980s, No. 598
EX $18   **NM** $29   **MIP** $49

❑ **John Deere 400**, 1:16-scale, Ertl, green, 1980s, No. 591
EX $16   **NM** $28   **MIP** $46

❑ **John Deere 400**, 1:16-scale, Ertl, green, light bar decal, 1980s, No. 591
EX $16   **NM** $28   **MIP** $46

❑ **John Deere 4310**, 1:16-scale, Ertl, green, w/mower deck and snow tiller, 2002, No. 15198
EX $8   **NM** $13   **MIP** $24

❑ **John Deere 4410 w/Mower Set**, 1:16-scale, Ertl, w/roll bar, 2007, No. 15967
EX $7   **NM** $12   **MIP** $18

❑ **John Deere AMT 600**, 1:16-scale, Ertl, green, came w/decals applied upside down, 1980s, No. 5597
EX $6   **NM** $11   **MIP** $18

❑ **John Deere AMT 600**, 1:16-scale, Ertl, green, 1980s, No. 5597
EX $6   **NM** $11   **MIP** $18

❑ **John Deere Gator**, 1:16-scale, Ertl, green, 2001, No. 15278
EX $7   **NM** $11   **MIP** $16

❑ **John Deere Gator**, 1:16-scale, Ertl, dark green, trial version w/fisherman, 2002, No. 15394
EX $8   **NM** $11   **MIP** $18

❑ **John Deere Gator**, 1:16-scale, Ertl, yellow, work site version, 2003, No. 15516
EX $7   **NM** $11   **MIP** $16

❑ **John Deere Gator, CX**, 1:16-scale, Ertl, green, 2004, No. 15637
EX $6   **NM** $9   **MIP** $14

❑ **John Deere Gator, CX Compact**, 1:16-scale, Ertl, two seats, short bed, 2004, No. 15637
EX $5   **NM** $10   **MIP** $15

❑ **John Deere Gator, CX Compact**, 1:16-scale, Ertl, 2005, No. 15637
EX $8   **NM** $12   **MIP** $16

❑ **John Deere Gator, HPX**, 1:16-scale, Ertl, dark green, 2004, No. 15636
EX $6   **NM** $9   **MIP** $14

❑ **John Deere Gator, HPX**, 1:16-scale, Ertl, 4 x 4, 2005, No. 15636
EX $8   **NM** $12   **MIP** $18

❑ **John Deere Gator, HPX 4x4**, 1:16-scale, Ertl, two seats, four wheels, 2004, No. 15636

❑ **John Deere Gator, XUV 620i**, 1:16-scale, Ertl, w/cage, 2007, No. 15932
EX $7   **NM** $12   **MIP** $18

❑ **John Deere L & G**, 1:16-scale, Ertl, green, plastic trailer w/friction dump latch, 1970s, No. 598
EX $49 **NM** $84 **MIP** $222

❑ **John Deere L110**, 1:16-scale, Ertl, tractor w/attachments, 2004, No. 15531
EX $5 **NM** $10 **MIP** $15

❑ **John Deere SST-16**, 1:16-scale, Ertl, green, zero turn, Collector Edition, 2001, No. 15223A
EX $7 **NM** $11 **MIP** $16

❑ **John Deere SST-18**, 1:16-scale, Ertl, green, zero turn, 2001, No. 15292
EX $4 **NM** $8 **MIP** $12

❑ **John Deere X-485**, 1:16-scale, Ertl, green, w/attachments, 2003, No. 15353
EX $7 **NM** $11 **MIP** $16

❑ **John Deere X-585**, 1:16-scale, Ertl, green, w/attachments, Collector Edition, 2003, No. 15340A
EX $8 **NM** $11 **MIP** $18

❑ **John Deere X-585**, 1:16-scale, Ertl, w/attachments, mower deck, wagon, rake, 2004, No. 15509
EX $5 **NM** $10 **MIP** $15

❑ **John Deere, RX-75**, 1:16-scale, Ertl, green, w/bagger, rear engine rider, 1990s, No. 5588
EX $6 **NM** $11 **MIP** $18

LAWN AND GARDEN 1:18-SCALE

❑ **John Deere Buck ATV**, 1:18-scale, Ertl, single seat, 2004, No. 15638
EX $5 **NM** $10 **MIP** $15

LAWN AND GARDEN 1:32-SCALE

❑ **John Deere 425**, 1:32-scale, Ertl, green, w/mower deck and snow blower, 1995, No. 5745
EX $2 **NM** $3 **MIP** $7

❑ **John Deere 425**, 1:32-scale, Ertl, w/gear, mower deck and front blade, 1995, No. 5740
EX $2 **NM** $3 **MIP** $7

❑ **John Deere 445**, 1:32-scale, Ertl, green, w/mower deck and roto tiller, 1995, No. 5742
EX $2 **NM** $3 **MIP** $5

❑ **John Deere 445**, 1:32-scale, Ertl, w/gear, 1995, No. 5741 *(Photo by Ertl)*
EX $2 **NM** $3 **MIP** $7

❑ **John Deere Buck ATV**, 1:32-scale, Ertl, single seat, 2004, No. 15640
EX $5 **NM** $10 **MIP** $15

❑ **John Deere Gator**, 1:32-scale, Ertl, green, reissued with stock #15254, 1995, No. 5748 *(Photo by Ertl)*
EX $2 **NM** $3 **MIP** $5

❑ **John Deere Gator**, 1:32-scale, Ertl, green, 2001, No. 15411
EX n/a **NM** n/a **MIP** $5

❑ **John Deere Gator, 6x4**, 1:32-scale, Ertl, two seats, six wheels, 2004, No. 15254
EX $5 **NM** $10 **MIP** $15

❑ **John Deere Gator, HPX**, 1:32-scale, Ertl, dark green, 2004, No. 15692
EX $2 **NM** $3 **MIP** $5

❑ **John Deere Gator, HPX 4x4**, 1:32-scale, Ertl, two seats, 2004, No. 15692
EX $5 **NM** $10 **MIP** $15

❑ **John Deere Lawn and Garden Assortment**, 1:32-scale, Ertl, Gator, Mower, Tractor, attachments, 2004, No. 36518
EX $10 **NM** $20 **MIP** $30

❑ **John Deere X485 Lawn and Garden Tractor**, 1:32-scale, Ertl, w/attachments, 2004, No. 15691
EX $7 **NM** $14 **MIP** $21

❑ **John Deere Z-Trak**, 1:32-scale, Ertl, green, zero turn, w/mower deck, 1999, No. 15018
EX $2 **NM** $3 **MIP** $5

LAWN AND GARDEN 12" LONG

❑ **John Deere Gator**, 12" long, Ertl, green, 2004, No. 15393
EX $4 **NM** $6 **MIP** $11

MISCELLANEOUS 1:03-SCALE

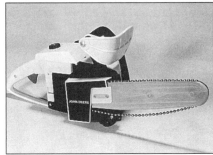

❑ **John Deere Chain Saw**, 1:03-scale, Ertl, yellow, working, 1970s, No. 523
EX $22 **NM** $53 **MIP** $68

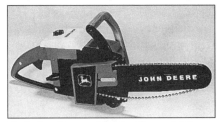

❑ **John Deere Chain Saw**, 1:03-scale, Ertl, green, working, 1970s, No. 526
EX $36 **NM** $92 **MIP** $118

❏ **John Deere Circular Saw**, 1:03-scale, Ertl, black, working, 1980s, No. 5503

EX $18   **NM** $33   **MIP** $42

MISCELLANEOUS 1:10-SCALE

❏ **John Deere 440 Snowmobile**, 1:10-scale, Suttle, metallic green, battery operated, 1970s, No. 8111

EX $59   **NM** $112   **MIP** $172

❏ **John Deere 440 Snowmobile**, 1:10-scale, Suttle, metallic green, push type, can also be found w/JDX skis, 1970s, No. 8111

EX $59   **NM** $112   **MIP** $172

❏ **John Deere Snowmobile**, 1:10-scale, Normatt, black, battery operated, 1970s, No. 7000

EX $98   **NM** $187   **MIP** $356

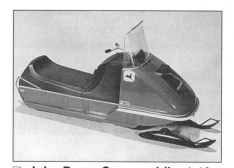

❏ **John Deere Snowmobile**, 1:10-scale, Normatt, green, battery operated, 1970s, No. 7000

EX $72   **NM** $137   **MIP** $272

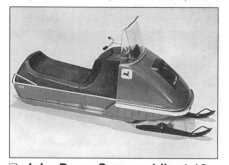

❏ **John Deere Snowmobile**, 1:10-scale, Normatt, green, push type, 1970s, No. 7000

EX $72   **NM** $137   **MIP** $272

❏ **John Deere Trail Fire Snowmobile**, 1:10-scale, Ertl, silver and gray, battery operated, 1980s, No. 573

EX $48   **NM** $82   **MIP** $112

MISCELLANEOUS 1:87-SCALE

❏ **John Deere 150th Anniversary Plaque**, 1:87-scale, Ertl, bronze plated on wood plaque, 1980s, No. 5519

EX $6   **NM** $27   **MIP** $32

MISCELLANEOUS 14" TALL

❏ **Little Johnnie Dearest**, 14" tall, B.J. Toy Company, green and yellow, stuffed toy, 1980s

EX npf   **NM** npf   **MIP** npf

❏ **Little Johnnie Dearest**, 14" tall, B.J. Toy Company, brown and tan, stuffed toy, 1980s

EX npf   **NM** npf   **MIP** npf

MISCELLANEOUS 2-7/8" LONG

❏ **John Deere Anvil**, 2-7/8" long, lead, did not come in box, 1937

EX $24   **NM** $83   **MIP** n/a

MISCELLANEOUS 36" TALL, APPROX.

❏ **John Deere Boy**, 36" tall, approx., Ertl, self-standing cardboard, did not come in box, 1980s
EX $19   NM $64   MIP n/a

MISCELLANEOUS 7" LONG

❏ **Original John Deere Story Books**, 7" long, John Deere, did not come in box, 1950s
EX $19   NM $62   MIP n/a

MISCELLANEOUS 8-1/2" LONG

❏ **Reproduction John Deere Story Books**, 8-1/2" long, John Deere, did not come in box, 1980s
EX $6   NM $9   MIP n/a

MISCELLANEOUS

❏ **Harvest Days Puzzle**, John Deere, 1970s
EX n/a   NM n/a   MIP $38

❏ **John Deere 225G Power Washer**, SpecCast, yellow, special for John Deere, limited to 200 units, 1990s
EX $19   NM $57   MIP $89

❏ **John Deere Anvil**, SpecCast, Parts Expo 1990, 1990s
EX $16   NM $27   MIP $33

❏ **John Deere Bears**, Korea, brown, 1990s
EX npf   NM npf   MIP npf

❏ **John Deere Farm Set**, Ertl, 1990s, No. 5995
EX $6   NM $8   MIP $19

❏ **John Deere Hanging Lamp**, white and yellow, plastic shade, 1980s

❏ **John Deere Puzzle**, John Deere, 1970s
EX n/a   NM n/a   MIP $57

❏ **John Deere Service Center**, Ertl, 1990s, No. 5996
EX $6   NM $8   MIP $19

❑ **John Deere Table Lamp**, green and yellow, glass shade, 1980s
EX npf   **NM** npf   **MIP** npf

❑ **John Deere Table Lamp**, white and yellow, plastic shade, 1980s
EX npf   **NM** npf   **MIP** npf

❑ **John Deere Table Lamp**, green and yellow, plastic shade, 1980s
EX npf   **NM** npf   **MIP** npf

PEDAL TRACTORS

❑ **John Deere 10**, Ertl, green, four holes in engine casting, original tractor restored, 1960s
EX $442   **NM** $769   **MIP** n/a

❑ **John Deere 10**, Ertl, green, three holes in engine casting, original tractor restored, 1960s
EX $412   **NM** $692   **MIP** n/a

❑ **John Deere 130**, Eska, green, one small hole in engine casting, original tractor restored; 1:16-scale tractor in foreground, 1970s, No. 531
EX $689   **NM** $1583   **MIP** n/a

❑ **John Deere 130**, Eska, green, variation in body casting, one large hole in engine casting, tractor in original condition, 1970s, No. 531
EX $689   **NM** $882   **MIP** n/a

❑ **John Deere 130**, Eska, green, two holes in upper part of engine casting, original tractor restored, 1970s, No. 531
EX $689   **NM** $882   **MIP** n/a

❑ **John Deere 130 Umbrella**, Detail: This photo shows the approximate mounting location for umbrellas on all pedal tractors made by Eska in the 1950's.

❑ **John Deere 20**, Ertl, green, no holes in engine casting, 1963 casting designs are slightly different than 1965 castings, they will not interchange, tractor in original condition, 1960s, No. 532
EX $198   **NM** $368   **MIP** $692

❑ **John Deere 30**, Ertl, green, can be found w/metal or plastic, front wheel rims, seat and steering wheels, tractor in original condition, 1970s, No. 520
EX $128   **NM** $268   **MIP** $458

❏ **John Deere 3140**, Rolly Toys of Germany, green, not marketed in the USA, tractor in original condition
EX $338   **NM** $462   **MIP** n/a

❏ **John Deere 3140**, Rolly Toys of Germany, green, not market in the USA, tractor in original condition
EX $389   **NM** $472   **MIP** n/a

❏ **John Deere 3650**, Ertl, WF
EX $43   **NM** $62   **MIP** $98

❏ **John Deere 3650**, Ertl, w/loader, 1991, No. 5675
EX $52   **NM** $78   **MIP** $146

❏ **John Deere 3650**, Rolly Toys of Germany, green, not marketed in the USA, tractor in original condition
EX $98   **NM** $153   **MIP** $178

❏ **John Deere 3650**, Rolly Toys of Germany, green, not marketed in the USA, tractor in original condition
EX $143   **NM** $189   **MIP** $221

❏ **John Deere 40**, Ertl, green, tractor in original condition, 1978, No. 520
EX $128   **NM** $239   **MIP** $406

❏ **John Deere 4020**, Ertl, WF, 1991, No. 5682 *(Photo by Ertl)*
EX $173   **NM** $322   **MIP** $396

❏ **John Deere 4300**, Ertl, 2000, No. 34380 *(Photo by Ertl)*
EX $32   **NM** $47   **MIP** $82

❏ **John Deere 50**, Ertl, green, tractor in original condition (40) Series tractor with a (50) Series decal, No. 520
EX $128   **NM** $229   **MIP** $388

❏ **John Deere 50**, Ertl, green, casting change, tractor in original condition, 1982, No. 520
EX $128   **NM** $229   **MIP** $388

❏ **John Deere 5020**, Ertl, green, 2004, No. 15502
EX $78   **NM** $102   **MIP** $163

❏ **John Deere 60**, Eska, green, restored; seat mounting bracket about 2-1/2" from rear of main tractor casting. Other version, about 1", small version, 1950s
EX $463   **NM** $743   **MIP** n/a

❏ **John Deere 60**, Eska, green, original tractor restored; 1:16-scale tractor in foreground, large version, 1950s
EX $427   **NM** $627   **MIP** n/a

❏ **John Deere 620**, Eska, green, original tractor restored 1:16-scale; tractor in foreground, 1950s
EX $478   **NM** $829   **MIP** n/a

❏ **John Deere 6400**, Ertl, green, 1997, No. 15046
EX $53   **NM** $74   **MIP** $127

❏ **John Deere 6410**, Ertl, 1999, No. 15060
EX $53   **NM** $74   **MIP** $127

❏ **John Deere 730**, Eska, several variations, 1950s
EX $432   **NM** $689   **MIP** $882

❑ **John Deere 7410**, Ertl, green, 1997, No. 5828
EX $78   **NM** $102   **MIP** $163

❑ **John Deere 7600**, Ertl, green, 1994, No. 552 *(Photo by Ertl)*
EX $98   **NM** $145   **MIP** $168

❑ **John Deere 8310**, Ertl, green, 2000, No. 15067
EX $82   **NM** $113   **MIP** $178

❑ **John Deere 8400**, Ertl, green, 1999, No. 5099
EX $78   **NM** $102   **MIP** $163

❑ **John Deere 8520**, Ertl, green, 2002, No. 15392
EX $78   **NM** $102   **MIP** $163

❑ **John Deere A**, Ertl, green, 1999, No. 15035
EX $121   **NM** $147   **MIP** $233

❑ **John Deere A**, Eska, red w/yellow wheels, block-type engine design, tractor in original condition, 1949
EX $16000   **NM** $18000   **MIP** n/a

❑ **John Deere A**, Eska, green, tractor in original condition, 1950s
EX $3398   **NM** $4698   **MIP** n/a

❑ **John Deere LGT**, Ertl, green, plastic grille, tin fenders and seat, tractor in original condition, 1970s, No. 531
EX $472   **NM** $772   **MIP** n/a

❑ **John Deere Roll Guard**, Ertl, fits 3010/3020 tractors, no sub frame or rain gutters, roof rivet, No. 548
EX $98   **NM** $123   **MIP** $198

❑ **John Deere Umbrella**, Heltrick, yellow, in original condition
EX $118   **NM** $277   **MIP** $348

TRACTORS 1:08-SCALE

❑ **John Deere 10**, 1:08-scale, Ertl, '97 National Farm Toy Museum, 1997, No. 5081MA *(Photo by Bossen Implement)*
EX $12   **NM** $32   **MIP** $58

❑ **John Deere 20**, 1:08-scale, Ertl, replica, 1997, No. 5917
EX $8   **NM** $16   **MIP** $32

❑ **John Deere 4010**, 1:08-scale, Scale Models, green, NF, 1999, No. FY-1001
EX $82   **NM** $107   **MIP** $153

❑ **John Deere 4020**, 1:08-scale, Scale Models, green, WF, 2001, No. FY-1021
EX $82   **NM** $107   **MIP** $153

❑ **John Deere 4430**, 1:08-scale, Scale Models, green, 2001, No. FY-1019
EX $113   **NM** $156   **MIP** $213

❑ **John Deere 70**, 1:08-scale, Scale Models, green, NF, 1997, No. FY-1005
EX $82   **NM** $107   **MIP** $153

❑ **John Deere A**, 1:08-scale, Scale Models, green, NF, unstyled, 2000, No. FY-1016A
EX $82   **NM** $107   **MIP** $153

❑ **John Deere B**, 1:08-scale, Scale Models, green, NF, styled on rubber, 1997, No. FY-1000
EX $82   **NM** $107   **MIP** $153

❑ **John Deere B**, 1:08-scale, Scale Models, green, WF, 1999, No. FY-1010
EX $82   **NM** $107   **MIP** $153

❑ **John Deere D**, 1:08-scale, Scale Models, green, unstyled on rubber, 1998, No. FY-1008
EX $82   **NM** $107   **MIP** $153

TRACTORS 1:128-SCALE

❑ **John Deere Micros**, 1:128-scale, Micro Machines, green, out of set, 1990s
EX $1   **NM** $2   **MIP** npf

❑ **John Deere Micros Set**, 1:128-scale, Ertl, green, w/tractor, wagon and disk, 1990s, No. 5572
EX npf   **NM** npf   **MIP** $9

TRACTORS 1:12-SCALE

❑ **John Deere 3010**, 1:12-scale, Auburn Rubber, red, 1960s
EX $16   **NM** $42   **MIP** $73

❑ **John Deere 830**, 1:12-scale, Kruse (Custom), green, did not come in box, 1970s-1980s
EX $72   **NM** $89   **MIP** n/a

❑ **John Deere G**, 1:12-scale, Kruse (Custom), green, 1970s-1980s
EX $27   **NM** $48   **MIP** n/a

❑ **John Deere GP**, 1:12-scale, Kruse (Custom), green, did not come in box, 1970s-1980s
EX $28   **NM** $47   **MIP** n/a

TRACTORS 1:16-SCALE

❑ **John Deere 2010**, 1:16-scale, Argentina (Sigomac), green, Utility, 1960s
EX $72   **NM** $93   **MIP** $127

❑ **John Deere 2010**, 1:16-scale, Ertl, green, 1970s, No. 516
EX $18   **NM** $42   **MIP** $66

❑ **John Deere 2010**, 1:16-scale, Ertl, green, w/Loader, 1970s, No. 517
EX $28   **NM** $76   **MIP** $103

❑ **John Deere 2010**, 1:16-scale, Sigomac, green, recast of obsolete model, 1980s
EX $68   **NM** $83   **MIP** $106

❑ **John Deere 2030**, 1:16-scale, Ertl, green, solid yellow decal, 1970s, No. 516
EX $12   **NM** $27   **MIP** $38

❑ **John Deere 2030**, 1:16-scale, Ertl, green, w/Loader, diecast bucket, 1970s, No. 517
EX $12   **NM** $28   **MIP** $42

❑ **John Deere 2030**, 1:16-scale, Ertl, green, w/Loader, stamped steel bucket, solid yellow decal, 1970s, No. 517
EX $12   **NM** $28   **MIP** $48

❑ **John Deere 2020**, 1:16-scale, Wader (Custom), green, 1960s
EX $636   **NM** $1382   **MIP** npf

❏ **John Deere 2040**, 1:16-scale, Ertl, green strobe decal, 1980s, No. 516

EX $9   **NM** $12   **MIP** $18

❏ **John Deere 2040**, 1:16-scale, Ertl, green, w/Loader, 1980s, No. 517

EX $9   **NM** $18   **MIP** $22

❏ **John Deere 2040**, 1:16-scale, Ertl, yellow, 40-series tractor w/50-series loader, 1980s, No. 517

EX $9   **NM** $18   **MIP** $22

❏ **John Deere 2520**, 1:16-scale, Scale Models, 1994 Farm Progress Show Edition, 1994, No. FB-2354

(Photo by Scale Models)

EX $33   **NM** $68   **MIP** $87

❏ **John Deere 2550**, 1:16-scale, Ertl, green, MFD, 1980s, No. 501

EX $12   **NM** $19   **MIP** $28

❏ **John Deere 2550**, 1:16-scale, Ertl, green, Collectors Edition, available w/open and closed rear fenders, 1980s, No. 510DA

EX $22   **NM** $28   **MIP** $42

❏ **John Deere 2640**, 1:16-scale, Ertl, green, "Field of Dreams" Dyersville, Iowa 1990 Special Edition, 1990s, No. 516DA

EX $16   **NM** $24   **MIP** $37

❏ **John Deere 2650**, 1:16-scale, Ertl, Utility, 1980s, No. 516 *(Photo by Ertl)*

EX $6   **NM** $11   **MIP** $17

❏ **John Deere 2650**, 1:16-scale, Ertl, w/loader, 1980s, No. 517 *(Photo by Ertl)*

EX $6   **NM** $12   **MIP** $18

❏ **John Deere 2650**, 1:16-scale, Ertl, w/wagon set, 1990s, No. 518

(Photo by Ertl)

EX $8   **NM** $14   **MIP** $28

❏ **John Deere 2275**, 1:16-scale, Ertl, green, MFD, cab, 1980s, No. 5579

EX $12   **NM** $27   **MIP** $39

❏ **John Deere 2755**, 1:16-scale, Ertl, green, w/Loader, 1980s, No. 5578

EX $12   **NM** $24   **MIP** $32

❏ **John Deere 2755**, 1:16-scale, Ertl, green, w/loader, 2004, No. 15538

EX $8   **NM** $18   **MIP** $28

❑ **John Deere 2755**, 1:16-scale, Ertl, green, 2004, No. 15537
EX $8   **NM** $23   **MIP** $28

❑ **John Deere 3010**, 1:16-scale, Ertl, green, three-point hitch, no fuel filters, first casting made, 1960s
EX $92   **NM** $198   **MIP** $538

❑ **John Deere 3010**, 1:16-scale, Ertl, green, NF, 1992, No. 5635
EX $14   **NM** $22   **MIP** $32

❑ **John Deere 3010**, 1:16-scale, Ertl, green, WF, Collector Edition, 1992, No. 5635DA
EX $17   **NM** $28   **MIP** $47

❑ **John Deere 3010**, 1:16-scale, Ertl, green, #20 Precision Series, 2001, No. 15210
EX $62   **NM** $88   **MIP** $122

❑ **John Deere 3010**, 1:16-scale, Ertl, Precision Classics #20, NF, 2004, No. 15210
EX $40   **NM** $80   **MIP** $120

❑ **John Deere 3010**, 1:16-scale, Scale Models, green, ROPS, Agricultural Safety Center, 1997, No. FY-1002
EX $23   **NM** $38   **MIP** $64

❑ **John Deere 3010**, 1:16-scale, Scale Models, green, Beckman High School Edition, 2000
EX $22   **NM** $32   **MIP** $48

❑ **John Deere 3020**, 1:16-scale, Argentina (Sigomac), green, 1960s
EX $256   **NM** $382   **MIP** npf

❑ **John Deere 3020**, 1:16-scale, Ertl, green, two long fuel filters, wide front end, 1960s
EX $52   **NM** $128   **MIP** $283

❑ **John Deere 3020**, 1:16-scale, Ertl, green, two long fuel filters, wide front end, 1960s
EX $52   **NM** $128   **MIP** $283

❑ **John Deere 3020**, 1:16-scale, Ertl, green, two short fuel filters, wide front end, 1960s, No. 547
EX $42   **NM** $152   **MIP** $263

❑ **John Deere 3020**, 1:16-scale, Ertl, green, two long fuel filters, wide plastic wheels, 1960s, No. 530
EX $36   **NM** $52   **MIP** $172

❑ **John Deere 3020**, 1:16-scale, Ertl, green, no muffler hole, fenders, or decals, 1960s
EX $36   **NM** $52   **MIP** $189

❑ **John Deere 3020**, 1:16-scale, Ertl, green, two long fuel filters, two trans. filters, two dash levers, narrow plastic wheels, 1960s
EX $36   **NM** $52   **MIP** $147

❑ **John Deere 3020**, 1:16-scale, Ertl, green, all wide plastic tires, 1960s
EX $33   **NM** $58   **MIP** $237

❑ **John Deere 3020**, 1:16-scale, Ertl, green, die-cast wide rear wheels, wide plastic front wheels, 1960s
EX $84   **NM** $156   **MIP** $384

❏ **John Deere 3020**, 1:16-scale, Ertl, green, die-cast wide rear wheels, narrow plastic front wheels, 1960s
EX $84   **NM** $156   **MIP** $384

❏ **John Deere 3020**, 1:16-scale, Ertl, green, die-cast wheels, short fillers, 1960s
EX $36   **NM** $98   **MIP** $319

❏ **John Deere 3020**, 1:16-scale, Ertl, green, three-point hitch, die-cast wheels, 1960s
EX $87   **NM** $163   **MIP** $389

❏ **John Deere 3020**, 1:16-scale, Ertl, green, two long fuel filters, narrow front, 1960s
EX $36   **NM** $52   **MIP** $172

❏ **John Deere 3020**, 1:16-scale, Ertl, green, all plastic wheels, 1960s
EX $34   **NM** $67   **MIP** $172

❏ **John Deere 3020**, 1:16-scale, Ertl, green, w/sub-frame in ROPS, two short fuel filters, two trans. filters, four dash levers, 1960s
EX $89   **NM** $206   **MIP** $476

❏ **John Deere 3020**, 1:16-scale, Ertl, green, WF, '94 Summer Toy Show Edition, 1994, No. 5059TA
EX $24   **NM** $36   **MIP** $68

❏ **John Deere 3020**, 1:16-scale, Ertl, green, NF, 2003, No. 15483
EX $11   **NM** $16   **MIP** $23

❏ **John Deere 3020**, 1:16-scale, Ertl, green, all plastic wheels, 1960s
EX $36   **NM** $96   **MIP** $243

❏ **John Deere 3020**, 1:16-scale, Ertl, green, two short fuel filters, two trans. filters, four dash levers, ROPS, 1960s
EX $89   **NM** $206   **MIP** $426

❏ **John Deere 320**, 1:16-scale, E-Tee's, green, Plow City Show Tractor 1989, 1980s
EX $23   **NM** $37   **MIP** $43

❏ **John Deere 3020**, 1:16-scale, Ertl, green, die-cast rear wheels, plastic front wheels, 1960s
EX $36   **NM** $97   **MIP** $246

❏ **John Deere 3020**, 1:16-scale, Ertl, green, two long fuel filters, two trans. filters and two dash levers, ROPS, 1960s
EX $89   **NM** $206   **MIP** $476

❏ **John Deere 320**, 1:16-scale, Trumm (Custom), green and yellow, 1980s
EX $19   **NM** $29   **MIP** $42

❏ **John Deere 330**, 1:16-scale, NB&K, green, "1989 Ozarks Show", 1980s
EX $88   **NM** $129   **MIP** $149

❏ **John Deere 330**, 1:16-scale, Trumm/DeBallie (Custom), green, '90 Plow City Toy Show 1990, 1990s
EX $19   **NM** $27   **MIP** $43

❏ **John Deere 40**, 1:16-scale, American Model Toys, green, did not come in box, 1980s
EX $26   **NM** $42   **MIP** n/a

❏ **John Deere 40**, 1:16-scale, American Sandcasting, green, did not come in box, 1980s
EX $24   **NM** $38   **MIP** n/a

❏ **John Deere 40**, 1:16-scale, Dave Nolt (Custom), green and yellow, 8th Annual Back East Farm Toy Show, 1990s
EX $189   **NM** $276   **MIP** $312

❏ **John Deere 40**, 1:16-scale, Ertl, green, 2004, No. 15600
EX $9   **NM** $14   **MIP** $28

❏ **John Deere 40**, 1:16-scale, Ertl, green, WF, fenders, 2004, No. 15600
EX $10   **NM** $17   **MIP** $25

❏ **John Deere 40**, 1:16-scale, Ertl, WF, 2005, No. 15600
EX $12   **NM** $18   **MIP** $24

❏ **John Deere 40/70**, 1:16-scale, Ertl, green, Collector Edition Set, 2003, No. 15469A
EX n/a   **NM** n/a   **MIP** $113

❏ **John Deere 4000**, 1:16-scale, Ertl, green, #5 Precision Series, 1994, No. 5684
EX $131   **NM** $162   **MIP** $236

❏ **John Deere 4010**, 1:16-scale, Ertl, green, WF, 1990, No. 5716 (Photo by Ertl)
EX $23   **NM** $34   **MIP** $48

❏ **John Deere 4010**, 1:16-scale, Ertl, green, '93 National Farm Toy Show, 1993, No. 5716DA
EX $27   **NM** $42   **MIP** $63

❏ **John Deere 4010**, 1:16-scale, Ertl, green, NF, 1997, No. 5716DP
(Photo by Ertl)
EX $22   **NM** $33   **MIP** $38

❏ **John Deere 4010**, 1:16-scale, Ertl, green, '97 Plow City Show Edition, 1997, No. 5506TA
EX $23   **NM** $38   **MIP** $58

❏ **John Deere 4010**, 1:16-scale, Ertl, green, '99 Iowa State Fair Edition, w/umbrella, 1999, No. 16028A
EX $53   **NM** $77   **MIP** $98

❏ **John Deere 4010**, 1:16-scale, Ertl, green, w/cab, 40th Anniversary, 2000, No. 15111A
EX $23   **NM** $38   **MIP** $58

❏ **John Deere 4010**, 1:16-scale, Ertl, green, high crop, '03 National Farm Toy Museum, 2003, No. 16109A
EX $27   **NM** $36   **MIP** $53

❏ **John Deere 4010**, 1:16-scale, Ertl, green, diesel, high crop, 2004, No. 15602
EX $10   **NM** $17   **MIP** $25

❏ **John Deere 4010**, 1:16-scale, Ertl, high crop, 2005, No. 15602
EX $12   **NM** $18   **MIP** $24

❏ **John Deere 4010**, 1:16-scale, Ertl, duals, 2006, No. 15856
EX $12   **NM** $18   **MIP** $24

❏ **John Deere 4020**, 1:16-scale, C & M Farm Toys, green, narrow front end, 1990s
EX $147   **NM** $193   **MIP** $243

❏ **John Deere 4020**, 1:16-scale, C & M Farm Toys, green, wide front end w/cab, 1990s
EX $163   **NM** $202   **MIP** $253

❏ **John Deere 4020**, 1:16-scale, C & M Farm Toys, green, narrow front end w/ROPS, 1990s
EX $147   **NM** $193   **MIP** $243

❏ **John Deere 4020**, 1:16-scale, C & M Farm Toys, green, wide front end, 1990s
EX $147   **NM** $193   **MIP** $243

❏ **John Deere 4020**, 1:16-scale, C & M Farm Toys, green, wide front end w/ROPS, 1990s
EX $163   **NM** $202   **MIP** $256

❏ **John Deere 4020**, 1:16-scale, Ertl, green, FFA Edition, Precision Series, 1992, No. 4992RO
EX $254   **NM** $333   **MIP** $489

❏ **John Deere 4020**, 1:16-scale, Ertl, green, NF, #3 Precision Series, 1992, No. 5638
EX $131   **NM** $162   **MIP** $213

❏ **John Deere 4020**, 1:16-scale, Ertl, green, WF, power shift, #4 Precision Series, 1993, No. 5549
EX $267   **NM** $361   **MIP** $562

❏ **John Deere 4020**, 1:16-scale, Ertl, green, w/237 corn picker, #14 Precision Series, 1999, No. 5083
EX $131   **NM** $162   **MIP** $178

❏ **John Deere 4020**, 1:16-scale, Ertl, green, ROPS, 2003, No. 15480
EX $21   **NM** $33   **MIP** $42

❏ **John Deere 4020**, 1:16-scale, Ertl, Collectors Edition, w/DVD, 2007, No. 15871A
EX $20   **NM** $40   **MIP** $60

❏ **John Deere 4020**, 1:16-scale, Scale Models, green, 1980s
EX $12   **NM** $21   **MIP** $28

❏ **John Deere 4020**, 1:16-scale, Scale Models, green, row crop tractor, "1988 World Ag Expo", 1980s
EX $12   **NM** $21   **MIP** $28

❏ **John Deere 4020**, 1:16-scale, Scale Models, green, row crop tractor, 3rd Summer Toy Festival Show Tractor, 1980s
EX $12   **NM** $21   **MIP** $28

❏ **John Deere 4040**, 1:16-scale, Ertl, green, 2WD, cab, 1999, No. 5133
EX $14   **NM** $23   **MIP** $32

❏ **John Deere 4040**, 1:16-scale, Ertl, green, duals, '01 Toy Tractor Times Anniversary, #16; 2,500 produced, 2001, No. 29174P
EX $26   **NM** $32   **MIP** $58

❏ **John Deere 4040**, 1:16-scale, Ertl, green, no cab, duals, 2003, No. 15478
EX $21   **NM** $33   **MIP** $42

❏ **John Deere 420**, 1:16-scale, Ertl, green, high crop, '03 Two Cylinder Club Edition, 2003, No. 16101A
EX $28   **NM** $53   **MIP** $88

❏ **John Deere 420**, 1:16-scale, Ertl, green, NF, 2004, No. 15481

❏ **John Deere 420**, 1:16-scale, Ertl, WF, 2007, No. 15964
EX $12   **NM** $19   **MIP** $24

❏ **John Deere 4230**, 1:16-scale, Ertl, green, '98 National Farm Toy Show, 1998, No. 5130PA
EX $42   **NM** $62   **MIP** $92

❏ **John Deere 4230**, 1:16-scale, Ertl, green, Collector Edition, 1999, No. 5132DA
EX $18 **NM** $28 **MIP** $42

❏ **John Deere 4230**, 1:16-scale, Ertl, green, 2001, No. 15202
EX $21 **NM** $33 **MIP** $42

❏ **John Deere 4250**, 1:16-scale, Ertl, green, National Farm Toy Show Tractor 1982, 1982, No. 5507AA
EX $238 **NM** $422 **MIP** $563

❏ **John Deere 4255**, 1:16-scale, Ertl, another image of the 4255, 1980s, No. 5583
EX $23 **NM** $44 **MIP** $66

❏ **John Deere 4255**, 1:16-scale, Ertl, green, 1980s, No. 5583
EX $23 **NM** $44 **MIP** $66

❏ **John Deere 430**, 1:16-scale, Ertl, green, w/o three-point hitch and w/new style rear wheels, 1950s
EX $488 **NM** $872 **MIP** $2277

❏ **John Deere 430**, 1:16-scale, Ertl, green, w/o decals, 1950s
EX npf **NM** npf **MIP** npf

❏ **John Deere 430**, 1:16-scale, Ertl, green, w/three-point hitch and old style rear rims, 1950s
EX $473 **NM** $748 **MIP** $1932

❏ **John Deere 430**, 1:16-scale, Ertl, blue, prototype—did not come in box, 1960s
EX $438 **NM** $862 **MIP** n/a

❏ **John Deere 430**, 1:16-scale, Nygren (Custom), green, did not come in box, 1980s
EX $132 **NM** $282 **MIP** n/a

❏ **John Deere 435**, 1:16-scale, Argentina (Sigomac), green, 1950s
EX $433 **NM** $682 **MIP** $1189

❏ **John Deere 435**, 1:16-scale, Engles, green, 1989 Lebanon, PA show, limited to 1500 untis, 1980s
EX $148 **NM** $183 **MIP** $237

❏ **John Deere 4430**, 1:16-scale, Argentina, green, plastic axle cap, three-point hitch, 1970s
EX $53 **NM** $74 **MIP** $86

❏ **John Deere 4430**, 1:16-scale, Argentina, green, three-point hitch, 1970s
EX $53 **NM** $74 **MIP** $86

❑ **John Deere 4430**, 1:16-scale, Ertl, green, pre-production sample, 1970s
EX $126   **NM** $289   **MIP** npf

❑ **John Deere 4430**, 1:16-scale, Ertl, green, 1970s, No. 512
EX $28   **NM** $56   **MIP** $88

❑ **John Deere 4430**, 1:16-scale, Ertl, green, small John Deere decal, International Harvester spindles, 1970s, No. 512
EX $28   **NM** $56   **MIP** $88

❑ **John Deere 4430**, 1:16-scale, Ertl, green, no filler caps on hood, 1970s, No. 512
EX $28   **NM** $52   **MIP** $79

❑ **John Deere 4430**, 1:16-scale, Ertl, green, inside of front wheels are all black, 1970s, No. 512
EX $28   **NM** $56   **MIP** $88

❑ **John Deere 4440**, 1:16-scale, Ertl, green, 1970s, No. 512
EX $24   **NM** $42   **MIP** $67

❑ **John Deere 4440**, 1:16-scale, Ertl, green, International Harvester front spindles, 1970s, No. 512
EX $24   **NM** $42   **MIP** $67

❑ **John Deere 4440**, 1:16-scale, Ertl, green, 5020-style front tires, duals, 1980s, No. 542
EX $28   **NM** $48   **MIP** $78

❑ **John Deere 4440**, 1:16-scale, Ertl, green, plastic, radio controlled, 1980s, No. 31
EX $16   **NM** $33   **MIP** $42

❑ **John Deere 4440**, 1:16-scale, Ertl, green, front weights, radio controlled, 1980s, No. 31
EX $16   **NM** $33   **MIP** $42

❑ **John Deere 4440**, 1:16-scale, Ertl, green, '95 Iowa State Fair, 1995, No. 5820TA
EX $56   **NM** $74   **MIP** $113

❑ **John Deere 4440**, 1:16-scale, Ertl, green, #17 Precision Series, 2000, No. 15077
EX $67   **NM** $88   **MIP** $148

❑ **John Deere 4440**, 1:16-scale, Pace Setter, green, glass decanter w/Pacesetter decal, 1980s
EX $22   **NM** $37   **MIP** $48

❏ **John Deere 4440**, 1:16-scale, Pace Setter, green, glass decanter w/Pacesetter decal, 1980s
EX $22   **NM** $37   **MIP** $48

❏ **John Deere 4440**, 1:16-scale, Pace Setter, green, glass decanter w/John Deere decal, 1980s
EX $26   **NM** $39   **MIP** $52

❏ **John Deere 4450**, 1:16-scale, Ertl, green, brown interior, black window frames, engine casting changed, 1980s, No. 541
EX $16   **NM** $22   **MIP** $27

❏ **John Deere 4450**, 1:16-scale, Ertl, green, yellow seat, 1980s, No. 5506
EX $21   **NM** $37   **MIP** $52

❏ **John Deere 4450**, 1:16-scale, Ertl, green, brown seat, 1980s, No. 5507
EX $24   **NM** $43   **MIP** $67

❏ **John Deere 4450**, 1:16-scale, Ertl, green, brown seat, 1980s, No. 5506
EX $21   **NM** $37   **MIP** $52

❏ **John Deere 4450**, 1:16-scale, Ertl, green, no holes for cab mounting in fenders, 1980s
EX $33   **NM** $74   **MIP** npf

❏ **John Deere 4450**, 1:16-scale, Ertl, green, yellow seat, duals, 1980s, No. 5507
EX $24   **NM** $43   **MIP** $67

❏ **John Deere 4450**, 1:16-scale, Ertl, green, 1980s, No. 541 *(Photo by Ertl)*
EX $16   **NM** $22   **MIP** $27

❏ **John Deere 4450**, 1:16-scale, Ertl, green, die-cast rims to commemorate Syracuse branch, 1980s, No. 541TA
EX $43   **NM** $64   **MIP** $98

❏ **John Deere 4450**, 1:16-scale, Ertl, green, Replica 15th Anniversary, 1996, No. 2544PA
EX $24   **NM** $32   **MIP** $48

❏ **John Deere 4450**, 1:16-scale, Ertl, green, 2000, No. 15160
EX $8   **NM** $13   **MIP** $18

❏ **John Deere 4455**, 1:16-scale, Ertl, green, MFD, 1980s, No. 5584
EX $24   **NM** $46   **MIP** $68

❏ **John Deere 4455**, 1:16-scale, Ertl, green, 1980s, No. 5584
EX $24   **NM** $46   **MIP** $68

❏ **John Deere 4520**, 1:16-scale, Ertl, green, '02 National Farm Toy Show, 2001, No. 16087A
EX $32   **NM** $62   **MIP** $106

❏ **John Deere 4620**, 1:16-scale, Ertl, cab, Collectors Edition, 2002, No. 15283A
EX $22   **NM** $32   **MIP** $42

❏ **John Deere 4620**, 1:16-scale, Ertl, green, ROPS, 2002, No. 15283
EX $23   **NM** $31   **MIP** $42

❏ **John Deere 4620**, 1:16-scale, Ertl, green, '03 Iowa State Fair, 1 of 3500, 2003, No. 16099A
EX $56   **NM** $73   **MIP** $98

❏ **John Deere 4630**, 1:16-scale, Ertl, '06 Plow City Show Edition, 2006, No. 16148A
EX $28   **NM** $43   **MIP** $69

❏ **John Deere 4640**, 1:16-scale, Ertl, Dealers Edition, 2006, No. 15823
EX $25   **NM** $45   **MIP** $60

❏ **John Deere 4640**, 1:16-scale, Ertl, Collector Edition, 2006, No. 15822A
EX $25   **NM** $40   **MIP** $55

❏ **John Deere 4760**, 1:16-scale, Ertl, green, MFD, 2002, No. 15349
EX $22   **NM** $37   **MIP** $48

❏ **John Deere 4850**, 1:16-scale, Ertl, green, pre-production run, did not come in box, 1980s
EX $49   **NM** $97   **MIP** n/a

❏ **John Deere 4850**, 1:16-scale, Ertl, green, Collector Edition, 1980s, No. 584DA
EX $32   **NM** $68   **MIP** $114

❏ **John Deere 4850**, 1:16-scale, Ertl, green, Collector Edition, 1980s, No. 584DA
EX $32   **NM** $68   **MIP** $114

❏ **John Deere 4850**, 1:16-scale, Ertl, green, large diameter front drive shaft, 1980s, No. 584
EX $22   **NM** $42   **MIP** $57

❏ **John Deere 4850**, 1:16-scale, Ertl, black, pre-production run, did not come in box, 1980s
EX $49   **NM** $97   **MIP** n/a

❏ **John Deere 4955**, 1:16-scale, Ertl, green, 1980s, No. 5587
EX $26   **NM** $47   **MIP** $88

❏ **John Deere 4960**, 1:16-scale, Ertl, duals, MFD, 1992, No. 5709 *(Photo by Ertl)*
EX $33   **NM** $47   **MIP** $88

❏ **John Deere 50**, 1:16-scale, Ertl, WF, 2007, No. 15890
EX $7   **NM** $14   **MIP** $24

❏ **John Deere 50**, 1:16-scale, Standi (Custom), green, 1980s
EX $24   **NM** $49   **MIP** $66

❏ **John Deere 50**, 1:16-scale, Standi (Custom), green, 1980s
EX $24   **NM** $49   **MIP** $66

❏ **John Deere 50/60**, 1:16-scale, Ertl, green, Collector Edition Set, 2003, No. 15344A
EX n/a   **NM** n/a   **MIP** $133

❏ **John Deere 5010**, 1:16-scale, Ertl, Precision Classics #25, WF, last release in PC series, 2004, No. 15608
EX $45   **NM** $90   **MIP** $130

❏ **John Deere 5020**, 1:16-scale, Ertl, green, no hole for air cleaner, 1960s, No. 555
EX $33   **NM** $57   **MIP** $87

❏ **John Deere 5020**, 1:16-scale, Ertl, green, two-piece air cleaner, angle brace in front axle, 1960s, No. 555
EX $47   **NM** $78   **MIP** $142

❏ **John Deere 5020**, 1:16-scale, Ertl, green, one-piece air cleaner, no brace in front axle, 1960s, No. 555
EX $52   **NM** $98   **MIP** $226

❏ **John Deere 5020**, 1:16-scale, Ertl, green, two-piece air cleaner, no brace in front axle, 1960s, No. 555
EX $47   **NM** $78   **MIP** $142

❏ **John Deere 5020**, 1:16-scale, Ertl, green, no air cleaner, angle brace in front axle w/rib support, 1970s, No. 555
EX $33   **NM** $57   **MIP** $87

❏ **John Deere 5020**, 1:16-scale, Ertl, green, no air cleaner, angle brace in front axle, has long decal, 1970s, No. 555
EX $33   **NM** $57   **MIP** $87

❏ **John Deere 5020**, 1:16-scale, Ertl, green, no air cleaner, angle brace in front axle, 1970s, No. 555
EX $38   **NM** $67   **MIP** $93

❏ **John Deere 5020**, 1:16-scale, Ertl, green, 150th Anniversary, Canadian Farm Show, 1980s, No. 555DA
EX $102   **NM** $163   **MIP** $237

❏ **John Deere 5020**, 1:16-scale, Ertl, green, no air cleaner, closed angle brace in front axle, 1984 models have shift lever on again, 1980s, No. 555
EX $33   **NM** $52   **MIP** $72

❏ **John Deere 5020**, 1:16-scale, Ertl, green, new frame detail, 1980s, No. 555
EX $38   **NM** $67   **MIP** $86

❏ **John Deere 5020**, 1:16-scale, Ertl, green, duals, '91 National Farm Toy Museum, 1991, No. 555PA
EX $59   **NM** $92   **MIP** $162

❏ **John Deere 5020**, 1:16-scale, Ertl, Precision Series, 40th Anniversary, 2006, No. 15881
EX $55   **NM** $85   **MIP** $120

❏ **John Deere 520**, 1:16-scale, Ertl, green, WF, 2002, No. 15360
EX $8   **NM** $16   **MIP** $23

❏ **John Deere 520**, 1:16-scale, Ertl, green, high crop, single front wheel, '02 Two Cylinder Club Edition, 2002, No. 16089A
EX $48   **NM** $67   **MIP** $98

❏ **John Deere 520**, 1:16-scale, Ertl, green, NF, 2004, No. 15599
EX $10   **NM** $17   **MIP** $25

❏ **John Deere 520**, 1:16-scale, Ertl, NF, 2005, No. 15599
EX $12   **NM** $18   **MIP** $24

❑ **John Deere 520**, 1:16-scale, Standi (Custom), green, 1980s
EX $32   **NM** $49   **MIP** $66

❑ **John Deere 520**, 1:16-scale, Standi (Custom), green, 1980s
EX $32   **NM** $49   **MIP** $66

❑ **John Deere 5200**, 1:16-scale, Ertl, MFD, Collectors Edition, 1995, No. 5845DA *(Photo by Ertl)*
EX $22   **NM** $37   **MIP** $47

❑ **John Deere 530**, 1:16-scale, Standi (Custom), chrome, 1980s
EX $32   **NM** $49   **MIP** $86

❑ **John Deere 530**, 1:16-scale, Standi (Custom), green, 1980s
EX $24   **NM** $49   **MIP** $66

❑ **John Deere 530**, 1:16-scale, Standi (Custom), green, 1980s
EX $24   **NM** $49   **MIP** $66

❑ **John Deere 530**, 1:16-scale, Trumm, green, '87 Plow City Show Edition, 1987
EX $16   **NM** $28   **MIP** $38

❑ **John Deere 5400**, 1:16-scale, Ertl, green, 1995, No. 5846 *(Photo by Ertl)*
EX $13   **NM** $28   **MIP** $36

❑ **John Deere 5400**, 1:16-scale, Ertl, green, revised, 1997, No. 5846DP
EX $13   **NM** $28   **MIP** $36

❑ **John Deere 5420**, 1:16-scale, Ertl, green, cab, w/loader, 2002, No. 15357
EX $18   **NM** $23   **MIP** $36

❑ **John Deere 60**, 1:16-scale, Ertl, green, light on rear of seat, 1950s
EX $121   **NM** $249   **MIP** $683

❑ **John Deere 60**, 1:16-scale, Ertl, green, LP, orchard versioin, Collector Edition, 1993, No. 5679DA
EX $24   **NM** $36   **MIP** $68

❑ **John Deere 60**, 1:16-scale, Ertl, green, NF, 2001, No. 15189
EX $6   **NM** $11   **MIP** $18

❑ **John Deere 60**, 1:16-scale, Ertl, green, standard, '01 Two Cylinder Club Edition, 2001, No. 16071
EX $43   **NM** $62   **MIP** $98

❑ **John Deere 60 w/227 Picker**, 1:16-scale, Ertl, picker is attached, 2006, No. 15816
EX $24   **NM** $36   **MIP** $42

❑ **John Deere 6030**, 1:16-scale, Ertl, WF, duals, 2007, No. 15907
EX $12   **NM** $24   **MIP** $33

❑ **John Deere 62**, 1:16-scale, SpecCast, green, 2002, No. JDM172
EX $16   **NM** $23   **MIP** $33

❑ **John Deere 620**, 1:16-scale, Ertl, green, three-point hitch, no light on seat, 1950s
EX $183   **NM** $367   **MIP** $1092

❑ **John Deere 620**, 1:16-scale, Ertl, green, light on rear of seat, 1950s
EX $132   **NM** $293   **MIP** $853

❑ **John Deere 620**, 1:16-scale, Ertl, green, orchard version, '92 Two Cylinder Club Edition, 1992, No. 5678DA
EX $26   **NM** $39   **MIP** $62

❏ **John Deere 620**, 1:16-scale, Ertl, green, high crop, Collector Edition, 2001, No. 15188A
EX $22   **NM** $31   **MIP** $48

❏ **John Deere 620**, 1:16-scale, Ertl, green, WF, 2002, No. 15428
EX $8   **NM** $13   **MIP** $26

❏ **John Deere 620**, 1:16-scale, Ertl, green, standard, '02 Summer Toy Show Edition, 2002, No. 16091A
EX $22   **NM** $33   **MIP** $62

❏ **John Deere 620**, 1:16-scale, Ertl, green, w/umbrella, '03 Iowa FFA Edition, 2003, No. 16107A
EX $24   **NM** $32   **MIP** $49

❏ **John Deere 620 LP High Crop**, 1:16-scale, Ertl, Precision #5, 2007, No. 15904
EX $65   **NM** $90   **MIP** $120

❏ **John Deere 6200**, 1:16-scale, Ertl, green, MFD, 1994, No. 5667

(Photo by Ertl)
EX $13   **NM** $18   **MIP** $27

❏ **John Deere 6200**, 1:16-scale, Ertl, green, 2WD, 1994, No. 5666
EX $13   **NM** $18   **MIP** $27

❏ **John Deere 630**, 1:16-scale, Ertl, green, LP, Collectors Edition, 1980s, No. 5590DA
EX $22   **NM** $28   **MIP** $32

❏ **John Deere 630**, 1:16-scale, Ertl, green, LP, 1980s, No. 5590
EX $16   **NM** $22   **MIP** $28

❏ **John Deere 630**, 1:16-scale, Ertl, green, LP, 1988 National Show Edition, 1988, No. 5590PA
EX $22   **NM** $37   **MIP** $48

❏ **John Deere 630**, 1:16-scale, Ertl, green, high crop, John Deere, Collector Edition, Precision Series #1, 2002, No. 15427A
EX $298   **NM** $422   **MIP** $633

❏ **John Deere 630**, 1:16-scale, Ertl, green, #21 in Precision Series, 2002, No. 15364
EX $63   **NM** $82   **MIP** $118

❏ **John Deere 630**, 1:16-scale, Ertl, Precision Classics #21, NF, 2004, No. 15364
EX $45   **NM** $90   **MIP** $130

❏ **John Deere 6320**, 1:16-scale, Ertl, green, '02 Farm Show Edition, 2002, No. 15346A
EX $28   **NM** $42   **MIP** $67

❏ **John Deere 6400**, 1:16-scale, Bruder, MFD, w/loader, 1990s, No. 00301
EX $18   **NM** $22   **MIP** $27

❏ **John Deere 6400**, 1:16-scale, Bruder, green, MFD, 1990s, No. 00300
EX $17   **NM** $21   **MIP** $24

❏ **John Deere 6400**, 1:16-scale, Ertl, green, MFD, ROPS, Collector Edition, 1993, No. 5667DA
EX $18   **NM** $27   **MIP** $38

❏ **John Deere 6400**, 1:16-scale, Ertl, green, 2WD, ROPS, Collector Edition, 1993, No. 5666DA
EX $18   **NM** $27   **MIP** $38

❏ **John Deere 6400**, 1:16-scale, Ertl, green, w/Loader, 1996, No. 5916 *(Photo by Ertl)*
EX $17   **NM** $28   **MIP** $37

❏ **John Deere 6410**, 1:16-scale, Ertl, green, w/loader, 1999, No. 5069
EX $18   **NM** $27   **MIP** $38

❏ **John Deere 6420**, 1:16-scale, Ertl, green, w/loader, 2002, No. 15208
EX $18   **NM** $27   **MIP** $38

❏ **John Deere 6430**, 1:16-scale, Ertl, Dealer Edition, 2007, No. 15951
EX $20   **NM** $40   **MIP** $65

❏ **John Deere 6920**, 1:16-scale, Bruder, green, MFD, duals, 2002, No. 02054
EX $23   **NM** $32   **MIP** $36

❏ **John Deere 6920**, 1:16-scale, Bruder, green, MFD, 2002, No. 02050
EX $21   **NM** $26   **MIP** $32

❏ **John Deere 6920**, 1:16-scale, Bruder, green, MFD, duals, w/loader, 2002, No. 02053
EX $24   **NM** $34   **MIP** $41

❏ **John Deere 6920**, 1:16-scale, Bruder, green, MFD, w/loader, 2002, No. 02052
EX $23   **NM** $32   **MIP** $36

❏ **John Deere 70**, 1:16-scale, Ertl, green, high crop, Collector Edition, 1991, No. 5611DA
EX $23   **NM** $32   **MIP** $47

❏ **John Deere 70**, 1:16-scale, Ertl, green, NF, 1991, No. 5611 *(Photo by Ertl)*
EX $13   **NM** $23   **MIP** $33

❏ **John Deere 70**, 1:16-scale, Ertl, green, #7 Precision Series, 1995, No. 5788 *(Photo by Ertl)*
EX $73   NM $121   MIP $173

❏ **John Deere 70**, 1:16-scale, Ertl, green, w/umbrella, '96 National Farm Toy Museum, 1995, No. 1219PA
EX $22   NM $33   MIP $53

❏ **John Deere 70**, 1:16-scale, Ertl, green, w/umbrella, '98 Iowa FFA Edition, 1998, No. 16002A
EX $23   NM $32   MIP $47

❏ **John Deere 70**, 1:16-scale, Ertl, green, high crop, '00 National Farm Toy Museum, 2000, No. 16048A
EX $26   NM $36   MIP $57

❏ **John Deere 70**, 1:16-scale, Ertl, green, standard, #23 in Precision Series, 2003, No. 15366
EX $67   NM $82   MIP $116

❏ **John Deere 70 Set**, 1:16-scale, Ertl, green, w/Wagon set, 1997, No. 5166 *(Photo by Kate Bossen)*
EX $14   NM $22   MIP $29

❏ **John Deere 70 Standard Tractor**, 1:16-scale, Ertl, Precision Classics #23, WF, first JD Precision Standard Tractor, 2004, No. 15366
EX $45   NM $90   MIP $125

❏ **John Deere 720**, 1:16-scale, Ertl, green, High Crop, wide front end, "Two Cylinder Club Expo. II 1990", 1990s, No. 5610TA
EX $32   NM $47   MIP $68

❏ **John Deere 720**, 1:16-scale, Ertl, green, High Crop, Collectors Edition, 1990s, No. 5610DA
EX $23   NM $34   MIP $56

❏ **John Deere 720**, 1:16-scale, Ertl, green, '94 Toy Tractor Times Edition, #9; 1,900 produced, 1994, No. 5844TA
EX $23   NM $32   MIP $48

❏ **John Deere 720**, 1:16-scale, Ertl, WF, Precision Classic #10, 1996, No. 5832 *(Photo by Ertl)*
EX $78   NM $109   MIP $183

❏ **John Deere 720**, 1:16-scale, Ertl, green, NF, 1997, No. 5007 *(Photo by Ertl)*
EX $9   NM $16   MIP $22

❏ **John Deere 720**, 1:16-scale, Ertl, green, w/#45 loader and #80 rear blade, #18 Precision Series, 2001, No. 15165
EX $66   NM $92   MIP $143

❏ **John Deere 720**, 1:16-scale, Ertl, green, w/rear blade, 2004, No. 15601
EX $11   NM $16   MIP $29

❏ **John Deere 720**, 1:16-scale, Yoder (Custom), green, 1980s
EX $33   NM $49   MIP $63

❏ **John Deere 720**, 1:16-scale, Yoder (Custom), green, 1980s
EX $33   NM $49   MIP $63

❏ **John Deere 720**, 1:16-scale, Yoder (Custom), green, 1990s
EX $33   NM $49   MIP $63

❏ **John Deere 720**, 1:16-scale, Yoder (Custom), green, diesel, 1990s
EX $33   NM $49   MIP $63

❑ **John Deere 720 w/Blade**, 1:16-scale, Ertl, 2005, No. 15601
EX $12   **NM** $18   **MIP** $24

❑ **John Deere 720 w/Blade set**, 1:16-scale, Ertl, green, single rear blade, 2004, No. 15601
EX $10   **NM** $17   **MIP** $25

❑ **John Deere 730**, 1:16-scale, Ertl, green, w/three-point hitch and smooth front tires, 1950s
EX $162   **NM** $389   **MIP** $872

❑ **John Deere 730**, 1:16-scale, Ertl, green, w/three-point hitch and ribbed front tires, 1950s
EX $162   **NM** $389   **MIP** $872

❑ **John Deere 730**, 1:16-scale, Ertl, green, w/o three-point hitch, w/o ribbed front tires, w/o hole for muffler, w/o power steering decal, 1950s
EX $162   **NM** $736   **MIP** $1352

❑ **John Deere 730**, 1:16-scale, Ertl, red, w/white International Harvester wheels, w/o three-point hitch or muffler hole, 1950s
EX $316   **NM** $748   **MIP** npf

❑ **John Deere 730**, 1:16-scale, Ertl, red, w/muffler, 1950s
EX $316   **NM** $748   **MIP** npf

❑ **John Deere 730**, 1:16-scale, Ertl, green, #13 in Precision Series, 1998, No. 5766
EX $82   **NM** $118   **MIP** $198

❑ **John Deere 730**, 1:16-scale, Ertl, Collector Edition, 2006, No. 15820A
EX $25   **NM** $40   **MIP** $55

❑ **John Deere 730**, 1:16-scale, Ertl, NF, Collectors Edition, 2007, No. 15820A
EX $8   **NM** $16   **MIP** $24

❑ **John Deere 730**, 1:16-scale, Sigomac, green, w/Firestone tires and three-point hitch, 1960s
EX $377   **NM** $686   **MIP** npf

❑ **John Deere 730**, 1:16-scale, Uruguay, green, 1950s
EX $377   **NM** $686   **MIP** npf

❑ **John Deere 730**, 1:16-scale, Yoder (Custom), green, 1980s
EX $33   **NM** $49   **MIP** $63

❑ **John Deere 730**, 1:16-scale, Yoder (Custom), green, 1980s
EX $33   **NM** $49   **MIP** $63

❑ **John Deere 730**, 1:16-scale, Yoder (Custom), red, 1980s
EX $98   **NM** $152   **MIP** $222

❑ **John Deere 730**, 1:16-scale, Yoder (Custom), red, 1980s
EX $98   **NM** $152   **MIP** $222

❑ **John Deere 7510**, 1:16-scale, Ertl, MFD, '01 Farm Show Edition, 2001
EX $38   **NM** $62   **MIP** $118

❏ **John Deere 7520**, 1:16-scale, Ertl, green, w/o air cleaner, 1970s
EX $314   **NM** $577   **MIP** $962

❏ **John Deere 7520**, 1:16-scale, Ertl, green, w/air cleaner, 1970s
EX $233   **NM** $336   **MIP** $563

❏ **John Deere 7520**, 1:16-scale, Ertl, MFD, Waterloo Works, 2004, No. 15584A
EX $27   **NM** $36   **MIP** $58

❏ **John Deere 7520**, 1:16-scale, Precision Engineering, green, Central Ohio Toy Show, 1980s
EX $324   **NM** $489   **MIP** $667

❏ **John Deere 7600**, 1:16-scale, Ertl, MFD, 1994, No. 5619 *(Photo by Ertl)*
EX $22   **NM** $37   **MIP** $43

❏ **John Deere 7600**, 1:16-scale, Ertl, 2WD, 1994, No. 5627
EX $22   **NM** $37   **MIP** $43

❏ **John Deere 7610**, 1:16-scale, Ertl, MFD, 2000, No. 15128
EX $23   **NM** $38   **MIP** $44

❏ **John Deere 7710**, 1:16-scale, Ertl, MFD, 1998, No. 5167 *(Photo by Kate Bossen)*
EX $22   **NM** $34   **MIP** $42

❏ **John Deere 7800**, 1:16-scale, Ertl, MFD, Waterloo works employee modular kit, 1992, No. 5718QA
EX $14   **NM** $33   **MIP** $58

❏ **John Deere 7800**, 1:16-scale, Ertl, MFD, Collector Edition, 1992, No. 5619DA
EX $32   **NM** $42   **MIP** $78

❏ **John Deere 7800**, 1:16-scale, Ertl, MFD, modular kit, 1992, No. 5719
EX $14   **NM** $23   **MIP** $28

❏ **John Deere 7800**, 1:16-scale, Ertl, MFD, demonstrator, 1992, No. 5739
EX $14   **NM** $23   **MIP** $28

❏ **John Deere 7800**, 1:16-scale, Ertl, MFD, Waterloo works modular kit, 1992, No. 5681QA
EX $21   **NM** $36   **MIP** $58

❏ **John Deere 7800**, 1:16-scale, Ertl, MFD, Mannheim modular kit, 1992, No. 5717QA
EX $21   **NM** $36   **MIP** $58

❏ **John Deere 7800**, 1:16-scale, Ertl, 2WD, Collector Edition, 1992, No. 5627CA
EX $29   **NM** $41   **MIP** $73

❏ **John Deere 7810**, 1:16-scale, Ertl, MFD, 1997, No. 5200
EX $23   **NM** $32   **MIP** $48

❏ **John Deere 7820**, 1:16-scale, Ertl, MFD, 2003, No. 15435
EX $23   **NM** $32   **MIP** $48

❏ **John Deere 7820**, 1:16-scale, Ertl, 2005, No. 15435
EX $12   **NM** $18   **MIP** $25

❏ **John Deere 7830**, 1:16-scale, Ertl, Dealer Edition, 2007, No. 15875
EX $25   **NM** $45   **MIP** $65

❏ **John Deere 7920**, 1:16-scale, Ertl, MFD, duals, Collector Edition, 2003, No. 15470A
EX $33   **NM** $48   **MIP** $72

❏ **John Deere 7920**, 1:16-scale, Ertl, MFD, duals, Waterloo Employee Edition, 2003, No. 15521A
EX $34   **NM** $67   **MIP** $123

❏ **John Deere 80**, 1:16-scale, Ertl, gold colored, 80th Anniversary of Columbus Branch, 1992, No. 5704YA
EX $72   **NM** $112   **MIP** $179

❏ **John Deere 80**, 1:16-scale, Ertl, green, 80th Anniversary of Columbus Branch, 1992, No. 5704PA
EX $27   **NM** $43   **MIP** $68

❏ **John Deere 80**, 1:16-scale, Ertl, WF, 2007, No. 15934
EX $20   **NM** $34   **MIP** $42

❏ **John Deere 80**, 1:16-scale, Stephan, green, 500 units made, 1993
EX $132   **NM** $189   **MIP** $266

❏ **John Deere 80**, 1:16-scale, Trumm (Custom), green, did not come in box, 1980s
EX $33   **NM** $68   **MIP** n/a

❏ **John Deere 80**, 1:16-scale, Trumm (Custom), green, did not come in box, 1980s
EX $33   **NM** $68   **MIP** n/a

❑ **John Deere 8010**, 1:16-scale,
E-Tee's, green, 1980s
EX $384 **NM** $434 **MIP** $673

❑ **John Deere 8020**, 1:16-scale,
Ertl, 4WD, #22 Precision Series,
2002, No. 15365
EX $88 **NM** $118 **MIP** $148

❑ **John Deere 8020**, 1:16-scale,
Ertl, Precision Classics #22, diesel,
4WD, 2004, No. 15365
EX $50 **NM** $100 **MIP** $150

❑ **John Deere 8020**, 1:16-scale,
E-Tee's, green, 1980s
EX $283 **NM** $434 **MIP** $593

❑ **John Deere 820**, 1:16-scale, Ertl,
green, 1993, No. 5705 *(Photo by Ertl)*
EX $27 **NM** $46 **MIP** $64

❑ **John Deere 820**, 1:16-scale,
Stephan Manufacturing, green,
limited to 500 units, 1991
EX $293 **NM** $422 **MIP** $682

❑ **John Deere 820**, 1:16-scale,
Trumm (Custom), green, did not
come in box, 1980s
EX $28 **NM** $62 **MIP** n/a

❑ **John Deere 820**, 1:16-scale,
Trumm (Custom), green, did not
come in box, 1980s
EX $28 **NM** $62 **MIP** n/a

❑ **John Deere 8200**, 1:16-scale,
Ertl, 1995, No. 5840 *(Photo by Ertl)*
EX $22 **NM** $33 **MIP** $42

❑ **John Deere 8200**, 1:16-scale,
Ertl, 2WD, revised graphics, 1996,
No. 5840CP
EX $22 **NM** $33 **MIP** $42

❑ **John Deere 8200**, 1:16-scale,
Ertl, radio control, 1997, No. 5196
EX $13 **NM** $28 **MIP** $42

❑ **John Deere 8210**, 1:16-scale,
Ertl, MFD, floatation tires, 2003,
No. 15476
EX $23 **NM** $34 **MIP** $48

❑ **John Deere 830**, 1:16-scale, Ertl,
green, Rice Special, '04 Two
Cylinder Club Edition, 2004,
No. 16075A
EX $38 **NM** $57 **MIP** $98

❑ **John Deere 830**, 1:16-scale,
Stephan Manufacturing, green and
yellow, limited to 500 units, 1990s
EX $302 **NM** $483 **MIP** $780

❑ **John Deere 830**, 1:16-scale,
Trumm (Custom), green, did not
come in box, 1980s
EX $28 **NM** $82 **MIP** n/a

❑ **John Deere 8300**, 1:16-scale,
Ertl, 1995, No. 5786 *(Photo by Ertl)*
EX $23 **NM** $34 **MIP** $48

❑ **John Deere 8300**, 1:16-scale,
Ertl, MFD, revised graphics, 1996,
No. 5786CP
EX $23 **NM** $34 **MIP** $48

❑ **John Deere 8300**, 1:16-scale,
Ertl, radio control, 1997, No. 5197
EX $13 **NM** $28 **MIP** $42

❑ **John Deere 8300T**, 1:16-scale,
Ertl, track tractor, 1999, No. 5182
EX $23 **NM** $34 **MIP** $48

❑ **John Deere 8310**, 1:16-scale, Ertl, MFD, '99 Farm Show Edition, 1999, No. 15117A
EX $79　　**NM** $109　　**MIP** $148

❑ **John Deere 8310T**, 1:16-scale, Ertl, track tractor, 2003, No. 15072
EX $21　　**NM** $32　　**MIP** $43

❑ **John Deere 8320**, 1:16-scale, Ertl, MFD, '03 Farm Show Edition, 2003, No. 15513A
EX $42　　**NM** $62　　**MIP** $92

❑ **John Deere 8400**, 1:16-scale, Ertl, duals, MFD, Collectors Edition, 1994, No. 5786DA *(Photo by Ertl)*
EX $34　　**NM** $52　　**MIP** $83

❑ **John Deere 8400T**, 1:16-scale, Ertl, track tractor, Collector Edition, 1998, No. 5181CA
EX $33　　**NM** $58　　**MIP** $87

❑ **John Deere 8400T**, 1:16-scale, Ertl, track tractor, Waterloo Employee Edition, 1998, No. 5176CA
EX $43　　**NM** $82　　**MIP** $178

❑ **John Deere 8410**, 1:16-scale, Ertl, MFD, duals, 1999, No. 15061
EX $23　　**NM** $34　　**MIP** $47

❑ **John Deere 8420**, 1:16-scale, Ertl, MFD, duals, 2002, No. 15200
EX $23　　**NM** $34　　**MIP** $56

❑ **John Deere 8420T**, 1:16-scale, Ertl, track tractor, 2002, No. 15207
EX $21　　**NM** $32　　**MIP** $43

❑ **John Deere 8430**, 1:16-scale, Ertl, MFD, 2006, No. 15787
EX $23　　**NM** $34　　**MIP** $63

❑ **John Deere 8430T**, 1:16-scale, Ertl, track tractor, 2006, No. 15130
EX $23　　**NM** $34　　**MIP** $63

❑ **John Deere 8520**, 1:16-scale, Ertl, MFD, floatation tires, European version, 2002, No. 15406
EX $23　　**NM** $34　　**MIP** $48

❑ **John Deere 8520**, 1:16-scale, Ertl, MFD, Waterloo Employee Edition, 2002, No. 15192
EX $43　　**NM** $82　　**MIP** $178

❑ **John Deere 8520**, 1:16-scale, Ertl, MFD, triples, Collector Edition, 2002, No. 15192A
EX $52　　**NM** $73　　**MIP** $128

❑ **John Deere 8560**, 1:16-scale, Ertl, green, 1980s, No. 5595
EX $42　　**NM** $68　　**MIP** $87

❑ **John Deere 8630**, 1:16-scale, Ertl, green, 1970s, No. 597
EX $64　　**NM** $122　　**MIP** $218

❑ **John Deere 8640**, 1:16-scale, Ertl, green, 1970s, No. 597
EX $64　　**NM** $104　　**MIP** $172

❑ **John Deere 8640**, 1:16-scale, Ertl, green, 40-series tractor w/50-series cab, 1980s, No. 597
EX $83　　**NM** $147　　**MIP** $214

❑ **John Deere 8650**, 1:16-scale, Ertl, green, 1980s, No. 5508
EX $42　　**NM** $73　　**MIP** $97

❑ **John Deere 8650**, 1:16-scale, Ertl, green, four-wheel drive w/old style cab, muffler on hood, 1980s, No. 5508
EX $44　　**NM** $89　　**MIP** $138

❑ **John Deere 8650**, 1:16-scale, Ertl, green, Collectors Edition, 1980s, No. 5508CA
EX $76　　**NM** $102　　**MIP** $178

❑ **John Deere 8650**, 1:16-scale, Gottman, 4WD, Kinze power conversion, 1991
EX $432　　**NM** $657　　**MIP** $992

❑ **John Deere 8760**, 1:16-scale, Ertl, green, Collectors Edition, cab glass, 1988, No. 5595BA
EX $42　　**NM** $67　　**MIP** $88

❑ **John Deere 8760**, 1:16-scale, Ertl, 4WD, 1992, No. 5715
EX $38 **NM** $59 **MIP** $78

❑ **John Deere 8870**, 1:16-scale, Ertl, 4WD w/duals, 1994, No. 5762

(Photo by Ertl)

EX $43 **NM** $57 **MIP** $77

❑ **John Deere 8870**, 1:16-scale, Ertl, 4WD, duals, 2004, No. 15598
EX $43 **NM** $57 **MIP** $78

❑ **John Deere 8870**, 1:16-scale, Ertl, 4WD, 2005, No. 15598
EX $15 **NM** $22 **MIP** $30

❑ **John Deere 8960**, 1:16-scale, Ertl, 4WD, Denver dealer edition, 1980s, No. 5595DA
EX $283 **NM** $389 **MIP** $594

❑ **John Deere 9200**, 1:16-scale, Ertl, 4WD, triples, wide tires, 1998, No. 15009
EX $63 **NM** $82 **MIP** $118

❑ **John Deere 9200**, 1:16-scale, Ertl, 4WD, triples, narrow tires, 1998, No. 15009
EX $63 **NM** $82 **MIP** $128

❑ **John Deere 9300**, 1:16-scale, Ertl, duals, 4WD w/duals, 1997, No. 5915 *(Photo by Ertl)*
EX $42 **NM** $63 **MIP** $88

❑ **John Deere 9300T**, 1:16-scale, Ertl, track tractor, 2000, No. 15007
EX $29 **NM** $32 **MIP** $53

❑ **John Deere 9300T**, 1:16-scale, Ertl, track tractor, '00 Farm Show Edition, 2000, No. 15112A
EX $38 **NM** $58 **MIP** $88

❑ **John Deere 9320**, 1:16-scale, Ertl, 4WD, duals, 2006, No. 15838
EX $33 **NM** $48 **MIP** $78

❑ **John Deere 9400**, 1:16-scale, Ertl, duals, 4WD, Collectors Edition, w/3 point hitch, 1997, No. 5914BA

(Photo by Ertl)

EX $63 **NM** $128 **MIP** $188

❑ **John Deere 9400T**, 1:16-scale, Ertl, track tractor, Waterloo Employee Edition, 2000, No. 15005N
EX $42 **NM** $63 **MIP** $88

❑ **John Deere 9400T**, 1:16-scale, Ertl, track tractor, Collector Edition, 2000, No. 15005A
EX $32 **NM** $53 **MIP** $63

❑ **John Deere 9420**, 1:16-scale, Ertl, 4WD, duals, 2001, No. 15205
EX $43 **NM** $67 **MIP** $83

❑ **John Deere 9420T**, 1:16-scale, Ertl, track tractor, 2004, No. 15206
EX $29 **NM** $32 **MIP** $53

❑ **John Deere 9520**, 1:16-scale, Ertl, 4WD, triples, 2003, No. 15479
EX $44 **NM** $68 **MIP** $88

❑ **John Deere 9520T**, 1:16-scale, Ertl, track, cab glass, die-cast front weights, 2006, No. 15839
EX $28 **NM** $38 **MIP** $68

❑ **John Deere 9620 Set**, 1:16-scale, Ertl, 4WD, w/1/64 gold 9620, Collector Edition, 2004, No. 15676A
EX $43 **NM** $67 **MIP** $83

❑ **John Deere A**, 1:16-scale, Arcade, green w/nickel plated driver, solid rubber tires, 1940s
EX $257 **NM** $762 **MIP** $3082

❑ **John Deere A**, 1:16-scale, Arcade, green, all aluminum wheels, man bolts on, separate stacks like the cast iron version, 1940s
EX $493 **NM** $1092 **MIP** $3382

❑ **John Deere A**, 1:16-scale, Ertl, green, "Ertl Toy" stamped on the side of gear shift case, 1940s
EX $62 **NM** $178 **MIP** $507

❑ **John Deere A**, 1:16-scale, Ertl, green, closed flywheel, smoothed side ribbed surface front tires, 1940s
EX $82 **NM** $198 **MIP** $677

❑ **John Deere A**, 1:16-scale, Ertl, green, closed flywheel, Arcade front tires, 1940s
EX $62　　**NM** $178　　**MIP** $507

❑ **John Deere A**, 1:16-scale, Ertl, green, rubber rear tires, Arcade front tires, open flywheel, headlights, 1940s
EX $162　　**NM** $348　　**MIP** $792

❑ **John Deere A**, 1:16-scale, Ertl, green, all aluminum wheels, no headlights, open fly wheel, 1940s
EX $493　　**NM** $1092　　**MIP** npf

❑ **John Deere A**, 1:16-scale, Ertl, brass, High Post, 1950s
EX $264　　**NM** $348　　**MIP** $889

❑ **John Deere A**, 1:16-scale, Ertl, red, High Post, 1950s
EX $226　　**NM** $656　　**MIP** n/a

❑ **John Deere A**, 1:16-scale, Ertl, green, High Post, 1950s
EX $114　　**NM** $268　　**MIP** $689

❑ **John Deere A**, 1:16-scale, Ertl, green, short stacks, 1980s, No. 539
EX $11　　**NM** $16　　**MIP** $19

❑ **John Deere A**, 1:16-scale, Ertl, green, long stacks, 50th Anniversary Edition, 1980s, No. 538DA
EX $22　　**NM** $36　　**MIP** $42

❑ **John Deere A**, 1:16-scale, Ertl, green, long stacks, 1980s, No. 539
EX $11　　**NM** $16　　**MIP** $19

❑ **John Deere A**, 1:16-scale, Ertl, green, Ertl 40th Anniversary Tractor, 1980s, No. 557DA
EX $23　　**NM** $42　　**MIP** $58

❑ **John Deere A**, 1:16-scale, Ertl, green, no collector engraving, front wheels steer, prototype; did not come in box, 1980s
EX $23　　**NM** $47　　**MIP** n/a

❑ **John Deere A**, 1:16-scale, Ertl, green, no collector engraving, unpainted stacks, prototype; did not come in box, 1980s
EX npf　　**NM** npf　　**MIP** npf

Photos by Jon Jacobson unless otherwise noted.

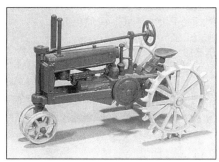

❏ **John Deere A**, 1:16-scale, Ertl, green, pre-production shelf model w/collector steel wheels, 1980s
EX $22   **NM** $48   **MIP** npf

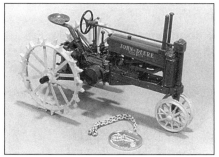

❏ **John Deere A**, 1:16-scale, Ertl, green and yellow, Precision Classics, The Ultimate Model A, 1990s, No. 560
EX $68   **NM** $93   **MIP** $173

❏ **John Deere A**, 1:16-scale, Ertl, w/cultivator, #2 Precision Series, 1991, No. 5633
EX $187   **NM** $267   **MIP** $453

❏ **John Deere A**, 1:16-scale, Ertl, gold plated, 125th Anniversary Kansas City Branch, 1995, No. 5046PA
EX $63   **NM** $108   **MIP** $188

❏ **John Deere A**, 1:16-scale, Ertl, Foxfire Farm, w/Red McCune, 1996, No. 5702
EX $18   **NM** $26   **MIP** $33

❏ **John Deere A**, 1:16-scale, Ertl, WWKI We Car Inc, 5000 unites, 1997, No. A047TO
EX $8   **NM** $18   **MIP** $27

❏ **John Deere A**, 1:16-scale, Ertl, hi-crop, '00 Two Cylinder Club Expo, 2000, No. 16038A
EX $32   **NM** $53   **MIP** $88

❏ **John Deere A**, 1:16-scale, Ertl, styled, NF, 2000, No. 15071
EX $8   **NM** $12   **MIP** $18

❏ **John Deere A**, 1:16-scale, Ertl, green, styled with man, 2003, No. 15571
EX $8   **NM** $16   **MIP** $23

❏ **John Deere A**, 1:16-scale, Ertl, gold plated, styled with man, 2003, No. 15569A
EX $26   **NM** $42   **MIP** $58

❏ **John Deere A**, 1:16-scale, Freiheit (Custom), green, did not come in box, 1980s
EX $219   **NM** $289   **MIP** n/a

❏ **John Deere A**, 1:16-scale, Lee/Hosch (Custom), green, solid rubber tires, no headlights, did not come in box, 1970s
EX $26   **NM** $89   **MIP** n/a

❏ **John Deere A**, 1:16-scale, Lincoln, green, 1950s
EX $146   **NM** $357   **MIP** $732

❏ **John Deere A**, 1:16-scale, Luck and Friesen (Custom), green, chrome man and steering post, available w/rubber tires, no box, 1970s
EX $18   **NM** $43   **MIP** n/a

❏ **John Deere A**, 1:16-scale, Parker (Custom), green, did not come in box, 1970s
EX $102   **NM** $147   **MIP** n/a

❏ **John Deere A**, 1:16-scale, Riecke (Custom), green, rubber tires, did not come in box, 1990s
EX $289   **NM** $353   **MIP** n/a

❏ **John Deere A**, 1:16-scale, Scale Models, green, all aluminum wheels, Anniversary Edition, 1980s
EX $26   **NM** $37   **MIP** $49

❏ **John Deere A**, 1:16-scale, Scale Models, green, steel wheels, No. 7 in Collector Series, 1980s
EX $21   **NM** $37   **MIP** $48

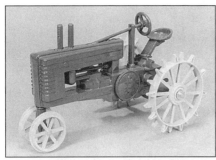

❑ **John Deere A**, 1:16-scale, Scale Models, green, No. 7 in Collector Series I, limited to 3000 units, 1980s
EX $34   **NM** $48   **MIP** $57

❑ **John Deere A**, 1:16-scale, Scale Models, green, Dyersville Show Tractor, 1980s
EX $22   **NM** $37   **MIP** $57

❑ **John Deere A**, 1:16-scale, Scale Models, slanted dash, Beckman High School Edition, 1989
EX $22   **NM** $37   **MIP** $58

❑ **John Deere A**, 1:16-scale, Scale Models, green, w/fenders "1890-1990 Wyoming Centennial-Lasting Legacy", 1990s
EX $23   **NM** $42   **MIP** $54

❑ **John Deere A**, 1:16-scale, Scale Models, on steel w/fenders, '92 World Ag Expo, 1992, No. FB-1594
EX $21   **NM** $37   **MIP** $48

❑ **John Deere A**, 1:16-scale, Scale Models, w/farmhand hay loader, 1995
EX $123   **NM** $167   **MIP** $233

❑ **John Deere A**, 1:16-scale, SpecCast, amoured tractor, replica of WWII tractor, 2002, No. CUST746
(Photo by Bossen Implement)
EX $78   **NM** $126   **MIP** $178

❑ **John Deere A**, 1:16-scale, SpecCast, on base "Best of Show", 2002, No. JDM167
EX $18   **NM** $32   **MIP** $47

❑ **John Deere A Set**, 1:16-scale, Ertl, green and yellow, Tractors of the Past set, 1980s, No. 5632
EX $22   **NM** $32   **MIP** $47

❑ **John Deere A, Unstyled**, 1:16-scale, Ertl, NF, 2007, No. 15869
EX $7   **NM** $14   **MIP** $21

❑ **John Deere AO**, 1:16-scale, Stephan, orchard, 1995
EX $133   **NM** $189   **MIP** $267

❑ **John Deere AR**, 1:16-scale, Dingman (Custom), green, did not come in box, 1980s
EX $189   **NM** $253   **MIP** n/a

❑ **John Deere AR**, 1:16-scale, Ertl, 1993, No. 5680
EX $18   **NM** $27   **MIP** $48

❑ **John Deere AR**, 1:16-scale, Ertl, Foxfire Farm, w/Elery, 1998, No. 5093
EX $19   **NM** $26   **MIP** $37

❑ **John Deere AR**, 1:16-scale, Scale Models, '94 Farm Progress Show Edition, 1994, No. FB-2353
EX $17   **NM** $24   **MIP** $46

❑ **John Deere AR**, 1:16-scale, Stephan, 1994
EX $133   **NM** $189   **MIP** $267

❑ **John Deere AW**, 1:16-scale, Ertl, w/umbrella, Collector Edition, 2000, No. 15070A
EX $17   **NM** $26   **MIP** $37

❑ **John Deere B**, 1:16-scale, Ertl
EX $22   **NM** $28   **MIP** $42

❑ **John Deere B**, 1:16-scale, Ertl, green, eight-bolt, 1996, No. 5904
(Photo by Ertl)
EX $16   **NM** $26   **MIP** $43

❑ **John Deere B**, 1:16-scale, Ertl, green, four bolt, Collector Edition, 1996, No. 5822DA
EX $26   **NM** $37   **MIP** $58

❑ **John Deere B**, 1:16-scale, Ertl, w/umbrella, '97 Iowa FFA Edition, 1997, No. 4833TA
EX $28   **NM** $43   **MIP** $57

❑ **John Deere B**, 1:16-scale, Ertl, sytled, #12 Precision Series, 1997, No. 5107
EX $123   **NM** $167   **MIP** $233

❑ **John Deere B**, 1:16-scale, Ertl, Foxfire Farm, w/corn loaded flare box wagon, 1997, No. 5341
EX $24   **NM** $32   **MIP** $48

❑ **John Deere B**, 1:16-scale, Ertl, unstyled, #24 Precision Series, 2003, No. 15487
EX $62   **NM** $89   **MIP** $113

❑ **John Deere B**, 1:16-scale, NB & K, green, Florida Show Tractor, 1980s
EX $43   **NM** $78   **MIP** $112

❑ **John Deere B**, 1:16-scale, Riecke (Custom), green, did not come in box, 1980s
EX $247   **NM** $322   **MIP** n/a

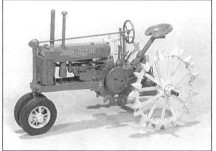

❑ **John Deere B**, 1:16-scale, Riecke (Custom), green, did not come in box, 1980s
EX $247   **NM** $322   **MIP** n/a

❑ **John Deere B**, 1:16-scale, Scale Models, 1994 Farm Progress Show Edition, 1994, No. FB-2352

(Photo by Kate Bossen)

EX $55   **NM** $92   **MIP** $127

❑ **John Deere B, Unstyled**, 1:16-scale, Ertl, Precision Classics #24, NF, spoked wheels, 2004, No. 15487
EX $45   **NM** $90   **MIP** $125

❑ **John Deere BN**, 1:16-scale, Ertl, single front wheel, 2000, No. 5902
EX $8   **NM** $16   **MIP** $28

❑ **John Deere BO**, 1:16-scale, SpecCast, green, on rubber, 1999, No. JDM117
EX $23   **NM** $32   **MIP** $42

❑ **John Deere BO**, 1:16-scale, SpecCast, green, on steel, 2001, No. JDM151
EX $18   **NM** $27   **MIP** $36

❑ **John Deere BR**, 1:16-scale, Ertl, green, Collectors Edition, 1980s, No. 5586DA
EX $21   **NM** $29   **MIP** $37

❑ **John Deere BR**, 1:16-scale, Ertl, green, on rubber, 1980s, No. 5586
EX $21   **NM** $27   **MIP** $36

❑ **John Deere BR**, 1:16-scale, Riecke (Custom), green, did not come in box, 1980s
EX $267   **NM** $322   **MIP** n/a

❑ **John Deere BR Set**, 1:16-scale, Ertl, w/wagon set, 1997, No. 5761

(Photo by Ertl)

EX $19   **NM** $28   **MIP** $37

❑ **John Deere BW**, 1:16-scale, Ertl, green, unstyled on rubber, 2002, No. 15348
EX $8   **NM** $16   **MIP** $24

❑ **John Deere BW**, 1:16-scale, Ertl, green, on steel w/umbrella, JD Founder's 200th Birthday, 2004, No. 15645A
EX $12   **NM** $22   **MIP** $48

❑ **John Deere BW-40**, 1:16-scale, Ertl, green, '96 Two Cylinder Club Expo, 5000 made, 1996, No. 5824TA
EX $63   **NM** $98   **MIP** $132

❑ **John Deere BWH**, 1:16-scale, Ertl, green, high crop, '03 JD Collector Center Precision #2, 2003, No. 15512A
EX $63   **NM** $98   **MIP** $152

❑ **John Deere C**, 1:16-scale, Ertl, green, '93 Two Cylinder Club Expo, 1993, No. 5700TA
EX $24   **NM** $37   **MIP** $67

❑ **John Deere D**, 1:16-scale, Dingman (Custom), green, did not come in box, 1980s
EX $258   **NM** $289   **MIP** n/a

❑ **John Deere D**, 1:16-scale, Dingman (Custom), green, did not come in box, 1980s
EX $258   **NM** $289   **MIP** n/a

❑ **John Deere D**, 1:16-scale, Dingman (Custom), green, did not come in box, 1980s
EX $258   **NM** $289   **MIP** n/a

❑ **John Deere D**, 1:16-scale, Dingman (Custom), green, did not come in box, 1980s
EX $279   **NM** $326   **MIP** n/a

❑ **John Deere D**, 1:16-scale, Dingman (Custom), green, did not come in box, 1980s
EX $258   **NM** $289   **MIP** n/a

❑ **John Deere D**, 1:16-scale, Dingman (Custom), gold, 50th Anniversary of John Deere, 1980s
(Photo by Lyle Dingman)
EX $443   **NM** $538   **MIP** $597

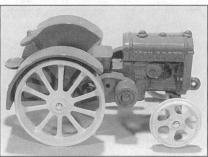

❑ **John Deere D**, 1:16-scale, Ertl, green, hole in seat, unstyled, 1970s, No. 500
EX $8   **NM** $17   **MIP** $26

❑ **John Deere D**, 1:16-scale, Ertl, green, unstyled, 1980s, No. 500
EX $8   **NM** $16   **MIP** $24

❑ **John Deere D**, 1:16-scale, Ertl, green and yellow, rubber tires, styled, 1990s, No. 5596
EX $18   **NM** $27   **MIP** $38

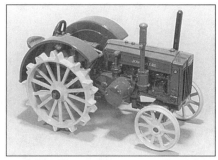

❑ **John Deere D**, 1:16-scale, Ertl, green, Collectors Edition, styled, 1990s, No. 5596DA
EX $22   **NM** $29   **MIP** $38

❑ **John Deere D**, 1:16-scale, Ertl, styled green, 100th Anniversary of Minneapolis Branch, 1994, No. 5817PA
EX $32   **NM** $47   **MIP** $78

❑ **John Deere D**, 1:16-scale, Ertl, gold plated, 100th Anniversary of Minneapolis Branch, styled, 1994, No. 5817PA
EX $76   **NM** $112   **MIP** $178

❑ **John Deere D**, 1:16-scale, Ertl, green, '98 Two Cylinder Club Exp, unstyled, 1998, No. 5995TA
EX $42   **NM** $67   **MIP** $98

❑ **John Deere D**, 1:16-scale, Ertl, green, unstyled on steel, 1999, No. 5179
EX $9   **NM** $18   **MIP** $28

❑ **John Deere D**, 1:16-scale, Ertl, green, '75 Anniversary Edition, 1999, No. 5198DA
EX $21   **NM** $29   **MIP** $48

❑ **John Deere D**, 1:16-scale, Keith (Custom), green, Land of Lincoln Show Tractor, 1980s
EX $32   **NM** $47   **MIP** $74

❏ **John Deere D**, 1:16-scale, Old Time Collectables (Custom), green, 1970s
EX $12   **NM** $26   **MIP** $37

❏ **John Deere D**, 1:16-scale, Scale Models, green, No. 15 in Collectors Series I, limited to 5000, 1980s
EX $18   **NM** $37   **MIP** $44

❏ **John Deere D**, 1:16-scale, Scale Models, green, reproduction of D, made by Vindex, cast of urian, 1998, No. 05450
EX $122   **NM** $156   **MIP** $226

❏ **John Deere D**, 1:16-scale, SpecCast, green, North Dakota Show Tractor, on steel, 1980s
EX $12   **NM** $38   **MIP** $48

❏ **John Deere D**, 1:16-scale, Vindex, green w/yellow wheels, nickel-plated drive, 1930s
EX $582   **NM** $1257   **MIP** npf

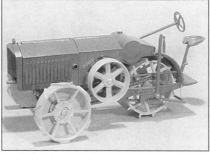

❏ **John Deere Dain**, 1:16-scale, Hansen, green, 1980s
EX $282   **NM** $463   **MIP** $659

❏ **John Deere Dain**, 1:16-scale, Scale Models, green, 2000, No. FY-0029 *(Photo by Bossen Implement)*
EX $32   **NM** $56   **MIP** $78

❏ **John Deere Froelich**, 1:16-scale, Cox (Custom), red and gray, did not come in box, 1970s
EX $2289   **NM** $3563   **MIP** n/a

❏ **John Deere Froelich**, 1:16-scale, Ertl, gray and red, Millenium Edition, 2000, No. 15008
EX $32   **NM** $56   **MIP** $78

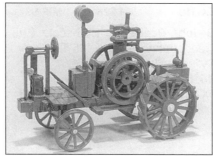

❏ **John Deere Froelich**, 1:16-scale, Scale Models, red and gray, 1980s
EX $68   **NM** $93   **MIP** $118

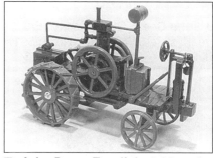

❏ **John Deere Froelich**, 1:16-scale, Scale Models, gray and red, No. 7 in Threshers Series, 1980s
EX $68   **NM** $93   **MIP** $118

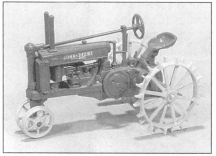

❏ **John Deere G**, 1:16-scale, Ertl, green, Collectors Edition, unstyled on steel, 1980s, No. 548DA
EX $23   **NM** $37   **MIP** $43

❏ **John Deere G**, 1:16-scale, Ertl, green, unstyled on rubber, 1980s, No. 548
EX $23   **NM** $36   **MIP** $43

❏ **John Deere G**, 1:16-scale, Ertl, green, styled, Collector Edition, 1997, No. 5103DA
EX $23   **NM** $38   **MIP** $48

❏ **John Deere G**, 1:16-scale, Ertl, green, high-crop, '97 Two Cylinder Club Expo, 1997, No. 5000TA
EX $53   **NM** $82   **MIP** $107

❏ **John Deere G**, 1:16-scale, Ertl, green, styled, 1998, No. 5104
EX $8   **NM** $12   **MIP** $18

❏ **John Deere G**, 1:16-scale, Ertl, green, '99 Iowa FFA Edition, 1999, No. 16011A
EX $21   **NM** $32   **MIP** $58

❏ **John Deere G**, 1:16-scale, Ertl, green, styled, WF, 2003, No. 15591
EX $8   **NM** $17   **MIP** $24

❏ **John Deere G**, 1:16-scale, Freiheit (Custom), green, fenders, did not come in box, 1980s
EX $248   **NM** $378   **MIP** n/a

❏ **John Deere G**, 1:16-scale, Freiheit (Custom), green, did not come in box, 1980s
EX $247   **NM** $372   **MIP** n/a

❏ **John Deere G**, 1:16-scale, Freiheit (Custom), green, fenders, did not come in box, 1980s
EX $247   **NM** $372   **MIP** n/a

❏ **John Deere G**, 1:16-scale, Freiheit (Custom), green, did not come in box, 1980s
EX $248   **NM** $376   **MIP** n/a

❏ **John Deere G**, 1:16-scale, Scale Models, green, No. 1 in Collectors Series II, limited to 5000 units, 1980s
EX $27   **NM** $44   **MIP** $58

❏ **John Deere GP**, 1:16-scale, Ertl, Standard, No. 5801 *(Photo by Ertl)*
EX $13   **NM** $27   **MIP** $26

❏ **John Deere GP**, 1:16-scale, Ertl, green, '94 Two Cylinder Club Edition, 1994, No. 5706TA
EX $23   **NM** $42   **MIP** $53

❏ **John Deere GP**, 1:16-scale, Ertl, green, Standard, Collectors Edition, 1994, No. 5767DA *(Photo by Ertl)*
EX $18   **NM** $26   **MIP** $37

❏ **John Deere GP**, 1:16-scale, Ertl, green, potato version, '95 Two Cylinder Club Edition, 1995, No. 5794TA
EX $21   **NM** $31   **MIP** $43

❏ **John Deere GP**, 1:16-scale, Ertl, green, wide tread version, 1995, No. 5787 *(Photo by Ertl)*
EX $13   **NM** $18   **MIP** $27

❏ **John Deere GP**, 1:16-scale, Ertl, green, wide tread version, Collector Edition, 1996, No. 5798DA
EX $13   **NM** $27   **MIP** $38

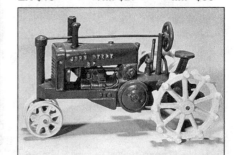

❏ **John Deere GP**, 1:16-scale, Gray (Custom), green, no box, 1970s
EX $23   **NM** $36   **MIP** n/a

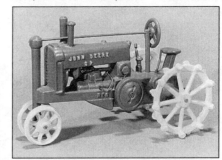

❏ **John Deere GP**, 1:16-scale, Gray (Custom), green, no box, 1970s
EX $23   **NM** $36   **MIP** n/a

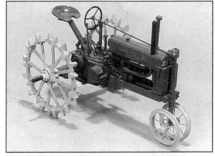

❏ **John Deere GP**, 1:16-scale, Riecke (Custom), green, did not come in box, 1990s
EX $189   **NM** $253   **MIP** n/a

❑ **John Deere GP**, 1:16-scale, Riecke (Custom), green, did not come in box, 1990s
EX $189   **NM** $253   **MIP** n/a

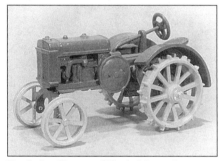

❑ **John Deere GP**, 1:16-scale, Scale Models, green, Standard Tread, No. 9 in Collectors Series I, limited to 3000 units, 1980s
EX $22   **NM** $37   **MIP** $44

❑ **John Deere GP Set**, 1:16-scale, Ertl, w/wagon set, 1996, No. 5062

(Photo by Ertl)
EX $16   **NM** $23   **MIP** $34

❑ **John Deere H**, 1:16-scale, Dingman (Custom), green, did not come in box, 1980s
EX $173   **NM** $219   **MIP** n/a

❑ **John Deere H**, 1:16-scale, Dingman (Custom), green, fenders and lights, did not come in box, 1980s
EX $173   **NM** $219   **MIP** n/a

❑ **John Deere H**, 1:16-scale, Dingman (Custom), green, did not come in box, 1980s
EX $154   **NM** $206   **MIP** n/a

❑ **John Deere H**, 1:16-scale, Ertl, green, '99 Two Cylinder Club Edition, 1999, No. 16006A
EX $32   **NM** $53   **MIP** $78

❑ **John Deere H**, 1:16-scale, Ertl, green, single front wheel, 2000, No. 15034
EX $12   **NM** $16   **MIP** $23

❑ **John Deere H**, 1:16-scale, Ertl, green, single front wheel, Collector Edition, 2000, No. 15033A
EX $14   **NM** $26   **MIP** $37

❑ **John Deere H**, 1:16-scale, Ertl, green, '00 Iowa FFA Edition, w/umbrella, 2000, No. 16043A
EX $16   **NM** $28   **MIP** $42

❑ **John Deere H**, 1:16-scale, NB & K, green and black, East Show Tractor, 1980s
EX $67   **NM** $106   **MIP** $128

❑ **John Deere H w/Hay Wagon Set**, 1:16-scale, Ertl, NF, hay wagon w/square bales, 2007, No. 15867
EX $12   **NM** $24   **MIP** $33

❑ **John Deere L**, 1:16-scale, SpecCast, green, '90 Toy Tractor Times, #5; 3,450 produced, 1990, No. TTT010
EX $16   **NM** $27   **MIP** $38

❑ **John Deere L**, 1:16-scale, SpecCast, green, unstyled, 2001, No. JDM171
EX $16   **NM** $22   **MIP** $33

❑ **John Deere L**, 1:16-scale, SpecCast, green, styled, w/John Deere engine, 2003, No. JDM174

(Photo by SpecCast)
EX $16   **NM** $22   **MIP** $33

❑ **John Deere L**, 1:16-scale, SpecCast, green, styled, w/Hercules engine, 2004, No. JDM176
EX $16   **NM** $22   **MIP** $33

❏ **John Deere L**, 1:16-scale, Stern (Custom), green, did not come in box, 1980s
EX $168   **NM** $236   **MIP** n/a

❏ **John Deere LA**, 1:16-scale, NB & K, green, Southern Indiana Show Tractor, 1980s
EX $23   **NM** $46   **MIP** $63

❏ **John Deere LA**, 1:16-scale, Riecke (Custom), yellow, did not come in box, 1980s
EX $198   **NM** $289   **MIP** n/a

❏ **John Deere LA**, 1:16-scale, Riecke (Custom), green, did not come in box, 1980s
EX $198   **NM** $289   **MIP** n/a

❏ **John Deere LA**, 1:16-scale, SpecCast, green, 1994, No. JDM045
EX $13   **NM** $21   **MIP** $28

❏ **John Deere LA**, 1:16-scale, SpecCast, green, 1994, No. JDM045
(Photo by SpecCast)
EX $13   **NM** $21   **MIP** $28

❏ **John Deere LA**, 1:16-scale, SpecCast, green, 2002, No. JDM173
EX $16   **NM** $22   **MIP** $33

❏ **John Deere LI**, 1:16-scale, SpecCast, yellow, 1995, No. JDM069
(Photo by SpecCast)
EX $18   **NM** $24   **MIP** $32

❏ **John Deere M**, 1:16-scale, Ertl, green, 1980s, No. 540
EX $12   **NM** $27   **MIP** $31

❏ **John Deere M**, 1:16-scale, Ertl, green, Collectors Edition, 1980s, No. 540TA
EX $13   **NM** $28   **MIP** $36

❏ **John Deere M**, 1:16-scale, Riecke (Custom), green, did not come in box, 1980s
EX $186   **NM** $237   **MIP** n/a

❏ **John Deere M**, 1:16-scale, S & K Sandcasting, green, 1983
EX $18   **NM** $33   **MIP** $47

❏ **John Deere M**, 1:16-scale, SpecCast, green, '96 Plow City Show Edition, 1996, No. CUST396
EX $16   **NM** $28   **MIP** $37

❏ **John Deere M w/Plow**, 1:16-scale, SpecCast, WF, 2 bottom plow, 2007, No. 200 *(Photo by SpecCast)*
EX $15   **NM** $30   **MIP** $48

❏ **John Deere MI**, 1:16-scale, Ertl, orange, 1980s, No. 5628
EX $16   **NM** $27   **MIP** $32

❑ **John Deere MT**, 1:16-scale, L & J, green, Lafayette Show Tractor, 1989
EX $32　　**NM** $63　　**MIP** $82

❑ **John Deere MT**, 1:16-scale, Riecke (Custom), green, did not come in box, 1980s
EX $183　　**NM** $247　　**MIP** n/a

❑ **John Deere MT**, 1:16-scale, Riecke (Custom), green, did not come in box, 1980s
EX $183　　**NM** $247　　**MIP** n/a

❑ **John Deere MT**, 1:16-scale, Riecke (Custom), green, did not come in box, 1980s
EX $183　　**NM** $247　　**MIP** n/a

❑ **John Deere MT**, 1:16-scale, SpecCast, green, NF, 1995, No. JDM056 *(Photo by SpecCast)*
EX $16　　**NM** $23　　**MIP** $33

❑ **John Deere MT**, 1:16-scale, SpecCast, green, WF, 1996, No. JDM073 *(Photo by SpecCast)*
EX $16　　**NM** $23　　**MIP** $33

❑ **John Deere OP**, 1:16-scale, Taiwan, red or green, really a GP, Deere misspelled, 1980s
EX $11　　**NM** $16　　**MIP** $22

❑ **John Deere OP**, 1:16-scale, Taiwan, green, really a GP, Deere misspelled, 1980s
EX $11　　**NM** $16　　**MIP** $22

❑ **John Deere Overtime**, 1:16-scale, Ertl, off colored green, 1994, No. 5811 *(Photo by Ertl)*
EX $13　　**NM** $18　　**MIP** $27

❑ **John Deere Pedal Tractor**, 1:16-scale, Riecke (Custom), green, did not come in box, 1990s
EX $19　　**NM** $28　　**MIP** n/a

❑ **John Deere R**, 1:16-scale, Ertl, green, Collectors Edition, 1980s, No. 544DA
EX $26　　**NM** $36　　**MIP** $46

❑ **John Deere R**, 1:16-scale, Ertl, green, 1980s, No. 544
EX $22　　**NM** $33　　**MIP** $42

❏ **John Deere R**, 1:16-scale, Ertl, green, both stacks green, 1980s, No. 544
EX $22   **NM** $33   **MIP** $42

❏ **John Deere R**, 1:16-scale, Trumm (Custom), green, 1980s
EX $22   **NM** $36   **MIP** $56

❏ **John Deere WA-14**, 1:16-scale, E-Tee's, green, 1980s
EX $426   **NM** $576   **MIP** $822

❏ **John Deere WA-17**, 1:16-scale, E-Tee's, green, 1980s
EX $446   **NM** $592   **MIP** $832

❏ **John Deere Waterloo Boy**, 1:16-scale, Cox (Custom), green, did not come in box, only 19 made, 1970s
EX $2189   **NM** $3472   **MIP** n/a

❏ **John Deere Waterloo Boy**, 1:16-scale, Ertl, green w/red engine, Collectors Edition, 1980s, No. 559DA
EX $23   **NM** $34   **MIP** $46

❏ **John Deere Waterloo Boy**, 1:16-scale, Ertl, green w/red engine, 1980s, No. 559
EX $22   **NM** $31   **MIP** $39

❏ **John Deere Waterloo Boy**, 1:16-scale, Ertl, gold, 70th Anniversary Collectors Edition, 1990s
EX $178   **NM** $283   **MIP** $326

❏ **John Deere Waterloo Boy**, 1:16-scale, Ertl, green, #15 in Precision Series, 1999, No. 15013
EX $66   **NM** $87   **MIP** $128

❏ **John Deere Waterloo Boy**, 1:16-scale, Scale Models, green, #3 in Thresher Series, 1980s
EX $18   **NM** $34   **MIP** $37

❏ **John Deere, 950**, 1:16-scale, Ertl, green, Compact Utility, No Model #5, 1980s, No. 581
EX $9   **NM** $12   **MIP** $18

❏ **John Deere, 950**, 1:16-scale, Ertl, green, Compact Utility, No Model #5, 1980s, No. 581
EX $9   **NM** $12   **MIP** $18

TRACTORS 1:20-SCALE

❏ **John Deere 6410**, 1:20-scale, Ertl, green, w/loader, 2002, No. 15424
EX $4   **NM** $8   **MIP** $11

TRACTORS 1:25-SCALE

❏ **John Deere 4430**, 1:25-scale, Ertl, green, model kit, reissued under stock #15006, 1970s, No. 8005
EX $12   **NM** $29   **MIP** $56

❏ **John Deere Lanz 3120**, 1:25-scale, Kovap, green, windup, 3 forward speeds, 1 reverse and retual, 2000, No. 3501
EX $16   **NM** $28   **MIP** $42

TRACTORS 1:32-SCALE

❏ **John Deere 3020**, 1:32-scale, Lee Aluminum, red and silver, 1970s
EX $13   **NM** $26   **MIP** $37

❏ **John Deere 3020**, 1:32-scale, Lee Aluminum, green, 1970s
EX $13   **NM** $26   **MIP** $37

❏ **John Deere 3020**, 1:32-scale, Lee Aluminum, green, 1970s
EX $13   **NM** $26   **MIP** $37

❏ **John Deere 3020**, 1:32-scale, Lee Aluminum, green, 1970s
EX $13   **NM** $26   **MIP** $37

❏ **John Deere 3020**, 1:32-scale, Lee Aluminum, green and red, 1970s
EX $13   **NM** $26   **MIP** $37

❏ **John Deere 3020**, 1:32-scale, Lee Aluminum, red and silver, 1970s
EX $13   **NM** $26   **MIP** $37

❏ **John Deere 3020**, 1:32-scale, Lee Aluminum, red, 1970s
EX $13   **NM** $26   **MIP** $37

❏ **John Deere 3140**, 1:32-scale, Ertl, green, MFD, w/loader, No. 5743
EX $4   **NM** $11   **MIP** $17

❏ **John Deere 3140**, 1:32-scale, Ertl, green, rear wheel rims inside diameter is 1-15/16", outside diameter is 1-1/4", 1970s, No. 1635
EX $14   **NM** $26   **MIP** $36

❏ **John Deere 3140**, 1:32-scale, Ertl, green, rear wheel rims are 1-1/4" diameter inside and outside, 1970s, No. 1635
EX $14   **NM** $26   **MIP** $36

❏ **John Deere 3140**, 1:32-scale, Ertl, green, plastic hitch extension, 1980s, No. 5512
EX $4   **NM** $7   **MIP** $12

❏ **John Deere 3140**, 1:32-scale, Ertl, green, 1980s, No. 5512
EX $4   **NM** $7   **MIP** $12

❏ **John Deere 3140**, 1:32-scale, Ertl, green, not marked "3140", 1980s, No. 5512
EX $4   **NM** $7   **MIP** $12

❏ **John Deere 3140**, 1:32-scale, Ertl, green, no muffler, 1980s, No. 5512
EX $4   **NM** $7   **MIP** $12

❏ **John Deere 3140**, 1:32-scale, Ertl, green, three-point hitch, note new decal, 1980s, No. 5580
EX $4   **NM** $8   **MIP** $13

❏ **John Deere 3140**, 1:32-scale, Ertl, green, MFD, 1982, No. 5537
EX $4   **NM** $8   **MIP** $13

❏ **John Deere 3140**, 1:32-scale, Ertl, green, MFD, w/loader and attachments, 1991, No. 5648
EX $11   **NM** $18   **MIP** $27

❏ **John Deere 3200**, 1:32-scale, Siku, green, limited run, 1994
EX $27   **NM** $52   **MIP** $78

❏ **John Deere 3350**, 1:32-scale, Ertl, green, black radiator screens, 1980s, No. 5580
EX $4   **NM** $8   **MIP** $13

❏ **John Deere 3350 Set**, 1:32-scale, Ertl, green, MFD, w/baler, 2002, No. 15369
EX $6   **NM** $12   **MIP** $18

❏ **John Deere 4020 w/FWA and Cab**, 1:32-scale, Ertl, 2006, No. 15840
EX $4   **NM** $12   **MIP** $18

❏ **John Deere 4430**, 1:32-scale, Argentina, green, 1980s
EX $12   **NM** $28   **MIP** $34

❏ **John Deere 4430**, 1:32-scale, Argentina, yellow, 1980s
EX $12   **NM** $23   **MIP** $34

❏ **John Deere 4430**, 1:32-scale, Ertl, green, NF, w/cab, 1973, No. 66
EX $3   **NM** $6   **MIP** $12

❏ **John Deere 4430 Set**, 1:32-scale, Ertl, green, std. drawbar, "2-stake" wagon; "Ertl" stamped on gate, 1970s
EX n/a   **NM** n/a   **MIP** $26

❏ **John Deere 4430 Set**, 1:32-scale, Ertl, green, high drawbar, "4-stake" wagon, 3-bottom plow, disc, drag, 1970s
EX npf   **NM** npf   **MIP** $44

❏ **John Deere 4430 Set**, 1:32-scale, Ertl, green, yellow rims on front of tractor and wagon, 1980s, No. 70
EX n/a   **NM** n/a   **MIP** $21

❏ **John Deere 4440**, 1:32-scale, Ertl, green, Strob decal on tractor, yellow rims on tractor, no cab, 1980s
EX $4   **NM** $12   **MIP** $16

❑ **John Deere 4440**, 1:32-scale, Pace Setter, green, glass decanter w/Pacesetter decals, 1980s
EX $16   **NM** $27   **MIP** $42

❑ **John Deere 4440 Set**, 1:32-scale, Ertl, Strob, yellow rims tractor front & wagon; "Ertl" stamped gate, 1980s, No. 70
EX n/a   **NM** n/a   **MIP** $19

❑ **John Deere 4450**, 1:32-scale, Ertl, green, 1980s, No. 66
EX $3   **NM** $11   **MIP** $14

❑ **John Deere 5410**, 1:32-scale, Ertl, green, MFD, w/cab, 2002, No. 40545
EX $4   **NM** $7   **MIP** $13

❑ **John Deere 5820**, 1:32-scale, Siku, green, MFD, 2004, No. 3050
EX $4   **NM** $8   **MIP** $23

❑ **John Deere 6210**, 1:32-scale, Ertl, green, w/loader, 1999, No. 176
EX $6   **NM** $13   **MIP** $18

❑ **John Deere 6210**, 1:32-scale, Ertl, w/loader and manure spreader, 2004, No. 15488
EX $7   **NM** $14   **MIP** $25

❑ **John Deere 6400**, 1:32-scale, Ertl, 1990s, No. 5668 *(Photo by Ertl)*
EX $4   **NM** $6   **MIP** $9

❑ **John Deere 6400**, 1:32-scale, Ertl, w/loader, 1995, No. 5720 *(Photo by Ertl)*
EX $6   **NM** $11   **MIP** $18

❑ **John Deere 6410**, 1:32-scale, Ertl, green, 1999, No. 175
EX $4   **NM** $14   **MIP** $18

❑ **John Deere 6820**, 1:32-scale, Siku, green, '03 LCN European Show Edition, 2003 *(Photo by Bossen Implement)*
EX $22   **NM** $32   **MIP** $48

❑ **John Deere 6920**, 1:32-scale, Siku, green, front hitch, 2002, No. 3252
EX $4   **NM** $8   **MIP** $21

❑ **John Deere 6920**, 1:32-scale, Siku, green, w/front weights, Mannheim Employee Edition, 2003, No. 3252 *(Photo by Bossen Implement)*
EX $22   **NM** $32   **MIP** $57

❑ **John Deere 6920**, 1:32-scale, Siku, green, extra painted details, w/display case, 2004, No. 4455
EX $22   **NM** $32   **MIP** $37

❑ **John Deere 7020**, 1:32-scale, Ertl, green, w/duals, '03 National Farm Toy Show Edition, 2003, No. 16105A
EX $21   **NM** $42   **MIP** $78

❑ **John Deere 7020**, 1:32-scale, Ertl, green, single wheels, 2004, No. 15610
EX $6   **NM** $11   **MIP** $23

❑ **John Deere 7020**, 1:32-scale, Ertl, 4WD, 2005, No. 15610
EX $8   **NM** $14   **MIP** $18

❑ **John Deere 7410**, 1:32-scale, Ertl, battery-operated w/wire control, 1997, No. 5204 *(Photo by Ertl)*
EX $4   **NM** $8   **MIP** $18

❑ **John Deere 7410**, 1:32-scale, Ertl, reissued under stock #34507, 1997, No. 5329 *(Photo by Ertl)*
EX $4   **NM** $8   **MIP** $12

❑ **John Deere 7520**, 1:32-scale, Ertl, green, w/duals, Collector Editions, 2004, No. 15578A
EX $16   **NM** $27   **MIP** $48

❑ **John Deere 7800**, 1:32-scale, Ertl, green, wire control, 1994, No. 5724
EX $4   **NM** $8   **MIP** $18

❑ **John Deere 7920**, 1:32-scale, Ertl, green, MFD, European version, 2004, No. 15525
EX $4   **NM** $8   **MIP** $13

❑ **John Deere 7920**, 1:32-scale, Ertl, 2005, No. 15525
EX $12   **NM** $18   **MIP** $24

❑ **John Deere 7930**, 1:32-scale, Ertl, duals, 2006, No. 15857
EX $8   **NM** $14   **MIP** $18

❑ **John Deere 8230T w/Trailed Sprayer Set**, 1:32-scale, Ertl, track tractor, 2007, No. 15877
EX $18   **NM** $28   **MIP** $38

❑ **John Deere 8400**, 1:32-scale, Ertl, green, MFD, #8 Precision Series, 1995, No. 5259
EX $34   **NM** $53   **MIP** $118

❑ **John Deere 8400**, 1:32-scale, Ertl, revised graphics, Precision Series, 1997, No. 5259CP *(Photo by Ertl)*
EX $34   **NM** $53   **MIP** $118

❑ **John Deere 8430**, 1:32-scale, Ertl, Series II Precision #4, duals, 2007, No. 15905
EX $55   **NM** $80   **MIP** $100

❑ **John Deere 8530**, 1:32-scale, Ertl, #3 in Precision Series II, 2006, No. 15305
EX $28   **NM** $48   **MIP** $72

❑ **John Deere 8640**, 1:32-scale, Pace Setter, green, glass decanter w/Pacesetter decals, 4WD, 1980s
EX $16   **NM** $27   **MIP** $48

❑ **John Deere 8960**, 1:32-scale, Ertl, green, battery operated w/P.T.O., 1980s, No. 5582
EX $13   **NM** $22   **MIP** $46

❑ **John Deere 9420T**, 1:32-scale, Ertl, green, track tractor, #2 in Precision Series II, 2002, No. 15286
EX $33   **NM** $54   **MIP** $98

❑ **John Deere 9420T**, 1:32-scale, Ertl, Precision Series II #2, trac, 2004, No. 15286

❑ **John Deere A**, 1:32-scale, Arcor, red or blue, 1950s
EX $17   **NM** $36   **MIP** $57

❑ **John Deere A**, 1:32-scale, Auburn Rubber, green, blue, red w/silver engine, 5" long, 1950s
EX $16   **NM** $38   **MIP** $56

❑ **John Deere A**, 1:32-scale, Scale Models, green, 1980s
EX $4   **NM** $9   **MIP** $14

❑ **John Deere A**, 1:32-scale, Scale Models, green, 1980s
EX $4   **NM** $9   **MIP** $14

❑ **John Deere B**, 1:32-scale, Brown's Models, green, model kit, 1980s
EX $22   **NM** $37   **MIP** $48

❑ **John Deere B**, 1:32-scale, Brown's Models, green, model kit, 1980s
EX $22   **NM** $37   **MIP** $48

❑ **John Deere B**, 1:32-scale, Brown's Models, green, model kit, 1980s
EX $22   **NM** $37   **MIP** $48

❏ **John Deere B**, 1:32-scale, Brown's Models, green, model kit, 1980s
EX $22   **NM** $37   **MIP** $48

❏ **John Deere B**, 1:32-scale, Brown's Models, green, model kit, 1980s
EX $22   **NM** $37   **MIP** $48

❏ **John Deere B**, 1:32-scale, Brown's Models, green, model kit, 1980s
EX $22   **NM** $37   **MIP** $48

❏ **John Deere Lanz**, 1:32-scale, Rex of West Germany, yellow, w/Loader, 1960s
EX $286   **NM** $447   **MIP** $838

❏ **John Deere Lanz**, 1:32-scale, Rex of West Germany, green, two square designs on hood, 1960s
EX $247   **NM** $353   **MIP** $493

❏ **John Deere Lanz**, 1:32-scale, Rex of West Germany, green, three-point hitch, square labels on hood, round design above tank, 1960s
EX $268   **NM** $372   **MIP** $546

❏ **John Deere Lanz Set**, 1:32-scale, Rex, green, made for World's Fair, very rare, 1960s
EX npf   **NM** npf   **MIP** $1326

❏ **John Deere Overtime**, 1:32-scale, Ertl, green, British Version of Waterloo Boy, 1990s, No. 5907
EX $3   **NM** $6   **MIP** $11

❏ **John Deere Overtime**, 1:32-scale, Ertl, green, Collectors Edition, British Version of Waterloo Boy, collector insert on radiator, 1990s, No. 5907EA
EX $4   **NM** $7   **MIP** $12

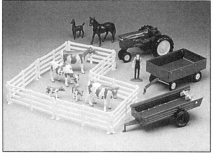

❏ **John Deere Set**, 1:32-scale, Ertl, set w/tractors and implements, 1990s, No. 5673 *(Photo by Ertl)*
EX n/a   **NM** n/a   **MIP** $22

❏ **Waterloo Boy**, 1:32-scale, Ertl, green, reissued under stock #15613, 1993, No. 5744 *(Photo by Ertl)*
EX $3   **NM** $6   **MIP** $11

❏ **John Deere 730**, 1:32-scale, Auburn Rubber, red, 1950s
EX $12   **NM** $27   **MIP** $52

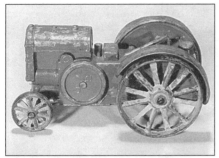

❑ **John Deere D**, 1:32-scale, Kansas Toy Company, green, 1930s
EX $119   **NM** $446   **MIP** npf

❑ **John Deere M**, 1:32-scale, Auburn Rubber, orange, blue, red, pink, light green, dark green and orange w/plastic wheels, 1950s
EX $16   **NM** $38   **MIP** $56

TRACTORS 1:43-SCALE

❑ **John Deere 3185**, 1:43-scale, Hong Kong, green, yellow decal, 1980s
EX $2   **NM** $6   **MIP** $9

❑ **John Deere 3185**, 1:43-scale, Hong Kong, green, orange decal w/o John Deere, 1980s
EX $2   **NM** $6   **MIP** $9

❑ **John Deere 3185**, 1:43-scale, Hong Kong, yellow, yellow decal, 1980s
EX $2   **NM** $6   **MIP** $9

❑ **John Deere 3185**, 1:43-scale, Hong Kong, yellow, orange decal w/o John Deere, 1980s
EX $2   **NM** $6   **MIP** $9

❑ **John Deere 4010**, 1:43-scale, Ertl, green, Broadstrike Edition, 1990s, No. 025
EX $9   **NM** $16   **MIP** $28

❑ **John Deere 4010**, 1:43-scale, Ertl, green, '93 National Farm Toy Show Edition, 1993
EX $8   **NM** $14   **MIP** $23

❑ **John Deere 4010**, 1:43-scale, Ertl, green, 1994, No. 5725
EX $4   **NM** $8   **MIP** $12

❑ **John Deere 4010**, 1:43-scale, SpecCast, 1990s
EX $6   **NM** $8   **MIP** $12

❑ **John Deere 4230**, 1:43-scale, Ertl, green, '98 LCN European Show Edition, 1998
EX $8   **NM** $14   **MIP** $32

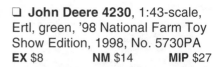

❑ **John Deere 4230**, 1:43-scale, Ertl, green, '98 National Farm Toy Show Edition, 1998, No. 5730PA
EX $8   **NM** $14   **MIP** $27

❑ **John Deere 4320**, 1:43-scale, Ertl, green, '93 LCN European Show Edition, 1993, No. 5725MA
EX $21   **NM** $38   **MIP** $98

❑ **John Deere 60**, 1:43-scale, SpecCast, 1990s
EX $6   **NM** $8   **MIP** $12

❑ **John Deere 630**, 1:43-scale, Ertl, red, LP, pre-production run, did not come in box, 1980s
EX $8   **NM** $12   **MIP** n/a

❑ **John Deere 630**, 1:43-scale, Ertl, green, LP, reissued under stock #33522, 1980s, No. 5599
EX $4   **NM** $8   **MIP** $11

❑ **John Deere 630**, 1:43-scale, Ertl, green, LP, '88 National Farm Toy Show Tractor, 1988, No. 5599MA
EX $8 **NM** $17 **MIP** $26

❑ **John Deere 730**, 1:43-scale, SpecCast, 1990s
EX $6 **NM** $8 **MIP** $12

❑ **John Deere A**, 1:43-scale, Ertl, all green, pre-production run, did not come in box, 1980s
EX $8 **NM** $12 **MIP** n/a

❑ **John Deere A**, 1:43-scale, Ertl, green w/yellow wheels, reissued under stock #33532, 1980s, No. 5598
EX $4 **NM** $8 **MIP** $11

❑ **John Deere A**, 1:43-scale, Ertl, green, part of Tractors of the Past Set—did not come in individual box, 1980s
EX $7 **NM** $14 **MIP** n/a

❑ **John Deere A**, 1:43-scale, Ertl, yellow w/white rims, pre-production run, did not come in box, 1980s
EX $8 **NM** $12 **MIP** n/a

❑ **John Deere B**, 1:43-scale, SpecCast, 1990s
EX $6 **NM** $8 **MIP** $12

❑ **John Deere D**, 1:43-scale, SpecCast, 1990s
EX $6 **NM** $8 **MIP** $12

❑ **John Deere H**, 1:43-scale, SpecCast, 1990s
EX $6 **NM** $8 **MIP** $12

❑ **John Deere Waterloo Boy**, 1:43-scale, SpecCast, 1990s
EX $6 **NM** $8 **MIP** $12

TRACTORS 1:50-SCALE

❑ **John Deere 2120**, 1:50-scale, Nacoral, 1960s
EX $387 **NM** $489 **MIP** $693

TRACTORS 1:64-SCALE

❑ **John Deere 20 Series Set**, 1:64-scale, Ertl, 3 tractors, 2006, No. 15853
EX $5 **NM** $9 **MIP** $12

❑ **John Deere 2510**, 1:64-scale, Ertl, green and yellow, 1996, No. 5756 *(Photo by Ertl)*
EX $4 **NM** $5 **MIP** $6

❏ **John Deere 2510**, 1:64-scale, Matsen (Custom), green and yellow, did not come in box, 1980s
EX $6   **NM** $22   **MIP** n/a

❏ **John Deere 30 Series Set**, 1:64-scale, Ertl, 3 tractors, 2006, No. 15789
EX $5   **NM** $8   **MIP** $12

❏ **John Deere 3010**, 1:64-scale, Matsen (Custom), green and yellow, did not come in box, 1980s
EX $6   **NM** $22   **MIP** n/a

❏ **John Deere 330**, 1:64-scale, Ertl, green, on furrow magazine card, 2000, No. 15158
EX $4   **NM** $5   **MIP** $6

❏ **John Deere 4010**, 1:64-scale, Ertl, green and yellow, plastic fenders, w/ or w/o hook-hitch, did not come in box, 1980s
EX $4   **NM** $12   **MIP** n/a

❏ **John Deere 4010**, 1:64-scale, Ertl, green and yellow, metal fenders, did not come in box, 1980s
EX $6   **NM** $12   **MIP** n/a

❏ **John Deere 4010**, 1:64-scale, Ertl, green, w/corn picker, 2002, No. 15377
EX $4   **NM** $6   **MIP** $11

❏ **John Deere 4010**, 1:64-scale, Ertl, green, '03 National Farm Toy Museum Edition, 2003, No. 16110A
EX $4   **NM** $5   **MIP** $7

❏ **John Deere 4010**, 1:64-scale, Keith (Custom), green and yellow, did not come in box, 1980s
EX $6   **NM** $22   **MIP** n/a

❏ **John Deere 4010**, 1:64-scale, Keith (Custom), green and yellow, Apache-Mall 1988 Show Tractor, did not come in box, 1980s
EX $6   **NM** $22   **MIP** n/a

❏ **John Deere 4020**, 1:64-scale, Ertl, green, MFD, w/cab, 2002, No. 15218
EX $4   **NM** $5   **MIP** $6

❏ **John Deere 4020**, 1:64-scale, Ertl, duals, ROPS, 2007, No. 15936
EX $2   **NM** $4   **MIP** $6

❏ **John Deere 4020**, 1:64-scale, Keith (Custom), green and yellow, did not come in box, 1980s
EX $6   **NM** $22   **MIP** n/a

❏ **John Deere 4020**, 1:64-scale, Matsen (Custom), green and yellow, did not come in box, 1980s
EX $6   **NM** $22   **MIP** n/a

❏ **John Deere 4020**, 1:64-scale, Matsen (Custom), green and yellow, did not come in box, 1980s
EX $6   **NM** $22   **MIP** n/a

❏ **John Deere 430**, 1:64-scale, Ertl, green, NF, 1996, No. 5620
EX $4   **NM** $5   **MIP** $6

❏ **John Deere 430**, 1:64-scale, Keith (Custom), green and yellow, 1988 New Ulm Show Tractor, did not come in box
EX $6   **NM** $22   **MIP** n/a

❑ **John Deere 430**, 1:64-scale, Keith (Custom), green and yellow, did not come in box, 1980s
EX $6   **NM** $22   **MIP** n/a

❑ **John Deere 430 w/Hay Rake**, 1:64-scale, Ertl, 2006, No. 15793
EX $4   **NM** $6   **MIP** $9

❑ **John Deere 4320**, 1:64-scale, Gunning (Custom), green and yellow, did not come in box, 1980s
EX $6   **NM** $22   **MIP** n/a

❑ **John Deere 4320**, 1:64-scale, Gunning (Custom), green and yellow, did not come in box, 1980s
EX $6   **NM** $22   **MIP** n/a

❑ **John Deere 4320**, 1:64-scale, Gunning (Custom), green and yellow, did not come in box, 1980s
EX $6   **NM** $22   **MIP** n/a

❑ **John Deere 4430**, 1:64-scale, Argentina, industrial yellow and black, 1980s
EX $27   **NM** $41   **MIP** $57

❑ **John Deere 4430**, 1:64-scale, Argentina, industrial yellow and black, 1980s
EX $27   **NM** $41   **MIP** $57

❑ **John Deere 4430**, 1:64-scale, Argentina, green and yellow, 1980s
EX $27   **NM** $41   **MIP** $57

❑ **John Deere 4430**, 1:64-scale, Argentina, green and yellow, 1980s
EX $27   **NM** $41   **MIP** $57

❑ **John Deere 4430**, 1:64-scale, Ertl, green and yellow, small wheels, rivet used for rear axle, on blue print card, 1980s, No. 1308
EX $4   **NM** $6   **MIP** $9

❑ **John Deere 4430**, 1:64-scale, Ertl, green and yellow, spun-on rear axle, on blue print card, 1980s, No. 1308
EX $4   **NM** $6   **MIP** $9

❑ **John Deere 4430**, 1:64-scale, Ertl, green and yellow, pushed-on front wheels, 1980s, No. 1619
EX $4   **NM** $6   **MIP** $9

❑ **John Deere 4430**, 1:64-scale, Ertl, green and yellow, spun-on front wheels, 1980s, No. 1619
EX $4   **NM** $6   **MIP** $9

❑ **John Deere 4430**, 1:64-scale, Ertl, green and yellow, (single) front cab post, rivet used for rear axle, 1980s, No. 1308
EX $4   **NM** $6   **MIP** $9

❑ **John Deere 4430**, 1:64-scale, Ertl, green and yellow, (single) front cab post, small wheels, on blue print card, 1980s, No. 1308
EX $4   **NM** $6   **MIP** $9

❑ **John Deere 4430**, 1:64-scale, Ertl, green & yellow, double front cab post, rivet rear axle, no box, 1980s, No. 1308
EX $4   **NM** $6   **MIP** $9

❑ **John Deere 4430**, 1:64-scale, Ertl, green and yellow, (double) front cab post, small wheels, on blue print card, 1980s, No. 1308
EX $4   **NM** $6   **MIP** $9

❑ **John Deere 4440**, 1:64-scale, Ertl, green and yellow, 1980s, No. 1619
EX $4   **NM** $6   **MIP** $9

❑ **John Deere 4440**, 1:64-scale, Ertl, green and yellow, 1980s, No. 1619
EX $4   **NM** $6   **MIP** $9

❑ **John Deere 4440**, 1:64-scale, Ertl, duals, 2007, No. 15939
EX $4   **NM** $6   **MIP** $9

❑ **John Deere 4450**, 1:64-scale, Ertl, green and yellow, 1980s, No. 5516
EX $4   **NM** $6   **MIP** $9

❑ **John Deere 4450**, 1:64-scale, Ertl, green and yellow, Pow-R-Pull, different tires, 1980s, No. 4092
EX $4   **NM** $6   **MIP** $9

❑ **John Deere 4450**, 1:64-scale, Ertl, green and yellow, Pow-R-Pull, 1980s, No. 4092
EX $4   **NM** $6   **MIP** $9

❑ **John Deere 4450**, 1:64-scale, Ertl, green and yellow, MFD, 1980s, No. 5517
EX $4   **NM** $6   **MIP** $9

❑ **John Deere 4450**, 1:64-scale, Ertl, green and yellow, 1980s, No. 5509
EX $4   **NM** $6   **MIP** $9

❑ **John Deere 4450**, 1:64-scale, Ertl, green and yellow, 1980s, No. 5509
EX $4   **NM** $6   **MIP** $9

❏ **John Deere 4450**, 1:64-scale, Ertl, green and yellow, 1980s, No. 5509
EX $4   **NM** $6   **MIP** $9

❏ **John Deere 4450**, 1:64-scale, Ertl, green and black, w/Loader, 1986, No. 587
EX $4   **NM** $6   **MIP** $9

❏ **John Deere 4455**, 1:64-scale, Ertl, green, 2WD, 1989, No. 5571
EX $4   **NM** $6   **MIP** $9

❏ **John Deere 4455**, 1:64-scale, Ertl, green, MFD, 1990, No. 5612
EX $4   **NM** $6   **MIP** $9

❏ **John Deere 4455**, 1:64-scale, Ertl, green, w/duals, 1990, No. 5606
EX $4   **NM** $6   **MIP** $9

❏ **John Deere 4455**, 1:64-scale, Ertl, green, MFD, 1990, No. 5612
EX $4   **NM** $6   **MIP** $9

❏ **John Deere 4455**, 1:64-scale, Ertl, green, w/loader, 1990, No. 5613
EX $4   **NM** $6   **MIP** $9

❏ **John Deere 4520**, 1:64-scale, Ertl, green, '01 National Farm Toy Show Edition, 2001
EX $4   **NM** $9   **MIP** $16

❏ **John Deere 4520**, 1:64-scale, Ertl, green, 2WD, duals, Hiniker cab, 2002, No. 15438
EX $4   **NM** $5   **MIP** $6

❏ **John Deere 4930 Dry Box Spreader**, 1:64-scale, Ertl, singles, 2007, No. 15941
EX $3   **NM** $6   **MIP** $8

❏ **John Deere 50**, 1:64-scale, Ertl, green, 1997, No. 5168
EX $4   **NM** $5   **MIP** $6

❏ **John Deere 5010**, 1:64-scale, Ertl, green, 2000, No. 15138
EX $4   **NM** $5   **MIP** $6

❏ **John Deere 5020**, 1:64-scale, Ertl, prototype, 1996, No. 5776
(Photo by Ertl)
EX $4   **NM** $6   **MIP** n/a

❏ **John Deere 5020**, 1:64-scale, Ertl, green, '97 National Farm Toy Museum Edition, 1997, No. 3051MA
EX $4   **NM** $5   **MIP** $7

❏ **John Deere 5020**, 1:64-scale, Ertl, green, on furrow magazine card, 2000, No. 15155
EX $4   **NM** $5   **MIP** $6

❏ **John Deere 5020**, 1:64-scale, Keith (Custom), green and yellow, did not come in box, 1980s
EX $6   **NM** $22   **MIP** n/a

❏ **John Deere 5020**, 1:64-scale, Keith (Custom), green and yellow, did not come in box, 1980s
EX $6   **NM** $22   **MIP** n/a

❏ **John Deere 5020**, 1:64-scale, Matsen (Custom), Industrial-yellow, did not come in box, 1980s
EX $6   **NM** $22   **MIP** n/a

❏ **John Deere 5020 w/Sheep's Foot**, 1:64-scale, Ertl, 2006, No. 15910
EX $4   **NM** $6   **MIP** $8

❏ **John Deere 5020 w/Spreader**, 1:64-scale, Ertl, 2006, No. 15827
EX $5   **NM** $9   **MIP** $12

❏ **John Deere 520**, 1:64-scale, Ertl, green, WF, 1997, No. 5193
EX $4   **NM** $5   **MIP** $6

❏ **John Deere 520**, 1:64-scale, Ertl, green, '99 Iowa FFA Edition, 1999, No. 16013A
EX $4   **NM** $5   **MIP** $8

❏ **John Deere 530**, 1:64-scale, Ertl, green, duals, 1997, No. 5194
EX $4   **NM** $5   **MIP** $6

❏ **John Deere 60**, 1:64-scale, Ertl, green and yellow, w/ or w/o hook-hitch, on blue print card, 1970s, No. 1305
EX $4   **NM** $6   **MIP** $89

❏ **John Deere 60**, 1:64-scale, Ertl, green, WF, '00 National Farm Toy Museum Edition, 2000, No. 16047A
EX $4   **NM** $5   **MIP** $6

❏ **John Deere 60**, 1:64-scale, Ertl, green, NF, 2000, No. 15331
EX $4   **NM** $5   **MIP** $6

❏ **John Deere 620**, 1:64-scale, Ertl, green, NF, 1999, No. 5205
EX $4   **NM** $5   **MIP** $6

❑ **John Deere 6200**, 1:64-scale, Ertl, green, 2WD, 1994, No. 5733
EX $4   **NM** $5   **MIP** $6

❑ **John Deere 6200**, 1:64-scale, Ertl, green, w/duals, 1995, No. 5734
EX $4   **NM** $5   **MIP** $6

❑ **John Deere 6200**, 1:64-scale, Ertl, green, '96 John Deere Parts Expo, 1996, No. 5912MA
EX $4   **NM** $5   **MIP** $6

❑ **John Deere 6210**, 1:64-scale, Ertl, green, MFD, 1998, No. 5170
EX $4   **NM** $5   **MIP** $6

❑ **John Deere 630**, 1:64-scale, Ertl, green, WF on furrow magazine card, 2000, No. 15153
EX $4   **NM** $5   **MIP** $6

❑ **John Deere 630**, 1:64-scale, Ertl, green, w/corn picker and wagon, 2000, No. 15086
EX $4   **NM** $5   **MIP** $6

❑ **John Deere 6400**, 1:64-scale, Ertl, green, w/loader, 1994, No. 5732
EX $4   **NM** $5   **MIP** $6

❑ **John Deere 6400**, 1:64-scale, Ertl, 1994, No. 5729 *(Photo by Ertl)*
EX $4   **NM** $5   **MIP** $6

❑ **John Deere 6400**, 1:64-scale, Ertl, green, w/revised loader, 1996, No. 5929
EX $4   **NM** $5   **MIP** $6

❑ **John Deere 6410**, 1:64-scale, Ertl, green, w/loader, 1998, No. 5169
EX $4   **NM** $5   **MIP** $6

❑ **John Deere 6420**, 1:64-scale, Ertl, green, MFD, 2002, No. 15226
EX $4   **NM** $5   **MIP** $6

❑ **John Deere 7020**, 1:64-scale, Ertl, green, '03 National Farm Toy Show Edition, 2003, No. 16106A
EX $6   **NM** $12   **MIP** $18

❑ **John Deere 7020**, 1:64-scale, Ertl, green, 2004, No. 15621
EX $4   **NM** $5   **MIP** $6

❑ **John Deere 7020**, 1:64-scale, Ertl, 4WD, 2005, No. 15621
EX $4   **NM** $6   **MIP** $8

❑ **John Deere 730**, 1:64-scale, Baker (Custom), green and yellow, did not come in box, 1980s
EX $6   **NM** $22   **MIP** n/a

❑ **John Deere 730**, 1:64-scale, Ertl, green and yellow, metal fenders, on blue print card, 1970s, No. 1306
EX $4   **NM** $6   **MIP** $89

❑ **John Deere 730**, 1:64-scale, Ertl, green and yellow, on blue print card, no mudel numbers on tractor, 1980s, No. 1306
EX $9   **NM** $18   **MIP** $89

❑ **John Deere 730**, 1:64-scale, Ertl, green and yellow, plastic fenders, w/ or w/o hook-hitch, on blue print card, 1980s, No. 1306
EX $4   **NM** $6   **MIP** $12

❑ **John Deere 730**, 1:64-scale, Keith (Custom), green and yellow, 1998 Lafayette Show Tractor, did not come in box
EX $6   **NM** $22   **MIP** n/a

❑ **John Deere 730**, 1:64-scale, Keith (Custom), green and yellow, 1998 Lafayette Show Tractor, did not come in box
EX $6   **NM** $22   **MIP** n/a

❑ **John Deere 730**, 1:64-scale, Keith (Custom), green and yellow, Wheatland fenders, did not come in box, 1980s
EX $6   **NM** $22   **MIP** n/a

❑ **John Deere 730**, 1:64-scale, Keith (Custom), green and yellow, did not come in box, 1980s
EX $6   **NM** $22   **MIP** n/a

❏ **John Deere 730**, 1:64-scale, Keith (Custom), green and yellow, did not come in box, 1980s
EX $6   **NM** $22   **MIP** n/a

❏ **John Deere 7520**, 1:64-scale, Baker (Custom), green and yellow, did not come in box, 1980s
EX $36   **NM** $47   **MIP** n/a

❏ **John Deere 7520**, 1:64-scale, Walters (Custom), green and yellow, 1980s
EX $36   **NM** $47   **MIP** n/a

❏ **John Deere 7520 w/Grain Drill**, 1:64-scale, Ertl, 2006, No. 15894
EX $5   **NM** $9   **MIP** $12

❏ **John Deere 7600**, 1:64-scale, Ertl, green, w/sound chip, 1994, No. 5750
EX $4   **NM** $5   **MIP** $6

❏ **John Deere 7600**, 1:64-scale, Ertl, green, friction drive, 1994, No. 5672
EX $4   **NM** $5   **MIP** $6

❏ **John Deere 7610**, 1:64-scale, Ertl, green, w/sound chip, 1996, No. 5206
EX $4   **NM** $5   **MIP** $6

❏ **John Deere 7610**, 1:64-scale, Ertl, green, friction drive, reissued under #15668, 1999, No. 5203
EX $4   **NM** $5   **MIP** $6

❏ **John Deere 7710**, 1:64-scale, Ertl, green, MFD, row crop duals, 2001, No. 15316
EX $4   **NM** $5   **MIP** $6

❏ **John Deere 7800**, 1:64-scale, Ertl, green, 2WD, 1992, No. 5538
EX $4   **NM** $5   **MIP** $6

❏ **John Deere 7800**, 1:64-scale, Ertl, green, MFD, 1992, No. 5651
EX $4   **NM** $5   **MIP** $6

❏ **John Deere 7800**, 1:64-scale, Ertl, green, w/loader, 1992, No. 5652
EX $4   **NM** $5   **MIP** $6

❏ **John Deere 7800**, 1:64-scale, Ertl, green, w/duals, 1992, No. 5649
EX $4   **NM** $5   **MIP** $6

❏ **John Deere 7800 Set**, 1:64-scale, Ertl, three-piece set, No. 5747
(Photo by Ertl)
EX n/a   **NM** n/a   **MIP** $9

❏ **John Deere 7810**, 1:64-scale, Ertl, green, MFD, 1996, No. 5702
EX $3   **NM** $4   **MIP** $6

❏ **John Deere 7820**, 1:64-scale, Ertl, green, MFD, w/row crop duals, 2003, No. 15493
EX $4   **NM** $5   **MIP** $6

❏ **John Deere 7830**, 1:64-scale, Ertl, 2006, No. 15916
EX $4   **NM** $6   **MIP** $8

❏ **John Deere 7920**, 1:64-scale, Ertl, green, MFD, '03 Farm Show Edition, 2003, No. 15541A
EX $4   **NM** $8   **MIP** $17

❏ **John Deere 7930 w/Grain Cart**, 1:64-scale, Ertl, 2006, No. 15858
EX $4   **NM** $6   **MIP** $8

❏ **John Deere 80**, 1:64-scale, Ertl, green, '96 National Farm Toy Museum Edition, 1996, No. 1213MA
EX $4   **NM** $5   **MIP** $6

❏ **John Deere 8000T 10th Anniversary Set**, 1:64-scale, Ertl, four track tractors, 2007, No. 15880
EX $7   **NM** $14   **MIP** $21

❏ **John Deere 8010**, 1:64-scale, Keith/Buhler (Custom), green and yellow, did not come in box
EX $28   **NM** $37   **MIP** n/a

❏ **John Deere 8020**, 1:64-scale, Ertl, green, 2004, No. 15616
EX $5   **NM** $6   **MIP** $8

❏ **John Deere 8020**, 1:64-scale, Ertl, diesel, 4WD, 2005, No. 15616
EX $4   **NM** $6   **MIP** $8

❏ **John Deere 8100**, 1:64-scale, Ertl, green, MFD, 1998, No. 5065
(Photo by Ertl)
EX $4   **NM** $5   **MIP** $6

❏ **John Deere 820**, 1:64-scale, Ertl, green, 2000, No. 15317
EX $4   **NM** $5   **MIP** $6

❏ **John Deere 820**, 1:64-scale, Ertl, green, 2000, No. 15137
EX $4   **NM** $5   **MIP** $6

❏ **John Deere 8200**, 1:64-scale, Ertl, green, 2WD, 1997, No. 5064
(Photo by Ertl)
EX $4   **NM** $5   **MIP** $6

❏ **John Deere 8210**, 1:64-scale, Ertl, green, 2WD, 1999, No. 15064
EX $4   **NM** $5   **MIP** $6

❏ **John Deere 8220**, 1:64-scale, Ertl, green, MFD, floation tires, 2003, No. 15496
EX $4　　**NM** $5　　**MIP** $6

❏ **John Deere 8230 w/Planter**, 1:64-scale, Ertl, 2006, No. 15797
EX $5　　**NM** $9　　**MIP** $12

❏ **John Deere 830**, 1:64-scale, Keith (Custom), green and yellow, did not come in box, 1980s
EX $6　　**NM** $22　　**MIP** n/a

❏ **John Deere 830**, 1:64-scale, Keith (Custom), green and yellow, 1987 New Ulm Show Tractor, did not come in box, 1980s
EX $6　　**NM** $22　　**MIP** n/a

❏ **John Deere 8300**, 1:64-scale, Ertl, green, MFD, 1996, No. 5063
EX $4　　**NM** $5　　**MIP** $6

❏ **John Deere 8300**, 1:64-scale, Ertl, green, MFD, 1996, No. 5063
EX $4　　**NM** $5　　**MIP** $6

❏ **John Deere 8310**, 1:64-scale, Ertl, green, 2WD, 2002, No. 15334
EX $4　　**NM** $5　　**MIP** $6

❏ **John Deere 8330**, 1:64-scale, Ertl, 2006, No. 15920
EX $4　　**NM** $6　　**MIP** $8

❏ **John Deere 8400**, 1:64-scale, Ertl, green, MFD and duals, 1996, No. 5927
EX $4　　**NM** $5　　**MIP** $6

❏ **John Deere 8400T**, 1:64-scale, Ertl, green, track tractor, 1997, No. 5051
EX $4　　**NM** $5　　**MIP** $6

❏ **John Deere 8400T**, 1:64-scale, Ertl, green, '97 Waterloo Works Edition, 1997, No. 5195EA

(Photo by Bossen Implement)
EX $8　　**NM** $22　　**MIP** $33

❏ **John Deere 8410**, 1:64-scale, Ertl, green, MFD, duals, 1999, No. 15062
EX $4　　**NM** $5　　**MIP** $6

❏ **John Deere 8410**, 1:64-scale, Ertl, green, MFD, '99 Farm Show Edition, 1999, No. 15118A
EX $6　　**NM** $16　　**MIP** $22

❏ **John Deere 8410T**, 1:64-scale, Ertl, green, track tractor, 2000, No. 15100
EX $4　　**NM** $5　　**MIP** $6

❏ **John Deere 8420**, 1:64-scale, Ertl, green, MFD, front and rear duals, 2002, No. 15225
EX $4　　**NM** $5　　**MIP** $6

❏ **John Deere 8420**, 1:64-scale, Ertl, green, 2002, No. 15413
EX $4　　**NM** $5　　**MIP** $6

❏ **John Deere 8420**, 1:64-scale, Ertl, green, MFD, European version, 2002, No. 15409
EX $4　　**NM** $5　　**MIP** $6

❏ **John Deere 8420T**, 1:64-scale, Ertl, green, '02 Farm Show Edition, 2002, No. 15347A
EX $4　　**NM** $5　　**MIP** $6

❏ **John Deere 8430T**, 1:64-scale, Ertl, 2006, No. 15919
EX $4　　**NM** $6　　**MIP** $8

❏ **John Deere 8520T**, 1:64-scale, Ertl, green, track tractor, 2002, No. 15224
EX $4　　**NM** $5　　**MIP** $6

❏ **John Deere 8560**, 1:64-scale, Ertl, green, 4WD, 1989, No. 5603
EX $4　　**NM** $5　　**MIP** $6

❏ **John Deere 8560**, 1:64-scale, Ertl, w/planter set, 1990s, No. 5805

(Photo by Ertl)
EX $4　　**NM** $5　　**MIP** $6

❏ **John Deere 8560**, 1:64-scale, Ertl, green, 4WD, 1993, No. 5603EP
EX $4　　**NM** $5　　**MIP** $6

❏ **John Deere 8630**, 1:64-scale, Baker (Custom), green and yellow, did not come in box, 1980s
EX $16　　**NM** $22　　**MIP** n/a

❏ **John Deere 8630**, 1:64-scale, Baker (Custom), green and yellow, 1988 GCD Show Tractor, 1980s
EX $22　　**NM** $29　　**MIP** $58

❏ **John Deere 8770**, 1:64-scale, Ertl, w/triples, 2007, No. 15935
EX $3　　**NM** $6　　**MIP** $8

Photos by Jon Jacobson unless otherwise noted.

❑ **John Deere 8850**, 1:64-scale, Ertl, light green and yellow, 1980s, No. 575
EX $12 **NM** $18 **MIP** $27

❑ **John Deere 8850**, 1:64-scale, Ertl, green and yellow, 1980s, No. 575
EX $12 **NM** $16 **MIP** $19

❑ **John Deere 8850**, 1:64-scale, Ertl, green and yellow, friction-motor, 1980s, No. 551
EX $8 **NM** $11 **MIP** $16

❑ **John Deere 8870**, 1:64-scale, Ertl, green, 4WD w/duals, reissued under stock #15322, 1995, No. 5791
(Photo by Ertl)
EX $4 **NM** $5 **MIP** $6

❑ **John Deere 9300T**, 1:64-scale, Ertl, green, track tractor, '00 Farm Show Edition, 2000, No. 15113A
EX $6 **NM** $16 **MIP** $22

❑ **John Deere 9320**, 1:64-scale, Ertl, green, model kit, 2002, No. 15429
EX $4 **NM** $5 **MIP** $6

❑ **John Deere 9400**, 1:64-scale, Ertl, green, 4WD, w/triples, 1997, No. 5937
EX $4 **NM** $5 **MIP** $6

❑ **John Deere 9400**, 1:64-scale, Ertl, green, model kit, 2001, No. 15294
EX $4 **NM** $5 **MIP** $6

❑ **John Deere 9400**, 1:64-scale, Ertl, green, 4WD, w/duals, 2001, No. 15321
EX $4 **NM** $5 **MIP** $6

❑ **John Deere 9400T**, 1:64-scale, Ertl, green, track tractor, 2000, No. 15015
EX $4 **NM** $5 **MIP** $6

❑ **John Deere 9420**, 1:64-scale, Ertl, green, 4WD, w/triples, reissued under stock #13553, 2002, No. 15222
EX $4 **NM** $5 **MIP** $6

❑ **John Deere 9420 w/2 Scrapers Set**, 1:64-scale, Ertl, duals, 2 yellow scrapers, 2007, No. 15929
EX $4 **NM** $8 **MIP** $12

❑ **John Deere 9420T**, 1:64-scale, Ertl, green, track tractor, 2002, No. 15223
EX $4 **NM** $5 **MIP** $6

❑ **John Deere 9620**, 1:64-scale, Ertl, green, 4WD, w/singles, 2004, No. 15678
EX $4 **NM** $5 **MIP** $6

❑ **John Deere 9620**, 1:64-scale, Ertl, 4WD, 2005, No. 15678
EX $4 **NM** $6 **MIP** $8

❑ **John Deere 9620**, 1:64-scale, Ertl, 2006, No. 15917
EX $4 **NM** $6 **MIP** $8

❑ **John Deere 9620T**, 1:64-scale, Ertl, green, track tractor, 2004, No. 15679
EX $4 **NM** $5 **MIP** $6

❑ **John Deere 9620T**, 1:64-scale, Ertl, track tractor, 2005, No. 15679
EX $4 **NM** $6 **MIP** $8

❑ **John Deere A**, 1:64-scale, Ertl, green and yellow, tall oil-breather, on blue print card, 1970s, No. 1304
EX $4 **NM** $5 **MIP** $89

❑ **John Deere A**, 1:64-scale, Ertl, green and yellow, w/ or w/o hook-hitch, on blue print card, 1970s, No. 1304
EX $4 **NM** $5 **MIP** $89

❑ **John Deere A**, 1:64-scale, Ertl, green, in wood box, Ertl 50th Anniversary, 1995, No. 5305
EX $4 **NM** $5 **MIP** $6

❑ **John Deere A**, 1:64-scale, Ertl, green, w/man on furrow magazine card, 2000, No. 15154
EX $4 **NM** $5 **MIP** $6

❑ **John Deere A**, 1:64-scale, Ertl, green, w/man, 2003, No. 15572A
EX $4 **NM** $5 **MIP** $6

❑ **John Deere A**, 1:64-scale, Nygren (Custom), green, w/Loader, tractor is by Ertl, did not come in box, 1980s
EX $9 **NM** $24 **MIP** n/a

❏ **John Deere A**, 1:64-scale, Scale Models, five different chrome colors, sold as a Christmas Ornament, 1980s
EX $3   **NM** $4   **MIP** $6

❏ **John Deere A**, 1:64-scale, Scale Models, green and yellow, 1980s
EX $3   **NM** $4   **MIP** $6

❏ **John Deere A**, 1:64-scale, Scale Models, green and yellow, 1980s
EX $3   **NM** $4   **MIP** $6

❏ **John Deere A**, 1:64-scale, Taiwan, red, sold as a Christmas Ornament, did not come in box, 1980s
EX $3   **NM** $4   **MIP** n/a

❏ **John Deere A w/'50 Chevy Truck Set**, 1:64-scale, Ertl, truck hauls styled A tractor, 2007, No. 15876
EX $6   **NM** $12   **MIP** $16

❏ **John Deere D**, 1:64-scale, Ertl, green and yellow, smooth rear wheels, on blue print card, No. 1303
EX $4   **NM** $5   **MIP** $89

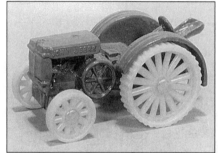

❏ **John Deere D**, 1:64-scale, Ertl, green and yellow, ribbed rear wheels, w/ or w/o hook hitch, on blue print card, No. 1303
EX $4   **NM** $5   **MIP** $12

❏ **John Deere D**, 1:64-scale, Ertl, gold, styled, 1 yr JD Commons, 1 of 5000, 1999, No. 15051A
EX $4   **NM** $5   **MIP** $22

❏ **John Deere D**, 1:64-scale, Ertl, green, styled, on furrow magazine card, 2000, No. 15157
EX $4   **NM** $5   **MIP** $6

❏ **John Deere D**, 1:64-scale, Ertl, green, styled, 2000, No. 15136
EX $4   **NM** $5   **MIP** $6

❏ **John Deere Froelich**, 1:64-scale, Ertl, green and yellow, on blue print card, 1970s, No. 1301
EX $4   **NM** $5   **MIP** $89

❏ **John Deere Froelich**, 1:64-scale, RB, very crude, came in set—did not come in individual box, 1980s
EX $3   **NM** $4   **MIP** n/a

❏ **John Deere G**, 1:64-scale, Scale Models, green and yellow, 1980s
EX $3   **NM** $4   **MIP** $6

❏ **John Deere G**, 1:64-scale, Scale Models, green and yellow, 1980s
EX $3   **NM** $4   **MIP** $6

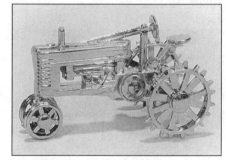

❏ **John Deere G**, 1:64-scale, Scale Models, five different chrome colors, sold as a Christmas Ornament, 1980s
EX $2   **NM** $4   **MIP** $6

❏ **John Deere GP**, 1:64-scale, Scale Models, green and yellow, 1980s
EX $6   **NM** $9   **MIP** $14

❏ **John Deere GP**, 1:64-scale, Scale Models, green and yellow, 1980s
EX $3   **NM** $4   **MIP** $6

❏ **John Deere GP**, 1:64-scale, Scale Models, green and yellow, 1980s
EX $6   **NM** $9   **MIP** $14

❏ **John Deere GP**, 1:64-scale, Scale Models, green and yellow, 1980s
EX $3   **NM** $4   **MIP** $6

❏ **John Deere Haying Set**, 1:64-scale, Ertl, tractor, square baler, bale wagon, mower conditioner, 2007, No. 15968
EX $9   **NM** $14   **MIP** $19

❏ **John Deere LA**, 1:64-scale, Custom Cast (Custom), green and yellow, did not come in box, 1980s
EX $16   **NM** $33   **MIP** n/a

❏ **John Deere Lanz 700**, 1:64-scale, Matchbox, green and yellow w/black tires, 1960s
EX $22   **NM** $46   **MIP** $67

❏ **John Deere Lanz 700**, 1:64-scale, Matchbox, green and yellow w/gray tires, 1960s
EX $22   **NM** $46   **MIP** $67

❏ **John Deere Set**, 1:64-scale, Ertl, green, Waterloo Boy, M, G, R, No. 5523
EX n/a   **NM** n/a   **MIP** $13

❏ **John Deere Set**, 1:64-scale, Ertl, five-piece tractor and implement set, 1990s, No. 5626 *(Photo by Ertl)*
EX n/a   **NM** n/a   **MIP** $17

❏ **John Deere Set**, 1:64-scale, Ertl, Revised, Overtime, MI, G, 80, 1995, No. 5523ER *(Photo by Ertl)*
EX n/a   **NM** n/a   **MIP** $12

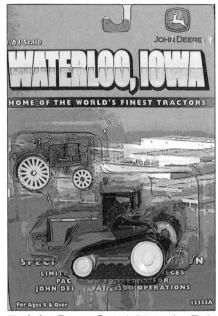

❏ **John Deere Set**, 1:64-scale, Ertl, green, 9400T and Waterloo Boy, 1 of 3000, JD Waterloo Works, 2001, No. 15335A *(Photo by Bossen Implement)*
EX n/a   **NM** n/a   **MIP** $33

❏ **John Deere Set**, 1:64-scale, Ertl, green, 4010 NF, 4020, 4320, 4620, 2001, No. 15216
EX n/a   **NM** n/a   **MIP** $18

❏ **John Deere Set**, 1:64-scale, Ertl, green, 4430, 4440, 4450 on card, 2003, No. 15492
EX n/a   **NM** n/a   **MIP** $18

❏ **John Deere Set**, 1:64-scale, Ertl, green, 72, 720, 730, 2003, No. 15565
EX n/a   **NM** n/a   **MIP** $13

❏ **John Deere Set**, 1:64-scale, Ertl, green, stacker set of 4020's, 2003, No. 15522
EX n/a   **NM** n/a   **MIP** $18

❏ **John Deere Set**, 1:64-scale, Ertl, green, 80, 820, 830, 2004, No. 15615
EX n/a   **NM** n/a   **MIP** $13

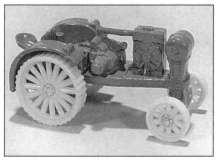

❑ **John Deere Waterloo Boy**, 1:64-scale, Ertl, green and yellow, ribbed rear wheels, large water pipe, on blue print card, 1970s, No. 1302
EX $4   **NM** $5   **MIP** $12

❑ **John Deere Waterloo Boy**, 1:64-scale, Ertl, green and yellow, ribbed rear wheels, small water pipe, on blue print card, 1970s, No. 1302
EX $4   **NM** $5   **MIP** $12

❑ **John Deere Waterloo Boy**, 1:64-scale, Ertl, green and yellow, smooth rear wheels, on blue print card, 1970s, No. 1302
EX $4   **NM** $5   **MIP** $89

TRUCKS 1:16-SCALE

❑ **John Deere Dealer Truck**, 1:16-scale, Ertl, white, 1980s, No. 5531
EX $12   **NM** $17   **MIP** $23

❑ **John Deere Dealer Truck**, 1:16-scale, Ertl, white, 1980s, No. 543
EX $12   **NM** $17   **MIP** $23

❑ **John Deere Ford F-150 Pickup**, 1:16-scale, Ertl, No. 5793 *(Photo by Ertl)*
EX $7   **NM** $13   **MIP** $19

❑ **John Deere Implement Truck**, 1:16-scale, Ertl, white, w/plastic front bumper, 1970s, No. 594
EX $72   **NM** $98   **MIP** $153

❑ **John Deere Implement Truck**, 1:16-scale, Ertl, white, w/die-cast front bumper, 1970s, No. 594
EX $78   **NM** $102   **MIP** $176

TRUCKS 1:25-SCALE

❑ **John Deere 57 Chevy Stake Truck**, 1:25-scale, Ertl, Prestige Series, No. 5049 *(Photo by Ertl)*
EX $12   **NM** $26   **MIP** $29

❑ **John Deere Dealer Truck**, 1:25-scale, Ertl, white, 1970s, No. 3827
EX $12   **NM** $17   **MIP** $24

❑ **John Deere Equipment Hauler**, 1:25-scale, Ertl, white and black w/1:32-scale yellow tractor backhoe, 1980s, No. 5570
EX $17   **NM** $32   **MIP** $43

❑ **John Deere Log Truck**, 1:25-scale, Ertl, white, w/ and w/o International lettering in grille, 1980s, No. 3180
EX $22   **NM** $46   **MIP** $52

Photos by Jon Jacobson unless otherwise noted.

❏ **John Deere Log Truck**, 1:25-scale, Ertl, white, w/o International lettering in grille, 1980s, No. 3180
EX $22   **NM** $46   **MIP** $52

❏ **John Deere Log Truck**, 1:25-scale, Ertl, white, w/International lettering in grille, 1980s, No. 3180
EX $36   **NM** $57   **MIP** $76

❏ **John Deere Parts Express Semi**, 1:25-scale, Ertl, white, 1970s, No. 3124
EX $11   **NM** $16   **MIP** $33

❏ **John Deere Parts Express Semi**, 1:25-scale, Ertl, white, 1980s, No. 3124
EX $11   **NM** $16   **MIP** $33

❏ **John Deere Truck w/Waterloo Boy on Back**, 1:25-scale, Ertl, No. 5768 *(Photo by Ertl)*
EX $9   **NM** $14   **MIP** $26

TRUCKS 1:43-SCALE

❏ **John Deere Dain Truck**, 1:43-scale, SpecCast, 1990s
EX $6   **NM** $8   **MIP** $12

❏ **John Deere Ford Truck**, 1:43-scale, SpecCast, 1990s
EX $6   **NM** $8   **MIP** $12

❏ **Semi w/John Deere Van Trailer**, 1:43-scale, Ertl, No. 5401 *(Photo by Ertl)*
EX $9   **NM** $18   **MIP** $23

TRUCKS 1:64-SCALE

❏ **John Deere '50 Chevy Grain Truck**, 1:64-scale, Ertl, No. 4633
(Photo by Ertl)
EX $3   **NM** $4   **MIP** $8

❏ **John Deere Dealer '50 Chevy Pickup**, 1:64-scale, Ertl, No. 5936
(Photo by Ertl)
EX $1   **NM** $2   **MIP** $3

❏ **John Deere Hauling Set**, 1:64-scale, Ertl, No. 5831 *(Photo by Ertl)*
EX $9   **NM** $13   **MIP** $22

❏ **John Deere Hauling Set**, 1:64-scale, Ertl, w/John Deere backhoe, No. 5574 *(Photo by Ertl)*
EX $9   **NM** $14   **MIP** $22

❏ **John Deere Hauling Set w/7810s**, 1:64-scale, Ertl, No. 5207
(Photo by Ertl)

EX $9   **NM** $16   **MIP** $23

❏ **John Deere Pickup w/John Deere MI on trailer**, 1:64-scale, Ertl, No. 5924 *(Photo by Ertl)*

EX $4   **NM** $7   **MIP** $12

❏ **John Deere Pickup w/Trailer and John Deere D**, 1:64-scale, Ertl, No. 5924 *(Photo by Kate Bossen)*

EX $4   **NM** $6   **MIP** $11

❏ **John Deere Straight Truck w/John Deere A '50 Chevy**, 1:64-scale, Ertl, No. 5933 *(Photo by Kate Bossen)*

EX $4   **NM** $6   **MIP** $11

❏ **Semi John Deere Consumer Products Van trailer**, 1:64-scale, Ertl, No. 5032 *(Photo by Ertl)*

EX $6   **NM** $12   **MIP** $18

❏ **Semi w/John Deere GT Van Box**, 1:64-scale, Ertl, No. 5814
(Photo by Ertl)

EX $6   **NM** $11   **MIP** $16

❏ **Semi w/John Deere Parts Van Box**, 1:64-scale, Ertl, No. 5714
(Photo by Kate Bossen)

EX $4   **NM** $8   **MIP** $16

KASTEN

IMPLEMENTS 1:64-SCALE

❏ **Kasten Manure Spreader**, 1:64-scale, Ertl, black

EX $6   **NM** $11   **MIP** $16

❏ **Kasten Wagon, Forage**, 1:64-scale, Ertl, black, 1980s, No. 9112

EX $6   **NM** $11   **MIP** $21

❏ **Kasten Wagon, Forage**, 1:64-scale, Ertl, black, 1980s, No. 9112

EX $6   **NM** $11   **MIP** $21

KILLBROS

IMPLEMENTS 1:64-SCALE

❏ **Killbros Wagon, Gravity**, 1:64-scale, Ertl, orange, No. 9413

EX $12   **NM** $18   **MIP** $26

KINZE

IMPLEMENTS 1:16-SCALE

❏ **Kinze Planter, 3600**, 1:16-scale, SpecCast, blue, 16 row w/interplants, 2006, No. GPR1283
(Photo by SpecCast)

EX $132   **NM** $227   **MIP** $328

❏ **Kinze Wagon, Auger 1050**, 1:16-scale, SpecCast, blue, duals, 2004, No. GPR1212
EX $63 **NM** $96 **MIP** $143

❏ **Kinze Wagon, Auger 1050**, 1:16-scale, SpecCast, blue, tracks, 2004, No. GPR1214
EX $63 **NM** $96 **MIP** $143

❏ **Kinze Wagon, Auger 1050**, 1:16-scale, SpecCast, blue, wide tread, 2004, No. CPR1213
EX $63 **NM** $96 **MIP** $143

❏ **Kinze Wagon, Auger 840**, 1:16-scale, Gottman, blue, diamond tread tires, serial numbered, 2002
EX $218 **NM** $267 **MIP** $333

❏ **Kinze Wagon, Auger 840**, 1:16-scale, Gottman, blue, tracks, serial numbered, 2002
EX $218 **NM** $267 **MIP** $333

IMPLEMENTS 1:64-SCALE

❏ **Kinze Grain Cart, 840**, 1:64-scale, Scale Models, blue and white, may be 1st or regular edition, No. 1802
EX $6 **NM** $9 **MIP** $14

❏ **Kinze Grain Cart, 840**, 1:64-scale, Scale Models, blue and white, Western Kansas Machinery Show "1988," 1st Edition, 1988
EX $6 **NM** $9 **MIP** $14

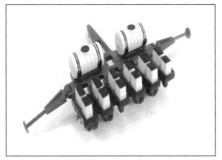

❏ **Kinze Planter, 2000**, 1:64-scale, SpecCast, blue, 6 row, No. CUST301 *(Photo by Bossen Implement)*
EX $6 **NM** $11 **MIP** $18

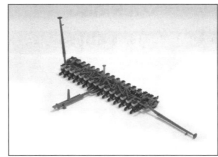

❏ **Kinze Planter, 3600**, 1:64-scale, SpecCast, blue, 16 row, 2002, No. GPR1205 *(Photo by Bossen Implement)*
EX $16 **NM** $22 **MIP** $33

❏ **Kinze Planter, 3600**, 1:64-scale, SpecCast, blue, 12 row, 2002, No. GPR1204
EX $17 **NM** $23 **MIP** $39

❏ **Kinze Planter, Set**, 1:64-scale, SpecCast, blue, 3600 12 and 16 row, '02 Farm Show Edition, 2002, No. GPR1203
EX n/a **NM** n/a **MIP** $78

❏ **Kinze Wagon, Auger 840**, 1:64-scale, Scale Models, blue, duals, No. 1806
EX $6 **NM** $11 **MIP** $18

❏ **Kinze Wagon, Auger 840**, 1:64-scale, Scale Models, blue, tracks, No. 1807 *(Photo by Bossen Implement)*
EX $6 **NM** $11 **MIP** $18

TRACTORS 1:16-SCALE

❏ **Kinze Big Blue**, 1:16-scale, SpecCast, 4WD, duals, this is one large tractor!, 2007, No. 921
(Photo by SpecCast)
EX $100 **NM** $150 **MIP** $200

KNUDSON

TRACTORS 1:16-SCALE

❏ **Knudson 310**, 1:16-scale, Precision Engineering, green, Hillside, 1997
EX $218 **NM** $267 **MIP** $333

❏ **Knudson 310**, 1:16-scale, Precision Engineering, green, serial numbered, 250 units, 1997
EX $218 **NM** $267 **MIP** $333

❏ **Knudson 360**, 1:16-scale, Precision Engineering, green, serial numbered, 250 units, 1997
EX $218 **NM** $267 **MIP** $333

❏ **Knudson 360**, 1:16-scale, Value Cast, green, Hillside
EX $13 **NM** $26 **MIP** $36

TRACTORS 1:64-SCALE

❏ **Knudson 310**, 1:64-scale, Value Cast, green, 1994 *(Photo by Bossen Implement)*
EX $13 **NM** $26 **MIP** $38

❑ **Knudson 310**, 1:64-scale, Value Cast, green, w/dozer blade, '96 Crosby, ND Toy Show Edition, 1996
(Photo by Bossen Implement)
EX $13   **NM** $26   **MIP** $43

❑ **Knudson 310H**, 1:64-scale, Value Cast, green, Hillside Model, 1994
EX $17   **NM** $26   **MIP** $38

❑ **Knudson 360**, 1:64-scale, Value Cast, yellow
EX $16   **NM** $23   **MIP** $43

❑ **Knudson 360**, 1:64-scale, Value Cast, green, w/triples
EX $13   **NM** $26   **MIP** $38

❑ **Knudson 360**, 1:64-scale, Value Cast, green, w/triples, 1995
EX $16   **NM** $17   **MIP** $38

❑ **Knudson 360**, 1:64-scale, Value Cast, white, w/duals, "Mendota Mama", 2002 *(Photo by Bossen Implement)*
EX $16   **NM** $26   **MIP** $38

❑ **Knudson 360H**, 1:64-scale, Value Cast, green, w/duals, Hillside Model, 1995
EX $16   **NM** $17   **MIP** $38

❑ **Knudson 4360**, 1:64-scale, Value Cast, yellow, singles, 1991
EX $16   **NM** $17   **MIP** $36

❑ **Knudson 4400**, 1:64-scale, Value Cast, yellow, w/duals, Collector Edition, 1991
EX $16   **NM** $19   **MIP** $38

❑ **Knudson 4400**, 1:64-scale, Value Cast, yellow, w/duals, 1991
(Photo by Bossen Implement)
EX $16   **NM** $17   **MIP** $36

KOEHRING

IMPLEMENTS 1:16-SCALE

❑ **Koehring Fox 3000 Forage Harvester "Fox Chopper"**, 1:16-scale, SpecCast, w/corn and hay head, 2007, No. 894 *(Photo by SpecCast)*
EX $85   **NM** $125   **MIP** $160

KORY

IMPLEMENTS 1:64-SCALE

❑ **Kory Wagon, Gravity**, 1:64-scale, Ertl, orange, No. 9520
EX $9   **NM** $16   **MIP** $24

❑ **Kory Wagon, Gravity**, 1:64-scale, Ertl, orange, No. 9520
EX $9   **NM** $16   **MIP** $24

❑ **Kory Wagon, Gravity**, 1:64-scale, Moore's, orange, 1997
EX $4   **NM** $5   **MIP** $8

KUBOTA

CONSTRUCTION EQUIPMENT 1:24-SCALE

❑ **Kubota Backhoe, BX-22**, 1:24-scale, China, orange, 2003, No. 0358
EX $14   **NM** $23   **MIP** $44

❑ **Kubota Mini-Excavator U-35**, 1:24-scale, China, orange, 2003, No. 0362
EX $11   **NM** $16   **MIP** $28

LAWN AND GARDEN 1:16-SCALE

❑ **Kubota 1560**, 1:16-scale, Scale Models, orange, No. FK-618
EX $8   **NM** $11   **MIP** $22

LAWN AND GARDEN 1:24-SCALE

❑ **Kubota RTY-900**, 1:24-scale, China, orange, 2003, No. 0500
EX $13   **NM** $22   **MIP** $39

❑ **Kubota T-1870**, 1:24-scale, China, orange, w/mower deck, 2003, No. 0356
EX $9   **NM** $14   **MIP** $29

❑ **Kubota ZD-28F**, 1:24-scale, China, orange, zero turn, w/mower deck, 2003, No. 0357
EX $13   **NM** $22   **MIP** $39

PEDAL TRACTORS

❑ **Kubota M-120**, Scale Models, orange, MFD, 2001, No. FK-627
EX $87   **NM** $121   **MIP** $153

❑ **Kubota M-6950**, Scale Models, orange, tractor in original condition
EX $148   **NM** $313   **MIP** $362

Photos by Jon Jacobson unless otherwise noted.

❑ **Kubota M-9000**, Scale Models, orange, 1999, No. FK-621
EX $87   **NM** $121   **MIP** $153

TRACTORS 1:16-SCALE

❑ **Kubota L-2850**, 1:16-scale, Scale Models, orange, 1988, No. FK-601
EX $8   **NM** $16   **MIP** $28

❑ **Kubota L-3410**, 1:16-scale, Scale Models, orange, MFD, grand, No. FK-619
EX $11   **NM** $22   **MIP** $36

❑ **Kubota L-5030**, 1:16-scale, Scale Models, orange, MFD, decal sheet included, L-3140, L-3430, L-3830, L-4330, L-4630, L-5030, 2003, No. FK-630
EX $9   **NM** $18   **MIP** $33

❑ **Kubota M-120**, 1:16-scale, Scale Models, orange, 2001, No. FK-622
(Photo by Bossen Implement)
EX $12   **NM** $24   **MIP** $43

TRACTORS 1:20-SCALE

❑ **Kubota M**, 1:20-scale, Diapet, orange, MFD, 1984
EX $11   **NM** $22   **MIP** $36

TRACTORS 1:24-SCALE

❑ **Kubota M-120**, 1:24-scale, China, orange, 2003, No. 0360
EX $13   **NM** $23   **MIP** $46

TRACTORS 1:64-SCALE

❑ **Kubota L-2850**, 1:64-scale, Scale Models, orange, No. FK-0602
(Photo by Bossen Implement)
EX $4   **NM** $6   **MIP** $6

❑ **Kubota L-2850**, 1:64-scale, Scale Models, orange, '91 Farm Progress Show Edition, 1991, No. FB-1583
(Photo by Bossen Implement)
EX $4   **NM** $6   **MIP** $9

❑ **Kubota L-2850**, 1:64-scale, Scale Models, orange, '93 Farm Progress Show Edition, 1993, No. FB-1632
EX $4   **NM** $6   **MIP** $9

M&W

IMPLEMENTS 1:64-SCALE

❑ **M&W Earthmaster**, 1:64-scale, Awe (Custom), M&W Red and cream, did not come in box
EX $9   **NM** $12   **MIP** n/a

❑ **M&W Gravity Wagon**, 1:64-scale, Ertl, red and silver, No. 9277
EX $12   **NM** $16   **MIP** $22

MASSEY-FERGUSON

CONSTRUCTION EQUIPMENT 1:16-SCALE

❑ **Massey-Ferguson Tractor, 3165**, 1:16-scale, Ertl, yellow, 1960s
EX $168   **NM** $324   **MIP** $918

❑ **Massey-Ferguson Tractor, 50 E**, 1:16-scale, Ertl, yellow, 1980s, No. 1123
EX $17   **NM** $32   **MIP** $43

❑ **Massey-Ferguson Tractor, 50 E**, 1:16-scale, Ertl, yellow, Collectors Edition, 1980s, No. 1123TA
EX $22   **NM** $38   **MIP** $48

CONSTRUCTION EQUIPMENT 1:32-SCALE

❑ **Massey-Ferguson Tractor, 135**, 1:32-scale, Britains, yellow, 1970s
EX $38   **NM** $48   **MIP** $82

❑ **Massey-Ferguson Wheel Loader**, 1:32-scale, Gamma, yellow, 1980s
EX $57   **NM** $74   **MIP** $98

CONSTRUCTION EQUIPMENT 1:43-SCALE

❏ **Massey-Ferguson Tractor, 50 B**, 1:43-scale, Corgi, yellow and red or orangeand white, also yellow w/o loader, 1970s
EX $38 **NM** $52 **MIP** $76

CONSTRUCTION EQUIPMENT 1:50-SCALE

❏ **Massey-Ferguson Crawler**, 1:50-scale, Brasileria, yellow, 1980s
EX $97 **NM** $128 **MIP** $193

❏ **Massey-Ferguson Crawler, 300**, 1:50-scale, NZG, yellow, 1970s
EX $72 **NM** $104 **MIP** $158

❏ **Massey-Ferguson Excavator**, 1:50-scale, NZG, yellow or white, 1970s
EX $33 **NM** $48 **MIP** $77

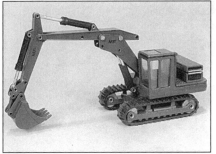

❏ **Massey-Ferguson Excavator**, 1:50-scale, NZG, military, 1970s
EX $33 **NM** $48 **MIP** $77

❏ **Massey-Ferguson Tractor, 50 B**, 1:50-scale, Conrad, yellow, w/Loader, 1980s
EX $43 **NM** $56 **MIP** $82

❏ **Massey-Ferguson Tractor, 50 D**, 1:50-scale, Conrad, yellow, Elite, 1980s
EX $43 **NM** $56 **MIP** $82

❏ **Massey-Ferguson Tractor, 50 D**, 1:50-scale, Conrad, yellow, w/Loader, 1980s
EX $43 **NM** $56 **MIP** $82

❏ **Massey-Ferguson Wheel Loader 600 C**, 1:50-scale, Cursor, yellow, 1970s
EX $48 **NM** $64 **MIP** $88

❏ **Massey-Ferguson Wheel Loader, 66 C**, 1:50-scale, Cursor, yellow, 1970s
EX $68 **NM** $88 **MIP** $113

CONSTRUCTION EQUIPMENT

❏ **Massey-Ferguson Crawler, 294 C**, red, 1980s
EX $96 **NM** $148 **MIP** $289

IMPLEMENTS 1:16-SCALE

❏ **Massey-Ferguson Disk**, 1:16-scale, Ertl, red, w/wheels, 1965, No. 439
EX $16 **NM** $33 **MIP** $58

❏ **Massey-Ferguson Disk**, 1:16-scale, Ertl, red, w/folding wings, 1979, No. 171
EX $18 **NM** $47 **MIP** $83

❏ **Massey-Ferguson Minimum Tillage Plow**, 1:16-scale, Ertl, red, 1982
EX $22 **NM** $43 **MIP** $78

❑ **Massey-Ferguson Mixer Mill**, 1:16-scale, Ertl, red, 1980s, No. 1112
EX $22   **NM** $38   **MIP** $48

❑ **Massey-Ferguson Plow**, 1:16-scale, Ertl, red, 7 bottom, metal bottoms, 1971, No. 172
(Photo by Bossen Implement)
EX $23   **NM** $56   **MIP** $88

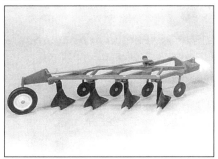

❑ **Massey-Ferguson Plow**, 1:16-scale, Ertl, red, 4 bottom, metal bottoms, 1980s
EX $21   **NM** $36   **MIP** n/a

❑ **Massey-Ferguson Plow**, 1:16-scale, Ertl, red, 4 bottom, plastic bottoms, 1989
EX $16   **NM** $23   **MIP** $33

❑ **Massey-Ferguson Wagon, Barge**, 1:16-scale, Ertl, red, 1965, No. 178 *(Photo by Bossen Implement)*
EX $12   **NM** $33   **MIP** $67

❑ **Massey-Ferguson Wagon, Barge**, 1:16-scale, Ertl, red, 1980s, No. 1113
EX $8   **NM** $24   **MIP** $38

❑ **Massey-Ferguson Wagon, Flare Box**, 1:16-scale, Ertl, red, 1965, No. 12
EX $9   **NM** $23   **MIP** $38

IMPLEMENTS 1:20-SCALE

❑ **Massey-Ferguson Combine, 510**, 1:20-scale, Borchardt (Custom), red, 1980s
EX $387   **NM** $426   **MIP** $473

❑ **Massey-Ferguson Combine, 760**, 1:20-scale, Ertl, red, square air intake screen, 1970s, No. 182
EX $58   **NM** $116   **MIP** $208

❑ **Massey-Ferguson Combine, 760**, 1:20-scale, Ertl, red, gray rims, round air intake screen, 1970s, No. 182
EX $56   **NM** $114   **MIP** $198

❑ **Massey-Ferguson Combine, 760**, 1:20-scale, Ertl, red, yellow rims, round air intake screen, 1970s, No. 182
EX $64   **NM** $126   **MIP** $208

❑ **Massey-Ferguson Combine, 850**, 1:20-scale, Ertl, red, 1980s, No. 1111
EX $46   **NM** $94   **MIP** $156

❑ **Massey-Ferguson Combine, 860**, 1:20-scale, Ertl, red, 1980s, No. 169
EX $48   **NM** $104   **MIP** $188

IMPLEMENTS 1:24-SCALE

❑ **Massey-Ferguson Combine, 8780**, 1:24-scale, Scale Models, red, AGCO Dealer Meeting 150th Anniversary, 1997, No. FT-0838
EX $26   **NM** $43   **MIP** $78

❑ **Massey-Ferguson Combine, 8780XP**, 1:24-scale, Scale Models, red, Collector Edition, 1997, No. FT-0867
EX $26   **NM** $43   **MIP** $78

❏ **Massey-Ferguson Combine,
9790**, 1:24-scale, Scale Models, red,
Collector Edition, 2002, No. FT-0882

(Photo by Bossen Implement)

EX $22 **NM** $33 **MIP** $68

❏ **Massey-Ferguson Combine,
9790**, 1:24-scale, Scale Models, red,
2003, No. FT-0883

EX $22 **NM** $33 **MIP** $68

IMPLEMENTS 1:25-SCALE

❏ **Massey-Ferguson Wagon,
Barge**, 1:25-scale, Ertl, red, model
kit, 1974, No. 8007

EX $11 **NM** $18 **MIP** $43

IMPLEMENTS 1:32-SCALE

❏ **Massey-Ferguson Combine**,
1:32-scale, Gamma, red, 1980s

EX $17 **NM** $28 **MIP** $47

❏ **Massey-Ferguson Combine,
7200**, 1:32-scale, Britians, red, 1999,
No. 00054

EX $23 **NM** $38 **MIP** $62

❏ **Massey-Ferguson Combine,
7278**, 1:32-scale, Siku, red, 2002,
No. 4254

EX $21 **NM** $33 **MIP** $53

❏ **Massey-Ferguson Combine,
760**, 1:32-scale, Britains, red, 1980s,
No. 9570

EX $14 **NM** $26 **MIP** $33

❏ **Massey-Ferguson Plow**, 1:32-
scale, Ertl, red, 6 bottom, 1980s

EX $4 **NM** $8 **MIP** $14

IMPLEMENTS 1:43-SCALE

❏ **Massey-Ferguson Combine**,
1:43-scale, Corgi, red, 1960s

EX $17 **NM** $32 **MIP** $68

❏ **Massey-Ferguson Combine**,
1:43-scale, Corgi, red, 1960s

EX $17 **NM** $32 **MIP** $68

IMPLEMENTS 1:64-SCALE

❏ **Massey Combine, 8590**, 1:64-
scale, Scale Models, red and silver,
Massey-Ferguson decals on the
front and back, No. 815

EX $9 **NM** $17 **MIP** $23

❏ **Massey Combine, 8590**, 1:64-
scale, Scale Models, red and silver,
No. 815

EX $9 **NM** $17 **MIP** $23

❏ **Massey Combine, 8590**, 1:64-
scale, Scale Models, red and silver,
National Toy Show "1987", No. 815

EX $9 **NM** $17 **MIP** $27

❏ **Massey-Ferguson Anhydrous
Ammonia**, 1:64-scale, Ertl, red,
1993, No. 7392

EX $3 **NM** $4 **MIP** $8

❏ **Massey-Ferguson Auger**, 1:64-
scale, Ertl, red, 1986, No. 606

EX $3 **NM** $4 **MIP** $8

❏ **Massey-Ferguson Baler**, 1:64-
scale, Ertl, red, round, 1980,
No. 1758

EX $3 **NM** $4 **MIP** $12

❏ **Massey-Ferguson Combine,
8590**, 1:64-scale, Scale Models,
w/grain head only, No. FT-0815

(Photo by Scale Models)

EX $8 **NM** $12 **MIP** $23

❏ **Massey-Ferguson Combine,
8680**, 1:64-scale, Ertl, red, 1998,
No. 230

EX $8 **NM** $12 **MIP** $18

Photos by Jon Jacobson unless otherwise noted.

❑ **Massey-Ferguson Combine, 8680**, 1:64-scale, Ertl, red, w/duals, Collector Edition, 1998, No. 2499UA

(Photo by Bossen Implement)

EX $18   NM $27   MIP $48

❑ **Massey-Ferguson Disk**, 1:64-scale, Ertl, red, w/wings, no wheels, 1982, No. 1862

EX $3   NM $4   MIP $6

❑ **Massey-Ferguson Minimum Tillage Plow**, 1:64-scale, Ertl, red, 1982, No. 1863

EX $8   NM $13   MIP $18

❑ **Massey-Ferguson Mix Mill**, 1:64-scale, Ertl, red, 1983, No. 1998

EX $3   NM $4   MIP $16

❑ **Massey-Ferguson Plow**, 1:64-scale, Ertl, red, 6 bottom, 1980, No. 1757

EX $8   NM $13   MIP $22

LAWN AND GARDEN 1:16-SCALE

❑ **Massey-Ferguson 2616H**, 1:16-scale, Scale Models, red, w/mower deck, 1996, No. FT-0505

EX $8   NM $13   MIP $22

❑ **Massey-Ferguson 2925H**, 1:16-scale, Scale Models, w/mower deck, 1998, No. FT-0545 *(Photo by Scale Models)*

EX $8   NM $13   MIP $22

MISCELLANEOUS 1:43-SCALE

❑ **Massey-Ferguson Farm Set**, 1:43-scale, Dinky, red, 1960s

EX n/a   NM n/a   MIP $104

PEDAL TRACTORS

❑ **Massey-Ferguson 1100**, Ertl, red w/gray decal, Massey Ferguson on decal towards the front, tractor in original condition

EX $198   NM $348   MIP $398

❑ **Massey-Ferguson 1100**, Ertl, red w/gray decal, Massey Ferguson on decal back by steering wheel, tractor in original condition

EX $198   NM $348   MIP $427

❑ **Massey-Ferguson 3270**, Ertl, red, 1999, No. 13055

EX $79   NM $102   MIP $168

❑ **Massey-Ferguson 3650**, Ertl, red, 1990

EX $76   NM $109   MIP $168

❑ **Massey-Ferguson 390**, Ertl, red, tractor in original condition

EX $168   NM $268   MIP $333

❑ **Massey-Ferguson 398**, Ertl, red, No. 1100

EX $143   NM $188   MIP $247

❑ **Massey-Ferguson 4270**, Scale Models, red, 2002, No. FT-0857

EX $108   NM $127   MIP $153

❑ **Massey-Ferguson 4370**, Scale Models, red, 2003, No. FT-0877

EX $108   NM $127   MIP $153

❑ **Massey-Ferguson 8160**, Scale Models, red, dynashift, 1996, No. FT-0822 *(Photo by Scale Models)*

EX $98   NM $127   MIP $153

TRACTORS 1:128-SCALE

❑ **Massey-Ferguson Micros**, 1:128-scale, Ertl, red, w/tractor, wagon and disk, 1990s, No. 1536

EX $3   NM $4   MIP $8

TRACTORS 1:16-SCALE

❑ **Massey-Ferguson 1080**, 1:16-scale, Ertl, red, V-8 engine, 1970s, No. 180
EX $97   **NM** $176   **MIP** $333

❑ **Massey-Ferguson 1080**, 1:16-scale, Ertl, red, 1970s, No. 180
EX $87   **NM** $166   **MIP** $313

❑ **Massey-Ferguson 1100**, 1:16-scale, Scale Models, red, WF, 1995, No. FT-0824
EX $18   **NM** $23   **MIP** $42

❑ **Massey-Ferguson 1100**, 1:16-scale, Scale Models, gold plated, WF, Employee Christmas Present from Joe Ertl, 1995, No. FT0824
EX $102   **NM** $153   **MIP** $202

❑ **Massey-Ferguson 1100**, 1:16-scale, Scale Models, red, NF, 1996, No. FT-0804 *(Photo by Scale Models)*
EX $11   **NM** $17   **MIP** $26

❑ **Massey-Ferguson 1105**, 1:16-scale, Ertl, red, red rims, 1970s, No. 161
EX $48   **NM** $93   **MIP** $158

❑ **Massey-Ferguson 1105**, 1:16-scale, Ertl, red, silver rims, 1970s, No. 161
EX $52   **NM** $113   **MIP** $178

❑ **Massey-Ferguson 1130**, 1:16-scale, Scale Models, No. FT-0823
(Photo by Scale Models)
EX $18   **NM** $24   **MIP** $32

❑ **Massey-Ferguson 1130**, 1:16-scale, Scale Models, red, '94 Fall Open House Edition, 1994, No. FB-2371
EX $19   **NM** $26   **MIP** $36

❑ **Massey-Ferguson 1130**, 1:16-scale, Scale Models, red, NF, 1997, No. FT-0823
EX $18   **NM** $24   **MIP** $32

❑ **Massey-Ferguson 1130**, 1:16-scale, Scale Models, red, WF, cab, '99 Fall Open House Edition, 1999, No. FB-2535
EX $21   **NM** $28   **MIP** $38

❑ **Massey-Ferguson 1130**, 1:16-scale, Scale Models, red, WF, duals, cab, '01 Louisville Show Edition, 2001, No. FB-2584
EX $21   **NM** $28   **MIP** $38

❑ **Massey-Ferguson 1150**, 1:16-scale, Ertl, red, 6 cylinder engine, 1970, No. 180
EX $133   **NM** $268   **MIP** $456

❑ **Massey-Ferguson 1150**, 1:16-scale, Ertl, red, V-8 engine, 1970s, No. 179
EX $138   **NM** $263   **MIP** $442

❑ **Massey-Ferguson 1150**, 1:16-scale, Scale Models, red, NF, '95 Fall Open House Edition, 1995, No. FB-2404
EX $21   **NM** $28   **MIP** $38

❑ **Massey-Ferguson 1150**, 1:16-scale, Scale Models, red, WF, w/duals, V8 engine, '96 Summer Open House Edition, 1996, No. FB-2436
EX $21   **NM** $27   **MIP** $48

❑ **Massey-Ferguson 1150**, 1:16-scale, Scale Models, red, WF, 1997, No. FT-0830 *(Photo by Scale Models)*
EX $18   **NM** $24   **MIP** $37

❑ **Massey-Ferguson 1150**, 1:16-scale, Scale Models, red, '03 Louisville Show Edition, 2003, No. FB-2631
EX $23   **NM** $32   **MIP** $48

❏ **Massey-Ferguson 1155**, 1:16-scale, Ertl, red, red rims, 1970s, No. 183
EX $52   **NM** $103   **MIP** $178

❏ **Massey-Ferguson 1155**, 1:16-scale, Ertl, red, silver rims, 1970s, No. 183
EX $48   **NM** $93   **MIP** $148

❏ **Massey-Ferguson 1155**, 1:16-scale, Ertl, red, Spirit of America, '00 National Farm Toy Show Edition, 2000, No. 16050A
EX $32   **NM** $48   **MIP** $87

❏ **Massey-Ferguson 1155**, 1:16-scale, Ertl, red, 2WD, cab, 2001, No. 13170
EX $21   **NM** $28   **MIP** $48

❏ **Massey-Ferguson 1250**, 1:16-scale, Scale Models, red, MFD, ROPS, 1997, No. FT-0831
EX $16   **NM** $23   **MIP** $31

❏ **Massey-Ferguson 1250**, 1:16-scale, Scale Models, red, MFD, ROPS, '97 Louisville Show Edition, 1997, No. FB-2456
EX $17   **NM** $26   **MIP** $36

❏ **Massey-Ferguson 135**, 1:16-scale, G&M Farm Toys, red, 2003
EX $278   **NM** $323   **MIP** n/a

❏ **Massey-Ferguson 135**, 1:16-scale, Scale Models, w/wagon Set, No. FT-0812 *(Photo by Scale Models)*
EX n/a   **NM** n/a   **MIP** $27

❏ **Massey-Ferguson 135**, 1:16-scale, Scale Models, red, upright exhaust, '92 Louisville Show Edition, 1990s, No. FB-1609
EX $16   **NM** $28   **MIP** $42

❏ **Massey-Ferguson 135**, 1:16-scale, Scale Models, red, under slung exhaust, Collector Edition, 1991, No. FB-2485
EX $16   **NM** $28   **MIP** $48

❏ **Massey-Ferguson 135**, 1:16-scale, Scale Models, red, w/canopy, 2000, No. FT-0597
EX $18   **NM** $23   **MIP** $42

❏ **Massey-Ferguson 1433**, 1:16-scale, Scale Models, red, MFD, ROPS, 2002, No. FT-0879
EX $12   **NM** $17   **MIP** $27

❏ **Massey-Ferguson 165**, 1:16-scale, Argentina, red, w/three-point hitch, 1980s, No. 175
EX $198   **NM** $432   **MIP** $722

❏ **Massey-Ferguson 175**, 1:16-scale, Ertl, red, die-cast rear rims, 1960s, No. 175
EX $63   **NM** $122   **MIP** $268

❏ **Massey-Ferguson 175**, 1:16-scale, Ertl, red, plastic red rims, w/muffler, 1960s, No. 175
EX $43   **NM** $82   **MIP** $143

❏ **Massey-Ferguson 175**, 1:16-scale, Ertl, red, no weight bar, no muffler, plastic rims, 1960s, No. 175
EX $63   **NM** $102   **MIP** $143

❏ **Massey-Ferguson 270**, 1:16-scale, Ertl, red, Collectors Edition, Phoenix, 1980s, No. 1104TA
EX $22   **NM** $36   **MIP** $42

❏ **Massey-Ferguson 270**, 1:16-scale, Ertl, red, 1980s, No. 1104
EX $18   **NM** $34   **MIP** $37

❑ **Massey-Ferguson 275**, 1:16-scale, Ertl, red, 1970s, No. 1103
EX $22   **NM** $38   **MIP** $63

❑ **Massey-Ferguson 275**, 1:16-scale, Ertl, red, 1970s, No. 1103
EX $22   **NM** $38   **MIP** $63

❑ **Massey-Ferguson 290**, 1:16-scale, Strike, red, 1980s
EX $22   **NM** $42   **MIP** $57

❑ **Massey-Ferguson 3070**, 1:16-scale, Ertl, red, MFD, 1980s, No. 1128
EX $18   **NM** $28   **MIP** $39

❑ **Massey-Ferguson 3070**, 1:16-scale, Ertl, red, 1980s, No. 1127
EX $18   **NM** $28   **MIP** $36

❑ **Massey-Ferguson 3070**, 1:16-scale, Ertl, red, Collectors Edition, 1980s, No. 1127DA
EX $22   **NM** $33   **MIP** $48

❑ **Massey-Ferguson 3070**, 1:16-scale, Ertl, red, Collectors Edition, MFD, 1980s, No. 1128DA
EX $22   **NM** $33   **MIP** $48

❑ **Massey-Ferguson 35**, 1:16-scale, G&M Farm Toys, red, 35X, diesel engine, 2002
(Photo by Bossen Implement)
EX $278   **NM** $323   **MIP** n/a

❑ **Massey-Ferguson 35**, 1:16-scale, G&M Farm Toys, red, diesel engine, 2002
EX $278   **NM** $323   **MIP** n/a

❑ **Massey-Ferguson 35**, 1:16-scale, Scale Models, red, special, 1998, No. FT-0856
EX $17   **NM** $23   **MIP** $32

❑ **Massey-Ferguson 35**, 1:16-scale, SpecCast, red, 1995, No. SCT-115
EX $17   **NM** $26   **MIP** $38

❑ **Massey-Ferguson 35**, 1:16-scale, SpecCast, green, 2000, No. SCT-185
EX $18   **NM** $27   **MIP** $42

❑ **Massey-Ferguson 3630**, 1:16-scale, Ertl, MFD, 1999, No. 13005
EX $17   **NM** $28   **MIP** $44

❑ **Massey-Ferguson 3650**, 1:16-scale, Ertl, red, MFD, 1992, No. 1345
EX $17   **NM** $24   **MIP** $36

❑ **Massey-Ferguson 3660**, 1:16-scale, Scale Models, red, 1994, No. FT-0803 *(Photo by Scale Models)*
EX $16   **NM** $23   **MIP** $36

❑ **Massey-Ferguson 398**, 1:16-scale, Ertl, red and silver, w/ROPS, 1980s, No. 1179
EX $16   **NM** $26   **MIP** $38

Photos by Jon Jacobson unless otherwise noted.

❑ **Massey-Ferguson 398**, 1:16-scale, Ertl, red and silver, FWA w/ROPS, 1980s, No. 1181
EX $16   **NM** $26   **MIP** $38

❑ **Massey-Ferguson 4225**, 1:16-scale, Scale Models, red, MFD, 1999, No. FT-0861
EX $17   **NM** $28   **MIP** $46

❑ **Massey-Ferguson 4225**, 1:16-scale, Scale Models, red, MFD, Collector Edition, 2001, No. FT-0868
(Photo by Bossen Implement)
EX $19   **NM** $32   **MIP** $48

❑ **Massey-Ferguson 4243**, 1:16-scale, Scale Models, red, MFD, 1998, No. FT-0855
EX $17   **NM** $28   **MIP** $46

❑ **Massey-Ferguson 4255**, 1:16-scale, Scale Models, red, MFD, ROPS, 2001, No. FT-0872
EX $17   **NM** $28   **MIP** $46

❑ **Massey-Ferguson 4270**, 1:16-scale, Scale Models, red, MFD, '97 Kansas City Dealer Meeting, 1997, No. FT-0834
EX $22   **NM** $33   **MIP** $48

❑ **Massey-Ferguson 4270**, 1:16-scale, Scale Models, red, MFD, 1998, No. FT-0873
EX $17   **NM** $28   **MIP** $46

❑ **Massey-Ferguson 4270**, 1:16-scale, Scale Models, gold, MFD, Employee Christmas Present from Joe Ertl, 1998, No. 1123
EX $122   **NM** $153   **MIP** $202

❑ **Massey-Ferguson 4270**, 1:16-scale, Scale Models, red, MFD, 1998, No. FT-0847
EX $17   **NM** $28   **MIP** $46

❑ **Massey-Ferguson 4325**, 1:16-scale, Scale Models, red, MFD, 2002, No. FT-0878
EX $17   **NM** $28   **MIP** $46

❑ **Massey-Ferguson 4370**, 1:16-scale, Scale Models, red, MFD, 2002, No. FT-0876
EX $17   **NM** $28   **MIP** $46

❑ **Massey-Ferguson 4370**, 1:16-scale, Scale Models, red, MFD, '02 Louisville Farm Show Edition, 2002, No. FB-2606 *(Photo by Bossen Implement)*
EX $18   **NM** $27   **MIP** $42

❑ **Massey-Ferguson 590**, 1:16-scale, Ertl, red, 1970s, No. 1106
EX $22   **NM** $33   **MIP** $53

❑ **Massey-Ferguson 590**, 1:16-scale, Ertl, red, '80 National Farm Toy Show Tractor, 1980, No. A103
EX $228   **NM** $362   **MIP** $476

❑ **Massey-Ferguson 595**, 1:16-scale, Ertl, red, 1970s, No. 1106
EX $36   **NM** $82   **MIP** $116

❑ **Massey-Ferguson 6170**, 1:16-scale, Ertl, red, MFD, '96 Louisville Farm Show Edition, 1996, No. FB-2411
EX $18   **NM** $29   **MIP** $48

❑ **Massey-Ferguson 7480**, 1:16-scale, Bruder, red, MFD, w/loader, 2003, No. 02042
EX $11   **NM** $22   **MIP** $28

❑ **Massey-Ferguson 7480**, 1:16-scale, Bruder, red, MFD, 2003, No. 02040
EX $9   **NM** $13   **MIP** $22

❑ **Massey-Ferguson 7480**, 1:16-scale, Bruder, red, MFD, w/duals and loader, 2003, No. 02043
EX $13   **NM** $26   **MIP** $32

❑ **Massey-Ferguson 8120**, 1:16-scale, Scale Models, 1995, No. FT-0820 *(Photo by Scale Models)*
EX $22   **NM** $33   **MIP** $52

❑ **Massey-Ferguson 8160**, 1:16-scale, Scale Models, 1997, No. FT-0825 *(Photo by Scale Models)*
EX $22   **NM** $33   **MIP** $52

❏ **Massey-Ferguson 8160**, 1:16-scale, Scale Models, red, MFD, '97 Kansas City Dealer Meeting, 1997, No. FT-0833
EX $22   **NM** $33   **MIP** $52

❏ **Massey-Ferguson 8270**, 1:16-scale, Scale Models, red, MFD, CST, 1999, No. FT-0864
EX $22   **NM** $33   **MIP** $52

❏ **Massey-Ferguson 8270**, 1:16-scale, Scale Models, red, MFD, '00 Louisville Farm Show Edition, 2000, No. FB-2554
EX $24   **NM** $36   **MIP** $58

❏ **Massey-Ferguson 8280**, 1:16-scale, Scale Models, red, MFD, Collector Edition, 2001, No. FT-0869
EX $24   **NM** $36   **MIP** $66

❏ **Massey-Ferguson 97**, 1:16-scale, Mohr (Custom), red and silver, 1980s
EX $148   **NM** $197   **MIP** $212

❏ **Massey-Ferguson 97**, 1:16-scale, Mohr (Custom), red and silver, MFD, 1980s
EX $163   **NM** $197   **MIP** $238

TRACTORS 1:20-SCALE

❏ **Massey-Ferguson 2775**, 1:20-scale, Ertl, red, 1970s, No. 1107
EX $18   **NM** $36   **MIP** $47

❏ **Massey-Ferguson 2805**, 1:20-scale, Ertl, red, 1970s, No. 1108
EX $18   **NM** $36   **MIP** $47

❏ **Massey-Ferguson 3070**, 1:20-scale, Scale Models, eight versions, 1990s
EX $36   **NM** $62   **MIP** $78

❏ **Massey-Ferguson 3070**, 1:20-scale, Scale Models, eight versions, 1990s
EX $36   **NM** $62   **MIP** $78

❏ **Massey-Ferguson 3070**, 1:20-scale, Scale Models, eight versions, 1990s
EX $36   **NM** $62   **MIP** $78

❏ **Massey-Ferguson 3070**, 1:20-scale, Scale Models, eight versions, 1990s
EX $36   **NM** $62   **MIP** $78

❏ **Massey-Ferguson 670**, 1:20-scale, Ertl, red, 1980s, No. 1105
EX $12   **NM** $27   **MIP** $42

❏ **Massey-Ferguson 690**, 1:20-scale, Ertl, red, duals, cab, '93 Phoenix Collector Edition, 1983, No. 1102DA
EX $13   **NM** $28   **MIP** $43

❏ **Massey-Ferguson 698**, 1:20-scale, Ertl, red, 1980s, No. 1102
EX $12   **NM** $28   **MIP** $48

❏ **Massey-Ferguson 699**, 1:20-scale, Ertl, red, 1980s, No. 1124
EX $12   **NM** $27   **MIP** $43

❑ **Massey-Ferguson 699**, 1:20-scale, Ertl, red, Collectors Edition, 1980s, No. 1102DA
EX $18   **NM** $36   **MIP** $47

TRACTORS 1:25-SCALE

❑ **Massey-Ferguson 1155**, 1:25-scale, Ertl, red, model kit, 1970s, No. 8007
EX $12   **NM** $32   **MIP** $78

❑ **Massey-Ferguson 1155**, 1:25-scale, Ertl, red, white, and blue; model kit, 1970s, No. 8016
EX $12   **NM** $32   **MIP** $78

❑ **Massey-Ferguson 35**, 1:25-scale, Morgan, red, 1970s
EX $26   **NM** $48   **MIP** $63

TRACTORS 1:32-SCALE

❑ **Massey-Ferguson**, 1:32-scale, Lone Star, red, 1980s
EX $6   **NM** $12   **MIP** $22

❑ **Massey-Ferguson**, 1:32-scale, Micro Models, gray, 1950s
EX $26   **NM** $48   **MIP** $63

❑ **Massey-Ferguson 1200**, 1:32-scale, Brian Norman, red, 4WD, cab, 3 point hitch, 2003 *(Photo by Bossen Implement)*
EX $178   **NM** $267   **MIP** $323

❑ **Massey-Ferguson 135**, 1:32-scale, Britains, red, 1970s
EX $28   **NM** $47   **MIP** $67

❑ **Massey-Ferguson 2640**, 1:32-scale, Gamma, red, 1980s
EX $6   **NM** $22   **MIP** $32

❑ **Massey-Ferguson 2680**, 1:32-scale, Britains, red, MFD, 1999, No. 09504
EX $6   **NM** $9   **MIP** $18

❑ **Massey-Ferguson 284 S**, 1:32-scale, Siku, red, 1980s, No. 2550
EX $6   **NM** $9   **MIP** $18

❑ **Massey-Ferguson 3050**, 1:32-scale, Ertl, red and silver, w/2 point hitch, 1990s, No. 1139
EX $4   **NM** $8   **MIP** $13

❑ **Massey-Ferguson 3050**, 1:32-scale, Ertl, red, MFD, w/loader, 1991, No. 1114
EX $9   **NM** $16   **MIP** $22

❑ **Massey-Ferguson 362**, 1:32-scale, Britains, red, MFD, 2001, No. 09502
EX $9   **NM** $18   **MIP** $26

❑ **Massey-Ferguson 3680**, 1:32-scale, Britains, red, MFD, w/duals, 2001, No. 09501
EX $8   **NM** $17   **MIP** $22

❑ **Massey-Ferguson 4270**, 1:32-scale, Siku, red, MFD, 2001, No. 2654
EX $6   **NM** $9   **MIP** $18

❏ **Massey-Ferguson 4880**, 1:32-scale, Ertl, red, Collectors Edition, also available in non-collectors series, 1980s, No. 1691EA
EX $27   **NM** $52   **MIP** $73

❏ **Massey-Ferguson 4880**, 1:32-scale, Ertl, 4WD, duals, 1982, No. 1691
EX $16   **NM** $32   **MIP** $53

❏ **Massey-Ferguson 4900**, 1:32-scale, Ertl, red, 4WD, duals, 1980s, No. 1691
EX $22   **NM** $32   **MIP** $48

❏ **Massey-Ferguson 4900**, 1:32-scale, Ertl, red, 4WD, singles, 1980s, No. 1691
EX $18   **NM** $28   **MIP** $43

❏ **Massey-Ferguson 6140**, 1:32-scale, Britains, red, MFD, 2001, No. 09449
EX $8   **NM** $17   **MIP** $23

❏ **Massey-Ferguson 6140**, 1:32-scale, Britains, red, MFD, w/loader, 2001, No. 09450
EX $9   **NM** $19   **MIP** $32

❏ **Massey-Ferguson 6180**, 1:32-scale, Britains, red, MFD, 1999, No. 09491
EX $6   **NM** $9   **MIP** $18

❏ **Massey-Ferguson 6270**, 1:32-scale, Britains, red, MFD, w/loader, 2004, No. 40512
EX $6   **NM** $9   **MIP** $18

❏ **Massey-Ferguson 6290**, 1:32-scale, Britains, red, MFD, 2002, No. 40511
EX $4   **NM** $8   **MIP** $16

❏ **Massey-Ferguson 8270**, 1:32-scale, Siku, red, MFD, w/duals, '02 LCN European Show Edition, 2002

(Photo by Bossen Implement)

EX $17   **NM** $24   **MIP** $36

❏ **Massey-Ferguson 8270**, 1:32-scale, Siku, red, MFD, w/extra paint detail and display case, 2004, No. 4454
EX $17   **NM** $24   **MIP** $36

❏ **Massey-Ferguson 8280**, 1:32-scale, Siku, red, MFD, 2002, No. 3251
EX $9   **NM** $12   **MIP** $22

❏ **Massey-Ferguson 9240**, 1:32-scale, Siku, red, MFD, 2001, No. 2868
EX $9   **NM** $13   **MIP** $26

TRACTORS 1:43-SCALE

❏ **Massey-Ferguson**, 1:43-scale, Corgi, red, 1970s
EX $24   **NM** $42   **MIP** $62

❏ **Massey-Ferguson**, 1:43-scale, Mini Mac, red, 1970s
EX $26   **NM** $48   **MIP** $63

❏ **Massey-Ferguson 1014**, 1:43-scale, Yaxon, red, 1980s
EX $6   **NM** $9   **MIP** $17

❏ **Massey-Ferguson 1134**, 1:43-scale, Yaxon, red, 1980s
EX $6   **NM** $9   **MIP** $17

❏ **Massey-Ferguson 1134**, 1:43-scale, Yaxon, red, 1980s
EX $6   **NM** $9   **MIP** $17

❏ **Massey-Ferguson 1134**, 1:43-scale, Yaxon, red, 1980s
EX $6   **NM** $9   **MIP** $17

❏ **Massey-Ferguson 135**, 1:43-scale, SpecCast, 1990s

EX $6   NM $8   MIP $12

❏ **Massey-Ferguson 165**, 1:43-scale, Corgi, red, 1970s

EX $37   NM $53   MIP $77

❏ **Massey-Ferguson 165**, 1:43-scale, Matchbox, red, 1970s

EX $17   NM $36   MIP $53

❏ **Massey-Ferguson 275**, 1:43-scale, Mini Mac, red, 1970s

EX $38   NM $58   MIP $102

❏ **Massey-Ferguson 595**, 1:32-scale, Britains, red, 1970s

EX $6   NM $9   MIP $18

❏ **Massey-Ferguson 595**, 1:32-scale, Britains, red, 1970s

EX $6   NM $9   MIP $18

❏ **Massey-Ferguson 65**, 1:43-scale, Corgi, red, steering wheel is missing, 1960s

EX $23   NM $48   MIP $73

❏ **Massey-Ferguson 65**, 1:43-scale, Triang Spot-On, red, 1960s

EX $4   NM $26   MIP $38

❏ **Massey-Ferguson Farm Set**, 1:43-scale, Mercury, red, 1960s

EX n/a   NM n/a   MIP $543

❏ **Massey-Ferguson Loader**, 1:43-scale, Corgi, silver, 1960s

EX $26   NM $52   MIP $78

❏ **Massey-Ferguson Loader**, 1:43-scale, Corgi, red, 1970s

EX $26   NM $52   MIP $78

TRACTORS 1:64-SCALE

❏ **Massey-Ferguson 1100**, 1:64-scale, Scale Models, 1995, No. FT-0810 *(Photo by Scale Models)*

EX $4   NM $8   MIP $9

❏ **Massey-Ferguson 1150**, 1:64-scale, Scale Models, red, '03 Louisville Farm Show Edition, 2003, No. FB-2632

EX $4   NM $8   MIP $9

❏ **Massey-Ferguson 1155**, 1:64-scale, Ertl, red, w/small wheels, 1970s, No. 1350
EX $28   **NM** $43   **MIP** $127

❏ **Massey-Ferguson 1155**, 1:64-scale, Ertl, gold, issued by ERTL as an employee award—did not come in box, 1970s
EX $63   **NM** $198   **MIP** n/a

❏ **Massey-Ferguson 1155**, 1:64-scale, Ertl, red and white, spun-on rear wheels, 1970s, No. 1350
EX $18   **NM** $33   **MIP** $72

❏ **Massey-Ferguson 1155**, 1:64-scale, Ertl, red and white, 1970s, No. 1350
EX $18   **NM** $33   **MIP** $72

❏ **Massey-Ferguson 1155**, 1:64-scale, Ertl, red and white, rivet used for rear axle, 1970s, No. 1350
EX $18   **NM** $33   **MIP** $72

❏ **Massey-Ferguson 1155**, 1:64-scale, Ertl, red, '00 National Farm Toy Show Edition, 2000, No. 16051
EX $6   **NM** $9   **MIP** $16

❏ **Massey-Ferguson 1155**, 1:64-scale, Ertl, red, 2004, No. 13437
EX $4   **NM** $6   **MIP** $8

❏ **Massey-Ferguson 2775**, 1:64-scale, Ertl, red and silver, pushed-on or spun-on front rims, rear axle, rivet or steel pin, 1970s, No. 1622
EX $4   **NM** $6   **MIP** $12

❏ **Massey-Ferguson 2775**, 1:64-scale, Ertl, red and silver, dome rear wheels, pushed-on or spun-on front rims, 1970s, No. 1622
EX $23   **NM** $44   **MIP** $93

❏ **Massey-Ferguson 2800**, 1:64-scale, Ertl, red and silver, 1970s, No. 1622
EX $6   **NM** $32   **MIP** $68

❏ **Massey-Ferguson 2800**, 1:64-scale, Ertl, red and silver, dome rear wheels, 1970s, No. 1622
EX $23   **NM** $44   **MIP** $93

❏ **Massey-Ferguson 3070**, 1:64-scale, Ertl, red, 2WD, w/duals, 1989, No. 1176
EX $4   **NM** $6   **MIP** $8

❏ **Massey-Ferguson 3070**, 1:64-scale, Ertl, red, MFD, 1989, No. 1107
EX $4   **NM** $6   **MIP** $8

❏ **Massey-Ferguson 3070**, 1:64-scale, Ertl, red, 2WD, w/loader, 1989, No. 1109
EX $4   **NM** $6   **MIP** $8

❏ **Massey-Ferguson 3070**, 1:64-scale, Ertl, red, 2WD, 1989, No. 1177
EX $4   **NM** $6   **MIP** $8

❏ **Massey-Ferguson 3070**, 1:64-scale, Scale Models, gold, sold as a Christmas ornament, 1980s
EX $3   **NM** $4   **MIP** $6

❏ **Massey-Ferguson 3070**, 1:64-scale, Scale Models, silver, sold as a Christmas ornament, 1980s
EX $3　　**NM** $4　　**MIP** $6

❏ **Massey-Ferguson 3120**, 1:64-scale, Ertl, red, 2WD, 1992, No. 1177FP
EX $3　　**NM** $4　　**MIP** $6

❏ **Massey-Ferguson 3120**, 1:64-scale, Ertl, red, 2WD, w/loader, 1992, No. 1109FP
EX $4　　**NM** $6　　**MIP** $8

❏ **Massey-Ferguson 3140**, 1:64-scale, Ertl, red, 2WD, w/duals, 1992, No. 1176FP
EX $3　　**NM** $4　　**MIP** $6

❏ **Massey-Ferguson 3140**, 1:64-scale, Ertl, red, MFD, 1992, No. 1107FP
EX $3　　**NM** $4　　**MIP** $6

❏ **Massey-Ferguson 3140**, 1:64-scale, Ertl, red, MFD, '96 Farm Show Edition, 1996, No. 2712MA
EX $3　　**NM** $4　　**MIP** $6

❏ **Massey-Ferguson 399**, 1:64-scale, Scale Models, red, MFD and ROPS, Kansas City, 150th Anniversary, 1997, No. FT-0837
EX $4　　**NM** $6　　**MIP** $8

❏ **Massey-Ferguson 399**, 1:64-scale, Scale Models, red, MFD and ROPS, 1998, No. FT-0849
EX $4　　**NM** $6　　**MIP** $8

❏ **Massey-Ferguson 4880**, 1:64-scale, Ertl, red and silver, rivets are used for axles, 1980s, No. 1727
EX $22　　**NM** $27　　**MIP** $36

❏ **Massey-Ferguson 4880**, 1:64-scale, Ertl, red and silver, hood decal is backwards, 1980s, No. 1727
EX $22　　**NM** $27　　**MIP** $36

❏ **Massey-Ferguson 4880**, 1:64-scale, Ertl, red and silver, spun-on wheels, rear decal can be silver or white, 1980s, No. 1727
EX $22　　**NM** $27　　**MIP** $36

❏ **Massey-Ferguson 4880 Tractors**, 1:64-scale, Ertl, Detail: tractor on left, silver rear decal; tractor on right, white rear decal

❏ **Massey-Ferguson 699**, 1:64-scale, Ertl, red and silver, 2WD, 1980s, No. 1120
EX $3　　**NM** $4　　**MIP** $6

❏ **Massey-Ferguson 699**, 1:64-scale, Ertl, red and silver, MFD, 1980s, No. 1130
EX $3　　**NM** $4　　**MIP** $6

❏ **Massey-Ferguson 699**, 1:64-scale, Ertl, red and silver, 2WD & duals, 1980s, No. 1129
EX $3　　**NM** $4　　**MIP** $6

❏ **Massey-Ferguson 699**, 1:64-scale, Ertl, red and silver, w/Loader, 1980s, No. 1125
EX $4　　**NM** $6　　**MIP** $7

❏ **Massey-Ferguson 699**, 1:64-scale, Ertl, red and silver, 1980s
EX $3　　**NM** $4　　**MIP** $6

❏ **Massey-Ferguson 8160**, 1:64-scale, Scale Models, red, MFD, 1997, No. FT-0821
EX $4　　**NM** $6　　**MIP** $9

❑ **Massey-Ferguson 8160**, 1:64-scale, Scale Models, red, MFD, Kansas City, 150th Anniversary, 1997, No. FT-0836
EX $4   **NM** $6   **MIP** $9

❑ **Massey-Ferguson 8270**, 1:64-scale, Ertl, red, MFD, w/wide single tires, 2003, No. 13404
EX $4   **NM** $6   **MIP** $8

❑ **Massey-Ferguson 8280**, 1:64-scale, Ertl, red, MFD, w/duals, 2000, No. 13052
EX $4   **NM** $6   **MIP** $8

❑ **Massey-Ferguson 8280**, 1:64-scale, Ertl, red, MFD, w/triples, Collector Edition, 2000, No. 13101A
EX $4   **NM** $6   **MIP** $8

❑ **Massey-Ferguson 8280**, 1:64-scale, Siku, red, MFD, w/5 bottom plow, No. 1621
EX n/a   **NM** n/a   **MIP** $9

TRUCKS 1:25-SCALE

❑ **Parts Express**, 1:25-scale, white, 1980s, No. 1152
EX $18   **NM** $37   **MIP** $48

TRUCKS 1:43-SCALE

❑ **Massey-Ferguson Ford Model T Van**, 1:43-scale, SpecCast, w/Massey Ferguson logo, 1990s
EX $6   **NM** $8   **MIP** $12

TRUCKS 1:64-SCALE

❑ **Massey-Ferguson Hauling Set**, 1:64-scale, Ertl, No. 7079 *(Photo by Ertl)*
EX $9   **NM** $12   **MIP** $18

❑ **Semi w/Massey-Ferguson Van Box**, 1:64-scale, Ertl, No. 1804
(Photo by Ertl)
EX $8   **NM** $12   **MIP** $18

MASSEY-HARRIS

BANKS 1:25-SCALE

❑ **Bank**, 1:25-scale, Ertl, yellow, 1980s
EX $4   **NM** $12   **MIP** $18

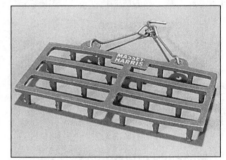

❑ **Massey-Harris Truck Bank**, 1:25-scale, Ertl, No. 1868 *(Photo by Kate Bossen)*
EX $6   **NM** $8   **MIP** $18

CONSTRUCTION EQUIPMENT 1:16-SCALE

❑ **Massey-Harris Crawler**, 1:16-scale, Lincoln, red, 1950s
EX $189   **NM** $292   **MIP** $506

IMPLEMENTS 1:08-SCALE

❑ **Massey-Harris Disc**, 1:08-scale, Scale Models, red, drag type, 1998, No. FT-0854
EX $32   **NM** $57   **MIP** $83

❑ **Massey-Harris Wagon, Flare Box**, 1:08-scale, Scale Models, red, 1998, No. FT-0853
EX $32   **NM** $57   **MIP** $83

IMPLEMENTS 1:16-SCALE

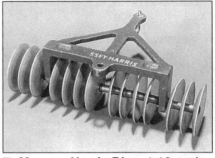

❑ **Massey-Harris Disc**, 1:16-scale, Lincoln, red, single gang, drag type, 1950s, No. 903
EX $18   **NM** $46   **MIP** $74

❑ **Massey-Harris Harrow**, 1:16-scale, Lincoln, red, drag type, 1950s, No. 905
EX $18   **NM** $46   **MIP** $74

❑ **Massey-Harris Mower**, 1:16-scale, Lincoln, red, 1950s, No. 907
EX $48   **NM** $71   **MIP** $143

❑ **Massey-Harris Spreader, No. 11**, 1:16-scale, King, red, spring drive, silver beaters, 1950s
EX $42   **NM** $98   **MIP** $207

❑ **Massey-Harris Combine, 80**, 1:20-scale, Reuhl, red, wide feeder house, seat on grain tank, 1950s
EX $384   **NM** $772   **MIP** $1162

❑ **Massey-Harris Combine, Clipper**, 1:20-scale, Reuhl, red, 1950s
EX $167   **NM** $323   **MIP** $687

❑ **Massey-Harris Spreader, No. 11**, 1:16-scale, Slik, red, ground drive, 1950s
EX $34   **NM** $89   **MIP** $167

❑ **Massey-Harris Combine, Clipper**, 1:20-scale, Lincoln, red, 1950s
EX $123   **NM** $238   **MIP** $492

❑ **Massey-Harris Combine, Clipper**, 1:20-scale, Reuhl, red, 1950s
EX $167   **NM** $323   **MIP** $687

IMPLEMENTS 1:20-SCALE

❑ **Massey-Harris Combine**, 1:20-scale, King, red, Harvest Brigade, wood reel, driver, 1950s
EX $143   **NM** $256   **MIP** $487

❑ **Massey-Harris Combine, Clipper**, 1:20-scale, Plymth, red, 1950s
EX $123   **NM** $238   **MIP** $492

❑ **Massey-Harris Disc**, 1:20-scale, Reuhl, red, wheel disc, 1950s, No. 35
EX $176   **NM** $312   **MIP** $502

❑ **Massey-Harris Combine, 70**, 1:20-scale, Reuhl, red, narrow feeder house, free standing seat, 1950s
EX $354   **NM** $672   **MIP** $1162

❑ **Massey-Harris Combine, Clipper**, 1:20-scale, Reuhl, red, 1950s
EX $167   **NM** $323   **MIP** $627

❑ **Massey-Harris Loader**, 1:20-scale, Reuhl, red, fits Reuhl 44, 1950s, No. 11
EX $177   **NM** $311   **MIP** $522

❑ **Massey-Harris Plow**, 1:20-scale, Reuhl, red, 3 bottom mounted, 1950, No. 37
EX $153   **NM** $287   **MIP** $462

❑ **Massey-Harris Wagon, Barge**, 1:20-scale, Reuhl, red, 1950s
EX $128   **NM** $211   **MIP** $388

IMPLEMENTS 1:43-SCALE

❑ **Massey-Harris Spreader**, 1:43-scale, Dinky, red, 1950s
EX $6   **NM** $22   **MIP** $43

❑ **Massey-Harris Spreader**, 1:43-scale, Dinky, red, 1950s
EX $6   **NM** $22   **MIP** $43

PEDAL TRACTORS

❑ **Massey-Harris 333**, Scale Models, red, NF, Collector Edition, 2004, No. FT-0670
EX $108   **NM** $132   **MIP** $163

❑ **Massey-Harris 44**, Eska, Large version, red, closed grille, tractor in original condition, No. 1953
EX $1198   **NM** $2223   **MIP** n/a

❑ **Massey-Harris 44**, Lambert, Small version, red, open grille, tractor in original condition, No. 1951
EX $2889   **NM** $4343   **MIP** n/a

❑ **Massey-Harris 44**, Scale Models, red, NF, 2001, No. FT-0596
EX $106   **NM** $128   **MIP** $153

❑ **Massey-Harris 44**, Scale Models, red, NF, Collector Edition, 2001, No. FT-0504
EX $108   **NM** $132   **MIP** $168

❑ **Massey-Harris Umbrella**, Heltrick, yellow, in original condition, No. 1957
EX $79   **NM** $179   **MIP** $318

TRACTORS 1:16-SCALE

❑ **Massey-Harris 101**, 1:16-scale, SpecCast, red, steel wheels, Collectors Edition, 1990s, No. 2693
EX $18   **NM** $26   **MIP** $37

❑ **Massey-Harris 101**, 1:16-scale, SpecCast, red, 1990 Summer Toy Festival, 1990s, No. 2691
EX $22   **NM** $36   **MIP** $42

❑ **Massey-Harris 101**, 1:16-scale, SpecCast, red, on rubber, Collector Edition, 1991, No. 2509
EX $18   **NM** $26   **MIP** $37

❑ **Massey-Harris 101**, 1:16-scale, SpecCast, red, NF on rubber, 1995, No. SCT-136
EX $18   **NM** $26   **MIP** $37

❑ **Massey-Harris 101**, 1:16-scale, SpecCast, red, '96 Great American Toy Show, 1996, No. CUST 397
EX $18   **NM** $26   **MIP** $37

❑ **Massey-Harris 101**, 1:16-scale, SpecCast, red, WF, w/side shields, 1998, No. SCT-145
EX $18   **NM** $26   **MIP** $37

❑ **Massey-Harris 101**, 1:16-scale, SpecCast, red, NF, w/side shields, 2001, No. SCT-198 *(Photo by SpecCast)*
EX $18   **NM** $26   **MIP** $37

❏ **Massey-Harris 101**, 1:16-scale, SpecCast, red, NF, on steel, 2003, No. SCT-206 (Photo by SpecCast)
EX $18   **NM** $26   **MIP** $37

❏ **Massey-Harris 102**, 1:16-scale, SpecCast, red, G & M EURO 1990, 1990s, No. CUST 118
EX $36   **NM** $78   **MIP** $98

❏ **Massey-Harris 102**, 1:16-scale, SpecCast, red, Tractor Classics Canada, 1990s
EX $22   **NM** $36   **MIP** $48

❏ **Massey-Harris 102**, 1:16-scale, SpecCast, red, WF, 1992, No. 2454
EX $18   **NM** $26   **MIP** $37

❏ **Massey-Harris 102**, 1:16-scale, SpecCast, red, puller, '99 Louisville Machinery Show Edition, 1999, No. SCT-166
EX $18   **NM** $26   **MIP** $37

❏ **Massey-Harris 15-22**, 1:16-scale, Scale Models, gray, 4WD, #11 in Collector Series, 1984
EX $43   **NM** $82   **MIP** $143

❏ **Massey-Harris 22**, 1:16-scale, SpecCast, red, NF, 2001, No. SCT-192
EX $18   **NM** $27   **MIP** $42

❏ **Massey-Harris 22**, 1:16-scale, SpecCast, red, WF, 2001, No. SCT-188
EX $18   **NM** $27   **MIP** $42

❏ **Massey-Harris 25**, 1:16-scale, Scale Models, red, 1991, No. FT-0805 (Photo by Scale Models)
EX $22   **NM** $33   **MIP** $44

❏ **Massey-Harris 25**, 1:16-scale, Scale Models, red, on rubber, '95 New York Farm Show, 1995, No. FB-2366
EX $16   **NM** $24   **MIP** $38

❏ **Massey-Harris 33**, 1:16-scale, Ertl, red, National Farm Toy Show 1987, 1987, No. 1172PA
EX $33   **NM** $47   **MIP** $89

❏ **Massey-Harris 33**, 1:16-scale, Scale Models, red, NF, 1991, No. 1109
EX $24   **NM** $33   **MIP** $47

❏ **Massey-Harris 333**, 1:16-scale, Scale Models, red, NF, 1992, No. FT-0801 (Photo by Scale Models)
EX $18   **NM** $33   **MIP** $43

❏ **Massey-Harris 333**, 1:16-scale, Scale Models, red, NF, '92 Farm Progress Show Edition, 1992, No. FB-1603
EX $24   **NM** $36   **MIP** $47

❏ **Massey-Harris 44**, 1:16-scale, Ertl, red, Collectors Edition, WF, 1980s, No. 1133DA
EX $37   **NM** $57   **MIP** $82

❏ **Massey-Harris 44**, 1:16-scale, Ertl, red, NF, 1980s, No. 1133
EX $23   **NM** $37   **MIP** $48

❏ **Massey-Harris 44**, 1:16-scale, Ertl, red, 1/16 and 1/43 tractors of the past set, 1990, No. 1110
EX n/a   **NM** n/a   **MIP** $48

❏ **Massey-Harris 44**, 1:16-scale, Ertl, red, "Canadian" C.I.F.E.S. 1991, 1990s
EX $23   **NM** $37   **MIP** $48

❏ **Massey-Harris 44**, 1:16-scale, Ertl, red, red stacks, 1990s, No. 1133
EX $23   **NM** $37   **MIP** $48

❑ **Massey-Harris 44**, 1:16-scale, Ertl, red, Foxfire Farm, w/Matt, 1998, No. 2046
EX $18   **NM** $27   **MIP** $43

❑ **Massey-Harris 44**, 1:16-scale, Ertl, red, WF, 2000, No. 13168
EX $14   **NM** $22   **MIP** $38

❑ **Massey-Harris 44**, 1:16-scale, Ertl, red, NF, #9 in Precision Series, 2002, No. 13082
EX $67   **NM** $82   **MIP** $148

❑ **Massey-Harris 44**, 1:16-scale, King, red, molded in 2 halves, separate driver, wears hat, 1950s
EX $53   **NM** $132   **MIP** $323

❑ **Massey-Harris 44**, 1:16-scale, Lincoln, red, Standard, 8 slots in grille, 1950s
EX $98   **NM** $296   **MIP** $638

❑ **Massey-Harris 44**, 1:16-scale, Scale Models, red, No. 4 in Antique Series, 1985
EX $22   **NM** $36   **MIP** $48

❑ **Massey-Harris 44**, 1:16-scale, Scale Models, red, w/Farmhand loader, 1990s
EX $123   **NM** $198   **MIP** $258

❑ **Massey-Harris 44**, 1:16-scale, Scale Models, red, special, 1992, No. 1115
EX $18   **NM** $23   **MIP** $48

❑ **Massey-Harris 44**, 1:16-scale, Slik, red, rubber tires and rims, 1950s
EX $72   **NM** $163   **MIP** $418

❑ **Massey-Harris 44**, 1:16-scale, Slik, red, tin rims, 1950s
EX $72   **NM** $163   **MIP** $418

❑ **Massey-Harris 44-6**, 1:16-scale, Stephan, red, NF, 6 cylinder engine, 1992
EX $127   **NM** $143   **MIP** $268

❑ **Massey-Harris 55**, 1:16-scale, Ertl, red, '92 National Farm Toy Show Edition, 1992, No. 1292PA
EX $22   **NM** $34   **MIP** $53

❑ **Massey-Harris 55**, 1:16-scale, Ertl, red, gas, Wheatland fenders, 1993, No. 1292TA
EX $18   **NM** $23   **MIP** $42

❑ **Massey-Harris 55**, 1:16-scale, Ertl, red, gas, clam shell fenders, 1994, No. 1292 *(Photo by Ertl)*
EX $12   **NM** $18   **MIP** $27

❑ **Massey-Harris 55**, 1:16-scale, Ertl, w/plow set, 1995, No. 7074

(Photo by Ertl)

EX n/a   **NM** n/a   **MIP** $44

❑ **Massey-Harris 555**, 1:16-scale, Ertl, red, 1994, No. 1105 *(Photo by Ertl)*
EX $17   **NM** $22   **MIP** $38

❑ **Massey-Harris 555**, 1:16-scale, Ertl, red, WF, Collector Edition, 1994, No. 1105DA
EX $22   **NM** $34   **MIP** $48

❑ **Massey-Harris 555**, 1:16-scale, Ertl, red, WF, '96 Sugar Valley Farm Toy Show Edition, 1996, No. 2673TA
EX $21   **NM** $32   **MIP** $48

❏ **Massey-Harris 744 D**, 1:16-scale, Marbil, red, 1980s
EX $67   **NM** $102   **MIP** $152

❏ **Massey-Harris 744 D**, 1:16-scale, Marbil, red, 1980s
EX $67   **NM** $102   **MIP** $152

❏ **Massey-Harris 744 D**, 1:16-scale, Marbil, red, 1980s
EX $67   **NM** $102   **MIP** $152

❏ **Massey-Harris 745 D**, 1:16-scale, Lesney, red, 1950s
EX $138   **NM** $312   **MIP** $627

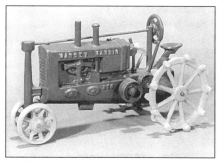

❏ **Massey-Harris Challenger**, 1:16-scale, Bob Gray (Custom), red, did not come in box, 1970s
EX $22   **NM** $38   **MIP** n/a

❏ **Massey-Harris Challenger**, 1:16-scale, Bob Gray (Custom), red, did not come in box, 1970s
EX $22   **NM** $44   **MIP** n/a

❏ **Massey-Harris Challenger**, 1:16-scale, Ertl, green, on rubber, 1991, No. 1103 *(Photo by Bossen Implement)*
EX $18   **NM** $32   **MIP** $43

❏ **Massey-Harris Challenger**, 1:16-scale, Ertl, green, on steel, Collector Edition, 1991, No. 1103TA
EX $18   **NM** $32   **MIP** $43

❏ **Massey-Harris Challenger**, 1:16-scale, Ertl, green, NF, on rubber, 1995, No. SCT-135
EX $18   **NM** $32   **MIP** $43

❏ **Massey-Harris Colt**, 1:16-scale, SpecCast, red, NF, 2001, No. SCT-189
EX $18   **NM** $32   **MIP** $43

❏ **Massey-Harris Colt**, 1:16-scale, SpecCast, red, WF, 2002, No. SCT-201 *(Photo by Bossen Implement)*
EX $18   **NM** $32   **MIP** $43

❏ **Massey-Harris Colt**, 1:16-scale, SpecCast, NF, w/umbrella, 2007, No. 287 *(Photo by SpecCast)*
EX $15   **NM** $28   **MIP** $42

❏ **Massey-Harris Mustang**, 1:16-scale, SpecCast, red, WF, 2002, No. SCT-191
EX $18   **NM** $32   **MIP** $43

❏ **Massey-Harris Mustang**, 1:16-scale, SpecCast, red, NF, 2002, No. SCT-202 *(Photo by Bossen Implement)*
EX $18   **NM** $32   **MIP** $43

❏ **Massey-Harris No. 1**, 1:16-scale, Scale Models, red, '93 Farm Progress Show Edition, 1993, No. FB-1617 *(Photo by Bossen Implement)*
EX $23   **NM** $36   **MIP** $57

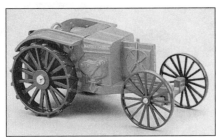

❑ **Massey-Harris No. 1**, 1:16-scale, Scale Models, red, 1993, No. FT-0807 *(Photo by Scale Models)*
EX $23   **NM** $36   **MIP** $57

❑ **Massey-Harris Pacemaker**, 1:16-scale, SpecCast, red and yellow, rubber tires, 1990s
EX $22   **NM** $36   **MIP** $48

❑ **Massey-Harris Pacemaker**, 1:16-scale, SpecCast, red and yellow, on steel, 1990s
EX $22   **NM** $36   **MIP** $48

❑ **Massey-Harris Pony**, 1:16-scale, Pioneer Collectables, red, '86 Toy Tractor Times Edition; 1,740 produced, 1986, No. PC1986
EX $26   **NM** $42   **MIP** $78

❑ **Massey-Harris Pony**, 1:16-scale, Scale Models, red, 1989, No. FT-0802
EX $9   **NM** $13   **MIP** $22

❑ **Massey-Harris Pony**, 1:16-scale, Scale Models, red, "1st Edition", 1990s, No. 2599
EX $13   **NM** $18   **MIP** $28

❑ **Massey-Harris Pony**, 1:16-scale, Scale Models, red, '94 Oklahoma Farm Show Edition, 1994, No. FB-2356
EX $13   **NM** $18   **MIP** $28

❑ **Massey-Harris Pony**, 1:16-scale, Scale Models, red, '94 Farmer Stockman Show Edition, 1994, No. FB-2373
EX $13   **NM** $18   **MIP** $28

❑ **Massey-Harris Pony**, 1:16-scale, Scale Models, red, '94 Husker Harvest Days Edition, 1994, No. FB-2372
EX $13   **NM** $18   **MIP** $28

❑ **Massey-Harris Pony**, 1:16-scale, Scale Models, red, '94 New York Farm Show Edition, 1994, No. FB-1640
EX $13   **NM** $18   **MIP** $28

❑ **Massey-Harris Twin Power**, 1:16-scale, SpecCast, red and yellow, rubber tires, 1989, No. 2685
EX $22   **NM** $36   **MIP** $48

TRACTORS 1:20-SCALE

❑ **Massey-Harris**, 1:20-scale, Raphael, blue or red, 1950s
EX $28   **NM** $73   **MIP** $123

❑ **Massey-Harris 44**, 1:20-scale, Lincoln, red, Standard, 4 slots in grille, 1950s
EX $78   **NM** $176   **MIP** $382

❑ **Massey-Harris 44**, 1:20-scale, Lincoln, red, Standard, 4 slots in grille, clam shell fenders, 1950s
EX $78   **NM** $176   **MIP** $382

❑ **Massey-Harris 44**, 1:20-scale, Reuhl, red, plastic rear rims, axle cap, 1950s
EX $287   **NM** $472   **MIP** $864

❑ **Massey-Harris 44**, 1:20-scale, Reuhl, red, plastic rear rims, 1950s
EX $287   **NM** $472   **MIP** $864

❑ **Massey-Harris 44**, 1:20-scale, Reuhl, red, all die-cast rims, 1950s
EX $287   **NM** $472   **MIP** $864

❑ **Massey-Harris 745**, 1:20-scale, Lincoln Micro, red, w/yellow loader, 1950s
EX $82   **NM** $223   **MIP** $437

❑ **Massey-Harris 745**, 1:20-scale, Lincoln Micro, red, 1950s
EX $78   **NM** $206   **MIP** $382

TRACTORS 1:32-SCALE

❑ **Massey-Harris 333**, 1:32-scale, Scale Models, red, 1991, No. FT-0800 *(Photo by Scale Models)*
EX $4   **NM** $6   **MIP** $9

❑ **Massey-Harris 44**, 1:32-scale, Scale Models, red, 1990 Farm Progress Show, 1990s
EX $6   **NM** $12   **MIP** $18

TRACTORS 1:43-SCALE

❑ **Massey-Harris 101**, 1:43-scale, SpecCast, 1990s
EX $6   **NM** $8   **MIP** $12

❑ **Massey-Harris 33**, 1:43-scale, Ertl, red, National Farm Toy Show 1987, 1987, No. 2515MA
EX $18   **NM** $33   **MIP** $48

❑ **Massey-Harris 33**, 1:43-scale, SpecCast, 1990s
EX $6   **NM** $8   **MIP** $12

❑ **Massey-Harris 44**, 1:43-scale, Dinky, red, metal wheels, tan driver, 1948, No. 300
EX $32   **NM** $63   **MIP** $119

❑ **Massey-Harris 44**, 1:43-scale, Ertl, red, 1980s, No. 2528
EX $4   **NM** $8   **MIP** $11

❑ **Massey-Harris 55**, 1:43-scale, Ertl, red, '92 National Farm Toy Show Edition, 1992, No. 1131EA
EX $9   **NM** $13   **MIP** $22

❑ **Massey-Harris 55**, 1:43-scale, Ertl, red, 1994, No. 1131 *(Photo by Ertl)*
EX $4   **NM** $8   **MIP** $11

❑ **Massey-Harris Challenger**, 1:43-scale, Ertl, green, 1980s, No. 2511
EX $4   **NM** $8   **MIP** $11

❑ **Massey-Harris Pony**, 1:43-scale, SpecCast, 1990s
EX $6   **NM** $8   **MIP** $12

❑ **Massey-Harris Twin Power**, 1:43-scale, SpecCast, 1990s
EX $6   **NM** $8   **MIP** $12

❑ **Massey-Harris Twin Power**, 1:43-scale, SpecCast, 1990s
EX $6   **NM** $8   **MIP** $12

TRACTORS 1:64-SCALE

❑ **Massey-Harris 33**, 1:64-scale, Scale Models, red, '91 Farm Progress Show Edition, 1991, No. FB-1556
EX $4   **NM** $6   **MIP** $8

❑ **Massey-Harris 33**, 1:64-scale, Scale Models, red, 1991, No. FC-1110
EX $4   **NM** $6   **MIP** $8

❑ **Massey-Harris 33**, 1:64-scale, Scale Models, red, '92 Farm Progress Show Edition, 1992, No. FB-1605
EX $4   **NM** $6   **MIP** $8

❑ **Massey-Harris 333**, 1:64-scale, Scale Models, red, '93 Farm Progress Show Edition, 1993
EX $4   **NM** $6   **MIP** $8

❑ **Massey-Harris 333**, 1:64-scale, Scale Models, 1994, No. FT-0811
(Photo by Scale Models)
EX $4   **NM** $6   **MIP** $8

❑ **Massey-Harris 44**, 1:64-scale, Scale Models, red and yellow, No. FJ-PS2651
EX $4   **NM** $6   **MIP** $8

❑ **Massey-Harris 44**, 1:64-scale, Scale Models, silver, sold as a Christmas ornament, 1980s
EX $2   **NM** $3   **MIP** $6

❑ **Massey-Harris 44**, 1:64-scale, Scale Models, gold, sold as a Christmas ornament, 1980s
EX $3   **NM** $4   **MIP** $6

❑ **Massey-Harris 44**, 1:64-scale, Scale Models, red, '90 Farm Progress Show Edition, 1990
EX $4   **NM** $6   **MIP** $8

❑ **Massey-Harris 44**, 1:64-scale, Scale Models, red, Kansas City 150th Anniversary, 1997, No. FT-0843
EX $4   **NM** $6   **MIP** $8

❑ **Massey-Harris No. 1**, 1:64-scale, Scale Models, red, '93 Farm Progress Show Edition, 1993, No. FB-1618
EX $4   **NM** $6   **MIP** $8

❑ **Massey-Harris No. 1**, 1:64-scale, Scale Models, red, 1995, No. FT-0808
(Photo by Scale Models)
EX $4   **NM** $6   **MIP** $8

❑ **Massey-Harris No. 1**, 1:64-scale, Scale Models, red, Kansas City 150th Anniversary, 1997, No. FT-0841
EX $4   **NM** $6   **MIP** $8

❑ **Massey-Harris Pony**, 1:64-scale, SpecCast, red and yellow
EX $6   **NM** $12   **MIP** $18

MELROE

IMPLEMENTS 1:16-SCALE

❑ **Spra-Coupe**, 1:16-scale, Scale Models, white, WF, 1990s
EX $34   **NM** $68   **MIP** $142

❑ **Spra-Coupe**, 1:16-scale, Scale Models, white, NF, 1990s
EX $34   **NM** $68   **MIP** $142

MINNEAPOLIS-MOLINE

BANKS 1:25-SCALE

❑ **Minneapolis-Moline Truck Bank**, 1:25-scale, Ertl, 1980s, No. 2224
(Photo by Ertl)
EX $4   **NM** $12   **MIP** $18

CONSTRUCTION EQUIPMENT 1:16-SCALE

❑ **Minneapolis-Moline Crawler 2 Star**, 1:16-scale, SpecCast, '04 National Toy Truck N Construction Show, 2004, No. CUST812
EX $23   **NM** $38   **MIP** $67

❑ **Minneapolis-Moline Crawler 2 Star**, 1:16-scale, SpecCast, w/bucket, metal tracks, 2005, No. SCT244
EX $23   **NM** $37   **MIP** $62

❑ **Minneapolis-Moline Crawler 2 Star**, 1:16-scale, SpecCast, w/blade, metal tracks, 2005, No. SCT233
EX $23   **NM** $37   **MIP** $62

❑ **Minneapolis-Moline Pan Scraper**, 1:16-scale, Mohr (Custom), yellow, 1980s
EX $392   **NM** $589   **MIP** $654

IMPLEMENTS 1:12-SCALE

❑ **Minneapolis-Moline Wood Wagon**, 1:12-scale, Werner, prairie gold, did not come in box, 1940s
EX $33   **NM** $47   **MIP** n/a

IMPLEMENTS 1:16-SCALE

❑ **Minneapolis-Moline Baler**, 1:16-scale, Koob (Custom), yellow, 760, 2001
EX $321   **NM** $362   **MIP** n/a

❑ **Minneapolis-Moline Combine**, 1:16-scale, Koob (Custom), yellow, Model 88, w/PTO, 2001
EX $321   **NM** $362   **MIP** n/a

❑ **Minneapolis-Moline Combine**, 1:16-scale, Koob (Custom), yellow, Model 88, w/wisconsin engine, 2001
EX $321   **NM** $362   **MIP** n/a

❑ **Minneapolis-Moline Combine**, SP, 1:16-scale, Cottonwood Acres, yellow, 1980s
EX $189   **NM** $433   **MIP** $512

❑ **Minneapolis-Moline Corn Sheller**, 1:16-scale, Cottonwood Acres, yellow, 1980s
EX $323   **NM** $382   **MIP** $433

❑ **Minneapolis-Moline Corn Sheller**, 1:16-scale, Cottonwood Acres, yellow, on IHC R-1Truck, 1990s
EX $387   **NM** $622   **MIP** $678

❑ **Minneapolis-Moline Corn Sheller**, 1:16-scale, Koob (Custom), yellow, Model D, 2000
EX $321   **NM** $362   **MIP** n/a

❑ **Minneapolis-Moline Corn Sheller**, 1:16-scale, Koob (Custom), yellow, Model E, 2000
EX $321   **NM** $362   **MIP** n/a

❑ **Minneapolis-Moline Corn Sheller**, 1:16-scale, Koob (Custom), yellow, Model E on truck, 2001
EX $489   **NM** $567   **MIP** n/a

❑ **Minneapolis-Moline Disc**, 1:16-scale, Slik, red, 1950s, No. 9855
EX $168   **NM** $338   **MIP** $588

❑ **Minneapolis-Moline Picker**, 1:16-scale, Cottonwood Acres, yellow, 2-row deluxe, 1990s
EX $289   **NM** $388   **MIP** $439

❏ **Minneapolis-Moline Plow**, 1:16-scale, Carter, red w/yellow wheel rims, 1950s
EX $98   **NM** $212   **MIP** $476

❏ **Minneapolis-Moline Uni-System**, 1:16-scale, Koob (Custom), yellow, husker, 2000
EX $289   **NM** $313   **MIP** n/a

❏ **Minneapolis-Moline Uni-System**, 1:16-scale, Koob (Custom), brown, Power Unit, 2000
EX $88   **NM** $126   **MIP** n/a

❏ **Minneapolis-Moline Uni-System**, 1:16-scale, Koob (Custom), brown, Transfer Cart, 2000
EX $22   **NM** $52   **MIP** n/a

❏ **Minneapolis-Moline Uni-System**, 1:16-scale, Koob (Custom), yellow, harvestor, w/reel, 2000
EX $289   **NM** $313   **MIP** n/a

❏ **Minneapolis-Moline Uni-System**, 1:16-scale, Koob (Custom), yellow, baler, 2000
EX $289   **NM** $313   **MIP** n/a

❏ **Minneapolis-Moline Uni-System**, 1:16-scale, Koob (Custom), yellow, picker-sheller, 2000
EX $289   **NM** $313   **MIP** n/a

❏ **Minneapolis-Moline Uni-System**, 1:16-scale, Koob (Custom), yellow, harvestor, w/pickup head, 2000
EX $48   **NM** $64   **MIP** n/a

❏ **Minneapolis-Moline Uni-System**, 1:16-scale, Koob (Custom), yellow, forage harvestor, w/corn head, 2001
EX $289   **NM** $363   **MIP** n/a

❏ **Minneapolis-Moline Uni-System**, 1:16-scale, Koob (Custom), yellow, forage harvestor pickup head, 2001
EX $48   **NM** $64   **MIP** n/a

❏ **Minneapolis-Moline Uni-System**, 1:16-scale, Koob (Custom), yellow, forage harvestor cutter bar head, 2001
EX $289   **NM** $313   **MIP** n/a

IMPLEMENTS 1:24-SCALE

❏ **Minneapolis-Moline Combine 69**, 1:24-scale, Slik, prairie gold, 1950s, No. 9831
EX $138   **NM** $342   **MIP** $743

❏ **Minneapolis-Moline Corn Sheller**, 1:24-scale, Hosch (Custom), yellow, reproduction of Slik, 1970s
EX $38   **NM** $77   **MIP** n/a

❏ **Minneapolis-Moline Corn Sheller**, 1:24-scale, Slik, yellow, 1950s
EX $238   **NM** $444   **MIP** $887

❏ **Minneapolis-Moline Corn Sheller**, 1:24-scale, Slik, prairie gold, original sheller sold through Minneapolis Moline Dealers in the 1950s, 1950s
EX $238   **NM** $444   **MIP** $887

❏ **Minneapolis-Moline Spreader**, 1:24-scale, Slik, prairie gold, 1950s
EX $68   **NM** $182   **MIP** $328

❏ **Minneapolis-Moline Wagon**, 1:24-scale, Slik, prairie gold, 1950s
EX $22   **NM** $73   **MIP** $142

IMPLEMENTS 1:64-SCALE

❏ **Minneapolis-Moline Corn-Sheller**, 1:64-scale, Nygren (Custom), Prairie Gold, did not come in box, 1980s
EX $9   **NM** $22   **MIP** n/a

❏ **Minneapolis-Moline Thresher**, 1:64-scale, Scale Models, silver and red, 1980s
EX $4   **NM** $8   **MIP** $12

PEDAL TRACTORS

❑ **Minneapolis-Moline**, orange and silver, "Shuttle Shift," tractor in original condition, missing spark plug and wires
EX $342   **NM** $716   **MIP** $918

❑ **Minneapolis-Moline**, orange, "TOT Tractor," tractor in original condition
EX $282   **NM** $483   **MIP** $833

❑ **Minneapolis-Moline Spirit of MM**, Scale Models, yellow, Signature Series, 1999, No. FU-0616
EX $11   **NM** $132   **MIP** $168

❑ **Minneapolis-Moline Spirit of MM**, Scale Models, yellow, 2000, No. FU-0617
EX $102   **NM** $123   **MIP** $153

TRACTORS 1:12-SCALE

❑ **Minneapolis-Moline**, 1:12-scale, Werner, prairie gold, did not come in box, 1940s
EX $93   **NM** $148   **MIP** n/a

TRACTORS 1:16-SCALE

❑ **Minneapolis-Moline 445**, 1:16-scale, SpecCast, WF, gas, fenders, 2007, No. 273 *(Photo by SpecCast)*
EX $15   **NM** $30   **MIP** $45

❑ **Minneapolis-Moline 5 Star**, 1:16-scale, Mohr (Custom), yellow, custom, available in Row Crop, wide front end and LP gas, 1980s
EX $98   **NM** $153   **MIP** $283

❑ **Minneapolis-Moline 5 Star**, 1:16-scale, Mohr (Custom), yellow, custom, available in Row Crop, wide front end and LP gas, 1980s
EX $98   **NM** $152   **MIP** $283

❑ **Minneapolis-Moline 5 Star**, 1:16-scale, Mohr (Custom), yellow, custom, available in Row Crop, wide front end and LP gas, 1980s
EX $98   **NM** $152   **MIP** $283

❑ **Minneapolis-Moline 5 Star**, 1:16-scale, Mohr (Custom), yellow, custom, available in Row Crop, wide front end and LP gas, 1980s
EX $98   **NM** $152   **MIP** $283

❑ **Minneapolis-Moline A4T-1600**, 1:16-scale, Berg (Custom), yellow, diesel, 1980s
EX $287   **NM** $577   **MIP** n/a

❑ **Minneapolis-Moline A4T-1600**, 1:16-scale, Berg (Custom), yellow, LP, 1980s
EX $287   **NM** $577   **MIP** n/a

❑ **Minneapolis-Moline A4T-1600**, 1:16-scale, Berg (Custom), red, did not come in box, diesel, 1980s
EX $289   **NM** $577   **MIP** n/a

❑ **Minneapolis-Moline A4T-1600**, 1:16-scale, Cottonwood Acres, red, 1980s

EX $463   **NM** $562   **MIP** $622

❑ **Minneapolis-Moline Experimental**, 1:16-scale, SpecCast, NF, experimental tractor, 2007, No. 271

EX $15   **NM** $30   **MIP** $45

❑ **Minneapolis-Moline G**, 1:16-scale, Cottonwood Acres, yellow, LP, 1980s

EX $98   **NM** $152   **MIP** $183

❑ **Minneapolis-Moline G-1000**, 1:16-scale, Cottonwood Acres, yellow and brown, LP, 1980s

EX $163   **NM** $189   **MIP** $263

❑ **Minneapolis-Moline G-1000**, 1:16-scale, Cottonwood Acres, yellow over brown, 1980s

EX $163   **NM** $189   **MIP** $263

❑ **Minneapolis-Moline G-1000**, 1:16-scale, Ertl, yellow w/yellow rims, 1960s, No. 17

EX $122   **NM** $226   **MIP** $492

❑ **Minneapolis-Moline G-1000**, 1:16-scale, Ertl, yellow w/white rims, 1960s, No. 17

EX $122   **NM** $266   **MIP** $592

❑ **Minneapolis-Moline G-1000**, 1:16-scale, Ertl, Mighty Minnie, dark gold w/chrome rims and large tires, chrome engine, 1970s, No. 2702

EX $78   **NM** $216   **MIP** $263

❑ **Minneapolis-Moline G-1000**, 1:16-scale, Ertl, Mighty Minnie, light gold w/chrome rims and large tires, chrome engine, 1970s, No. 2702

EX $78   **NM** $216   **MIP** $263

❑ **Minneapolis-Moline G-1000**, 1:16-scale, Ertl, Mighty Minnie, gold w/chrome rims and small tires, chrome engine, 1970s, No. 2702

EX $78   **NM** $216   **MIP** $263

❑ **Minneapolis-Moline G-1000**, 1:16-scale, Ertl, Mighty Minnie, gold w/chrome rims and small tires, black engine, 1970s, No. 2702

EX $78   **NM** $216   **MIP** $233

❑ **Minneapolis-Moline G-1000 Vista**, 1:16-scale, Parker/Lowry (Custom), yellow and white, did not come in box, 1980s

EX $163   **NM** $263   **MIP** n/a

❑ **Minneapolis-Moline G-1000 Vista**, 1:16-scale, Parker/Lowry (Custom), yellow and white, did not come in box, 1980s
EX $163   **NM** $263   **MIP** n/a

❑ **Minneapolis-Moline G-1335**, 1:16-scale, Ertl, yellow w/white rims, 1970s, No. 19
EX $122   **NM** $188   **MIP** $292

❑ **Minneapolis-Moline G-550**, 1:16-scale, Ertl, yellow, Collectors Edition, No. 4382DA *(Photo by Ertl)*
EX $17   **NM** $27   **MIP** $38

❑ **Minneapolis-Moline G-550**, 1:16-scale, Ertl, yellow, '96 Sugar Valley Farm Toy Show, 1996, No. 3043TA
EX $23   **NM** $32   **MIP** $48

❑ **Minneapolis-Moline G-550**, 1:16-scale, Ertl, yellow, MFD, diesel, 1996, No. 7057 *(Photo by Ertl)*
EX $13   **NM** $22   **MIP** $38

❑ **Minneapolis-Moline G-705**, 1:16-scale, Mohr (Custom), yellow and brown, 1980s
EX $148   **NM** $189   **MIP** $233

❑ **Minneapolis-Moline G-706**, 1:16-scale, Mohr (Custom), yellow and brown, 1980s
EX $148   **NM** $189   **MIP** $233

❑ **Minneapolis-Moline G-706**, 1:16-scale, Mohr (Custom), FWA, yellow and brown, 1980s
EX $148   **NM** $182   **MIP** $233

❑ **Minneapolis-Moline G-750**, 1:16-scale, Ertl, yellow, '94 National Farm Toy Show Edition, 1994, No. 4375PA
EX $18   **NM** $28   **MIP** $43

❑ **Minneapolis-Moline G-750**, 1:16-scale, Ertl, yellow, NF, 1995, No. 4375 *(Photo by Ertl)*
EX $18   **NM** $27   **MIP** $33

❑ **Minneapolis-Moline G-750**, 1:16-scale, Ertl, yellow, 2WD, Collectors Edition, 1995, No. 4375DA *(Photo by Ertl)*
EX $18   **NM** $28   **MIP** $48

❑ **Minneapolis-Moline G-750**, 1:16-scale, Ertl, yellow, '95 Prairie Gold Edition, 1998, No. 2288TA
EX $23   **NM** $32   **MIP** $53

❑ **Minneapolis-Moline G-750**, 1:16-scale, Ertl, yellow, w/Hiniker cab, Collector Edition, 2000, No. 13105A
EX $23   **NM** $32   **MIP** $53

❑ **Minneapolis-Moline G-750**, 1:16-scale, Ertl, yellow, '02 Western MN Steam Threshers Reunion, 2002
EX $23   **NM** $32   **MIP** $53

❑ **Minneapolis-Moline G-850**, 1:16-scale, Scale Models, yellow, Louisville Show puller, 1980s
EX $22   **NM** $33   **MIP** $48

❑ **Minneapolis-Moline G-850**, 1:16-scale, Scale Models, yellow, 1988
EX $22   **NM** $31   **MIP** $47

❏ **Minneapolis-Moline G-850**, 1:16-scale, Scale Models, yellow, w/cab and duals, '97 November Open House Edition, 1997, No. FB-2473
EX $22   **NM** $31   **MIP** $47

❏ **Minneapolis-Moline G-900**, 1:16-scale, Cottonwood Acres, yellow and white, LP, 1980s
EX $163   **NM** $189   **MIP** $263

❏ **Minneapolis-Moline G-900**, 1:16-scale, Cottonwood Acres, yellow and white, 1980s
EX $163   **NM** $189   **MIP** $263

❏ **Minneapolis-Moline G-940**, 1:16-scale, Scale Models, yellow, OSLO Lions Club 4-2-89, 1980s
EX $22   **NM** $33   **MIP** $43

❏ **Minneapolis-Moline G-940**, 1:16-scale, Scale Models, 1991, No. FF-0292 *(Photo by Scale Models)*
EX $18   **NM** $21   **MIP** $28

❏ **Minneapolis-Moline G-940**, 1:16-scale, Scale Models, yellow, '92 Husker Huske's and Days Edition, 1992, No. FB-1599
EX $22   **NM** $31   **MIP** $47

❏ **Minneapolis-Moline G-940**, 1:16-scale, Scale Models, yellow, '92 Minnesota State Fair Edition, 1992, No. FB-1593
EX $22   **NM** $31   **MIP** $47

❏ **Minneapolis-Moline G-940**, 1:16-scale, Scale Models, yellow, WF, w/stacks, 1992, No. FU-0555
EX $23   **NM** $32   **MIP** $53

❏ **Minneapolis-Moline G-940**, 1:16-scale, Scale Models, yellow, '92 June Open House, 1992 *(Photo by Bossen Implement)*
EX $22   **NM** $31   **MIP** $47

❏ **Minneapolis-Moline GB**, 1:16-scale, Cottonwood Acres, yellow, 1980s
EX $98   **NM** $152   **MIP** $183

❏ **Minneapolis-Moline GB**, 1:16-scale, Cottonwood Acres, yellow, LP, 1980s
EX $98   **NM** $152   **MIP** $183

❏ **Minneapolis-Moline GTB**, 1:16-scale, Cottonwood Acres, yellow, first tractor, 1980s
EX $98   **NM** $152   **MIP** $183

❏ **Minneapolis-Moline GTS**, 1:16-scale, Mohr (Custom), yellow, 1980s
EX $123   **NM** $189   **MIP** $228

❏ **Minneapolis-Moline GTS**, 1:16-scale, Mohr (Custom), yellow, 1980s
EX $123   **NM** $189   **MIP** $228

❏ **Minneapolis-Moline GTS**, 1:16-scale, Mohr (Custom), yellow, 1980s
EX $123   **NM** $189   **MIP** $228

❑ **Minneapolis-Moline J**, 1:16-scale, Scale Models, yellow, 8th Annual Gateway Mid-America Toy Show, 1980s
EX $23   **NM** $56   **MIP** $72

❑ **Minneapolis-Moline J**, 1:16-scale, Scale Models, antique brass, 1980s
EX $42   **NM** $166   **MIP** $189

❑ **Minneapolis-Moline J**, 1:16-scale, Scale Models, yellow, 1980s
EX $23   **NM** $56   **MIP** $72

❑ **Minneapolis-Moline Jet Star**, 1:16-scale, Riecke (Custom), yellow/brown, did not come in box, 1990s
EX $248   **NM** $289   **MIP** n/a

❑ **Minneapolis-Moline Jet Star**, 1:16-scale, Riecke (Custom), brown, did not come in box, 1990s
EX $248   **NM** $289   **MIP** n/a

❑ **Minneapolis-Moline M-5**, 1:16-scale, Mohr (Custom), yellow and brown, 1980s
EX $98   **NM** $153   **MIP** $183

❑ **Minneapolis-Moline M-5**, 1:16-scale, Mohr (Custom), Standard, yellow and brown, 1980s
EX $98   **NM** $153   **MIP** $183

❑ **Minneapolis-Moline M-5**, 1:16-scale, Mohr (Custom), yellow and brown, 1980s
EX $98   **NM** $153   **MIP** $183

❑ **Minneapolis-Moline M-602**, 1:16-scale, Mohr (Custom), yellow and brown, row crop front end, 1980s
EX $123   **NM** $168   **MIP** $208

❑ **Minneapolis-Moline M-602**, 1:16-scale, Mohr (Custom), yellow and brown, wide front end, 1980s
EX $123   **NM** $168   **MIP** $208

❑ **Minneapolis-Moline M-604**, 1:16-scale, Mohr (Custom), FWA, yellow and brown, 1980s
EX $123   **NM** $168   **MIP** $208

❑ **Minneapolis-Moline M-604**, 1:16-scale, Mohr (Custom), yellow and brown, 1980s
EX $123   **NM** $168   **MIP** $208

❏ **Minneapolis-Moline M-670 Super**, 1:16-scale, Cottonwood Acres, yellow and brown, limited to a production run of 1500, 1980s
EX $98   **NM** $152   **MIP** $223

❏ **Minneapolis-Moline R**, 1:16-scale, Arcor, red, 1940s
EX $22   **NM** $52   **MIP** $74

❏ **Minneapolis-Moline R**, 1:16-scale, Arcor, prairie gold, 1940s
EX $38   **NM** $118   **MIP** $223

❏ **Minneapolis-Moline R**, 1:16-scale, Auburn Rubber, red w/silver engine and wheel hubs, 7-3/8" long
EX $22   **NM** $52   **MIP** $74

❏ **Minneapolis-Moline R**, 1:16-scale, Auburn Rubber, red, 8" long, 1950s
EX $22   **NM** $52   **MIP** $74

❏ **Minneapolis-Moline R**, 1:16-scale, Cottonwood Acres, CAB, yellow, 1980s
EX $98   **NM** $148   **MIP** $222

❏ **Minneapolis-Moline R**, 1:16-scale, Hosch (Custom), yellow, reproduction of Slik, 1980s
EX $36   **NM** $62   **MIP** $73

❏ **Minneapolis-Moline R**, 1:16-scale, Mohr (Custom), yellow, narrow front, 1980s
EX $68   **NM** $89   **MIP** $219

❏ **Minneapolis-Moline R**, 1:16-scale, Mohr (Custom), yellow, w/cab, 1980s
EX $98   **NM** $148   **MIP** $262

❏ **Minneapolis-Moline R**, 1:16-scale, Mohr (Custom), yellow, w/cab, 1980s
EX $98   **NM** $148   **MIP** $262

❏ **Minneapolis-Moline R**, 1:16-scale, Parker (Custom), yellow, did not come in box, 1980s
EX $148   **NM** $189   **MIP** n/a

❏ **Minneapolis-Moline R**, 1:16-scale, Scale Models, yellow, Mankato Show 1989, limited to 1090 units, 1980s
EX $27   **NM** $36   **MIP** $47

❏ **Minneapolis-Moline R**, 1:16-scale, Scale Models, yellow, 1989 National Farm Toy Show, 1980s
EX $27   **NM** $36   **MIP** $47

❑ **Minneapolis-Moline R**, 1:16-scale, Scale Models, yellow, Prairie Gold Rush, Port Hope, Michigan 7-1-1989, w/rubber tires, 1989
EX $27   **NM** $36   **MIP** $47

❑ **Minneapolis-Moline R**, 1:16-scale, Slik, prairie gold w/red rear wheel centers, 1950s
EX $348   **NM** $782   **MIP** $1867

❑ **Minneapolis-Moline R**, 1:16-scale, Slik, yellow, rubber tires, 1950s
EX $348   **NM** $782   **MIP** $1867

❑ **Minneapolis-Moline RTS**, 1:16-scale, Cottonwood Acres, Standard, yellow, 1980s
EX $98   **NM** $148   **MIP** $183

❑ **Minneapolis-Moline RTU**, 1:16-scale, Mohr (Custom), yellow, 1980s
EX $98   **NM** $116   **MIP** $143

❑ **Minneapolis-Moline Steam Engine**, 1:16-scale, Scale Models, black, 1987 *(Photo by Bossen Implement)*
EX $123   **NM** $189   **MIP** $233

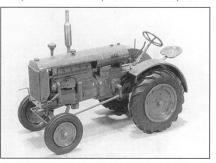

❑ **Minneapolis-Moline Twin City**, 1:16-scale, Mohr (Custom), gray, 1980s
EX $167   **NM** $189   **MIP** $232

❑ **Minneapolis-Moline Twin City**, 1:16-scale, Mohr (Custom), gray, 1980s
EX $167   **NM** $189   **MIP** $232

❑ **Minneapolis-Moline Twin City J**, 1:16-scale, Mohr (Custom), gray, 1980s
EX $167   **NM** $189   **MIP** $232

❑ **Minneapolis-Moline Twin City J**, 1:16-scale, Scale Models, gray, 1980s
EX $28   **NM** $48   **MIP** $78

❑ **Minneapolis-Moline Twin City J**, 1:16-scale, Scale Models, gray, Prairie Gold Rush model, 1980s
EX $28   **NM** $48   **MIP** $78

❑ **Minneapolis-Moline U**, 1:16-scale, Mohr (Custom), yellow, Standard, 1980s
EX $123   **NM** $189   **MIP** $228

❏ **Minneapolis-Moline U**, 1:16-scale, SpecCast, yellow, '93 Turtle River Toy News Edition, 1993, No. CUST 244
EX $16   **NM** $22   **MIP** $33

❏ **Minneapolis-Moline U**, 1:16-scale, SpecCast, yellow, NF, 1994, No. SCT118 *(Photo by SpecCast)*
EX $16   **NM** $22   **MIP** $33

❏ **Minneapolis-Moline U**, 1:16-scale, SpecCast, yellow, TSC Tractor Supply Company, 1994, No. CUST 279
EX $16   **NM** $22   **MIP** $33

❏ **Minneapolis-Moline U**, 1:16-scale, SpecCast, yellow, '95 Louisville Show Edition, 1995, No. SCT-3012
EX $16   **NM** $22   **MIP** $33

❏ **Minneapolis-Moline U**, 1:16-scale, SpecCast, yellow, '95 Great American Toy Show Edition, 1995, No. CUST 349
EX $16   **NM** $22   **MIP** $33

❏ **Minneapolis-Moline U**, 1:16-scale, SpecCast, yellow, on steel, 1995
EX $16   **NM** $22   **MIP** $33

❏ **Minneapolis-Moline U**, 1:16-scale, SpecCast, yellow, WF, 1995, No. SCT123 *(Photo by Kate Bossen)*
EX $16   **NM** $22   **MIP** $33

❏ **Minneapolis-Moline U**, 1:16-scale, SpecCast, yellow, puller, '97 Louisville Show Edition, 1997, No. SCT-144
EX $16   **NM** $22   **MIP** $33

❏ **Minneapolis-Moline U**, 1:16-scale, SpecCast, yellow, w/umbrella, '97 Farm Progress Show Edition, 1997, No. SCT-148
EX $16   **NM** $22   **MIP** $33

❏ **Minneapolis-Moline U**, 1:16-scale, SpecCast, yellow, single front wheel, 2001, No. SCT-196
EX $16   **NM** $22   **MIP** $33

❏ **Minneapolis-Moline U**, 1:16-scale, SpecCast, yellow, puller, '02 Louisville Show Edition, 2002, No. SCT-203
EX $16   **NM** $22   **MIP** $33

❏ **Minneapolis-Moline U**, 1:16-scale, SpecCast, yellow, NF, 2003, No. SCT-219 *(Photo by Bossen Implement)*
EX $21   **NM** $28   **MIP** $43

❏ **Minneapolis-Moline U-302**, 1:16-scale, Cottonwood Acres, yellow and white, 1990s
EX $98   **NM** $152   **MIP** $183

❏ **Minneapolis-Moline UB**, 1:16-scale, Cottonwood Acres, yellow, 1980s
EX $98   **NM** $152   **MIP** $183

❏ **Minneapolis-Moline UB**, 1:16-scale, Hosch (Custom), yellow, reproduction of Slik, 1980s
EX $22   **NM** $48   **MIP** $68

❏ **Minneapolis-Moline UB**, 1:16-scale, Hosch (Custom), yellow, reproduction of Slik, 1980s
EX $22   **NM** $48   **MIP** $68

❏ **Minneapolis-Moline UB**, 1:16-scale, Slik, yellow, 1950s
EX $122   **NM** $253   **MIP** $487

❏ **Minneapolis-Moline UB**, 1:16-scale, Slik, prairie gold w/red rims, 1950s
EX $123   **NM** $266   **MIP** $486

Photos by Jon Jacobson unless otherwise noted.

❏ **Minneapolis-Moline UB Special**, 1:16-scale, Mohr (Custom), yellow, 1980s

EX $123   **NM** $189   **MIP** $228

❏ **Minneapolis-Moline UDLX**, 1:16-scale, Mohr (Custom), yellow, 1980s

EX $123   **NM** $189   **MIP** $228

❏ **Minneapolis-Moline UDLX**, 1:16-scale, Scale Models, prairie gold w/red rims, comfort tractor, 1980s, No. 1303

EX $22   **NM** $33   **MIP** $42

❏ **Minneapolis-Moline UDLX**, 1:16-scale, Scale Models, Prairie Gold Rush, Greenville, Ohio, July 4, 1984, comfort tractor, 1984

EX $22   **NM** $33   **MIP** $48

❏ **Minneapolis-Moline Universal Tractor**, 1:16-scale, Bloomstrand Models (Custom), red, type 2, style A, 1990s

EX $123   **NM** $286   **MIP** n/a

❏ **Minneapolis-Moline Universal Tractor**, 1:16-scale, Bloomstrand Models (Custom), red, type 3, style B w/extension rims, 1990s

EX $123   **NM** $286   **MIP** n/a

❏ **Minneapolis-Moline Universal Tractor**, 1:16-scale, Bloomstrand Models (Custom), red, type 1, style A, 1990s

EX $123   **NM** $286   **MIP** n/a

❏ **Minneapolis-Moline Universal Tractor**, 1:16-scale, Bloomstrand Models (Custom), red, type 3, style B, 1990s

EX $123   **NM** $286   **MIP** n/a

❏ **Minneapolis-Moline UTC**, 1:16-scale, Mohr (Custom), yellow, Cane, 1980s

EX $123   **NM** $189   **MIP** $228

❏ **Minneapolis-Moline UTS**, 1:16-scale, Cottonwood Acres, yellow, wide front end, 1980s

EX $98   **NM** $152   **MIP** $183

❏ **Minneapolis-Moline UTS**, 1:16-scale, SpecCast, yellow, rubber tires, 1980s

EX $22   **NM** $33   **MIP** $43

❏ **Minneapolis-Moline UTS**, 1:16-scale, SpecCast, yellow, accompanied w/belt buckle, 1980s

EX $22   **NM** $33   **MIP** $43

❏ **Minneapolis-Moline UTS**, 1:16-scale, SpecCast, yellow, wide front end, 1980s
EX $22　　**NM** $33　　**MIP** $43

❏ **Minneapolis-Moline UTU**, 1:16-scale, Cottonwood Acres, yellow, 1980s
EX $98　　**NM** $152　　**MIP** $183

❏ **Minneapolis-Moline UTU**, 1:16-scale, Mohr (Custom), yellow, 1980s
EX $123　　**NM** $189　　**MIP** $228

❏ **Minneapolis-Moline V**, 1:16-scale, Pioneer Collectible, '88 Toy Tractor Times Anniversary, #3; 1,038 produced, 1988, No. PC1988
EX $25　　**NM** $50　　**MIP** $76

❏ **Minneapolis-Moline Z**, 1:16-scale, Cottonwood Acres, yellow, 1980s
EX $98　　**NM** $152　　**MIP** $183

❏ **Minneapolis-Moline Z**, 1:16-scale, Mohr (Custom), yellow, 1980s
EX $98　　**NM** $116　　**MIP** $163

❏ **Minneapolis-Moline Z**, 1:16-scale, Mohr (Custom), yellow, 1980s
EX $98　　**NM** $116　　**MIP** $163

❏ **Minneapolis-Moline Z**, 1:16-scale, Mohr (Custom), yellow, 1980s
EX $98　　**NM** $116　　**MIP** $163

❏ **Minneapolis-Moline ZB**, 1:16-scale, Mohr (Custom), yellow, 1980s
EX $98　　**NM** $116　　**MIP** $243

❏ **Minneapolis-Moline, Spirit**, 1:16-scale, Scale Models, yellow, Spirit of Moline, 1990s
EX $27　　**NM** $38　　**MIP** $48

TRACTORS 1:24-SCALE

❏ **Minneapolis-Moline 4 Star**, 1:24-scale, Slik, brown belly w/yellow wheel centers, 1950s
EX $33　　**NM** $78　　**MIP** $182

❏ **Minneapolis-Moline 445**, 1:24-scale, Slik, prairie gold w/red wheel centers, also w/brown belly, w/new style Moline decal, 1950s
EX $72　　**NM** $223　　**MIP** $396

❏ **Minneapolis-Moline R**, 1:24-scale, Slik, prairie gold, 1950s
EX $14　　**NM** $23　　**MIP** $37

❏ **Minneapolis-Moline R**, 1:24-scale, Slik, red, green or yellow, plastic tires, 1950s to 1980s
EX $14   **NM** $23   **MIP** $37

❏ **Minneapolis-Moline R**, 1:24-scale, Slik, red or green, rubber tires, 1950s to 1980s
EX $14   **NM** $23   **MIP** $37

TRACTORS 1:25-SCALE

❏ **Minneapolis-Moline Jr.**, 1:25-scale, Ertl, yellow, 1960s, No. 15
EX $68   **NM** $138   **MIP** $288

❏ **Minneapolis-Moline Jr.**, 1:25-scale, Ertl, yellow, Thermogas decals, 1960s, No. 15
EX $68   **NM** $238   **MIP** $388

❏ **Minneapolis-Moline Jr.**, 1:25-scale, Ertl, yellow, LPG, 1960s, No. 15
EX $58   **NM** $127   **MIP** $288

❏ **Minneapolis-Moline Jr.**, 1:25-scale, Ertl, yellow and brown, LPG, 1960s, No. 15
EX $58   **NM** $127   **MIP** $288

❏ **Minneapolis-Moline Jr.**, 1:25-scale, Ertl, yellow and brown, 1960s, No. 15
EX $68   **NM** $138   **MIP** $338

❏ **Minneapolis-Moline Jr.**, 1:25-scale, Ertl, yellow, steerable, LPG, 1970s, No. 15
EX $28   **NM** $48   **MIP** $142

TRACTORS 1:32-SCALE

❏ **Minneapolis-Moline Z**, 1:32-scale, Auburn Rubber, red or green w/black tires, 4" long, 1940s
EX $12   **NM** $23   **MIP** $47

❏ **Minneapolis-Moline Z**, 1:32-scale, Auburn Rubber, prairie gold w/white, red tires, 1940s
EX $28   **NM** $56   **MIP** $128

TRACTORS 1:43-SCALE

❏ **Minneapolis-Moline G-1050**, 1:43-scale, Ertl, yellow, MFD, Replica Edition, 1995, No. 2291YP
EX $8   **NM** $13   **MIP** $22

❏ **Minneapolis-Moline G-750**, 1:43-scale, Ertl, yellow, '94 National Farm Toy Show Edition, 1994, No. 2291YA
EX $8   **NM** $13   **MIP** $22

❏ **Minneapolis-Moline G-750**, 1:43-scale, Ertl, yellow, 1995, No. 2291
(Photo by Ertl)
EX $4   **NM** $8   **MIP** $11

❏ **Minneapolis-Moline G-950**, 1:43-scale, Ertl, yellow, '94 LCN European Show Edition, 1994, No. 2291YR
EX $12   **NM** $27   **MIP** $38

TRACTORS 1:64-SCALE

❏ **Minneapolis-Moline 670**, 1:64-scale, Cottonwood Acres, yellow, 1980s
EX $9   **NM** $17   **MIP** $27

❏ **Minneapolis-Moline 670**, 1:64-scale, Cottonwood Acres, yellow, 1980s
EX $9   **NM** $17   **MIP** $27

❏ **Minneapolis-Moline A4T-1600**, 1:64-scale, Berg (Custom), red and white, LP, 1980s
EX $22   **NM** $28   **MIP** $38

❏ **Minneapolis-Moline A4T-1600**, 1:64-scale, Berg (Custom), red and white, 1980s
EX $22   **NM** $28   **MIP** $38

❏ **Minneapolis-Moline A4T-1600**, 1:64-scale, Berg (Custom), yellow and white, 1980s
EX $22   **NM** $28   **MIP** $38

❏ **Minneapolis-Moline A4T-1600**, 1:64-scale, Cottonwood Acres, red and white, LP, 1980s
EX $22   **NM** $28   **MIP** $38

❏ **Minneapolis-Moline A4T-1600**, 1:64-scale, Cottonwood Acres, red and white, 1980s
EX $22   **NM** $28   **MIP** $38

❏ **Minneapolis-Moline A4T-1600**, 1:64-scale, Cottonwood Acres, yellow and white, 1980s
EX $22   **NM** $28   **MIP** $38

❏ **Minneapolis-Moline A4T-1600**, 1:64-scale, Cottonwood Acres, yellow and white, LP, 1980s
EX $22   **NM** $28   **MIP** $38

❏ **Minneapolis-Moline A4T-1600**, 1:64-scale, Scale Models, yellow, no cab, Collector Edition, 2001, No. FB-2586 *(Photo by Bossen Implement)*
EX $6   **NM** $9   **MIP** $14

❏ **Minneapolis-Moline A4T-1600**, 1:64-scale, Scale Models, yellow, 2001, No. FU-0605
EX $6   **NM** $9   **MIP** $14

❏ **Minneapolis-Moline A4T-1600**, 1:64-scale, Scale Models, yellow, '04 Louisville Farm Show Edition, 2004, No. FB-2638
EX $6   **NM** $9   **MIP** $14

❏ **Minneapolis-Moline G-1000**, 1:64-scale, Berg (Custom), yellow and white, 1980s
EX $16   **NM** $22   **MIP** $28

Photos by Jon Jacobson unless otherwise noted.

❑ **Minneapolis-Moline G-1000**, 1:64-scale, Berg (Custom), yellow and white, LP, 1980s

EX $16   **NM** $22   **MIP** $28

❑ **Minneapolis-Moline G-1000**, 1:64-scale, Walters (Custom), yellow and white, 1990s

EX $6   **NM** $17   **MIP** $27

❑ **Minneapolis-Moline G-1350**, 1:64-scale, Pro Tractor Replicas, yellow and white, 1990s

EX $6   **NM** $17   **MIP** $27

❑ **Minneapolis-Moline G-1000**, 1:64-scale, Cottonwood Acres, yellow and white, 1980s

EX $9   **NM** $17   **MIP** $27

❑ **Minneapolis-Moline G-1000**, 1:64-scale, Walters (Custom), yellow and white, 1990s

EX $6   **NM** $17   **MIP** $27

❑ **Minneapolis-Moline G-1355**, 1:64-scale, Cottonwood Acres, yellow and white, 1990s

EX $6   **NM** $17   **MIP** $27

❑ **Minneapolis-Moline G-1000**, 1:64-scale, Walters (Custom), yellow and white, 1990s

EX $6   **NM** $17   **MIP** $27

❑ **Minneapolis-Moline G-1050**, 1:64-scale, Pro Tractor Replicas, yellow and white, 1980s

EX $6   **NM** $17   **MIP** $27

❑ **Minneapolis-Moline G-850**, 1:64-scale, Scale Models, yellow and white, 1988 World Ag-Expo, 1988

EX $3   **NM** $4   **MIP** $6

❑ **Minneapolis-Moline G-1000**, 1:64-scale, Walters (Custom), yellow and white, 1990s

EX $6   **NM** $17   **MIP** $27

❑ **Minneapolis-Moline G-1350**, 1:64-scale, Pro Tractor Replicas, red, white and blue, 1990s

EX $6   **NM** $17   **MIP** $27

❑ **Minneapolis-Moline G-850**, 1:64-scale, Scale Models, yellow and white, NF, 1988

EX $3   **NM** $4   **MIP** $6

❏ **Minneapolis-Moline G-850**, 1:64-scale, Scale Models, yellow, WF, 1992, No. FC-1111 *(Photo by Bossen Implement)*
EX $4   **NM** $6   **MIP** $8

❏ **Minneapolis-Moline G-900**, 1:64-scale, Berg (Custom), yellow and white, LP

❏ **Minneapolis-Moline G-900**, 1:64-scale, Berg (Custom), yellow and white, 1980s
EX $9   **NM** $17   **MIP** $27

❏ **Minneapolis-Moline G-900**, 1:64-scale, Cottonwood Acres, yellow and white, 1980s
EX $9   **NM** $17   **MIP** $27

❏ **Minneapolis-Moline G-940**, 1:64-scale, Scale Models, yellow, NF, 1991
EX $9   **NM** $17   **MIP** $27

❏ **Minneapolis-Moline G-950**, 1:64-scale, Pro Tractor Replicas, yellow and white, 1990s
EX $6   **NM** $17   **MIP** $27

❏ **Minneapolis-Moline G-950**, 1:64-scale, Pro Tractor Replicas, yellow and white, 1990s
EX $6   **NM** $17   **MIP** $27

❏ **Minneapolis-Moline G-950**, 1:64-scale, Scale Models, yellow and white, No. FU-0546 *(Photo by Scale Models)*
EX $4   **NM** $6   **MIP** $8

❏ **Minneapolis-Moline J**, 1:64-scale, Scale Models, five different chrome-colors, sold as a Christmas ornament, 1980s
EX $2   **NM** $3   **MIP** $6

❏ **Minneapolis-Moline J**, 1:64-scale, Scale Models, yellow and red, 1980s
EX $3   **NM** $4   **MIP** $6

❏ **Minneapolis-Moline J**, 1:64-scale, Scale Models, yellow and red, 1980s
EX $3   **NM** $4   **MIP** $6

❏ **Minneapolis-Moline J**, 1:64-scale, Scale Models, yellow and red, 1980s
EX $3   **NM** $4   **MIP** $6

❏ **Minneapolis-Moline J**, 1:64-scale, Scale Models, yellow and red, 1980s
EX $3   **NM** $4   **MIP** $6

❏ **Minneapolis-Moline J**, 1:64-scale, Scale Models, gray, 1985
EX $3   **NM** $4   **MIP** $6

❏ **Minneapolis-Moline J**, 1:64-scale, Scale Models, gray, 1985
EX $3   **NM** $4   **MIP** $6

❏ **Minneapolis-Moline Set**, 1:64-scale, Ertl, yellow, G-750 and 5 Star, 2002, No. 13084
EX n/a   **NM** n/a   **MIP** $13

❏ **Minneapolis-Moline Steam Engine**, 1:64-scale, Scale Models, black and red, 1987
EX $4   **NM** $7   **MIP** $13

❏ **Minneapolis-Moline Steam Engine**, 1:64-scale, Scale Models, black and red, Minneapolis Expo 1987, 1987
EX $4   **NM** $7   **MIP** $13

❏ **Minneapolis-Moline U**, 1:64-scale, Scale Models, yellow, 1991, No. FU-3056
EX $3   **NM** $4   **MIP** $6

❏ **Minneapolis-Moline UB**, 1:64-scale, Baker (Custom), yellow and red, did not come in box, 1980s
EX $6   **NM** $12   **MIP** n/a

❏ **Minneapolis-Moline UB**, 1:64-scale, Baker (Custom), yellow and red, did not come in box, 1980s
EX $6   **NM** $12   **MIP** n/a

❏ **Minneapolis-Moline UB**, 1:64-scale, Baker (Custom), yellow and red, did not come in box, 1980s
EX $6   **NM** $12   **MIP** n/a

❏ **Minneapolis-Moline UB**, 1:64-scale, Baker (Custom), yellow and red, did not come in box, 1980s
EX $6   **NM** $12   **MIP** n/a

❏ **Minneapolis-Moline UB**, 1:64-scale, Baker (Custom), yellow and red, did not come in box, 1980s
EX $6   **NM** $12   **MIP** n/a

❏ **Minneapolis-Moline UB**, 1:64-scale, Baker (Custom), yellow and red, 1988 St. Louis Show Tractor (Note: a few were painted gold), 1988
EX $6   **NM** $12   **MIP** $18

❏ **Minneapolis-Moline UDLX**, 1:64-scale, Mohr (Custom), yellow and red, did not come in box, 1980s
EX $8   **NM** $18   **MIP** n/a

❏ **Minneapolis-Moline UDLX**, 1:64-scale, Mohr (Custom), yellow and red, did not come in box, 1980s
EX $8   **NM** $18   **MIP** n/a

❑ **Minneapolis-Moline UDLX**, 1:64-scale, Scale Models, yellow and red, 1986
EX $4   **NM** $9   **MIP** $18

❑ **Minneapolis-Moline UDLX**, 1:64-scale, Scale Models, yellow and red, 1986
EX $4   **NM** $9   **MIP** $18

❑ **Minneapolis-Moline UDLX**, 1:64-scale, Scale Models, yellow and red, 1986, No. FU-3303 (Photo by Scale Models)
EX $4   **NM** $9   **MIP** $18

❑ **Minneapolis-Moline ZBE**, 1:64-scale, SpecCast, yellow and red, red decal
EX $6   **NM** $9   **MIP** $18

❑ **Minneapolis-Moline ZBE**, 1:64-scale, SpecCast, yellow and red, black decal
EX $6   **NM** $9   **MIP** $18

❑ **Minneapolis-Moline ZBU**, 1:64-scale, SpecCast, yellow and red, red decal
EX $6   **NM** $9   **MIP** $18

❑ **Minneapolis-Moline ZBU**, 1:64-scale, SpecCast, yellow and red, black decal
EX $6   **NM** $9   **MIP** $18

TRUCKS 1:25-SCALE

❑ **Minneapolis-Moline Dain Antique Truck**, 1:25-scale, Scale Models, yellow, 1990s
EX $6   **NM** $12   **MIP** $17

MISCELLANEOUS

CONSTRUCTION EQUIPMENT 1:130-SCALE

❑ **Pay Loader**, 1:130-scale, Mercury, yellow, 1960s
EX $22   **NM** $53   **MIP** $78

CONSTRUCTION EQUIPMENT

❑ **Pay Loader**, Hong Kong, 3" long, white, 1970s
EX $4   **NM** $17   **MIP** $27

❑ **Pay Loader**, Hong Kong, 2" long, white, 1970s
EX $4   **NM** $14   **MIP** $27

IMPLEMENTS 1:16-SCALE

❑ **Arcade Farm Set**, 1:16-scale, Arcade, tractor, disc harrow, corn planter, hay mower, drag harrow; black rubber wheels, 1939, No. 686
EX n/a   **NM** n/a   **MIP** n/a

❑ **Farm Wagon and Horse Team**, 1:16-scale, Arcade, 2 grey horses, blue driver, red wagon, black rubber wheels w/silver centers, 11" long, 1941, No. 4080
EX n/a   **NM** n/a   **MIP** n/a

❏ **Wheel Scraper**, 1:16-scale, Arcade, gray w/red cast-iron wheels, 8-1/4" long, 1929, No. 287
EX n/a   **NM** n/a   **MIP** n/a

IMPLEMENTS 1:24-SCALE

❏ **Hay Loader**, 1:24-scale, Slik, prairie gold, 1950s
EX $74   **NM** $123   **MIP** n/a

IMPLEMENTS 1:25-SCALE

❏ **Corn Harvester**, 1:25-scale, Arcade, green body, yellow seat, black rubber wheels w/red centers, 5" long, 1939, No. 4180
EX n/a   **NM** n/a   **MIP** n/a

❏ **Corn Harvester**, 1:25-scale, Arcade, green w/red and yellow parts, rubber wheels w/blue centers, 6-1/2" long, 1939, No. 702
EX n/a   **NM** n/a   **MIP** n/a

❏ **Hay Loader**, 1:25-scale, Slik, green, 1950s
EX $74   **NM** $123   **MIP** n/a

❏ **Hay Rake**, 1:25-scale, Arcade, red, nickeled wheels, 10 wire rakes, 4-3/4" wide, 1939, No. 417
EX $72   **NM** $98   **MIP** $323

❏ **Tandem Disc Harrow**, 1:25-scale, Arcade, front has 16 discs, rear has 18 discs, 6-3/4" long, 1939, No. 704
EX n/a   **NM** n/a   **MIP** n/a

IMPLEMENTS 1:32-SCALE

❏ **Seeder**, 1:32-scale, Auburn Rubber, plow seeder w/driver, 3-1/2" long
EX n/a   **NM** n/a   **MIP** n/a

❏ **Seeder**, 1:32-scale, Auburn Rubber, red w/black wheels, 3" long
EX n/a   **NM** n/a   **MIP** n/a

❏ **Spreader**, 1:32-scale, Auburn Rubber, green, 4-3/4" long
EX n/a   **NM** n/a   **MIP** n/a

❏ **Thresher**, 1:32-scale, Auburn Rubber, red w/white wheels, 5-1/2" long
EX n/a   **NM** n/a   **MIP** n/a

IMPLEMENTS 1:64-SCALE

❏ **Anhydrous Tank**, 1:64-scale, Ertl, various colors, 1980s
EX $4   **NM** $6   **MIP** $8

❏ **Anhydrous Tank**, 1:64-scale, Ertl, various colors, 1980s
EX $4   **NM** $6   **MIP** $8

❏ **Anhydrous Tank**, 1:64-scale, Mini Toys, various colors, 1980s
EX $3   **NM** $4   **MIP** $8

❏ **Bale Grinder**, 1:64-scale, Ertl, various colors, 1980s
EX $3   **NM** $4   **MIP** $9

❏ **Bale Mover**, 1:64-scale, Hurley's, green, did not come in box, 1980s
EX $3   **NM** $9   **MIP** n/a

❏ **Bale Mover**, 1:64-scale, Matsen (Custom), red, did not come in box, 1980s
EX $2   **NM** $3   **MIP** n/a

❏ **Combine Trailer**, 1:64-scale, Van Hove (Custom), black, did not come in box, 1980s
EX $12   **NM** $32   **MIP** n/a

Photos by Jon Jacobson unless otherwise noted.

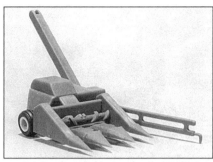

❏ **Corn Picker**, 1:64-scale, Standi (Custom), green or red, 1980s
EX $3   **NM** $4   **MIP** $6

❏ **Disc**, 1:64-scale, Standi (Custom), various colors, 1980s
EX $3   **NM** $4   **MIP** $6

❏ **Grain Auger**, 1:64-scale, Variation photo: Rubber tire on left, plastic tire on right, 1980s

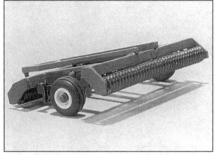

❏ **Cultimulcher**, 1:64-scale, Gunning (Custom), red and black, did not come in box, 1980s
EX $6   **NM** $14   **MIP** n/a

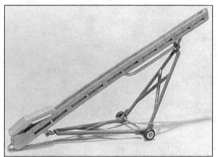

❏ **Elevator**, 1:64-scale, Standi (Custom), various colors, 1980s
EX $3   **NM** $4   **MIP** $6

❏ **Grain Auger**, 1:64-scale, Ertl, various colors, plastic tires, 1980s
EX $4   **NM** $6   **MIP** $8

❏ **Disc**, 1:64-scale, Ertl, various colors, 1980s
EX $3   **NM** $4   **MIP** $9

❏ **Field Cultivator**, 1:64-scale, Ertl, various colors, 1980s
EX $9   **NM** $16   **MIP** $22

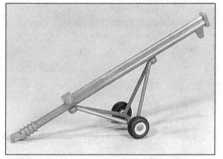

❏ **Grain Auger**, 1:64-scale, Mini Toys, various colors, rubber tires, 1980s
EX $4   **NM** $6   **MIP** $8

❏ **Disc**, 1:64-scale, Standi (Custom), various colors, 1980s
EX $3   **NM** $4   **MIP** $7

❏ **Forage Wagon**, 1:64-scale, Ertl, red and gray, can have either gray or red-rims, 1980s
EX $4   **NM** $6   **MIP** $8

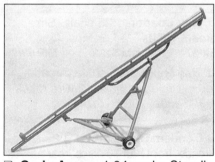

❏ **Grain Auger**, 1:64-scale, Standi (Custom), various colors, 1980s
EX $4   **NM** $6   **MIP** $8

❑ **Grain Cart**, 1:64-scale, Ertl, various colors, 1980s
EX $3   **NM** $6   **MIP** $8

❑ **Grain Drill**, 1:64-scale, Standi (Custom), various colors, 1980s
EX $3   **NM** $4   **MIP** $6

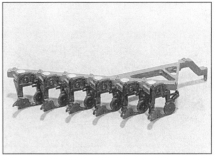

❑ **Plow**, 1:64-scale, Ertl, various colors, 1980s
EX $12   **NM** $18   **MIP** $24

❑ **Grain Cart**, 1:64-scale, Mini Toys, various colors, 1980s
EX $3   **NM** $6   **MIP** $8

❑ **Grain Dryer**, 1:64-scale, Standi (Custom), various colors, 1980s
EX $3   **NM** $4   **MIP** $7

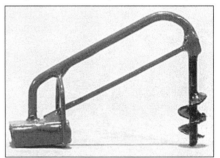

❑ **Post Hole Auger**, 1:64-scale, Van Hove (Custom), red and black, did not come in box, 1980s
EX $3   **NM** $9   **MIP** n/a

❑ **Grain Drill**, 1:64-scale, Matsen (Custom), various colors, did not come in box, 1980s
EX $4   **NM** $12   **MIP** n/a

❑ **Manure Spreader**, 1:64-scale, Mini Toys, various colors, 1980s
EX $3   **NM** $4   **MIP** $8

❑ **Rear Blade**, 1:64-scale, Van Hove (Custom), various colors, did not come in box, 1980s
EX $3   **NM** $6   **MIP** n/a

❑ **Round Baler**, 1:64-scale, Die-Cast Promotions, Gehl 2580 Silage Special round baler, red w/"Gehl" decal, w/1 bale, 2002, No. 40021
EX $4   **NM** $8   **MIP** 12

❑ **Mixmill**, 1:64-scale, Ertl, various colors, 1980s
EX $4   **NM** $6   **MIP** $8

❑ **Grain Drill**, 1:64-scale, Nygren (Custom), various colors, did not come in box, 1980s
EX $4   **NM** $12   **MIP** n/a

❑ **Round Baler**, 1:64-scale, Ertl, various colors, 1980s
EX $3   **NM** $4   **MIP** $9

❏ **Shredder**, 1:64-scale, Scale Models, yellow or red, 1980s
EX $1   **NM** $2   **MIP** $4

❏ **Snow Blower**, 1:64-scale, Standi (Custom), various colors, 1980s
EX $3   **NM** $4   **MIP** $5

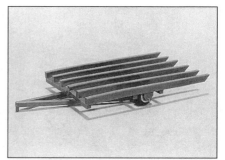

❏ **Stack-Mover**, 1:64-scale, Standi (Custom), various colors, 1980s
EX $2   **NM** $3   **MIP** $4

❏ **Sickle Mower NI**, 1:64-scale, Nygren (Custom), green, orange and silver, did not come in box, 1980s
EX $3   **NM** $9   **MIP** n/a

❏ **Spray-Caddy**, 1:64-scale, Matsen (Custom), various colors, did not come in box, 1980s
EX $3   **NM** $6   **MIP** n/a

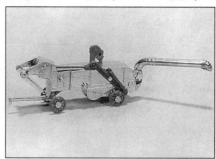

❏ **Thresher**, 1:64-scale, Scale Models, silver and red, 1980s
EX $4   **NM** $8   **MIP** $12

❏ **Silage Blower**, 1:64-scale, Speicher, green, did not come in box
EX $3   **NM** $9   **MIP** n/a

❏ **Sprayer**, 1:64-scale, Ertl, various colors, 1980s
EX $3   **NM** $4   **MIP** $6

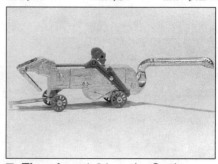

❏ **Thresher**, 1:64-scale, Scale Models, silver and red, 1st Case Expo 1987, 1980s
EX $4   **NM** $8   **MIP** $12

❏ **Silage Blower**, 1:64-scale, Standi (Custom), various colors, 1980s
EX $2   **NM** $3   **MIP** $4

❏ **Stacker**, 1:64-scale, Standi (Custom), various colors, 1980s
EX $3   **NM** $4   **MIP** $6

❏ **Thresher**, 1:64-scale, Scale Models, silver and red, Summer Toy Fest 1987, 1980s
EX $4   **NM** $8   **MIP** $12

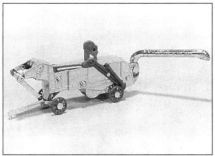

❏ **Thresher**, 1:64-scale, Scale Models, silver and red, 9th Toy Show 1986, 1980s
EX $4   **NM** $8   **MIP** $12

❏ **V-Ripper**, 1:64-scale, Matsen (Custom), various colors, did not come in box, 1980s
EX $9   **NM** $12   **MIP** n/a

❏ **Wagon, Forage**, 1:64-scale, Standi (Custom), black and orange, 1980s
EX $3   **NM** $4   **MIP** $9

❏ **Wagon, Forage**, 1:64-scale, Standi (Custom), various colors, 1980s
EX $3   **NM** $4   **MIP** $9

IMPLEMENTS

❏ **Hay Rake**, Arcade, 2 black horses, steel rakes, red and yellow frame, 4-3/4" long, 7" wide, 1939, No. 703
EX $123   **NM** $223   **MIP** $623

❏ **Seeder and Mower**, Ideal, seeder has 2 bins, 5-1/4" long; mower 5-1/2" long, late 1940s, No. STR-60
EX n/a   **NM** n/a   **MIP** n/a

❏ **Trailer**, Arcade, red w/nickel-plated disc wheels, 3-3/4" long, 1929, No. 289
EX n/a   **NM** n/a   **MIP** n/a

❏ **Trailer**, Arcade, red w/nickel-plated disc wheels, 4-5/8" long, 1929, No. 288
EX n/a   **NM** n/a   **MIP** n/a

❏ **Trailer**, Arcade, red w/nickel-plated disc wheels, 6-3/8" long, 1929, No. 286
EX n/a   **NM** n/a   **MIP** n/a

MISCELLANEOUS 1:64-SCALE

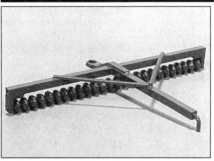

❏ **Packer**, 1:64-scale, Speicher, green, did not come in box, 1980s
EX $6   **NM** $14   **MIP** n/a

❏ **Snow Blower**, 1:64-scale, Van Hove (Custom), various colors, did not come in box, 1980s
EX $3   **NM** $12   **MIP** n/a

PEDAL TRACTORS

❏ **Trailer for Pedal Tractors**, Detail: Close-up of straight-sided and flare-sided fenders

❏ **Trailer for Pedal Tractors**, Ertl, trailer w/o fenders, came in colors to match different brands of tractors, metal wheel rims, 1970s to present
EX $12   **NM** $22   **MIP** $38

❏ **Trailer for Pedal Tractors**, Eska, flare sided fenders, can be found in colors to match different brands of tractors, metal wheel rims, 1950s
EX $123   **NM** $233   **MIP** $303

❏ **Trailer for Pedal Tractors**, Eska, w/fenders, lug tires, can be found in colors to match different brands of tractors, 1960s
EX $123   **NM** $233   **MIP** $303

❏ **Trailer for Pedal Tractors**, Eska, straight sided fenders, can be found in colors to match different brands of tractors, metal wheel rims, 1960s
EX $123   **NM** $233   **MIP** $289

TRACTORS 1:16-SCALE

❏ **Tractor and Dump Trailer**, 1:16-scale, Arcade, red tractor, red driver w/flesh face/hands, trailer in aluminum finish w/red stripe, black rubber wheels w/silver centers, 15-1/2" long, 1940, No. 7300
EX n/a   **NM** n/a   **MIP** n/a

TRACTORS

❏ **Climbing Caterpillar Tractor**, Marx, wind-up, silver, red and silver wheels, black treads, blade in front, driver, 9-1/2" long, 1950s
EX $100   **NM** $275   **MIP** $450

❏ **Climbing Tractor**, Marx, wind-up, red plastic and tin, blue driver, black treads, 5-1/2" long, 1950s, No. 1312
EX $45   **NM** $90   **MIP** $150

❏ **Climbing Tractor**, Marx, wind-up, sparkling, 8-1/2" long, 1960s

❏ **Farm Tractor and Wagon**, Hubley, red, uses #472 Tractor, 10-1/4" long, 1961-62, No. 474
EX n/a   **NM** n/a   **MIP** $58

❏ **Farm Tractor and Wagon**, Hubley, uses #472 Tractor, 10-1/4" long, 1963-65, No. 474
EX n/a   **NM** n/a   **MIP** $58

❏ **Fix-All Tractor**, Marx, 40+ pieces, tools, removable driver, battery and radiator filled from water can, 9" long, 1953
EX n/a   **NM** n/a   **MIP** n/a

❏ **Highboy Climbing Tractor**, Marx, wind-up, 10-1/2" long, 1950s
EX $100   **NM** $200   **MIP** $300

❏ **Hi-Lift Tractor**, Marx, wind-up, orange, NF w/ loader, 1950s, No. 1840
EX $40   **NM** $80   **MIP** $125

❏ **Hubley Jr. Tractor**, Hubley, red, yellow rear wheel hubs marked "Hubley Jr.," 7-1/4" long, 1955, No. 473
EX $2   **NM** $6   **MIP** $27

❏ **Hubley Jr. Tractor**, Hubley, red, orange; yellow rear wheel hubs marked "Hubley Jr.," 7-1/4" long, 1956, No. 473
EX $2   **NM** $6   **MIP** $27

❏ **Tractor**, Arcade, assorted colors, wooden black wheels, 4-1/4" long, 1941, No. 7321X
EX n/a   **NM** n/a   **MIP** n/a

❏ **Tractor**, Arcade, assorted colors, rubber wheels, 3-1/8" long, 1941, No. 7240X
EX n/a   **NM** n/a   **MIP** n/a

❏ **Tractor**, Arcade, red, green, orange, wooden black wheels, 3-1/8" long, 1941, No. 7260X
EX n/a   **NM** n/a   **MIP** n/a

❏ **Tractor**, Hubley, red, blue cast-iron driver, yellow rear wheel hubs, 6-3/4" long, 1948, No. 475
EX $22   **NM** $38   **MIP** $78

❏ **Tractor**, Hubley, red, nickel-plated driver, yellow rear wheel hubs, 6-3/4" long, 1949, No. 475
EX $22   **NM** $38   **MIP** $78

❏ **Tractor**, Hubley, red, nickel-plated driver, yellow rear wheel hubs, 7-1/4" long, 1950-51, No. 473
EX $2   **NM** $4   **MIP** $28

❏ **Tractor**, Hubley, red, green, or orange; 4-3/4" long, 1951-58, No. 309
EX $2   **NM** $4   **MIP** $27

❏ **Tractor**, Hubley, green, black rear wheel hubs, 5-1/2" long, 1952, No. 328
EX $4   **NM** $18   **MIP** $48

❏ **Tractor**, Hubley, red, yellow rear wheel hubs, 7" long, 1952-53, No. 472
EX $2   **NM** $4   **MIP** $28

❏ **Tractor**, Hubley, red, green, orange; black rear wheel hubs, 5-1/2" long, 1953-55, No. 328
EX $4   **NM** $18   **MIP** $48

❏ **Tractor**, Hubley, red, functional steering, spoked rear wheel hubs, spring seat, 9-1/2" long, 1953-56, No. 490
EX $9   **NM** $32   **MIP** $73

❏ **Tractor**, Hubley, red, orange; yellow rear wheel hubs marked "Hubley Jr.," 7-1/4" long, 1954, No. 473
EX $2   **NM** $4   **MIP** $28

❏ **Tractor**, Hubley, red; black rear wheel hubs, 5-1/2" long, 1954-55, No. 456
EX $2   **NM** $4   **MIP** $28

❏ **Tractor**, Hubley, red, green, orange; yellow rear wheel hubs, 5-1/2" long, 1956, No. 337
EX $4   **NM** $18   **MIP** $48

❏ **Tractor**, Hubley, red, orange; yellow rear wheel hubs, 5-1/2" long, 1956-58, No. 451
EX $2   **NM** $4   **MIP** $28

❏ **Tractor**, Hubley, red, orange; black rear wheel hubs marked "Hubley Jr.," 7-1/4" long, 1957-58, No. 472
EX $4   **NM** $18   **MIP** $48

❏ **Tractor**, Hubley, red, functional steering, 9-1/4" long, 1957-64, No. 496
EX $18   **NM** $53   **MIP** $73

❏ **Tractor**, Hubley, red, black rear wheel hubs marked "Hubley Jr.," 7-1/4" long, 1959-62, No. 472
EX $2   **NM** $4   **MIP** $28

❏ **Tractor**, Hubley, red, yellow, or orange; 4-3/4" long, 1959-65, No. 309
EX $2   **NM** $4   **MIP** $28

❏ **Tractor**, Hubley, red; black rear wheel hubs, 5-1/2" long, 1962, No. 456
EX $2   **NM** $4   **MIP** $28

❏ **Tractor**, Hubley, black rear wheel hubs marked "Hubley Jr.," 7-1/4" long, 1963, No. 472
EX $2   **NM** $4   **MIP** $28

❏ **Tractor**, Hubley, black rear wheel hubs marked "Hubley Jr.," 7-1/4" long, 1964, No. 1472
EX n/a   **NM** n/a   **MIP** n/a

❏ **Tractor**, Hubley, red rear wheel hubs, 7-1/4" long, 1965, No. 472
EX $2   **NM** $4   **MIP** $28

❏ **Tractor**, Hubley, red, 9-1/4" long, 1965, No. 1520
EX $4   **NM** $8   **MIP** $48

❏ **Tractor**, Renwal, assorted color combinations, driver, 5-1/4" long, 1953-55, No. 186
EX $12   **NM** $24   **MIP** $42

❏ **Tractor and Hay-Rake**, Ideal, functional steering wheel, hayrake moves up and down when pulled, assorted colors, 9" long, 1947-49, No. HTR-100
EX $15   **NM** $32   **MIP** $48

❏ **Tractor and Mower**, Ideal, functional steering wheel, mower cuts when pulled, 9" long, 1948-49, No. MTR-100
EX $15   **NM** $31   **MIP** $42

❏ **Tractor and Seeder**, Ideal, functional steering wheel, seeder hoppers open and close, 9" long, late 1940s
EX $12   **NM** $24   **MIP** $40

❏ **Tractor Loader**, Hubley, red, movable loader, 12-1/4" long, 1965, No. 1502
EX $27   **NM** $52   **MIP** $83

❏ **Tractor Sales & Service Farm Machinery Set**, Marx, 4 pieces, 11-1/2" tractor in red, yellow and blue; hay rake, plow, mower, 1950s
EX $100   **NM** $200   **MIP** $300

❏ **Tractor with Cultivator**, Hubley, red, functional steering, cultivator rake detaches, 9-1/4" long, 1957-59, No. 502
EX $63   **NM** $97   **MIP** $143

❏ **Tractor with Stake Trailer**, Hubley, red, 1502 Tractor w/stake trailer, 18-1/2" long, 1965, No. 1504
EX n/a   **NM** n/a   **MIP** $87

❏ **Tractor-Loader**, Hubley, red, functional steering, spring seat, movable loader, 13" long, 1954-56, No. 500
EX $22   **NM** $67   **MIP** $128

❏ **Tractor-Loader**, Hubley, orange, functional steering, fixed seat, movable loader, 12-3/4" long, 1957-64, No. 501
EX $21   **NM** $63   **MIP** $98

MISCELLANEOUS IMPLEMENTS

IMPLEMENTS 1:64-SCALE

❏ **Hay Rack**, 1:64-scale, Ertl, various colors
EX $3   **NM** $4   **MIP** $6

❏ **Hay Rack**, 1:64-scale, Mini Toys, various colors
EX $3   **NM** $4   **MIP** $6

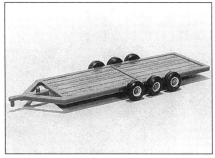

❏ **Machinery Trailer**, 1:64-scale, Ertl, various colors, plastic tires
EX $4   **NM** $6   **MIP** $8

❏ **Machinery Trailer**, 1:64-scale, Mini Toys, various colors, rubber tires
EX $4   **NM** $6   **MIP** $8

❏ **Wagon, Bale Throw**, 1:64-scale, Standi (Custom), various colors
EX $3   **NM** $4   **MIP** $6

MITSUBISHI

TRACTORS 1:64-SCALE

❏ **Mitsubishi MT 3000**, 1:64-scale, Variation photo: square and round front axles on tractors

❏ **Mitsubishi MT 3000**, 1:64-scale, Mini Toys, white and blue, front axle can be round or square, 1980s, No. 600
EX $3   **NM** $6   **MIP** $8

MUSTANG

CONSTRUCTION EQUIPMENT 1:16-SCALE

❏ **Mustang Skid Loader**, 1:16-scale, Ertl, yellow, 1980s, No. 152301
EX $26   **NM** $48   **MIP** $72

CONSTRUCTION EQUIPMENT 1:25-SCALE

❏ **Mustang Mini Excavator ME-6002**, 1:25-scale, DCP, yellow, issued also under part #699990, 2002, No. 40010 *(Photo by Bossen Implement)*
EX $9   **NM** $16   **MIP** $23

❏ **Mustang Skid Loader 2042**, 1:25-scale, DCP, yellow, 2002, No. 641990
EX $9   **NM** $16   **MIP** $23

❏ **Mustang Skid Loader 2050**, 1:25-scale, DCP, yellow, issued also under part #605990, 2002, No. 20005 *(Photo by Bossen Implement)*
EX $9   **NM** $16   **MIP** $23

❏ **Mustang Skid Loader 2050**, 1:25-scale, NZG, yellow, 2003, No. 351
EX $9   **NM** $16   **MIP** $23

NEW HOLLAND

BANKS 1:25-SCALE

❏ **New Holland Truck Bank**, 1:25-scale, Ertl, No. 390 *(Photo by Ertl)*
EX $4   **NM** $12   **MIP** $18

❏ **New Holland Truck Bank**, 1:25-scale, Ertl, yellow, 1980s, No. 379
EX $4   **NM** $12   **MIP** $18

❏ **New Holland Truck Bank**, 1:25-scale, Ertl, red and yellow, 1980s
EX $4   **NM** $12   **MIP** $18

CONSTRUCTION EQUIPMENT 1:16-SCALE

❏ **New Holland Skid Loader**, 1:16-scale, Ertl, yellow, 1980s, No. 320
EX $16   **NM** $27   **MIP** $31

❏ **New Holland Skid Loader**, 1:16-scale, Ertl, yellow, Collectors Edition, 1980s, No. 320DA
EX $17   **NM** $28   **MIP** $38

❏ **New Holland Wheel Loader TV-140**, 1:16-scale, Scale Models, yellow, bi-directional, 1999, No. JLE42705
EX $23   **NM** $32   **MIP** $53

CONSTRUCTION EQUIPMENT 1:25-SCALE

❏ **New Holland Skid Loader, 555**, 1:25-scale, NZG, yellow and black, no decal on front of ROPS, 1980s, No. 276
EX $14   **NM** $22   **MIP** $32

❏ **New Holland Skid Loader, 555**, 1:25-scale, NZG, yellow and black, roll guard decal, 1980s, No. 276
EX $14   **NM** $22   **MIP** $32

CONSTRUCTION EQUIPMENT 1:32-SCALE

❏ **New Holland Crawler DC-180**, 1:32-scale, ROS, yellow, w/blade, 2003, No. 667
EX $8   **NM** $16   **MIP** $23

❏ **New Holland Crawler TK-95M**, 1:32-scale, ROS, blue, 2002, No. 405035 *(Photo by Bossen Implement)*
EX $8   **NM** $16   **MIP** $33

❏ **New Holland Skid Loader**, 1:32-scale, Ertl, yellow, 1990s, No. 358
EX $4   **NM** $6   **MIP** $12

❏ **New Holland Skid Loader LS-170**, 1:32-scale, Ertl, yellow, 2000, No. 13563
EX $4   **NM** $6   **MIP** $12

❏ **New Holland Tractor 9030**, 1:32-scale, Scale Models, yellow, bi-directional, 1997, No. 414

Photo by Kate Bossen)

EX $6   **NM** $12   **MIP** $22

❏ **New Holland Wheel Loader LW-190**, 1:32-scale, ROS, yellow, 2003, No. 668

EX $8   **NM** $16   **MIP** $23

CONSTRUCTION EQUIPMENT 1:50-SCALE

❏ **New Holland Crawler DC-180**, 1:50-scale, Ertl, yellow, 2003, No. 13645

EX $9   **NM** $16   **MIP** $22

❏ **New Holland Skid Loader**, 1:50-scale, Ertl, yellow and black, 1980s, No. 378

EX $4   **NM** $6   **MIP** $9

❏ **New Holland Skid Loader**, 1:50-scale, Ertl, yellow, 1980s, No. 378

EX $4   **NM** $6   **MIP** $8

CONSTRUCTION EQUIPMENT 1:64-SCALE

❏ **New Holland Skid Loader LS-170**, 1:64-scale, Ertl, yellow, 2000, No. 13562

EX $4   **NM** $6   **MIP** $8

IMPLEMENTS 1:08-SCALE

❏ **New Holland Engine**, 1:08-scale, Ertl, red, 1-1/2 HP, 1995, No. 321

EX $6   **NM** $11   **MIP** $26

❏ **New Holland Engine**, 1:08-scale, Ertl, 100th Anniversary of New Holland, 1-1/2 HP, 1995, No. 321DA

(Photo by Ertl)

EX $8   **NM** $12   **MIP** $28

IMPLEMENTS 1:16-SCALE

❏ **New Holland 66 Baler**, 1:16-scale, SpecCast, engine powered, 2007, No. 1506

EX $50   **NM** $85   **MIP** $110

❏ **New Holland Baler**, 1:16-scale, Ertl, red, square, 1970s

EX $48   **NM** $87   **MIP** $173

❏ **New Holland Baler**, 1:16-scale, Ertl, red, square, reissued under part #13671, 1980s, No. 318

EX $14   **NM** $22   **MIP** $28

❏ **New Holland Baler**, 1:16-scale, Ertl, red, square, New Holland's 100th Anniversary, 1995, No. 335DA

EX $12   **NM** $22   **MIP** $47

❏ **New Holland Baler 668**, 1:16-scale, Scale Models, red, round, w/bale, 1999, No. JLE429DS

EX $8   **NM** $16   **MIP** $28

❏ **New Holland Baler 77**, 1:16-scale, Riecke (Custom), red, some were powered by electric moto, 1992

EX $389   **NM** $623   **MIP** n/a

❏ **New Holland Baler, 660**, 1:16-scale, Scale Models, red, round w/bale, 1996, No. FF-0223

(Photo by Scale Models)

EX $14   **NM** $22   **MIP** $32

❏ **New Holland Baler, 664**, 1:16-scale, Scale Models, red, round w/bale, 1997, No. FF-0393

(Photo by Scale Models)

EX $12   **NM** $21   **MIP** $29

❏ **New Holland Baler, BR-780**, 1:16-scale, Scale Models, red, round, w/bale, Collector Edition, 2004, No. JLE522DS

EX $14   **NM** $23   **MIP** $42

❏ **New Holland Disc**, 1:16-scale, Ertl, red, 1999, No. 13505

EX $8   **NM** $13   **MIP** $22

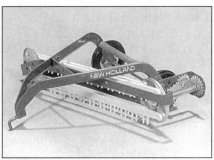

❑ **New Holland Hay Rake**, 1:16-scale, Ertl, red, 1980s, No. 316
EX $9　　**NM** $18　　**MIP** $23

❑ **New Holland Mixer Mill**, 1:16-scale, Ertl, red, 1999, No. 3039
EX $8　　**NM** $13　　**MIP** $28

❑ **New Holland Mixer Mill, 358**, 1:16-scale, Ertl, red, 1980s, No. 323
EX $12　　**NM** $22　　**MIP** $38

❑ **New Holland Mower**, 1:16-scale, Ertl, blue, rotary cutter, 2002, No. 13587
EX $7　　**NM** $12　　**MIP** $22

❑ **New Holland Mower Conditioner**, 1:16-scale, Scale Models, red and yellow, 1990s, No. 394
EX $7　　**NM** $14　　**MIP** $27

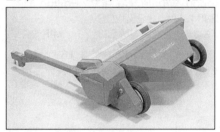

❑ **New Holland Mower Conditioner**, 1:16-scale, Scale Models, red and yellow, 25th Anniversary, 1990s, No. 312
EX $8　　**NM** $16　　**MIP** $23

❑ **New Holland Spreader**, 1:16-scale, Ertl, red, 1970s
EX $36　　**NM** $73　　**MIP** $248

❑ **New Holland Spreader**, 1:16-scale, Ertl, red, 1988, No. 314
EX $7　　**NM** $12　　**MIP** $26

❑ **New Holland Spreader**, 1:16-scale, Ertl, red and yellow, 2007, No. 13721
EX $18　　**NM** $24　　**MIP** $35

❑ **New Holland Square Baler**, 1:16-scale, Ertl, w/4 square bales, 2005, No. 13671
EX $8　　**NM** $14　　**MIP** $22

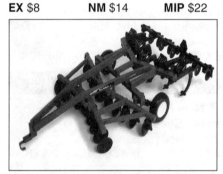

❑ **New Holland Tillage Tool**, 1:16-scale, Ertl, blue, ST-770 Ecolo-Tiger, 2003, No. 13612 *(Photo by Bossen Implement)*
EX $16　　**NM** $23　　**MIP** $42

❑ **New Holland Wagon, Bale**, 1:16-scale, Ertl, red and yellow, 1980s, No. 319
EX $8　　**NM** $18　　**MIP** $28

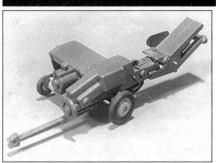

❑ **New Holland Wagon, Forage**, 1:16-scale, Ertl, red, 1970s
EX $47　　**NM** $142　　**MIP** $288

IMPLEMENTS 1:25-SCALE

❑ **New Holland Baler**, 1:25-scale, Advanced, red, 1960s
EX $106　　**NM** $213　　**MIP** $353

❑ **New Holland Wagon, Bale**, 1:25-scale, Advanced, red, 1960s
EX $76　　**NM** $188　　**MIP** $352

IMPLEMENTS 1:32-SCALE

❑ **New Holland Baler**, 1:32-scale, Britains, red, 1980s
EX $4　　**NM** $7　　**MIP** $12

❑ **New Holland Baler**, 1:32-scale, Britains, yellow, 1980s
EX $3   **NM** $6   **MIP** $9

❑ **New Holland Baler**, 1:32-scale, Ertl, red, also issued under part #9556, 1997, No. 3020
EX $3   **NM** $6   **MIP** $9

❑ **New Holland Baler, 376**, 1:32-scale, Britains, red, 1980s
EX $4   **NM** $7   **MIP** $12

❑ **New Holland Baler, 377**, 1:32-scale, Britains, red, 1980s
EX $4   **NM** $7   **MIP** $12

❑ **New Holland Baler, 940**, 1:32-scale, Britains, yellow, 1980s
EX $3   **NM** $6   **MIP** $9

❑ **New Holland Big Baler**, 1:32-scale, Ertl, w/3 large bales, 2006, No. 13668
EX $8   **NM** $14   **MIP** $18

❑ **New Holland Combine**, 1:32-scale, Ertl, red, 1970s, No. 750
EX $68   **NM** $152   **MIP** $328

❑ **New Holland Combine, 8070**, 1:32-scale, Yaxon, yellow, 1980s
EX $17   **NM** $28   **MIP** $33

❑ **New Holland Combine, CR9060**, 1:32-scale, Ertl, Dealer Edition, 2 heads, 2007, No. 13724
EX $4   **NM** $8   **MIP** $15

❑ **New Holland Combine, CR-960**, 1:32-scale, Ertl, yellow, w/corn and grain heads, 2003, No. 13628
EX $16   **NM** $24   **MIP** $43

❑ **New Holland Combine, CR-970**, 1:32-scale, Ertl, yellow, w/corn and grain heads, Collector Edition, 2003, No. 13625A
EX $18   **NM** $31   **MIP** $48

❑ **New Holland Combine, CR980**, 1:32-scale, Ertl, yellow, 2006, No. 13694
EX $8   **NM** $14   **MIP** $18

❑ **New Holland Combine, CX-880**, 1:32-scale, Ertl, yellow, grain head only, European version, no SMV sign, 2002, No. 40449
EX $19   **NM** $32   **MIP** $63

❑ **New Holland Combine, CX-880**, 1:32-scale, Ertl, yellow, grain head only, 2002, No. 40449A
EX $19   **NM** $33   **MIP** $53

❑ **New Holland Combine, CX-880**, 1:32-scale, Ertl, yellow, grain head only, revised graphics, 2004, No. 40527
EX $18   **NM** $31   **MIP** $49

❑ **New Holland Combine, TR-85**, 1:32-scale, Britains, yellow, 1980s, No. 9571
EX $19   **NM** $31   **MIP** $43

❑ **New Holland Combine, TR-96**, 1:32-scale, Ertl, yellow, Collectors Edition, 1980s, No. 375DA
EX $26   **NM** $39   **MIP** $57

❑ **New Holland Combine, TR-96**, 1:32-scale, Ertl, yellow, red decals, 1987, No. 375 *(Photo by Ertl)*
EX $22   **NM** $36   **MIP** $47

❑ **New Holland Combine, TR-97**, 1:32-scale, Ertl, yellow, black decals, 1994, No. 375DP
EX $18   **NM** $28   **MIP** $44

❑ **New Holland Combine, TR-98**, 1:32-scale, Ertl, yellow, w/corn and grain heads, 1998, No. 13519
EX $18   **NM** $28   **MIP** $44

❏ **New Holland Swather**, 1:32-scale, Ertl, red and yellow, 1970s
EX $68   **NM** $162   **MIP** $323

IMPLEMENTS 1:43-SCALE

❏ **New Holland Baler, 940**, 1:43-scale, NZG, yellow, 1980s
EX $3   **NM** $6   **MIP** $9

❏ **New Holland Combine GT**, 1:43-scale, Burbon, yellow, 1980s
EX $53   **NM** $78   **MIP** $108

❏ **New Holland Combine, Clayson**, 1:43-scale, Burbon, yellow, 1980s
EX $53   **NM** $78   **MIP** $108

❏ **New Holland Combine, TF-42**, 1:43-scale, NZG, yellow, 1980s
EX $18   **NM** $36   **MIP** $53

IMPLEMENTS 1:64-SCALE

❏ **New Holland Baler**, 1:64-scale, Ertl, red and yellow, square, 1987, No. 337
EX $4   **NM** $5   **MIP** $6

❏ **New Holland Baler**, 1:64-scale, Ertl, red, square, New Holland's 100th Anniversary, 1995, No. 356FA
EX $4   **NM** $6   **MIP** $11

❏ **New Holland Baler**, 1:64-scale, Nygren (Custom), red and yellow, did not come in box, 1980s
EX $3   **NM** $9   **MIP** n/a

❏ **New Holland Baler**, 1:64-scale, Scale Models, red, round, 1999, No. JLE430DS
EX $4   **NM** $6   **MIP** $8

❏ **New Holland Baler, 660**, 1:64-scale, Scale Models, red, round, 1996, No. 347 *(Photo by Scale Models)*
EX $4   **NM** $6   **MIP** $8

❏ **New Holland Baler, 664**, 1:64-scale, Scale Models, red, round, 1997, No. 396 *(Photo by Scale Models)*
EX $4   **NM** $6   **MIP** $8

❏ **New Holland Combine, CR-960**, 1:64-scale, Ertl, yellow, w/2 heads, 2002, No. 13595
EX $6   **NM** $9   **MIP** $18

❏ **New Holland Combine, CR-970**, 1:64-scale, Ertl, yellow, w/2 heads, Dealer Edition, 800 Units, Serial Numbered, enclosed box, 2002, No. 13594A
EX $123   **NM** $178   **MIP** $349

❏ **New Holland Combine, CR-970**, 1:64-scale, Ertl, yellow, w/2 heads, Collector Edition, 2002, No. 13594
EX $8   **NM** $23   **MIP** $43

❏ **New Holland Combine, CR99070**, 1:64-scale, Ertl, 2 heads, 2007, No. 13733
EX $4   **NM** $8   **MIP** $12

❏ **New Holland Combine, TR-97**, 1:64-scale, Ertl, yellow, red decals, 1980s, No. 815
EX $8   **NM** $12   **MIP** $27

❏ **New Holland Combine, TR-97**, 1:64-scale, Ertl, yellow, black decals, 1995, No. 815EP
EX $8   **NM** $19   **MIP** $26

❏ **New Holland Combine, TR-98**, 1:64-scale, Ertl, yellow, 1998, No. 13500
EX $8   **NM** $19   **MIP** $26

❏ **New Holland Disc**, 1:64-scale, Ertl, blue, 2007, No. 13735
EX $2   **NM** $4   **MIP** $7

❏ **New Holland Disk**, 1:64-scale, Ertl, blue, w/wheels, 2004, No. 13662
EX $4   **NM** $5   **MIP** $6

❏ **New Holland Field Cultivator**, 1:64-scale, Ertl, 2007, No. 13734
EX $4   **NM** $8   **MIP** 12

❏ **New Holland Forage Blower, 40**, 1:64-scale, Ertl, red, 1996, No. 343
(Photo by Ertl)
EX $2   **NM** $3   **MIP** $4

❏ **New Holland Forage Chopper, 900**, 1:64-scale, Ertl, red and yellow, w/interchangeable heads, 1990s, No. 372
EX $4   **NM** $5   **MIP** $6

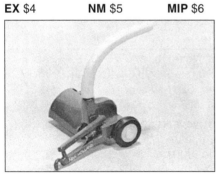

❏ **New Holland Forage Harvester**, 1:64-scale, Nygren (Custom), red and yellow, did not come in box, 1980s
EX $3   **NM** $9   **MIP** n/a

❏ **New Holland Ginder Mixer**, 1:64-scale, Ertl, 1996, No. 351 *(Photo by Ertl)*
EX $4   **NM** $6   **MIP** $8

❏ **New Holland Hay Rake**, 1:64-scale, Ertl, blue, 1990s, No. 369
EX $3   **NM** $4   **MIP** $6

❏ **New Holland Hay Rake**, 1:64-scale, Van Hove (Custom), red and yellow, did not come in box, 1990s
EX $6   **NM** $9   **MIP** n/a

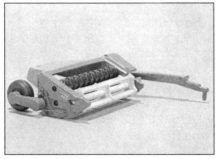

❏ **New Holland Mower-Conditioner**, 1:64-scale, Ertl, red and yellow, 1980s, No. 322
EX $3   **NM** $4   **MIP** $6

❏ **New Holland Planter, SP-580**, 1:64-scale, Ertl, blue, 16 row, 2003, No. 13631
EX $4   **NM** $6   **MIP** $9

❏ **New Holland Sickle Mower**, 1:64-scale, Matsen (Custom), red and yellow, did not come in box
EX $3   **NM** $9   **MIP** n/a

❏ **New Holland Spreader, 145**, 1:64-scale, Ertl, red, 1994, No. 308
EX $4   **NM** $5   **MIP** $6

❏ **New Holland Spreader, 308**, 1:64-scale, Ertl, red, V-tank, 1996, No. 346
EX $3   **NM** $4   **MIP** $6

❏ **New Holland Swather**, 1:64-scale, Scale Models, yellow and red, 1980s
EX $18   **NM** $27   **MIP** $37

❏ **New Holland Tillage Tool, ST-740**, 1:64-scale, Ertl, blue, 2003, No. 13639
EX $4   **NM** $6   **MIP** $9

❏ **New Holland Wagon, Forage**, 1:64-scale, Ertl, red and yellow, 1980s, No. 373
EX $4   **NM** $6   **MIP** $8

❏ **New Holland Wagon, Forage**, 1:64-scale, Ertl, red and gray, 1980s, No. 373
EX $4   **NM** $6   **MIP** $8

IMPLEMENTS

❏ **New Holland Baler**, Advanced, chrome, 1960s
EX $192   **NM** $344   **MIP** $419

❏ **New Holland Baler**, Advanced, red, removable bale throwers, 1960s
EX $58   **NM** $117   **MIP** $253

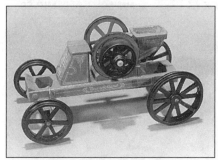

❏ **New Holland Engine**, Scale Models, red, 1980s
EX $8   **NM** $16   **MIP** $24

LAWN AND GARDEN 1:16-SCALE

❏ **New Holland 95 GT**, 1:16-scale, Scale Models, w/mower deck, 1996, No. 397 *(Photo by Scale Models)*
EX $6   **NM** $12   **MIP** $21

PEDAL TRACTORS

❏ **New Holland 6640**, Ertl, 2WD, WF, 1996, No. 357 *(Photo by Ertl)*
EX $89   **NM** $123   **MIP** $152

❏ **New Holland 8560**, Ertl, blue, WF, gemini, 1998, No. 3326
EX $89   **NM** $132   **MIP** $153

❏ **New Holland Construction**, Scale Models, yellow, Collector Edition, 2002, No. JLE469DS
EX $89   **NM** $132   **MIP** $168

❏ **New Holland Construction**, Scale Models, yellow, 2002, No. JLE479DS
EX $87   **NM** $123   **MIP** $153

❏ **New Holland TC-33D**, Scale Models, blue, Boomer, 1999, No. JLE423DC
EX $87   **NM** $123   **MIP** $153

❏ **New Holland TJ-425**, Scale Models, blue, 4WD, 2002, No. JLE478DS
EX $98   **NM** $146   **MIP** $202

❏ **New Holland TJ-450**, Scale Models, blue, 4WD, w/duals, Collector Edition, 2002, No. JLE470DS
EX $122   **NM** $162   **MIP** $243

❏ **New Holland TM-165**, Ertl, blue, MFD, 2002, No. 13557
EX $89   **NM** $132   **MIP** $153

❏ **New Holland TM-190**, Ertl, blue, 2003, No. 13635
EX $87   **NM** $123   **MIP** $153

TRACTORS 1:16-SCALE

❏ **New Holland 3930**, 1:16-scale, Scale Models, blue, w/ROPS, 1996, No. JLE391DS
EX $13   **NM** $22   **MIP** $32

❏ **New Holland 3930**, 1:16-scale, Scale Models, blue, '96 Agland Expo, 1996, No. FB-2447
EX $13   **NM** $22   **MIP** $32

❏ **New Holland 5635**, 1:16-scale, Scale Models, blue, '96 Farm Progress Show Edition, 1996, No. FB-2430
EX $17   **NM** $26   **MIP** $42

❏ **New Holland 5635**, 1:16-scale, Scale Models, blue, 2WD w/ROPS, 1997, No. 406 *(Photo by Scale Models)*
EX $18   **NM** $23   **MIP** $36

❏ **New Holland 5635**, 1:16-scale, Scale Models, blue, '97 New York Farm Show Edition, 1997, No. FB-2460
EX $17   **NM** $26   **MIP** $42

❏ **New Holland 5635**, 1:16-scale, Scale Models, blue, MFD, 2000, No. JLE428DS
EX $14   **NM** $24   **MIP** $38

❏ **New Holland 7740**, 1:16-scale, Ertl, blue, w/loader, 1996, No. 3389
EX $18   **NM** $26   **MIP** $46

❏ **New Holland 7740**, 1:16-scale, Ertl, blue, MFD, w/ROPS, 1996-97, No. 329 *(Photo by Ertl)*
EX $22   **NM** $37   **MIP** $46

❏ **New Holland 7840**, 1:16-scale, Ertl, blue, MFD, w/cab, 1997, No. 3601
EX $14   **NM** $23   **MIP** $42

❏ **New Holland 7840**, 1:16-scale, Ertl, blue, w/cab and loader, 2002, No. 13588
EX $16   **NM** $28   **MIP** $46

❏ **New Holland 8260**, 1:16-scale, Ertl, blue, MFD, '97 National Farm Toy Show Edition, 1997, No. 3031PA
EX $23   **NM** $32   **MIP** $43

❏ **New Holland 8340**, 1:16-scale, Ertl, blue, 2WD, w/7411 loader, 1997, No. 3389 *(Photo by Kate Bossen)*
EX $22 **NM** $33 **MIP** $46

❏ **New Holland 8340**, 1:16-scale, Ertl, blue, MFD, w/loader, 1999, No. 13530
EX $17 **NM** $26 **MIP** $42

❏ **New Holland 8360**, 1:16-scale, Ertl, blue, MFD, w/ROPS, gemini, 1998, No. 3037
EX $17 **NM** $26 **MIP** $42

❏ **New Holland 8560**, 1:16-scale, Ertl, blue, MFD, gemini, Collector Edition, 1998, No. 3036DA
EX $22 **NM** $34 **MIP** $48

❏ **New Holland 8670**, 1:16-scale, SpecCast, blue, 2WD, w/duals, genesis, 1997, No. 9673686
EX $22 **NM** $34 **MIP** $58

❏ **New Holland 8770**, 1:16-scale, SpecCast, blue, 2WD, genesis, 1998, No. 9623760
EX $22 **NM** $34 **MIP** $58

❏ **New Holland 8770A**, 1:16-scale, SpecCast, blue, genesis, "End of an Era", 2001, No. 10000
EX $22 **NM** $34 **MIP** $63

❏ **New Holland 8970**, 1:16-scale, SpecCast, blue, MFD, genesis, 1999, No. 9673911
EX $22 **NM** $34 **MIP** $63

❏ **New Holland 9384**, 1:16-scale, Scale Models, blue, 4WD, '99 Farm Progress Show Edition, 1999, No. JLE434DS
EX $88 **NM** $112 **MIP** $146

❏ **New Holland 9384**, 1:16-scale, Scale Models, blue 4WD, 2000, No. JLE437DS
EX $52 **NM** $67 **MIP** $122

❏ **New Holland 9682**, 1:16-scale, Scale Models, blue, 4WD, triples, '97 Orlando Edition, 1997, No. JLE416DS
EX $92 **NM** $114 **MIP** $149

❏ **New Holland 9682**, 1:16-scale, Scale Models, blue, 4WD, triples, 1998, No. JLE418DS
EX $67 **NM** $89 **MIP** $132

❏ **New Holland 9882**, 1:16-scale, Scale Models, blue, 4WD, w/duals, 1996, No. 402 *(Photo by Scale Models)*
EX $62 **NM** $88 **MIP** $127

❏ **New Holland Set**, 1:16-scale, Ertl, blue, 8160, w/hay rake, 1998, No. 3320
EX n/a **NM** n/a **MIP** $48

❏ **New Holland Set**, 1:16-scale, Ertl, blue, TS-135A, w/backhoe and rear blade, 2004, No. 13652
EX n/a **NM** n/a **MIP** $53

❏ **New Holland T6070**, 1:16-scale, Ertl, Dealer Edition, 2007, No. 13727

❏ **New Holland TC-33D**, 1:16-scale, Scale Models, blue, MFD, 1998, No. JLE424DS
EX $16 **NM** $22 **MIP** $32

❏ **New Holland TG-285 MFD**, 1:16-scale, Scale Models, blue, MFD, Collector Edition, 2004, No. JLE497DS
EX $27 **NM** $37 **MIP** $56

❏ **New Holland TJ-375**, 1:16-scale, Scale Models, blue, 4WD, triples, "01 Farm Progress Show Edition, 2001, No. JLE456DS
EX $93 **NM** $121 **MIP** $178

❏ **New Holland TJ-425**, 1:16-scale, Scale Models, blue, 4WD, 2002, No. JLE475DS
EX $82 **NM** $107 **MIP** $154

❏ **New Holland TJ-450**, 1:16-scale, Scale Models, blue, 4WD, wide duals, Collector Edition, 2002, No. JLE466DS
EX $87 **NM** $112 **MIP** $166

❏ **New Holland TJ-480**, 1:16-scale, Ertl, blue, 4WD, '06 Farm Progress Show, 2006, No. 13675
(Photo by Bossen Implement)
EX $48 **NM** $72 **MIP** $97

❏ **New Holland TJ-530**, 1:16-scale, Ertl, blue, 4WD, duals, Collector Edition, 2006, No. 13673A
EX $49 **NM** $73 **MIP** $98

❏ **New Holland TL-100**, 1:16-scale, Scale Models, blue, MFD, 1999, No. JLE451
EX $14 **NM** $23 **MIP** $39

❏ **New Holland TL-80**, 1:16-scale, Scale Models, blue, 2002, No. JLE430 *(Photo by Bossen Implement)*
EX $14 **NM** $23 **MIP** $39

❏ **New Holland TM-150**, 1:16-scale, Ertl, blue, MFD, 2002, No. 13560
EX $17 **NM** $26 **MIP** $47

❏ **New Holland TM-165**, 1:16-scale, Ertl, blue, MFD, 2002, No. 13577
EX $19 **NM** $33 **MIP** $52

❏ **New Holland TN-75**, 1:16-scale, Scale Models, blue, 2WD, w/foldable ROPS, 2000, No. JLE444DS
EX $14 **NM** $23 **MIP** $39

❏ **New Holland TS-115A**, 1:16-scale, Ertl, blue, MFD, w/cab and loader, 2003, No. 13620A
EX $16 **NM** $24 **MIP** $42

❏ **New Holland TS-125A**, 1:16-scale, Ertl, blue, MFD, cab glass, Dealer Edition, 2003, No. 13619A
EX $43 **NM** $66 **MIP** $88

❑ **New Holland TS-125A**, 1:16-scale, Ertl, blue, MFD, European Version, 2004, No. 13621
EX $16   **NM** $24   **MIP** $42

❑ **New Holland TS-135A**, 1:16-scale, Ertl, blue, MFD, cab glass, Collector Edition, 2003, No. 13626A
EX $18   **NM** $27   **MIP** $49

❑ **New Holland TV-140**, 1:16-scale, Scale Models, blue, Bi-Directional, 1998, No. JLE409A
(Photo by Bossen Implement)
EX $19   **NM** $28   **MIP** $53

❑ **New Holland TV-145**, 1:16-scale, Scale Models, blue, Bi-Directional, No. JLE409 *(Photo by Scale Models)*
EX $21   **NM** $32   **MIP** $57

TRACTORS 1:32-SCALE

❑ **New Holland 6635**, 1:32-scale, Britains, blue, MFD, 1999, No. 9487
EX $4   **NM** $8   **MIP** $12

❑ **New Holland 8560**, 1:32-scale, Ertl, blue, MFD, 1999, No. 9488
EX $4   **NM** $8   **MIP** $12

❑ **New Holland 8670**, 1:32-scale, Ertl, blue, MFD, 1997, No. 313
EX $4   **NM** $7   **MIP** $11

❑ **New Holland 9682**, 1:32-scale, Ertl, blue, 4WD, w/duals, 1997, No. 3021
EX $9   **NM** $17   **MIP** $38

❑ **New Holland 9880**, 1:32-scale, Ertl, blue, 4WD, w/duals, 2003, No. 13654
EX $8   **NM** $14   **MIP** $28

❑ **New Holland 9882**, 1:32-scale, Ertl, blue, 4WD, w/triples, Collector Edition, 1997, No. 3017DA
(Photo by Bossen Implement)
EX $29   **NM** $43   **MIP** $88

❑ **New Holland T6070**, 1:32-scale, Ertl, 2007, No. 13729
EX $4   **NM** $8   **MIP** $12

❑ **New Holland T7050**, 1:32-scale, Ertl, Dealer Edition, duals, 2007, No. 13718
EX $12   **NM** $18   **MIP** $24

❑ **New Holland TD-95**, 1:32-scale, Ertl, blue, MFD, No. 40580
EX $4   **NM** $12   **MIP** $22

❑ **New Holland TG**, 1:32-scale, Ertl, tractor w/applicator and tank, 2006, No. 13692
EX $8   **NM** $14   **MIP** $18

❑ **New Holland TG275**, 1:32-scale, Ertl, duals, 2007, No. 13729
EX $4   **NM** $8   **MIP** $13

❑ **New Holland TG-285**, 1:32-scale, Ertl, blue, MFD, w/duals, Dealer Intro Edition, 2002, No. 13614
EX $46   **NM** $72   **MIP** $123

❑ **New Holland TG-285**, 1:32-scale, Ertl, blue, MFD, w/duals, Collector Edition, 2003, No. 13655A
EX $14   **NM** $28   **MIP** $42

❑ **New Holland TG305**, 1:32-scale, Ertl, 2006, No. 13683
EX $8   **NM** $14   **MIP** $18

❑ **New Holland TJ-375**, 1:32-scale, Scale Models, blue, 4WD, w/triples, '01 Farm Progress Show, 2001, No. JLE457DS
EX $17   **NM** $26   **MIP** $48

❑ **New Holland TJ-425**, 1:32-scale, Scale Models, blue, 4WD, w/duals, 2002, No. JLE476DS
EX $17   **NM** $26   **MIP** $46

❑ **New Holland TJ-450**, 1:32-scale, Scale Models, blue, 4WD, w;duals, Collector Edition, 2002, No. JLE466DS
EX $17   **NM** $26   **MIP** $48

❑ **New Holland TM-165**, 1:32-scale, Ertl, blue, MFD, 2002, No. 40522
EX $4   **NM** $12   **MIP** $23

❑ **New Holland TS-135A**, 1:32-scale, Ertl, blue, MFD, 2003, No. 40785
EX $4   **NM** $9   **MIP** $18

❑ **New Holland TSA125**, 1:32-scale, Ertl, 2006, No. 13698
EX $8   **NM** $14   **MIP** $18

TRACTORS 1:64-SCALE

❑ **New Holland 7840**, 1:64-scale, Ertl, blue, w/loader, 1997, No. 3297
EX $4   **NM** $6   **MIP** $8

❑ **New Holland 7840**, 1:64-scale, Ertl, blue, w/loader, revised, 1998, No. 3297
EX $4   **NM** $6   **MIP** $8

❑ **New Holland 8770**, 1:64-scale, Ertl, blue, 2WD, 1996, No. 391
(Photo by Ertl)
EX $4   **NM** $5   **MIP** $6

❑ **New Holland 8870**, 1:64-scale, Ertl, blue, MFD, cab glass, 1996, No. 392 *(Photo by Ertl)*
EX $4   **NM** $5   **MIP** $6

❏ **New Holland 8970**, 1:64-scale, Ertl, blue, MFD w/duals, 1996, No. 394 *(Photo by Ertl)*
EX $4　　**NM** $5　　**MIP** $6

❏ **New Holland 8970A**, 1:64-scale, Ertl, duals, decal sheet, 2007, No. 13732
EX $3　　**NM** $6　　**MIP** $9

❏ **New Holland 9384**, 1:64-scale, Scale Models, blue, 4WD, w/duals, '99 Farm Progress Show Edition, 1999, No. JLE435DS
EX $6　　**NM** $8　　**MIP** $13

❏ **New Holland 9384**, 1:64-scale, Scale Models, blue, 4WD, w/duals, 2000, No. JLE438DS
EX $6　　**NM** $8　　**MIP** $13

❏ **New Holland 9682**, 1:64-scale, Scale Models, blue, 4WD, w/triples, 1997, No. JLE417DS
EX $6　　**NM** $8　　**MIP** $13

❏ **New Holland 9682**, 1:64-scale, Scale Models, blue, 4WD, w/duals, 1998, No. JLE419DS
EX $6　　**NM** $8　　**MIP** $13

❏ **New Holland 9882**, 1:64-scale, Scale Models, blue, 4WD, w/duals, 1996, No. JLE390DS *(Photo by Scale Models)*
EX $6　　**NM** $8　　**MIP** $13

❏ **New Holland 9882**, 1:64-scale, Scale Models, blue, 4WD, w/duals, '98 Farm Progress Show Edition, 1998, No. FB-2508
EX $6　　**NM** $8　　**MIP** $13

❏ **New Holland Set**, 1:64-scale, Ertl, blue, MFD, w/grain cart, 2003, No. 13633
EX n/a　　**NM** n/a　　**MIP** $11

❏ **New Holland T7050**, 1:64-scale, Ertl, 2007, No. 13717
EX $3　　**NM** $4　　**MIP** $6

❏ **New Holland TG-255**, 1:64-scale, Ertl, blue, MFD, '03 Farm Progress Show Edition, 2003, No. 13666X
EX $6　　**NM** $14　　**MIP** $22

❏ **New Holland TG-255**, 1:64-scale, Ertl, blue, MFD, 2003, No. 13617
EX $4　　**NM** $5　　**MIP** $6

❏ **New Holland TG-285**, 1:64-scale, Ertl, blue, MFD, w/duals, Collector Edition, 2002, No. 13616
EX $6　　**NM** $14　　**MIP** $22

❏ **New Holland TJ-375**, 1:64-scale, Scale Models, blue, 4WD, w/triples, '01 Farm Progress Show Edition, 2001, No. JLE458DS
EX $6　　**NM** $8　　**MIP** $13

❏ **New Holland TJ-425**, 1:64-scale, Scale Models, blue, 4WD, w/duals, 2002, No. JLE477DS
EX $6　　**NM** $8　　**MIP** $13

❏ **New Holland TJ-450**, 1:64-scale, Scale Models, blue, 4WD, w/duals, Collector Edition, 2002, No. JLE468DS
EX $6　　**NM** $8　　**MIP** $13

❏ **New Holland TJ-450**, 1:64-scale, Scale Models, blue, 4WD, w/duals, yellow and red decal, 2004, No. JLE450DS *(Photo by Bossen Implement)*
EX $6　　**NM** $8　　**MIP** $13

❏ **New Holland Tractor w/Grain Cart**, 1:64-scale, Ertl, 2005, No. 13670
EX $4　　**NM** $6　　**MIP** $9

TRUCKS 1:16-SCALE

❏ **New Holland Pickup**, 1:16-scale, Ertl, No. 368 *(Photo by Ertl)*
EX $8　　**NM** $12　　**MIP** $18

TRUCKS 1:32-SCALE

❏ **New Holland Pickup**, 1:32-scale, Ertl, No. 382 *(Photo by Ertl)*
EX $4　　**NM** $6　　**MIP** $11

❏ **New Holland Pickup w/Skid Steer on Trailer**, 1:32-scale, Ertl, No. 367 *(Photo by Ertl)*
EX $8　　**NM** $16　　**MIP** $27

TRUCKS 1:64-SCALE

❏ **New Holland Pickup w/Ford 8N on trailer**, 1:64-scale, Ertl, No. 384
(Photo by Ertl)
EX $4　　**NM** $6　　**MIP** $11

❑ **Semi w/New Holland Van Box**,
1:64-scale, Ertl, No. 345 *(Photo by Ertl)*
EX $8   **NM** $12   **MIP** $18

NEW IDEA

BANKS 1:43-SCALE

❑ **New Idea Dime Bank**, 1:43-scale,
Ertl, white, 1990s
EX $2   **NM** $3   **MIP** $6

IMPLEMENTS 1:16-SCALE

❑ **New Idea Baler, 4665**, 1:16-scale,
Ertl, red, round, 2002, No. 13400
EX $13   **NM** $22   **MIP** $33

❑ **New Idea Baler, 484**, 1:16-scale,
Scale Models, orange, collector's
edition and non-collector's edition,
1980s
EX $17   **NM** $32   **MIP** $47

❑ **New Idea Corn Picker**, 1:16-
scale, Ertl, silver, mounted on AC
D-17, 2001, No. 13191
EX $118   **NM** $163   **MIP** $263

❑ **New Idea Corn Picker**, 1:16-scale,
Topping, green and silver, 1950s
EX $128   **NM** $316   **MIP** $562

❑ **New Idea Mower**, 1:16-scale,
Topping, green and orange, 1950s
EX $78   **NM** $172   **MIP** $283

❑ **New Idea Planter**, 1:16-scale,
Scale Models, 4 row, 1991, No. 9100
EX $18   **NM** $32   **MIP** $53

❑ **New Idea Spreader**, 1:16-scale,
Scale Models, orange and green,
1980s
EX $12   **NM** $22   **MIP** $43

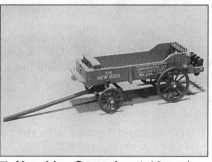

❑ **New Idea Spreader**, 1:16-scale,
Scale Models, orange and green,
Commemorative Edition 85th
Anniversary, 1980s
EX $12   **NM** $28   **MIP** $43

❑ **New Idea Spreader**, 1:16-scale,
Topping, orange, green & silver,
slant cross bar, 1950s
EX $68   **NM** $183   **MIP** $336

❑ **New Idea Spreader**, 1:16-scale,
Topping, orange and green, straight
cross bar, 1950s
EX $68   **NM** $183   **MIP** $346

❑ **New Idea Spreader, 350**, 1:16-
scale, Scale Models, silver and
orange, 1980s
EX $12   **NM** $26   **MIP** $53

❑ **New Idea Spreader, 3622**, 1:16-
scale, Scale Models, 1980s,
No. FF-0250 *(Photo by Scale Models)*
EX $12   **NM** $28   **MIP** $48

IMPLEMENTS 1:32-SCALE

❏ **New Idea UNI System**, 1:32-scale, Scale Models, orange and silver, 20th anniversary 1965 to 1985, 1980s
EX $16   **NM** $58   **MIP** $97

❏ **New Idea UNI System, 800c**, 1:32-scale, Scale Models, silver and gray, collector's edition and non-collector's edition, 1980s
EX $18   **NM** $43   **MIP** $78

IMPLEMENTS 1:64-SCALE

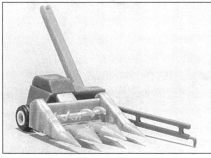

❏ **New Idea Corn Picker**, 1:64-scale, Standi (Custom), green, silver and orange, 1980s
EX $3   **NM** $4   **MIP** $6

OLIVER

BANKS 1:25-SCALE

❏ **Oliver Hart-Parr Truck Bank**, 1:25-scale, Ertl, No. 2304 *(Photo by Ertl)*
EX $4   **NM** $12   **MIP** $18

BANKS

❏ **Oliver Mail Box Bank**, Ertl, green, 1960s
EX $68   **NM** $98   **MIP** $127

CONSTRUCTION EQUIPMENT 1:16-SCALE

❏ **Oliver Crawler, HG**, 1:16-scale, Ertl, green, green metal tracks, Collector Edition, 1999, No. 13002A
EX $18   **NM** $26   **MIP** $47

❏ **Oliver Crawler, HG**, 1:16-scale, Ertl, green, green rubber tracks, red seat, 2002, No. 13079
EX $12   **NM** $17   **MIP** $27

❏ **Oliver Crawler, OC-3**, 1:16-scale, Ertl, yellow, metal tracks, '99 Toy Truck & Construction Edition Show, 1999, No. 16014A *(Photo by Bossen Implement)*
EX $27   **NM** $46   **MIP** $62

❏ **Oliver Crawler, OC-3**, 1:16-scale, Ertl, green, rubber tracks, 2000, No. 13007
EX $12   **NM** $17   **MIP** $27

❏ **Oliver Crawler, OC-6**, 1:16-scale, Slik, yellow, 1960s
EX $298   **NM** $482   **MIP** $982

❏ **Oliver OC-12 Crawler**, 1:16-scale, SpecCast, gas, w/umbrella, 2007, No. 288 *(Photo by SpecCast)*
EX $20   **NM** $40   **MIP** $60

❏ **Oliver Tractor, 550**, 1:16-scale, SpecCast, yellow, '97 Great American Toy Show Edition, 1997, No. CUST 429
EX $16   **NM** $24   **MIP** $43

❏ **Oliver Tractor, 550**, 1:16-scale, SpecCast, yellow, Collector Edition, 2003, No. SCT-216
EX $16   **NM** $24   **MIP** $43

❏ **Oliver Tractor, 77 Super**, 1:16-scale, SpecCast, yellow, w/duals, '96 LaCrosse Toy Fest Edition, 1996, No. CUST 404
EX $16   **NM** $24   **MIP** $43

❏ **Oliver Tractor, 770**, 1:16-scale, SpecCast, yellow, 1995, No. SCT-131
EX $14   **NM** $22   **MIP** $33

❏ **Oliver Tractor, 770**, 1:16-scale, SpecCast, yellow, '96 Louisville Farm Show Edition, 1996, No. CUST 386
EX $14   **NM** $22   **MIP** $33

❏ **Oliver Tractor, 880**, 1:16-scale, SpecCast, yellow, '97 LaCrosse Toy Fest Edition, 1997, No. CUST 437
EX $16   **NM** $24   **MIP** $48

CONSTRUCTION EQUIPMENT

❏ **Cletrac**, Ronsen (Custom), dirty gray, 1920s
EX $988   **NM** $1133   **MIP** npf

IMPLEMENTS 1:08-SCALE

❑ **Oliver Wagon, Flare Box**, 1:08-scale, Scale Models, green, '97 Farm Progress Show Edition, 1997, No. FB-2464
EX $32   **NM** $48   **MIP** $77

IMPLEMENTS 1:12-SCALE

❑ **Oliver Plow**, 1:12-scale, Slik, green, made for Super 55 tractor, 1950s, No. 9866
EX $138   **NM** $333   **MIP** $472

IMPLEMENTS 1:16-SCALE

❑ **Oliver Baler**, 1:16-scale, Koob (Custom), green, w/PTO, 2001
EX $273   **NM** $303   **MIP** n/a

❑ **Oliver Baler**, 1:16-scale, Koob (Custom), green, w/wisconsin engine, 2001
EX $298   **NM** $357   **MIP** n/a

❑ **Oliver Baler**, 1:16-scale, Slik, green, w/motor, 1950s, No. 9851
EX $96   **NM** $182   **MIP** $333

❑ **Oliver Baler**, 1:16-scale, Slik, green, PTO driven, 1950s, No. 9829
EX $138   **NM** $262   **MIP** $633

❑ **Oliver Combine**, 1:16-scale, Slik, green, pull type, 1950s
EX $88   **NM** $188   **MIP** $376

❑ **Oliver Corn Picker**, 1:16-scale, Slik, green and silver, picker is removable from tractor, 1950s
EX $126   **NM** $247   **MIP** $568

❑ **Oliver Corn Picker**, 1:16-scale, Slik, green and silver w/green tips on snouts, picker is removable from tractor, 1950s
EX $126   **NM** $247   **MIP** $568

❑ **Oliver Corn Picker**, 1:16-scale, Slik, green, pull type, 1950s
EX $78   **NM** $142   **MIP** $298

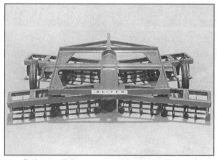

❑ **Oliver Disc**, 1:16-scale, Ertl, green, 1960s, No. 28
EX $22   **NM** $68   **MIP** $168

❑ **Oliver Disc**, 1:16-scale, Ertl, green, 1970s, No. 28
EX $22   **NM** $68   **MIP** $168

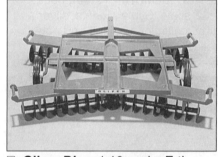

❑ **Oliver Disc**, 1:16-scale, Ertl, green, 1970s, No. 628
EX $22   **NM** $68   **MIP** $168

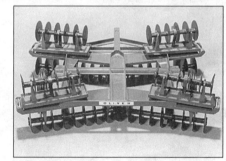

❑ **Oliver Disc**, 1:16-scale, Ertl, green, w/wings, 1970s, No. 649
EX $68   **NM** $198   **MIP** $428

❑ **Oliver Disc**, 1:16-scale, Slik, green, 1950s
EX $92   **NM** $223   **MIP** $442

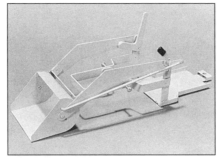

❑ **Oliver Loader**, 1:16-scale, Ertl, green, fits 1800 series, 1970s
EX $58   **NM** $159   **MIP** $256

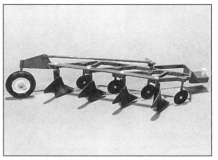

❑ **Oliver Plow**, 1:16-scale, Ertl, green. 4 bottom, 1970s, No. 27
EX $26   **NM** $68   **MIP** $168

❑ **Oliver Drill**, 1:16-scale, Slik, green, 1950s
EX $68   **NM** $158   **MIP** $448

❑ **Oliver Mower**, 1:16-scale, Slik, green, 1950s
EX $37   **NM** $89   **MIP** $188

❑ **Oliver Plow**, 1:16-scale, Slik, green, 1950s, No. 9850
EX $98   **NM** $189   **MIP** $389

❑ **Oliver Drill**, 1:16-scale, Slik, green, 1950s
EX $68   **NM** $158   **MIP** $448

❑ **Oliver Plow**, 1:16-scale, Arcade, red, No. 7, 1925
EX $78   **NM** $168   **MIP** $523

❑ **Oliver Rake**, 1:16-scale, Slik, green, 1950s
EX $88   **NM** $224   **MIP** $546

❑ **Oliver Hay Rake**, 1:16-scale, Ertl, 1990s, No. 2706 *(Photo by Ertl)*
EX $12   **NM** $18   **MIP** $27

❑ **Oliver Plow**, 1:16-scale, Arcade, red, 1940s
EX $78   **NM** $168   **MIP** $523

❑ **Oliver Spreader**, 1:16-scale, Arcade, yellow, "Oliver 7 Superior" decal, 10-1/4" long, 1941, No. 7140
EX $228   **NM** $582   **MIP** $1189

❑ **Oliver Spreader**, 1:16-scale, Ertl, green, belt drive, 1960s, No. 626
EX $48   **NM** $116   **MIP** $212

❑ **Oliver Spreader**, 1:16-scale, Ertl, green, chain drive, 1960s, No. 26
EX $22   **NM** $48   **MIP** $169

❑ **Oliver Spreader**, 1:16-scale, Slik, green, gear drive, 1950s, No. 9836
EX $78   **NM** $166   **MIP** $368

❑ **Oliver Spreader**, 1:16-scale, Slik, green, belt drive, 1950s, No. 9836
EX $68   **NM** $126   **MIP** $278

❑ **Oliver Trailer**, 1:16-scale, Slik, green or red, 1950s
EX $6   **NM** $18   **MIP** $38

❑ **Oliver Wagon**, 1:16-scale, Slik, green, 1950s, No. 9840
EX $16   **NM** $63   **MIP** $168

❑ **Oliver Wagon**, 1:16-scale, Slik, green, 1950s, No. 9840
EX $16   **NM** $63   **MIP** $168

❑ **Oliver Wagon Barge**, 1:16-scale, Ertl, green, plastic rims, 1960s, No. 623
EX $23   **NM** $68   **MIP** $158

❑ **Oliver Wagon Barge**, 1:16-scale, Ertl, green, die-cast rims, 1960s, No. 23
EX $33   **NM** $78   **MIP** $176

❑ **Oliver Wagon Barge**, 1:16-scale, Ertl, green, die-cast rims, 1960s, No. 23
EX $33   **NM** $78   **MIP** $176

❑ **Oliver Wagon, Flare Box**, 1:16-scale, Ertl, green, 1960s, No. 12
EX $18   **NM** $42   **MIP** $128

❑ **Oliver Wagon, Gravity**, 1:16-scale, Ertl, green, 1960s, No. 605
EX $68   **NM** $172   **MIP** $493

IMPLEMENTS 1:25-SCALE

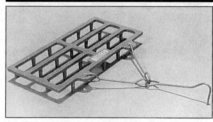

❑ **Oliver Harrow**, 1:25-scale, Slik, red or green, 1940s
EX $6   **NM** $18   **MIP** $38

❑ **Oliver Mower**, 1:25-scale, Arcade, red, green, blue; yellow cutter bar moves, 4" long, 1939, No. 4210X
EX $48   **NM** $93   **MIP** $178

❑ **Oliver Mower**, 1:25-scale, Arcade, red or green, 1950s
EX $48   **NM** $93   **MIP** $178

❑ **Oliver Mower**, 1:25-scale, Slik, green, 1950s
EX $6   **NM** $18   **MIP** $48

❑ **Oliver Planter**, 1:25-scale, Arcade, red, green, blue; 4-1/2" long, 1939, No. 4220X
EX $78   **NM** $112   **MIP** $188

❑ **Oliver Planter**, 1:25-scale, Arcade, red or green, 1940s
EX $78   **NM** $112   **MIP** $188

❑ **Oliver Plow**, 1:25-scale, Arcade, red, blue or green; black rubber tires, 6-1/4" long, 1940s, No. 4230X
EX $69   **NM** $138   **MIP** $339

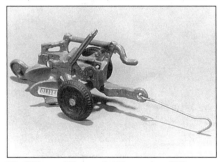

❑ **Oliver Plow**, 1:25-scale, Slik, green, 1940s
EX $6   **NM** $18   **MIP** $38

IMPLEMENTS 1:25-SCALE

❑ **Oliver Disc**, 1:25-scale, Slik, green or red, 1940s
EX $6   **NM** $18   **MIP** $38

❑ **Oliver Rake**, 1:25-scale, Slik, green, 1950s
EX $6   **NM** $18   **MIP** $38

MISCELLANEOUS 1:32-SCALE

❑ **Oliver Pen Set**, 1:32-scale, Scale Models, antique brass, 1980s
EX $4   **NM** $9   **MIP** $16

MISCELLANEOUS

❑ **Oliver Outboard Boat Motor**
EX $513   **NM** $983   **MIP** $3388

PEDAL TRACTORS

❑ **Oliver 1800**, Ertl, green w/white wheels, plastic grille, original tractor restored, 1960s
EX $738   **NM** $1389   **MIP** n/a

❑ **Oliver 1800**, Eska, green w/white wheels, decal over cast grille, tractor in original condition
EX $1937   **NM** $3189   **MIP** n/a

❑ **Oliver 1850**, Ertl, green w/white wheels, plastic grille, tractor in original condition, 1964
EX $648   **NM** $833   **MIP** $1433

❑ **Oliver 1855 White**, Ertl, green w/white wheels, plastic grille, original tractor restored
EX $648   **NM** $833   **MIP** $1423

❑ **Oliver 70**, Scale Models, green, NF, '99 Farm Progress Show Edition, 1999, No. FU-0618
EX $96   **NM** $123   **MIP** $168

❑ **Oliver 70**, Scale Models, green, NF, 2003, No. FU-0621
EX $88   **NM** $112   **MIP** $153

❑ **Oliver 88**, Scale Models, green, NF, w/fenders, Collector Edition, 2003, No. FU-0638
EX $88   **NM** $112   **MIP** $153

❑ **Oliver 88 Small Version**, Eska, green w/red wheels, closed grille, original; wheels replaced, rear seat bracket 2-1/2" from rear of main casting; other version, 1", 1947
EX $1533   **NM** $2033   **MIP** n/a

❑ **Oliver 88 Small Version**, Eska, green w/red wheels, open grill, tractor in original condition, 1947
EX $1533   **NM** $2722   **MIP** n/a

❑ **Oliver 880**, Eska, green w/white wheels, tractor in original condition, 1958
EX $922   **NM** $1533   **MIP** n/a

❑ **Oliver Spirit**, Scale Models, green, WF, Collector Edition, 1999, No. FU-0608
EX $102   **NM** $136   **MIP** $188

❑ **Oliver Spirit**, Scale Models, green, WF, 2000, No. FU-0610
EX $89   **NM** $122   **MIP** $159

❑ **Oliver Super 88**, Eska, green w/red wheels, tractor in original condition, 1954
EX $1022   **NM** $1633   **MIP** n/a

❑ **Oliver Umbrella**, Heltrick, yellow, in original condition
EX $128   **NM** $168   **MIP** $343

TRACTORS 1:08-SCALE

❑ **Oliver 1800**, 1:08-scale, Scale Models, green, NF, 1998, No. FU-0603
EX $73   **NM** $122   **MIP** $173

❑ **Oliver 1850**, 1:08-scale, Scale Models, green, NF, '97 Farm Progress Show Edition, 1997, No. FB-2463
EX $73   **NM** $122   **MIP** $173

❑ **Oliver 1850**, 1:08-scale, Scale Models, green, NF, 1998, No. FU-0594
EX $73   **NM** $122   **MIP** $173

TRACTORS 1:12-SCALE

❑ **Oliver 55, Super**, 1:12-scale, Slik, green w/green rims, 1950s
EX $268   **NM** $542   **MIP** $1192

❑ **Oliver 99**, 1:12-scale, Franklin Mint, green, 2000
EX $93   **NM** $124   **MIP** $153

❑ **Oliver 99 Super**, 1:12-scale, Franklin Mint, green, 2003
EX $89   **NM** $117   **MIP** $133

TRACTORS 1:16-SCALE

❑ **Oliver 1555**, 1:16-scale, Ertl, green, NF, diesel, 1994, No. 2223
(Photo by Ertl)
EX $19   **NM** $32   **MIP** $53

❑ **Oliver 1555**, 1:16-scale, Ertl, green, gas, WF, w/swept back axle, Collector Edition, 1994, No. 2223DA
(Photo by Bossen Implement)
EX $22   **NM** $34   **MIP** $58

❑ **Oliver 1555**, 1:16-scale, Ertl, green, WF, ROPS, '94 National Farm Toy Museum Edition, 1994, No. 2389PA *(Photo by Bossen Implement)*
EX $21   **NM** $33   **MIP** $56

❑ **Oliver 1555**, 1:16-scale, Ertl, green, NF, w/Hiniker cab, '03 Summer Toy Show Edition, 2003, No. 16104A
EX $19   **NM** $32   **MIP** $53

❑ **Oliver 1655**, 1:16-scale, Ertl, green, WF, diesel, 1994, No. 4472

(Photo by Ertl)

EX $16   **NM** $28   **MIP** $42

❑ **Oliver 1655**, 1:16-scale, Ertl, green, MFD, duals, '95 Sugar Valley Farm Toy Show Edition, 1995, No. 2273CA

EX $37   **NM** $48   **MIP** $93

❑ **Oliver 1655**, 1:16-scale, Ertl, green, MFD, ROPS, Collector Edition, 1995, No. 4472DA

EX $22   **NM** $34   **MIP** $58

❑ **Oliver 1655**, 1:16-scale, Ertl, green, WF, ROPS, diesel, '95 Penn State Farm Toy Show, 1995, No. 2313DA *(Photo by Bossen Implement)*

EX $22   **NM** $34   **MIP** $58

❑ **Oliver 1655**, 1:16-scale, Ertl, green, WF, swept back axle, w/Hiniker cab, 2001, No. 13186

EX $16   **NM** $28   **MIP** $42

❑ **Oliver 1655 White**, 1:16-scale, Ertl, green, WF, swept back axle, diesel, 1997, No. 4474 *(Photo by Ertl)*

EX $19   **NM** $32   **MIP** $47

❑ **Oliver 1655 White**, 1:16-scale, Ertl, red, Heritage '97 Farm Show Edition, 1997, No. 2031TA

EX $16   **NM** $28   **MIP** $47

❑ **Oliver 1655 White**, 1:16-scale, Ertl, green, WF, '02 CIFES Edition, 2002

EX $16   **NM** $28   **MIP** $47

❑ **Oliver 1755**, 1:16-scale, Scale Models, green, NF, 1980s

EX $16   **NM** $28   **MIP** $38

❑ **Oliver 1755**, 1:16-scale, Scale Models, green, NF, "87 Farm Progress Show Edition, 1987

EX $16   **NM** $28   **MIP** $38

❑ **Oliver 1755**, 1:16-scale, Scale Models, green, WF, Summer Toy Fest 1990, 1990

EX $16   **NM** $28   **MIP** $39

❑ **Oliver 1755**, 1:16-scale, Scale Models, green, '91 Penn State Farm Show, 1991

EX $16   **NM** $28   **MIP** $38

❑ **Oliver 1755**, 1:16-scale, Scale Models, green, WF, fender tanks, '91 National Show Edition, 1991

EX $16   **NM** $28   **MIP** $53

❑ **Oliver 1755 White**, 1:16-scale, Scale Models, green, Turtle River Toy Show 7-9-89, 1989

EX $16   **NM** $28   **MIP** $38

❑ **Oliver 1800**, 1:16-scale, Ertl, green, die-cast rims, 1960s, No. 604

EX $98   **NM** $198   **MIP** $573

❑ **Oliver 1800**, 1:16-scale, Ertl, green, die-cast rims, long checkerboard decal, 1960s, No. 604

EX $142   **NM** $378   **MIP** $922

❑ **Oliver 1800**, 1:16-scale, Ertl, green, die-cast rims, MFD, 1960s, No. 606

EX $132   **NM** $298   **MIP** $718

❑ **Oliver 1800**, 1:16-scale, Ertl, green, die-cast rims, checkerboard decal w/Keystone, 1960s, No. 604

EX $142   **NM** $378   **MIP** $922

❏ **Oliver 1800**, 1:16-scale, Scale Models, NF, gold plated employee Christmas gift from Joe Ertl, no box, 2006 *(Photo by Bossen Implement)*
EX $173 **NM** $248 **MIP** n/a

❏ **Oliver 1800**, 1:16-scale, Scale Models, NF, '06 Farm Progress, 2006, No. FT-1331
EX $16 **NM** $22 **MIP** $41

❏ **Oliver 1850**, 1:16-scale, Ertl, green, plastic rims, 1960s, No. 604
EX $42 **NM** $113 **MIP** $243

❏ **Oliver 1850**, 1:16-scale, Ertl, green, plastic rims, no fenders, 1960s, No. 604
EX $38 **NM** $98 **MIP** $234

❏ **Oliver 1850**, 1:16-scale, Ertl, green, die-cast rims, 1960s, No. 604
EX $68 **NM** $148 **MIP** $273

❏ **Oliver 1850**, 1:16-scale, Ertl, green, plastic rear rims, die-cast front rims, MFD, 1960s, No. 606
EX $112 **NM** $222 **MIP** $468

❏ **Oliver 1850**, 1:16-scale, Ertl, green, all die-cast rims, MFD, 1960s, No. 606
EX $112 **NM** $252 **MIP** $488

❏ **Oliver 1850**, 1:16-scale, Scale Models, green, 1989
EX $16 **NM** $28 **MIP** $43

❏ **Oliver 1855**, 1:16-scale, Ertl, green, die-cast front rims, plastic rear rims, MFD, 1970s, No. 606
EX $112 **NM** $222 **MIP** $488

❏ **Oliver 1855**, 1:16-scale, Ertl, green, duals, w/ROPS, 1970s, No. 610
EX $112 **NM** $188 **MIP** $228

❏ **Oliver 1855**, 1:16-scale, Ertl, green, wide front, 1970s, No. 609
EX $98 **NM** $189 **MIP** $382

❏ **Oliver 1855**, 1:16-scale, Ertl, green, NF, 1970s, No. 604
EX $48 **NM** $98 **MIP** $224

❏ **Oliver 1855**, 1:16-scale, Ertl, green, NF, plastic rims, no fenders, 1970s, No. 604
EX $42 **NM** $82 **MIP** $188

❏ **Oliver 1855**, 1:16-scale, Scale Models, green, 10th National Farm Toy Show Nov. 7, 1987, 1987
EX $16 **NM** $28 **MIP** $38

❏ **Oliver 1855**, 1:16-scale, Scale Models, green, "91 Penn State Farm Show, 1991
EX $16 **NM** $28 **MIP** $43

❏ **Oliver 1855**, 1:16-scale, Scale Models, green, w/wide front end, 1991, No. FU-1318
EX $22   **NM** $33   **MIP** $43

❏ **Oliver 1855**, 1:16-scale, Scale Models, green, WF, 1997, No. FU-0537
EX $16   **NM** $28   **MIP** $43

❏ **Oliver 1855**, 1:16-scale, Scale Models, green, WF, 1997, No. FF-0201 *(Photo by Scale Models)*
EX $16   **NM** $22   **MIP** $43

❏ **Oliver 1855 White**, 1:16-scale, Ertl, green, die-cast front rims, plastic rear rims, MFD, 1970s, No. 606
EX $98   **NM** $239   **MIP** $478

❏ **Oliver 1855 White**, 1:16-scale, Ertl, green, WF, 1970s, No. 609
EX $98   **NM** $189   **MIP** $454

❏ **Oliver 1855 White**, 1:16-scale, Ertl, green, NF, fenders, 1970s, No. 604
EX $42   **NM** $112   **MIP** $242

❏ **Oliver 1855 White**, 1:16-scale, Ertl, green, NF, no fenders, 1970s, No. 604
EX $38   **NM** $92   **MIP** $212

❏ **Oliver 1855 White**, 1:16-scale, Scale Models, green, Heritage Series, 1980s
EX $22   **NM** $33   **MIP** $43

❏ **Oliver 1855 White**, 1:16-scale, Scale Models, green, WF, 1992, No. FU-0556
EX $16   **NM** $28   **MIP** $43

❏ **Oliver 1950T**, 1:16-scale, Ertl, green, MFD, '02 National Farm Toy Show Edition, 2002, No. 16094A
EX $77   **NM** $93   **MIP** $122

❏ **Oliver 1950T**, 1:16-scale, Ertl, green, MFD, w/Hiniker cab, 2003, No. 13382
EX $16   **NM** $28   **MIP** $43

❏ **Oliver 1955**, 1:16-scale, Scale Models, green, NF, 1980s
EX $16   **NM** $28   **MIP** $38

❏ **Oliver 1955**, 1:16-scale, Scale Models, green, Mankato Farm Toy Show, 1987
EX $22   **NM** $33   **MIP** $43

❏ **Oliver 1955**, 1:16-scale, Scale Models, green, w/wide rear tires, Louisville Farm Machinery Show 2-13-88 National Tractor Pull, 1988
EX $16   **NM** $28   **MIP** $38

❏ **Oliver 1955**, 1:16-scale, Scale Models, green, St. Louis Toy Show 2-7-88, 1988
EX $22   **NM** $33   **MIP** $43

❑ **Oliver 1955**, 1:16-scale, Scale Models, green, '90 Farm Progress Show Edition, 1990
EX $16   **NM** $28   **MIP** $43

❑ **Oliver 1955**, 1:16-scale, Scale Models, gold plated employee christmas gift from Joe Ertl, 1990
EX $142   **NM** $173   **MIP** $206

❑ **Oliver 1955**, 1:16-scale, Scale Models, green, '91 New York Farm Show Edition, 1991
EX $16   **NM** $28   **MIP** $43

❑ **Oliver 1955**, 1:16-scale, Scale Models, green, WF, 1991, No. FU-0137
EX $16   **NM** $28   **MIP** $43

❑ **Oliver 1955**, 1:16-scale, Scale Models, green, WF, fender tanks, '91 National Show Edition, 1991, No. FB-1566 *(Photo by Bossen Implement)*
EX $19   **NM** $32   **MIP** $53

❑ **Oliver 1955**, 1:16-scale, Scale Models, green, '92 Oklahoma Farm Show Edition, 1992
EX $16   **NM** $28   **MIP** $43

❑ **Oliver 1955**, 1:16-scale, Scale Models, green, WF, w/fender tanks, 1992, No. FU-0554 *(Photo by Scale Models)*
EX $22   **NM** $32   **MIP** $53

❑ **Oliver 1955**, 1:16-scale, Scale Models, green, WF, cab, '97 Spring Open House Edition, 1997, No. FB-2470
EX $16   **NM** $28   **MIP** $43

❑ **Oliver 1955**, 1:16-scale, Scale Models, green, WF, cab, 1998, No. FU-0597
EX $16   **NM** $28   **MIP** $43

❑ **Oliver 2150**, 1:16-scale, Berg (Custom), green, did not come in box, 1980s

❑ **Oliver 2150**, 1:16-scale, Berg (Custom), green, several variations, did not come in box, 1980s
EX $289   **NM** $473   **MIP** n/a

❑ **Oliver 2255**, 1:16-scale, Berg (Custom), green, did not come in box, 1980s
EX $327   **NM** $422   **MIP** n/a

❑ **Oliver 2255**, 1:16-scale, Berg (Custom), green, did not come in box, 1980s
EX $289   **NM** $473   **MIP** n/a

❑ **Oliver 2255**, 1:16-scale, Scale Models, green, '97 AGCO July Dealer Meeting, Kansas City, 1997, No. FU-0590
EX $19   **NM** $32   **MIP** $48

❑ **Oliver 2255**, 1:16-scale, Scale Models, green, WF, cab, 1998, No. FU-0599
EX $19   **NM** $32   **MIP** $48

❑ **Oliver 2255**, 1:16-scale, Scale Models, green, WF, '03 Farm Progress Show Edition, 2003, No. FU-0640
EX $19   **NM** $32   **MIP** $48

❑ **Oliver 2455**, 1:16-scale, Berg (Custom), green and white, 1980s
EX $343   **NM** $533   **MIP** n/a

❑ **Oliver 2455**, 1:16-scale, Scale Models, green, 4WD, w/duals, no cab, Collector Edition, 2001, No. FU-0608
EX $76   **NM** $98   **MIP** $148

❑ **Oliver 2455**, 1:16-scale, Scale Models, green, 4WD, w/cab, '03 Louisville Farm Show Edition, 2003, No. FB-2628
EX $76   **NM** $98   **MIP** $158

❑ **Oliver 2455**, 1:16-scale, Scale Models, green, 4WD, cab, 2003, No. FU-0635
EX $76   **NM** $98   **MIP** $148

❑ **Oliver 2655**, 1:16-scale, Berg (Custom), green, 1980s
EX $343   **NM** $533   **MIP** n/a

❑ **Oliver 2655**, 1:16-scale, Berg (Custom), green, w/cab, did not come in box, 1980s
EX $389   **NM** $589   **MIP** n/a

❑ **Oliver 2655**, 1:16-scale, Berg (Custom), green, did not come in box, 1980s
EX $389   **NM** $589   **MIP** n/a

❑ **Oliver 2655**, 1:16-scale, Cottonwood Acres, green, w/cab, 1980s
EX $327   **NM** $482   **MIP** $589

❑ **Oliver 44**, 1:16-scale, SpecCast, green, Farm and Construction Show in California, 1990
EX $18   **NM** $38   **MIP** $48

❑ **Oliver 44 Super**, 1:16-scale, SpecCast, green, Lafayette Show Tractor, 1987
EX $18   **NM** $28   **MIP** $48

❑ **Oliver 44 Super**, 1:16-scale, SpecCast, green, '89 Toy Tractor Times, #4; 2,535 produced, 1989, No. TTT009
EX $22   **NM** $38   **MIP** $48

❑ **Oliver 44 Super**, 1:16-scale, SpecCast, green, '94 Crossroads USA Show Edition, 1994, No. CUST 278
EX $18   **NM** $26   **MIP** $48

❑ **Oliver 44 Super**, 1:16-scale, SpecCast, green, '96 Paxton-Buckley-Loda FFA Show Edition, 1996, No. CUST 376
EX $18   **NM** $28   **MIP** $48

❑ **Oliver 44 Super**, 1:16-scale, SpecCast, green, 1998, No. SCT-161
EX $16   **NM** $26   **MIP** $48

❑ **Oliver 44 Super**, 1:16-scale, SpecCast, green, '99 Lake Region Thresher Assn. Edition, 1999
EX $18   **NM** $28   **MIP** $48

❑ **Oliver 44 Super**, 1:16-scale, SpecCast, green, 2002, No. SCT-204
EX $16   **NM** $26   **MIP** $48

❑ **Oliver 440**, 1:16-scale, SpecCast, green, Collector Edition, 1989, No. SCT-044
EX $16   **NM** $36   **MIP** $43

❑ **Oliver 440**, 1:16-scale, SpecCast, green, 30th Anniversary of White's Purchase of Oliver, 1990, No. SCW006
EX $16   **NM** $36   **MIP** $43

❑ **Oliver 440**, 1:16-scale, SpecCast, green, '90 Crossroads USA Show Edition, 1990, No. CUST 108
EX $16   **NM** $36   **MIP** $43

❑ **Oliver 440**, 1:16-scale, SpecCast, green, '94 Crossroads USA Show Edition, 1994
EX $16   **NM** $26   **MIP** $43

❑ **Oliver 440**, 1:16-scale, SpecCast, green, '94 Louisville Farm Show Edition, 1994, No. 3000
EX $16   **NM** $26   **MIP** $43

❑ **Oliver 440**, 1:16-scale, SpecCast, green, Central Tractor Grand Opening, 1994, No. CUST 276
EX $16   **NM** $26   **MIP** $43

❑ **Oliver 440**, 1:16-scale, SpecCast, green, Spec Cast 20th Anniversary 1974-1994, 1994, No. CUST 334
EX $16   **NM** $26   **MIP** $43

❑ **Oliver 440**, 1:16-scale, SpecCast, green, red wheels and weights, 1995, No. SCT-134
EX $16   **NM** $26   **MIP** $43

❑ **Oliver 440**, 1:16-scale, SpecCast, green, 2003, No. SCT-218
EX $16   **NM** $26   **MIP** $43

❑ **Oliver 55 Super**, 1:16-scale, Yoder (Custom), green, 1980s
EX $48   **NM** $83   **MIP** $98

❑ **Oliver 550**, 1:16-scale, SpecCast, green, Collector Edition, 1996, No. SCT-141
EX $14   **NM** $22   **MIP** $38

❑ **Oliver 550**, 1:16-scale, SpecCast, green, '97 Bloomington Show Edition, 1997, No. CUST 427
EX $14   **NM** $22   **MIP** $38

❑ **Oliver 550**, 1:16-scale, SpecCast, 1997, No. SCT143 *(Photo by SpecCast)*
EX $14   **NM** $22   **MIP** $38

❑ **Oliver 550**, 1:16-scale, SpecCast, green, '96 Crossroads USA Show Edition, 1997, No. CUST 419
EX $14   **NM** $22   **MIP** $38

❑ **Oliver 550**, 1:16-scale, Yoder (Custom), green, 1980s
EX $48   **NM** $83   **MIP** $98

❑ **Oliver 550**, 1:16-scale, Yoder (Custom), green, 1980s
EX $48   **NM** $83   **MIP** $98

❑ **Oliver 60**, 1:16-scale, Howell, green, regular issue, did not come in box, 1980s
EX $48   **NM** $73   **MIP** n/a

❑ **Oliver 60**, 1:16-scale, Howell, green, custom issue, did not come in box, 1980s
EX $89   **NM** $113   **MIP** n/a

❑ **Oliver 60**, 1:16-scale, SpecCast, green, on rubber, No. SCT-182
EX $16   **NM** $22   **MIP** $38

❑ **Oliver 60**, 1:16-scale, SpecCast, green, on steel, 1996, No. SCT-165
EX $16   **NM** $22   **MIP** $38

❑ **Oliver 60**, 1:16-scale, SpecCast, green, '00 Crossroads USA Show Edition, 2000, No. CUST 662
EX $16   **NM** $22   **MIP** $38

❑ **Oliver 60**, 1:16-scale, SpecCast, green, puller, '00 Louisville Farm Show Edition, 2000, No. SCT-180
EX $18   **NM** $26   **MIP** $43

❑ **Oliver 66**, 1:16-scale, Howell, green, did not come in box
EX $48   **NM** $73   **MIP** n/a

❑ **Oliver 66**, 1:16-scale, SpecCast, green, '92 Dairy Nationals, 1992, No. CUST 177
EX $16   **NM** $26   **MIP** $48

❑ **Oliver 66**, 1:16-scale, SpecCast, green, '95 Crossroads USA Show Edition, 1995, No. CUST 348
EX $16   **NM** $26   **MIP** $48

❑ **Oliver 66**, 1:16-scale, SpecCast, green, WF, '01 Crossroads USA Show Edition, 2001, No. CUST 712
EX $16   **NM** $26   **MIP** $48

❑ **Oliver 70**, 1:16-scale, Arcade, Row Crop, red w/bronze striping, black rubber wheels w/yellow centers, 7-1/2" long, 1937, No. 356
EX n/a   **NM** n/a   **MIP** n/a

❑ **Oliver 70**, 1:16-scale, Arcade, red, blue, green; white rubber wheels, 5-1/2" long, 1937, No. 359
EX n/a   **NM** n/a   **MIP** n/a

❑ **Oliver 70**, 1:16-scale, Arcade, green, 1940s
EX $148   **NM** $329   **MIP** $1392

❏ **Oliver 70**, 1:16-scale, Arcade, green w/white wheel centers, 1940s
EX $148   **NM** $329   **MIP** $1392

❏ **Oliver 70**, 1:16-scale, Gray (Custom), green, did not come in box, 1970s
EX $22   **NM** $37   **MIP** n/a

❏ **Oliver 70**, 1:16-scale, Gray (Custom), green, 10th anniversary 1968-1978, did not come in box, 1978
EX $22   **NM** $37   **MIP** n/a

❏ **Oliver 70**, 1:16-scale, Scale Models, green, NF, on steel, #3 in Collectors Series I, 1979
EX $18   **NM** $26   **MIP** $37

❏ **Oliver 70**, 1:16-scale, Scale Models, green, 1980s
EX $18   **NM** $26   **MIP** $37

❏ **Oliver 70**, 1:16-scale, Scale Models, green, Row crop, 1980s
EX $18   **NM** $26   **MIP** $37

❏ **Oliver 70**, 1:16-scale, Scale Models, green, NF, on steel, Antique Series, 1983
EX $18   **NM** $26   **MIP** $37

❏ **Oliver 70**, 1:16-scale, Scale Models, green, NF, on rubber, Antique Series, 1986
EX $18   **NM** $26   **MIP** $37

❏ **Oliver 70**, 1:16-scale, Scale Models, green, NF, on rubber, w/farmhand hay loader, 1987
EX $113   **NM** $182   **MIP** $223

❏ **Oliver 70**, 1:16-scale, Scale Models, green, Summer Toy Festival Show Tractor, NF on steel, 1988
EX $18   **NM** $26   **MIP** $37

❏ **Oliver 70**, 1:16-scale, Scale Models, green, w/wide front end, National Show Tractor 1988, 1988
EX $18   **NM** $26   **MIP** $37

❏ **Oliver 70**, 1:16-scale, Scale Models, green, WF, on rubber, 1988
EX $18   **NM** $26   **MIP** $37

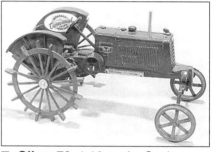

❏ **Oliver 70**, 1:16-scale, Scale Models, green, w/wide front end Montana Centennial, 1989
EX $18   **NM** $26   **MIP** $37

❏ **Oliver 70**, 1:16-scale, Scale Models, green, w/wide front end, and rubber tires, 1989 Summer Toy Fest, 1989
EX $18   **NM** $26   **MIP** $37

❏ **Oliver 70**, 1:16-scale, Scale Models, green, NF on rubber, green grille, 1997, No. FU-1309
(Photo by Scale Models)
EX $8   **NM** $12   **MIP** $18

❏ **Oliver 70**, 1:16-scale, Scale Models, green, NF, on rubber, swept back fenders, '97 Farm Progress Show Edition, 1997, No. FB-2465
EX $18　　　**NM** $26　　　**MIP** $37

❏ **Oliver 70**, 1:16-scale, Scale Models, green, '97 DuQuoin Farm Show Edition, 1997, No. FB-2479
EX $18　　　**NM** $26　　　**MIP** $37

❏ **Oliver 70**, 1:16-scale, Scale Models, green, NF, on rubber, swept back fenders, 2000, No. FU-0598
EX $18　　　**NM** $26　　　**MIP** $37

❏ **Oliver 70**, 1:16-scale, Slik, red, 1950s
EX $22　　　**NM** $58　　　**MIP** $72

❏ **Oliver 70**, 1:16-scale, Slik, red, 1950s
EX $22　　　**NM** $58　　　**MIP** $72

❏ **Oliver 70**, 1:16-scale, Slik, green, 1950s
EX $22　　　**NM** $58　　　**MIP** $72

❏ **Oliver 70**, 1:16-scale, SpecCast, green, NF, on rubber, 1999, No. SCT-164
EX $14　　　**NM** $22　　　**MIP** $38

❏ **Oliver 70**, 1:16-scale, SpecCast, green, NF, on steel, 2001, No. SCT-194
EX $14　　　**NM** $22　　　**MIP** $38

❏ **Oliver 70**, 1:16-scale, SpecCast, single front wheel, U.S. Flag tractor in red, white and blue, 2006, No. SCT276 *(Photo by Bossen Implement)*
EX $32　　　**NM** $53　　　**MIP** $98

❏ **Oliver 70 w/Cultivator**, 1:16-scale, Dingman, green, did not come in box, 1980s
EX $368　　　**NM** $543　　　**MIP** n/a

❏ **Oliver 77**, 1:16-scale, Ertl, green, NF, #4 in Precision Series, 1997, No. 2657 *(Photo by Ertl)*
EX $98　　　**NM** $132　　　**MIP** $177

❏ **Oliver 77**, 1:16-scale, Lincoln, green w/red wheel centers, 1950s
EX $289　　　**NM** $592　　　**MIP** $773

❏ **Oliver 77**, 1:16-scale, Slik, green w/red rims, steerable, Diesel, 1950s, No. 9852
EX $189　　　**NM** $362　　　**MIP** $763

❏ **Oliver 77**, 1:16-scale, Slik, green, open engine, 1950s
EX $233　　　**NM** $427　　　**MIP** $956

❏ **Oliver 77**, 1:16-scale, Slik, green, Diesel, open engine, 1950s
EX $233　　　**NM** $427　　　**MIP** $956

❏ **Oliver 77**, 1:16-scale, Slik, green w/red wheel centers, non-steerable, brown driver, 1950s
EX $98　　　**NM** $189　　　**MIP** $482

❑ **Oliver 77**, 1:16-scale, SpecCast, green, 1991, No. SCW-026
EX $14 **NM** $22 **MIP** $38

❑ **Oliver 77**, 1:16-scale, SpecCast, green, WF, 1992, No. SCT-058
EX $14 **NM** $22 **MIP** $38

❑ **Oliver 77**, 1:16-scale, SpecCast, green, '92 Manvel Pioneer Days, 1992
EX $14 **NM** $22 **MIP** $38

❑ **Oliver 77**, 1:16-scale, SpecCast, green, '92 Crossroads USA Show Edition, 1992
EX $14 **NM** $22 **MIP** $38

❑ **Oliver 77**, 1:16-scale, SpecCast, green, NF, Tractor Supply Company, 1993, No. CUST 171
EX $14 **NM** $22 **MIP** $38

❑ **Oliver 77**, 1:16-scale, SpecCast, green, '96 Crossroads USA Show Edition, 1996, No. CUST 391
EX $14 **NM** $22 **MIP** $38

❑ **Oliver 77**, 1:16-scale, SpecCast, green, NF, w/2-16 radex plow on plaque, '03 WI Farm Technology Days Edition, 2003, No. CUST 768
EX n/a **NM** n/a **MIP** $243

❑ **Oliver 77**, 1:16-scale, SpecCast, NF, diesel, 2007, No. 272
(Photo by SpecCast)
EX $15 **NM** $30 **MIP** $45

❑ **Oliver 77 Super**, 1:16-scale, Ertl, green, WF, #5 in Precision Series, 1998, No. 2658
EX $74 **NM** $116 **MIP** $178

❑ **Oliver 77 Super**, 1:16-scale, Ertl, green, NF, green rims, #10 in Precision Series, 2003, No. 13385
EX $63 **NM** $92 **MIP** $118

❑ **Oliver 77 Super**, 1:16-scale, SpecCast, green, NF, 1994, No. SCT-117
EX $14 **NM** $22 **MIP** $38

❑ **Oliver 77 Super**, 1:16-scale, SpecCast, green, puller, 1998, No. SCT-157
EX $14 **NM** $22 **MIP** $38

❑ **Oliver 77 Super**, 1:16-scale, SpecCast, green, '99 Crossroads USA Show Edition, 1999, No. CUST 630
EX $14 **NM** $22 **MIP** $38

❑ **Oliver 77 Super**, 1:16-scale, SpecCast, green, '01 Paxton-Buckley-Loda Show Edition, 2001, No. CUST 699
EX $14 **NM** $22 **MIP** $38

❑ **Oliver 77 Super**, 1:16-scale, SpecCast, green, NF, '04 FFA Edition, 2004, No. CUST 798
EX $18 **NM** $26 **MIP** $48

❑ **Oliver 77 Super**, 1:16-scale, SpecCast, green, high crop, '01 National Farm Toy Museum Edition, 2004, No. CUST 808
EX $22 **NM** $31 **MIP** $58

❑ **Oliver 77, Super**, 1:16-scale, Howell, green, did not come in box, 1980s
EX $48 **NM** $73 **MIP** n/a

❑ **Oliver 77, Super**, 1:16-scale, Howell, green, did not come in box, 1980s
EX $48 **NM** $73 **MIP** n/a

❑ **Oliver 77, Super**, 1:16-scale, Slik, green w/green rims, 1950s
EX $233 **NM** $427 **MIP** $956

❑ **Oliver 770**, 1:16-scale, SpecCast, green and white, wide front end, 1990s
EX $14 **NM** $22 **MIP** $38

❑ **Oliver 770**, 1:16-scale, SpecCast, green, '91 Crossroads USA Show Edition, 1991, No. CUST 123
EX $14 **NM** $22 **MIP** $38

❑ **Oliver 770**, 1:16-scale, SpecCast, green, '91 Farm Progress Show Edition, 1991
EX $14 **NM** $22 **MIP** $38

❑ **Oliver 770**, 1:16-scale, SpecCast, green, '91 Paxton-Buckley-Loda Show Edition, 1991
EX $14 **NM** $22 **MIP** $38

❑ **Oliver 770**, 1:16-scale, SpecCast, green, single front wheel, 1991
EX $14 **NM** $22 **MIP** $38

❑ **Oliver 770**, 1:16-scale, SpecCast, green, WF, '93 Oliver Collector News, 1992
EX $14 **NM** $22 **MIP** $38

❑ **Oliver 770**, 1:16-scale, SpecCast, green, '92 Penn State Farm Show, 1992
EX $14 **NM** $22 **MIP** $38

❑ **Oliver 770**, 1:16-scale, SpecCast, green, WF, Quality Farm and Fleet, 1992, No. CUST 182
EX $14 **NM** $22 **MIP** $38

❑ **Oliver 770**, 1:16-scale, SpecCast, green, NF, '93 Crossroads USA Show Edition, 1993, No. CUST 214
EX $14 **NM** $22 **MIP** $38

❑ **Oliver 770**, 1:16-scale, SpecCast, green, WF, '93 Farm Progress Show Edition, 1993, No. CUST 228
EX $14 **NM** $22 **MIP** $38

❑ **Oliver 770**, 1:16-scale, SpecCast, green, 1994, No. SCT-105
EX $14 **NM** $22 **MIP** $38

❏ **Oliver 80**, 1:16-scale, Scale Models, green, NF on steel, #3 in Collector Series I, 1979
EX $22 **NM** $36 **MIP** $48

❏ **Oliver 80**, 1:16-scale, Scale Models, green, Diesel, 1980
EX $22 **NM** $36 **MIP** $48

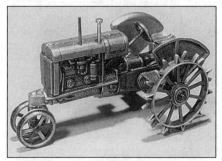

❏ **Oliver 80**, 1:16-scale, Scale Models, antique brass, 1980s
EX $42 **NM** $166 **MIP** $189

❏ **Oliver 80**, 1:16-scale, Scale Models, green, rubber tires, Diesel, 1980s
EX $22 **NM** $33 **MIP** $48

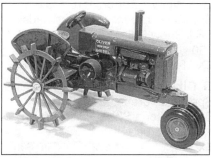

❏ **Oliver 80**, 1:16-scale, Scale Models, green, steel wheels, Diesel, #3 Collector Series II, 1986
EX $22 **NM** $33 **MIP** $48

❏ **Oliver 88**, 1:16-scale, Howell, Row crop, green, did not come in box, 1980s
EX $48 **NM** $73 **MIP** n/a

❏ **Oliver 88**, 1:16-scale, Howell, Row crop, green, did not come in box, 1980s
EX $48 **NM** $73 **MIP** n/a

❏ **Oliver 88**, 1:16-scale, Scale Models, green, NF, 2003, No. FU-0639
EX $22 **NM** $36 **MIP** $48

❏ **Oliver 88**, 1:16-scale, SpecCast, green, '92 National Pullers Assn. Edition, 1992, No. CUST 158
EX $14 **NM** $22 **MIP** $38

❏ **Oliver 88**, 1:16-scale, SpecCast, green, WF, '92 Louisville Farm Show Edition, 1992, No. SCW-029
EX $14 **NM** $22 **MIP** $38

❏ **Oliver 88**, 1:16-scale, SpecCast, green, '92 Turtle River News Edition, 1992
EX $14 **NM** $22 **MIP** $38

❏ **Oliver 88**, 1:16-scale, SpecCast, green, '93 Indy Superpull Edition, 1993
EX $14 **NM** $22 **MIP** $38

❏ **Oliver 88**, 1:16-scale, SpecCast, green, '95 Greensburg Power of the Past Toy Show Edition, 1995, No. CUST 399
EX $14 **NM** $22 **MIP** $38

❏ **Oliver 88**, 1:16-scale, SpecCast, green, single front wheel, '95 LaCrosse Show Edition, 1995, No. CUST 370
EX $14 **NM** $22 **MIP** $38

❏ **Oliver 88 Super**, 1:16-scale, SpecCast, green, diesel, '92 Farm Progress Show Edition, 1992, No. CUST 193
EX $14 **NM** $22 **MIP** $38

❏ **Oliver 88 Super**, 1:16-scale, SpecCast, green, Wheatland, '92 Michigan Show Edition, 1992, No. CUST 159
EX $14 **NM** $22 **MIP** $38

❏ **Oliver 88 Super**, 1:16-scale, SpecCast, green, '93 Louisville Farm Show Edition, 1993, No. SCW-030
EX $14 **NM** $22 **MIP** $38

❏ **Oliver 88 Super**, 1:16-scale, SpecCast, green, 1994, No. AGCO-001
EX $14 **NM** $22 **MIP** $38

❏ **Oliver 88 Super**, 1:16-scale, SpecCast, green, puller, '97 Louisville Farm Show Edition, 1997, No. SCT-157
EX $14 **NM** $22 **MIP** $38

❏ **Oliver 88 Super**, 1:16-scale, SpecCast, green, WF, 2001, No. SCT-195
EX $14 **NM** $22 **MIP** $38

❏ **Oliver 88, Super**, 1:16-scale, Howell, green, did not come in box, diesel
EX $48 **NM** $73 **MIP** n/a

Photos by Jon Jacobson unless otherwise noted.

❑ **Oliver 88, Super**, 1:16-scale, Howell, green, did not come in box, diesel, 1980s
EX $48   **NM** $73   **MIP** n/a

❑ **Oliver 880**, 1:16-scale, Scale Models, green, '91 World Ag Show Edition, 1991
EX $22   **NM** $36   **MIP** $48

❑ **Oliver 880**, 1:16-scale, Scale Models, green, 1991
EX $22   **NM** $36   **MIP** $48

❑ **Oliver 880**, 1:16-scale, Scale Models, green, '91 Mulberry Florida Toy Show, 1991, No. FB-1527
EX $22   **NM** $36   **MIP** $48

❑ **Oliver 880**, 1:16-scale, Slik, green w/white wheel centers, 1950s
EX $78   **NM** $162   **MIP** $383

❑ **Oliver 880**, 1:16-scale, SpecCast, green, WF, 1991, No. SCW-009
EX $14   **NM** $22   **MIP** $38

❑ **Oliver 880**, 1:16-scale, SpecCast, green, Central Tractor Edition, 1991
EX $14   **NM** $22   **MIP** $38

❑ **Oliver 880**, 1:16-scale, SpecCast, green, Wheatland, '91 Michigan Show Edition, 1991
EX $14   **NM** $22   **MIP** $38

❑ **Oliver 880**, 1:16-scale, SpecCast, green, '92 Tractor Classics Edition, 1992
EX $14   **NM** $22   **MIP** $38

❑ **Oliver 880**, 1:16-scale, SpecCast, green, '92 Fort Recovery Tractor Pull, 1992, No. CUST 176
EX $14   **NM** $22   **MIP** $38

❑ **Oliver 880**, 1:16-scale, SpecCast, green, NF, 1998, No. SCT-209
EX $14   **NM** $22   **MIP** $38

❑ **Oliver 90**, 1:16-scale, Scale Models, green, on steel, #19 in Collector Series I, 1991, No. FU-1019 *(Photo by Bossen Implement)*
EX $28   **NM** $48   **MIP** $98

❑ **Oliver 99, Super**, 1:16-scale, NB & K, dark green and yellow, Official 8th Annual Michigan Farm Toy Show, limited to 1128 units, 1988
EX $67   **NM** $96   **MIP** $123

❑ **Oliver Hart-Parr**, 1:16-scale, Gray (Custom), green, steel wheels, 1970s
EX $27   **NM** $42   **MIP** n/a

❑ **Oliver Hart-Parr**, 1:16-scale, Gray (Custom), green, 10th anniversary 1968-1978, did not come in box, 1978
EX $27   **NM** $42   **MIP** n/a

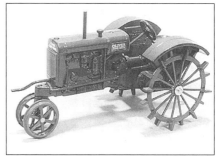

❑ **Oliver Hart-Parr**, 1:16-scale, Scale Models, green, 1990 Farm Progress Show, 1990
EX $22   **NM** $33   **MIP** $48

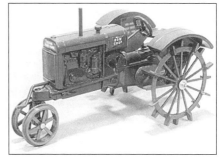

❑ **Oliver Hart-Parr**, 1:16-scale, Scale Models, dark green, Oliver anniversary, 1990s
EX $22   **NM** $33   **MIP** $48

❑ **Oliver Hart-Parr #3**, 1:16-scale, SpecCast, green, Hart-Parr Collector club Edition, 2003, No. CUST 778
EX $93   **NM** $122   **MIP** $178

❑ **Oliver Hart-Parr 28-44**, 1:16-scale, Scale Models, green, '94 Central States Thresherman's Reunion, 1992, No. FB-1598
EX $22   **NM** $36   **MIP** $63

❑ **Oliver Hart-Parr 28-44**, 1:16-scale, Scale Models, green, 1994, No. FU-0154 *(Photo by Bossen Implement)*
EX $22   **NM** $36   **MIP** $63

❑ **Spirit of Oliver**, 1:16-scale, Scale Models, green/chrome rims, 1980s
EX $27   NM $38   MIP $58

❑ **Spirit of Oliver**, 1:16-scale, Scale Models, green, 1980s
EX $27   NM $38   MIP $53

❑ **Spirit of Oliver**, 1:16-scale, Scale Models, green, new cab and top, 1990s
EX $27   NM $38   MIP $53

TRACTORS 1:25-SCALE

❑ **Oliver 1855**, 1:25-scale, Scale Models, green, 1990s, No. FU-0236
EX $3   NM $6   MIP $11

❑ **Oliver 1855**, 1:25-scale, Scale Models, green, '91 Husker Harvest Days Edition, 1991, No. FB-1547
EX $3   NM $6   MIP $11

❑ **Oliver 1855**, 1:25-scale, Scale Models, green, 1991, No. FU-0180
EX $3   NM $6   MIP $11

❑ **Oliver 1855**, 1:25-scale, Scale Models, green, '97 Farm Progress Show Edition, 1997, No. FB-2484
EX $3   NM $6   MIP $11

❑ **Oliver 70**, 1:25-scale, green
EX n/a   NM n/a   MIP n/a

❑ **Oliver 70**, 1:25-scale, Arcade, red and green, 1941, No. 3560
EX $48   NM $113   MIP $424

❑ **Oliver 70**, 1:25-scale, Arcor, green, 1940s
EX $12   NM $33   MIP $98

❑ **Oliver 70**, 1:25-scale, Arcor, green, 1940s
EX $12   NM $33   MIP $98

❑ **Oliver 70**, 1:25-scale, Auburn Rubber, green (rare), or red, 6-1/2" long, 1950s
EX $12   NM $33   MIP $98

❑ **Oliver 70**, 1:25-scale, Hubley, various colors, Orchard, 1930s
EX $78   NM $142   MIP $453

❑ **Oliver Style**, 1:25-scale, green

TRACTORS 1:32-SCALE

❑ **Oliver 2655**, 1:32-scale, Ertl, 4WD, duals, cab, 3-point hitch, '05 National Farm Toy Show, 2005, No. 16138A *(Photo by Ertl)*
EX $17   NM $28   MIP $53

❑ **Oliver 2655**, 1:32-scale, Ertl, 4WD, singles, cab, 2006, No. 13803

(Photo by Bossen Implement)

EX $16   **NM** $26   **MIP** $32

❑ **Oliver 70**, 1:32-scale, Scale Models, green, steel wheels, 1980s

EX $3   **NM** $4   **MIP** $8

❑ **Oliver 70**, 1:32-scale, Scale Models, green, rubber tires, 1980s

EX $3   **NM** $4   **MIP** $8

❑ **Oliver 70**, 1:32-scale, Scale Models, green, Iowa Sesquicentennial Edition, 1996, No. FB-1582

EX $3   **NM** $4   **MIP** $8

❑ **Oliver 80**, 1:32-scale, Scale Models, green, 1980s

EX $2   **NM** $3   **MIP** $6

❑ **Oliver 80**, 1:32-scale, Scale Models, green, 1980s

EX $2   **NM** $3   **MIP** $6

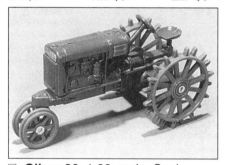

❑ **Oliver 80**, 1:32-scale, Scale Models, green, 1980s

EX $2   **NM** $3   **MIP** $6

❑ **Oliver 880**, 1:32-scale, Slik, green, 1960s

EX $72   **NM** $172   **MIP** $372

TRACTORS 1:43-SCALE

❑ **Oliver 60**, 1:43-scale, SpecCast, green, 1980s

EX $6   **NM** $8   **MIP** $12

❑ **Oliver 60**, 1:43-scale, SpecCast, 1990s

EX $6   **NM** $8   **MIP** $12

❑ **Oliver 70**, 1:43-scale, SpecCast, steel wheels, 1990s

EX $6   **NM** $8   **MIP** $12

❑ **Oliver 70**, 1:43-scale, SpecCast, green, 1990s

EX $6   **NM** $8   **MIP** $12

TRACTORS 1:64-SCALE

❑ **Oliver 1355**, 1:64-scale, Gentle Ben (Custom), green and white, 1980s

EX $4   **NM** $5   **MIP** n/a

❑ **Oliver 1555**, 1:64-scale, Ertl, green, NF, 1999, No. 2278

EX $4   **NM** $5   **MIP** $6

❑ **Oliver 1600**, 1:64-scale, Walters (Custom), green and white, did not come in box, 1980s
EX $4 **NM** $16 **MIP** n/a

❑ **Oliver 1650**, 1:64-scale, Walters (Custom), green and white, did not come in box, 1980s
EX $4 **NM** $16 **MIP** n/a

❑ **Oliver 1800**, 1:64-scale, Walters (Custom), green and white, did not come in box, 1980s
EX $4 **NM** $16 **MIP** n/a

❑ **Oliver 1600**, 1:64-scale, Walters (Custom), green and white, did not come in box, 1980s
EX $4 **NM** $16 **MIP** n/a

❑ **Oliver 1650**, 1:64-scale, Walters (Custom), green and white, did not come in box, 1980s
EX $4 **NM** $16 **MIP** n/a

❑ **Oliver 1800**, 1:64-scale, Walters (Custom), green and white, did not come in box, 1980s
EX $4 **NM** $16 **MIP** n/a

❑ **Oliver 1650**, 1:64-scale, Gentle Ben (Custom), green and white, did not come in box, 1980s
EX $4 **NM** $16 **MIP** n/a

❑ **Oliver 1755**, 1:64-scale, Scale Models, green and white, 1980s
EX $4 **NM** $4 **MIP** $6

❑ **Oliver 1800**, 1:64-scale, Walters (Custom), green and white, did not come in box, 1980s
EX $4 **NM** $16 **MIP** n/a

❑ **Oliver 1650**, 1:64-scale, Gentle Ben (Custom), green and white, did not come in box, 1980s
EX $4 **NM** $16 **MIP** n/a

❑ **Oliver 1800**, 1:64-scale, Gentle Ben (Custom), green and white, did not come in box, 1980s
EX $4 **NM** $16 **MIP** n/a

❑ **Oliver 1800 TT**, 1:64-scale, Gentle Ben (Custom), green and white, did not come in box, 1980s
EX $4 **NM** $16 **MIP** n/a

❑ **Oliver 1850**, 1:64-scale, Berg (Custom), LP, green and white, did not come in box, 1980s
EX $4   **NM** $16   **MIP** n/a

❑ **Oliver 1850**, 1:64-scale, Berg (Custom), green and white, did not come in box, 1980s
EX $4   **NM** $16   **MIP** n/a

❑ **Oliver 1850**, 1:64-scale, Berg (Custom), green and white, 1980s
EX $4   **NM** $16   **MIP** n/a

❑ **Oliver 1850**, 1:64-scale, Berg (Custom), green and white, w/gray rims, did not come in box, 1980s
EX $4   **NM** $16   **MIP** n/a

❑ **Oliver 1850**, 1:64-scale, Gentle Ben (Custom), green and white, did not come in box, 1980s
EX $4   **NM** $16   **MIP** n/a

❑ **Oliver 1850**, 1:64-scale, Gentle Ben (Custom), green and white, did not come in box, 1980s
EX $4   **NM** $16   **MIP** n/a

❑ **Oliver 1850**, 1:64-scale, Walters (Custom), green and white, did not come in box, 1980s
EX $4   **NM** $16   **MIP** n/a

❑ **Oliver 1850**, 1:64-scale, Walters (Custom), green and white, did not come in box, 1980s
EX $4   **NM** $16   **MIP** n/a

❑ **Oliver 1850**, 1:64-scale, Walters (Custom), green and white, did not come in box, 1980s
EX $4   **NM** $16   **MIP** n/a

❑ **Oliver 1855**, 1:64-scale, Ertl, green, '94 National Farm Toy Museum Edition, 1994, No. 1243MA
EX $4   **NM** $5   **MIP** $6

❑ **Oliver 1855**, 1:64-scale, Scale Models, same as FU-1113, No. FU-0548 *(Photo by Scale Models)*
EX $2   **NM** $3   **MIP** $4

❑ **Oliver 1855**, 1:64-scale, Scale Models, green and white
EX $3   **NM** $4   **MIP** $6

❑ **Oliver 1855**, 1:64-scale, Scale Models, green and white, 1987 Dyersville Show Tractor, 1987
EX $3   **NM** $4   **MIP** $6

❑ **Oliver 1855**, 1:64-scale, Scale Models, green and white, 1988 World Ag-Expo, 1988
EX $3   **NM** $4   **MIP** $6

❑ **Oliver 1855**, 1:64-scale, Walters (Custom), green and white, did not come in box
EX $4   **NM** $16   **MIP** n/a

❑ **Oliver 1855**, 1:64-scale, Walters (Custom), green and white, did not come in box
EX $4   **NM** $16   **MIP** n/a

❑ **Oliver 1855**, 1:64-scale, Walters (Custom), green and white, did not come in box
EX $4   **NM** $16   **MIP** n/a

❑ **Oliver 1950T**, 1:64-scale, Ertl, green, MFD, '02 National Farm Toy Show Edition, 2002, No. 16095A
EX $6   **NM** $12   **MIP** $27

❑ **Oliver 1950T**, 1:64-scale, Ertl, green, MFD, 2003, No. 13386
EX $4   **NM** $5   **MIP** $6

❑ **Oliver 1955**, 1:64-scale, Scale Models, green and white
EX $3   **NM** $4   **MIP** $6

❑ **Oliver 1955**, 1:64-scale, Scale Models, green and white, 1988 Louisville, 1988
EX $3   **NM** $4   **MIP** $6

❑ **Oliver 2455**, 1:64-scale, Berg (Custom), green and white
EX $13   **NM** $26   **MIP** n/a

❑ **Oliver 2455**, 1:64-scale, Gentle Ben (Custom), LP, green and white, did not come in box
EX $13   **NM** $26   **MIP** n/a

❑ **Oliver 2455**, 1:64-scale, Gentle Ben (Custom), green and white, did not come in box
EX $13   **NM** $26   **MIP** n/a

❑ **Oliver 2455**, 1:64-scale, Scale Models, green, 4WD, '02 Louisville Farm Show Edition, 2002, No. FB-2608
EX $4   **NM** $6   **MIP** $13

❑ **Oliver 2455**, 1:64-scale, Scale Models, green, 4WD, 2002, No. FU-0634
EX $4   **NM** $6   **MIP** $13

❑ **Oliver 2455**, 1:64-scale, Scale Models, green, 4WD, w/cab, '03 Louisville Farm Show Edition, 2003, No. FB-2629
EX $4   **NM** $6   **MIP** $13

❑ **Oliver 2455**, 1:64-scale, Scale Models, green, 4WD, w/cab, 2003, No. FU-0636
EX $4   **NM** $6   **MIP** $13

❑ **Oliver 70**, 1:64-scale, Scale Models, green and red, C.L.A.T.S. "1988"
EX $3   **NM** $4   **MIP** $6

❑ **Oliver 70**, 1:64-scale, Scale Models, green and red
EX $3   **NM** $4   **MIP** $6

Photos by Jon Jacobson unless otherwise noted.

❑ **Oliver 70**, 1:64-scale, Scale Models, green and red
EX $3 **NM** $4 **MIP** $6

❑ **Oliver 70**, 1:64-scale, Scale Models, five different chrome-colors, sold as a Christmas ornament
EX $3 **NM** $4 **MIP** $6

❑ **Oliver 70**, 1:64-scale, Scale Models, green and red
EX $3 **NM** $4 **MIP** $6

❑ **Oliver 70**, 1:64-scale, Scale Models, green and red, 1985
EX $3 **NM** $4 **MIP** $6

❑ **Oliver 77**, 1:64-scale, Baker (Custom), green and red, did not come in box, 1980s
EX $6 **NM** $22 **MIP** n/a

❑ **Oliver 77**, 1:64-scale, Baker (Custom), green and red, did not come in box, 1980s
EX $6 **NM** $22 **MIP** n/a

❑ **Oliver 77**, 1:64-scale, SpecCast, green, NF, 1993, No. 95002
EX $4 **NM** $6 **MIP** $9

❑ **Oliver 77**, 1:64-scale, SpecCast, green, WF, 1994, No. 95006
EX $4 **NM** $6 **MIP** $9

❑ **Oliver 77**, 1:64-scale, Walters (Custom), green and red and yellow, did not come in box, 1980s
EX $6 **NM** $22 **MIP** n/a

❑ **Oliver 770**, 1:64-scale, Gentle Ben (Custom), green and white, did not come in box
EX $6 **NM** $22 **MIP** n/a

❑ **Oliver 770**, 1:64-scale, Gentle Ben (Custom), green and white, did not come in box
EX $6 **NM** $22 **MIP** n/a

❑ **Oliver 770**, 1:64-scale, Scale Models, green and white
EX $4 **NM** $6 **MIP** $9

❑ **Oliver 770**, 1:64-scale, Scale Models, green and white
EX $4 **NM** $6 **MIP** $9

❑ **Oliver 770**, 1:64-scale, Scale Models, green and white
EX $4 **NM** $6 **MIP** $9

❏ **Oliver 770**, 1:64-scale, Scale Models, green and white
EX $4   **NM** $6   **MIP** $9

❏ **Oliver 770**, 1:64-scale, SpecCast, green and white
EX $4   **NM** $6   **MIP** $12

❏ **Oliver 770**, 1:64-scale, SpecCast, green and white
EX $4   **NM** $6   **MIP** $12

❏ **Oliver 80**, 1:64-scale, Scale Models, five different chrome colors, sold as a Christmas ornament
EX $2   **NM** $3   **MIP** $4

❏ **Oliver 80**, 1:64-scale, Scale Models, green and red
EX $3   **NM** $4   **MIP** $6

❏ **Oliver 80**, 1:64-scale, Scale Models, green and red
EX $3   **NM** $4   **MIP** $6

❏ **Oliver 88**, 1:64-scale, SpecCast, green, WF, 1993, No. 95003
EX $4   **NM** $6   **MIP** $9

❏ **Oliver 88**, 1:64-scale, SpecCast, green, NF, 1994, No. 95007
EX $4   **NM** $6   **MIP** $9

❏ **Oliver 880**, 1:64-scale, Gentle Ben (Custom), green and white, did not come in box
EX $6   **NM** $22   **MIP** n/a

❏ **Oliver 880**, 1:64-scale, Gentle Ben (Custom), green and white, did not come in box
EX $6   **NM** $22   **MIP** n/a

❏ **Oliver 880**, 1:64-scale, Gentle Ben (Custom), green and white, did not come in box
EX $6   **NM** $22   **MIP** n/a

❏ **Oliver 880**, 1:64-scale, Scale Models, green and white
EX $4   **NM** $6   **MIP** $8

❏ **Oliver 880**, 1:64-scale, Scale Models, green and white
EX $4   **NM** $6   **MIP** $8

❏ **Oliver 880**, 1:64-scale, Scale Models, green and white
EX $4   **NM** $6   **MIP** $8

❑ **Oliver 880**, 1:64-scale, Scale Models, green and white
EX $4   **NM** $6   **MIP** $8

❑ **Oliver 880**, 1:64-scale, SpecCast, green and white
EX $4   **NM** $6   **MIP** $12

❑ **Oliver 880**, 1:64-scale, SpecCast, green and white
EX $4   **NM** $6   **MIP** $12

❑ **Oliver 880 Twin**, 1:64-scale, Lozmack and Hoag (Custom), industrial yellow and white, did not come in box
EX $9   **NM** $23   **MIP** n/a

❑ **Oliver 99**, 1:64-scale, Keith (Custom), green and red and yellow, did not come in box
EX $6   **NM** $22   **MIP** n/a

❑ **Oliver 99, Super**, 1:64-scale, Keith/Gentle-Ben (Custom), green and yellow, 1988 South Bend Show Tractor, 1988
EX $6   **NM** $22   **MIP** n/a

❑ **Oliver Hart-Parr**, 1:64-scale, Ertl, green, 1999, No. 13012
EX $4   **NM** $6   **MIP** $8

❑ **Oliver Hart-Parr**, 1:64-scale, Scale Models, green, '90 Farm Progress Show Edition, 1990
EX $4   **NM** $6   **MIP** $8

❑ **Oliver Hart-Parr**, 1:64-scale, Scale Models, green, 1991, No. FU-0469
EX $4   **NM** $6   **MIP** $8

❑ **Oliver Set**, 1:64-scale, Ertl, green, Oliver 1655 and Hart Parr, 2002, No. 13083
EX n/a   **NM** n/a   **MIP** $11

❑ **Spirit of Oliver**, 1:64-scale, Scale Models, green and white, W. Brooklyn IL. 1988, 1st Edition
EX $4   **NM** $5   **MIP** $9

❑ **Spirit of Oliver**, 1:64-scale, Scale Models, green and white, Moultrie, GA 1988, 1st Edition, 1988
EX $4   **NM** $5   **MIP** $9

TRUCKS 1:25-SCALE

❑ **Oliver Dain Antique Truck**, 1:25-scale, Scale Models, green, 1990s
EX $6   **NM** $11   **MIP** $18

OMC

CONSTRUCTION EQUIPMENT 1:16-SCALE

❑ **OMC Skid Loader**, 1:16-scale, Ertl, Mustang, 1980s, No. 355
EX $18   **NM** $38   **MIP** $58

PARKER

IMPLEMENTS 1:16-SCALE

❑ **Parker Gravity Wagon**, 1:16-scale, Ertl, Parker Green, 1990s, No. 2214DA
EX $16   **NM** $27   **MIP** $43

IMPLEMENTS 1:64-SCALE

❏ **Parker Gravity Wagon**, 1:64-scale, Ertl, Parker Green
EX $9   **NM** $16   **MIP** $24

❏ **Parker Gravity Wagon**, 1:64-scale, Ertl, Parker Green
EX $9   **NM** $16   **MIP** $24

PIERCE

TRUCKS 1:64-SCALE

❏ **Pierce 55 Aerial Ladder Fire Truck**, 1:64-scale, Ertl, red and white, No. 2401
EX $5   **NM** $8   **MIP** $12

❏ **Pierce Pumper Fire Truck**, 1:64-scale, Ertl, all red, No. 2403
EX $5   **NM** $8   **MIP** $12

❏ **Pierce Pumper Fire Truck**, 1:64-scale, Ertl, white cab w/red body, No. 2403
EX $6   **NM** $9   **MIP** $13

❏ **Pierce Tanker Fire Truck**, 1:64-scale, Ertl, all red, No. 2402
EX $8   **NM** $13   **MIP** $17

❏ **Pierce Tanker Fire Truck**, 1:64-scale, Ertl, white cab w/red body, No. 2402
EX $7   **NM** $12   **MIP** $15

PLAY SETS

FARM COUNTRY 1:32-SCALE

❏ **John Deere Value Playset**, 1:32-scale, Ertl, tractor, plow, fencing, animals, 2003, No. 15474
EX n/a   **NM** n/a   **MIP** $23

FARM COUNTRY 1:64-SCALE

❏ **Accessory Set**, 1:64-scale, Ertl, 4-piece grain bin w/30 animals, 1990
EX n/a   **NM** n/a   **MIP** $10

❏ **Accessory Set**, 1:64-scale, Ertl, silo, grain bin, propane tank, bunk, 1991, No. 4305
EX n/a   **NM** n/a   **MIP** $15

❏ **AGCO Value Playset**, 1:64-scale, Ertl, 40 pieces, Allis-Chalmers DT180 tractor, pickup truck, shed, animals, fencing, disc, 2003, No. 13405
EX n/a   **NM** n/a   **MIP** $35

❏ **Barn & Silo Set**, 1:64-scale, Ertl, 117 pieces, barn door reads "Blueberry Hill Farm," animals, fencing, 1995
EX n/a   **NM** n/a   **MIP** $22

❏ **Big Farm Barn Playset**, 1:64-scale, Ertl, 40 pieces, 1993, No. 4316
EX n/a   **NM** n/a   **MIP** $22

❏ **Big Farm Farm House Playset**, 1:64-scale, Ertl, 56 pieces, 1995, No. 4417
EX n/a   **NM** n/a   **MIP** $25

❏ **Case-IH Value Playset**, 1:64-scale, Ertl, 2 tractors, pickup w/horse trailer, animals, fencing, shed, 2005, No. 14470
EX n/a   **NM** n/a   **MIP** $20

❏ **Cattle Shed Set**, 1:64-scale, Ertl, 64 pieces, 1991, No. 4238
EX n/a   **NM** n/a   **MIP** $20

❏ **County Fair Set**, 1:64-scale, Ertl, 1996
EX n/a   **NM** n/a   **MIP** $20

❏ **Dairy Barn Playset**, 1:64-scale, Ertl, barn, fencing, animals, 2002, No. 12279
EX n/a   **NM** n/a   **MIP** $28

❏ **Deluxe Farm Set**, 1:64-scale, Ertl, 169 pieces, house and out buildings, 1990
EX n/a   **NM** n/a   **MIP** $45

❏ **Farm Dealership Set**, 1:64-scale, Ertl, 34 pieces, No. 4231
EX n/a   **NM** n/a   **MIP** $30

❏ **Farm House Set**, 1:64-scale, Ertl, 40 pieces, 2-story house w/green roof, fence, furniture, 1991
EX n/a   **NM** n/a   **MIP** $22

❏ **Freight Train Set**, 1:64-scale, Ertl, 42 pieces, battery powered, 1990
EX n/a   **NM** n/a   **MIP** $35

❏ **Gable Barn Set**, 1:64-scale, Ertl, 65 pieces, gable barn, fencing, animals, 2002, No. 12277
EX n/a   **NM** n/a   **MIP** $30

❏ **Garage Set**, 1:64-scale, Ertl, 40 pieces, red garage w/overhead door, fencing, ladder, ducks, pickup truck, flagpole, dog, 1990
EX n/a   **NM** n/a   **MIP** $40

❏ **Hog Confinement Set**, 1:64-scale, Ertl, 2 hog buildings, fencing, hogs, 2002, No. 12291
EX n/a   **NM** n/a   **MIP** $20

❏ **Hog Lot Set**, 1:64-scale, Ertl, 86 pieces, 3-door white barn w/red roof
EX n/a   **NM** n/a   **MIP** $17

❏ **Horse Stable Playset**, 1:64-scale, Ertl, 45 pieces, stable, fences, horses, 2002, No. 12290
EX n/a   **NM** n/a   **MIP** $20

❏ **Longhorn Ranch Set**, 1:64-scale, Ertl, 121 pieces, log home, 1999
EX n/a   **NM** n/a   **MIP** $35

❏ **Machine Shed and Garage Set**, 1:64-scale, Ertl, 1998
EX n/a   **NM** n/a   **MIP** $20

❏ **Ranch Action Rodeo Set**, 1:64-scale, Ertl, 57 pieces, 1994
EX n/a   **NM** n/a   **MIP** $30

❏ **Sale Barn Set, Country Kids**, 1:64-scale, Ertl, 100 pieces, auction building, animals, fences, furniture
EX n/a   **NM** n/a   **MIP** $75

❏ **Single Story House Set**, 1:64-scale, Ertl, house, porch, swingset, people, 2002
EX n/a   **NM** n/a   **MIP** $18

❏ **Vintage Building Set**, 1:64-scale, Ertl, 42 pieces, corn crib, granary, chicken coop, 5 ducks, 10 chickens & roosters, 3 farmers, 1 dog, 1993
EX n/a   **NM** n/a   **MIP** $22

❏ **Western Barn Set**, 1:64-scale, Ertl, red barn, windmill, fencing, animals, 2002
EX n/a   **NM** n/a   **MIP** $28

MARX PLAY SETS

❏ **Farm Set**, Marx, No. 6050
EX $50   **NM** $180   **MIP** $275

❏ **Farm Set**, Marx, No. 6006
EX $50   **NM** $195   **MIP** $300

❏ **Farm Set**, Marx, Series 2000, 100 pieces, 1958, No. 3948
EX $80   **NM** $250   **MIP** $400

❏ **Farm Set**, Marx, 20" steel barn, 14 farm animals, 5 sections of fence, 4 rows of crops, plastic tractor w/7 attachments, farm tools, feed boxes, 1965, 1968-73, No. 5942
EX $55   **NM** $165   **MIP** $290

❏ **Farm Set**, Marx, Deluxe, 1969, No. 3953
EX $75   **NM** $225   **MIP** $375

❏ **Happi-Time Farm Set**, Marx, Sears, No. 3480
EX $35   **NM** $95   **MIP** $150

❏ **Happi-Time Farm Set**, Marx, Sears, barn, silo, no figures, 60mm animals and implements, 1953, No. 3940
EX $65   **NM** $150   **MIP** $275

❏ **Happi-Time Farm Set**, Marx, Sears, Series 2000, 100 pieces, w/chicken shed, 1958, No. 3943
EX $65   **NM** $150   **MIP** $260

❏ **Happi-Time Farm Set**, Marx, Deluxe set, Sears, Series 2000, tin litho barn and silo, 1958, No. 3949
EX $50   **NM** $150   **MIP** $250

❏ **Happi-Time Farm Set**, Marx, Sears, Deluxe platform farm, barn and 2 silos on raised platform, 2-wheel cart pictured on box never included, 1959-60, No. 5931
EX $100   **NM** $225   **MIP** $375

❏ **Lazy Day Farm Set**, Marx, Montgomery Wards, 60mm people and animals, no silo, barn, 1951, No. 3931
EX $60   **NM** $150   **MIP** $250

❏ **Lazy Day Farm Set**, Marx, Montgomery Wards, Series 1000, no silo, 54mm people and animals, 1958, No. 3942
EX $50   **NM** $150   **MIP** $250

❏ **Lazy Day Farm Set**, Marx, Montgomery Wards, 100 pieces, 1960, No. 3945
EX $60   **NM** $165   **MIP** $275

❏ **Modern Farm Set**, Marx, 54mm, plastic and tin, 1951, No. 3931
EX $50   **NM** $150   **MIP** $250

❏ **Modern Farm Set**, Marx, 1967, No. 3932
EX $65   **NM** $185   **MIP** $310

❏ **Modern Farm Set**, Marx, metal barn, fence, tractor, animals, c.1951, No. 3925
EX $50   **NM** $150   **MIP** $250

POCLAIN

CONSTRUCTION EQUIPMENT 1:50-SCALE

❏ **Poclain 1000 Front Loader, 1000**, 1:50-scale, Sijam, red and gray, 1970s
EX $53   **NM** $74   **MIP** $97

❏ **Poclain 1000 Front Loader, 1000**, 1:50-scale, Sijam, red and gray, 1970s
EX $53   **NM** $74   **MIP** $97

❏ **Poclain Clam Shell Bucket, 90**, 1:50-scale, Gescha, red and gray, 1970s
EX $38   **NM** $48   **MIP** $72

❏ **Poclain Clam Shell Bucket, 90**, 1:50-scale, Gescha, red and gray, 1970s
EX $38   **NM** $48   **MIP** $72

❏ **Poclain Clam Shell Bucket, 90 B**, 1:50-scale, Conrad, red and gray die-cast, 1980s
EX $34   **NM** $42   **MIP** $72

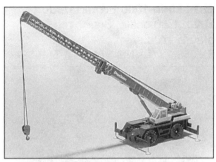

❏ **Poclain Crane**, 1:50-scale, Sijam, red and gray, 1970s
EX $78   **NM** $104   **MIP** $142

❏ **Poclain Excavator, 1000**, 1:50-scale, Sijam, red and gray, 1970s
EX $53   **NM** $74   **MIP** $97

❏ **Poclain Excavator, 1000**, 1:50-scale, Sijam, red and gray, 1980s
EX $53   **NM** $74   **MIP** $97

❏ **Poclain Excavator, 160**, 1:50-scale, Conrad, red and gray, 1980s
EX $52   **NM** $87   **MIP** $129

❏ **Poclain Excavator, 350**, 1:50-scale, Conrad, red and gray (also in brown), 1980s
EX $98   **NM** $143   **MIP** $197

❏ **Poclain Excavator, 60**, 1:50-scale, Gescha, Barriquand, yellow and blue, 1970s
EX $172   **NM** $289   **MIP** $394

❏ **Poclain Excavator, 90**, 1:50-scale, Gescha, red and gray, 1970s
EX $44   **NM** $69   **MIP** $114

❏ **Poclain Excavator, 90 B**, 1:50-scale, Conrad, red and gray, 1980s
EX $42   **NM** $68   **MIP** $98

❏ **Poclain Excavator, GC 120**, 1:50-scale, Bourbon, red and white, old style cab, 1960s
EX $98   **NM** $139   **MIP** $197

❏ **Poclain Excavator, GC 120**, 1:50-scale, Bourbon, red and white, 1960s
EX $98   **NM** $139   **MIP** $197

❏ **Poclain Excavator, GC 120**, 1:50-scale, Bourbon, red and white or off-white, 1960s
EX $98   **NM** $139   **MIP** $197

❏ **Poclain Excavator, HC 300**, 1:50-scale, Bourbon, red and white, 1960s
EX $183   **NM** $264   **MIP** $298

❏ **Poclain Excavator, HC 300**, 1:50-scale, Bourbon, red and white or off white, chrome cyliner rams, 1960s
EX $183 **NM** $264 **MIP** $298

❏ **Poclain Excavator, LC 80**, 1:50-scale, Bourbon, red and white, chrome cylinder rams, 1960s
EX $137 **NM** $174 **MIP** $234

❏ **Poclain Excavator, LC 80**, 1:50-scale, Bourbon, red and white, white cylinder rams, 1960s
EX $98 **NM** $139 **MIP** $197

❏ **Poclain Excavator, SC 150**, 1:50-scale, Gescha, red and gray, 1970s
EX $86 **NM** $124 **MIP** $166

❏ **Poclain Excavator, TC 45**, 1:50-scale, Bourbon, red and white, 1960s
EX $137 **NM** $174 **MIP** $234

❏ **Poclain Excavator, TC 45**, 1:50-scale, Bourbon, red and white, 1960s
EX $137 **NM** $174 **MIP** $234

❏ **Poclain Excavator, TC 45**, 1:50-scale, Bourbon, red and white, 1960s
EX $137 **NM** $174 **MIP** $134

❏ **Poclain Excavator, TC B**, 1:50-scale, Bourbon, red and white or off white, 1960s
EX $137 **NM** $174 **MIP** $234

❏ **Poclain Excavator, TC S**, 1:50-scale, Bourbon, red and white or off white, 1960s
EX $137 **NM** $174 **MIP** $234

❏ **Poclain Excavator, TY S**, 1:50-scale, Bourbon, red and white, 1960s
EX $137 **NM** $174 **MIP** $234

❏ **Poclain Front Loader, GC 120**, 1:50-scale, Bourbon, red and white, large cab, 1960s
EX $137 **NM** $174 **MIP** $234

❏ **Poclain Front Loader, HC 300**, 1:50-scale, Bourbon, red and white, 1960s
EX $223 **NM** $248 **MIP** $298

❑ **Poclain Front Shovel**, 1:50-scale, Bourbon, red and gray, 1960s
EX $76   **NM** $97   **MIP** $138

❑ **Poclain Wheel Excavator**, 1:50-scale, Bourbon, red and white, 1960s
EX $137   **NM** $174   **MIP** $234

❑ **Poclain Wheel Excavator, LY2P**, 1:50-scale, Bourbon, red and white, chrome cylinder rams, 1960s
EX $137   **NM** $174   **MIP** $234

❑ **Poclain Front Shovel, GC 120**, 1:50-scale, Bourbon, red and white, 1960s
EX $137   **NM** $174   **MIP** $234

❑ **Poclain Wheel Excavator, 90**, 1:50-scale, Gescha, red and gray, 1970s
EX $38   **NM** $54   **MIP** $87

❑ **Poclain Wheel Excavator, LY2P**, 1:50-scale, Bourbon, red and white, 1960s
EX $137   **NM** $174   **MIP** $234

❑ **Poclain Front Shovel, GC 120**, 1:50-scale, Bourbon, red and white, small cab, 1960s
EX $137   **NM** $174   **MIP** $234

❑ **Poclain Wheel Excavator, GY 120**, 1:50-scale, Bourbon, red and white, 1960s
EX $137   **NM** $174   **MIP** $234

❑ **Poclain Wheel Excavator, TX**, 1:50-scale, Bourbon, red and white, 1960s
EX $137   **NM** $174   **MIP** $234

❑ **Poclain Wheel Excavator**, 1:50-scale, Bourbon, red and white, 1960s
EX $137   **NM** $174   **MIP** $234

❑ **Poclain Wheel Excavator, LY2P**, 1:50-scale, Bourbon, Detail photo: red & white plastic; this view could be found on either of the two excavators, 1960s

❑ **Poclain Wheel Excavator, TY 45**, 1:50-scale, Bourbon, red and white, 1960s
EX $137   **NM** $174   **MIP** $234

Photos by Jon Jacobson unless otherwise noted.

❑ **PPM Crane**, 1:50-scale, Sijam, red and gray, 1970s
EX $78   **NM** $104   **MIP** $142

CONSTRUCTION EQUIPMENT 1:56-SCALE

❑ **Poclain Wheel Excavator, 90**, 1:56-scale, Majorette, red and gray, 1980s
EX $8   **NM** $16   **MIP** $22

CONSTRUCTION EQUIPMENT 1:90-SCALE

❑ **Poclain TY 45 Wheel Excavator**, 1:90-scale, Tomica, red and white, 1970s
EX $38   **NM** $46   **MIP** $52

❑ **Poclain TY 45 Wheel Excavator**, 1:90-scale, Tomica, red and white, 1970s
EX $38   **NM** $46   **MIP** $52

CONSTRUCTION EQUIPMENT

❑ **Poclain Wheel Excavator**, red, hand made
EX npf   **NM** npf   **MIP** npf

MISCELLANEOUS 1:35-SCALE

❑ **Poclain Long Mount Clam Ice Tongs**, 1:35-scale, Bourbon, red, 1960s
EX $98   **NM** $137   **MIP** $196

MISCELLANEOUS

❑ **Poclain Clam Shell Bucket, TY 45**, red, battery operated, 1960s
EX $137   **NM** $174   **MIP** $234

REX

TRUCKS 1:64-SCALE

❑ **Rex Cement Mixer**, 1:64-scale, Ertl, red and cream, plastic drum, rivet in frame behind cab, No. 370
EX $71   **NM** $92   **MIP** $110

❑ **Rex Cement Mixer**, 1:64-scale, Ertl, red and cream, plastic drum, No. 370
EX $49   **NM** $74   **MIP** $88

❑ **Rex Cement Mixer**, 1:64-scale, Ertl, blue and silver, plastic drum, No. 370
EX $48   **NM** $72   **MIP** $89

❑ **Rex Cement Mixer Mid-1960s Wheel**, 1:64-scale, Ertl, close-up, only found on Rex mixer

RUMELY

IMPLEMENTS 1:43-SCALE

❑ **Rumely Oil Pull Water Wagon**, 1:43-scale, SpecCast, 1990s
EX $6   **NM** $8   **MIP** $12

TRACTORS 1:16-SCALE

❑ **Rumely Oil Pull**, 1:16-scale, Scale Models, black, 1990s
EX $67   **NM** $122   **MIP** $183

TRACTORS 1:43-SCALE

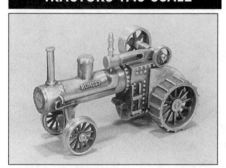

❑ **Rumely Oil Pull**, 1:43-scale, SpecCast, 1990s
EX $6   **NM** $8   **MIP** $12

TRACTORS 1:64-SCALE

❑ **Rumely Oil Pull**, 1:64-scale, Scale Models, green, '91 Farm Progress Show Edition, 1991, No. FB-1536
EX $4   **NM** $6   **MIP** $8

❑ **Rumely Oil Pull**, 1:64-scale, Scale Models, green, 1991, No. FF-0135
EX $4   **NM** $6   **MIP** $8

❑ **Rumely Oil Pull**, 1:64-scale, Scale Models, green, '96 Farm Progress Show Edition, 1996, No. FB-2441
EX $4   **NM** $6   **MIP** $8

SHEPARD

TRACTORS 1:16-SCALE

❑ **Shepard**, 1:16-scale, Scale Models
EX $27   **NM** $52   **MIP** $82

❑ **Shepard SD-3**, 1:16-scale, Nolt, '93 Pennsylvania State Farm Show, 1993
EX $33   **NM** $54   **MIP** $96

❑ **Shepard SD-3**, 1:16-scale, Nolt, '98 Farm Science Review, 1998
EX $33   **NM** $54   **MIP** $96

❑ **Shepard SD-3**, 1:16-scale, Scale Models, NF, 1995
EX $27   **NM** $52   **MIP** $82

❑ **Shepard SD-4**, 1:16-scale, Scale Models, 60th Annniversary of Shepard Mfg. Co., 1996
EX $27   **NM** $52   **MIP** $82

SILVER KING

TRACTORS 1:16-SCALE

❑ **Silver King**, 1:16-scale, Rock Ridge Casting, WF, 1980s
EX $68   **NM** $93   **MIP** $112

❑ **Silver King**, 1:16-scale, Siegel (Custom), silver, 1980s
EX $93   **NM** $178   **MIP** n/a

❑ **Silver King 41**, 1:16-scale, SpecCast, NF, Continental engine, 2006, No. CUST893

Photo by Bossen Implement)
EX $63   **NM** $82   **MIP** $133

❑ **Silver King 42**, 1:16-scale, SpecCast, single front wheel, 2005, No. CUST854 *(Photo by SpecCast)*
EX $63   **NM** $82   **MIP** $113

SIMPLICITY

LAWN AND GARDEN 1:16-SCALE

❑ **Simplicity GT**, 1:16-scale, Scale Models, w/mower deck, legacy 20 H, 1997, No. 542 *(Photo by Scale Models)*
EX $8   **NM** $12   **MIP** $18

STEIGER

CONSTRUCTION EQUIPMENT 1:32-SCALE

❑ **Steiger Panther III**, 1:32-scale, Ertl, industrial yellow, 1982, No. 1939
EX $32   **NM** $57   **MIP** $78

❑ **Steiger Panther III**, 1:32-scale, Ertl, industrial yellow, Toy Farmer Series, 1983, No. 3091
EX $16   **NM** $52   **MIP** $78

❑ **Steiger Wildcat II**, 1:32-scale, Ertl, yellow, 4WD, Toy Farmer Series, 2004, No. 14329A
EX $17   **NM** $27   **MIP** $33

CONSTRUCTION EQUIPMENT 1:64-SCALE

❏ **Steiger Industrial**, 1:64-scale, Ertl, industrial yellow and black, 1980, No. 1980
EX $28   **NM** $48   **MIP** $73

IMPLEMENTS 1:64-SCALE

❏ **Steiger Disc**, 1:64-scale, Matsen (Custom), green and black, did not come in box, 1980
EX $12   **NM** $27   **MIP** n/a

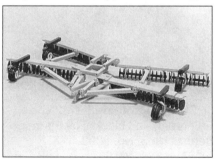

❏ **Steiger Disc**, 1:64-scale, Matsen (Custom), green and black, did not come in box, 1980s
EX $12   **NM** $27   **MIP** n/a

TRACTORS 1:12-SCALE

❏ **Steiger Bearcat III**, 1:12-scale, Valley Patterns, green and black, limited to 100 units, 1970s
EX $653   **NM** $934   **MIP** $1042

❏ **Steiger Cougar II**, 1:12-scale, Valley Patterns, green and black, limited to 150 units, 1970s
EX $653   **NM** $934   **MIP** $1242

❏ **Steiger Panther 1000**, 1:12-scale, Valley Patterns, green & black, various letter & number designations below Panther decal, 1980s
EX $653   **NM** $934   **MIP** $1042

TRACTORS 1:16-SCALE

❏ **Steiger**, 1:16-scale, Berg (Custom), green, did not come in box, 1980s
EX $389   **NM** $689   **MIP** n/a

❏ **Steiger 2200**, 1:16-scale, Scale Models, green, 4WD, w/red rims, Collector Edition, First Steiger Built, 2001, No. ZSM915
EX $78   **NM** $118   **MIP** $153

❏ **Steiger 2200**, 1:16-scale, Scale Models, green, 4WD, w/red rims, First Steiger built, 2002, No. ZSM950
EX $78   **NM** $118   **MIP** $153

❏ **Steiger 2200**, 1:16-scale, Scale Models, green, 4WD, Second Steiger built, 2004, No. ZSM1024
EX $78   **NM** $118   **MIP** $153

❏ **Steiger Panther 1000**, 1:16-scale, Scale Models, green and black, CP-1400, 1983
EX $98   **NM** $122   **MIP** $143

❏ **Steiger Panther 1000**, 1:16-scale, Scale Models, green, 4WD, w/triples, '95 Heritage, Fargo, ND, 1995, No. ZSM830 *(Photo by Bossen Implement)*
EX $78   **NM** $118   **MIP** $153

❏ **Steiger Panther 1000**, 1:16-scale, Scale Models, green, duals, 4WD, CP-1400, 1996, No. ZSM849
(Photo by Scale Models)
EX $73   **NM** $114   **MIP** $143

TRACTORS 1:32-SCALE

❏ **Steiger Bearcat I**, 1:32-scale, Ertl, green, 4WD, Toy Farmer Series, 2000, No. 2018
EX $12   **NM** $16   **MIP** $33

❏ **Steiger Bearcat II**, 1:32-scale, Ertl, green, 4WD, Toy Farmer Series, 2002, No. 2021
EX $12   **NM** $16   **MIP** $33

❑ **Steiger Bearcat II**, 1:32-scale, Ertl, green, 4WD, Toy Farmer Series, 2003, No. 2020
EX $12   **NM** $16   **MIP** $33

❑ **Steiger Cougar 1000**, 1:32-scale, Ertl, green, Special Edition, 1980s, No. 256DA
EX $22   **NM** $43   **MIP** $73

❑ **Steiger Cougar 1000**, 1:32-scale, Ertl, green, 4WD, duals, POFI (German tractor magazine), 1990s, No. 256 *(Photo by Bossen Implement)*
EX $28   **NM** $46   **MIP** $93

❑ **Steiger Cougar III**, 1:32-scale, Ertl, gold, Steiger Classic Cougar, did not come in box, 1980s
EX $98   **NM** $192   **MIP** $289

❑ **Steiger Cougar III**, 1:32-scale, Ertl, green and black, collector's and

non-collector's series available, 1981, No. 1930
EX $22   **NM** $37   **MIP** $68

❑ **Steiger Lion 1000**, 1:32-scale, Scale Models, green, last edition, 1987
EX $323   **NM** $533   **MIP** $689

❑ **Steiger Panther 1000**, 1:32-scale, Scale Models, green and black, 1980s
EX $18   **NM** $26   **MIP** $37

❑ **Steiger Panther 1000**, 1:32-scale, Scale Models, green, CP1400, Collectors Edition, 1980s, No. 1900
EX $28   **NM** $47   **MIP** $68

❑ **Steiger Panther 1000**, 1:32-scale, Scale Models, green, duals, CP1400, 1997, No. ZSM839 *(Photo by Scale Models)*
EX $18   **NM** $24   **MIP** $36

❑ **Steiger Panther III**, 1:32-scale, Ertl, red, white and blue, Toy Farmer Series, Spirit of 76, 1980s, No. 3090
EX $23   **NM** $53   **MIP** $78

❑ **Steiger Panther III**, 1:32-scale, Ertl, green and black, collector's and non-collector's available, 1980s, No. 1925
EX $28   **NM** $57   **MIP** $78

❑ **Steiger Panther III**, 1:32-scale, Ertl, green and black, Toy Farmer Series, 1983, No. 3093
EX $23   **NM** $53   **MIP** $78

❑ **Steiger Panther IV**, 1:32-scale, Scale Models, green and black, CP1400, 1980s, No. 1905
EX $26   **NM** $32   **MIP** $48

❏ **Steiger Puma 1000**, 1:32-scale, Scale Models, green, Collector & Non Collectors, 1987
EX $22   **NM** $33   **MIP** $53

❏ **Steiger Titan**, 1:32-scale, Ertl, yellow, 4WD, STR-360, Toy Farmer Series, 1998, No. 2014
EX $12   **NM** $16   **MIP** $33

❏ **Steiger Wildcat I**, 1:32-scale, Ertl, green, 4WD, Toy Farmer Series, 1998, No. 2015 *(Photo by Ertl)*
EX $12   **NM** $16   **MIP** $33

❏ **Steiger Wildcat I**, 1:32-scale, Ertl, green, 4WD, Series I, 1999, No. 14082A
EX $12   **NM** $16   **MIP** $33

❏ **Steiger Wildcat, Super I**, 1:32-scale, Ertl, green, 4WD, Toy Farmer Series, 1999, No. 2016 *(Photo by Ertl)*
EX $12   **NM** $16   **MIP** $33

❏ **Steiger Wildcat, Super II**, 1:32-scale, Ertl, green, 4WD, Toy Farmer Series, 2002, No. 2019
EX $12   **NM** $16   **MIP** $33

TRACTORS 1:64-SCALE

❏ **Steiger Cougar**, 1:64-scale, Ertl, green and black, dark windows, 1981, No. 1945
EX $27   **NM** $46   **MIP** $64

❏ **Steiger Cougar**, 1:64-scale, Ertl, green and black, clear windows, 1981, No. 1945
EX $27   **NM** $46   **MIP** $64

❏ **Steiger Panther**, 1:64-scale, Scale Models, green and black, 1st edition, on Steiger card, 1984
EX $6   **NM** $9   **MIP** $28

❏ **Steiger Panther**, 1:64-scale, Scale Models, green and black, on Steiger card, regular edition, 1985
EX $6   **NM** $9   **MIP** $29

❏ **Steiger Panther**, 1:64-scale, Scale Models, green, 4WD, '89 Heart of America Show, 1989
EX $8   **NM** $18   **MIP** $37

❏ **Steiger Panther**, 1:64-scale, Scale Models, green, 4WD, on Case-IH card, 1996, No. ZSM845
EX $6   **NM** $9   **MIP** $16

TOY FARMER

IMPLEMENTS 1:64-SCALE

❏ **Toy Farmer Anhydrous Tank**, 1:64-scale, Mini Toys, white and red, rubber tires
EX $3   **NM** $4   **MIP** $6

❏ **Toy Farmer Anhydrous Tank**, 1:64-scale, Mini Toys, white w/various wheel-colors, rubber tires
EX $3   **NM** $4   **MIP** $6

❏ **Toy Farmer Fertilizer Spreader**, 1:64-scale, Ertl, various colors
EX $3   **NM** $4   **MIP** $9

❏ **Toy Farmer Fertilizer Spreader**, 1:64-scale, Mini Toys, various colors
EX $3   NM $4   MIP $9

❏ **Toy Farmer Fertilizer Spreader**, 1:64-scale, Mini Toys, various colors
EX $3   NM $4   MIP $9

❏ **Toy Farmer Liquid Spreader**, 1:64-scale, Mini Toys, various colors
EX $3   NM $4   MIP $9

❏ **Toy Farmer Liquid Spreader**, 1:64-scale, Mini Toys, various colors
EX $3   NM $4   MIP $9

TRU-SCALE

IMPLEMENTS 1:16-SCALE

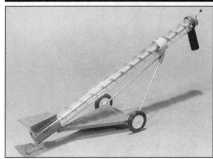

❏ **Tru-Scale Auger**, 1:16-scale, Carter/Ertl, red, 1970s, No. 414
EX $27   NM $43   MIP $98

❏ **Tru-Scale Baler**, 1:16-scale, Carter, red, yellow rims
EX $23   NM $112   MIP $243

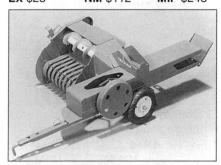

❏ **Tru-Scale Baler**, 1:16-scale, Carter, red, cream rims, 1956, No. 408
EX $37   NM $86   MIP $189

❏ **Tru-Scale Baler**, 1:16-scale, Carter, red, green rims, 1960s, No. 408
EX $137   NM $283   MIP $442

❏ **Tru-Scale Combine**, 1:16-scale, Carter, red, 1960s, No. 406
EX $68   NM $142   MIP $283

❏ **Tru-Scale Combine**, 1:16-scale, Carter, red or green, 1970s, No. 406
EX $68   NM $142   MIP $283

❏ **Tru-Scale Corn Picker**, 1:16-scale, Carter, red, fits Tru-Scale 560, 1960s, No. 411
EX $107   NM $173   MIP $289

❏ **Tru-Scale Corn Picker**, 1:16-scale, Carter, red, fits Tru-Scale 560, 1970s
EX $107   NM $173   MIP $289

❏ **Tru-Scale Disc**, 1:16-scale, Carter, red, no wheels, 1960s, No. 405
EX $33   NM $82   MIP $153

❑ **Tru-Scale Disc**, 1:16-scale, Carter, red, 2 wheels, strap holds it up, 1970s, No. 412
EX $58 **NM** $163 **MIP** $284

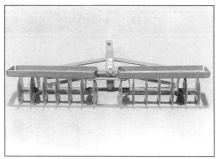

❑ **Tru-Scale Disc**, 1:16-scale, Carter, red, single gang, 1970s
EX $23 **NM** $48 **MIP** $103

❑ **Tru-Scale Elevator**, 1:16-scale, Carter, red, tin rims, 1960s, No. 410
EX $18 **NM** $48 **MIP** $112

❑ **Tru-Scale Forage Harvester**, 1:16-scale, Carter, red, 1970s, No. 415
EX $58 **NM** $122 **MIP** $326

❑ **Tru-Scale Grain Drill**, 1:16-scale, Carter, red, 1960s, No. 409
EX $48 **NM** $98 **MIP** $182

❑ **Tru-Scale Grain Drill**, 1:16-scale, Carter, red, 1970s, No. 409
EX $48 **NM** $98 **MIP** $182

❑ **Tru-Scale Loader**, 1:16-scale, Carter, red, fits Tru-Scale 560, 1970s, No. 407
EX $33 **NM** $72 **MIP** $112

❑ **Tru-Scale Mower**, 1:16-scale, Carter, red, 1970s, No. 416
EX $33 **NM** $72 **MIP** $142

❑ **Tru-Scale Plow**, 1:16-scale, Carter, red, 2 bottom, yellow wheels, 1960s, No. 404
EX $33 **NM** $119 **MIP** $332

❑ **Tru-Scale Plow**, 1:16-scale, Carter, red, 4 bottom, 1970s, No. 418
EX $33 **NM** $89 **MIP** $177

❑ **Tru-Scale Plow**, 1:16-scale, Carter, red or green, 2 bottom, white wheels, 1970s, No. 404
EX $33 **NM** $79 **MIP** $142

❑ **Tru-Scale Side Rake**, 1:16-scale, Carter, red, 1970s, No. 419
EX $27 **NM** $62 **MIP** $142

❑ **Tru-Scale Spreader**, 1:16-scale, Carter, red, 1960s, No. 403
EX $22   **NM** $58   **MIP** $112

❑ **Tru-Scale Spreader**, 1:16-scale, Carter, red, white fenders, 1970s, No. 403
EX $22   **NM** $58   **MIP** $132

❑ **Tru-Scale Spreader**, 1:16-scale, Carter, red, white fenders, 1970s, No. 403
EX $22   **NM** $58   **MIP** $132

❑ **Tru-Scale Trailer**, 1:16-scale, Carter, red, white wheels, utility, 1960s, No. 302
EX $22   **NM** $48   **MIP** $72

❑ **Tru-Scale Trailer**, 1:16-scale, Carter, red, tilt bed, winch, 1970s, No. 303
EX $22   **NM** $68   **MIP** $122

❑ **Tru-Scale Trailer**, 1:16-scale, Carter, red, Service, 1970s, No. 304
EX $133   **NM** $323   **MIP** $588

❑ **Tru-Scale Wagon**, 1:16-scale, Carter, red, yellow wheels, Flare box, 1960s, No. 402
EX $38   **NM** $46   **MIP** $127

❑ **Tru-Scale Wagon**, 1:16-scale, Carter, red, white wheels, Flare box, 1970s, No. 402
EX $22   **NM** $46   **MIP** $127

❑ **Tru-Scale Wagon**, 1:16-scale, Carter, red, Barge box, 1970s, No. 417
EX $22   **NM** $58   **MIP** $112

TRACTORS 1:16-SCALE

❑ **Tru-Scale 560**, 1:16-scale, Carter, red, plastic wheel rims, 1960s, No. 401
EX $22   **NM** $46   **MIP** $189

❑ **Tru-Scale 560**, 1:16-scale, Carter, red, metal grille, IH decal, metal wheels, 1960s, No. 401
EX $22   **NM** $76   **MIP** $289

❑ **Tru-Scale 560**, 1:16-scale, Carter, red, metal wheels, 1960s, No. 401
EX $22   **NM** $56   **MIP** $219

❏ **Tru-Scale 890**, 1:16-scale,
Carter, red, green or yellow, 1970s,
No. 890
EX $33   **NM** $119   **MIP** $286

❏ **Tru-Scale 891**, 1:16-scale,
Carter, red, green or yellow, 1970s,
No. 891
EX $43   **NM** $189   **MIP** $389

❏ **Tru-Scale M**, 1:16-scale, Carter,
red, two variations: raised Pat.
Pending lettering, and engraved
lettering, 1950s
EX $48   **NM** $162   **MIP** $489

TRACTORS 1:32-SCALE

❏ **Tru-Scale Tractor**, 1:32-scale,
Ertl, red or blue, plastic tires and
rims, 1970s
EX $3   **NM** $8   **MIP** $28

Photos by Jon Jacobson unless otherwise noted.

TWIN CITY

TRACTORS 1:16-SCALE

❏ **Twin City 12-20**, 1:16-scale,
SpecCast, gray, steel wheel, limited
to 1500 units, 1987
EX $37   **NM** $62   **MIP** $78

❏ **Twin City 12-20**, 1:16-scale,
SpecCast, gray, '89 Old Time Tractor
Pull, LaMoure, ND, 1989
EX $28   **NM** $42   **MIP** $73

❏ **Twin City 12-20**, 1:16-scale,
SpecCast, gray, on rubber, 1989
EX $28   **NM** $42   **MIP** $73

❏ **Twin City 17-28**, 1:16-scale,
Scale Models, gray, #17 in Collector
Series I, 1988 *(Photo by Bossen Implement)*
EX $28   **NM** $42   **MIP** $73

TRACTORS 1:64-SCALE

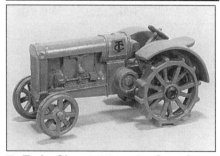

❏ **Twin City**, 1:64-scale, SpecCast,
gray
EX $6   **NM** $9   **MIP** $18

TRACTORS

❏ **Twin City 60-90**, Gray (Custom),
gray, 1978
EX $112   **NM** $193   **MIP** n/a

UNVERFERTH

IMPLEMENTS 1:64-SCALE

❏ **Unverferth Wagon Gravity**,
1:64-scale, Ertl, red, No. 9365
EX $9   **NM** $16   **MIP** $24

❏ **Unverferth Wagon Gravity**,
1:64-scale, Ertl, red, No. 9365
EX $9   **NM** $16   **MIP** $24

❏ **Unverferth Wagon Gravity 630**,
1:64-scale, SpecCast, green, 1998
(Photo by Bossen Implement)
EX $11   **NM** $23   **MIP** $37

❏ **Unverferth Wagon Gravity 630**,
1:64-scale, SpecCast, red, 1998
EX $11   **NM** $23   **MIP** $37

VERMEER

IMPLEMENTS 1:64-SCALE

❑ **Vermeer Baler, 605J**, 1:64-scale, Ertl, yellow and black, No. 4301
EX $6   **NM** $12   **MIP** $18

VERSATILE

IMPLEMENTS 1:16-SCALE

❑ **Versatile Combine, 2000**, 1:16-scale, Scale Models, red & yellow, designed w/removable grain tank to show inner workings, 1980s
EX $123   **NM** $178   **MIP** $268

IMPLEMENTS 1:64-SCALE

❑ **Versatile Combine, 2000**, 1:64-scale, Scale Models, red and silver, regular edition, 1980s
EX $4   **NM** $12   **MIP** $18

❑ **Versatile Combine, 2000**, 1:64-scale, Scale Models, red and silver, 1st Edition, 1980s
EX $4   **NM** $12   **MIP** $18

❑ **Versatile Combine, 2000**, 1:64-scale, Scale Models, red and silver, Alleman, Iowa FPS 1986, 1980s
EX $4   **NM** $12   **MIP** $18

❑ **Versatile Combine, 2000**, 1:64-scale, Scale Models, red and silver, Louisville 1986, 1980s
EX $4   **NM** $12   **MIP** $18

❑ **Versatile Swather, 4700**, 1:64-scale, Scale Models, red, black, and yellow, 1980s
EX $6   **NM** $11   **MIP** $18

❑ **Versatile Swather, 4700**, 1:64-scale, Scale Models, red, black, and yellow, Winnipeg MB 1986, 1980s
EX $6   **NM** $11   **MIP** $18

TRACTORS 1:16-SCALE

❑ **Versatile**, 1:16-scale, Scale Models, red, black and rust, 825, 895, 936 decalls included in packaging, 1980s
EX $98   **NM** $133   **MIP** $163

❑ **Versatile 1150**, 1:16-scale, Scale Models, red, black and yellow, Phonex tractor, on Plague, 1980s
EX $158   **NM** $343   **MIP** $473

❑ **Versatile 1150**, 1:16-scale, Scale Models, red, black and yellow, triples, rubber stack, 1982
EX $158   **NM** $277   **MIP** $328

❑ **Versatile 1156**, 1:16-scale, Scale Models, Designation 6, red, black and yellow, 1991, No. 302
EX $98   **NM** $133   **MIP** $163

❑ **Versatile 118**, 1:16-scale, Scale Models, red, Collector Edition, 2000, No. JLE445DS
EX $67   **NM** $88   **MIP** $133

❑ **Versatile 500**, 1:16-scale, Scale Models, duals, 1997, No. 412

(Photo by Scale Models)
EX $62   **NM** $83   **MIP** $133

❑ **Versatile 825**, 1:16-scale, Scale Models, red and yellow, plastic wheels, 1984, No. 324FT
EX $67   **NM** $98   **MIP** $128

❑ **Versatile 825**, 1:16-scale, Scale Models, red, w/duals, rubber tires, 2001, No. 305
EX $63   **NM** $82   **MIP** $123

❑ **Versatile 895**, 1:16-scale, Scale Models, red and black and yellow, metal muffler and oil cooler, no planatary hubs, 1992
EX $148   **NM** $182   **MIP** $278

❑ **Versatile 895**, 1:16-scale, Scale Models, red and black and yellow, metal muffler w/o oil cooler, no planatary hubs, 1992
EX $148   **NM** $182   **MIP** $278

❑ **Versatile 895**, 1:16-scale, Scale Models, red, black and yellow, w/planatary hubs, rubber muffler, 1992
EX $148   **NM** $182   **MIP** $278

❑ **Versatile 935**, 1:16-scale, Scale Models, red, coming on strong Boston, 1991, No. 318

(Photo by Bossen Implement)
EX $98   **NM** $133   **MIP** $153

❑ **Versatile 935**, 1:16-scale, Scale Models, red, duals, 1997, No. 324

(Photo by Scale Models)
EX $98   **NM** $133   **MIP** $153

❑ **Versatile 936**, 1:16-scale, Scale Models, duals, same as FF-0245, 1996, No. 388 *(Photo by Scale Models)*
EX $93   **NM** $127   **MIP** $143

❑ **Versatile Big Roy**, 1:16-scale, Sharp (Custom), red and yellow, did not come in box, 1980s
EX $389   **NM** $589   **MIP** n/a

❑ **Versatile D-100**, 1:16-scale, Scale Models, red, Collector Edition, 1999, No. JLE436DS
EX $67   **NM** $88   **MIP** $122

❑ **Versatile D-100**, 1:16-scale, Scale Models, red, 2000, No. JLE440DS
EX $62   **NM** $83   **MIP** $118

TRACTORS 1:32-SCALE

❑ **Versatile 1150**, 1:32-scale, Scale Models, red, black and rust, dual wheels, 1983
EX $28   **NM** $56   **MIP** $67

❏ **Versatile 1150**, 1:32-scale, Scale Models, red, black and rust, triple wheels, 1983
EX $28   **NM** $56   **MIP** $72

❏ **Versatile 1150**, 1:32-scale, Scale Models, red, black and yellow, triple wheels, 1983
EX $37   **NM** $62   **MIP** $88

❏ **Versatile 1156**, 1:32-scale, Scale Models, Designation 6, red, black and yellow, 1980s
EX $28   **NM** $56   **MIP** $63

❏ **Versatile 256**, 1:32-scale, Scale Models, red, black and rust, 1980s
EX $4   **NM** $12   **MIP** $23

❏ **Versatile 256**, 1:32-scale, Scale Models, red, black and rust, available w/ and w/o 1st edition, 1980s
EX $4   **NM** $12   **MIP** $23

❏ **Versatile 276**, 1:32-scale, Scale Models, red, black and rust, comes w/duals, planter and cultivator, kit, 1980s
EX $18   **NM** $28   **MIP** $52

❏ **Versatile 276**, 1:32-scale, Scale Models, industrial yellow, 1980s
EX $4   **NM** $12   **MIP** $23

❏ **Versatile 836**, 1:32-scale, Scale Models, Designation 6, red, black, rust, collector's & non-collector's available, 1984
EX $18   **NM** $28   **MIP** $43

❏ **Versatile 936**, 1:32-scale, Scale Models, red, black and yellow, 1996, No. 395 *(Photo by Scale Models)*
EX $11   **NM** $22   **MIP** $32

❏ **Versatile Big Roy**, 1:32-scale, Die-Cast Promotions, red, black & rust, Museum version, 2005, No. 40051
EX $53   **NM** $77   **MIP** $123

❏ **Versatile Big Roy**, 1:32-scale, Die-Cast Promotions, red, black & rust, Factory version, 2005, No. 40050
EX $53   **NM** $77   **MIP** $123

TRACTORS 1:64-SCALE

❏ **Versatile 836**, 1:64-scale, Scale Models, red, black and rust, 1st edition
EX $27   **NM** $33   **MIP** $43

❏ **Versatile 836**, 1:64-scale, Scale Models, red, black and rust
EX $27   **NM** $33   **MIP** $43

Photos by Jon Jacobson unless otherwise noted.

❑ **Versatile 836**, 1:64-scale, Scale Models, red, black and rust
EX $27   **NM** $33   **MIP** $43

❑ **Versatile 836**, 1:64-scale, Scale Models, Designation 6, red, black and rust, 1980s
EX $22   **NM** $36   **MIP** $43

❑ **Versatile 836**, 1:64-scale, Scale Models, red, black and rust, 1986 Louisville, 1986
EX $27   **NM** $33   **MIP** $43

❑ **Versatile 836**, 1:64-scale, Scale Models, red, black and rust, 1986 Alleman F.P.S., 1986
EX $27   **NM** $33   **MIP** $43

❑ **Versatile 876**, 1:64-scale, Scale Models, red, black and rust, 1st edition
EX $27   **NM** $33   **MIP** $43

❑ **Versatile 876**, 1:64-scale, Scale Models, red, black and rust
EX $27   **NM** $33   **MIP** $43

❑ **Versatile 876**, 1:64-scale, Scale Models, red, black and rust
EX $27   **NM** $33   **MIP** $43

❑ **Versatile 876**, 1:64-scale, Scale Models, Designation 6, red, black and rust, 1980s
EX $22   **NM** $36   **MIP** $48

❑ **Versatile 876**, 1:64-scale, Scale Models, red, black and rust, 1986 Alleman F.P.S., 1986
EX $27   **NM** $33   **MIP** $43

❑ **Versatile 876**, 1:64-scale, Scale Models, red, black and rust, 1986 Louisville, 1986
EX $27   **NM** $33   **MIP** $43

❑ **Versatile 895**, 1:64-scale, Clifton (Custom), red, yellow and black, did not come in box
EX $22   **NM** $33   **MIP** n/a

❑ **Versatile 936**, 1:64-scale, Scale Models, red, black and rust, 1st edition
EX $27   **NM** $33   **MIP** $43

❏ **Versatile 936**, 1:64-scale, Scale Models, red, black and rust
EX $27   NM $33   MIP $43

❏ **Versatile 936**, 1:64-scale, Scale Models, red, black and rust
EX $27   NM $33   MIP $43

❏ **Versatile 936**, 1:64-scale, Scale Models, Designation 6, red, black and rust, 1980s
EX $22   NM $36   MIP $43

❏ **Versatile 936**, 1:64-scale, Scale Models, red, black and rust, 1986 Louisville, 1986
EX $27   NM $33   MIP $43

❏ **Versatile 936**, 1:64-scale, Scale Models, red, black and rust, 1986 Alleman F.P.S., 1986
EX $27   NM $33   MIP $43

❏ **Versatile Big Roy**, 1:64-scale, Die-Cast Promotions, red, black & rust, Museum version, 2006, No. 40063 *(Photo by Die-Cast Promotions)*
EX $16   NM $22   MIP $33

❏ **Versatile Big Roy**, 1:64-scale, Die-Cast Promotions, red, black & rust, Factory version, 2006, No. 40062
(Photo by Die-Cast Promotions)
EX $16   NM $22   MIP $33

WALLIS

TRACTORS 1:16-SCALE

❏ **Wallis 20-30**, 1:16-scale, Scale Models, made for Farmhand Promotions 1989, 1980s
EX $26   NM $52   MIP $88

❏ **Wallis 20-30**, 1:16-scale, Scale Models, green, #6 in Collector Series I, 1981 *(Photo by Bossen Implement)*
EX $23   NM $42   MIP $88

TRACTORS 1:43-SCALE

❏ **Wallis**, 1:43-scale, SpecCast, 1990s
EX $6   NM $8   MIP $12

TRACTORS 1:64-SCALE

❏ **Wallis 20-40**, 1:64-scale, Scale Models, gray
EX $4   NM $6   MIP $12

WHITE

BANKS 1:25-SCALE

❏ **White T Bank**, 1:25-scale, Ertl, red/white, 1990s
EX $4   NM $12   MIP $18

BANKS 1:32-SCALE

❏ **White 160 Bank**, 1:32-scale, Scale Models, silver, 1980s
EX $2 **NM** $4 **MIP** $8

IMPLEMENTS 1:16-SCALE

❏ **White Disc**, 1:16-scale, Scale Models, No. FU-0960 *(Photo by Scale Models)*
EX $8 **NM** $13 **MIP** $18

❏ **White Disc**, 1:16-scale, Scale Models, red, 1980s
EX $8 **NM** $13 **MIP** $18

❏ **White Planter 6100**, 1:16-scale, Scale Models, red, 4 row, No. FF-0216 *(Photo by Scale Models)*
EX $12 **NM** $27 **MIP** $52

❏ **White Planter 6100**, 1:16-scale, Scale Models, red, plastic markers, 1980s
EX $12 **NM** $27 **MIP** $52

❏ **White Planter 6100**, 1:16-scale, Scale Models, red, die-cast markers, 1980s
EX $12 **NM** $27 **MIP** $52

❏ **White Wagon, Center Pump**, 1:16-scale, Scale Models, red, 1980s
EX $6 **NM** $13 **MIP** $23

IMPLEMENTS 1:24-SCALE

❏ **White Combine, 9700**, 1:24-scale, Scale Models, red, 1980s
EX $68 **NM** $127 **MIP** $182

❏ **White Combine, 9700**, 1:24-scale, Scale Models, red, Collectors Edition, 1983
EX $88 **NM** $142 **MIP** $206

❏ **White Combine, 9700**, 1:24-scale, Scale Models, red, 1983
EX $68 **NM** $127 **MIP** $182

❏ **White Combine, 9720**, 1:24-scale, Scale Models, red, 1990
EX $88 **NM** $156 **MIP** $238

PEDAL TRACTORS

❏ **White**, Scale Models, gray, NF, tractor in original condition, 1986
EX $126 **NM** $206 **MIP** $362

❏ **White**, Scale Models, gray, NF, new grille decal, 1987
EX $126 **NM** $206 **MIP** $362

❑ **White 145**, Scale Models, gray, WF, 2WD, workhorse, 1991
EX $103   **NM** $143   **MIP** $213

❑ **White 145**, Scale Models, black, WF, 2WD, workhorse, 1992
EX $103   **NM** $143   **MIP** $213

❑ **White 145**, Scale Models, gray, NF, workhorse, 1992
EX $103   **NM** $143   **MIP** $213

❑ **White 145**, Scale Models, gray, NF, 2WD, workhorse, '97 Farm Progress Show Edition, 1997
EX $78   **NM** $126   **MIP** $188

❑ **White 2-70**, Scale Models, silver, WF, MFD, '00 Farm Progress Show Edition, 2000, No. FB-2569
EX $73   **NM** $122   **MIP** $178

❑ **White 6215**, Scale Models, WF 2WD, silver, 1995, No. FT-0585

(Photo by Scale Models)
EX $98   **NM** $148   **MIP** $172

❑ **White American**, Scale Models, gray and silver, NF, 1990
EX $96   **NM** $155   **MIP** $205

TRACTORS 1:16-SCALE

❑ **White 160**, 1:16-scale, Scale Models, silver, 1st Edition, 1988
EX $18   **NM** $27   **MIP** $38

❑ **White 170**, 1:16-scale, Scale Models, silver, 1988
EX $18   **NM** $27   **MIP** $38

❑ **White 185**, 1:16-scale, Scale Models, silver, 1st edition, w/duals, 1988
EX $18   **NM** $27   **MIP** $38

❑ **White 185**, 1:16-scale, Scale Models, silver, w/duals, 1988
EX $18   **NM** $27   **MIP** $38

❑ **White 195**, 1:16-scale, Scale Models, silver, w/duals, 1990s
EX $18   **NM** $27   **MIP** $38

❑ **White 2-135**, 1:16-scale, Scale Models, gray w/silver strips, on plaque, Dealer Edition, 1978
EX $27   **NM** $42   **MIP** $59

❑ **White 2-135**, 1:16-scale, Scale Models, gray w/silver stripes, FWA, 1979
EX $27   **NM** $38   **MIP** $48

❑ **White 2-135**, 1:16-scale, Scale Models, gray w/silver stripes, on plaque, 1979
EX $22   **NM** $36   **MIP** $59

❑ **White 2-135**, 1:16-scale, Scale Models, gray w/silver stripes, FWA, 1980
EX $27   **NM** $38   **MIP** $48

❑ **White 2-135**, 1:16-scale, Scale Models, gray w/silver stripes, 1980
EX $27   **NM** $38   **MIP** $48

❏ **White 2-135**, 1:16-scale, Scale Models, gray w/silver stripes, 1980
EX $27   **NM** $38   **MIP** $48

❏ **White 2-135**, 1:16-scale, Scale Models, gray w/red stripes, 1982
EX $24   **NM** $38   **MIP** $48

❏ **White 2-155**, 1:16-scale, Scale Models, gray w/silver stripes, 1979
EX $27   **NM** $47   **MIP** $58

❏ **White 2-135**, 1:16-scale, Scale Models, gray w/red stripes, planter vase, 1980s
EX $3   **NM** $8   **MIP** $16

❏ **White 2-135**, 1:16-scale, Scale Models, gray w/red stripes, Series III, 1985
EX $24   **NM** $38   **MIP** $48

❏ **White 2-155**, 1:16-scale, Scale Models, gray w/silver stripes, on plaque, Collectors Edition, 1979
EX $28   **NM** $48   **MIP** $63

❏ **White 2-135**, 1:16-scale, Scale Models, gray w/red stripes, 1982
EX $24   **NM** $38   **MIP** $48

❏ **White 2-135**, 1:16-scale, Scale Models, gray w/red stripes, Series III, 1985
EX $24   **NM** $38   **MIP** $48

❏ **White 2-155**, 1:16-scale, Scale Models, gray w/silver stripes, 1979
EX $27   **NM** $47   **MIP** $58

❏ **White 2-135**, 1:16-scale, Scale Models, gray w/red stripes, Collectors Edition, 1982
EX $36   **NM** $53   **MIP** $78

❏ **White 2-135**, 1:16-scale, Scale Models, silver, 25th Anniversary of JLE, Inc., 1995, No. FB-2402

(Photo by Bossen Implement)
EX $18   **NM** $28   **MIP** $43

❏ **White 2-155**, 1:16-scale, Scale Models, gray w/red stripes, 1982
EX $24   **NM** $47   **MIP** $58

❑ **White 2-155**, 1:16-scale, Scale Models, gray w/red stripes, Collectors Edition, 1982
EX $27   **NM** $47   **MIP** $58

❑ **White 2-155**, 1:16-scale, Scale Models, gray w/red stripes, Series III, 1985
EX $24   **NM** $47   **MIP** $58

❑ **White 2-180**, 1:16-scale, Scale Models, gray w/silver stripes, 1979
EX $27   **NM** $57   **MIP** $78

❑ **White 2-180**, 1:16-scale, Scale Models, gray w/silver stripes, 1979
EX $27   **NM** $57   **MIP** $78

❑ **White 2-180**, 1:16-scale, Scale Models, gray w/silver stripes, wide rear tires, 1979
EX $27   **NM** $53   **MIP** $78

❑ **White 2-180**, 1:16-scale, Scale Models, gray w/red stripes, 1982
EX $27   **NM** $48   **MIP** $68

❑ **White 2-180**, 1:16-scale, Scale Models, gray w/silver stripes, Series III, 1985
EX $27   **NM** $53   **MIP** $78

❑ **White 2-44**, 1:16-scale, SpecCast, '98 Crossroads USA Show, 1998, No. CUST 596
EX $16   **NM** $27   **MIP** $47

❑ **White 2-44**, 1:16-scale, SpecCast, Collector Edition, 1998, No. SCT-162
EX $16   **NM** $27   **MIP** $47

❑ **White 4-175**, 1:16-scale, Scale Models, gray w/silver stripes, 1980
EX $166   **NM** $227   **MIP** $368

❑ **White 4-175**, 1:16-scale, Scale Models, gray w/red stripes, 1981
EX $97   **NM** $138   **MIP** $173

❑ **White 4-210**, 1:16-scale, Scale Models, gray w/red stripes, 1980
EX $78   **NM** $106   **MIP** $136

❑ **White 4-210**, 1:16-scale, Scale Models, gray w/silver strips, 1980
EX $88   **NM** $118   **MIP** $147

❑ **White 4-225**, 1:16-scale, Scale Models, gray w/red stripes, 1983
EX $78   **NM** $106   **MIP** $136

❑ **White 4-270**, 1:16-scale, Scale Models, gray w/red stripes, 1984
EX $88   **NM** $118   **MIP** $147

❑ **White 4-270**, 1:16-scale, Scale Models, gray w/red stripes, Louisville, KY, 1984
EX $98   **NM** $148   **MIP** $193

❑ **White 700**, 1:16-scale, Scale Models, gray w/gray stripes, engraved, 7th annual toy show, 1984
EX $18   **NM** $34   **MIP** $48

❑ **White American 60**, 1:16-scale, Scale Models, red, w/ROPS, 1989, No. 131
EX $13   **NM** $26   **MIP** $34

❑ **White American 60**, 1:16-scale, Scale Models, green, w/ROPS, 1989, No. 129
EX $13   **NM** $26   **MIP** $34

❑ **White American 60**, 1:16-scale, Scale Models, silver, w/ROPS, 1989, No. 128
EX $13   **NM** $26   **MIP** $34

❑ **White American 60**, 1:16-scale, Scale Models, yellow, w/ROPS, 1989, No. 130
EX $13   **NM** $26   **MIP** $34

❑ **White American 60**, 1:16-scale, Scale Models, red, no ROPS or fenders, 1990
EX $8   **NM** $18   **MIP** $22

❑ **White American 60**, 1:16-scale, Scale Models, silver, no ROPS or fenders, 1990
EX $8   **NM** $18   **MIP** $22

❑ **White American 60**, 1:16-scale, Scale Models, green, no ROPS or fenders, 1990
EX $8   **NM** $18   **MIP** $22

❑ **White American 60**, 1:16-scale, Scale Models, yellow, no ROPS or fenders, 1990
EX $8   **NM** $18   **MIP** $22

❑ **White American 80**, 1:16-scale, Scale Models, green, w/cab, 1990s
EX $14   **NM** $27   **MIP** $38

❑ **White American 80**, 1:16-scale, Scale Models, red, w/cab, 1990s
EX $14   **NM** $27   **MIP** $38

❑ **White American 80**, 1:16-scale, Scale Models, yellow, w/cab, 1990s
EX $14   **NM** $27   **MIP** $38

❑ **White American 80**, 1:16-scale, Scale Models, silver, w/cab, 1990s
EX $14   **NM** $27   **MIP** $38

❑ **White American Set 60**, 1:16-scale, Scale Models, Collector Set, 1989
EX n/a   **NM** n/a   **MIP** $233

❑ **White American Set 80**, 1:16-scale, Scale Models, Collector Set, 1990 *(Photo by Bossen Implement)*
EX n/a   **NM** n/a   **MIP** $263

❑ **White Plainsman AT-1400**, 1:16-scale, Scale Models, red, 4WD, Collector Edition, 2000, No. FU-0582
EX $73   **NM** $106   **MIP** $153

❑ **White Plainsman AT-1400**, 1:16-scale, Scale Models, red, 4WD, 2000, No. FU-0589
EX $73   **NM** $106   **MIP** $153

TRACTORS 1:32-SCALE

❑ **White**, 1:32-scale, Scale Models, gray w/red stripes, 1980s
EX $2   **NM** $4   **MIP** $8

❑ **White**, 1:32-scale, Scale Models, gray w/red stripes, Farm Progress Show, Marion, Iowa Sept. 27-29, 1983, 1980s
EX $2   **NM** $4   **MIP** $8

❑ **White**, 1:32-scale, Scale Models, gray w/red stripes, National Farm Machinery Show, Louisville, Kentucky Feb. 15-18, 1984, 1980s
EX $2   **NM** $4   **MIP** $8

❑ **White 160**, 1:32-scale, Scale Models, silver, 1st edition, 1980s
EX $2   **NM** $8   **MIP** $12

❑ **White 185**, 1:32-scale, Scale Models, gray, Field Boss, 1986
EX $3   **NM** $8   **MIP** $12

❑ **White 185**, 1:32-scale, Scale Models, gray, Field Boss, 1986
EX $3   **NM** $8   **MIP** $12

❑ **White 2-135**, 1:32-scale, Scale Models, silver w/silver decals, 10th Anniversary 1977-1987
EX $2   **NM** $8   **MIP** $12

❑ **White 2-135**, 1:32-scale, Scale Models, gray w/red stripes, w/ or w/o 1st edition, 1980s
EX $3   **NM** $8   **MIP** $12

❑ **White 2-155**, 1:32-scale, Scale Models, silver w/silver decals, 10th Anniversary 1977-1987
EX $2   **NM** $8   **MIP** $12

❑ **White 2-155**, 1:32-scale, Scale Models, gray w/red stripes, w/ or w/o 1st edition, 1980s
EX $3   **NM** $8   **MIP** $12

❑ **White 2-32**, 1:32-scale, Scale Models, red and silver, 1980s
EX $4   **NM** $12   **MIP** $22

❑ **White 2-32**, 1:32-scale, Scale Models, gray w/red stripes, 1986 Louisville Farm Show, 1980s
EX $4   **NM** $12   **MIP** $22

❑ **White 2-35**, 1:32-scale, Scale Models, gray w/red stripes, 1980s
EX $4   **NM** $12   **MIP** $22

❏ **White 37**, 1:32-scale, Scale Models, Field Boss, gray, 1980s
EX $4　　NM $12　　MIP $24

❏ **White Iseki 2-35**, 1:32-scale, Scale Models, gray, 1986
EX $4　　NM $12　　MIP $27

❏ **White Isski**, 1:32-scale, Scale Models, silver, pen set, 1980s
EX $4　　NM $12　　MIP $18

TRACTORS 1:64-SCALE

❏ **White**, 1:64-scale, Scale Models, Field Boss, silver and gray, 1st Edition, 1980s
EX $4　　NM $5　　MIP $9

❏ **White 145**, 1:64-scale, Scale Models, gray, workhorse, 1992, No. FU-0545
EX $4　　NM $5　　MIP $6

❏ **White 160**, 1:64-scale, Scale Models, silver and gray, 1st Edition, 1980s
EX $4　　NM $6　　MIP $9

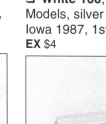

❏ **White 160**, 1:64-scale, Scale Models, silver and gray, 1980s
EX $4　　NM $6　　MIP $9

❏ **White 160**, 1:64-scale, Scale Models, chrome, Bahamas 1987, 1987
EX $4　　NM $6　　MIP $18

❏ **White 160**, 1:64-scale, Scale Models, chrome, Christmas 1987, 1987
EX $4　　NM $6　　MIP $9

❏ **White 160**, 1:64-scale, Scale Models, silver and gray, Alleman, Iowa 1987, 1st Edition, 1987
EX $4　　NM $6　　MIP $9

❏ **White 160**, 1:64-scale, Scale Models, silver and gray, 1988 World Ag-Expo, 1st Edition, 1988
EX $4　　NM $6　　MIP $9

❏ **White 160**, 1:64-scale, Scale Models, chrome, 1988 Parts Conference, 1988
EX $4　　NM $6　　MIP $9

❏ **White 160**, 1:64-scale, Scale Models, chrome, Christmas 1988, can be either first or regular edition, 1988
EX $4　　NM $6　　MIP $9

❏ **White 160**, 1:64-scale, Scale Models, silver and gray, 1988 Minnesota State Fair, 1st Edition, 1988
EX $4   **NM** $6   **MIP** $9

❏ **White 160**, 1:64-scale, Scale Models, silver and gray, 1st Edition, 1988
EX $4   **NM** $6   **MIP** $9

❏ **White 160**, 1:64-scale, Scale Models, silver and gray, Louisville 1988, 1st Edition, 1988
EX $4   **NM** $5   **MIP** $9

❏ **White 170**, 1:64-scale, Scale Models, gray, workhorse, 1992, No. FU-0540
EX $4   **NM** $6   **MIP** $9

❏ **White 185**, 1:64-scale, Scale Models, silver and gray, w/oil-filters, 1980s
EX $4   **NM** $6   **MIP** $9

❏ **White 185**, 1:64-scale, Scale Models, silver and gray, w/o oil-filters, 1980s
EX $4   **NM** $6   **MIP** $9

❏ **White 185**, 1:64-scale, Scale Models, Field Boss, silver and gray, 1st Edition, 1986
EX $4   **NM** $6   **MIP** $9

❏ **White 185**, 1:64-scale, Scale Models, Field Boss, silver and gray, Alleman, Iowa 1986, 1st Edition, 1986
EX $4   **NM** $6   **MIP** $9

❏ **White 185**, 1:64-scale, Scale Models, Field Boss, chrome, Christmas 1986, 1986
EX $4   **NM** $6   **MIP** $9

❏ **White 185**, 1:64-scale, Scale Models, silver and gray, w/o oil-filters, 1st Edition, 1986
EX $4   **NM** $6   **MIP** $9

❏ **White 185**, 1:64-scale, Scale Models, Field Boss, silver and gray, Alleman, Iowa, 1986, 1st Edition, 1986
EX $4   **NM** $6   **MIP** $9

❏ **White 185**, 1:64-scale, Scale Models, Field Boss, silver and gray, 1st Edition, 1986
EX $4   **NM** $6   **MIP** $9

❏ **White 185**, 1:64-scale, Scale Models, Field Boss, silver and gray, Merrillville, Indiana, 1986, 1st Edition, 1986
EX $4   **NM** $6   **MIP** $9

❏ **White 185**, 1:64-scale, Scale Models, silver and gray, w/oil-filters, 1st Edition, 1986
EX $4   **NM** $6   **MIP** $9

❏ **White 185**, 1:64-scale, Scale Models, Field Boss, silver and gray, Louisville 1987, 1st Edition, 1987
EX $4   **NM** $6   **MIP** $9

❏ **White 185**, 1:64-scale, Scale Models, silver and gray, Alleman, Iowa 1987, 1st Edition, 1987
EX $4   **NM** $6   **MIP** $9

❏ **White 185**, 1:64-scale, Scale Models, Field Boss, chrome, W. Dubuque FFA 1988, 1988
EX $4   **NM** $6   **MIP** $9

❏ **White 195**, 1:64-scale, Scale Models, gray, workhorse, 1992, No. FU-0541
EX $4   **NM** $6   **MIP** $9

❏ **White 2-135**, 1:64-scale, Scale Models, silver and gray
EX $4   **NM** $7   **MIP** $14

❏ **White 2-135**, 1:64-scale, Scale Models, silver and gray, 1st Edition
EX $4   **NM** $7   **MIP** $14

❏ **White 2-135**, 1:64-scale, Scale Models, chrome, National Canadian Toy Show 1985, 1st Edition, 1985
EX $4   **NM** $14   **MIP** $23

❏ **White 2-135**, 1:64-scale, Scale Models, chrome, Kansas City 1985, 1st Edition, 1985
EX $4   **NM** $14   **MIP** $23

❏ **White 2-135**, 1:64-scale, Scale Models, chrome, Louisville 1985 1st Edition, 1985
EX $4   **NM** $14   **MIP** $23

❏ **White 2-135**, 1:64-scale, Scale Models, chrome, Scottsdale 1985 1st Edition, 1985
EX $4   **NM** $14   **MIP** $23

❏ **White 2-135**, 1:64-scale, Scale Models, silver and gray, 1978-1988, 1988
EX $4   **NM** $7   **MIP** $14

❑ **White 2-155**, 1:64-scale, Scale Models, silver and gray
EX $4　　NM $7　　MIP $14

❑ **White 2-155**, 1:64-scale, Scale Models, silver and gray, 1st Edition
EX $4　　NM $7　　MIP $14

❑ **White 2-155**, 1:64-scale, Scale Models, silver and gray, 1978-1988, 1988
EX $4　　NM $7　　MIP $14

❑ **White 2-180**, 1:64-scale, Scale Models, silver and gray
EX $4　　NM $7　　MIP $14

❑ **White 2-180**, 1:64-scale, Scale Models, silver and gray
EX $4　　NM $7　　MIP $14

❑ **White 2-180**, 1:64-scale, Scale Models, silver and gray
EX $4　　NM $7　　MIP $14

❑ **White 2-180**, 1:64-scale, Scale Models, silver and gray, 1st Edition
EX $4　　NM $7　　MIP $14

❑ **White 2-180**, 1:64-scale, Scale Models, silver and gray, 1st Edition
EX $4　　NM $7　　MIP $14

❑ **White 2-180**, 1:64-scale, Scale Models, chrome, Christmas 1985, 1st Edition, 1985
EX $3　　NM $4　　MIP $6

❑ **White 2-180**, 1:64-scale, Scale Models, chrome, Knightstown, Indiana 1985, 1st Edition, 1985
EX $4　　NM $14　　MIP $23

❑ **White 2-180**, 1:64-scale, Scale Models, silver and gray, Louisville Farm Show 1986, 1st Edition, 1986
EX $4　　NM $7　　MIP $14

❑ **White 2-180**, 1:64-scale, Scale Models, silver and gray, Dyersville Summer Toy Festival 1986, 1st Edition, 1986
EX $4　　NM $7　　MIP $14

❑ **White 4-270**, 1:64-scale, Scale Models, silver and gray, Alleman, Iowa 1987, 1987
EX $18   **NM** $24   **MIP** $34

❑ **White 4-270**, 1:64-scale, Scale Models, silver and gray, 1991
EX $18   **NM** $24   **MIP** $34

❑ **White American 60**, 1:64-scale, Ertl, silver, w/ROPS, 1990s, No. 4269
EX $4   **NM** $5   **MIP** $6

❑ **White American 60**, 1:64-scale, Ertl, silver, w/cab, 1990s, No. 4275
EX $4   **NM** $5   **MIP** $6

❑ **White American 60**, 1:64-scale, Ertl, yellow, w/cab, 1990s, No. 4275
EX $4   **NM** $5   **MIP** $6

❑ **White American 60**, 1:64-scale, Ertl, green, w/cab, 1990s, No. 4275
EX $4   **NM** $5   **MIP** $6

❑ **White American 60**, 1:64-scale, Ertl, yellow, w/ROPS, 1990s, No. 4269
EX $4   **NM** $5   **MIP** $6

❑ **White American 60**, 1:64-scale, Ertl, red, w/ROPS, 1990s, No. 4269
EX $4   **NM** $5   **MIP** $6

❑ **White American 60**, 1:64-scale, Ertl, green, w/ROPS, 1990s, No. 4269
EX $4   **NM** $5   **MIP** $6

❑ **White American 60**, 1:64-scale, Ertl, red, w/cab, 1990s, No. 4275
EX $4   **NM** $5   **MIP** $6

❑ **White American 80**, 1:64-scale, Ertl, yellow, w/cab, 1990s, No. 4285
EX $4   **NM** $5   **MIP** $6

❑ **White American 80**, 1:64-scale, Ertl, green, w/cab, 1990s, No. 4285
EX $4   **NM** $5   **MIP** $6

❑ **White American 80**, 1:64-scale, Ertl, green, w/ROPS, 1990s, No. 4280
EX $4   **NM** $5   **MIP** $6

❑ **White American 80**, 1:64-scale, Ertl, silver, w/ROPS, 1990s, No. 4280
EX $4   **NM** $5   **MIP** $6

❑ **White American 80**, 1:64-scale, Ertl, silver, w/cab, 1990s, No. 4285
EX $4   **NM** $5   **MIP** $6

❑ **White American 80**, 1:64-scale, Ertl, yellow, w/ROPS, 1990s, No. 4280
EX $4   **NM** $5   **MIP** $6

❑ **White American 80**, 1:64-scale, Ertl, red, w/ROPS, 1990s, No. 4280
EX $4   **NM** $5   **MIP** $6

❑ **White American 80**, 1:64-scale, Ertl, red, w/cab, 1990s, No. 4285
EX $4   **NM** $5   **MIP** $6

❑ **White American Set 60**, 1:64-scale, Ertl, boxed set of 4 colors, green, red, yellow, silver, 1990s, No. 4287EA
EX n/a   **NM** n/a   **MIP** $18

❑ **White American Set 80**, 1:64-scale, Ertl, boxed set of 4 colors, green, red, yellow, silver, 1990s, No. 4286EA
EX n/a   **NM** n/a   **MIP** $18

TRUCKS 1:16-SCALE

❑ **White Dealer Pickup**, 1:16-scale, Scale Models, white, 1970s
EX $8   **NM** $16   **MIP** $28

❑ **White Truck**, 1:16-scale, Ertl, white and red, 1970s
EX $242   **NM** $516   **MIP** $982

❑ **White Truck**, 1:16-scale, Ertl, brown, 1970s
EX $242   **NM** $516   **MIP** $982

WHITEHEAD & KALES

IMPLEMENTS 1:16-SCALE

❑ **Stake Trailer**, 1:16-scale, Arcade, red, later models in gray, rubber tires, "W&K" cast into wheels, 1923
EX n/a   **NM** n/a   **MIP** n/a

INDEX

Photos by Jon Jacobson unless otherwise noted.

Case Disc, 80-81
Case Dump Truck 330, 78
Case Excavator 1085 B Cruz-Air, 76
Case Excavator 125 B, 76
Case Excavator 1280, 76
Case Excavator 688, 78
Case Excavator 9030B, 78
Case Excavator 980 B, 76
Case Excavator CX-130, 78
Case Excavator CX-210, 78
Case Excavator, Drott 50, 76
Case Hammer Mill, 80
Case Hay Loader, 80
Case L, 83, 91, 95-96, 98
Case LA, 91, 96
Case Mack Truck Bank, 73
Case Minimum Tillage Plow, 80-81
Case Pace Setter, 94
Case Pickup, 99
Case Plow80
Case Plow, 80-81
Case RC, 91
Case RC, 96
Case Roller 1102, 76
Case Roller 1601, 76
Case SC, 83, 91-92
Case Semi, 99-100
Case Skid Loader 1845, 77
Case Skid Loader 1845 B, 77
Case Skid Loader 1845 C, 79
Case Spreader, 80
Case Steam Engine, 92, 96, 98-99
Case Steam Roller, 74
Case Thresher, 81-82
Case Trencher 760, 77
Case Trencher DH4 B, 77
Case VA, 92
Case VAC, 82, 92, 96
Case Wagon, 81
Case Wagon, Barge, 81
Case Wagon, Flare Box, 81
Case Wagon, Gravity, 81
Case Water Wagon, 81
Case Wheel Loader, 74
Case Wheel Loader 621, 78

Case Wheel Loader 621B, 79
Case Wheel Loader 621C, 79
Case Wheel Loader 621D, 79
Case Wheel Loader 740, 77
Case Wheel Loader W20 B, 77
Case Wheel Loader W20 C, 77
Case Wheel Loader W30, 74, 78
Case-IH 2294, 109
Case-IH 2394, 104, 111
Case-IH 245, 104, 109
Case-IH 2594, 104, 109, 111-12, 114
Case-IH 305, 109
Case-IH 3294, 104, 112
Case-IH 335 Magnum, 104
Case-IH 3394, 112
Case-IH 4230, 104-5, 112
Case-IH 4694, 112
Case-IH 480 Quad Trac, 112
Case-IH 480, 105
Case-IH 4894, 109, 112
Case-IH 4994, 105, 110-11
Case-IH 5120, 105, 110, 112
Case-IH 5130, 105, 110, 112
Case-IH 5140, 105, 110, 112
Case-IH 5150, 105
Case-IH 5230, 110
Case-IH 5240, 110
Case-IH 5250, 105-6
Case-IH 685, 106
Case-IH 7120, 106, 112-13
Case-IH 7130, 104, 106, 113
Case-IH 7140, 106, 113
Case-IH 7150, 106, 113
Case-IH 7210, 106, 113
Case-IH 7220, 106, 113
Case-IH 7240, 106, 113
Case-IH 7250 and MX-285, 113
Case-IH 7250, 104, 106, 113
Case-IH 8920, 106, 113
Case-IH 8940, 106, 113
Case-IH 8950, 106, 113
Case-IH 8950, 104
Case-IH 9150, 110
Case-IH 9250 w/Planter Set, 114
Case-IH 9250, 113
Case-IH 9260, 114
Case-IH 9270, 107, 110
Case-IH 9280, 107
Case-IH 9370, 107, 110, 114
Case-IH 9380, 107, 110, 114
Case-IH 9390, 107, 110-11, 114
Case-IH 94 Series, 104
Case-IH 956 XL, 111
Case-IH Air Drill, 102
Case-IH Air Drill 8500, 102
Case-IH Baler, 100, 102
Case-IH Baler, 8465 Round, 100

Case-IH Baler, 8575 Big Square, 100
Case-IH Big Baler, 101
Case-IH C-100, 107
Case-IH C-80, 107
Case-IH C-90, 107
Case-IH Combine 8010AFX, 101
Case-IH Combine 1660, 102
Case-IH Combine 1666, 102
Case-IH Combine 1680, 101
Case-IH Combine 2166, 102
Case-IH Combine 2188, 102
Case-IH Combine 2366, 102-3
Case-IH Combine 2388, 100, 102-3
Case-IH Combine, 7010 Axial Flow, 102
Case-IH Combine 7010, 103
Case-IH Combine 8010, 102
Case-IH Combine, AFX-8010, 102-3
Case-IH Cotton Picker 1844, 103
Case-IH Cotton Picker 2155, 103
Case-IH Cotton Picker 2555, 100, 103
Case-IH Cultivator 1840, 100
Case-IH CVT-170, 107
Case-IH Disc, 100, 103
Case-IH DX-33, 104, 107
Case-IH Farm Set, 103
Case-IH Forage Harvestor, 100, 103
Case-IH Ford F-150 Pickup, 114
Case-IH Grain Drill 5100, 100
Case-IH Hauling Set, 115
Case-IH Hay Rake, 100-1
Case-IH Historical Toy Set, 114
Case-IH Magnum, 111
Case-IH Magnum 305, 114
Case-IH Manure Spreader, 101
Case-IH Maxxum 140; 107, 111, 114
Case-IH Mixer Mill, 101, 103
Case-IH Mower Conditioner, 103
Case-IH Mower, Rotary, 101
Case-IH MX-110, 107
Case-IH MX-120, 107
Case-IH MX-125, 108
Case-IH MX-135, 108
Case-IH MX-170, 104
Case-IH MX-210, 108
Case-IH MX-220, 108
Case-IH MX-230, 108
Case-IH MX-235, 108
Case-IH MX-240, 104, 108
Case-IH MX-255, 104, 108
Case-IH MX-270, 104, 108
Case-IH MX-275 w/Disc Harrow, 111
Case-IH MX-275, 108
Case-IH MX-285, 104, 108
Case-IH MX-305, 104, 108, 111
Case-IH MXU-125, 108
Case-IH MXU-135, 111

Photos by Jon Jacobson unless otherwise noted.

John Deere 4320, 348, 351
John Deere 435, 319
John Deere 440 Snowmobile, 308
John Deere 440, 271
John Deere 4410 w/Mower Set, 306
John Deere 4430 Set, 344
John Deere 4430, 312
John Deere 4430, 271, 319-20, 343-44, 351-52
John Deere 4440 Set, 345
John Deere 4440, 320-21, 344-45, 352
John Deere 445, 307
John Deere 4450, 321, 345, 352-53
John Deere 4455, 321-22, 353
John Deere 4520, 322, 353
John Deere 4620, 322
John Deere 4630, 322
John Deere 4640, 322
John Deere 4760, 322
John Deere 4850, 322
John Deere 4930 Dry Box Spreader, 353
John Deere 4955, 322
John Deere 4960, 322
John Deere 50, 311, 322, 353
John Deere 50/60, 322
John Deere 5010, 323, 353
John Deere 5020, 311, 323, 353
John Deere 520, 323-24, 353
John Deere 5200, 324
John Deere 530, 324, 353
John Deere 5400, 324
John Deere 5410, 345
John Deere 5420, 324
John Deere 57 Chevy Stake Truck, 360
John Deere 5820, 345
John Deere 60, 311, 324, 348, 353
John Deere 6030, 324
John Deere 62, 324
John Deere 620, 311, 324-25, 353
John Deere 6200, 325, 354
John Deere 6210, 345, 354
John Deere 630, 325, 348-49, 354
John Deere 6320, 325
John Deere 637 Disc, 298
John Deere 6400, 311, 325, 345, 354
John Deere 6410, 311, 325, 342, 345, 354
John Deere 6420, 325, 354
John Deere 6430, 325
John Deere 6820, 345
John Deere 6920, 325, 345
John Deere 70 Set, 326
John Deere 70, 312, 325-26
John Deere 7020, 345, 354
John Deere 720, 326-27

John Deere 730, 311, 327, 347, 349, 354
John Deere 7410, 312, 345
John Deere 7510, 327, 355
John Deere 7520, 328, 345, 355
John Deere 7600, 312, 328, 355
John Deere 7610, 328, 355
John Deere 7710, 328, 355
John Deere 7800 Set, 355
John Deere 7800, 328, 345, 355
John Deere 7810, 328, 355
John Deere 7820, 328, 355
John Deere 7830, 328, 355
John Deere 7920, 328, 345, 355
John Deere 7930, 346, 355
John Deere 80, 328, 355
John Deere 8000T 10th Anniversary Set, 355
John Deere 8010, 329, 355
John Deere 8020, 329, 355
John Deere 8100, 355
John Deere 820, 329, 355
John Deere 8200, 329, 355
John Deere 8210, 329, 355
John Deere 8220, 356
John Deere 8230, 346, 356
John Deere 830, 313, 329, 356
John Deere 8300, 329, 356
John Deere 8300T, 329
John Deere 8310, 312, 330, 356
John Deere 8310T, 330
John Deere 8320, 330
John Deere 8330, 356
John Deere 8400, 312, 330, 346, 356
John Deere 8400T, 330, 356
John Deere 8410, 330, 356
John Deere 8410T, 356
John Deere 8420, 330, 356
John Deere 8420T, 330, 356
John Deere 8430, 330, 346
John Deere 8430T, 330, 356
John Deere 8520, 312, 330
John Deere 8520T, 356
John Deere 8530, 346
John Deere 8560, 330, 356
John Deere 8630, 330, 356
John Deere 8640, 330, 346
John Deere 8650, 330
John Deere 8760, 330-31
John Deere 8770, 356
John Deere 8850, 357
John Deere 8870, 331, 357
John Deere 8960, 331, 346
John Deere 9200, 331
John Deere 9300, 331
John Deere 9300T, 331, 357
John Deere 9320, 331, 357

John Deere 9400, 331, 357
John Deere 9400T, 331, 357
John Deere 9420, 331, 357
John Deere 9420T, 331, 346, 357
John Deere 9520, 331
John Deere 9520T, 331
John Deere 9620 Set, 331
John Deere 9620, 357
John Deere 9620T, 357
John Deere A Set, 334, 358
John Deere A, 312, 331-34, 346, 349, 357-58
John Deere Ammonia Tank, 280
John Deere AMT 600, 306
John Deere Anvil, 308-9
John Deere AO, 334
John Deere AR, 334
John Deere Auger, 280
John Deere AW, 334
John Deere B, 312, 334-35, 346-47, 349
John Deere Backhoe Loader 310SJ, 277
John Deere Backhoe, 271, 276-78, 280
John Deere Bale Mover, 280
John Deere Bale-Grinder, 298
John Deere Baler, 280-81, 298-99
John Deere BN, 335
John Deere BO, 335
John Deere Boy, 309
John Deere BR, 335
John Deere Buck ATV, 307
John Deere Bulldozer 650J, 277
John Deere BW, 335
John Deere BW-40, 335
John Deere BWH, 335
John Deere C, 335
John Deere Carry Scraper K9, 281
John Deere Chain Saw, 307
John Deere Circular Saw, 308
John Deere Combine, 279, 281-82, 295-99, 303
John Deere Commodity Cart 1900, 299
John Deere Corn Picker, 282, 299
John Deere Corn-Sheller, 300
John Deere Cotton Picker, 282, 300, 303
John Deere Crawler, 271-74, 277-79
John Deere D Bank, 270
John Deere D, 312, 335-37, 348-49, 358
John Deere Dain Truck, 361
John Deere Dain, 337
John Deere Dealer í50 Chevy Pickup, 361
John Deere Dealer Truck, 360

John Deere Disc, 279, 282-84, 300, 303

John Deere Drag, 284

John Deere Drum Bank, 270

John Deere Dump Truck 400 D, 277

John Deere Elevator, 284

John Deere Equipment Hauler, 360

John Deere Excavator, 276-78

John Deere Farm Set, 309

John Deere Feller Bucher 843L, 277

John Deere Flail Chopper, 284

John Deere Forage Blower, 300

John Deere Forage Harvester, 284, 297, 300

John Deere Forage Wagon, 284

John Deere Ford F-150 Pickup, 360

John Deere Ford Truck, 361

John Deere Froelich, 337, 358

John Deere Frontier Blade, 284

John Deere G, 313, 337-38, 358

John Deere Gator, 304, 306-7

John Deere GP Set, 339

John Deere GP, 313, 338-39, 359

John Deere Grader, 274, 276-78

John Deere Grain Binder, 284

John Deere Grain Cart 500, 300

John Deere Grain Drill, 284-85, 300

John Deere Gravity Wagon, Frontier, 285

John Deere Grinder Mixer, 285

John Deere H, 339, 349

John Deere Hammer Mill, 285

John Deere Hauling Set w/7810s, 362

John Deere Hauling Set, 361

John Deere Hay Elevator, 285

John Deere Hay Loader, 285

John Deere Hay Rake, 285, 300

John Deere Hay Wagon, 285

John Deere Haying Set, 359

John Deere Hayrack and Team, 285

John Deere Hydra Spreader, 286

John Deere Implement Trailer, 286

John Deere Implement Truck, 360

John Deere L & G, 307

John Deere L, 339-40

John Deere L110, 307

John Deere LA, 340, 359

John Deere Lanz 3120, 343

John Deere Lanz 700, 359

John Deere Lanz Combine, 297

John Deere Lanz Set, 347

John Deere Lanz, 347

John Deere Lawn and Garden Assortment, 307

John Deere LGT, 312

John Deere LI, 340

John Deere Loader, 286

John Deere Log Skidder 648 E, 274, 277-78

John Deere Log Truck, 360-61

John Deere M, 340, 348

John Deere Machinery Trailer, 286

John Deere Manure Spreader, 279, 286-88, 297-98, 300-1

John Deere Marston Trailer, 297

John Deere Material Handler 3200, 277

John Deere MC Crawler, 274

John Deere Mechanical Bank, 270

John Deere MI, 340

John Deere Micros Set. 312

John Deere Mix Mill, 301

John Deere Mower Conditioner, 288-89, 301

John Deere Mower, 288-89, 297, 301

John Deere MT, 341

John Deere Mulch Master, 289, 301

John Deere Mulch Ripper 2700, 289, 301

John Deere Mulch-Tiller, 301

John Deere OP, 341

John Deere Overtime, 341, 347

John Deere Parts Express Semi, 361

John Deere Pedal Tractor, 341

John Deere Pickup, 362

John Deere Planter, 289, 301

John Deere Plow, 279, 289-91, 296

John Deere R, 341-42

John Deere Rake, 297

John Deere Roll Guard, 312

John Deere Round Baler 567, 291

John Deere Scraper, 276

John Deere Semi w/Log Skidder 648G III Set, 278

John Deere Service Center, 309

John Deere Set, 347, 359

John Deere Shredder, 297, 301-2

John Deere Skid Loader, 274-78

John Deere Snowmobile, 308

John Deere Sprayer 4700, 302

John Deere SST-16, 307

John Deere SST-18, 307

John Deere Stationary Engine Waterloo Boy Engine, 279-80

John Deere Stationary Gas Engine, 279-80, 291-92, 296

John Deere Straight Truck w/John Deere A '50 Chevy, 362

John Deere Thresher, 292, 296

John Deere Tool Bar Cultivator, 292

John Deere Tool Bar Rotary Hoe, 292

John Deere Tractor 2755, 275

John Deere Tractor, 3185, 277

John Deere Tractor, 440, 275

John Deere Tractor, 5010, 275, 279

John Deere Tractor, 6410 Set, 275

John Deere Tractor, 720, 275

John Deere Tractor, 730, 275

John Deere Tractor, 80, 275

John Deere Tractor, 820, 275

John Deere Tractor, 830, 275

John Deere Tractor, BI, 275

John Deere Tractor, D, 271

John Deere Tractor, LA, 275

John Deere Tractor, LI, 275

John Deere Tractor, MI, 275-76

John Deere Trail Fire Snowmobile, 308

John Deere Truck Prestige Series, 270

John Deere Truck w/Waterloo Boy on Back, 361

John Deere Value Playset, 450

John Deere WA-14, 342

John Deere WA-17, 342

John Deere Wagon Buckboard, 292

John Deere Wagon Running Gear, 292

John Deere Wagon, 296

John Deere Wagon, Bale Throw, 302

John Deere Wagon, Bale, 292

John Deere Wagon, Barge, 292-93, 297-98, 302

John Deere Wagon, Chuck, 293

John Deere Wagon, Flare Box, 279, 293-94, 298, 302

John Deere Wagon, Forage, 294, 302-3

John Deere Wagon, Grain, 294-95

John Deere Wagon, Gravity, 295, 303

John Deere Wagon, Hay, 295, 298

John Deere Walking Plow w/Team, 304

John Deere Walking Plow, 304

John Deere Waterloo Boy, 342, 349, 360

John Deere Wheel Loader, 276-79

John Deere X485 Lawn and Garden Tractor, 307

John Deere X-485, 307

John Deere Z-Trak, 307

John Deere, 950, 342

John Deere, RX-75, 307

John Deere/Bauer Built Planter, 36 Row, 303

K

Kasten Manure Spreader, 362

Kasten Wagon, Forage, 362

Killbros Wagon, Gravity, 362

Massey-Harris Truck Bank, 380
Massey-Harris Twin Power, 386, 388
Massey-Harris Wagon, Barge, 382
Massey-Harris Wagon, Flare Box, 380
McCormick 10-20, 219-20, 226
McCormick 15-30, 220
McCormick 22-36, 220
McCormick 624, 197
McCormick B-250, 224
McCormick B-434, 222
McCormick Baler, 192
McCormick C-100, 220
McCormick C-70, 220
McCormick Combine, 184
McCormick Crawler, 181
McCormick CX-100, 223
McCormick Deering 10-20, 220
McCormick Deering Box Wagon, 184
McCormick Deering Combine 20, 184
McCormick Deering Combine 22, 185
McCormick Deering Cream Separator, 185
McCormick Deering Plow, 185
McCormick Deering Spreader, 185
McCormick Deering Thresher, 185, 190
McCormick Deering Wagon, 186
McCormick Disc, 186
McCormick Elevator 456, 186
McCormick Engine, 181
McCormick F-20, 226
McCormick Farmall M, 223
McCormick Farmall Regular, 234
McCormick International Baler, 186
McCormick International Disc, 186
McCormick International Mower, 186
McCormick Loader Long, 187
McCormick Loader Short, 187
McCormick Loader, 187
McCormick Mower, 27, 187
McCormick MTX-140, 196, 220
McCormick MTX-175, 224
McCormick Picker, 192
McCormick Plow, 187-88
McCormick Reaper, 188
McCormick Spreader, 188
McCormick Thresher, 189
McCormick Trac-Tractor, 176
McCormick W-30, 220
McCormick W-4, 220
McCormick W-6, 220
McCormick W-6 Super, 220
McCormick W-9, 221
McCormick Wagon, 188-89
McCormick Wagon, Flare Box, 192

McCormick WD-9, 221, 226
Minneapolis-Moline 4 Star, 400
Minneapolis-Moline 445, 391, 400
Minneapolis-Moline 5 Star, 391
Minneapolis-Moline 670, 402
Minneapolis-Moline A4T-1600, 391-92, 402
Minneapolis-Moline Baler, 389
Minneapolis-Moline Combine, 389-90
Minneapolis-Moline Corn Sheller, 389-90
Minneapolis-Moline Crawler 2 Star, 389
Minneapolis-Moline Dain Antique Truck, 406
Minneapolis-Moline Disc, 389
Minneapolis-Moline Experimental, 392
Minneapolis-Moline G, 392
Minneapolis-Moline G-1000 Vista, 392-93
Minneapolis-Moline G-1000, 392, 402-3
Minneapolis-Moline G-1050, 401, 403
Minneapolis-Moline G-1335, 393
Minneapolis-Moline G-1350, 403
Minneapolis-Moline G-1355, 403
Minneapolis-Moline G-550, 393
Minneapolis-Moline G-705, 393
Minneapolis-Moline G-706, 393
Minneapolis-Moline G-750, 393, 401
Minneapolis-Moline G-850, 393-94, 403-4
Minneapolis-Moline G-900, 394, 404
Minneapolis-Moline G-940, 394, 404
Minneapolis-Moline G-950, 401, 404
Minneapolis-Moline GB, 394
Minneapolis-Moline GTB, 394
Minneapolis-Moline GTS, 394
Minneapolis-Moline J, 395, 404-5
Minneapolis-Moline Jet Star, 395
Minneapolis-Moline Jr., 401
Minneapolis-Moline M-5, 395
Minneapolis-Moline M-602, 395
Minneapolis-Moline M-604, 395
Minneapolis-Moline M-670 Super, 396
Minneapolis-Moline Pan Scraper, 389
Minneapolis-Moline Picker, 389
Minneapolis-Moline Plow, 390
Minneapolis-Moline R, 396-97, 400-1
Minneapolis-Moline RTS, 397
Minneapolis-Moline RTU, 397
Minneapolis-Moline Set, 405
Minneapolis-Moline Spirit of MM, 391
Minneapolis-Moline Spreader, 390

Minneapolis-Moline Steam Engine, 397, 405
Minneapolis-Moline Thresher, 390
Minneapolis-Moline Truck Bank, 389
Minneapolis-Moline Twin City, 397
Minneapolis-Moline U, 397-98, 405
Minneapolis-Moline U-302, 398
Minneapolis-Moline UB Special, 399
Minneapolis-Moline UB, 398, 405
Minneapolis-Moline UDLX, 399, 405-6
Minneapolis-Moline Uni-System, 390
Minneapolis-Moline Universal Tractor, 399
Minneapolis-Moline UTC, 399
Minneapolis-Moline UTS, 399-400
Minneapolis-Moline UTU, 400
Minneapolis-Moline V, 400
Minneapolis-Moline Wagon, 389-90
Minneapolis-Moline Z, 400-1
Minneapolis-Moline ZB, 400
Minneapolis-Moline ZBE, 406
Minneapolis-Moline ZBU, 406
Minneapolis-Moline, Spirit, 400
Mitsubishi MT 3000, 413
Mixmill, 409
Modern Farm Set, 451
Mogul 10-20, 221
Mogul 12-25, 221
Mogul 8-16, 221
Monarch Crawler, 3546 Mower, 125
Mustang Mini Excavator ME-6002, 413
Mustang Skid Loader 2042, 414
Mustang Skid Loader 2050, 413-14
Mustang Skid Loader, 413

N

New Holland 3930, 420
New Holland 5635, 420
New Holland 66 Baler, 415
New Holland 6635, 422
New Holland 6640, 420
New Holland 7740, 420
New Holland 7840, 420, 422
New Holland 8260, 420

Photos by Jon Jacobson unless otherwise noted.

Photos by Jon Jacobson unless otherwise noted.

Farm Frenzy

American Farm Collectibles

Identification and Price Guide, 2nd Ed.

by Russell E. Lewis

Experience America's rural history and role in society in this full-color enhanced edition devoted to farming, in all it's glory. From rarely seen implement advertisements to kitchen collectibles, tools and vintage toy tractors, this book contains a nice cross section of this popular collecting arena.

Softcover • 8-1/4 x 10-7/8 • 288 pages
1,000 color photos
Item# Z0722 • $24.99

Toys & Prices 2008

15th Edition

Edited by Karen O'Brien

Quickly locate and accurately price and identify items with this top-selling annual post-war toy guide. Within the 32,000 toy listings you'll discover information about everything from Barbie to Western Toys and ViewMaster, plus, 95,000 values for your favorite collectible toys. In addition, you gain insight about the latest toy trends and top ten lists for each category.

Softcover • 7 x 10-1/2 • 824 pages

2,000 b&w photos • 16-page color sect
Item# Z0971 • $21.99

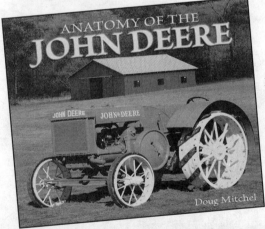

Anatomy of the John Deere

by Doug Mitchel

Feed your interest in the king of the fields with this lavishly illustrated guide to everything John Deere. This guide covers more than 40 tractors, featured in brilliatn color photos, along with historical and performance details.

Hardcover • 10-1/4 x 10-1/4 • 256 pages
300+ color photos
Item# Z0982 • $35.00

Photos by Jon Jacobson unless otherwise noted.

Public Health

As a paramedic, you will encounter ethical dilemmas on an almost daily basis. It is best to work through these issues as they arise by communicating calmly and directly with everyone involved.

Matching

Part I

Match each of the definitions in the left column to the appropriate term in the right column.

_____ 1. A way of measuring and comparing the overall impact of deaths resulting from different causes; calculated based on a fixed age minus the age at death.

_____ 2. Injuries that occur without intent to harm (commonly called accidents); examples are motor vehicle crashes, poisonings, drownings, falls, and most burns.

_____ 3. Monitoring and comparing the current number and nature of medical cases against the expected volume of these cases at a given time and place in the community.

_____ 4. The ongoing systematic collection, analysis, and interpretation of injury data essential to the planning, implementation, and evaluation of public health practice.

_____ 5. Reducing the effects of an injury or illness that has already happened.

_____ 6. Deaths caused by injury and disease usually expressed as a rate; the number of deaths in a certain population in a given time period divided by the size of the population.

_____ 7. Number of nonfatally injured or disabled people, usually expressed as a rate; the number of nonfatal injuries in a certain population in a given time period divided by the size of the population.

_____ 8. In the context of prevention, specific measures or activities designed to meet a program objective; categories include education/behavior change, enforcement/legislation, engineering/technology, and economic incentives.

_____ 9. Injuries that are purposefully inflicted by a person on himself or herself or on another person; examples include suicide or attempted suicide, homicide, rape, assault, domestic abuse, elder abuse, and child abuse.

_____ 10. Collection of the methods, skills, and activities necessary to determine whether a service or program is needed, is likely to be used, is conducted as planned, and actually helps people.

_____ 11. The study of the causes, patterns, prevalence, and control of disease in groups of people.

_____ 12. A potentially hazardous situation that puts people in a position in which they could be harmed.

A. Epidemiology

B. Evaluation

C. Intentional injuries

D. Interventions

E. Morbidity

F. Mortality

G. Passive interventions

H. Primary prevention

I. Process objectives

J. Public health

K. Risk

L. Secondary prevention

_____ **13.** An industry whose mission is to prevent disease and promote good health within groups of people.

M. Surveillance

_____ **14.** Statements of how a program will be implemented, describing the service to be provided, the nature of the service, and to whom it will be directed.

N. Syndromic surveillance

_____ **15.** Keeping an injury or illness from occurring.

O. Unintentional injuries

_____ **16.** Something that offers automatic protection from injury or illness, often without requiring any conscious change of behavior by the person; child-resistant bottles and airbags are examples.

P. Years of potential life lost

Part II

Match the following prevention methods with the correct situation.

_____ **1.** New guardrails are installed on a road in the area because a lot of crashes have occurred there.

A. Education

_____ **2.** The emergency medical services (EMS) agency holds a free "Learn CPR Week" for residents of the town.

B. Enforcement

_____ **3.** A vehicle insurance company offers a discounted rate to 16-year-olds for taking driver's education.

C. Engineering/ environment

_____ **4.** The police stop students on the way to school and hand out coupons for a free iTunes music download to students who are wearing their seat belts.

D. Economic incentives

_____ **5.** A car dealership offers a free child car seat check this weekend.

_____ **6.** An adolescent is stopped for speeding in a work zone and is given a ticket that costs him $250.

_____ **7.** The new car seats available have a five-point harness system instead of a bar that holds the child in the seat.

_____ **8.** The ambulance crew offers to do an inspection of any elderly person's home to determine potential risk areas. This service is provided free of charge.

_____ **9.** Because of the law, all poisons must be listed on the front of every container that contains products that can cause poisoning.

_____ **10.** Homeowners receive a discount on their home insurance because they have a smoke alarm and carbon monoxide (CO) monitor on every floor of the house.

Multiple Choice

Read each item carefully, and then select the best response.

_____ **1.** Fred is on the roof, trying to reposition the "dish" during the big game. He falls off and hurts his back. This is considered a(n) _____ injury.
- **A.** intentional
- **B.** unintentional
- **C.** secondary
- **D.** environmental

_____ **2.** Which of the following is NOT an intentional injury?
- **A.** Rape
- **B.** Motor vehicle crash
- **C.** Suicide
- **D.** Elder abuse

_____ **3.** When choosing objectives as you build an implementation plan, the _S_ in SMART stands for:
- **A.** signs.
- **B.** swelling.
- **C.** simple.
- **D.** success.